# THE STERN GANG

# THE
# STERN GANG
## Ideology, Politics and Terror, 1940–1949

## JOSEPH HELLER
Department of International Relations
Hebrew University of Jerusalem

## FRANK CASS
### LONDON

*First published in 1995 in Great Britain by*
FRANK CASS & CO. LTD.
Newbury House, 900 Eastern Avenue,
London IG2 7HH

*and in the United States of America by*
FRANK CASS
ISBS, 5804 N.E. Hassalo Street, Portland, Oregon 97213-3644

British Library Cataloguing in Publication Data

Heller, Joseph
   Stern Gang: Ideology, Politics and Terror,
   1940–49
   I. Title
   956.9494

   ISBN 0-7146-4558-3 (cloth)
   ISBN 0-7146-4106-5 (paper)

Library of Congress Cataloging-in-Publication Data

Heller, Joseph, 1937–
   [Leḥi. English]
   The Stern Gang : ideology, politics, and terror, 1940–1949 /
Joseph Heller.
     p.  cm.
   Includes bibliographical references and index.
   ISBN 0-7146-4558-3 : — ISBN 0-7146-4106-5 (pbk.)
   1. Loḥame ḥerut Yiśra'el. 2. Palestine—History—1929–1948.
   3. Revisionist Zionism—Palestine—History. I. Title.
DS150.R56H4513   1995
956.94′04—dc20                         94-17641
                                                   CIP

Typeset by Vitaset, Paddock Wood
Printed in Great Britain by
Bookcraft (Bath) Ltd, Midsomer Norton

# Contents

# List of Illustrations

# Preface

This book does not purport to provide a narrative history of the Stern Gang from its foundation in 1940 and its revival in 1943 until its ultimate disappearance in 1949. Rather, it constitutes an attempt to reveal and analyse the ideological and political development of the group during those years. This is a neglected aspect of its history. Hitherto, writings on the Stern Gang – most of them by its own former members – have been typified by idealised heroism. Alternatively, emphasis has been placed on its terrorism. A closer examination of the source material, both public and secret, reveals an entirely different (and far more fascinating) aspect of the group: its obsession with Great Powers inimical to Britain and amenable to its own ideology. It is this which ranks it as an extremely radical movement.

The basic thesis of this study is that the Stern Gang was not an ideological offshoot of the *Irgun Zvai Leumi* (IZL) of the 1930s, but of 'maximalist' Zionist Revisionism, which was itself an offspring of the inter-war European radical right. After its revival in 1943, the group created a new ideology which is here designated National Bolshevism.

The latter term is derived from the ideology developed in Weimar Germany, principally by Moeller van den Bruck and Ernst Jünger in the 1920s and by Karl Otto Paetel and Ernst Niekisch in the early 1930s. These men, fearing Germany's collapse under the Republic and its submission to the Western Powers after the 1919 Versailles settlement, developed an ideology which was paradoxical because it attempted to combine elements of both the right and the left. Simultaneously, it supported anti-capitalism, state planning and an obviously pro-Soviet foreign policy as well as the notion of the organic unity of the nation *(Volksgemeinschaft)*. Thus presented, National Bolshevism symbolised an ideology of distress, itself characteristic of some fringe circles within the German radical right. It expressed a desire to create a 'third force' which would bridge the gap between communism and Nazism. Its failure, however, was inherent in the dynamics of polarisation which led to the collapse of the Weimar Republic.[1]

Unaware of the German precedent, the Stern Gang developed a Hebrew version of National Bolshevism, projecting a form of leftist chauvinism. This, too, originated as an ideology of distress: faced with the revival of the IZL in 1944, the Sternists had to prove their own *raison d'être*. If the Jewish kingdom of Stern's aspirations could not be established with the help of the Axis powers (to whom he originally appealed), then it was necessary to turn to the Soviet Union. The important point was to accelerate Britain's expulsion from *Eretz Israel* (Hebrew: land of Israel) by forging alliances with victorious powers.

Thus began the Sternists' process of 'leftism', which was to generate profound changes in its ideological position on matters domestic as well as foreign. Rather like the right-wing National Bolsheviks of Weimar, the Sternists also believed that, even though rejecting the notion of a class war and adopting that of the organic unity of the nation, they could win the sympathy of the working class and attract the support of the Soviet Union. The former would be promised the leadership of the emergent state (provided workers participated in the war against British foreign rule), and the latter would be won over by the pronouncement of anti-imperialist slogans. It is the manner in which those positions were worked out and presented that is the principal theme of this book.

I would like to thank the former members of the Stern Gang who assisted me in my attempt to shed new light on its history. Foremost among these are Dr Israel Eldad (Scheib), who never tired of replying to my enquiries; Mr A Spielman, Director of the *Beit-Yair* Archives (YHA), though he was well aware of the 'danger' that some Sternist myths might be destroyed; Mr David and Mrs Amira Stern, who allowed me to inspect 'Yair's Churn' Archives (YCA); Professor Uzi Ornan; the late Mr Haggai Eshed; Messrs Hayim Dviri, Mordechai Shalev, Aharon Haichman, Benjamin Zeroni, Pinhas Genosar and Yitzchak Zelnick; Mrs Roni Zamir; and 'Avidan', who still insists on keeping his true identity a secret. Unfortunately, I was unable to gain access to the papers of either Nathan Yellin-Mor or Mosheh Sneh, or to see as much of the relevant private correspondence as I would have wished.

I would also like to thank the late Professor Shemuel Ettinger, Professor Shlomo Avineri who was first to bring to my attention the affinity between the later *Lehi* and Weimar's National Bolshevism, Dr Shmuel Almog, Professor E. Mendelsohn, Professor Y. Porath and the late Professor M. Stern for their criticism and encouragement. Responsibility for the arguments and conclusions presented in this book is, however, mine alone. Professor Israel Gutman and Mr A. Shnaidovski kindly helped me by providing translations from material in Polish.

I owe a deep debt of gratitude to the faculties of Humanities and Social Sciences, and to the Davis Institute for International Relations and the Institute for Contemporary Jewry (all of the Hebrew University, Jerusalem) for their financial support, and to Professor Stuart Cohen and Mr Barry Davis, who helped me to translate and edit the original Hebrew version of the book for an English-speaking audience.

NOTE

1. On the radical right, see Stanley G. Payne, *Fascism: Comparison and Definition* (Madison, Wisconsin and London, 1980); on National Bolshevism, see O-E. Schüddekopf, *Linke leute von Rechts* (Stuttgart, 1960) and Louis Dupeux, *Stratégie communiste et dynamique conservatrice: Essai sur les différents sens de l'espression 'National Bolchévisme' en Allemagne, 1919–1933* (Paris, 1976).

# Abbreviations

| | |
|---|---|
| CID | Criminal Investigation Department |
| CO | Colonial Office |
| CZA | Central Zionist Archives |
| FO | Foreign Office |
| GOC | General Officer in Command |
| HA | Haganah Archives |
| HH | Haganah History |
| HIAS | Hebrew Sheltering and Immigrants Aid Society |
| JI | Jabotinsky Institute |
| IDF | Israel Defence Force |
| IGP | Inspector General of Police |
| IZL | *Irgun Zvai Leumi* |
| *Ketavim* | Collected Writings of the Stern Gang (*Lehi*) |
| *Lehi* | Fighters for the Freedom of Israel (the Stern Group or Stern Gang) |
| LPA | Labour Party Archives |
| *Maki* | Communist Party of Israel |
| *Mapai* | Labour Party of *Eretz Israel* (Social Democratic Party) |
| *Mapam* | United Workers' Party (Marxist Zionist Party) |
| *Mizrachi* | National Religious Party |
| NILI | 'The Eternity of Israel Shall Not Die' (Zionist Underground in the First World War) |
| NZO | New Zionist Organisation (Revisionist Party after 1935) |
| NWU | National Workers' Union |
| PKP | Communist Party of Palestine |
| PICME | Political Intelligence Center Middle East |
| SHAI | Haganah Secret Service |
| UNSCOP | United Nations Special Commission on Palestine |
| WIZO | Women's International Zionist Organisation |
| Yair | Avraham Stern |
| YCA | Yair (Milk) Churn Archives |
| YHA | Yair House Archives |
| *Yishuv* | Organised Jewish Community in Palestine (controlled by the Jewish Agency and the National Committee) |

# Introduction:
# The Revisionist Background

Though the programme and politics of the Stern Gang (*Lehi–Lohamei Herut Yisrael*, 'Freedom Fighters of Israel') changed radically between 1940 and 1949, there is little doubt that its origins lay in Revisionism. An understanding of the group therefore requires an analysis of the political and ideological character of Revisionism, and in particular of its internal struggles with regard to fascism and democracy, which eventually led to *Lehi*'s emergence.

The character of Revisionism was largely shaped by the charismatic personality of Zeev (Vladimir) Jabotinsky, who founded the movement in 1925 and led it until his death 15 years later. Born in Odessa in 1880, Jabotinsky was deeply influenced by that dynamic cosmopolitan centre of commerce and by its flourishing secular Jewish culture. Equally, if not more, influential were his university days in Rome (1898–1901). There he first became familiar with socialism and with Marxist doctrines, though he was far more powerfully drawn to nationalism, liberalism and individualism, romanticism and futurism. In particular he was attracted by Garibaldi and Mazzini. The former had a lasting impact on him, greater than that of any other historical figure. Jabotinsky, indeed, considered himself a Jewish Garibaldi, though his actions tended to recall Cavour. He adopted a pragmatic position, combining Herzl's political Zionism and his political visions, with Max Nordau's 'muscular Jewry'. It was with Herzl, however, that Jabotinsky identified most, admiring both his revolutionary leadership and his political and social beliefs. For him, *Altneuland* did indeed map out a new society. There is no doubt that Jabotinsky considered himself Herzl's successor and tried throughout his life to emulate him, by becoming the Zionist revolution's 'flywheel' and 'torch'.[1]

Actively involved in Zionist political work in Constantinople (1909–10), Jabotinsky projected the image of a calculating politician who understood the need for careful manoeuvring between Ottomanism and Arabism. The collapse of the Ottoman Empire and the rise of British imperial dominance, of which Jabotinsky was a staunch supporter, wrought a political revolution in the Middle East. It also generated a basic and lasting rift between Jabotinsky and Weizmann.

Jabotinsky believed that only after the formation of Jewish battalions
and their active participation in the war could the Zionists lay serious
claim to Palestine. Weizmann, though supporting the creation of such
units, advocated a political breakthrough, to be achieved by diplomatic efforts, such as the Balfour Declaration and a British Mandate
for Palestine. Jabotinsky's personal battlefield experience as an officer
in the British army led him to create the most important myth of his
life – the vital role played by the Jewish Legion, which his followers
would later liken to that of Pilsudksi's Legion in the liberation of
Poland. Since Palestine had supposedly been conquered by Jewish
blood, this feat could be repeated. Jabotinsky frankly discounted the
mounting objections to Zionism in the military and civil administration: he was in fact arrested in 1920 for attempting to organise illegal
Jewish defence during the first Arab pogrom. Jabotinsky regarded the
Jewish battalions as an essential element in a larger plan whereby
Britain would implement the Zionist colonisation of Palestine and
thus establish its most reliable bastion in the Middle East. In fact,
Jabotinsky's great expectations from Britain led, ultimately, to the
abandonment of the naive attitude towards Britain in the Revisionist
movement (and its affiliated bodies, *Betar* and IZL) and to the emergence of policies hostile to the Mandatory Power. But Jabotinsky's
initial belief in the 'mutual loyalty' between Britain and the Jewish
people was reflected in the principal document of the Revisionist
movement:

> Our attitude towards the Mandatory Government is based on two
> factors: we believe faithfully in the integrity and justice of the British
> people . . . but there is another factor: the cooperation of interest.
> It is not true that England is doing us a favour, without benefit to
> herself. With our assistance England gained a great deal and might
> obtain more in the future . . . there are powerful states in Western
> and Eastern Europe that are publicly envious of the cooperation of
> England with the Zionists . . . Moreover, in the Mediterranean –
> England's corridor to the East – where both on the eastern and
> southern shores there exists a danger of anti-European tendencies,
> the Jews are building the only mainstay which is morally affiliated
> with Europe and forever will be part and parcel of Europe . . .[2]

Throughout his life Jabotinsky considered himself a devout liberal,
and pro-British, but so did Weizmann, the leading Zionist politician
until the early 1930s. Why, then, did they differ so fundamentally?
Personal jealousy certainly played a part, but they also adopted radically different approaches towards operative politics. Jabotinsky's
liberalism constituted a political ideal in the service of his Zionist

programme; Weizmann took a contradictory approach. The latter had learned from the Zionist positivist thinker Ahad Ha-Am that liberalism was an empirical political philosophy. Hence his systematic collaboration with the general Zionists, the middle-class non-Revisionist conservative right, and with the labour movement. His 'synthetic' policy viewed both political endeavour and settlement as essential components of Zionism.

Jabotinsky, on the other hand, was contemptuous of the settlement policy. His Zionism emphasised bourgeois urban development and placed total and unconditional reliance on the British colonial system. Above all, he advocated political activisim. Jabotinsky's plan was in essence Herzl's charter, modelled on the Greeks who were expelled from Turkey (1919–22) and the white settlers in Southern Rhodesia.[3] But while Herzl's charter remained moribund, Jabotinsky put his faith in the Balfour Zionist document approved by the League of Nations. For him both documents had the force of international law. He clung to this policy until the end of his life. Yet Jabotinsky was obsessed with the idea that the Jews would never survive as a minority in Palestine, even if they succeeded in creating an indigenous culture of their own. Without a Jewish majority Palestine would never constitute a national territorial unit, as shown by the models of the German minority in the Baltic lands, the Greeks in Asia Minor and probably also, in the long run, the whites in southern Africa.[4]

It is a major paradox of Revisionism that within 15 years (1929–44) it veered from Anglophilia to bitter Anglophobia. This shift was generated by Jabotinsky's own stubborn adherence to the British connection, deriving from a misreading of Britain's *realpolitik* considerations in its foreign and colonial policies, even before it was threatened by the Axis powers; under his influence, it became a fundamental tenet of his Zionist faith, notwithstanding Britain's all-too-obvious retreat from Zionism. Jabotinsky's conception of the 'Seventh Dominion'[5] which he first expressed publicly in 1928, also gave rise to the unfounded hope that the establishment of a Jewish state was imminent.

More significantly, he also suggested that 'common' Anglo-Zionist interests in Palestine would lead the British to establish a 'colonising regime' there. By facilitating an annual influx of 40,000 Jews, within 25 years the British would have created a Jewish majority in a state on both sides of the Jordan. Inevitable Arab opposition would be unable to overcome the 'iron wall' to be created with British help. In accordance with good liberal principles, the Arabs would receive equal individual rights, though of course no national rights. Revisionism thus argued for the attainment of Jewish statehood in an ineluctable, evolutionary process. However, Britain's departure from its initial Zionist commitments, a policy which first emerged in the Passfield White Paper of 1930, as well as in the Report of the Shaw Commission of Inquiry a few months earlier and in the Hope-Simpson Report, sparked the first crisis between Jabotinsky and Britain. It was particularly acute because of the impact of the new maximalist wing which had just become the dominant element in the Revisionist movement in Palestine. Its leader, Abba Achimeir,[6] called on the Revisionist movement to revise its foreign policy orientation. Britain should no longer be relied upon as it was a declining imperial power. Moreover Achimeir, who believed in integral nationalism and admired Il Duce, rejected parliamentary democracy and demanded that Revisionism emulate the fascist model. Achimeir's pressure forced Jabotinsky to change his tactics and project himself as a radical politician. Consequently, he called for a 'final period of experiment, at the end of which the people of Israel could arrive at the right conclusions and clarify whether leaving the mandate in the hands of the British is compatible with the interests of Zionism'.[7] This was the first time, though not the last, that Jabotinsky had to cope with strong ideological and political opposition in his own movement. The crisis with the Achimeir faction reached its height in 1932–33, and only Achimeir's arrest staved off the Revisionist movement's internal disintegration. Achimeir made a come-back in 1936 but by then he was no longer a serious political rival to Jabotinsky. Yet his ideological influence remained formidable, and in 1937 the new exponents of maximalist views in Revisionism, such as Uriel Heilperin (later Ratosh), again attempted to revolutionise it by transforming it into a fighting liberation movement. Heilperin was followed by Begin and his colleagues in 1938, and finally by Avraham Stern in 1940.

Jabotinsky first parted company with the Zionist establishment in 1923, when he resigned from the Zionist executive. His complaint was that the executive, under Weizmann's leadership, had failed to extract from the British government an undertaking in favour of a more definitely pro-Zionist policy. Jabotinsky had his own views on how to secure British support. To realise them, he not only established a separate party in 1925 but, as early as 1923, set up a youth movement, *Betar*. Its prime function was educational: to forge the new Jewish personality and prepare recruits for future battalions which would protect the Jewish state from Arab interference during its formative periods. *Betar*'s twin symbols were Yosef Trumpeldor (who had died fighting the Arabs at Tel-Hai in 1920: the name *Betar* was an acronym of *Brit* [Alliance] Yosef Trumpeldor) and the city of Betar (the last Jewish stonghold of the Bar-Kochba rebellion, which fell to the

Romans in 135 CE). It was modelled on the Czech *Sokol* but was later also influenced by the Italian fascist *Ballila* and maintained a naval school at Civitavecchia. Its militarist leaders were strongly encouraged by Jabotinsky himself, attracted as he was to such heroic figures as Samson, Spartacus, Garibaldi and the Polish heroes Mickiewicz and Sienkiewicz. Still, Jabotinsky also tried to give it constructive functions, such as the 'recruiting troops' programme under which each *Betar* member was to volunteer to work for two years in Palestine to meet the needs of the coming Jewish state.[8]

By the 1930s Jabotinsky also found himself acting as supreme commander of the *Irgun Zvai Leumi* (IZL, National Military Organisation, also known as the *Irgun*) which had split from the *Haganah* in 1931 on purely military grounds. True, Jabotinsky did not originally intend the IZL to replace his dream of a revived, legal Jewish Legion. On the contrary, the Legion had a central standing in his ideology which the IZL never attained. For a while, he had even rejected the approaches of the IZL's founder and commander, Avraham Tehomi. But by 1936 Jabotinsky had come to appreciate that the IZL could become a useful tool in his overall campaign to achieve the leadership of the Zionist movement.

By 1937 the IZL was thus a purely Revisionist organisation. But neither it nor the later Stern Gang (*Lehi*) were products of the main body of evolutionary Revisionism. Rather, they were offshoots of its maximalist wing, which was dominated by three renegades from the Zionist Labour Movement. These were the historian-propagandist Abba Achimeir, already mentioned; the messianic prophet-poet Uri Zvi Greenberg[9]; and the right-radical journalist Yehoshua Heshel Yeivin[10] from *Ahdut Ha-Avodah* ('Unity of Labour'). What attracted them to Jabotinsky's movement was its leader's 'activist' image, gained by his adoption of views which originated in part with Max Nordau and Israel Zangwill.[11] Despite this infusion of former socialists, Jabotinsky's party remained firmly wedded to middle-class economic ideas, partly because of the social affiliation of his original supporters.

Virtually from the outset the labour movement saw the establishment of the Revisionist organisation as a direct provocation, not least because of its militant anti-working-class orientation. Thus it was no accident that Jabotinsky and his followers acquired the image of a fascist, and later Nazi, party. In large measure they themselves were responsible for that image. From its inception, Revisionism advocated the principle of 'Monism' – *Chad-Ness* (one banner) – and strongly rejected what Jabotinsky called the 'incongruous mixture' (*shaatnez*) of socialism and nationalism. Moreover, he claimed, the majority of the Jewish people belonged to the middle class and not the working class. Technological advances, he claimed, would lead to the disappearance of the proletariat. This 'modernising ideology', typical of the radical right of the inter-war era, went hand in hand with the advocacy of Italian fascist theories of corporatism and integralism. These included a legislature based on occupations, compulsory arbitration in labour disputes, the complete rejection of class war while the nation-building process continued, and last but not least the primacy of Nation over Class in all walks of life.[12]

In present-day Israel, Jabotinsky has once again become the subject of a trenchant ideological dispute. Shlomo Avineri described him as a disciple of integral nationalism and racism (that is, fascism), whereas Israel Eldad, the former *Lehi* ideologue, depicted him as a shining example of liberalism.[13]Jabotinsky himself seems to have behaved eclectically. He took from fascism what he found convenient, especially its socio-economic ideas; but his liberal heritage prevented him from adopting additional elements, as many of his adherents wished. For example, Jabotinsky remained a firm proponent of democracy; he also regarded reason as a surer guide to political action than either emotion or instinct. Furthermore, he formally – if not in practice – rejected the leadership principle so characteristic of fascism. He did not, before 1938, indulge in the glorification of violence by his maximalist followers, although in times of internal crisis he would encourage his followers by evoking myths and activist slogans such as 'to die or to conquer the mountain' (*Betar* anthem, March 1932) or recommending imitation of the Serbian national myth of Kossovo (*Betar* conference, Warsaw, September 1938); this was after the British hanged Shlomo Ben Yosef, a *Betar* member. If he was prone to use the word 'race' in connection with the Jews, it was meant, as so often during this period, more in the sense of 'people' or 'nation' than in the specific biological sense connoted by the German *Volk*.

Still, Revisionist ideology was reminiscent of the European radical right and was accompanied by violence, especially between 1930 and 1938, when Mussolini's racial legislation finally induced Revisionism to discard its pro-Italian orientation. Secretly, though, the *Irgun* in particular continued to flirt with Italy.

This was the period in which the Revisionist movement increased its proportion of the overall vote for delegates to the Zionist congress, from less than 7 per cent (18,000) in 1929 to 21 per cent (more than 55,000) in 1931. Zionism was then facing its most serious crisis to date – the 1929 riots and the 1930 White Paper. Numerically, Revisionism reached a peak in 1933, when it received more than 95,000 votes, though this represented a decline in its overall share. In 1935 the

Revisionists left the Zionist movement, claiming that the incipient New Zionist Organisation (NZO) could commmand the allegiance of 713,000 voters. This figure was certainly exaggerated.[14]

Jabotinsky ignored the dangers inherent in his assumption of three incompatible functions: president of the NZO, head of *Betar* and supreme commander of the IZL. Paradoxically, he also failed to foresee the coming crisis within Palestine, let alone that a world war was looming.[15] But these developments were to inject a completely new political-military mentality into Revisionism in general and into the IZL in particular. For many of his maximalist followers, Jabotinsky's pro-British orientation was now outdated. While he was still advocating his grand plan of establishing a 'colonising regime', they were being influenced by the concepts of war and liberation. Jabotinsky's concessions to the maximalists, such as the founding of a new Zionist organisation (1935), or the lip-service he paid by consenting to change the *Betar* oath in 1938, were of no avail, since the issue at stake was not organisational but ideological. The unbridgeable gap created in the Revisionist movement between its pro-British ideology and the political reality, especially after the White Paper of 1939, was bound to bring with it the final collapse of Revisionism, since its basic ethos was in ruins. Jabotinsky was fighting a losing battle, and his precipitate death in August 1940 signalled Revisionism's final collapse, parallel with that of its main bastion, Polish Jewry, now under Hitler's boot.

It was Begin who usurped power from Jabotinsky's political heirs, and not Stern and his disciples, since they, unlike Begin, totally rejected his leadership. Begin, rather than rebelling against the founding father, preferred to 'interpret' him in his own radical way, turning him into the 'Father of the Revolt'. In this sense the Sternists were far more intellectually honest. The price they paid for that honesty constitutes one of the main themes of this book.

*Lehi*, as it emerged in 1940, was a product of the sweeping crisis that engulfed the Revisionist movement at the moment of Jabotinsky's death. The founding father had been able to create the bridges necessary to maintain Revisionism as an unbroken movement in ideology and organisation, though always threatened by the maximalists. But none of his successors could keep it together. The cement, in the form of Jabotinsky's charismatic leadership, was missing. Yet Jabotinsky's dominance had extended only to the Revisionist movement as such; in *Betar* and in the IZL he had continuously lost ground since 1938, when his pro-British orientation failed to justify itself and the movement had to accept as a *fait accompli* the martyrs of *Betar* and of the IZL.

When Avraham Stern found that he could not succeed Jabotinsky he formed an underground movement which failed abysmally owing

to a lack of means and its faith in an Axis victory. However, its total
collapse in 1942 proved only temporary, though its revival the following year required a significant change of course. Unlike the IZL, it
tried to acquire legitimisation from the Zionist left. In external politics
it gradually leaned towards Soviet Russia, particularly after the Second
World War, a stance accompanied by the adoption of some elements
of communist ideology. This new vision of the world, in which Stalin
was to be the final moderator, did not alter *Lehi*'s radical right programme. Instead, it produced a new kind of ideology: a unique
amalgam of right and left, recalling the National Bolshevism of the
Weimar Republic, The Israeli public, though, was unconvinced, and
*Lehi* fared poorly in the elections to the first Knesset. Menachem
Begin's more simplistic interpretation of Jabotinsky's contradictory
messages was far more persuasive than the views propounded by the
trio of Nathan Yellin-Mor, Israel Eldad (Scheib) and Yitzchak Shamir.

This book describes and analyses the intense dialectical game
played by the *Lehi* leaders in their endeavour to preserve their original
heritage, together with their parallel and tireless effort to adapt to the
dramatically changing world around them. In fact, it was only the
relentless anti-British terrorist struggle that kept them together as the
ideological gaps within the leadership deepened between those who
sought reunification with the IZL and those who sought a *modus
vivendi* with the *Haganah*. The inevitable result was the movement's
disintegration. A final morale-boosting attempt – the assassination of
Count Bernadotte, the UN mediator – failed to achieve its purpose, as
was demonstrated by the outcome of the Knesset elections.

# PART ONE

# REVISIONISM IN THE 1930s

# 1

# The Revisionist Movement: A Revolutionary Liberation Movement?

Despite the hopes which he placed in the British, Jabotinsky had suffered disappointments from the beginning of their rule. These intensifed with the 'Wailing Wall' incident on the Day of Atonement (24 September) 1928, when the governor of Jerusalem, Keith-Roach, ordered the removal of the barrier separating men and women worshippers. Together with the subsequent riots of 1929, that event generated a traumatic change, not for Jabotinsky himself, but for the newly affiliated members of his Revisionist movement.

Both ideology and tactics began to change with the appearance on the scene of Abba Achimeir, Uri Zvi Greenberg and Yehoshua Heshel Yeivin. In 1927, before he joined the Revisionist movement, Achimeir had already claimed that England could have been relied on had its imperialism been a hundred years younger, but not now. Italian fascism had now to be the political model.[1] Both publicly and privately, Achimeir called upon Jabotinsky to adopt Mussolini's theory of power and his elitist doctrine ('Sir, why do you consult with us so excessively? Command us *more*.. We are obliged to obey you. Perhaps privately you desire to be a friend amongst friends . . . but fate has chosen you to lead, and you *must not* sidestep this role').[2] Unlike Jabotinsky, who was inclined to deflect his anger from England to the official Zionist leadership, Achimeir also regarded the British as the real culprits, accusing them of fomenting dissent between Arabs and Jews.[3] The leaders of the *Yishuv* (the Jewish community in Palestine) themselves displayed a cringing deference to the British authorities in Palestine. The *Yishuv* lacked the 'desire to rule' and would not be able to attain its goals unless cured of its three illnesses – the *haluka* (distribution of charity funds), socialist 'vegetarianism' and 'nativisation' by a handful of Englishmen. Instead it must follow the example of small peoples who had fought for their freedom and honour: the Boers in South Africa, those of the Tyrol who fought Napoleon, and above all the heroes of Yodepheth, the Temple Mount, Massada, Betar and Tel Hai.[4]

At this stage Jabotinsky avoided a confrontation with Achimeir, who was not challenging his leadership, merely his doctrine.[5] But the uprecedented bloodshed of the summer of 1929 (when 133 Jews were killed and 339 wounded) aggravated the tension within the Revisionist movement between Jabotinsky and his disciples. Jabotinsky regarded the events as 'a terrible insult for us and a disgrace for the British nation, but they are not a holocaust'.[6] Others, however, argued that England had now to decide whether she was for or against Zionism; otherwise Zionists might turn elsewhere.[7] Moreover, while Jabotinsky still emphasised the 'common [that is, the anti-Arab] interests' linking Britain and the Jews and continued to stress Britain's energetic and honourable role, Achimeir and Yeivin portrayed the British Prime Minister as a latter-day Tsar. Ramsay MacDonald covered up the massacre of Hebron just as Nicholas II had covered up the pogrom at Kishinev.[8] Lingering assumptions of 'common interests' received another blow with the publication of the report of the Shaw Commission of Inquiry. Could it be, Yeivin asked, that a vast empire, ruling 500 million human beings without asking for their agreement, could speak of annoying 'a handful of mutinous [Arabs] as a reason for violating international guarantees'?[9]

The sense of shock generated among Revisionist maximalists by the events of 1929, together with their disappointment towards England, is well expressed in Greenberg's poetry.

> You have deceived me, O King; we, the wounded people, called you:
> Cyrus the King, world champion of kings! . . .
> We loved no other flag in the world like yours!
> . . . We must have greatly erred in trusting the Gentile![10]

Greenberg's solution was a secular messianism: . . . *nation of Jews awaiting the Messiah . . .*

> . . . a beleaguered nation of Jews.
> Surrounded by armies of hate, both Christian and Moslem
> and from each drop of Jewish blood will a *bloodstone* be formed
> and out of one such stone and another an eternal wall for that nation
> until the advent of Messiah and the thunder of the wheel in time.[11]

The twofold confrontation with the Arabs and the British was a historical necessity; the British 'stand in our way like a barrier before the Messiah. They have consigned us to plunder and death at the hands of the filthiest people in the East'.[12]

Unlike Greenberg, Revisionist theoreticians did not ascribe a mystical-apocalyptic dimension to the situation of Jewry in general, or to that of Zionism in particular. But his fellow maximalists did believe that Jewry could only be saved by a meta-historical process of messianic salvation. Achimeir provides an example. Ordinarily, his Spenglerian outlook would have presupposed the decline of Judaism, but he was able to produce a gloss on the events of 1929 which saw them as a link in the chain of Jewish wars since Pharaoh, Rome, the Inquisition and the Tsar. They had all defeated the Jewish people, but where were they today? 'Can we not overcome a few dishonourable muftis, effendis and sheikhs . . .?' In his eyes the twentieth-century Arabs were no better than the Arameans, the Philistines, the descendants of Lot, the Canaanites, Prizzites and Girgashites, who had all disappeared from the stage of history. In contrast, the Jewish nation was a people distinguished by immortality. Theirs had not been a real defeat, but a transient one, which contained the seeds of future victory, like that of France in 1870.[13] The romance between 'perfidious Albion' and 'innocent Jewry' had now come to a very disappointing end. Promises stemming from political intrigue were not to be believed: 'Study the entirety of world history and find where the messiah of any nation whatsoever crossed over a bridge of paper [Jabotinsky's term]!'.[14] There was an ideal behind the suffering of the victims in their desire to overcome the trauma of persisting exile. Thus, they said 'It is good that this happened to us'. Here, then, was a decisive historical moment.[15]

Jabotinsky himself still refused to believe that all chances of a partnership with England were gone, though his faith had been weakened, and he too talked of seeking an alternative power.[16] None the less, in the summer of 1930, dismissing the 'hysterical' pessimism of his disciples, he called for England to be given 'a last chance', since the real blame lay with the errors of the official 'Zionist leadership.[17]

Achimeir, however, had been certain as early as 1928. The publication of the Shaw Commission Report and the 1930 Passfield White Paper had provided the impetus for his nationalistic theories. For the Jewish people, he reasoned, 'to whatever extent the goal is supreme, all kinds of suffering are indeed feasible'. The goal could be Mount Moriah, where the temple of the movement would be built, or it could be Golgotha, where its bearers would be crucified. He proposed transferring the centre of Zionist leadership to Paris and Warsaw. France had interests in the Middle East and was independent of England, whereas Warsaw housed the Jewish masses. Zionism was in a position comparable to that of France after 1871 and Russia after the 1905 revolution, whereas England was in the position of Rome in its decline in the fourth century. The Jewish people was not made up of ghetto dwellers, but of heroic millions.[18] Here was the source of those myths characteristic of maximalist thought in Revisionism – later to be inherited by Stern and his followers – for the lack of triumphant heroism was merely incidental, to be blamed on the leadership. Had the *Yishuv* been trained to take up arms when called upon, Hebron and Safed would still have been safe.[19]

The Passfield White Paper, with its harsh rulings on 'questions of life and death' for Zionism (immigration, land and the character of the regime) prompted Jabotinsky's disciples in Palestine to call for a war of liberation, even though he himself continued to adhere to the political option. Achimeir, however, rejected Jabotinsky's idea of a mass movement: 'In a liberation movement large numbers are value-less, human cannon fodder is valueless, herds are valueless; small numbers are valuable, as is activism, as are the youth.' A minority of heroes would establish the 'Kingdom of Israel', not within the borders prescribed by Herbert Samuel, but rather within those maintained by King David and Joab, his general.[20] These notions were inherited with only minor changes by the IZL and the Stern group. The new activism led, on 9 October 1930, to a demonstration against Dr Drummond Shiels, Under-Secretary for the Colonies, then on a visit to Palestine, during which Achimeir was beaten and arrested.[21] Now, for the first time, Jabotinsky explicitly rejected fascism.[22]

MacDonald's letter of 13 February 1931, a reversal of Passfield's White Paper on immigration and settlement, became a positive turning-point in the history of Zionism, since it facilitated the trans-formation of the Jewish *Yishuv* from a small settlement of about 170,000 in 1931 to one of 370,000 by the time of the Arab uprising of 1936. This could have become a turning-point in the development of Revisionism as well, had Jabotinsky considered it a positive document. He was, however, constrained by an ideology which expected the British to achieve greater Zionist ends by means of a classic colonial formula. Such a dogmatic ideology led eventually to extremist politics among his followers in Palestine, because of their high expectations. This explains the negative reception Jabotinsky awarded the letter: not only did it not abrogate the White Paper, but it actually made the achievement of Zionism conditional upon Arab acquiescence.[23]

Towards the end of 1931 Jabotinsky began secretly to look for an alternative country to put pressure on England. Achimeir had already openly talked to Italy the previous May. One did not have to be a fascist to admit that fascism had succeeded in removing distasteful social theories such as communism in the West. The Italian and the Jewish peoples had much in common – they each had high hopes of immigration, they were each proletarian and each possessed a super-fluous population.[24]

The seventeenth Zionist congress, convened in July 1931 in Basel, would, for Jabotinsky, determine who would hold sway in the Zionist organisation, he or those he termed 'the band of spiritual bastards', a group 'I despise coldly and greatly'.[25] The refusal of the majority at the congress to accept the resolution proposed by the Revisionists concerning the declaration of a Jewish state as Zionism's final goal was to cause Jabotinsky and his organisation to secede from the Zionist organisation within less than five years. Meanwhile the gap between Jabotinsky and his maximalist disciples in Palestine widened. He still relied upon the 'innocent' (his term) belief in 'the integrity of the world, in the power of justice'.[26] They, however, were becoming more radical. At Basel, Greenberg delivered a speech in full symbolic-messianic strain in which he accused the congress itself of making a mockery of the Jewish people and of placing them at the mercy of their English and Arab enemies.[27] In October 1931 Achimeir's circle of *Betar* youth established the 'League of *Sicarii*' as an expression of direct action.[28]

The radical trio – Achimeir, Greenberg and Yeivin – had indeed now reached a crisis in their relations with Jabotinsky. According to Achimeir, the difference between Jabotinsky and Weizmann was nothing more than an 'atmosphere of pressure'. Nevertheless Jabotinsky might yet be freed from the political functionaries of the Revisionist movement. According to one of the participants (Yaakov Orenstein, later a close aide of Avraham Stern) the first meeting of the League of *Sicarii* discussed whether to take up arms. Those who felt that the hour had not yet come, left. Decisions were then taken to recruit members, hoard arms and plan operations. Practically speaking, the League was a failure, though it played an important role in the formulation of Revisionist maximalist ideology, which was later to be expressed in practice by the IZL and the Stern group. The inner circle of the League adopted the view of Yosef Katznelson, a close associate of Achimeir (and later of Stern) who argued that the British constituted the greatest stumbling-block to the Jewish state and that the Arabs were merely an instrument in their hands. The other members were, like Jabotinsky, still of the opinion that Great Britain supported the Arabs because of their fighting spirit and that if the Jews attacked the Arabs, the British would change their minds.[29]

But despite the loud proclamations, no further anti-British activities were launched. The glorification of the League stems from the later nostalgia of its veterans and their jealousy of the propaganda and practical success of the IZL and Stern group. It was not the trial of the League members after the murder of Arlosoroff (Head of the Political Department of the Jewish Agency) in 1933 which prevented their launching the war of liberation, but the general lessening of tension. A real underground movement would not emerge until the 'Arab Uprising' of 1936–39 and the publication of MacDonald's White

Paper in 1939.[30] The League did, however, create the precedent of a revolutionary handful of people viewing themselves as activist pioneers, and of the cult of imprisonment: the road to the 'Kingdom of Israel' led through prison dungeons.[31]

Even Jabotinsky was carried along by this wave. Writing to Richard Lichtheim early in the summer of 1931, he disavowed the actions of Achimeir and his colleagues.[32] But he was forced to rule in favour of the founding of the League, lest he lose control of his own movement. This led to one of his most famous articles, *Oyfn Pripitshek* ('At the Fireside') in which he called upon the youth to learn to shoot, saying that without militarism there would be no hope for Zionism; for the first time he accused the British of 'treachery'.[33] The extremist trend was shown by disturbances at the Hebrew University when Norman Bentwich was appointed to the Chair of International Peace in February 1932. Within two days, his lecture was interrupted at the instigation of the Revisionist student unions (*El Al* and *Hulda)* which called for the foundation of a Jewish *military* academy. Fifteen of the people causing the disturbance were arrested, including Achimeir, Raziel, Perlmutter and Dviri. Raziel, Perlmutter and Stern (though he was not present) were expelled from the university, but were later re-admitted.[34] It was the League of *Sicarii* trials following the murder of Arlosoroff that were to save Jabotinsky from the final confrontation with the maximalists.

Notwithstanding their impressive showing in the elections to the seventeenth Zionist congress, in which they secured 21 per cent of the votes, the Revisionists failed to attain power. That defeat further encouraged the rejection of democracy among Achimeir's followers. Revisionism's mandate to speak for the nation did not come from the polls but from the 'tragedy, rage and hope . . the years of blood, shame and tears from Hebron of 1929 to the White Paper . . . and the torturing of Jews living throughout the diaspora . . .'. The Narodniks too had spoken in the name of the entire people in the face of a somnolent, stupid, apathetic and treacherous population.[35]

Still ambivalent, Jabotinsky did not bow to the radicals' pressure. But his position was shifting. For the first time, he praised the activities of Achimeir and his colleagues, prophesying that he would yet play an important part 'in our world affairs', adding: 'Greetings to you from afar, Abba Achimeir, our Teacher!'[36] He also called upon his followers to 'ignore' the immigration laws which violated 'morality and integrity', since curbs on immigration constituted a form of murder. The Mandatory Power had lost all legal rights to demand obedience to its laws. Using such language for the first time, he called the British authorities 'a gang of foreigners' trying to take control of Palestine by violating their word of honour – meaning the Balfour Declaration and the Mandate. He called for controlled disobedience, including the refusal to pay taxes and 'intolerance' towards the police. Overnight, so it seemed, Jabotinsky had become an adherent of the cult of imprisonment, with Gandhi as his symbol. Echoing Achimeir's style, Jabotinsky also asked whether 'it really is true that we are still a living nation'.[37] Events had now reached a climax. For the first time, Jabotinsky dropped the axiom of 'common interests' and was prepared to use Achimeir to strengthen revisionist *tactical* ideology.

Jabotinsky now analysed why a power other than Britain might lend Zionism its support. The imperial value of Palestine would be further enhanced were a waterway, parallel to the Suez Canal, to be constructed between Gaza and Aqaba; still more influential would be the transformation of the Bay of Acre into the largest harbour in the Mediterranean basin, servicing a formidable local economy. Only a Jewish state could facilitate the detachment of the land from its Arab environment and its permanent attachment to Europe, and its role as a Jewish refuge.[38] Jabotinsky's firmer attitude to England may have stemmed from his expectations of Mussolini; alternatively, he may have regarded such proclamations as a tactical means of putting pressure on England. Whatever the case, their influence upon the IZL, the Stern group and the Revisionists in later years was significant: these organisations transformed, in part, these tactics to strategy. During the next two weeks Jabotinsky was to encourage the strategic rather than the tactical interpretation, even floating the idea that the League of Nations directly administer the Mandate.[39] Such notions provided the League of *Sicarii* with further opportunities to direct its anger against Britain.[40]

It became evident at the national convention of the Revisionist movement in Palestine that it was only with regard to tactics that Achimeir and Jabotinsky had attained a meeting of minds. Achimeir spoke of two trends in the movement: one favouring salons, the other, imprisonment. The latter trend was not open to the masses who vote, but only to a sacrificial minority – the *sansculottes* who would realise Zionism. Jacob Weinschal (a leading Revisionist and later a biographer of Stern) accepted the educational value of the activities of such a group but argued for a mass movement. Jabotinsky tried to bridge the gap between the two, hoping that some combination of the two approaches would help show the world the tragic contrast between the Mandate and the regime.[41] On the one hand, he supported the idea of a mass petition to interested governments to make them more aware of the Jewish question. At the same time, however, he acknowledged the importance of the League of *Sicarii* to the wider movement:

We would simply be blind if we underestimated the great moral influence exercised by the 'Achimeir spirit' in the lands of the diaspora . . . Sometimes, to be sure, their activities are not carried out in the right way, and this is a pity, as the fact is that an ideology of resistance to ironed trousers is developing there rapidly. But I should not, for such a reason, advise us to dissolve this camp, even if we are able to do so.[42]

How, then, did the Revisionists maintain their unity? First, their basic assumption was that their differences with official Zionism were far greater than their internal disagreements. For thousands of years of Jewish history, Yeivin claimed, two doctrines had fought one another: one had viewed the Jewish nation as a nation like any other, seeking out conquests and a 'material life'; the other had favoured rising above earthly political accomplishment in order to become a 'priestly kingdom'. This argument had begun with the dispute between the prophet Samuel and the people concerning the need for a king, and had continued with the attempt of the Sages to obscure the heroism of Bar-Kochba, the Ahad Ha'am–Berdichevsky debate, and the attempts to belittle the achievements of Aharonson and Trumpeldor. Jabotinsky concurred; neither did he oppose the proposition that the main disaster was on the home front. The proponents of pacifist, socialist and bi-national doctrines were more dangerous than the external enemy. He did not disagree with the need for Achimeir's 'disobedient Zionism' to achieve its goals 'by all means', nor did he question the evils of the situation which allowed Jewish youth to be educated against a background of charity-seekers and emissaries instead of militant resistance.[43]

But Achimeir refused to confuse tactics with strategy. On the eve of the fifth world conference of the Revisionist movement, he rejected the idea of the petition ('There are more concrete ways [to raise the Palestine question] than occupying the youthful army of the movement of national revival in collecting signatures').[44] Shortly thereafter he even praised individual terrorism, applauding the assassination of the French President, Paul Doumer, at the hands of Pavel Gorgulov.[45] Achimeir had expressed such ideas as early as 1926, when he had written his 'Scroll of the *Sicarii*' which became so well known following the League of *Sicarii* trial in 1933. He even justified the assassination of the *Agudat Israel* leader, Jacob de Haan in 1924 and the attempt on Mussolini's life in 1926.[46]

Notwithstanding his search for a compromise formula, Jabotinsky could not accept these notions. *Betar*, he made clear, was a legal organisation striving to achieve a legal aim; the League of *Sicarii* had to refrain from violating 'the moral rule of the sanctity of human life, except in self-defence'.[47] Jabotinsky's position was, however, becoming increasingly difficult. He was now forced to admit that he himself had been guilty of encouraging the *sansculottes* ideology by calling Achimeir 'our teacher' (although he insisted that he had not thereby intended support of Achimeir's plan and ideology). He was prepared to accept parallel tactics, but not a parallel ideology. The ideology of 'only an underground, the rest is unnecessary!' he rejected as 'near-sighted, nervous impressionism. Sometimes diplomacy should be used, at other times adventurism; occasionally the spirit of peace, and on other occasions – the spirit of war.' As a general rule, Jabotinsky considered the Revisionist movement an 'orchestra', lacking both ideological collectivism and ideological pluralism – a movement of opportunism, changing tactics on the way to the final strategic goal.[48]

The differences in outlook became plain during the course of a secret argument between Jabotinsky and Yeivin in 1932. The latter claimed that the classical Revisionist outlook was dead and buried; Jabotinsky replied that the maximalist alternative lacked 99 per cent of the elements of Zionism, being based on 'forbidden romance'. Self-sacrifice was indeed a requirement, but not a sanctified one. The attempt to introduce into the heart of the Revisionist movement a *sansculottes* ideology was nothing less than an attempt to expel him from his own party. Were they to win, he would leave it, because it was a democratic party built on nineteenth-century lines. Its 'legionary revolutionary character', justifying '*karamola*' (rebellion), was only acceptable 'at necessary and proper times'.[49]

Assured that the maximalists would, for the time being, limit themselves to a political struggle,[50] Jabotinsky still tried to bridge his differences with them at the Vienna conference in the summer of 1932. As the 'moral' mandate given to the British had now been 'torn up', his 'petition movement' would force Britain to alter her policies. Under pressure from an aggressive maximalist delegation, he promised that in Palestine itself 'deeper and broader steps' would be taken. The *Yishuv* would not settle for verbal protests: 'Palestine shall develop into a country of *resistance*, with deep differences between the government and part of the populace, a profound and tangible difference'.[51] There was thus a contradiction in Jabotinsky's relations with the maximalists as well as in his expectations of the British. On the one hand, he expected England to make a change for the better – such as accepting the idea of a new Jewish Legion – while on the other he spoke pessimistically of the future of British rule in the Middle East.[52]

Altogether, in fact, Jabotinsky was standing on increasingly weak ground. Although the maximalists had aroused opposition in several circles, there was no open demand at the conference for their removal from the Revisionist movement – notwithstanding their image as supporters of Mussolini and Hitler.[53] Jabotinsky vehemently rejected Achimeir's demand for a dictatorship, emphasising the democracy of the Revisionist movement. But, as expected, he simultaneously announced that he would not expel Achimeir from his movement. With the future of the Revisionist movement at stake, Jabotinsky chose compromise. Achimeir, however, was still able to cling to his hopes of conquering the entire Revisionist movement.[54] The latter's programme was clear and unambiguous: Palestine did not belong to the Jewish nation because the Jews had not yet spilt their blood for it; it belonged to England for English soldiers had spilt their blood in its conquest.[55] Clearly, he would not be impressed with Jabotinsky's plan to establish a Jewish Legion. Jewish 'martyrs' or heroes in the service of foreign ideals were not the point.

Overshadowing these debates was Hitler's victory in the elections to the Reichstag on 31 July 1932, which transformed the Nazis into the largest German party. This event made a lasting impression on Achimeir and Yeivin. Just a few days before, Yeivin had written of 'Hitler, the builder of the new, Great Germany' (though in the same breath admitting he was the planner 'with great consistency of his Haman-programme to destroy the Jews'). The value of Nazism, in his eyes, was the 'terrible blow' it had struck against 'false Zionism' ('the Zionism of Ahad Ha-am' which controlled official Zionism both in Jerusalem and in Berlin).[56] For both Yeivin and Achimeir there was no distinction between Nazism and other movements of national liberation.[57] Hitler's triumph only fuelled Achimeir's praise of him and Mussolini. Their ideologies, he reasoned, were realistic romanticism. Just as Germany and Italy worshipped their past, so too did the Jews.

There were two reasons why Hitler's accession to the German chancellorship on 31 January 1933 did not serve as a warning of things to come to the revolutionaries of Achimeir's school. One was their convoluted conception that its real meaning was 'the bankruptcy of the whole system of [Jewish] assimilation';[59] the other was their blind hatred of socialism and communism, which was greater than their strictly limited hatred of Nazism.[60] Achimeir called upon the masses to learn from the success of Nazism – 'the German chauvinist movement'. He himself drew four 'healthy' conclusions: (1) it is forbidden to trample proudly on the soul of a nation; (2) complete 'anti-Dubnovism' – the bankruptcy of those schools of thought favouring the diaspora; (3) assimilation is hopeless, for healthy nations guard their own purity from 'national bastardy', both physically and intellectually; (4) Germany, the greatest of the gentile nations, is gradually being cured of communism. Hitler was thus the expression of the rage of a healthy people whose national pride had been violated. What the pogroms of 1881 did for the Jews of Russia, Nazism did for the Jews of Germany. Now only the possibility of a substantial alternative option for the Jews of the Soviet Union bothered him: 'Either the destiny of Russian Jewry or . . . the Kingdom of Israel in the Near East! There is no third possibility.'[61]

Neither Achimeir nor Yeivin was convinced by Jabotinsky's argument that Hitler might indeed put his anti-Semitic programmes, an integral part of his ideology, into practice.[62] Yeivin explained that Nazism was not a return to barbarism, but rather the abandonment of internationalist ideals and a return to the nationalist idea. Germany would inflict only 'material ruin' upon her Jews and would 'vomit' them out of herself. Hitler was no different from other European rulers who desired to bring the Jews of Europe to a state of hunger and rot.[63]

The maximalists now wanted to hasten the secession of the Revisionist movement from the Zionist organisation.[64] Achimeir took as a sign of victory the publication on 22 March 1933 of the Lodz Manifesto, in which Jabotinsky forced the moderates in his movement to accept his view in the face of the expected secession.[65] Three days later *Hazit Ha-Am* ('The People's Front') came out in open support of Nazism: 'The socialists and communists think that Hitler's movement is a mere shell – but we think it has both shell and content. The anti-Semitic shell should be discarded, but not its anti-Marxist content.'[66] The newspaper further called on the members of the Revisionist movement in Palestine to put themselves 'uniformly at the disposal of the leader!' who was finally assuming solitary control of his movement. Jabotinsky quickly dissociated himself from the title of dictator.[67]

Eventually, the Nazis' anti-Jewish boycott, initiated on 1 April, and the anti-Jewish legislation which followed, pushed *Hazit Ha-Am* into following Jabotinsky's boycott against Germany: 'If Germany is against Judaea, Judaea will be against Germany. Take fright, enemies of Israel in Berlin, as the God of the hosts of Israel rises up.'[68] Nevertheless, Jabotinsky attacked the maximalists: 'The articles and collages on Hitler and the Hitler movement appearing in *Hazit Ha-Am* are, for me and for us all, a stab in the back.' He warned the chairman of the Revisionist centre in Palestine, Dr Avraham Weinschal, of his intention to demand the expulsion of Achimeir and Yeivin from the Revisionist movement if one more line in praise of Nazism as a national liberation movement appeared, and demanded that they actively join the 'attacks' on Hitler.[69]

In fact, members of the League of *Sicarii* had begun to carry out anti-Nazi operations even before Jabotinsky sent his letter to Weinshal. On 13 May they set fire to the entrance of the German consulate in

Jerusalem, the next day they tore down the flag of the German consulate in Jaffa; two weeks later they did the same in Jerusalem.[70] One possible reason for the change may have been the Nazi boycott of 1 April and Jabotinsky's article, 'The Revisionist movement and Germany';[71] another might have been the forthcoming elections to the eighteenth Zionist congress.[72] The verbal struggle, punctuated by violent clashes between the Revisionists and labour movement, now reached a new climax following the murder of Arlosoroff on 16 June 1933. That very day, *Hazit Ha-Am* accused Arlosoroff of signing an agreement with Germany in return for Jewish rights.[73]

During the legal proceedings arising from the murder, the extremism of the League of the *Sicarii* was fully exposed. Achimeir, it seemed, wanted an armed revolution, not mere blasts of the *shofar*.[74] Yeivin declared himself prepared to achieve power over the bridge of blood libels.[75] Throughout the trial Achimeir and his colleagues received encouragement from their supporters and from Jabotinsky, and thus the ideological dispute between Jabotinsky and the maximalists came to a temporary halt. Achimeir did not come out openly against the British, but spoke highly of the late NILI (Zionist underground in the First World War) heroes, and especially of Sarah Aharonson, the Joan of Arc of Israel.[76] Yeivin, still adhering to the British partnership, none the less argued that the 'hunting of the terrorists' – the illegal immigrants – by the police, would only help Zionism because revolutionary movements are strengthened by persecution.[77]

Achimeir was acquitted of all charges in the Arlosoroff murder trial on 16 May 1934. On 12 July he, Yeivin, Lichter, Svorai, Dviri, Orenstein and Yosef Katznelson were charged with belonging to the League of *Sicarii*, and a week later five of them were sentenced to imprisonment.[78] The Arlosoroff affair was to inject further poison into the relations between the two wings of Zionism for some time. Indeed, both sides perceived it as part of a world struggle between right and left.[79] Achimeir and his colleagues lost their position as an activist faction within Revisionism; on the other hand, they became the martyrs of the entire movement. Not even the documents published during their trial early in the summer of 1933 could shake their new position.[80]

## THE ESTABLISHMENT OF THE *IRGUN ZVAI LEUMI* (IZL) AND ITS IDEOLOGICAL DEVELOPMENT

The events of 1929 also led to a split in the *Haganah*. This was instigated by Avraham Tehomi, who did not believe that the *Haganah* was militaristic enough. As early as the seventeenth congress, Tehomi tried to interest Jabotinsky in his new organisation – *Irgun Bet* (Organisation B) – *Ha-Haganah Ha-Leumit* (National Defence).[81] This constituted a clique of officers in Jerusalem (*Ha-Suhba* – the Association of Friends), formed around the commander of the local branch of *Irgun Bet* – Abraham Krichevsky, and including Avraham Stern, Hillel Kook and David Raziel. Although they stressed their non-political nature, most members of *Ha-Suhba* had no roots in *Betar*. They were drawn to maximalist Revisionism by its models of national liberation and adoration of the heroes of Jewish history.[82]

After 1929 Yeivin encouraged the members of *Ha-Haganah Ha-Leumit* to become the independent 'Jewish force in the homeland' to defend the settlements, thus facilitating further immigration and settlement. This notion arose from Jabotinsky's idea of the Legions, but was now to be applied in a radically different ideological context. As a result of frustration with British Zionist politics, the *Irgun* and automatically *Betar*, in the late 1930s, became a terrorist underground, contrary to Jabotinsky's own wishes.

Yeivin's writings in *Ha-Metsuda* ('The Fortress', which was *Ha-Suhba*'s bulletin) differed considerably from his articles in the public press. The Yeivin of *Doar Ha-Yom* ('Daily Mail') or of *Hazit Ha-Am* wrote in a mystical messianic vein. In *Ha-Metsuda* he was more realistic. With no foreseeable prospect of altering the demographic balance in Palestine (then four to one in favour of the Arabs), quality rather than quantity had to be emphasised. This could be attained by both technical and psychological training. The latter was more diffi-cult than the former because, in the first place the *Yishuv* tended to preach pacifism, with slogans like 'the life of your brotherly neighbour' is as valuable as that of 'your Jewish mother', and second, there was the feeling of distaste brought on by the concept of militarism.[83] This new force would rid the *Yishuv* of its dependence on 'costly' British military aid. Herzl himself had argued that an army was not a necessary evil, but should be *the* aim of the builders of the Jewish state, with all ready to die for the national flag. Raziel himself spoke of the need for sacrifice even before Stern. The hope was 'not . . . to die on some hospital cot, but rather to absorb the final bullet aimed at destroying the Jewish *Yishuv*'.[84]

Unlike Achimeir's circle, *Ha-Haganah Ha-Leumit* did not consider the Nazis to be a model national liberation movement, but felt that Jews should respond to Germany by forming a strong organisation to protect Jewish honour and life.[85] Yeivin sought to challenge Jabotinsky in the IZL's bulletin. The events of 1929 had destroyed the illusion that 'rights alone, with no active force visible at its side, can influence the nations of the world . . . only if we seem strong will this have any effect on the world.'[86]

Avraham Stern gave poetical expression to the IZL's viewpoint in his 'Unidentified Soldiers' which became the IZL's (and *Lehi's*) anthem. His central motif was personal sacrifice; 'Our desire is to be free men forever! Our dream: to die for our people!'[87] The IZL sought to reinterpret Jewish history, especially that of the Bar-Kochba period, from the radical national point of view, so as not to repeat the mistakes of 1929. Thus they recruited to their service Professor Joseph Klausner, whose qualifications as a historian of the Second Temple period were more nationalistic than scientific. Klausner judged national uprisings not by their result, but in the light of national liberty and honour. Though Bar-Kochba had brought about the destruction of Judaea and the annihilation of half a million Jews, the alternative was for the entire people to sink into slavery and degradation. This is what happened to the Samaritans, whereas the Jews survived as a great struggling nation – taking into exile Bar-Kochba's spirit of rebellion, which gave them the inner fortitude to resist oppressors and eventually attain national rebirth.[88] For Yeivin too, the insurrection had opened a glorious new page in the history of the nation. If Bar-Kochba's 'doctrine of flint' were adopted, his kingdom would rise again from the ashes.[89]

### THE EVE OF THE ARAB REBELLION

Apart from his poems and scattered hints in his private letters, few sources describe the development of Avraham Stern's political thinking before the first split in the IZL (April 1937). In 1929 Stern was a 21-year-old student who had four years earlier emigrated from his native Poland. He had been one of the first to respond to Achimeir's call: 'We love the land of Israel more than our own lives, for we are willing to dedicate ourselves and our lives to her', he wrote to his future mother-in-law.[90] Later testimony tells of his rejection of the faulty conspiracy of the League of the *Sicarii*.[91]

There was also something of Achimeir in Stern's response to the Passfield White Paper of 1931.[92] The analysis of Jewish history which he wrote in 1932 was clearly influenced by Yeivin and Achimeir. Jewish experience had wavered between heroism and persecution. Hatred of the Jew had begun with Pharaoh, Haman and Antiochus. Yet there had been the heroic tradition: Mattathias, Judas Maccabbaeus, Bar Giora, Yohanan of Giscala, Elazar Ben Yair (Stern's ideal Jewish figure throughout his life) and Bar-Kochba. He saw himself continuing in this essentially optimistic tradition: 'Israel was defeated, but not shamed: Judaea was subjugated, but not profaned.' Even in the Middle Ages, though the Jews rarely fought 'with a strong hand', they had always remained true to their faith and their nation and had died martyrs. Achimeir's less optimistic outlook saw martyrdom and self-sacrifice as incompatible concepts. For Stern a persecuted people is not vanquished, but maintains its solidarity. None the less, the incessant persecutions at the end of the Middle Ages had weakened the spirit of the people, with only momentary hopes of redemption. The last, that of Shabbetei Zvi, was followed by increased anti-Semitism and assimilation. Finally the pogroms of the 1880s in Russia opened the eyes of the assimilationist Jewish intelligentsia and aroused the people. Still the situation of the Jewish people was getting worse. Jews were persecuted everywhere. Racism had complemented political, religious and economic hatred. The assimilationists closed ranks with the enemies of the people, and communism tried to destroy the Jewish people in the diaspora as a separate entity. In Palestine the Jews were confronted with the Arab danger – 'the dissolution of generations' and 'eternal savagery'. However, there existed a solution: 'a unified and united organised body to become the army of redemption, standing ready along the iron front opposing every enemy and self hater; a body of free men striving to liberate the nation and build the state.'[93]

As regards the Arabs, they were not a nation fighting for their freedom, but an 'unruly mob', too easily incited against the Jews by the 'hidden criminal propaganda' of the Comintern. Their frequent attacks on Jews reflected their cruelty and a 'wonderful' expertise in the use of various weapons.[94] Unlike Jabotinsky, Stern could not see Great Britain or any other Mandatory Power forcing a Jewish state on the Arabs. They had to be overcome by Jewish heroic forces themselves.

At a later stage, *Lehi* was to obscure Stern's anti-communist ideology, and to replace it with a mythical pro-communism. In the early 1930s, however, Stern still held firmly to the conventional Revisionist concepts, somewhere between Jabotinsky and Achimeir and Yeivin. In February 1934, while studying in Florence, Italy, he organised the local Revisionist branch, seeking recruits from the fascist party. He even actively supported Jabotinsky's national petition, which had little in common with the martyrological tone of his contemporary poems.[95] In fact, it was not until 1936 that he completely absorbed Achimeir's ideas, when he was influenced by Uriel Heilperin (Ratosh) – an altogether more independent and systematic disciple of Achimeir.[96] Even his awareness of Britain's 'betrayal' post-dated 1934. Moreover, when the crisis with Jabotinsky and Revisionism finally broke, Stern and his associates still retained the main axioms they had inherited from Jabotinsky, Achimeir, Yeivin, Greenberg and Heilperin, minus the relationship with England.

\*

None of the available sources indicates when the paths trod by Zeev Jabotinsky and Avraham Stern converged and when they separated. What we do know is that at the beginning of 1935 Stern was in Krakow in connection with the sixth world convention of the Revisionist movement. He listened to Jabotinsky and admitted that his speech contained several good phrases. But he also remarked that Jabotinsky was ageing and was no longer the same person who had been able to arouse the masses.[97] It is impossible to say whether Stern already considered himself the alternative to what he regarded as Jabotinsky's fading leadership (as was certainly the case towards the end of the 1930s). It was still too early to speak of a confrontation between the two men.

In March 1934 the Revisionists renewed their interest in Italy. Mussolini seemed to be supporting a Jewish state, which would be 'most valuable' for the Revisionist petition, and to 'comprehend' that three million Jews would serve Italian interests better than 25 million Arabs. Even if the Jewish state had a population of 16 million, it would not be a military threat to Italian interests.[98] Jabotinsky again returned to the question of an Italian orientation in January 1935, though indirectly. He rejected fascism, ruling that the Jewish state should adopt a liberal constitution (this was apparently after Italian aggression in Ethiopia at the close of 1934).[99] However, at the end of March 1935, the Revisionist organ *Ha-Yarden* quoted Italian newspaper reports that Il Duce had himself indicated that the transformation of Palestine into an independent kingdom would solve the Jewish question. Not surprisingly, the Revisionist newspaper now began to take an openly pro-Italian line in the Ethiopian dispute.[100]

Poland also influenced the Revisionists and they took the opportunity of Pilsudski's death for *Betar* to hold a 'great' demonstration in honour of the Polish national hero, where Jabotinsky compared him to Trumpeldor. Each had sacrificed his life for the good of the homeland, though the one lived to complete his task, while the other lost his life at an early stage, his heritage being that Palestine could be redeemed only by sacrifice.[101] These Revisionist thoughts, which expressed a deep feeling that Poland's path to independence could be that of Zionism as well, could not have been too distant from the deepest longings of Avraham Stern, who uncompromisingly admired both Mussolini and Pilsudski.[102] He was also greatly influenced by Polish romantic poetry, especially that of Adam Mickiewicz.[103] Pilsudski's successors were also praised, despite their abrogation of the Minorities Pact, mainly because they supported the 'evacuation' of Polish Jewry – the main reservoir of the future 'Kingdom of Israel'.[104]

But it was not until the foundation of the New Zionist Organisation (NZO) in 1935 that Revisionism became truly radical. At the founding convention of the NZO, held in Vienna on 7 September 1935, Jabotinsky presented a plan to disband the diaspora by means of the immigration of a million and a half Jews in ten years.[105] Even though Jabotinsky still had some favourable things to say about the British, the wording of his plan was indeed radical. He spoke of three stages in its execution: (a) a Jewish state; (b) an exodus from the diaspora; (c) the creation of a national culture to affect the entire world. (In 1940 Stern was to formulate a plan of his own. This included Jabotinsky's three stages, but posited that they were to be preceded by another, more extreme, revolutionary stage: the redemption of the land by forced conquest from the foreign regime with the help of Britain's enemies.) Jabotinsky also proposed conquering Zionism by replacing the labour movement's 'fattening pioneer spirit' by the 'pride of sacrifice'.

All of this made no impression on the maximalists, whose spokesman was Dr Paul Haller (later to become supporter of the National Workers' Front and the *Sulam* club, though not of the Stern Gang). The founding convention, he complained, was hardly different from the old Zionist congresses, with their political manoeuvrings and organisational quarrels, and demonstrated the lack of a revolutionary national element within the Jewish people. Whereas previous demands had been made 'with a stammer', the new organisation resorted to 'theatrical pathos'. He addressed the religious nationalists, urging them to become fighters for 'the Kingdom of God and of Israel', and promising the workers social liberation parallel with their national liberation. Haller none the less concluded with an expression of trust in Jabotinsky.[106]

*

Even before the NZO's founding convention Uriel Heilperin (later Ratosh) had begun to enunciate his original views on Zionism and Revisionism. Though unsuccessful in the Revisionist movement, his views were to exert considerable influence on Stern during the coming years. Heilperin's thesis was that the international crisis centring on Ethiopia provided the Jews with an opportunity to benefit from the rivalries of the Powers. Within 20 years the Zionists could establish a state of ten million Jews which would serve as a European bastion on the Mediterranean shore, to prevent an attack by 'the desert peoples'. A Jewish Legion would be required to defend it. If England was not interested, Mussolini would be ready to replace her.[107] The Italian presence in Ethiopia was justified, for Africans were unable to rule themselves, and Mussolini, the heir to Diego Diaz, Vasco da Gama and European imperialism, was to be supported.[108] This was all the more so in view of the danger that the Arabs might exploit Britain's helplessness and attack the Jews. The Druze slaughter of the Lebanese Christians in 1860, the massacre of the Armenians by the Turks in the First World War, and the horrors of the Assyrian slaughter in Iraq (1933) were all warnings against Zionism's 'forced reliance' on 'British bayonets' which might abandon the *Yishuv*.[109]

Achimeir also now rejoined the pro-Italian chorus. Italy was a typically hungry power – like the Jews, the hungriest of nations. Il Duce's expansionist doctrines proved his realism. The balance of power had changed and Britain was in decline.[110] Berlin, rather than Rome, was the seat of the most dangerous enemy of world peace. It was gleefully noted that the *Volkischer Beobachter* had praised Weizmann and the labour movement for the 'Transfer Agreement' – 'The Hitlerite landowner praises his peasant.'[111] (The agreement, which appeared to almost all Revisionists to be 'a betrayal' of Zionism, was paradoxically later regarded positively by Avraham Stern himself, who saw in it a precedent for an agreement with Hitler in 1940–41.[112] Still, we can only presume that Stern agreed with Jabotinsky's scornful appraisal of Hitler at the founding convention, which led to his uncompromising rejection of the 'Transfer Agreement'.) Achimeir now called upon the British to co-operate with 'the vital forces in Judaism' (that is, the Revisionists), the 'bearers of the national conscience'. He promised a war to the finish against 'court Jews', the 'super moralists', the forces of 'exilic rot' and the 'red missionaries' in all their variations.[113] The nineteenth Zionist congress at Lucerne – the 'Hitlerian Congress' – was attacked.[114] There were 'two partners' to the plunder of the German Jewish diaspora: Nazism and Palestinian socialism.[115]

Altogether, the maximalists were dissatisfied with the NZO's founding convention. Jabotinsky remained tied to his pro-British orientation, and insisted on neutrality in the Ethiopian conflict, despite sympathy for Italian expansionism from within the NZO.[116] Jabotinsky's viewpoint on fascism was cautious, in light of the conflict developing between Mussolini and the West. His neutrality was ambivalent: he apparently rejected fascism at the beginning of 1935, but did not subsequently condemn it, sensing that he might be able to benefit from it.[117]

In 1935 Jabotinsky did not consider Achimeir, despite his immediate and distant past, at all dangerous. One reason was Jabotinsky's own essential pragmatism and tendency towards ideological pluralism.[118] Another was was his desire to compensate Achimeir after his release from prison, shattered in body and broken in spirit. Since Achimeir was now a martyr rather than the leader of an active opposition, it seemed appropriate to hug him to the bosom of the movement and exploit him for its need at a time of emergency and weakness in its London and Jerusalem centres. Achimeir did indeed adjust himself to the operative ideology of the Revisionist movement. The ideological differences between the two men dispersed, and Jabotinsky suggested that Achimeir join the leadership of the NZO, as head of the Training and Immigration Department.[119]

Achimeir thus ceased to play the part of a catalyst within the Revisionist movement, a role which might have led to a clash with Jabotinsky, and thence to a split. He unwillingly became a martyr, and his role in the Revisionist movement came to an end. Nevertheless, the growing ideological and strategic cleavage within the movement could not be papered over. New forces now surfaced in Revisionism: Heilperin and Begin in the movement itself, and Raziel and Stern in the IZL. It was their opposition to Jabotinsky in the years 1937–39 that was to be crucial. Indeed, those years closed one era in the history of the Revisionist movement, and opened another. The Arab rebellion, on the one hand, and Britain's simultaneous retreat from her support of Zionism, on the other, led dialectically to the gradual decomposition of the classical Revisionist movement and the loss of its ideological and organisational assets at the same time.

# 2

# Revisionism between Political Struggle and Fighting Underground, 1936–39

SELF-RESTRAINT (*HAVLAGAH*) AS A DIVISIVE ISSUE

The events of the years 1936–39 forced Jabotinsky to make dramatic tactical shifts while at the same time attempting to retain his fundamental assumptions. Once again, the NZO threatened to split. Shared hostility to the Zionist left and to Weizmann, even when combined with support for Jabotinsky's criticism of England, was insufficient: the increasing bloodshed demanded radical change, specifically the need for partisan and terrorist activity. To Jabotinsky's maximalist adherents, mainly in the IZL and its political adjunct, the 'Faction of Allegation and Faith', his supposed pro-British orientation seemed increasingly irrelevant. Even the British themselves found it barely credible. Throughout the period 1929–37, they considered Jabotinsky unreliable, in particular because of his reckless public statements, and prevented him from appearing in Palestine to testify before the Royal Commission of Inquiry.[1]

The weakness and ambiguity of Jabotinsky's leadership were especially evident once Arab rioting broke out in 1936. On the one hand, he claimed that the riots had been planned by the Arabs with the assistance of British officials; on the other hand he ridiculed those who held that the British were hostile towards Zionism.[2] The IZL was itself divided in its response: its commander, Tehomi, opposed retaliatory acts, such acts were nevertheless carried out by the commander of the Tel Aviv branch, A. Krichevsky, together with his subordinates, H. Kalay, A. Haichman and B. Zeroni (all to be deeply involved in the split of 1940).[3] Apart from re-emphasising the possibility of an Italian orientation, Jabotinsky once again sank into the ambiguity of supporting 'self-restraint', hoping that the Jewish Legions might yet materialise.

The confrontation with Achimeir had thus been postponed, not avoided. Even though a mere shadow of his former self, Achimeir clashed with his leader at the fourth national convention of *Betar* in Poland in June 1936.[4] There, Achimeir proclaimed that the era of 'the bridge of iron' had replaced that of 'a bridge of paper'. Using the model of insurgent Spanish fascism, he called for 'the Zionism of the Alcazar' and an end to 'the morass of self-restraint'. The victorious forces of the century were communism and fascism, not social democracy. Those doctrines were to fall on fertile soil within *Betar*.[5]

Within two months Jabotinsky's own private doubts about 'self-restraint' had grown. Although he still refused to succumb to the pressure applied by his followers in Palestine, he did revert to the Polish and Italian options, partly through fear of a British surrender to the Arabs. He envisaged that Poland and Italy would somehow lead a collective Mandate which would enforce a new version of the Nordau plan for the evacuation of the diaspora within two to three generations. Polish leaders, in particular, would be interested in evacuation because such a policy would bolster their demand for colonies.[6] This, however, was a forlorn hope. Jabotinsky's previous attempts to use the 'Alliance policy' with the smaller states of Eastern Europe as a means of pressure on Britain to open the gates of Palestine had been unsuccessful.[7] Moreover, he constantly underestimated Britain's Arab and Islamic interests, which were far more weighty than her Zionist considerations. In fact, and as was illustrated by his appearance before the Peel Commission, Jabotinsky still continued to place his confidence in the British.[8]

Jabotinsky had to make a clear decision on the question of 'self-restraint'. Ultimately, his control of the IZL depended on this issue, which was to split the organisation on 23 April 1937. Tehomi and his supporters became convinced by Ben-Gurion's thesis that 'self-restraint' was a vital policy if Jewish immigration was to be continued and civil war averted, and joined the *Haganah*. About 1,500 of the Revisionist IZL advocated retaliation against Arab terrorism, and maintained the existence of their independent organisation.[9]

## THE ESTABLISHMENT OF THE REVISIONIST IZL

The independent IZL established a committee comprising Raziel, Stern, Heilperin (Ratosh) and Chaim Lubinsky, who were mandated to draw up organisational principles. Their ideology focused on three main points: '(1) the fate of the Jewish nation will be decided by Jewish armed force on the soil of the homeland; (2) the IZL views as an ally any Jew supporting this aim; (3) the IZL views as an ally any non-Jew who recognises the right of the Jewish people to the independence of its homeland.'[10] A subsequent declaration, drawn up by Raziel and Stern, announced the establishment of the *Irgun*,[11] and spoke of the 'enslavement' of the Jewish Agency to 'foreign rule' and its 'betrayal' in accepting cantonisation. The IZL revealed its links with the NZO both by its choice of terminology and by castigating the *Haganah* as a 'leftist' organisation, interested not in unifying Jewish forces but rather in bringing the IZL to its knees. Nevertheless, the declaration also contained the seeds of the split of 1940. Military rather than political power would establish the future Jewish state – the *Irgun*, it was implied, would be the kernel of such a 'Jewish force' – and England was the real 'external enemy'.

Jabotinsky accepted his appointment as the IZL's supreme commander. Within a week he was also directing its followers: 'if the rioting continues and if it is characterised by a tendency to attack Jews, do not exercise self-restraint!' Jabotinsky attempted to resolve the expected clash between his various positions by declaring that 'no connection and no bridge' existed between the IZL and the NZO; the members of the one were not to be considered responsible for the activities of the other. Even 'Zeev [Jabotinsky], too, carries out his duties in this matter as a single individual.'[12] Nevertheless, it was undeniable that a split had indeed occurred.[13] Its primary cause was the evolution of two schools of thought. One, which advocated 'self-restraint', had always been pacifist; it wanted the *Haganah* to serve as no more than the army of a Jewish canton. The other, which rejected 'self-restraint', wanted the IZL to be the Legion of 'the Jewish state'. Advocates of the latter school established a command, consisting of Robert Bitker as commander-in-chief, Moshe Rosenberg as its head, David Raziel as commander of Jerusalem, Aharon Haichman as commander of Tel Aviv and Hanoch Kalay as commander of Haifa. Stern was the secretary and Lubinsky, H. Kook, Posak and Y. Paamoni were members of its temporary staff.[14]

One version of the IZL's history portrays an immediate split between Jabotinsky and Stern, evident at their confrontation in Alexandria in June 1937.[15] At this stage, however, the IZL seems still to have been closely supervised by the heads of the NZO and *Betar*. In fact, the first version of the Revisionist IZL was a failure. Bitker proved to be a poor choice; since he did not know Hebrew, he left the authority for retaliatory actions with the commanders of the branches. The IZL's financial difficulties also involved him in September 1937 in a robbery (termed an 'expropriation'), delegated to the *Sadan* group headed by A. Selman.[16]

## THE *SADAN* ('ANVIL') GROUP

It was the *Sadan* group (also termed 'the Faction for Ideological Criticism') which effectively continued the work of the maximalists. In the formulation drawn up by M.A. Perlmutter, one of its ideologists, Revisionist Zionism was no more than 'a separate demonstration of the lack of all political effort and a demonstration of the Jewish catastrophe'.[17] The leader of the group, Selman, attacked the ideology of self-restraint which he claimed had injected into the *Yishuv* a sense of despair concerning the Zionist solution and threatened to turn the Zionist movement into a false-messianism.[18] The NZO, instead of undertaking constructive political and educational work, had merely engaged in 'cheap competition' with the Zionist movement. The much admired League of *Sicarii*, the 'fighting sector', had been betrayed by 'the moderate, snobbish spirit' of the 'secondary leadership' – the authorised committee of the NZO too readily looked for agreements with the left, or with allies on the civilian right. The true justification for secession from the Zionist organisation was the creation of a 'fighting body', suited to the vital needs of the Jewish nation and its revolutionary course. This time, however, the movement should be one of 'the proletarian masses'. Other liberation movements indicated that the proletariat are the vanguard of any revolution, for they have nothing to lose. They have to be educated to the idea of 'the desire to rule'. These themes were to recur in *Lehi* formulations. So, too, did the *Sadan* group's clearly Nietzschean outlook: the Jewish people were a superior nation with exceptionally fine laws and customs.[19]

Confrontations between the Revisionist movement and the *Sadan* group occurred only in Palestine. Jabotinsky was never attacked at all. When temporarily expelled from the Revisionist movement, members of the group took refuge in the IZL. Here, however, they failed completely; their 'expropriations' were a shambles; the Revisionist movement in Palestine refused to support them when they were put on trial; one of their number, Zvi Frankel (ben Amram) was drowned by his comrades in the IZL who feared that he might violate their secrecy. These incidents concluded the first chapter in the history of the Revisionist IZL and led to the dismissal of Bitker from his command and his departure from the country.[20]

This failure had less effect on Jabotinsky's dual leadership than the more dramatic events surrounding the Peel Commission. Rumours spread that Jabotinsky was considering accepting the division of Palestine, though his tactics were inevitably limited by the extremist stance of his supporters in that country.[21] Dr Altman claimed that the proposed settlement favoured the Arabs, and could not therefore be implemented. An Arab rising could be quelled, but not a Jewish revolt: 'There is no limit to the destruction the genius of this nation shall cause if it finds no way to live. In this war the victors shall be those with nothing to lose . . . [and] there is no power on earth stronger than despair.'[22] Thus, with the publication of the Peel Report, Revisionism faced another test. This time the challenge was to come from Uriel Heilperin (Ratosh).

HEILPERIN'S 'DEMAND FOR AUTHORITY' – THE FAILURE
OF AN IDEOLOGICAL REVOLUTION WITHIN REVISIONISM

Shortly after the publication of the Peel Report (7 July 1937) Heilperin
(then on the editorial board of *Ha-Yarden*) challenged the idea of the
colonising regime so central to Jabotinsky's basic assumptions. The
era of 'common interests' between Zionism and England, he claimed,
had come to an end. England wanted to abandon its Mandate and join
an alliance with the future government of Palestine. Echoing Nordau
and Zangwill, he called for the immediate transfer of power to the
Jews. Although not a majority, they were a qualitative minority, sur-
passing the rest of the population in education, capital and energy.
Moreover, the percentage of young people among the Jews was greater
than that of the Arab majority. He reproved official Zionism for
demanding either a division of Palestine or the continuation of the
Mandate, as opposed to the Arabs who demanded the entire country.
This, he felt, proved the Jewish Agency's inferiority to the 'leadership
of strength' claimed by the Arabs of Palestine, who remained unaffec-
ted by any Jewish moderation. Like Achimeir (in his articles) and
Stern (in his poems), Heilperin shared Jabotinsky's call 'to die or
conquer the mountain'.[23]

Jabotinsky and Altman continued to adopt a public stand against
the continuation of 'self-restraint'. Nevertheless, the *Betar* leadership
gave Heilperin no support, and clung to the British orientation. Heilperin himself reiterated Jabotinsky's ideas of 1932 and 1936 in calling
for alternatives, and though he did not mention Italy explicitly, it was
clear that he had this country in mind.[24] Thus he called for a 'Legion of
the Bearers of the War of Liberation', established not by means of
education and 'objective', criteria (as Jabotinsky advocated) but in a
'subjective' way, by a 'call to war'.[25] The seriousness of Heilperin's
intent was shown when he submitted his proposal to the national
council of the NZO in Palestine as early as 17 December 1937.[26] His
argument, taken from the Royal Commission itself, was that the
*Yishuv* was capable of producing 50,000 soldiers who could take
control of the country. At the time of the rioting England maintained
in Palestine an army only half that size, while in 1920 France had
conquered Syria from the Arabs with 60,000 troops. Significantly, he
repeated his warning that if the NZO did not adjust itself to the spirit
of the youth striving to attain freedom, 'separatist growths' would
develop in it.[27] Heilperin was supported by a majority of 27 to eight.
The decision was now in the hands of the NZO convention which was
due to meet in Prague at the beginning of 1938. The sixth proposal put
to the convention declared that 'The Jewish government will establish

a network of pacts with the interested powers (taking especial note of Great Britain) concerning the guarantee of their special interests.[28]

Avraham Stern is known to have been influenced by Heilperin's series of articles. Even before the appearance of *Our Eyes are Lifted Up to Domination*, some 'secret cells' of the IZL had been established within branches of *Betar* in Poland (spring–summer 1937). These were not meant to be an underground within an underground, but rather a reservoir for the IZL in Palestine. Stern himself was not formally a member of either the NZO or *Betar*, but these did constitute his cultural political milieu. He hoped that, with the help of Avraham Amper and Nathan Friedman-Yellin, a force of 40,000 youths would eventually arise from the Jewish populations of Eastern Europe and the Balkans to raise 'the banner of rebellion' in Palestine against the British. According to Friedman-Yellin's later version, he no longer regarded Jabotinsky as the effective leader. The IZL was now an organisation of national liberation, striving for complete independence from the political overlordship of the NZO.[29]

At the same time, Heilperin was supported by the proclamation of 'the activist-Revisionist front' in Poland at the beginning of 1938. This attacked the Revisionist leadership for its failure to crusade against 'liquidatory Zionism' (meaning, the Jewish Agency) and its conciliatory policy towards the left. It had failed to support 'the fighting groups' of Revisionism and, with its imposed leadership from above, had ceased to be a real mass movement. The Revisionist movement could be rescued if it dropped its pro-English orientation, adopted 'active resistance' and waged war against the Agency as well as 'social communists' among the Jewish people. Its signatories were Menachem Begin, a commissioned officer of *Betar* and a member of the central committee of the Revisionist movement in Poland; Y. Virnick, who held similar positions; Z. Lerner, a member of the central committee; S. Merlin, the secretary of the executive committee and a member of the board of the Revisionist movement in Poland, later co-editor with Friedman-Yellin and Stern of *Di Tat*, the IZL newspaper in Poland; A. Stavsky; I. Epstein, a *Betar* commissioned officer; and Nathan Friedman – later the head of the *Lehi* centre, and at that time a member of the board of the Revisionist movement in Poland.[30]

Neither this group, nor Heilperin and Stern, were contemplating a complete split. In fact, in November 1937 Stern arrived in Warsaw with a letter of recommendation from Jabotinsky to the NZO representative in Poland, Dr J.B. Shechtman, with the message: 'Please do for the bearer anything you are ready to do for me.'[31] True, at the convention itself, Begin did demand a war of liberation against England, while Heilperin emphasised the need to look for alternative powers. But they were in a tiny minority. Even though Jabotinsky declared himself in favour of ending 'self-restraint', he still hoped that his 'ten-year plan' and a call for an international solution would unite both his movement and the Jewish people behind him. Ultimately, the convention closed with support for Jabotinsky's English orientation, though it expressed dissatisfaction at British policies in Palestine, and called for a 'fight with all the force it could command against the anti-Zionist regime'.[32]

Heilperin had met Jabotinsky in Alexandria in the summer of 1937. His impression was that Jabotinsky had an obsession about Wilson's 'fourteen points', and was inclined to allow the Arabs the right of self-determination. A generation later, Heilperin would state that Stern, also in Alexandria at the time, was similarly convinced of Jabotinsky's flawed understanding of the three key issues of the day – the British, the Arabs and the Jews.[33] Certainly, Stern and Heilperin became much closer during this period. Heilperin told Stern that the Revisionist movement was no different from the rest of Zionism; the problem was not the character of British policy, but their very rule; there was no choice but to wage war against them. The Arabs must be defeated only to prove to the British that the Jewish people was the preferable partner. They both expressed their reservations regarding the League of the *Sicarii* and its 'emotional' and 'unfocused' propaganda and activities. Both were decisively influenced by Achimeir's views without admitting this openly, just as they never admitted Jabotinsky's dialectical influence on them.

Now, in 1938, Stern and Heilperin realised that they had to bring about a final confrontation with Jabotinsky. Heilperin was to do this openly, and when he failed in the summer of 1938, he was to draw full ideological conclusions; he would withdraw and adopt a 'Canaanite' orientation. Stern, meanwhile, was to try to work behind the scenes in order to influence activist circles in the direction of his ideas.

In the summer of 1938, on the eve of the third world convention of *Betar*, Heilperin made a final attempt to break through the ideological walls of Revisionism. The convention met two weeks after the hanging of Shlomo Ben Yosef, and Heilperin's anti-British tone evoked a more favourable response. Like Stern, he viewed this first hanging as a decisive turning-point and now called on *Betar* to become a 'revolutionary military party'.[34] Denying a basic Revisionist axiom, he dismissed the Balfour Declaration, saying: 'Our very right to the country is *our own*, and the essence of our power is *our own power*.' The Jews would 'conquer' (rather than just 'take control of') the country, and he laid great stress on 'war potential'. Heilperin now revived and developed his 'Semitic' theory, which had lain dormant since 1935. The Jewish state would be a natural 'centre and shelter' for all the minority groups within the region. His negation of the diaspora was now extreme; so was his call to uproot the Jewish religion from Jewish nationality. The actual assumption of power would be carried out by a small number; the masses would remain passive until the very hour of decision. The crucial element was 'the power of sacrifice of the few' who, although a minority, 'represent the historical desire, the interest and all the vital forces of the nation'.[35]

Basic to Heilperin's thesis was the argument that the Arabs in Palestine were not a nation. Arab terrorism in Palestine was dependent on external support and relied on Jewish passivity. Large-scale Jewish immigration, capital investment and culture would lead to Jewish sovereignty which would bring stability and security to the Near East. This Hebrew nation (also called 'Canaan') would conclude alliances with Egypt, Saudi Arabia, Iran, an independent Druze principality and the minorities of Lebanon. It would indeed have to compete against Pan-Arabism for the favours of the powers, but the 'war potential' would be decisive.[36] On the economic front, Heilperin called for the adoption of the theory of corporations propounded by fascist Italy. The Jewish state would be a lever for the technical and economic development of all the nations of the region, the 'natural link' completing the process of liberation and rebirth of 'the glorious Ancient East'.[37] The 'negation of the diaspora' meant that all forms of life, language, thought patterns and leadership typical of the diaspora were to be uprooted.

Had it not been for Heilperin's call for the uprooting of religion from the Hebrew nationality, Stern would have been able to accept the entire platform. In his total rejection of socialism and Marxism as the fruit of 'the machine of strangulation and violence of the foreign regime ruling the country', Heilperin remained typical of the Zionist right. This, too, Stern accepted; it was his disciples who would gradually free themselves of the Revisionist anti-leftist heritage. Heilperin himself presented simply a somewhat obscure conception of the type of regime likely to arise after the establishment of the Hebrew state.

### THE MARTYRDOM OF SHLOMO BEN YOSEF AS A CATALYST IN THE RADICALISATION OF THE NZO

In the 'Instructions concerning the Organisation' which Jabotinsky sent to the IZL on 30 April 1937, it was clear that the re-established IZL would seek to end 'self-restraint'.[38] But Bitker, the commander-in-chief, and his successor, Moshe Rosenberg, were still irresolute. It was *Betar*'s unit in Rosh Pina that pushed the IZL into an uncompromising stand on this issue. Moreover, the IZL's counter-terrorist activities were the result of the renewal of Arab violence at the end of September 1937, which reached a peak with the murder of five Jews near Kiryat-Anavim. This led to the IZL reprisal under David Raziel on 14 November ('Black Sunday' – a turning-point in IZL history), when a number of Arabs were shot and killed in various places in Jerusalem.[39]

At the beginning of 1938 Raziel declared the motive for the actions to be the Arab success in deriving political benefit from terrorism. He rejected out of hand the fears of the Agency executive that the Jews would forfeit world public opinion. That attitude only reflected the lack of 'the desire and psychological willingness for war' and the 'defeatism' of the left, as had been demonstrated in the *Yishuv* in 1929, in Germany in 1933 and in Austria in 1934. This 'self-restraint' had affected the British army, when 20,000 soldiers were unable to control '700 barefoot Arabs', not to mention the 'passivity of the Ghafirs' (the Jewish Settlement police). As early as the beginning of 1938 the IZL convinced itself that the shame of 'self-restraint' had already been obliterated by its own few troops, and that the Arabs were finally alarmed.[40]

Though far away in London, Jabotinsky thought of his subordinates in Palestine. 'Tell them', he wrote to Moshe Rosenberg, 'that from afar I collect items of news about your lives, as if a precious treasure. I am aware of the impediments which do not daunt you. I am aware, too, of your actions. How good it is that I have been blessed with such disciples.'[41] Jabotinsky was thus giving his approval *after* the IZL retaliatory acts. It would seem that his concern with his own leadership left him with no choice. He had already demonstrated (with Achimeir and at the time of the Ben Yosef affair) – and was to do so with Stern – that tactical concerns of that nature predominated over ideological considerations.

At the beginning of February 1938, while the NZO convention was under way in Prague, sentence of death was passed on *Betar* Ghafir Yehezkeel Altman, who had killed an Arab child, and the policeman Mordechai Schwarz, who had killed an Arab policeman. Altman was pardoned but Schwartz was hanged on 16 August. An escalation in terrorist and anti-terrorist actions was bound to lead to further death sentences under the emergency laws of 11 November 1937. Accordingly, on 21 April (following the terrorist murder of Jews in Galilee), a reprisal – albeit ineffective – was carried out by three members of the *Betar* recruiting platoon in Rosh Pina. Jabotinsky and Binyamin Askin, his assistant on the NZO executive, tried to tone down the political element in the trial, so as to soften the expected verdict.[42]

These acts were facilitated by the ideological atmosphere of early 1938, expressed in Uri Zvi Greenberg's poem, 'Judaea Today, Judaea Tomorrow/Ballad of Sorrow and Joy'.[43] *The Book of Indictment and Faith* (which concludes with the above poem) was published over a year before the Rosh Pina action, and was widely applauded in Revisionist and related circles. Greenberg wrote what his followers wanted to read: 'Hebrew poetry has finally been blessed with a vision in compensation for the wilderness of the periods of prosperity and self-restraint.'[44] The book doubtless had a direct effect on *Betar*'s 'recruiting platoon' in Rosh Pina.[45]

The independent actions proved a serious challenge to the IZL's commanders. Irritated, the latter boasted that they had carried out similar and far more successful retaliatory actions, and had not even been deterred by the trial of Ben Yosef and his colleagues or by Jabotinsky's subsequent tireless efforts to obtain pardons. Jabotinsky himself took another route, attempting (unsuccessfully) to persuade the Colonial Secretary, Malcolm MacDonald, that Ben Yosef's execution would not prevent the Arabs from sabotaging the *Yishuv*; to the Jews he would become a martyr, and thus the symbol of a deep rift between the Jewish people and the British nation. Clearly Jabotinsky feared the impact of the execution on his movement.[46]

His fears were to prove to be well founded; the day after the execution a leaflet of 'the Sons of the Zealots' proclaimed that Ben Yosef 'had fallen because of the guilt of the people!' It also promised vengeance.[47] Jabotinsky appreciated that the hanging constituted a test of his position as leader, and that he had unhesitatingly to support Ben Yosef. He did so in a historic letter he wrote to his mother in Poland and to the members of his platoon in Rosh Pina: 'I was not the person who educated Ben Yosef . . . his followers, more than mine, will be the educators of an entire generation.' In public, Jabotinsky now rejected the pro-British orientation, which had favoured political legalism and the establishment of an army, rather then terrorism and an underground. 'Of his gallows we shall make a tower, of his grave a shrine, of his memory a religion.'[48] His private correspondence, however, reveals this to have been a tactical switch. His own preference was still for exerting pressure on the British, and he therefore sought to distance himself from the IZL.[49]

Jabotinsky knew that he would have to justify the ending of 'self-restraint' at the world convention of *Betar* in September 1938. Nevertheless, there were certain lines of his basic ideology that he would not cross. One was his fundamental attachment to England. Indeed, Jabotinsky still tried to reassure himself that Britain was at root supportive of Zionism and that if the NZO came to power, Britain would somehow keep her 'vow' – namely, the Balfour Declaration.[50] The IZL, on the other hand, opted for more anti-Arab action. At the same time its confrontation with the *Haganah* reached a dangerous and unprecedented peak, with an IZL member being imprisoned after mistakenly killing a Jew; in response a *Haganah* member was kidnapped (25 July–1 August). On 19 August, Stern met Jabotinsky in Warsaw, and pressed for more action and a stronger line against the *Haganah*. Jabotinsky refused, because the *Haganah* was fighting for its life and because of the IZL's weakness. But Stern demanded more help for 'the front' (Palestine) from 'the hinterland'. The hinterland, claimed Jabotinsky, was not capable of aiding the front: 'You are a unit which has crossed the front lines and been surrounded by the enemy on all sides. *You are cut off* . . .' Stern, however, demanded a call for action from the supreme commander, and for funds; failing those, he wanted at least moral support. Jabotinsky agreed to the latter request, and meanwhile gave an order to break up a *Mapai* gathering in Poland.[51]

Eventually, under pressure from the leadership of the NZO, Raziel, who had become head of the IZL command, agreed to open negotiations with the 'leftist devils' of the *Haganah*. These resulted in an agreement (although also in Raziel's resignation).[52] However, for its part, the IZL was convinced that its policy of ending 'self-restraint' had led to a clear victory; the number of Arabs killed in July 1938 amounted to 150, in contrast to 'only' 30 Jews.[53]

## THE THIRD WORLD CONVENTION OF BETAR

By the eve of the third *Betar* world convention in Warsaw, in September 1938, the establishment of IZL secret 'cells' in *Betar* branches in Poland was well under way. Dr Israel Scheib, then head of the *Betar* branch in Volkovisk, realised that paramilitary action was triumphing over ideological education. But, as he was later to write, the real choice had lain between disaffection from *Betar*, especially by its adolescent membership, and the adoption of a more activist line.[54] The international crisis over the Sudetenland further heightened tension on the eve of the convention; so, too, did the Anglophobia generated by the hanging of Mordechai Schwartz.[55]

At the convention itself, Jabotinsky denied the 'longings for arms and blood' within *Betar*, and in the same breath defended the reprisals. There was much discussion of the roles of military training and cultural work within the movement, leading to a confrontation between those who viewed *Betar* as the realisation of military Zionism and those who viewed militarism as merely one component of Zionism. The clash climaxed in the famous debate between Jabotinsky and Menachem

Begin. World conscience, claimed Begin, had ceased to react and the League of Nations was on the verge of dissolution. England had in fact decided in favour of the Arabs because they had national ambitions and were willing to fight, whereas only a part of the Jewish people were fighting. In a style reminiscent of Stern, he declared: 'We want to fight – to die or to triumph.' Begin announced that Zionism was on the threshold of the third period in its history. After 'practical Zionism' and 'political Zionism', the time had come for 'military Zionism', in accordance with the models of Cavour and Garibaldi.[56]

Thus was launched the third fundamental attack on Jabotinsky from within the Revisionist movement. This time he could not resort to the dialectical argument that he had employed in 1932; he had no choice but to engage in serious debate. He did make one tactical concession by agreeing to add to the *Betar* oath ('I shall not raise my arm except in self-defence') the words 'and for the conquest of my homeland'. Otherwise he was adamant that 'the question of entering Palestine *precedes* the outburst of bravery'. His position was based on a realistic appraisal of the situation. The Jewish position in Palestine was still so weak that

> no earthly strategist would say that in the present situation we are capable of performing the act of a Garibaldi or a de Valera. That is mere idle chatter. Our situation is far removed from that of the Italians or the Irish, and if you feel there is no alternative to the proposals made by Mr Begin and if you are armed – commit suicide. If there is no more world conscience, then there is the River Vistula and Communism.[57]

Less realistic was Jabotinsky's faith in world conscience and the British. In fact, his suggestion of support from an alternative power undermined his pro-British orientation, and encouraged Heilperin and Stern in their search for such an option. It thus hastened the final collapse of his own ideological position. The root fault lay in Jabotinsky's exaggerated self-confidence in his ability to maintain control of 'separatist growths' – as Ratosh put it. Jabotinsky's realism was undoubtedly greater than that of Begin. But the entire Revisionist movement, influenced by mystical-messianic and apocalyptic tendencies, could not by its very nature adapt itself to realistic thinking, neither in Zionist nor in international politics.

For tactical reasons, Jabotinsky attempted to paper over his differences with his critics. His debate with Begin was not published in the contemporary Revisionist press. Moreover, at a memorial ball some time later Jabotinsky delivered a militant speech, intended to obscure the existing differences of principle and display a homogenous movement before Jewish and world public opinion. He raised Ben Yosef to the level of 'a saint' and 'a pure man' and, of course, 'a hero'. God and fate had indeed selected Ben Yosef to be the teacher of the movement. Echoing Greenberg, he proclaimed: 'For the blood of insurrection is dew which fertilizes the soil.'[58] Jabotinsky was re-elected leader of *Betar*. Even so, the basic gulf remained. This was noted by Scheib, who in his own speech pointed to the wide gap between the nineteenth-century mentality of the leader of *Betar* and the twentieth-century mentality of his youthful followers. Jabotinsky's response was to leave the hall. Scheib had overstepped himself and the leader was not prepared for yet another confrontation with the activists in his movement.[59]

When Scheib met Stern behind the scenes during the convention, he asked for one last chance to capture *Betar* for activism. But Stern, too, had seen through Jabotinsky's Ben Yosef speech.[60] For the future founders of *Lehi* present at the convention – Stern, Friedman-Yellin and Scheib – the experience there was a turning-point. Yunitchman and Rosenfeld also felt that the gap could be bridged with Begin, but not with Jabotinsky.[61] Thus, despite Jabotinsky's re-election, the impending schism, in the IZL if not in the NZO or in *Betar*, was clearly imminent.[62]

### THE IZL AND THE NZO: FROM THE *BETAR* CONVENTION TO THE WHITE PAPER

The deterioration of the international political situation after Munich, together with the escalation of the Palestine crisis, ensured the use of a stronger and more vehement style of rhetoric on the part of the NZO (and *Betar*) and the IZL. It also prepared the ground for action on the part of the latter. Jabotinsky was determined to maintain his hold on both parts of the movement, but Stern foresaw that this would prove impossible. Thus, while Jabotinsky kept to his political struggle, Stern emphasised active liberation. However, he proceeded to transform the IZL in a quiet fashion, intending to present Jabotinsky and his followers with a *fait accompli*. Thus his newspapers in Poland, *Di Tat* (The Deed – in Yiddish) and *Jerozolima Wyzwolona* (Liberated Jerusalem – in Polish) attempted to obscure the ideological disagreements which were already very tangible. Although both began to introduce Stern's independent thoughts, most of the ideas expressed were acceptable to the NZO too. Stern also adopted many of Jabotinsky's models, often taken from Irish, Italian and Polish history. There was much admiration of Pilsudski,[63] and the quotations from Greenberg make it clear that Stern was still far from being the pro-leftist Yellin-Mor sought to depict in the late 1940s.[64] The anti-British tone, although steadily more strident, was also kept within bounds.[65]

Jabotinsky had not regarded the convention as a defeat for his political programme, which he now reiterated: (a) England was to be persuaded to veto any possible change in the Mandate; (b) an intergovernmental convention initiated by the US government and supported by Romania and Poland was to be convened to discuss the Jewish question; and (c) a 'Zion *Sejm*' of Eastern European Jewry was to be organised to apply appropriate pressure.[66] The example of Czechoslovakia was not applicable to Palestine, as the former lay near the throat of the 'Big Wolf', whereas Palestine lay surrounded by weak and divided states dependent on England.[67] By contrast Achimeir, though only a shell of his former self, served as a mouthpiece for the activists by claiming that the Czech disaster demonstrated that Zionism should not trust the Western democracies.[68] The behaviour of England and France surely proved that Spengler's prophecy concerning the decline of the West had come true. U.Z. Greenberg declared that London would be regarded as the Rome of the Jewish people, who were waiting for a 'leader of a liberation movement who is worthy of a miraculous moment'.[69]

Initially, Jabotinsky refused to believe that the IZL was acting independently. Later, however, he did complain that 'they' wanted to destroy *Betar* – 'my creation and choice'. He decided that the best response was reorganisation into a unified youth movement, with the 'military principle' operating in Palestine 'whereas in the diaspora *Betarism* will reign supreme'. There was to be no separate action.[70] Within less than three months he was to enforce this policy on the IZL in the 'Paris Agreement'. Even so, he was unable to prevent a split.

Meanwhile, the IZL boldly proclaimed that its activites had generated a shift in British policy, for the government was searching for ways to persuade the *Irgun* not to go 'completely wild'. But Raziel proclaimed that the IZL, unlike the *Haganah*, would not be tamed.[71] In any case, according to Yeivin, the British only really understood war with no compromise. That was why they had released the Arab leaders who had been expelled to the Seychelles and had eventually negotiated with Eamon de Valera.[72] Meanwhile (autumn 1938), Aharon Haichman, a member of the IZL high command, ran an officer course for Polish *Irgun* supporters in Zofjowka, Poland, in which 24 members of the secret 'cells' took part. Another course with Polish instructors took place in Andrychow. The participants were eventually to become the commanding core of Stern's 40,000-strong Palestine invasion plan.[73]

Acting in Jabotinsky's name, Dr S. Yunitchman, *Betar*'s senior figure in Palestine, tried to stem the tide. He noted the contribution maximalism had made in the past to the revitalisation of the Revisionist movement, and stressed that there was indeed room for its members in the movement – but only if they accepted Jabotinsky's political leadership and control of policy. After all, the man was a 'leader-prophet'.[74] Yeivin replied that the dispute between the Revisionist maximalists and minimalists was not insignificant; it would decide the fate of the nation and its homeland. The gap between the two was now even greater than that between the Revisionist minimalists and the parties of the 'old' Zionist organisation. Revisionism had lost its fighting character, and was now merely a 'poor' imitation of this 'old' and bankrupt organisation. The *Yishuv* was far stronger than in 1917, but none the less the Balfour Declaration was about to be taken away. Thus militant ideology rather than settlements was the only answer.[75] With positions at such variance, there was little point in continuing the debate. Despite further exchanges,[76] both sides remained adamant. A captive of his own earlier pronouncements, Jabotinsky was himself unwilling to accept any maximalist doctrine. His only possible counter was to revive, in January 1939, the possibility of the Italian option. Unlike Britain and France, he argued, the Italians would be unable to come to an agreement with the Arabs; neither was there any possibility of an Arab–Italian agreement based on hatred of the Jews.[77]

It is against this background that the 'Paris agreement' of 1 February 1939 must be considered. The meeting was intended to resolve the dispute between Jabotinsky and representatives of independent trends within the IZL. Stern, their chief ideologist, was not present; but other representatives of the *Irgun* were: Raziel, Hillel Kook, H. Lubinsky and H.S. Ha-Levy. They made no attempt to conceal the fact that the IZL sought independence. Primacy, they suggested, would be exercised by the IZL in the *Yishuv*, and by *Betar* in the diaspora. Moreover, 'the Department of Military Education' in the diaspora would contain IZL representatives, whose director would set up units of *Betar* graduates to serve as 'the reserve of the *Irgun*'[78] As anticipated, the conference in Paris appeared to end in a victory for Jabotinsky. But even Raziel viewed this as 'a necessary evil'; he was unhappy with the fact that Jabotinsky himself assumed the post of first director of the 'Department of Military Education'[79].

Stern was determined to reject the Paris agreement and to work for the complete independence of the IZL. The strength of his decision can be gauged from the press conference which he convened in Warsaw on 6 March 1939 with the participation of the editors of his newspapers in Poland – Friedman-Yellin, Merlin and Lily Strassmann. The background to the press conference was the news that matters had taken a turn for the worse at the St James's conference, in London. There was a danger that the Balfour Declaration might be abrogated and an Arab state established in Palestine. The Arabs reacted with demonstrations of joy, which were countered by the renewal of IZL anti-Arab terrorist acts.[80] England was warned, and at the Warsaw press conference a programme of four points was proclaimed for: (1) 'Shattering Arab armed resistance by means of armed punitive action'; (2) 'Steadily increasing the percentage of Jews in the country by means of natural immigration with neither certificates nor visas'; (3) 'Educating and organising the Jewish people as a reservoir and a cushion for the pioneer fighting on the Palestine front'; (4) 'Acquiring supporters and aid in states whose interests harmonise, directly or indirectly, with the realisation of the aims of the IZL.'[81]

On the surface, the declaration was compatible with Jabotinsky's basic assumptions. In fact, however, it was aimed at the IZL's complete political independence. Unlike his supreme commander, Stern wanted the organisation to draw operative conclusions from the new situation created on the eve of the publication of the British government's White Paper. As it was, Stern went much further than his leader in his public call for alternative alliances. 'Philanthropic Zionism', he claimed, had proved bankrupt, failing to make real headway in settling Jews in Palestine. Financed and aided by diaspora Jewry, thousands of young people could be sent there to provide greater military potential for the *Yishuv*. If England could not see the danger of 'German incitement and insurrectionist activities amongst the Arabs', then 'there are other countries, such as France and Turkey, that comprehend the dangers involved' and which were thus 'the potential allies of the Jewish national movement'. So were the states of Eastern Europe.[82] What made matters worse was that (as Jabotinsky learned from sources other than the IZL newspaper in Poland) he had been described at the press conference as 'an ex-activist and extremist political thinker now following policies which, in our opinion, preach complacency in Zionist matters, whereas we have finally decided to take matters into our own hands'.[83]

Raziel admitted to Jabotinsky that 'things which should not have been uttered' were said at the press conference. In a letter of December 1938 to A.F. Giles, assistant inspector-general of police in charge of the CID in Jerusalem, he had gone to considerable lengths to reassure the British of the IZL's loyalty. He had sought to overcome the issue of the IZL's anti-Arab terrorist act by claiming that it would in fact aid the government.[84]

Jabotinsky seems to have been unaware of the military courses the IZL was holding in Poland (and of the IZL's 'cells' in *Betar*'s branches). Raziel did not tell him, and he was to hear of them only from Count

Lubienski, the Director-General of the Polish Foreign Office.[85] Stern
even forbade those taking the course to visit Jabotinsky in Warsaw,
so that he would not learn of the preparations being made for a revolt.
According to Haichman and Lavstein, Stern had come to an agreement
with the Polish government whereby, in return for Polish assistance in
training, supplying arms and help in illegal immigration, the IZL
would see to it that Poland won an important position in the Middle
East and would arouse world Jewry to assist Poland in her struggle
against Germany. At the conclusion of the course Stern spoke of the
similarity between the Polish and Jewish wars of liberation. It is highly
unlikely that the Polish authorities, whose officers served as instructors
on the Andrychow course, would not have been aware of the ramifica-
tions it would have on their relations with Britain.[86] Stern was especially
impressed by the fact that Poland, whose rulers were anti-Semitic,
were prepared to assist in a Jewish war of liberation, thereby demonstrating that their concern for Polish national interests was stronger
than their anti-Semitism. This assumption, valid in the case of Poland,
made it possible for him to attempt a similar course with respect to
Germany at the end of 1940.

Jabotinsky also became increasingly out of touch with his supporters
in Palestine, for whom the St James's talks constituted 'the writing on
the wall'. The direction of their thoughts was expressed by M.A.
Perlmutter, a former follower of Achimeir, and Selman. He declared
that Germany had lost the First World War because it had not properly
evaluated the importance of Palestine, relying as it did on Jewish
hatred of Russia. England was now repeating this error. It was relying
on the Jews' hatred of Hitler without taking into account the Palestine
question. England might thus lose the next war. It could not be denied
that the Jews hated Hitler, but if England were to betray the Jewish
people, the Jews might say to themselves: 'Let us perish with the
Philistines!' and shout out 'Heil Hitler' in Jerusalem! In words which
foreshadowed Stern's declaration in 1940, Perlmutter stated on
1 March 1939:

> The Jews consider the Nazis and the supporters of Hitler relative
> enemies, but they view as their sworn foe the country that is pre-
> venting them from getting rid of all Hitler supporters once and for
> all. The country really hostile to the Jewish people is that country
> which prevents the Jewish people from freeing themselves from
> conditions of exile.[87]

Jabotinsky himself, however, still clung to his old 'policy of alliances'.
He was especially confident that, during his forthcoming visit to
London, the Polish Foreign Minister would find support for the

problem of the immigration of Polish Jews. Poland was as important as the USA and France in the European balance of power. Halifax, the British Foreign Secretary, and his advisers understood this. What had to be convened was a Zionist *Sejm*, a world Jewish convention in Poland, under the auspices of the Polish government.[88]

Nevertheless, the German occupation of Prague did convince Jabotinsky that the 'ten-year plan' should be implemented with greater speed. The first of the many millions should be transferred shortly, on the model of the 'population exchange' between Turkey and Greece in 1922, and a military unit of diaspora Jews should be set up for the defence of the Jewish state.[89] He confronted his impatient disciples by stating that 'Over the past few years it has seemed to me that the more horrible the catastrophe becomes, the shorter will be the roads of exile we shall still have to travel'.[90] In contrast, his followers in Palestine wavered between the IZL tendency to despair of England entirely and support of their leader's weakened orientation towards that country.

\*

Following the paths mapped out by Heilperin (Ratosh), the IZL was by this stage attempting to formulate a new Zionist philosophy. Zionism was not only a negative movement – a movement of those escaping 'from what was done to us by foreigners'. The Jewish people needed to be resurrected by a strong state, for Europe would shortly be controlled only by 'strong races'.[91] The IZL also cited Maimonides' teachings on obligatory warfare,[92] and the obligation to kill off the 'seven Canaanite peoples', as well as the prophet Jeremiah (48:10: 'Cursed is he who performs God's work deceitfully and keeps his sword from blood'). In Maimonides' name, they also guaranteed that the messianic king would restore the kingdom of David to its pristine glory.

Raziel, too, stiffened his attitude towards both England and the possibility of a union with the *Haganah*. Unlike Stern, however, he tried to maintain his loyalty to Jabotinsky within the framework of the 'Paris agreement'.[93] For his part, Jabotinsky emphasised his personal supervision over the IZL. Raziel assured the leader of complete loyalty: 'We hope and trust that with us you will be able to conquer not only the inheritance of the tribes of Reuben and Gad, but far beyond this, if necessary.'[94] He sought to implement the Paris agreement organisationally, but was obstructed by some of Jabotinsky's associates, who accused him of being the leader of an 'anti-Jabotinsky gang'. Those circumstances undermined Raziel's position, as he was caught between Jabotinsky and Stern, and also threatened by the schemes hatched by his own deputy in the *Betar* leadership, Dr Yunitchman.

Yet he promised Jabotinsky: 'You may rely on this staff [the IZL] with
security and pride, if only you let it grow with all its strength.'[95]

In actual fact, the IZL was not as powerful as it claimed to be –
numerically, technically or financially. For propaganda purposes it
exaggerated its own value, boasting that it was in possession of many
weapons, including cannon, that it was financially richer than its parent
movement and that it would bring thousands of its members to
Palestine from the diaspora should war break out. Its members con-
tinually underrated the effectiveness of Arab opposition, claiming
that attacks from Syria or Transjordan could easily be repelled. If
necessary, drastic measures (gas or microbes capable of wiping out an
'enormous' number of Arabs throughout the Near East) could be
used. Hitherto they had refrained from terrorist activities against the
British authorities, but warned that their policies could change.[96]

Jabotinsky still refused to admit that the 'partnership' with England
had reached its end. Only three days before the publication of the 1939
White Paper, he publicly stated that he believed that it would be
deferred, because the government understood that the time for such a
document was not ripe. Nevertheless, the ambivalence in his attitude
became plain when he at the same time argued that something so
precious as the Mandate over Palestine 'could not be kept by a
trembling hand'.[97] Clearly, Jabotinsky was being torn between his two
mutually contradictory roles as president of the NZO and as supreme
commander of the IZL.

FROM THE WHITE PAPER TO THE OUTBREAK OF WAR:
THE WIDENING OF THE BREACH BETWEEN JABOTINSKY AND
THE IZL

The ambivalence in Jabotinsky's position did not end when the publication of the White Paper became imminent. Now, however, he had
to contend with a challenge from Uri Zvi Greenberg, as well as from
the IZL. Visiting Vilna, Jabotinsky was confronted with the anti-
British slogan 'Acre-Gaza', coined by Greenberg.[98] The following day
he was also confronted by the *Betar* representatives – Epstein and
Scheib – and Greenberg. As a concession to the militant mood,
Jabotinsky proposed to organise and train 100,000 Jewish soldiers for
'immigration and conquest', as well as the 'Zion *Sejm*' plan. Scheib
contemptuously dismissed the *Sejm* idea as a waste of youthful energies;
he favoured the immigration and conquest idea alone. As was to be
the case with his insurrection plan of October 1939, Jabotinsky probably regarded this as a purely demonstrative proposal, a means of
bringing pressure to bear on the British.[99]

Thus, Jabotinsky continued to walk his tightrope. On the one hand, he admitted that the White Paper would leave 'deep wounds in our heart and in our soul'; however, it would be forgotten. His programme was now: (a) an end to 'self-restraint'; (b) illegal immigration; (c) a British-Polish-Romanian condominium until the establishment of the state; (d) the 'Zion *Sejm*'; and (e) a Jewish military unit in Poland for emergency use in Palestine.[100] His belief that he had healed the rift with Stern's group in Poland was clearly mistaken,[101] even though he had been behind the acquisition of arms, costing 212,000 zloty, for the IZL.[102] The IZL was unlikely to accept Jabotinsky's political programme, in which Britain still played a significant role. Its command announced on 16 May 1939, that 'blood and the sword', and not the White Paper, would be decisive. This was especially relevant on the eve of a world war, when the British were more likely to select as allies the 'fighting' Arabs than the Jews, who were 'exercising self-restraint'.[103] Jabotinsky, too, condemned the White Paper ('A holy thread has been snapped, a great altar destroyed . . .').[104] But he lost credibility in IZL circles. Although publicly and unreservedly identifying himself with the IZL, he sent them orders not to carry out any operations: 'I frankly fail to see any real and tangible [need] for actions and reactions in connection with the [White] Paper.'[105]

The test came on 29 May, when the IZL carried out a 'retaliatory' operation in the Arab village of Bir Ades, near Magdiel. Four Arab women were reported to have been killed. Incensed, Jabotinsky demanded that those responsible for the operation be punished, that in future the Arabs receive advance warning of impending attacks, and that the killing of the four women be denied, if it really was untrue.[106] But the IZL described the operation as a 'heroic' attack of 'great' educational value for its members, and as a turning-point because it was carried out in a 'purely' Arab district, far away from Jewish territory (*sic*!). Moreover, the operation marked a strategic shift, because for the first time the Arabs had requested arms from the government to defend their villages.[107] In short, the IZL had shown that the *Yishuv* was capable of competing with the Arabs in terrorism, and that counter-terrorism – unlike 'self-restraint' – was effective. Above all, however, the action had begun to change the Jewish self-image, itself a necessary precondition to the realisation of a large Jewish state. During their long exile, Jews had been contaminated by a feeling of 'civil inferiority', whereas in their independent homeland they had definitely known how to fight and kill, despite the hallowed tradition of 'thou shalt not murder'. The shattering of 'self-restraint' and the exercise of force would generate self-respect.[108] Co-operation with the Arabs as proposed by the Jewish

Agency was beside the point. Did the British migrate to America to co-operate with the American Indians? Did the Boers exchange Holland for the plains of South Africa in order to co-operate with the Zulu warriors, the Hottentots and the Bushmen? Achimeir and Heilperin's ideas had begun to make deep inroads into the IZL ideology.[109]

In parallel with the Bir Ades operation, and on the same day, the IZL attacked the Rex cinema In Jerusalem, using modern terrorist devices – an explosive jacket and explosive chocolates. Between 2 and 8 June they also blew up telephone lines, telephone booths and electric transformers in Jerusalem and Tel Aviv. These operations were described as being of an anti-British nature. Immediately thereafter the IZL tried to place a bomb among visitors to the prison in Jerusalem but IZL member Rachel Habshush (Ohevet-Ammi) was caught and sentenced to life imprisonment. The IZL also initiated the planting of a booby-trapped envelope at the Jerusalem central post office, causing the death of a British policeman, Constable Fred Clarke.[110]

The escalation of the operations troubled Jabotinsky, because he wanted to transform the struggle against Britain into a legalistic one.[111] He still believed that the ideological differences between himself and Stern and his followers could be bridged administratively, by adding them to the ruling bodies of the NZO and of *Betar* (a move which Stern rejected).[112] Furthermore, in conversation with Malcom Mac-Donald, Jabotinsky denied any connection with the terrorist incidents. He offered to go to Palestine, but admitted that he could guarantee nothing, because – as long as IZL members were being kidnapped by the police – his own influence was no more than moral.[113] In fact, despite further opposition from the Polish government and the IZL, Jabotinsky was still clinging to his 'Zion *Sejm*' idea. Indeed, this even clouded his views on the imminent danger of a world war. He dismissed Hitler and Mussolini as cowards, 'completely normal and unsophisticated businessmen'. The tension they generated was no more than 'a sensational conjuncture' and would calm down. Instead of war, Eastern Europe would be swept by a strongly anti-Semitic movement, mainly influenced by the White Paper. Mass emigration had to be demanded before that danger materialised.[114]

The IZL now went further. It called for the immediate resignation of the leaders of the Jewish Agency; the 'Fighters for the Freedom of Israel' would take the fate of the *Yishuv* into their own hands. They warned the British: 'The Ir[gun] does not consider itself obliged to fight at the side of the British as long as Great Britain remains the ally of the Mufti.' Its true aim was 'the conquest of Palestine within the borders of the Davidic Kingdom, the establishment of the Kingdom of

Israel by force . . . and [*Irgun*] will fight using *every* means against any enemy blocking its path to ultimate redemption'.[115]

For tactical reasons, Stern was at this point prepared to admit that the Arabs were the real enemy, and that Britain might eventually co-operate with an armed *Yishuv*.[116] Nevertheless, it was clear whom he saw as another possible enemy: 'The moment it becomes clear that Britain does not intend to fulfil this obligation [a Jewish state], the Jews will stop being loyal to Britain – the ally of the Arabs. In any case there will not be any other alternative – they will have to find other allies.'[117] This theme was echoed by the IZL's newspapers in Poland, where the emphasis on *raison d'état* alone was also stressed. If necessary, Jews would have to shed 'innocent' Arab blood. Only thus would they overcome the blind enthusiasm for morality, which had been the product of hundreds of years of Jewish slavery.[118] Anti-British sentiments increased even further after 12 July 1939, when the authorities – citing 'illegal' immigration activites – cancelled the immigration quota for the period October 1939–March 1940 and seized the ship *Colorado*.[119]

But the British were not the only targets of IZL attack. Adopting the line taken by the NZO, Stern and his followers pointed out that the failure of the Jewish Agency was now glaringly obvious. The country had been promised to the Mufti 'by means of a single stroke of the pen'. The shrinking of Zionist rights since 1917 was inversely proportional to the development of the *Yishuv*'s economic projects, a fact which proved that independence was not dependent '*to any extent whatsoever*' upon economic achievement. A 'thousand' examples in history demonstrated that independence was not attained through economic projects or wealth.[120] The Jewish Agency had failed to make political demands; instead it had transformed Zionism into a simple economic venture, a kind of Pithom and Raamses built in the ancestral homeland. Now those responsible for this disaster were to be replaced by those who knew how to lead a nation in its fight for full liberation.[121] The IZL's identification with the rightist ideology of the Revisionists is clear here, and cannot be denied, despite the fact that the IZL occasionally claimed that it was uninterested in questions of social import.[122] The 'leftist' national institutions and the *Histadrut* were profaning the sanctified concepts of 'war' and 'conquest': war does not mean an election campaign, as conquest does not mean taking control of labour of the soil. Salvation would only come through a war 'of fire and blood'.[123]

Jabotinsky now finally realised that Stern and his followers were trying to turn the *Irgun* into an independent body at any cost. He accepted that many of their complaints were real, and recognised their 'unique patriotism'; but he was not prepared to surrender to them. Surprisingly, he was prepared to accept the possibility of a split.[124] His immediate entourage, however, had not yet despaired. On 1 August Dr David Buckspan (the chairman of the 'committee of deputies' of the NZO in Palestine), apparently speaking on Jabotinsky's behalf, proposed representation on the executive for the IZL and its maxima-list supporters.[125] Jabotinsky considered the proposal lacked prestige ('terribly non-*salonfähig*'), but supported it notwithstanding. Within a few days he was optimistic about a split not being absolutely necessary – relations were 'bound to get worse before they got better'.[126]

According to one of the maximalist activists, Naftali Lubenchik, 'the [maximalist] Faction of Allegation and Faith' enjoyed consider-able influence over the IZL in the period following the White Paper. In his account, the IZL was merely a *'tabula rasa'* and he and his colleagues in the faction hoped that the *Irgun* would accept political direction. In the summer of 1939, frequent meetings were held between the maximalist faction headed by Yeivin and the IZL command.[127] Jabotinsky was now sure that Stern's 'separatist' mentality and orien-tation[128] weakened the movement in Palestine. He cautioned his followers not to 'exaggerate the importance of the Palestine front . . . Especially at this time when "Zionism" has once again become the movement of those who are forbidden to come to Palestine, let us not silence our voice in the Diaspora because of a local *va banque*.'[129] Thus the *Irgun* remained secondary in his political considerations.

But the IZL tried to cultivate its own anti-British image. In an interview given in the United States, it compared itself to the Irish Republican Army. Its doctrine was both military – the defence of Palestine, and political – attaining an absolute Jewish majority in Palestine by means of mass immigration. In both respects, the British were the 'direct enemy'. Numbers in themselves were unimportant, when it was borne in mind that 1,800 IRA members had successfully tied down 80,000 British soldiers. In any case, without hindrance, Palestine was capable of absorbing from eight to ten million Jews.[130] Clearly, an alternative ally had to be sought.

> In these days when every power is searching for allies, the *Irgun* will make contact with a power which could assist it more than any other, and which would give us a more reliable guarantee for the establishment of a Jewish fatherland. At the same time the *Irgun* will obstruct the military efforts of those powers who will prevent the Jewish people from returning to its homeland.[131]

In Palestine itself, attacks on England escalated. So too did IZL criticism of the official Zionist leadership. 'Self-restraint' was depicted as the root of all evil.[132] The *Irgun* were the new Hasmoneans, out to fight the assimilationists, who had entrenched themselves in the 'Haqra fortress' in Rehavia.[133] The members of the *Histadrut* should not be deceived by their leaders into becoming involved in a civil war. With an IZL victory, 'the worker will have bread and freedom, the settler will have land, the farmer will have security, the manufacturer and merchant will have a means of subsistence, and millions of Jews at present lost in foreign lands will have refuge, the entire nation will have honour and respect'.[134] The IZL was trying to project the image of an organisation above party differences and class disputes, and not merely the military arm of the Revisionists.

It was at this stage that Stern began to criticise more openly the Zionist ideas of his 'supreme commander'. In the process, he also began to formulate a new ideology of Zionism. He claimed that there were no great differences between Jabotinsky and the Jewish Agency (*Hovevei Zion*), because neither believed in the ability of the Jewish people to establish its state at any time with its own resources: 'Both viewed England as the decisive factor'; and both mistakenly assumed that world public opinion and the League of Nations were political factors. His alternative ideology was based on force: 'always decisive in the lives of conquerers and freedom fighters.' Rights were awarded only to the strong, who are allowed to take them by force if they are not given them legally: 'For the land and freedom and government are not given to the weak and are not ever purchased – they have always been conquered by bloodshed and the sword.' His rejection of both the Revisionist movement and the workers' movement was absolute. Neither the descendants of Borochov nor those of Herzl ever understood the meaning of an ideology of force. The only force which could break the power of the Arabs and suppress it completely was 'the Hebrew army of conquest, the army of freedom and of kingdom' – the IZL – which would establish 'the kingdom of Israel' on *all* of the land 'upon which the Jewish people had lived at some time in their past'.[135]

Unlike Jabotinsky, Stern believed that a world war would break out, and had taken this into account. Here his attack on Jabotinsky was unambiguous. No Jew would fight in 'foreign armies', there would be no 'foreign legion' or 'mercenary army', as in the First World War. Instead the IZL – 'a tribe of warriors' – would fight alongside the 'power which would recognise that the Jewish people were the sole owners of the country and that they would establish their kingdom in it'. What had happened to T.E. Lawrence and his Bedouin tribes would happen to the Jewish people: 'When the coming war breaks out, foreign statesmen and officers would approach us . . . and try to persuade us to join them . . .' Did Stern, at this early juncture, already regard Italy or Germany as a potential ally? Our sources do not provide an answer. But in view of Revisionist contacts with the Italians before the outbreak of the war, the possibility cannot be ruled out.

Stern was exercised by the fate of the 'Jewish Legions' after the First World War, and was determined that the experience of disbandment should not be repeated. In any case the future of the Jewish kingdom was one of permanent war:

> Our nation will yet fight in our land for a long time until it pours out its rule upon the nations and conquers new lands, and so for many more generations the children of Israel will go to school to learn the arts of war, and for many more generations the Jewish kingdom will resemble a military camp in the East-Arabian desert.[136]

Though outnumbered by the Arabs, the Jews remained qualitatively superior. They would be like the 70 million Japanese who had been able to overcome the 400 million Chinese.[137]

The *Irgun* expressed undisguised support for Poland, the supplier of arms and trainer of IZL members on her own soil. Poland became both an ally and a model for national liberation, and the sayings of Pilsudski, admired by the Revisionists and Stern in particular, were extensively cited. 'The blood shed today, life sinking today, will bestow the fruits of its blessing, but only in the future . . . [the] very same trends, so unpopular [and condemned] at first, were eventually victorious. This, too, was the fate of armed uprisings. Now they are considered utopian . . . '[138] The *Irgun* also expressed its unambiguous support for Poland in the summer of 1939 over the question of Danzig and the Polish Corridor. Particular emphasis was given to Polish disappointment at the lack of British support. The Poles regarded Britain as unreliable, and had therefore entered into negotiations with Hitler. Given the Polish people's readiness (unlike the Czechs) for a heroic war for their homeland until their last drop of blood, Hitler would make important concessions.[139]

The period prior to the outbreak of war witnessed an escalation of IZL violence against the British. Three retaliatory murders were carried out against British policemen, two of whom – Cairns and Barker – had been responsible for torturing an IZL commander, Binyamin Zeroni. The IZL defended the assassinations (carried out on 26 August) as 'legalistic' rather then 'political' actions. When criticised by the labour movement's newspaper *Davar* (speech), the *Irgun*'s command insisted that the actions did not of themselves illustrate its orientation *vis-à-vis* Britain.

> Our attitude towards Britain, for better or worse, is not determined by the behaviour of a single individual belonging to the British

nation. Our attitude towards Great Britain is determined by the attitude of the government to our fight for a large Jewish state in Palestine. But any detective, even if he is *British*, that dares torture a Jewish prisoner – will be put to death.[140]

The killing of Cairns and Barker led to a wave of arrests, and within a few days (31 August) the entire IZL command had been imprisoned. Its members had been taken by surprise at a meeting where they were discussing Jabotinsky's plan for 'armed rebellion'. This was to have included an illegal immigration operation, in which Jabotinsky himself was to have taken part, as the prelude to an 'armed rising' during which Jabotinsky would declare the establishment of a Jewish state in Palestine. Even if it failed immediately, so Jabotinsky felt, the operation would still have 'tremendous demonstrative value through-out the world'. Stern, surprisingly, seems to have felt that the entire plan 'would lead to the ruin of the *Irgun*'. There was other opposition, too. After his release from prison, Raziel explained to Jabotinsky that 'we were too thinly spread to consider such projects seriously'.[141]

Coming from Jabotinsky, this was a surprising plan – especially in view of his preoccupation with the 'Zion *Sejm*' and the formulation of a political solution. How can its content be explained? We must surely reject the claim, put forward by Jabotinsky's followers, that his funda-mental ideology underwent a sudden and complete metamorphosis. His letters, his articles and even his last book – *The Jewish War Front* – all indicate that he constantly held, both in secret and in public, that politics, not violence, were of primary importance. His plan may, indeed, have been a 'temporary, despairing leap';[142] but it is also pos-sible that Jabotinsky never really meant it to be implemented; he simply wanted to demonstrate his sympathy with maximalist ideas in Palestine, so as to prevent a split and a take-over of the IZL by Stern and his followers. As in 1937, Jabotinsky's proposals for 'a rebellion' cannot be taken seriously. His intention was to use the idea to gain greater credibility for himself as 'supreme commander' of the IZL and to stifle the independent strivings of the IZL for the benefit of the NZO. In fact, by the end of August the plan had already reverted to what it really was, a mere sheet of paper.

# PART TWO

# THE STERN PERIOD

# 3

# The Split in the IZL against the Background of the Outbreak of War

THE OPPOSITION TO WAR RECRUITMENT
AS AN ANTI-BRITISH CATALYST

After Raziel's imprisonment on 19 May, the IZL's political views had become more extreme; under Kalay's command, the organisation adopted a more anti-British guise. The White Paper had added Britain to its catalogue of enemies.[1] Only because of the international crisis over Danzig did reprisal activity against the Arabs cease after 20 July.[2] Nevertheless the IZL claimed that its actions – the assassination of Clarke (11 June), the operation at the government broadcasting studios (30 June) and the assassination of Cairns and Barker – had 'undermined the White Paper policies'.[3] This was in marked contrast to the policy adopted by the *Yishuv* establishment. Indeed, all the 'arguments' and 'debates' at the twenty-first Zionist congress in Geneva 'were actually nothing but a question of . . . surrender and acquiescence . . . and of abandoning the homeland'. By insisting that the Jews work 'within the framework of the White Paper', the head of the Jewish Agency had revealed himself to be a 'British Agent'.[4]

The outbreak of war revealed the extent to which the split within the IZL had widened. Unhesitatingly, Jabotinsky cabled immediate support to the President of Poland and ureservedly placed the NZO at the disposal of Britain and France.[5] Even though still in prison, David Raziel took a similar stand. Writing to the commanding officer of the British army in Palestine on 5 September, he unambiguously declared his allegiance to England: 'Our criticism of the methods of the Government regarding the fulfilment of the Mandate, was at no time meant to imply a hostile attitude to the British Government as such.'[6] But these sentiments did not reflect the mood of the IZL as a whole. Indeed, on the same day the national command (now controlled officially by Zeroni, but indirectly by Stern and Kalay) issued its Order No. 107, completely contradicting Raziel's statement and forbidding its members to join any volunteer service announced by the national institutions.

> Treacherous and idle hands are directing the potential energy of the people into unsuitable channels . . . IZL soldiers will not spill their

blood for concepts of democracy, justice or European culture aimed *merely* at the defence of *foreign* interests and totally incapable of bringing our redemption any nearer.[7]

In an attempt to obscure its own internal disagreements, the IZL, on 10 September, proclaimed a 'cessation of its aggressive operations' in Palestine. The purpose, it declared, was to 'avoid giving assistance to any degree whatsoever [to] the greatest enemy of the Jewish people in the entire world – German Nazism'. Indeed, it was the Nazis who were now castigated as 'Amalekite persecutors'.[8]Even so, the widening split could not be healed. Stern was himself 'extremely astonished' that the IZL had proclaimed a kind of unilateral armistice; his colleagues would have nothing to do with the notion of recruitment, calling on those IZL members who had joined the *Haganah* in 1937 to return to the fold.[9] They also attacked Jabotinsky's idea of forming a Jewish Legion. 'We shall not be led astray by the concept of an army which will be nothing but an updated version of the J.S.P. [Jewish Settlement police]'.[10] Besides, the British would surely have nothing to do with a military unit influenced by the Jewish Agency, whose pro-Soviet elements (*Ha-Shomer Ha-Tsair* and *Poale Zion Semol*) would not hesitate to assist the Russians, at that time allied to Hitler. The authorities, if they were at all interested in Jewish Legions, wanted only nationalist units, such as the IZL could form.[11]

Thus the IZL, cut off from Jabotinsky, needed a new father-figure, and one more suited to its members' feelings about Britain. This was found in the person of Aharon Aharonson, the myth of whose clandestine NILI organisation the IZL proceeded to resurrect. Quite apart from attributing the Balfour Declaration entirely to NILI's efforts, the IZL also outlined parallels between that organisation and itself. Both were ready for self-sacrifice; moreover, both shared the same axioms, basic to any Jewish liberation movement: (a) *'All means are acceptable* in the Jewish war of liberation as long as they lead to the attainment of the goal – the establishment of 'the Kingdom of Israel'; (b) 'the Jewish *sense of ownership and right to sovereignty* over Palestine exists both without *colonisation* and before a Jewish majority had been attained in Palestine'; (c)'The "Kingdom of Israel" will not be established through parliamentary and legal means, but rather by the devotion of Jewish youth and its willingness for ultimate self-sacrifice'.[12]

In keeping with that outlook, the IZL went on to maintain that the war provided the 'opportunity to dictate terms to governments and great powers' (a notion already expressed some two months earlier by Stern in his article, 'Principles and Conclusions'). By supporting

Britain, Jabotinsky and Weizmann had thrown away this opportunity and gained nothing in return. Afer all, the IZL argued, the Jews did have some cards to play.

> Even the handful of oppressed Jews in the Nazi hell might become troublesome or a useful force in time of war. It is also clear that the Jewish *Yishuv*, as well as world – and, especially American – Jewry, might well be either a troublesome and harmful factor to the British or a helpful and fruitful one.[13]

This totally unrealistic view of the situation is understandable only in terms of the particular brand of historicism favoured by Stern and Kalay. History, they maintained, was the outcome of constellations and opportunities stemming from the independent positions taken by particular peoples without reference to external factors. Indeed, all who supported 'foreign interests' were traitors – a category which now included not only the Jewish Agency but the NZO too.

### THE IZL BETWEEN RAZIEL AND STERN

By the third week of the war, Jabotinsky realised that Polish Jewry was no longer an active factor in Zionism; but he had no sense whatsoever of its impending destruction. Instead, he visualised 'an exodus of unprecedented magnitude' which, since the war was a transitory phenomenon, would precede the establishment of a large Jewish state.[14] Meanwhile, he cautioned the IZL within Palestine to be more moderate toward the British.[15] As his later correspondence revealed, Jabotinsky in fact wanted to transform the *Irgun* into 'the National Militiary Organisation of *Betar*', so that he could control it through Raziel, who also served as a Commissioner of *Betar*.[16]

David Raziel carried out Jabotinsky's commands *in toto*. Before his release from Sarafend on 24 October 1939 (arranged through the intervention of Pinhas Rutenberg), he apparently signed an agreement with the inspector-general of police, A. Saunders, whereby the *Irgun* would cease operations against England, would provide the authorities with intelligence and would assist them in operations in the Middle East, the Balkans and the Baltic countries. In return, *Irgun* would receive 3,000 Palestine pounds as the beginning of financial assistance 'with more to follow, depending on developments'. All remaining IZL prisoners would be released within a fortnight; the *Irgun* would be awarded 25 per cent of the certificates available under the fixed immigration quotas; Revisionist propaganda would not be interfered with and exit permits would be granted. Moreover, elections would be held for a representative assembly at an appropriate time and the 'National Workers' Union' would be given a share in government projects.[17]

Under the terms of the Raziel–Saunders agreement, Stern and his colleagues were also released from detention. Nevertheless, they considered it a treasonable document, and were now determined to remove Raziel from the command. Their own interpretation of the agreement was that their 'drawn-out' battle had led to embryonic signs of a change in English policy, which now favoured 'compromise' with the *Irgun*. The IZL had to take advantage of that situation, specifically by crossing the threshold of the third period in its history, that of 'large operations'. Moreover, it could do so despite the fact that the war had commenced before the IZL had managed to become the decisive force in the *Yishuv* and the nation at large.[18] This rhetoric obscured the bitter reality created by the circumstances under which the war had broken out: in fact, the Jewish people had no option but to adopt a pro-British and anti-German orientation. By declaring that, although it was in favour of overthrowing Hitler, the IZL's main purpose was the 'national territorial' redemption of the Jewish people, the *Irgun* laid the groundwork for an eventual anti-British orientation. It was no coincidence that the belief now spread that the IZL was the real heir of the League of the *Sicarii*.[19] The possibility already existed that Stern and his colleagues might consider an alliance with the Axis powers. Thus, at the very beginning of the Second World War, the IZL stood on the verge of a dangerous choice.

JABOTINSKY AND THE WAR

Sensitive to his geographical distance from Palestine, Jabotinsky did not consider himself to be more than an adviser to the NZO and the IZL there.[20] In fact, the IZL was a secondary factor in his calculations. In his book *The Jewish War Front*, written in February and March 1940, the emphasis was on political solutions, and the 'Supreme Commander' of the IZL made no mention of 'armed insurrection'. Unlike the IZL, he was preoccupied with the plight of the Jews in Poland under Nazi occupation. He could already envisage terrible pogroms and even massacres (though not, of course, the horrors of the Holocaust). Despite the scale of the killings, he regarded German actions as a continuation of earlier anti-Semitic traditions, though he dismissed any possibility of concluding a deal with the Nazis. He did not forget his hostility to the Soviet Union (reinforced by the conclusion of the Molotov–Ribbentrop pact); yet he regarded the anti-Zionist policy of the British government in Palestine to be in some ways worse than that of Tsarist Russia, because by arresting members of the *Haganah* and the IZL the British were preventing Jews from defending themselves against pogroms. Nevertheless, unlike Stern, Jabotinsky did not consider the 1939 White Paper to be an irrevocable document. After all, he argued, the Arabs were also disappointed with it, and it was they who would strive to have it abrogated.[21]

Thus, whereas Stern believed that Britian's 'solid wall' could only be breached by declaring war on Britain – and allying with the devil – Jabotinsky considered it to be only a temporary edifice which would indeed soon fall. Hence the ease with which he could formulate a post-war policy on the lines of the Nordau plan rather than the White Paper.[22] He foresaw a brilliant economic future for the Jewish state, whose real hinterland would be populous South-East Asia. It was obvious that Palestine would include the eastern bank of the Jordan River. Arab objections to its annexation were not to be feared, as that region contained no sites holy to Islam, only 300,000 Bedouins, and no large feudal families, intelligentsia or industrial and mercantile middle classes. Substantial population exchanges would take place, and the minorities would be protected.[23]

In his eagerness to 'sell' his post-war plan to the Allies, on the assumption of their ultimate victory, Jabotinsky made mutually contradictory declarations. On the one hand he spoke of a guaranteed Arab minority in a Jewish state; on the other, he traced the image of a bi-national state: any cabinet could sport a Jewish prime minister and an Arab deputy prime minister, or vice versa; it went without saying (in the later version of his plan) that there would be equality of rights and obligations in parliamentary elections, in military and civil service and in the allocation of budgets, as well as in the distribution of land.[24] Given this confusion, it is hardly surprising that Stern and his disciples regarded the bi-national elements in Jabotinsky's programme with disgust.

At the same time, Jabotinsky formulated his main goals for the Jewish people as a whole: (1) the establishment of a Jewish army on all Allied fronts; (2) recognition of a civilian world Jewish authority, with representation on all international bodies dealing with migration and rehabilitation as well as at the Peace Conference; (3) a Jewish state; and (4) the declaration that a pact guaranteeing international civil equality for the Jews should constitute an Allied war aim.[25] Reiterating his emphasis on the process of national liberation, Jabotinsky proposed that a Jewish army of 100,000 men could conquer Palestine with the full agreement of the Allies. Moreover, a *senatus populusque Judaeorum* (or a 'World Jewish Elected Assembly') would be convened, and the NZO would thereby gain control of the Jewish people.[26]

Early in the spring of 1940, Jabotinsky decided to move the executive

committee of the NZO to the USA, and to recruit American Jewry for
his movement. Palestine had become a secondary goal, since he could
not get there, and because his movement in Palestine was on the verge
of financial collapse. He made it publicly known that the NZO took no
responsibility for *Yishuv* policies adopted under conditons of crisis.[27]
His support for Britain in her darkest hour was unstinting, and in May
1940 he declared: 'It is clear that, in this war, we want England to win,
regardless of all her crimes against Zionism. She is decidedly the lesser
of the two evils.'[28] When Churchill became Prime Minister, Jabotinsky
wished him success in his 'historic mission', and pointed out how absurd
it was to ignore the Jewish problem. He proposed recruiting 130,000
Jews, on condition that the Jewish army receive the same status as that
of the Poles and that MacDonald's Palestine policies be revoked. The
Palestine problem should be left to consideration by the Peace
Conference.[29]

### THE NZO IN PALESTINE: THE CHALLENGE PRESENTED BY THE 'FACTION OF ALLEGATION AND FAITH'

Like the earlier Passfield White Paper, the MacDonald White Paper led
to a resurgence in Revisionist maximalism. Indeed, 'revolutionary
Zionism' now blamed 'the great political defeat' on the IZL as well as
on the 'official' Zionist leadership. The diplomatic alternatives
suggested by the NZO had also failed. Instead of exhorting the people
to oppose England's 'policies of annihilation', and following the revolutionary road 'by physical and military means', the national movement had become 'mere literature'. Of course, the major portion of the
blame rested with the 'criminal leadership' of *Mapai* which, never truly
desirous of a state, had established merely a disunited and disintegrating *Yishuv*, lacking both a national will and political power,
while the diaspora was on the threshold 'of disaster'. But the Revisionists had also failed to seize the opportunity to set up a state. They
had not created the necessary tools – a national newspaper network, a
complex propaganda apparatus, a publishing house and so on. Since
they relied on an evolutionary development, they also lacked dyna-
mism. The revolutionary method meant not only propaganda, but also
revolutionary action aimed at creating facts.[30]

Powerful though such statements were, they did not amount to an
all-out rebellion against Jabotinsky. For one thing, the maximalists still
retained several of his axioms (especially regarding the protection and
representation of the Arab minority) and did not (yet) openly favour
'armed insurrection' against Britain, believing that an offer to protect
British military and imperial interests in Palestine would still

provide the basis for an agreement. Moreover, and for tactical reasons arising out of conditions within the NZO, the maximalists also refrained from open attacks on Jabotinsky himself. They preferred to project the image of men who had remained faithful to Jabotinsky-style fundamentalism. Thus, they explained, within the Revisionist movement two souls were engaged in combat: the one belonging to Jabotinsky, which supported 'revolutionism' and strove to establish a new race, and another belonging to Grossman, which claimed to be correcting distortions by its 'preaching' and by joining the Zionist organisation. The split of 1933 in Katowice had led to the expulsion of the Grossman faction, but 'Grossmanism' had revived within the movement, where it was now represented by Altman and his NZO 'committee of deputies'.[31] Against that background, the maximalists claimed to be attempting to save the NZO rather than rebelling against it. In the past they had rescued the NZO by spreading the concept of revolutionism and war among the *Betar* youth, which had thus become 'Palestinocentric' in contrast to the Revisionist movement, which was 'diasporacentric'. They now had to return to the fray.[32]

Seen in this light, the war waged by Stern and Kalay against Raziel was only part of a broader front which the maximalists, headed by Yeivin and Greenberg, were bringing to bear against Altman. This opposition became clear to Raziel after his release from prison. At the same time the maximalists fiercely opposed the entry of the Revisionist movement into the national committee, headed by Rutenberg. This act, complained Yeivin and his colleagues, constituted '*treason*'. The true revolutionary path was not to try to take control of the *Yishuv* from within, by acting as a minority in the national committee, but to take 'control of the Jewish masses'. That goal could be attained by creating a large and courageous national force of 20,000 people who would paralyse the machinery of the national institutions, put an end to their operation, and accept control of the *Yishuv*. The entire Zionist movement would then also fall into its hands. The demonstration instigated by the IZL high command on 17 May 1939 had shown that with the help of 5,000 people it was possible to exercise authority over the masses while the 'criminals of the [Jewish] Agency' were hiding in their offices.[33]

Yeivin wanted to revive the *Hazit Ha'am* (People's Front). As far as he was concerned, nothing had changed. No concession was to be made to the most basic element of a revolutionary party: 'hatred of the enemy, absolute, raging hatred, which generates a chasm between itself and the old world, which has been condemned to death. This holy chasm is the most certain guarantee of the formulation and victory of the revolution, and cannot under any circumstances be conceded.'

The maximalists considered the communist model as one worthy of tactical – although not, of course, ideological – imitation: the communists took care to ensure that the chasm between themselves and the middle-class world remained unobscured by maintaining strained relations with it. That tactic was contrasted with the policy adopted by the social democrats, who resolved to live in peace with the middle class and to gain power, but then themselves imitated that very class and soon found themselves frightened by the spectre of revolution. Such was the fate awaiting Altman and his followers. The struggle would end only when the incumbent leadership – 'the hallucinationists' – were replaced.[34]

Maximalist confidence in ultimate victory stemmed from the belief that the *Yishuv* was united by abstract ideals rather than material interests. As Greenberg put it, without the Western Wall, there would be no bread. Ideals render human life orderly; in their absence, anarchy predominates, together with famine and want. The growing disintegration of the *Yishuv* was proof of this. The Revisionist movement had a right to exist only as a revolutionary party, and not as a party of interests. Yeivin and his disciples foresaw a situation in which 15,000–20,000 revolutionary youngsters would set up within the *Yishuv* a 'redeeming unity'; the *Yishuv* would hand over the government to them in order to put an end to anarchy.[35] Yeivin thus emphasised opposition to the organised *Yishuv* rather than to the British. In attempting to realise the ideas of the 'Faction of Allegation and Faith', however, Stern and Kalay reversed that order of priorities.

By the end of 1939, the 'Faction of Allegation and Faith' could reiterate that Altman and the accord with the national committee had failed, on both the economic and the political fronts. The maximalists demanded that the party council be convened to consider their participation in the committee. It was now a matter of survival. *Mapai* possessed money and institutions; the liberation movement had only the graves of its martyrs and the tears of those tortured. Were it to concede these, it would lose all its assets.[36]

## THE IZL ON THE EVE OF THE SPLIT

For all their ambitions, Yeivin, Achimeir, Greenberg and other members of the 'Faction of Allegation and Faith' lacked Jabotinsky's charisma. Hence, as long as the president of the NZO was alive, their chances were dim. On the other hand, Jabotinsky was isolated from events in Palestine. Moreover, Raziel's pro-British tendencies aroused unrest in the *Irgun*, and there was the possibility of the Stern–Kalay group seizing power in the IZL high command. The cement which had united the two wings of the IZL in the recent past – the war against Arab terrorism – had vanished. The IZL now encountered opposition not only in the *Yishuv*, but within the NZO too. The latter included 'the foxes' of the 'committee of deputies', headed by Altman, who 'mocked self-restraint, but dared not fight against it' and who 'lacked the spirit to withstand tension and . . . imprisonment'. It also included the 'procurers of the pen' who were trying to 'profit from the IZL's deeds and hitch a ride on its shoulders'. The *Irgun* warned that it would wield the 'cleansing axe' upon those 'dirty hands' extended to take hold of it.[37]

In thus emphasising the ideological–political dispute between itself and the 'committee of deputies', the IZL was able to conceal its own serious internal rift between Raziel and Stern and Kalay. During the few months between the Raziel–Saunders accord and the split in the summer of 1940, IZL publications spread abroad their ideology of zeal as if nothing was happening. Particularly praised were the efforts of the heroic Finns, who were engaged in a 'war of zealots' against the Soviet conqueror. The maximalists had already learned from Jabotinsky that zealotry needed no logical explanation: 'There are many questions to which the only answer is the unconvincing word "Because!" Why do you believe in God? "Because!" How can you prefer an impoverished life in your homeland and not accept luxury in a foreign land? "Because!" Why speak Hebrew? "Because!"' The Finnish example now also showed that 'Where the magnificence of a nation is concerned, its courage – and not its area and number of inhabitants – is decisive'. Unlike France in the 1930s, which had wallowed in a morass of petty calculations, Finland was now engaged in its passion to live. It might fall, but 'a fighting nation, even if defeated, acquires its historic right to independent and free existence'.[38]

The *Yishuv* had to draw the appropriate lesson. Zionism had been transformed from a national revolutionary project to a matter of 'business' and fund-raising. Its organised leaders could not contemplate military operations. They had therefore to be replaced. At the head of 'the Movement for the Rebirth of Israel' there could only stand a person blessed with three characteristics: (a) an unshakeable faith in the just nature and final victory of the Zionist idea; (b) a 'pure national consciousness' that only Palestine in its historical boundaries could solve the Jewish question; and (c) the 'boldness' needed to present the demands of the Jews in their entirety and to do so honourably.[39]

The IZL duly criticised the NZO for joining other sectors of the *Yishuv* in not voicing forceful protests against the publication of the land laws in February 1940.[40] Even if contemporary conditions did make it impossible to draw the sword from its scabbard, these 'Nuremberg laws' would be remembered with shame. When the time came, the IZL would make an end of all the enemies of Zion and of all the traitors to the Hebrew nation. The true implication of the land laws was evident from the statement made by the Colonial Secretary in Parliament, who had declared that the appeasement of the Arabs resulted from the danger that they would side with Hitler in the war, whereas the Jews had no choice but to side with England: 'The conclusion from his statement is extremely clear – England makes political concessions only to those who fight against her. Those who do not fight against her will receive nothing from her.'[41]

In February 1940, Stern and the other members of the command of the IZL who were still imprisoned were transferred from Sarafend to Mazra. Their split with Raziel and the 'committee of deputies' grew deeper, as they became convinced that the Revisionist movement had no interest in securing their release. They now resolved to detach themselves from the NZO, and to establish a political movement to support the IZL. Above all, they would not contact either of the belligerent sides in the war, except in return for political guarantees. This left them with the freedom to choose between sides. Stern regarded Zionist efforts to win the support of Germany and Turkey in the First World War as precedents for present approaches to the Axis powers.[42] In any case Germany was now likely to be victorious, and agreement with her would be necessary to save the *Yishuv*.[43] The poems which Stern wrote in prison during this period indicate the resilience of the central motifs of his life: the sacrificial theme, illustrated by Ben Yosef and possibly by himself in the future ('To our mothers'), and ideas of Jewish messianic redemption ('The Messiah').[44] His new conception was that:

> the Germans are indeed our present enemies. But the British are more dangerous, for they are our future enemies. If we succeed in persuading the Germans that we are prepared to view the British as our major foe, our losses in Poland and other occupied countries might be reduced to a minimum.[45]

Just before the release of the members of the high command on 18 June 1940, the heads of the *Irgun* not imprisoned tried to maintain a united ideological front. To that end, they emphasised the 'doctrine of the few'. Jewish history, as well as the victory of the Bolsheviks in Russia, proved that 'limited forces suffice as long as they enjoy the one decisive faculty in any war for domination: decisiveness, prepared-ness, faith and militarism'. The minority had 'to dare to be aggressive' and 'to dare *to use violence*'.[46] Raziel, however, who wanted to regain control of the IZL, favoured the idea of an army rather than an underground or a handful of revolutionaries. He argued that 'a sound connection' had to exist between the civilian-political and the military spheres. Hannibal had failed because of Carthage's rotten civilian structure, while Rome had triumphed because of its excellent civilian organisation. The IZL was already a 'fairly strong' kernel of a liberation movement, since it numbered thousands. But in order to become the main factor it would have to number tens of thousands; no army could be strong without a 'vast' hinterland – otherwise it would be defeated.[47]

The impending split did not prevent the NZO and the IZL from sharing a common attitude towards the *Yishuv* left and towards the Arabs. The former's emphasis on socialist revolution necessarily rendered them incapable of conquering their homeland, especially with ideas of friendship with the Arabs.[48] As for the Palestinians themselves, they were obviously uncompromising enemies, who supported the enemy camp (the Axis powers). Although currently incapable of insurrection, the Arabs might in the future pose a threat, a 'fifth column'. Indeed, the British might try to deflect Arab rage in the direction of the *Yishuv*, and give in to the Arabs at the expense of the Jewish people.[49]

Altogether, there was by now little support for England in the IZL; the predominant leaning was towards neutrality. In direct contradiction to Jabotinsky, the official organ of the IZL now stated that the Jewish people had no war goal. In fact, it now attacked Jabotinsky as well as the official leadership for encouraging Jews to enlist in British service; even in a 'special Jewish army', Jews would shed their blood 'for doubtful ideals or for dangerous experiments already proved bankrupt in the past'.[50] Admittedly, Stern did not yet wish to reveal the change in his orientation. Thus the underground newspaper, *Ba-Herev* (By the Sword), expressed its satisfaction with Hitler's great victories at the beginning of the war – not on an ideological basis, but because of a latent admiration for 'this evil man's' technical ability to overcome the Allies' material advantages in manufacturing ammunition by enlisting the entire German hinterland in support of Goering's call to place 'Guns before butter'. The success of Nazism lay in the fact that it had:

spread throughout the body of the German nation and created tens of millions of little Hitlers, who were nothing but miniature copies of their mentor. Like him they were fully dedicated to their cause, they showed a cynical attitude towards all moral values, a devilish hatred for their opponents and a fantastic inventive genius . . . The *political* preparations of the Nazi Movement not only made it possible for Germany to fight successfully; they also determined the strategic methods of the struggle.

The Jews had to learn from Hitler, and set up a 'vast hinterland' dedicated to the service of 'the great cause'.[51] Thus was the ideological ground being prepared within the IZL for Stern's alternative option.

### THE SPLIT – IN THEORY AND IN PRACTICE

Once released from prison, Raziel tried to wrest back the leadership of the high command from Zeroni, a member of the Stern–Kalay group. This move, together with a sharp letter from Kalay and the command, led to Raziel's resignation. Under pressure, he agreed to continue functioning until the release of the other members of the high command,[52] but his participation thereafter does not seem to have been very effective. Specifically, he seems to have taken no part in drafting the command's last communiqué before its dissolution, when the *Irgun* split. The latter document indicates that the IZL policy was now determined by the followers of Stern. It argued that Axis victories now made it possible to compel Britain to adopt a pro-Zionist policy, but 'demands' rather than 'concessions, appeasement and flattery' or a 'compromise . . . *without setting a price*' must be made. The IZL would fight against all 'those who would yield', all those willing to give up national interests in favour of 'insignificant matters'. The danger was that 'the trend towards compromise and appeasement gets ever stronger, even within the National movement in the *Yishuv*'. The reference to Raziel and Altman was implicit but clear.[53] The theory that it was possible to force England to make concessions may have been only tactical. Its formulators may not have believed in it at all, but merely wanted to pave the way to an accord with the Axis powers who (unlike Britain) were capable of guaranteeing the Jewish people a state in return. Whichever was the case, it seems that Stern could not withstand the temptation presented by Hitler's great victories in May and June 1940, the entry of Italy into the war on 10 June, and his own anticipation of England's final defeat in the Battle of Britain in the summer of 1940.

Jabotinsky was aware of what was happening, but could do little. Practically, he was only able to keep an eye on the IZL mission to the USA,[54] demanding that it desist from any direct or indirect political activity, especially in connection with the establishment of a Jewish army.[55] Thus, the gulf between Jabotinsky and Stern was now infinitely greater than that between Jabotinsky and the Zionist organisation from which he had resigned. Now, in the IZL's command, only Raziel clung to the leader's pro-British attitude. In a letter to Lord Lothian, the British Ambassador in Washington, Jabotinsky made it clear that he had never demanded the abrogation of MacDonald's White Paper as a precondition for the establishment of a Jewish army. He had merely advocated that its implementation be postponed. Typically, he claimed that (as had been the case in 1916), the Jewish leadership was more responsible than the British government for preventing the establishment of a Jewish fighting force.[56]

On 18 June, Stern was released from prison, together with Kalay, Haichman and Lubinsky, his colleagues in the command – ironically as a result of the intercession and guarantees made by Altman to the authorities (who seem to have known little of Stern's true political leanings). The following day, a 'stormy' meeting took place between Stern, Raziel and the other members of the command, where Raziel repeated his resignation: 'After your filthy letter I have no intention of working with you.' A new command was elected, headed by Avraham Stern, and with the participation of Kalay, Haichman and Lubinsky. After intervention by the 'committee of deputies', Raziel soon retracted his resignation, claiming that only Jabotinsky – the 'Supreme Commander' – was empowered to discharge him and appoint a replacement. Raziel was rejected by the new command, but Stern had not at this stage received his appointment from Jabotinsky. Not even Stern was yet willing to deny the latter's authority.[57]

On 26 June 1940 Stern and his command published their 'High Command Communiqué No. 112', generally accepted by *Lehi* veterans as the inception of their movement.[58] Not unexpectedly, this declared the central goal to be the establishment of 'the Kingdom of Israel' by force of arms within its historic boundaries. The distinction lay in its declared political orientation. In complete contrast to Communiqué No. 111, issued on 31 May 1940 under Raziel's command, Stern and his command openly called 'to evade by all possible means any foreign recruitment'. Familiar attacks were made on the *Haganah*, but Stern had no intention of sitting back; instead, he intended to take the political initiative: 'At this hour when nations fall, and states are destroyed, it is criminal to sit by and watch evil develop.' He assured his followers that victory was inevitable; but he also warned that it would be accompanied by death and torture, which was 'worse than death'. Thus the IZL – 'a tribe of freedom fighters' – had no room for those tired of war or of little faith, for the doubters and the soft-hearted.[59]

Immediately after the publication of the communiqué, the changes in the command were reported to Jabotinsky by Raziel and the leaders of the NZO. In his reply of 29 June, Jabotinsky empowered Altman to take decisions.[60] Although there is no reason to assume that Jabotinsky valued Stern more highly than Raziel, Stern tried to win the 'Supreme Commander's' confidence by establishing direct contact with him, hoping thereby to be appointed by Jabotinsky to be head of the command. He blamed Altman and Raziel for the situation, and listed no less than ten misdemeanours that had necessitated Raziel's removal: (1) his assumption of responsibility for the IZL while still in prison; (2) his personal guarantee that operations would cease after his release; (3) his public appearances in all NZO institutions; (4) his personal intervention in NZO matters and his attempt to take control of the entire movement by means of the 'National Workers' Union'; (5) his factional politics; (6) his removal of people inside and outside the IZL for criticising him; (7) his 'intentional' break of relations with the command as a result of his desire to run the IZL by himself; (8) 'his doing nothing and even *saying* nothing in reaction to the [government's] decrees' (stricter implementation of the immigration laws, severe sentences in courts martial, and the land laws); (9) his unsuccessful negotiations concerning the '*Yishuv* ransom' (*Kofer ha-Yishuv*) in connection with the IZL allowance, and his 'vain struggle' against it, so as to obtain funds by force; (10) his negotiations with British intelligence on the basis of 'payments and discounts' in matters of immigration and labour (that is, the Raziel–Saunders agreement).[61]

On the central issue which caused the split – the question of foreign orientation – Stern merely gave oblique hints. He hoped that Jabotinsky would conclude that his move expressed the lack of confidence which the IZL command and membership had in Raziel (which the latter had himself sensed when tendering his resignation in early 1940). Stern professed his loyalty to the movement: 'There is no place for a split which might break up the entire movement and bring down catastrophe upon us.' Raziel and Altman were 'dissatisfied trouble-makers taking his name in vain'. The question of the attitude to Britain was clouded over, perhaps because Stern hoped that – isolated from events in Palestine – the 'Supreme Commander' might yet overrule the 'committee of deputies'. Here Stern was undoubtedly deluding himself. Altman persuaded Raziel to return to his position as head of the IZL command. Confronted with Raziel's reluctance, and Stern's attacks, he then asked Jabotinsky to despatch an explicit order reappointing Raziel to his post and an additional command to Stern to accept this. In response, Stern argued within the IZL that the split would strengthen the movement ideologically and administratively, and again attacked Raziel for his inactivity. He intended to set up a political movement to serve as a public hinterland for the *Irgun* and have it led by the heads of the 'Faction of Allegation and Faith'.[62]

Stern's assessment of Jabotinsky's inability to dictate the turn of events in Palestine from the USA was not completely mistaken. Jabotinsky's mood at the time was extremely despondent. His main desire – a Jewish army – had not yet been realised, and he was awaiting America's entry into the war. Even thereafter, however, the battles might be long and drawn out, though he hoped they might end quickly, and that a peace conference would implement his Nordau plan. Of course, were Germany to win the war, there would indeed be no place for the Jews, either in Europe or in Palestine.[63]

Once Raziel was reappointed by Jabotinsky, Stern tried his luck with the IZL mission in New York. In letters to Shmuel Merlin, he blamed Raziel for turning his back on his friends and colluding with Altman. Unaware of Jabotinsky's authorisation, Stern pretended he could have reached an agreement with Raziel; the problem lay with Altman and his interference. The NZO and Altman wanted to turn the IZL 'into an empty vessel . . . which would dance according to his [Altman's] flute'.[64] Moreover, Altman and Raziel had misled Jabotinsky by constructing a tissue of 'distortions' and 'forgeries' designed to conceal the fact that Altman was even more of a collaborator than the *Haganah*. Again concealing the central issue of the IZL's foreign orientation, Stern declared that Pittman (Jabotinsky) would have to realise that:

> On the burning question, our stand is like his . . . Neumann [Altman], by his defeatism here, is destroying everything we now aspire to achieve. To our sorrow, Pittman did not hear our side. They misled him with distorted reports, and because of the confidence he once had in these people, he has helped them, I hope unwittingly, to tear apart the most precious thing we have . . . We have done everything to keep the body intact. The issues between us and Cantor [Raziel] were almost settled already . . . but Neumann blocked the way and aborted this settlement at the very last moment out of his desire to be in control.

Stern even suggested the (highly unlikely) possibility of his travelling to New York to meet Jabotinsky, perhaps feeling that the inevitability of an Axis victory was his clinching argument.[65]

At this point Raziel's patience ran out and he related the whole story to his friend Hillel Kook, now a member of the IZL mission in the US. Despite the strong words uttered against him by Stern, he had refrained from telling Jabotinsky that the main point at issue between them was the question of external orientation. He described to Kook the style and methods Stern had used against him in the struggle. He

had been made a victim of 'terrible horror propaganda' spread by
Stern and his supporters: 'If you lie down on your right side, you are a
traitor; on the left – you are a scoundrel. Lie on your stomach – you
have sold your birthright for a mess of lentils; on your back – you have
sold your soul to Satan.'[66] Altogether, Raziel admitted that he had
underestimated Jabotinsky's complaints against Stern in the 'Paris
agreement' period. Without specifying their differences, Raziel now
went on to vilify his former friend:

> Concerning Meir [Stern], this delicate playboy, hovering over this
> base, earthly world in holy piety, almost not touching the impurity
> of this world with his angel's wings, careful not to speak against a
> person so as not to dirty this overspreading sanctity – this charming
> boy has been revealed as an expert at intrigue the stench of which
> being unprecedented in . . . the house of Pittman [Jabotinsky] . . .
> One sees nothing before the decisive hour. When the time comes to
> show one's cards, the job is nice and clean, a delicate ivory statue
> wearing a tie in good taste and smart suit with the trousers precisely
> creased. In short, an unscrupulous, intelligent person, who so dis-
> torts the facts that the borders of reality mean nothing to him, and a
> super-demagogue . . . Where did he learn this pleasant skill? The
> devil only knows. Actually, I think it's not new to him. This is the
> way he has been from the start; it's just that the lion is not always
> recognised by its claws.[67]

Continuing in the same vein, Raziel claimed that 'the stinking
poison' Stern poured on him from prison had brought about his resignation. The IZL was then 'on wobbly legs'. Stern had tried to delay the
announcement of the appointment of a new command for six weeks,
but he himself had agreed to a delay of only ten days. Altman, however, had discovered what was afoot after only a few days, and Raziel
was then forced to accept the command again, especially after it
became clear that the 'dirty work' was Stern's alone, and not that of
the IZL rank and file. Now that he had returned to the command,
however, 'there is nothing of which I have not been accused . . .
(incidentally, they let it be known that I came down with a severe
nervous ailment and must not be contacted – not a bad method of
propaganda)'.[68]

So serious a rift could not even be repaired by Jabotinsky's sudden
death in August 1940. Although new negotiations between the sides
were initiated, their failure was virtually inevitable. Raziel realised
that Stern was only interested in gaining time so that he could blame
him even further. Raziel himself hoped that Stern would be isolated
'with a small circle of simple or rotten people'.[69] But this proved to be

a misreading of the situation: the split was far more serious than he had imagined. True, the majority did not follow Stern, but some ceased to be active altogether, and the IZL did not recover from the split until the appointment of Begin as commander-in-chief at the end of 1943.

Not all IZL members understood the reasons for the split. Many interpreted it as the result of tactical differences and personal quarrels, rather than ideological disagreement.[70] On the other hand, several knew that the split stemmed from Yair's new foreign external orientation; even if they were unaware of his flirtation with the Axis powers, they knew of his desire for a complete break with the British and a renewal of operations against them.[71] The disagreement over the question of orientation also encompassed the issue of the political authority of the NZO over the IZL; but that was not the primary matter at stake. In theory Stern would have accepted the authority of the NZO, had Jabotinsky and his supporters in the 'committee of deputies' refrained from coming out in support of Great Britain in the war.

Thus, it was not the axioms of either Jabotinsky or Achimeir which were of paramount importance to Stern, but rather the operative conclusions stemming from them. Stern might have preferred the 'clearer' Jabotinsky of the late 1920s and the early 1930s – 'To Die or Conquer the Mountain', 'Teach them to Shoot', 'Orientation' – to the Jabotinsky of 1937–39, ambivalent towards England. The Heilperin he tended to agree with was the man of 1937 – 'Our Eyes are Lifted up to Government' and 'the Speech to Members of the Sect' – not the one of 1940 (see below). The Achimeir of 1930–33 was acceptable to him as the preacher and ideologue of an uncompromising liberation war, but not as the head of the demonstrative 'League of the *Sicarii*', devoid of operational value. The central basic assumptions he imbibed from these three teachers were his unimpeachable faith in the role of force in the history of the nations and in Jewish history, on the one hand, and the desire for power, on the other. Hence, Stern can be described as a typical disciple of Nietzsche and of social Darwinism. Force, he held, is what controls nature and history. Life as a desire for power means constant violence where the strong overcome the weak, enslave them or annihilate them. Thus, the life of one is built on the ruins of others, and freedom is a characteristic of the strong to act while overcoming obstacles. To the basic outlook, expressed in his poems and his ideological and operative programme of the summer of 1939 – 'Principles and Conclusions', must be added the concept of an opportune hour in the life of a nation, which he also inherited from his teachers in the Revisionist movement. As soon as it is decided that the proper hour has arrived, the rule of the end justifying the means must be applied. The new organisation he set up – 'IZL in Israel' – is the story of the application of these axioms. Basically, it is one of tragedy, because of the enormous gap between the axioms themselves and their realisation. The rapid fall was inevitable, because the axioms were built on a messianic and irrational base, and the means of realising them were imaginary and vague.

In both theoretical and practical terms, what Stern had in mind was that he would succeed Jabotinsky as the new and charismatic leader of the national movement (the NZO). In accordance with the teachings of Achimeir and Heilperin, he had always viewed the NZO as a liberation movement, and not merely a parliamentary opposition to Weizmann's Zionist organisation. He felt that Jabotinsky's revolutionary impulse had failed him massively in 1939, when he supported the Allies unconditionally. The real and true leader, and the legitimate interpreter of the concept of the liberation movement, then became Stern himself. Hence his ambivalent reaction to Jabotinsky's death at the height of the crisis over the split in the IZL. Although sincerely mourning the death of the 'supreme commander', he condemned him as one who, at the end of his life, was inferior to the Mufti in terms of leadership. As his psychologically minded biographer has written:

> Jabotinsky's death, naturally, brought Yair to centre stage. For years he had carefully prepared himself for this task, but was he ready for it? Until now he had been revealed as a poet of the altar fire, as a tempting diplomat, as a deep thinker (*sic*). But now he had to come forward as a leader, and this was a somewhat different role. With Jabotinsky's death, all bridges of retreat were burnt, nobody could disturb or prevent him from carrying out his fundamental ideas. The freedom was perhaps too sudden for him, which was possibly why he reacted to Jabotinsky's death as he did. His conclusion was, however, inevitable: 'I go forward!'[72]

# 4

# 'The IZL in Israel': Political Movement or Revolutionary Underground?

The only reason for the creation of the new organisation was Stern's failure to wrest the *Irgun* from the Revisionist movement. Nevertheless, even during the course of the attempted take-over he had already come out against Jabotinsky, arguing that there existed no difference between Hitler and Chamberlain, between Dachau or Buchenwald and sealing the gates of *Eretz Israel*, or, for that matter, between the 'Nazo-Fascist' states and the 'democracies'. Stern regarded communists and social democrats as equal enemies, and could see no distinction in England between the socialists and the conservatives. Indeed, all nations of the world understood only 'the language of the bullet, the rifle and the bomb'.[1] National liberation would come from an armed Jewish youth, with its spiritual and physical strength, its high level of technology and culture and its readiness for sacrifice. What was now required was unity and preparations for war in the service of a purely Jewish cause. Nevertheless, Stern did not entirely abandon the Revisionist line: he too attacked the defeatist Zionist leadership and regarded the Arabs as the immediate foe. Moreover, and possibly with an eye to attracting IZL members, he declared that 'in the meantime we refrain from taking English lives'.[2]

Perhaps influenced by such tendencies, Raziel tried to play down the split. Beginning with his order No. 112 of 22 July 1940, he argued that the disagreement within the IZL was purely personal, and sought to reunify the organisation by warning of an imminent Arab attack. Suppressing the agreement with Saunders of October 1939, and rejecting the 'yoke of foreign rule', he emphasised the *Irgun*'s continuing 'liberty and freedom of action'.[3] In December 1940, by which time the IZL was completely paralysed, he was to declare the schism to be over.[4]

That was not the case. In its first announcement,[5] 'IZL in Israel' described the previous year as one of 'disaster and destruction' for both the distressed and exploited *Yishuv* and the ruined and imprisoned European diaspora. Stern, Kalay and Zeroni declared that the creation of a new organisation had been an act of purification, since the inadequate figures of the old organisation – Raziel, Haichman, Lubinsky and others – had been expelled. The new movement sought to unite all those ready for liberation, and posed as the sole representative of a fighting Jewry to be centred in *Eretz Israel* after the 'annihilation of the diaspora'. Its immediate task was an armed take-over of the country as soon as possible, and the war was to provide such an opportunity. It would indeed participate in the war, but only as a 'revolutionary underground', assisting 'the power' which would help set up the Jewish army and state. Although there was no explicit mention of fighting on the Axis side, Mussolini's Italy (always favoured by Jabotinsky, Achimeir and Ratosh) seemed to be implied.

## THE QUESTION OF THE ITALIAN CONNECTION:
## THE 'JERUSALEM AGREEMENT' OF 16 SEPTEMBER 1940

Stern's desire to align with Italy can be traced to several sources: lingering Revisionist pro-Italian sentiments, his own sojourn in Italy in 1933–34, and a belief that the NILI pattern of the First World War might be repeated. Stern had foreseen contacts on the Polish model in August 1939, and they were indeed instituted with the Italian consul in Jerusalem, Conte Quinto Mazzolini, although they ceased when Italy entered the war on 10 June 1940.

But matters soon took a new turn. Moshe Rothstein, a former IZL member, who was in 1940 working for both British intelligence and IZL intelligence, claimed that the Italians were interested in a fascist IZL Jewish state under their protection. Stern learned of this proposal, and felt that even if it was not serious, it would be useful for the British to be aware of his conditions for collaboration with either side.[6]

After 13 September, when the Italian army began to advance on Egypt, Stern thought that the opportune hour had indeed arrived. Meanwhile, he had also been impressed by the Italian bombing of Haifa and of Tel Aviv where, on 9 September, 117 people were killed and 140 injured. As he told a somewhat sceptical Ratosh, he foresaw an Axis victory which could lead to the fulfilment of Zionism.[7] That some arrangement could be made with a victorious Italy he hardly doubted. Influenced by Ratosh's extreme denial of the diaspora and by Jabotinsky's analysis of anti-semitism, Stern altogether underestimated the importance of Hitler's and Mussolini's anti-semitic ideology and chose to ignore Mussolini's anti-Jewish measures. Indeed, following the line taken by Jabotinsky in his last book (*The War Front of the Jewish People*), Stern even regarded Polish anti-semitism as stronger in some respects than its Nazi counterpart. The fascists were certainly amenable to an arrangement, based on evacuation.[8] Thus was laid the theoretical groundwork for the 'Jerusalem agreement' with Italy, which envisioned the possibility of such an eventual deal with Germany too.[9]

Under the terms of the proposed 'agreement' which the 'IZL in Israel' now drafted, Italy was to effect the transfer of Jews under Axis control to their homeland, and to help organise the army of the Hebrew state. The necessary ideological identity would be ensured by the establishment of a 'corporative regime' and the formulation of an identical foreign policy. Haifa was to serve as a base for the foreign power.[10] The Old City in Jerusalem, except for the sites holy to the Jews, would be under the Vatican, which would recognise the Hebrew state through Italian intercession. A Hebrew majority of 80 per cent would be guaranteed, together with the recognition of the Arab states.[11] There would be economic co-operation between the new state and the Arab countries and possibly with the Italians. In return for Jewish immigration and doubtful independence, Stern was thus prepared to turn the 'Kingdom of Israel' into a satellite of the Axis powers. Yet there is no evidence whatsoever of any likely response from Mussolini to all of this.[12] When Stern lost hope in Italy after its defeats on the Greek front and in the Western Desert in December 1940, he simply replaced a faltering Italy with a victorious Germany.

## 'THE PRINCIPLES OF REVIVAL' AND THE POLITICAL SITUATION (1940–41)

The ideological underpinnings of this extroardinary approach are best illustrated by the new group's writings of this period, and in particular by those which are collectively entitled 'The Principles of Revival'. Under Stern's inspiration, these insisted that not even the IZL had managed to 'shake the dust of the diaspora from its feet'.[13] What was required, he believed, was a revolutionary twist to the teachings which he had imbibed from Jabotinsky. Indeed, in order to carry them out a pact had to be concluded with the devil. Just as Jabotinsky had believed Petlura to be no worse then Plehve, of whom Herzl had apparently approved, so Stern felt that Hitler (not to mention Mussolini) was no worse than the Polish 'colonels' with whom he had negotiated with relative success.

Stern's only criterion for the definition of a 'Jewish war' was whether its aims included the establisment of an independent Hebrew state within its historic borders. A nation which lacked sovereignty, he believed, could not wage a struggle for personal liberties; social and individual rights were only possible within the sovereign nation. Citing an example also favoured by the NZO and IZL, he frequently drew inspiration from the Irish struggle during the First World War.

Indeed, the example of *Sinn Fein* in 1916 was particularly persuasive to Stern, who was convinced that the use of violence was a condition for national liberation among both the Jews and the Gentiles. The mistake of the British, in his analysis, lay in their failure to take advantage of the fact that the rebels themselves were a minority of the Irish people. It was by executing the freedom fighters, and thereby transmuting them into martyrs, that the British had in fact saved Ireland's soul. That, indeed, had been the aim of the rebels, who were aware in advance of their impending failure, but were willing to sacrifice their lives. The Irish people, three-quarters of whom had assimilated with the British, decided to remind the world that they were still a nation. The same morning that Thomas Clarke was placed before a firing-squad in Kilmainham, the old Ireland vanished without trace. The comparison with *Eretz Israel* was self-evident. Neither politics nor diplomacy would liberate the Jewish people, but rather 'the strong arm of fighting youth'.[14]

To say this was not to state that pacts with foreign powers were not feasible; but the 'opportune hour' for such agreements would come only if the 'IZL in Israel' could convince the potential ally of its strength and will to sovereignty by means of military operations and acts of vengeance. Thus all private interests must be subordinated 'to the requirements of the war of liberation'. Anyone interfering with this war would be considered an enemy and a traitor. The members of the new underground would simply be 'a cog in the war machine', but their desire for liberty would find expression in military and other actions directed against the Arabs and the British.[15] At the same time physical and financial pressure had to be applied in order to wrest control of the Jewish streets from the other, treacherous, elements in the *Yishuv*. Moreover, the NZO had failed to come to terms with Arab military strength.[16]

To all this Stern added another element. He had been taught by his maximalist teachers – such as Ratosh – that the masses were the sole instruments in the revolutionary war against the enemy. Aware that he possessed very few followers, he believed that the masses could be won over to uncompromising ideas and absolute demands by the zealous adherence of the revolutionary core to fundamental principles and final goals, expressed in conspiracy and illegal acts. (Thus, following the lessons of the *Narodnaya Volya*, the assassination of a prominent Englishman would serve as a model for the education of the *Yishuv*.)[17] It was the task of the leadership to set up exalted goals before the nation. The French, for example, had adored Napoleon – even in defeat – despite all the superhuman efforts and endless sacrifice he demanded of them. 'Who dares say that a nation hates making efforts and sacrifice? This is not so. One only needs to know how to stir them up. That accomplished, it is possible to do anything with a nation, anything.'[18]

Ratosh's influence was also clear in the first of the 'Principles', which emphasised the rights of the Hebrew race to the 'homeland' extending 'from the Nile to the Euphrates'. An 'Era of War and Conquest', the group proclaimed, would be characterised by an underground army and the preparation of the revolutionary masses for wars of liberation, culminating in the final conquest of the land. This would be followed by the 'Era of Sovereignty (*adnut*) and Redemption', with the establishment of a socio-economic regime in the spirit of the morality of the prophets and the promotion of mass immigration and population growth.

On other matters, however, there was some internal disagreement within the 'IZL in Israel'. In his own wording of 'The Principles of Revival', Hanoch Kalay spoke of the land of Israel as the 'living space' of all Jews.[19] (This insensitivity to a clearly Nazi term was to be corrected in the final version to 'life-land'.) He envisaged a state which would constitute a strong regional power and, following the inclination of maximalist Revisionism towards the fascist-authoritarian model, called for the establishment of 'a strong centralised national government which would see to the nation's conquests and put an end to the bickering and deceit of the political parties which tear the nation apart and distract it towards vain ideals and goals'. Stern wanted to omit this definition which might damage the non-party image that 'the Principles of Revival' tried to cultivate. But Kalay also advocated including the anti-leftist Revisionist heritage in the 'Principles', attacking groups which 'deny the nation's destiny of complete redemption and which fly foreign flags . . .'.[20] Indeed, he called for 'an end to class struggle', with labour disputes to be settled by compulsory national arbitration under a corporatist economic system.[21]

Kalay's draft was accepted in the sphere of foreign policy. Alliances with anyone were possible in order 'to annihilate' the diaspora and set up 'the Kingdom of Israel'. On other issues, however, matters were less straightforward. To solve the question of the Arabs, Kalay proposed their 'transfer', while Stern preferred a 'population exchange' with these 'foreigners'. Moreover, Kalay tended to be vague about the relationship between religion and state, stressing 'respect and honour' for religious Jewry which maintains a link between the nation and its God, while Stern called for a building of the Third Temple. For him, in any case, this was a symbol of Hebrew independence and not merely a religious matter, for Jewish wars had always been characterised by religion, and religion had protected the life of the nation in exile as a substitute for the state: the prayer book was a kind of passport, the *Torah* – a kind of constitution, the prayer shawl – a flag. Thanks to religious zealotry, 'the blood of the nation remained purely Hebrew'.[22] Religion was not, however, such a pressing issue since, as yet, only the 'Era of War and Conquest' was at hand. This was in accordance with the Revisionist tendency to leave the character of the regime to the period following the establishment of the state.

More significant, in retrospect, was the commitment which the 'Principles' made to the establishment of a 'righteous regime' under which, in accordance with the morality of the prophets, there would be neither hunger nor unemployment. This the 'IZL in Israel' inserted in order to emphasise the distinctiveness of its ideology from Revisionism. Nevertheless, here, too, the 'Principles' were sufficiently vague for the new group to remain within the Revisionist ideological ambit. Classless monism, with respect for all in the economy, was still predominant in the social ideology of the new body, and the social programme was subsumed under a declaration that there would be no 'starved and unemployed' people. It was, indeed, only in 1943 that the first real steps to the left would be made. In publishing 'The Principles of Revival', Stern and his followers committed themselves to ideas of the radical right and integral nationalism, as had Achimeir, Yeivin and Ratosh in their day. The main features of their ideology were historical determinism, social Darwinism, militarism, corporatism and imperialism, xenophobia, 'sacred egoism', suppression of opposition, subordination of the individual to the state, anti-liberalism, a denial of democracy and an internally centralised regime.[23]

Altogether, the 'Principles' were regarded as an attempt to 'uproot once and for all' the ideological confusion characteristic of the *Irgun*, and to prove the 'absolute independence' of the 'IZL in Israel'. In fact, ideological and practical unification was stressed in the absence of any real action. After their publication (in two parts – in October 1940 and February 1941), members were asked to subscribe to the 'Principles' or to leave the organisation, for they were considered immutable. Contrary to standard Revisionist teachings, they were explicitly informed that the Balfour Declaration was dead and thus any pro-British orientation must be defunct.[24] Any attempt by the right to create the 'uniform national front' called for by Pinhas Rutenberg was inevitably futile.[25] Stern supported his argument by reference to the examples of the Irish government and the Indian National Congress, both of which had refused to join Britain against Hitler. Abdullah and Fakhri Abd al-Hadi's 'peace gangs' were justified in collaborating with the British because the Arabs had been promised independence which, in accordance with the White Paper, Britain would indeed grant them within three years. The fate awaiting the Jews, however, was already indicated by the *Patria* disaster and the expulsions to Mauritius. Those drafted into the Polish and Czech armies would, on their return home, find anti-semitism. *Yishuv* recruits to Britain's army could expect an Arab state.[26]

In the absence of any alternative, ideology meanwhile became a substitute for action. The 'IZL in Israel' reverted to the familiar Revisionist recitation of the litany of historical heroes – from the Hasmoneans to NILI. The latter model particularly exercised Stern, who had day-dreamed of creating a new version of NILI while in Mazra prison. As he had told Yeivin, one of those who had shaped his own ideological thinking, just as NILI had struggled against the Turkish overlords of the land, so he would struggle against its British masters. Yeivin pointed out that the two situations could not be compared: NILI had waged war against the Turks who were hated by world Jewry, whereas at present the Jewish people viewed the British as their allies against Hitler: 'They will say of you that you assisted Hitler . . . they will cover your memory with spittle and disgrace. You will be hated and shamed by the very nation you desire to liberate.' His protests were to no avail. Stern replied 'simply': 'I know that. Nevertheless, I will do it.'[27]

The purpose of the NILI example was to help formulate an operative ideology for the underground revolutionary military organisation until practical conditions in *Eretz Israel* made national fulfilment possible. The Jewish messianic concept was the link between the Hasmoneans and NILI. A 'terrible' world war would ensue on the appearance of the herald of the Messiah, after which the Messiah himself would appear and establish the rule of the Hebrew nation over the entire world. 'Realists' believed that the Messiah must be helped by channelling the desire of the nation into the correct grooves and by awakening the people to correct action in order to throw off the foreign yoke.[28] Authorisation for this teaching was found in the writings of Maimonides, who had stated that the messianic king was not expected to work miracles such as the resurrection of the dead. Rather, he was to be judged according to his success in defeating the neighbouring peoples, rebuilding the Temple and gathering in the Jews who were scattered throughout the world.[29]

The religious element in Stern's thinking must not be underestimated. His partner in editing *Ba-Mahteret* would later testify that Stern had devoted his life to the underground not only out of cold political calculations, but because 'he seems to have had what mystics call a revelation'.[30] Alongside his messianic thinking, Stern wanted to entrench a new Zionist philosophy, detached from the diaspora. True

Zionism could never be realised by righteous gentiles, but rather by the Hebrew nation assisted by an ally – any ally. 'The desire to weaken the status of diaspora Jews, thus compelling them to migrate to another land does not harm the Hebrew freedom movement, and may even – in certain cases – assist it. A Jew-hater can in fact be pro-Zionist. A Judeophile may be anti-Zionist.'[31] Here, then, was his ideological basis for the secret pact he wanted to reach with Hitler.

Every power had to be judged with ruthless objectivity by what it actually *did* for the Hebrew people. For all the promises of Balfour, Ramsay MacDonald and others, Britain still prevented immigration.[32] Five million American Jews were doing nothing for the re-establishment of their homeland, whereas Roosevelt had promised a delegation from Lithuania that their country would once again be independent. Britain had not gone to war because of Hitler's attack on the freedom of Austria and Czechoslovakia, but in order to prevent Germany taking over the world at England's expense. Well might Britain appeal to 'justice' in defence of her cause, but so equally might the Soviet Union and Nazi Germany in pursuit of theirs. While Naftali Lubenchik, Stern's representative, was meeting with Otto Werner von Hentig, the emissary of the German Foreign Office in Beirut, Stern was publicly stating a clear position between the two world camps: 'We shall not recognize any old or new order. We shall not permit a world order to be reached as long as our own question is not put in order by setting up our Kingdom in its promised land . . .' This was not the neutral standpoint it appeared to be; in fact, Stern was adopting a pro-German line, especially in the light of his severe criticism of the Jewish Agency for its involvement in the war on the British side.[33] For the 'IZL in Israel' the situation was now clear. Britain's betrayal of Zionism disqualified her from being an ally. The denial of the legitimacy of the diaspora was absolute, and Jews should not give foreigners their strength by joining their armies, Czech as well as British, but channel all their energies into the war of liberation in their homeland.[34]

In sum, England was the real 'enemy', Germany a mere 'persecutor'. This was a distinction which Stern was repeatedly to emphasise. Hitler was in that respect akin to Haman (the arch-persecutor of Jewish historical memory); the 'enemy' was represented by the British conquerors of the Hebrew homeland. Thus, even the Nazi ghettos were merely the lesser of two evils. Many of their denizens would die of disease and hunger, but most would survive. Jews had also suffered persecution in the early years of the Soviet Union, and were even put in concentration camps because of their middle-class status. They had to adapt, as they had to in the pioneering conditions of the land of Israel. Despite the doom-laden prognostications of

Western Jews, 'Russian Jewry as a whole, in public, is still very much alive. It is possible that the Red assimilation had destroyed its spirit, but the body was strong'. The best of its youth would still join the underground. Moreover, the 'IZL in Israel' expressed great admiration for the maintenance of public and cultural services in the Warsaw ghetto, which was portrayed as 'a kind of small state, whose population was of the same dimensions as the Jewish community in *Eretz Israel*'.[35]Nevertheless, 'there is no redemption in the Diaspora'. Stern was exercised by the feeling that he was living through a decisive moment in Jewish history. Redemption would come about through taking the right political decisions and by increasing the moral strength of the fighters of the 'IZL in Israel' by 'purification' – designed to infect the masses with their faith.[36]

### THE FIRST ATTEMPT TO COMMUNICATE WITH NAZI GERMANY

The sources do not allow a clear picture of Naftali Lubenchik's mission to Beirut towards the end of 1940. It is not certain whether the intention was to make contact with the Germans alone, or if Stern had not yet entirely abandoned the Italian option.[37] What is clear, however, is that the idea of approaching Germany to propose an alliance was Stern's; there was no opposition from Kalay and Zeroni in the high command.

Lubenchik, a former candidate of the 'Faction of Allegation and Faith' for the leadership of the NZO, made his way to Beirut with the help of a Maronite and a Shi'ite agent, the latter a friend of David Siton, Stern's Arab expert.[38] In Beirut, Lubenchik met von Hentig, then the delegate of the German Foreign Office to the Italian armistice committee in Vichy Syria.[39] The memorandum arising from their conversation is an entirely authentic document, on which the stamp of the 'IZL in Israel' is clearly embossed.[40] The document's starting point is that Hitler had no intention of murdering Jews, but merely of encouraging them to migrate from Europe. Here was apparent common ground. Stern, however, understood that Hitler was not yet ready to transfer the Jewish masses to *Eretz Israel* in order to establish a Jewish state within its boundaries. He thus had to be convinced to act as follows:

(a) There may possibly be a collusion of interests between the aims of the 'New Order' in Europe as interpreted by the Germans and the true national aspirations of the Jewish people represented by the IZL. (b) Co-operation between the new Germany and the reborn *volkisch-nationalen Hebraertum* may be possible. (c) The

re-establishment of the Jewish state in its historic borders, on a
national and totalitarian basis, allied with the German Reich, does
not contradict the need for the protection and strengthening of the
future German positions of strength in the Near East.[41]

Doubtless sensing his hated enemy's imminent defeat (the Battle of
Britain was then at its height), Stern offered 'active participation in
the war on the German side. On the condition that the aforementioned
aspirations of the Israeli freedom movement are recognised'. Within
the framework of co-operation, Stern hoped he could recruit 40,000
men for the conquest of *Eretz Israel*. Taking his cue from a recent
speech by Hitler, in which the German dictator stressed that 'he would
exploit any combination and coalition to isolate England and smite
her', Stern emphasised that the 'moral' effect of the participation
of 'the Jewish liberation movement in the New Order . . . would
strengthen its moral foundations in the eyes of all humanity'.[42] He also
took the trouble to provide von Hentig with a somewhat slanted history
of the genesis of the 'IZL in Israel', obscuring the fact that it represented only a small proportion of the original IZL. He stressed that,
as demonstrated by its military collaboration with the Polish government, the IZL had been 'extremely close' to the totalitarian movements of Europe. He did, however, acknowledge the break with
Jabotinsky, claiming that his own ideology was original, and was
essentially realised in anti-British terrorism.[43]

In an attempt to recruit his spiritual mentor's public support for the
underground, Stern revealed the German connection to Achimeir
(who first made it public) at the end of the summer of 1941. Achimeir
tried to convince Stern that, even without the ghettos and Rommel's
advance, he did not see Britain as the number one enemy of the Jewish
people. In principle, he favoured a German connection, rather than
one with Vichy or Mussolini, but only in order to put an end to the
slaughter of European Jewry. Under the conditions of the summer of
1941, however, a connection with the Germans meant 'creating a fifth
column benefiting the Angel of Death'. Stern's reply was: 'We will
manage somehow with the Germans after they conquer *Eretz Israel* –
the Russians got along with them when it was necessary.' Achimeir
retorted: 'You remind me of the marksman who shoots first and then
draws a circle around the spot marked by the bullet hole.'[44]

Lubenchik reported that there was a conflict among the Nazi
leaders between those who advocated *realpolitik*, seeking to get rid of
the Jews by emigration, and those who advocated *idealpolitik*, want-
ing to annihilate them.[45] This lends some plausibility to the claim
advanced by Stern's disciples that he was seeking 'rescue'. In fact,

however, that was a secondary concern. 'Rescue' was a means of over-coming his colleagues' doubts on the alliance with Germany. Stern himself eventually admitted that his real motive was recruitment.

All we want of the Germans is to enable us to transfer this army to the coasts of *Eretz Israel*, and the war against the British to liberate the homeland will begin here. The Jews will attain a state, and the Germans will, incidentally, be rid of an important British base in the Middle East, and also solve the Jewish question in Europe . . .

In vain, Y. Orenstein tried to convince Stern that the German hatred of the Jews was so intense as to drive out any logical proposal, and that they were in any case weighing the number of Arabs against that of the Jews. Furthermore the *Yishuv* and the Jewish people would view the alliance attempt with disbelief. Stern replied that only movements which did not hesitate succeeded: witness the Bolshevik acceptance of the Brest-Litovsk Treaty in March 1918.[46]

The question of the German alignment became more urgent in the spring of 1941. On 14 April Rommel's troops reached the outskirts of Tobruk; on 21 April the British suffered another defeat at the hands of the Germans in Greece; at the end of April the uprising led by Rashid Ali broke out in Iraq. Clearly, Britain faced a severe crisis. The 'IZL in Israel' now came out with a provocative broadcast. Again, as with the memorandum to von Hentig, it claimed to speak for the Revisionist IZL. As representative of the 'Hebrew Freedom Movement', Stern attacked the Jewish Agency – 'this clique of ageing lobbyists . . . their authority is less than that of a Jewish community in territories conquered by Germany . . . The Agency has become a government recruiting office.' They had despatched 8,000 soldiers as cannon-fodder to various war fronts without receiving anything in return.[47] The situation was 'serious and critical', but there was 'no place for unfounded panic' and one should not be too pessimistic, for 'we must not ignore the possibilities latent in the political and military events which have taken place and which will take place in the East in the near future'. The *Yishuv* had to prepare for an attempted Arab riot and a German invasion, but not – as the 'National Institutions' would have it – by sitting and waiting. Instead they must now demonstrate to the Arabs the superiority of Hebrew force.

In reality, short of the proposed alliance, Stern had no immediate proposals in the event of a German invasion. All he could offer was a general exhortation to prepare for 'sacrifice and suffering' as 'all the nations of Europe . . . have faced and are facing all these tribulations caused by the War. We may hunger, but we will not die! We may suffer, but we will not perish! Our numbers may decline, but we will

not be destroyed! The Eternal One of Israel does not lie!' Stern talked
of national redemption, and the need to 'fight under all conditions for
this redemption'. The world had to know that 'a Hebrew in Zion is no
bound slave nor human dust . . . It is our Massada'. In other words: if
the proposed alliance did not materialise, Stern was ready for a last-
ditch stand. But he was opposed to the notice of general conscription
for all aged 20 to 30, which was issued by the 'National Institutions' on
2 May.[48]

Within 24 hours of the broadcast of 10 May the authorities had
responded. The police made extensive arrests of members of the 'IZL
in Israel'. According to the *Haganah* secret service (the Shai), sketches
of military targets were found on two of its members. Others were
closely watched by the police and by the Shai until their liquidation at
the beginning of 1942.[49] Meanwhile, Owen Tweedy, the director of the
government press office in Jerusalem, spoke of Goebbels' Ministry of
Propaganda waging a war of nerves from Baghdad and encouraging
the men of the 'Fifth Column' operating in the underground. *Ha-
Aretz*, thus prompted, spoke of the presence of a 'Quisling': 'Hitler
appointed him and his salary is high.'[50]

Members of the IZL were also shocked by the broadcast, as is
shown in a letter from Meridor to a friend. Already worried by the
arrests, he feared worse measures to come. His anxiety was deepened
because he believed that Stern and his associates were simply:

> ravenous for power, only for power, and hope to achieve it by all
> means and in all ways. Yair clearly hopes that when the Germans
> get here he will be deputy-governor of the Jews by virtue of his con-
> spiracy, but he forgets only one thing: just how little the promises of
> the Germans can be relied on at all. Meanwhile, Radio Berlin has
> already announced that the Jews in this country have already
> surrendered to the Germans, and that the Jews are praying for the
> Germans to get here. I am only looking for the logic in all this, but
> I cannot find it . . . [Arab] Riots are only started under the influence
> of German money and arms. If the IZL in Israel is also linked to the
> Axis, then they must be natural allies of the *Mufti* and his gang;
> logic can find no other solution. We always condemned the defeat-
> ists and the supporters of the idea of an Arab federation with the
> Jewish state in the middle. And here a new axis is developing in the
> Near East: the *Mufti*, Yair and Rashid Ali in Iraq. I am still walking
> about in a dream and I cannot believe my eyes.[51]

The Allied invasion of Syria, on 8 June 1941, and the suppression of
the pro-Nazi rising in Iraq had no effect on the standpoint of the 'IZL
in Israel'. The threat from Rommel had not yet passed and the Nazi

invasion of the Soviet Union on 22 June did not remove the danger from the north. On 14 June the 'IZL in Israel' issued a special appeal to Churchill,[52] presenting its 'conditions' for a political and military alliance with Britain. This involved the immediate cancellation of the White Paper, Hebrew self-government, with a Hebrew army to fight in and for *Eretz Israel*, and cast-iron guarantees for full independence at the end of the war. This was not an apparent reversal of Stern's tactics, but rather a propaganda exercise. He reiterated that this was not an ideological war, both sides were fighting for the sake of power and conquest. Not only the nations under German domination felt hatred for their conquerers; so did those under British domination. The Jewish Agency had not participated on the side of democracy against totalitarianism in Spain, so why was it suddenly a 'divine mission' to fight against the fascist army in Greece?[53]

Stern was anxious to stress the uniqueness of his new organisation and its ability to serve as a non-party alternative. Hence the condemnation of *both* the NZO and *Mapai*. Imitating the style of Achimeir and Yeivin, he condemned *Mapai* for having turned fund-raising from a means to an end, for creating 'Hottentot conditions' in all spheres, for having exploited mass emotions, for the creation of a bureaucratic apparatus and for having abandoned the masses to hunger and unemployment. The NZO was but a poor and even ridiculous imitation of *Mapai* and the Agency, with party more important than the nation. The IZL had rebelled against the party as at the time of the Ben Yosef affair, but the party had reasserted its authority with the outbreak of war, trying to turn the IZL into its own 'storm troops'.[54]

Stern also had a reason to attack the PKP when, after Hitler's invasion of the Soviet Union, the latter exhorted the youth to join the British army – 'armed brother of the Red Army' – even though the *Yevsektsia* opposed the release of 'Jews faithful to Zion' and '*Torah* giants' (meaning, great scholars and religious leaders) from prison in Siberia and Kazakhstan. Stern became obsessed with his war against recruitment. For the time being, he believed that he had been successful, as fewer than 500 men had registered. He claimed that anti-Semitism existed in the ranks of the British army, and that the Hebrew soldiers – referred to as 'Palestinians' – were abandoned on every front.[55]

### THE SCHISM IN THE 'IZL IN ISRAEL' AND A SECOND MISSION TO THE GERMANS

A year of propaganda had seen little in the way of actual operations. The first robbery at the APC bank in Tel Aviv (16 September 1940) succeeded – 4,400 Palestinian pounds were 'expropriated' – but it had been followed by arrests; besides, the money was soon spent. Even the explosion at the 'Immigration Department' after the *Patria* affair (19 December 1940) did not generate the desired public echo. In mid-July 1941 the attempted 'expropriation' at the Arab Bank failed. The arrest of Lubenchik and the failure of his mission became known, and then more news came of the worsening conditions of European Jewry. All this tarnished the prestige of the underground, and led to a crisis in the high command in the autumn of 1941. The first to rebel was Hanoch Kalay, Stern's second-in-command, who came to the conclusion that there was no chance of an alliance with Germany on the basis of enmity towards the British. 'If you think that when the Germans force you to become the head of the ghetto in *Eretz Israel*, I will be your deputy', he told Stern, 'you are very much mistaken.' Stern replied: 'The guarantee that I will not become the head of the ghetto under any conditions whatever is my readiness to die at any moment.'[56]

From the other side, such extremists within the 'IZL in Israel' as Yaakov Lavstein (Eliav) and Binyamin Zeroni, who was extremely critical of Stern, increased their pressure on him to commence anti-British operations. Kalay, however, feared that these would fail and would merely prompt an 'extermination' campaign by the *Yishuv*. The fundamental tactics of the group were misguided. NILI, after all, had managed to reach an agreement with the British, whereas the 'IZL in Israel' had failed, and had better disband, rejoin the *Irgun*, or even open negotiations with the *Haganah* (albeit for reasons of political tactics). Zeroni supported the idea of negotiations with the *Irgun*, and met with Meridor. Thus, by the autumn of 1941 the revolutionary underground was on the verge of another split. Lavstein declared that Kalay deserved 'physical extermination', and Stern was forced to put together a new high command. Lavstein and Yitzhak Zelnick became members, whilst the new chief-of-staff was Yehoshuah Zetler, commander of the 'expropriation' from the APK Bank. Stern rejected Kalay's accusation that the group's operations had failed.[57] Yet the messianic and self-sacrificial elements in Stern's outlook, which had intensified with the outbreak of war, meant that he could well accept failure as a necessary part of the process of redemption.[58] In order to purify the entire undergound from accusations of treason, he was even ready (according to Zelnick's later testimony) to be a Quisling, and to die at the hands of an anti-Quisling underground which might spring up amongst his followers.[59]

It was against this background that, at the end of 1941, Stern proposed another mission to the Germans. A German invasion from Egypt (he argued) was still feasible, and with it, the possibility of a Turkish surrender to Hitler in the north and a British evacuation in the east. This only underlined the futility of what had been the almost universal Jewish support for Britain in the war. Zionism had now to make a 'distinction between the desirable and the possible' and make 'precise calculations of profit and loss'. To this must be added the increasing flow of information concerning a worsening of the conditions of European Jewry under the Nazis, and the increasingly unfavourable policy of the British towards Zionism.

Friedman-Yellin set out on his mission to the Germans in December 1941. A generation later he was to claim that his primary motive had been 'rescue'; but that explanation is doubtful in the light of our knowledge that Stern's basic axioms had not changed. On the agenda this time were not the Jews of Poland, as had been the case with Lubenchick's abortive mission, but those of the Balkans and central Europe. 'The idea this time was that these Jews would overrun the country; Britain could not expel them because of a lack of shipping, and Germany would profit from this cleansing of Europe of Jews.'[60] Did Stern really suppose that the Germans would be attracted to his ideas even if he did not propose an active anti-British alliance? No definite answer to this question can be given. Even if Stern knew nothing of the extermination of the Jews already being carried out by the *Einsatzgruppen*, his plan was even less realistic than that at the end of 1940, when Lubenchik had proposed an active alliance. On this occasion it appears that Stern's model was Pilsudski's co-operation with Japan and Germany during the First World War. However, Friedman-Yellin's mission was even less successful than Lubenchik's had been. He was arrested near Aleppo, prior to reaching enemy territory, a few days before Stern's assassination.[61]

### SCHEIB'S 'COMMENTARY' ON 'THE PRINCIPLES OF REVIVAL'

When Germany invaded Poland, most *Betar* and IZL leaders managed to flee into Soviet-occupied territory. By the beginning of 1940 some 500 people had gathered there; about 100 were IZL members, who were organised into Unit C, which was headed by Avraham Amper, a Stern confidant. This unit, together with that in Vilna (headed by Yaakov Banai), were both disbanded, and only 30 of their combined number reached Palestine. A few rallied to Stern, while the rest did not join his group (by then named *Lehi*, an acronym for *Lohamei Herut Yisrael* – Fighters for the Freedom of Israel) until the summer of 1943.[62] Only in Palestine did they hear of the IZL's declaration of loyalty to the British authorities.

Begin, the most senior of the *Betar* officers (the others being Epstein, Yutan and Scheib) convened a council in which discussion revolved around issues raised during the Warsaw debate of September 1938. Two opinions were formulated. Virnick argued that there was no point in fighting England until Hitler had been defeated. Scheib, however, advocated Stern's line and demanded that England's present weakness be exploited; England should be fought and an alliance concluded with whoever was willing to help. Friedman-Yellin did not take a stand.[63]

Begin agreed in principle with Scheib, but apparently argued against looking for allies. Although not regarding the war as a Jewish war, he was nevertheless cautious. 'You are well aware that the hater of those who hate me is not *always* automatically my friend . . . There is a large gap between a common denial and a positive approach.' But at the same time he also attempted to reconcile his overall loyalty to Jabotinsky with his opposition to conscription under the existing conditions. Hence his argument that: 'We shall not fight as individuals in all kinds of foreign units . . . The Head of *Betar* has clearly stated that every volunteer for a mixed unit [the reference being to the 'mixed battalion' of Jews and Arabs] confirms the White Paper.'[64]

Scheib did not know of the attempt to make contact with the Germans until his arrival in Palestine in April 1941. He supported an Italian orientation and his outlook was closer to the 'Faction of Allegation and Faith'. Adopting a pragmatic line, he seemed to believe that the British – but for their intense anti-Zionism – were capable of implementing the mass transfer of Jews from the Nazi-occupied areas to *Eretz Israel* and thus preventing a great tragedy. However, in a manner reminiscent of Stern, he also took a stand on principle. 'From a purely Zionist point of view, pure and consistent, Hitler is not the enemy of the Kingdom of Israel and the return to Zion . . . but rather Britain alone . . .' As a practical measure, he proposed applying 'vast pressure' on the Mandatory Power while it was engaged in a decisive war: 'The Irish understood this . . . and if someone extends his hand to you at this moment – take it . . . There is no alternative: the hour has come, and if we miss it we are lost.'[65]

In Palestine, Scheib set up residence in Jerusalem, near the homes of his ideological mentors, Yeivin and Greenberg. He could now pour out his hatred of the 'English gentiles', surrounded by the 'Arab filth', laughing at the Western Wall. In his future vision, the Wall would either engulf the *Yishuv* in destruction or prove its salvation.[66] When he learnt of the split in the IZL, he immediately rejected the official line. With Stern's agreement, Scheib (using the pseudonym 'Ben David') wrote for the NZO organ *Ha-Mashkif* – as a form of camouflage and as proof of his worthiness. Thus placed, he could only hint at his support for the new ideological trend: 'We are passing our sons through the melting pot . . . to a Moloch not our own.'[67] Nevertheless, he did not hesitate to criticise Jabotinsky for openly deluding himself until the last that the world would recognise Jewish rights and would build them 'an orphanage'.[68]

With the 'IZL in Israel', Scheib's relationship was academic. Familiar with the historical sources of the ideology of the 'revolutionary underground', he had also become acquainted with Stern's concepts, such as 'the Kingdom of Israel by force', through reading Greenberg's poetry. It was with those materials to hand that 'Eldad' (the pseudonym which Scheib used in the underground) undertook to compose a comprehensive explanation of 'The Principles of Revival'.

Throughout, Eldad's 'commentary' preferred the term 'race' to 'chosen people'.[69] The former term expressed the essential biological unity of the Hebrews, which the Emancipation and the Enlightenment had – unsuccessfully – attempted to destroy. Ever since its foundation by Abraham, Eldad argued, the Hebrew race had evinced three central motifs: a desire for vengeance, hatred of the gentiles and love of 'the Kingdom'. It was not the blood of the brave martyrs which flowed in their veins, as Bialik claimed, but rather the tribal blood of Abraham the Patriarch, the pursuer of kings, the obeyer of the Divine command to bind Isaac. Throughout, the Hebrews were guided by destiny. The God of Israel (who was accorded an altogether more central position in Eldad's ideology than in that of Stern) had chosen His people, not they Him. Moreover, He desired to see the construction of His Temple and tens of millions of His children ruling from the Nile to the Euphrates. Their right to the land therefore stemmed not from international law, but rather from the desire of the nation to survive. Therein, Eldad impressed on Stern, lay the basic difference between true Zionism and that 'of refugees' preached by 'political' Zionists of the old school. They, having been nurtured on European liberal and socialist ideas, sought nothing more than a 'state', itself a gentile term, which would constitute but a means for organising public life. The 'IZL in Israel', however, demanded a 'Kingdom' (an authentic Hebrew category) – a goal in its own right, an expression of supreme material need which draws man closer to his God.

The first task of the liberation movement was to revive the messianic longings which had been undermined by timid leadership. Using the sword of authentic Judaism, it had to lay the groundwork for redemption amid blood and fire. A nation returning to its homeland did not require a charter, and the path to follow was that of Joshua, the Hasmoneans and Bar-Kochba. One inference was that calculation rather than emotion, should determine which outside forces to co-operate with when the conditions for redemption were favourable.

Another was that true Zionism stemmed not from compulsion, but from will (in the Nietzschean sense), from a racial destiny in which a 'blood force, a Divine force: the passion for sovereignty' was active. Therefore the goals of the freedom movement were not productivisation or a middle class, or an agricultural and industrial regime, but simply the conquest of the homeland and the establishment of the Kingdom. The problem of the socio-economic regime would be solved in the terms laid down by Jabotinsky: 'Neither liberalistic anarchy nor Bolshevik enslavement, but rather a life of liberty and freedom according to the laws of the *Torah*, the prophets and the sages, under the supervision of a *Sanhedrin* in Jerusalem.'

Eldad's 'commentary' was equally faithful to Revisionist maximalism in its discussion of the Arab question. Indeed, in this respect he was more influenced than Stern had been by Berdichevsky, Nietzsche and Greenberg. He did not advocate the destruction of the Arabs, but their 'transfer' out of *Eretz Israel*. He appreciated that the Arabs would not assimilate, but would declare war. Nevertheless, he proclaimed that his ultimate aim was a 'strong and eternal' alliance with the Arab kings. The return to Zion would be a condition of membership of the Jewish Nation. Because of the 'desire to rule' of the Hebrew race, and because of the cultural inferiority of the Middle East hitherto, the new Hebrew civilisation would dominate the area. Hebrew blood would be splattered on the altar of the war of liberation and true prophets would arise from the nation to purify it.

### THE REACTION OF THE NZO AND THE IZL TO THE SCHISM

The Revisionist establishment soon reacted to Scheib's criticisms, behind which they discerned Stern's influence. Dr Benyamin Lubotsky responded that: 'The Nazi programmes have . . . no place for any Zionism at all, neither that of Herzl and Jabotinsky nor that of the Foundation Fund, and not even that of Mr Ben David [Scheib].' Eri Jabotinsky, who had met Stern in prison after his own arrest for commanding the illegal immigrant boat *Sakaria*, was even more insistent on loyalty to his father. Although he sympathised with Stern, and agreed with him that the NZO was lamentably passive, he nevertheless argued that his tactics were endangering the overall effectiveness of *Betar* and the *Irgun*, particularly in the question of immigration.[70]

The prime targets of the campaign waged by the Revisionist leadership were the rank and file members of the 'IZL in Israel'. Their organisation, they were now informed, had degenerated into an 'ideological-spiritual sect', saturated with defeatism and despair; its foreign policy – the Italian 'agreement' – was in ruins; and Stern

himself was motivated by 'criminal careerism' and a 'passion for rule'.
In March 1941 the tone grew more strident. Falsehood, obscured by
poetic ideology, was leading Stern's comrades towards

> the service of a foreign master . . . You have been sold to our sworn
> enemy . . . your leaders . . . have turned you into a network of
> informers and slaves to slaves . . . Do you realise for which 'master'
> you are working? And why? And in return for what? In return for
> the 'council of elders' of the Ghetto in Warsaw or Lublin? . . . Stop
> this madness while you still can!!![71]

Clearly, the IZL was afraid that it might itself become tainted with the
mark of collaboration with the Axis.[72] Accordingly, and in contrast to
Stern, it sought to draw attention to German–Arab collaboration.[73]
Reluctantly, it conceded to NZO pressure on the question of recruitment to the British army;[74] more explicitly, it openly publicised and
attacked the 'Italian agreement'.[75] At a slightly later stage, it also
attempted to point out the futility of an alliance with Germany. Quite
apart from the fact that the Germans were no less an enemy than
the Arabs, there were pragmatic considerations. Unlike Stern, who
considered Rommel's victory to be imminent in May 1941, the IZL
believed that Wavell would prevail. In any case, did not the Rashid
Ali's uprising show the foolishness of any attempt to forge an alliance
with the Axis? 'Admit your fatal error and do not interfere with the
work of the *Irgun* and its renewed war against the forces of surrender
and self-restraint.'[76]

This direct style stemmed, of course, from the severe shocks
suffered by the IZL and the Revisionist movement in the wake of the
schism, and was part of the effort to revive the IZL. Now the IZL
sought – selectively – to emphasise the legacy of its two eminent
father-figures. First, the element of revolt in Pilsudski's teachings was
emphasised, while his revolutionary side and his system of personal
terrorism were played down.[77] Second, Jabotinsky was described not
as he had really been but as the IZL wished him to be remembered –
hence the stress on the Hebrew battalions, on the prison sentence in
Acre and on the slogan 'To die or conquer the mountain' as symbols of
his policy.[78] When Raziel met his death in Iraq in May 1941, a new and
necessary myth was constructed around him too: he had been made of
the same material as Pilsudski and Atatürk, and was equal in stature to
Judas Macabbaeus, Bar-Kochba, Trumpeldor and Jabotinsky.[79]

Stern swiftly returned the fire. The Revisionist movement, he
complained, had betrayed its own destiny. Thus, his response took
two forms. It opened with an admission of Revisionism's undoubted
contributions to the definition of the national goal and the revival

of the national idea. Specifically, it had been the NZO which had turned the Jewish question into an international one and developed contacts with Poland and Romania. Jabotinsky, too, had established *Betar* at a time when 'Agency Zionism' had supported pacifism and had become a British Agency. What followed, however, was altogether critical. Revisionist policy would be entirely bankrupt were Britain – 'despite everything' – to abrogate Jewish rights and set the Arabs over the land of Israel. Were this to happen, only 'war by force' would free the 'enslaved people' and 'establish the Kingdom of Israel'. So it had been with other liberated nations – Greece, Serbia, Bulgaria, Italy, Ireland, Poland and Czechoslovakia. Instead of offering resistance, Altman and his colleagues were trying to turn the IZL into a kind of 'leftist *Haganah*', which would take orders from Golomb, rather than from the 'Israeli Order of Liberation', which was waging the 'holy ideological war'.[80]

### THE LAST ACCORD: THE OBLITERATION OF THE 'IZL IN ISRAEL'

Stern was fighting with his back to the wall. His alternative ideology and policy made no impression on the vast majority of the public, including the Revisionist public, which regarded him and his supporters as traitors. Stern's response was to entrench himself even more deeply in his own ideology. For one thing, he likened Shertok and other leaders of the 'organised *Yishuv* to the Hellenisers of the Second Temple period, who had similarly bowed down to foreign authorities (in this case by supporting conscription).[81] Second, to the 'handful', he stressed even more the importance of fighting itself. Thus perceived, the 'IZL in Israel' – like Joshua, Gideon and the NILI – was bound to prevail.[82] Finally, and notwithstanding the news of German atrocities against the Jews, Stern insisted on retaining his basic ideological distinction between Jewry's 'persecutor' and its 'enemy'.[83] Convinced that the suffering of the Jews in *Eretz Israel* was infinitely greater than that in the diaspora,[84] his tone towards 'perfidious Albion' became even more hysterical.

After the arrest of Yehoshua Zetler, the chief-of-staff of the group, Stern took over direct control of its operations. He decided that the targets of attack were now to be the heads of the police and the CID in Palestine (Wilkin and Morton) as it was they, after all, rather than the British Minister of State resident in the Middle East, who were hunting his men.[85] In the event, the 'IZL in Israel' killed two Jewish officers (Schiff and Goldman – the former serving as chief of the Jewish Tel Aviv police) accompanied by a British officer (Turton). In another 'expropriation' (9 January) two Jewish passers-by were accidentally killed. Stern expressed his sorrow, but maintained that there had been no alternative – two members of his own group had been captured in the course of the action. The killing of Jewish 'hirelings' like Schiff and Goldman, and of Turton, was entirely justified, especially in view of the tortures to which arrested members of the 'IZL in Israel' were being subjected.[86]

Stern and his colleagues had now gone too far. The group's public image as fascists and Quislings led people to inform against them. On the day after the explosion at 8 Yael Street, their photographs were published in the press. On 27 January four of them were surprised by the police. Zack and Amper were killed and Svorai and Lavstein wounded. A few days later (12 February 1942) Stern's own hideout was discovered and he too was killed. In vain, the remnants of the 'IZL in Israel' attempted to wreak vengeance; most of them were arrested.[87]

In all the history of the underground movements in Palestine and Israel, never was there so wide a gap between the end and the means as existed in the case of the 'IZL in Israel'. None of its models proved suitable. *Lehi* would subsequently cultivate the myth of its fallen founders, but would also learn the lesson of their failures. The ideology would go on fertilising terrorist activity, but care would be taken to reduce the dimensions of the gap between the means and the end.

### THE REACTION OF THE 'ORGANISED *YISHUV*'

The executive of the Jewish Agency first considered the 'IZL in Israel' on 25 January 1942. Shertok made sure that his letter to the inspector-general of the police condemning the attack on 8 Yael Street was published. The consensus of the *Yishuv* was absolute; it was necessary to 'burn out the evil'. Shertok also accused those who 'had bred the serpents' (meaning, the NZO and the IZL), and who were now showing signs of repentance. The feeling was, however, that it was not wise to draw too much public attention to the matter, and that it should be kept within the confines of the *Yishuv*.[88] The chairman of the national committee, Yitzchak Ben-Zvi, the Mayor of Tel Aviv, Y. Rokah, and the chairman of the league of local councils, Gorodisky, met the Chief Secretary of the Government, Sir John MacPherson, his assistant, Robert Scott, and the Governor of the province of Lydda, R.E.H. Crosbie. Both sides agreed to co-operate in uprooting terrorism.[89] The central committee of *Mapai*, which discussed the subject on the same day, confirmed this approach. *Haganah* intelligence began kidnapping members of Stern's group, with the assistance of the *Palmach*.[90]

## THE NZO AND IZL REACTION TO THE EXTERMINATION OF
## THE STERN GROUP

*Ha-Mashkif* also joined the chorus which condemned Stern and his followers. The unsuccessful expropriation of 9 January 1942 was depicted as 'an abominable crime, which . . . aroused disgust in the hearts of all members of the community'; and the murder of Schiff and Goldman as 'a tragedy for the entire community', a 'terrible crime' at the very hour the Jewish people was making 'an effort to be a partner in this war of life and death for the survival of the world and for its own future'.[91] Moreover, and so as to demonstrate the absolute loyalty of the NZO (and the IZL) to the authorities, the newspaper published on 30 January a picture of Stern, the caption of which told of a reward of 1,000 Palestinian pounds for anyone bringing about his arrest and 2,000 pounds for the capture of those who laid the landmines which killed Schiff and his colleagues.[92]

However, the real campaign against the Stern group was conducted in an internal leaflet.[93] Like all groups which had left the NZO, this one was also destined for a quick demise, since it lacked any political programme or public morality. On the other hand, the murder of Stern and his comrades had surely been illegal – 'the customs of Nazis' – because they had not opposed their arrest. An investigation should be conducted and those guilty punished. Admittedly, a section of the NZO did support the 'IZL in Israel' when its members were kidnapped by the organised *Yishuv*. But, on the whole, the IZL was hardly able to conceal its joy at Stern's total failure. Members of the group had failed to hold their own in battle and thus 'once and for all the title of a Hebrew fighting force was removed from them'.[94] There followed a call for the reunification of all underground activities.[95]

In the absence of agreement on anti-British operations, this was impossible. True, IZL criticisms of Britain's 'murder' of Stern did increase in the wake of the *Struma* incident (24 February 1942), which sank in the Black Sea with 769 people on board. Stern's fate, it was now proclaimed, might be an unfortunate precedent. Moreover, Stern himself was now depicted in a more generous light; after all, he had been one of the IZL's key political figures during its finest years, 1937–39. Only later had a 'satanic force motivated him'. With his death, the Hebrew liberation movement had lost 'one of those who were capable of leading it to its goal at the decisive moment'.[96]

But all this had little operational effect. In fact, it was to be two more years before the IZL would shake off its political subordination to the NZO. Eri Jabotinsky's attempt to guide the Revisionists to a more activist line (somewhat reminiscent of Stern's) failed.[97] Thus, with Rommel continuing to constitute a threat to the *Yishuv*, and the Revisionists still committed to recruitment to the British army, the IZL was thwarted. 'Caught between the hammer and the anvil', all it could do was to prepare 'for the opportune moment'.[98]

## THE AUTHORITIES AND THE 'IZL IN ISRAEL'

The various agencies of the British government paid considerable attention to developments in the IZL and the NZO. They had noted as 'a most interesting point' that on the outbreak of the Second World War, Jabotinsky could promise that only 75 per cent of his supporters in Palestine could be relied upon to support the British in the conflict. This would not be the case were free immigration to be permitted. Jabotinsky's proposals to set up a Jewish legion in the USA and to work for anti-German propaganda were considered 'fantastic'. Nor was military intelligence much impressed by the relative moderation of the Revisionist movement, since it did not consider the average Palestinian Jew much prone to demonstrations and disorder.[99] It was well aware of the coming split, which it considered to be inevitable given the fact that the Revisionist leadership lacked the courage and strength to control the situation.[100]

Military intelligence was also well aware of Stern's moves towards Italy: 'Though not looking forward to finding themselves under Italian rule, they think by posing as a Jewish Fascist Organisation they may obtain better treatment should that distasteful situation arise.'[101] This and the 'expropriation' at the APC Bank in Tel Aviv on 16 September, led the authorities to consider the elimination of the new organisation as early as October 1940,[102] and by mid-November the arrest of its most important members was reported.[103] The British were not yet aware of Lubenchik's mission and its aims, nor of the contacts with the Germans.[104] Thus when Tweedy reacted to the Stern group broadcast on 10 May 1941, military intelligence did not mention that this was a signal to the Germans. It was more obsessed with the potential of the 80,000 German Jews as a 'fifth column'.[105] In October 1941 suspicion fell on the Stern group, because of its desperate shortage of funds.[106]

In mid-October the Stern group was first mentioned in the report of the High Commissioner to the Colonial Secretary, in a review of 'The Illegal Jewish Organisations'. The size of the *Haganah* (100,000 men) and the IZL (5,000–8,000 members), was exaggerated. The IZL was described as a 'criminal' anti-Arab terrorist organisation, a 'most dangerous' and 'formidable' group – and this at its nadir – which executed vengeance with no pangs of conscience or morality. No less negative was the depiction of the 'IZL in Israel':

With the Stern Group, ideology, responsibility and any pretence of helping to build up the National home are left behind. The moral translation is from a plane on which the utter destruction of the sinners of the Amalekites is a divine command, to the plane on which guys are merely bumped off, rubbed out or put on the spot.[107]

Their contacts with the Italians, and now with the Germans, were stressed, as was their anti-British propaganda, and they were evaluated as a threat to security, though politically insignificant. Numbering only 50 at the time of the schism, they were still fewer than 100. The IZL itself was regarded as the more immediately dangerous organisation, and the better candidate for suppression,[108] though in the long run the *Haganah* with its tens of thousands of members posed the greater threat.[109]

The Yael Street episode, however, prompted the decision to make a terminal attack on the 'IZL in Israel'.[110] The police, who had at first complained of the lack of co-operation on the part of the Hebrew public, now noted with satisfaction that they had received many letters informing on suspects – proof of the public opposition to the 'criminal' group. The inspector-general of police was aware of the ultimate threat of the secret military organisations of both right and left,[111] but now (January 1942) Stern was surely the worst of the Zionist leaders, a 'megalomaniac, fifth column gangster' – though no more than 300 men obeyed his orders.[112]

Thus Stern's death was considered a great success, for 'the brains' of the group had been eliminated, and even the Colonial Office expressed satisfaction.[113] In fact, however, of the few hundred members only 18 (admittedly the most prominent figures) had been arrested;[114] the remainder were still supported by the IZL, especially after Stern's elimination.[115] Nevertheless, the 'IZL in Israel' had suffered too severe a blow to react effectively. Hence military intelligence dismissed the efforts of the Stern group,[116] and turned its attention to the *Haganah* (estimated in the summer of 1942 to number 30,000–100,000 members) and the IZL (estimated at 1,200–1,500).[117]

## AVRAHAM STERN – MYTH AND REALITY

Avraham Stern was born on 23 December 1907 in the town of Suwalki in the province of Bialystok, then under Tsarist rule. Years of war, revolution and civil strife within Russia transported him to the Bashkiria region in the south-west Ural mountains for a period of about six years (1915–21). He spent only about four years in independent Poland, emigrating by himself to Palestine at the age of 18, and completing his studies at the Hebrew Gymnasia in Jerusalem. In 1927 he began studying Classics and Hebrew Literature at the Hebrew University. Both the Bolshevik revolution and the re-establishment of an independent Poland left a life-long impression, from which he would eventually try to draw lessons for the Zionist revolution. In the 1930s, as a result of the experience gained during the 1929 riots and their aftermath, he finalised his outlook on life – initially, within the Revisionist framework, but later mainly in rebellion against its axioms. The outbreak of the Second World War accelerated this process, but few were to follow him at the time of the schism, because this meant a complete break with the parent political movement and an orientation based on powers hostile to the Jewish people.

Stern's heirs and disciples never dared confront his true image publicly, because this would have meant admitting failure. Since they could accept his most central assumption – uncompromising war against the foreign regime – they could view his failure as purely operational.

The myth of the leader-founder began to be built in the summer of 1943, with the revival of the underground. It was then necessary to clear Stern of any connection with the Axis powers. He was portrayed as a man free of any real external orientations: 'He fought for the freedom of Israel. This was his egoistic interest . . . His eyes were raised to Jerusalem and only to Jerusalem.'[118] The accusation – originating from Reuters – that he had been a Nazi agent constituted 'incitement'. The myth-building reached a climax in February 1944, in reaction to Menachem Begin's proclamation of a 'revolt' which entirely ignored 'the proclamation' of Avraham Stern. The founder of *Lehi*, Stern's followers declared, had been 'the first of the Hebrew Freedom Fighters in the homeland'[119] while the IZL, along with the rest of the *Yishuv*, had been committed to recruitment for the British. He had dedicated his life on the altar of the homeland: 'He lost his body. The *Yishuv* lost . . . a personality of character and strength unprecedented in the *Yishuv*.'[120]

Even that did not suffice. *Lehi*'s leaders attributed to Stern's life mythological and meta-historical significance:

He was not one of those who live and die like other people. He was a Prometheus, appearing once in many generations and bringing fire to mankind. The fire is always reminiscent of the great incendiary, Prometheus, who sacrificed himself . . . After two thousand years of exile Yair once again ignited the flame of passion for freedom.[121]

His life, like that of Rabbi Judah Ha-Levi, throbbed with 'the internal drive for freedom'. His death made it clear to his disciples that there could be no compromise with the foreign regime, for 'Freedom demands a constant war and sacrifices'.[122] The main point that his heirs wished to get across to the public was that the 'founder' of the Hebrew freedom movement was neither Herzl nor Aharonson (of whom they wrote positively), nor Jabotinsky (of whom they wrote ambivalently), nor Begin, but rather Stern himself. 'The Euclid of National Geometry' and 'the symbol of perfection', he had merged 'vision' with 'material strength', and turned them 'into a political factor of the first order'.[123] Jabotinsky had erred in depicting Zionism as the problem of an exiled nation lacking territory, and in appealing for the sympathy of the nations of the world. Stern, by contrast, as the representative of 'the subjugated Hebrew homeland' stressed how useful the freedom of Israel might be to them, if they would only help in attaining it.[124] Since 1937 Stern had advocated an independent Hebrew army (based on the IZL), aimed at establishing the 'Kingdom of Israel', whereas Jabotinsky advocated the Legion, the colonising regime and petitions.[125]

To strengthen the thesis of Stern's exemplary leadership, his followers published his article, 'The Leader', written in the autumn of 1941 after the failures of Lubenchik, the Arab Bank 'expropriation' and the Kalay–Zeroni crisis. When the world is involved in wars and revolutions, the masses seek out a leader:

> As hope in the authority of the public falls, as trust in the power of the public collapses, man's primeval instinct, imprinted deeply on his heart, comes once again to the fore: total submission to a man of strength, blind following after the leader. The rot of Athenian democracy preceded the advent of Alexander of Macedonia. The loss of the French Revolution lifted up Napoleon. And in our day we bear witness to the hopelessness of many, to autocracy in many lands, from Soviet Russia and Nazi Germany to fascist Italy and democratic England.

Stern hoped for the coming of such a leader in *Eretz Israel* too:

> In the history of the Hebrew people the rule of the strong hand, of the man of war, of the judge and the king has become a tradition, a glorious link in the chain of government . . . Each generation and its own heroes. Now, too, the people raise their eyes to an anonymous leader who will lead them on the path of redemption.

Whether or not Stern was that leader was immaterial, for the freedom movement did not ascribe the existence of its destiny to any single person, since in any case only suffering and the scaffold await him. 'But you must surely know that if one falls, another will dedicate his life to the cause.'[126]

Begin was not, of course, willing to recognise Stern's 'copyright' when he proclaimed his own 'revolt' in 1944. With dripping sarcasm Begin wrote that the heirs of 'a great patriot' were trying to transform him into 'a sacred idol. A New Jesus. We can safely say that such an attempt would disgust Yair himself if he were alive.' *He-Hazit* was following the example of the Soviet Union, where Stalin had been transformed into a living idol in order to obliterate the memory of Trotsky.[127] Stern died without a gun in his room, without the possibility of a battle with the police because, Begin suggested, he wanted above all to have the opportunity of a trial, where he could voice his demands before the ears of the world. But fate in the form of a policeman's bullets kept him from his preferred destiny.[128]

As a political figure, Avraham Stern must undoubtedly be placed on the extreme right of the *Yishuv* and the Zionist movement, subject as he was to the influence of the European radical right of the inter-war period and its integral nationalism.[129] Though he grew up in the ambit of the political culture of Russia, Poland and Lithuania, his political awareness ripened in Palestine between 1929 and 1939, under the influence of Pilsudski, Mickiewicz, Lenin and Alexander Block, as well as Jabotinsky, Uri Zvi Greenberg, Achimeir and Ratosh. Though some of his heroes were of the Marxist left, he totally rejected communism. The left only influenced him, as it did Achimeir, by its technique of taking power. In Jewish history he was taken by biblical figures and by the Zealots and the Hasmoneans, Bar-Kochba and David Ha-Ruebeni.[130] In the early 1930s he already tended to ascribe decisive weight to force, and regarded social Darwinism as the decisive factor in the liberation of nations. Hence his simultaneous admiration of such different figures as Eleazar Ben-Yair of Massada, Avshalom Feinberg and Aharon Aharonson of NILI, the Russian social revolutionary Savinkov, Thomas Clarke of Ireland and – last but not least – Pilsudski. His outlook, like that of his spiritual Revisionist mentors, was romantic-élitist. Thus any nationalist movement could serve as his model. Heroism, however uncontrolled, was the key to final success, even if the failures on the road to the final goal be numerous. The demise of the messianic movements in Israel did not discourage him for, as he had learnt from Klausner, their outlook would eventually triumph.[131] Maimonides, too, encouraged him – victory in battle, the reconstruction of the Temple and the gathering in of the exiles sufficed for the belief that the 'IZL in Israel' was another link in the chain of activist messianic movements in Israel. These basic assumptions, he believed, could be realised by revolutionary activity – 'expropriations', terrorism and missions to foreign powers.

Stern's mystic and doctrinaire outlook clouded his understanding of political reality from 1939 to 1942. Both Weizmann and Jabotinsky had failed to grasp that force alone could achieve 'the Kingdom of Israel', and that meant an inevitable concentration on *Eretz Israel* to the exclusion of the diaspora. His theory of the 'persecutor' versus the 'enemy' was only possible because of this denial of the diaspora, and made even the worst anti-Semite into a potential ally. His spiritual mentors in the Revisionist movement had taught him to reject the English orientation, and to believe that Poland was a power capable of assisting in Jewish national liberation. The loss of Poland and the victories of the Axis powers led him to the idea of an alliance with them. Jabotinsky himself had taught that Nazi anti-Semitism was not final and that an understanding could be reached with it, though Stern overlooked his earlier reservations. Thus his political realism could counsel an alliance with any power – except Stalin's Russia – at the appropriate time.

Even more than Jabotinsky, Stern was alienated from the 'organised *Yishuv* and its political goals. When Yitzhak Sadeh of the *Palmach* met him in mid-October 1941, Sadeh said it was like talking to a wall. He tried to warn Stern that his tactics were likely to bring about a violent confrontation with the *Palmach*. Stern, however, only wanted to emphasise that he opposed neither right nor left, he believed in neither, only in force, and that he regarded the British as the main enemy of the Jews. He could not understand why the *Palmach* and the 'IZL in Israel' could not simply agree to leave each other alone.[132]

Stern's actions were intended to proceed in three stages: (1) terrorism – aimed at the heads of the government and their assistants, in order to undermine the foundations of the government of enslavement; (2) partisan warfare – striking at the structure of foreign rule; (3) insurrection and the expulsion of the enslaving power from the country, after which the sovereign rule of the Hebrew nation would be established in its homeland.[133] Whereas *Lehi*, and the IZL of 1944, attempted to put stage 2 into operation, Stern himself was never to leave stage 1. In practice, he could never break out of the limiting framework of a small terrorist faction, vulnerable to attack.

One method of forcing such a breakthrough was to undermine economic life, not in order to accomplish a social revolution, but in order to compel the national institutions to do as the revolutionary underground desired. It was suggested that terrorist operations be carried out in large factories to compel employers to pay their workers a cost-of-living allowance. In this way the 'IZL in Israel' would win the favour of thousands of workers and acquire the support of employers – through fear. They placed particular emphasis on their ability, in contrast to the Revisionist movement, to win over the workers. The communists in Russia had understood that in order to secure the support of the farmers they had to promise them land, just as Hitler knew how to promise each social caste what it wanted – work for the unemployed, profits for the industrialist. All this was not left-wing ideology, merely the tactics of a revolutionary underground trying to harness everyone to the accomplishment of national liberation. More practically there was talk of action against informers, such as Altman, or against the British High Commissioner, MacMichael, who was to blame for the sinking of the *Patria* and the expulsion of Jews to Mauritius.[134]

The 'IZL in Israel' was born of Revisionism and its monistic ideology, but Stern broke away when he abandoned the British orientation and opted for the violent war of liberation. Despite his failures, Stern could not admit the flaws in his basic assumptions, for he had begun to think in mystical rather than realistic political terms. Hence his unwillingness to accept asylum – on the very eve of his death – either from the right or from the left despite the fact that this could have saved him from the police. He did not wish, of course, to betray his comrades who were languishing in prisons, but there was another, more significant, factor: he had reserved for himself the position of the messiah Ben Yosef who would come before the messiah Ben David, and therefore his personal failure would not mean the failure of his movement.[135]

INTERMEZZO: SUMMER–AUTUMN 1942

The 'IZL in Israel' was eliminated as an organisation in the winter of 1942, but the few remnants which continued in existence tried at least to maintain their ideology. Hence the claim that these were only temporary 'troughs'.[136] When Rommel was poised at the gates of El-Alamein, and the NZO and the IZL proclaimed their support for conscription (which reached its climax with 1,908 men in July 1942), the 'IZL in Israel' – or more precisely two of its remnants, Eldad and Prunin – continued to preach energetically against the 'mad conscription' in the service of a 'collapsing' empire. It was not the possibility of German victory that alarmed them, but rather the fact that these recruits would surely return to Palestine 'shattered . . . and disarmed'.[137] On 15 June 1942, Ballantine and Giles, while threatening exile and extinction, also made an offer to the members of the underground remanded in Mazra prison; two of them would be released and Yehoshua Cohen (one of the 'remnant' not yet arrested) would be persuaded to cease terrorist activity. This approach was seen as evidence of the group's continuing ability to threaten the British, and though some could see tactical advantages in such co-operation, the main response was a reiteration of their own conditions for ceasing terrorist activity. These included: the transfer of authority to the 'Hebrew nation', immediate Jewish control over immigration and the transfer of the arsenals to the Jews in the event of a German advance and a British withdrawal: 'We will fight the invader and any foreign ruler of this country.'[138]

Thus perceived, the negotiations were hardly likely to meet with success; indeed, they were not even noted by the British themselves. But uppermost in the minds of the remnants of the 'IZL in Israel' was the need to rid themselves of the stain of their vain attempt to link themselves with the Axis. Hence Avraham Selman's plaint from Mazra prison to Moshe Shertok, director of the political department of the Jewish Agency, blaming the British, assisted by Altman and his colleagues, for inventing that charge in order to obscure the pro-Nazi trend of the Arabs. The Government only wanted to hold a trial of Jewish 'Quislings' so that it could discredit all the Jewish groups, and launch a fierce campaign against the underground. Meanwhile there was a danger that the remnants of the group, 'immature youth persecuted for a long time like wolves by everybody and with every means' and 'surrounded by hate and suffocation . . . might be tempted by a real unscrupulous Nazi agent'.[139]

The remnants of the group were not, however, able to cleanse themselves in the eyes of the national institutions, nor in those of their ex-comrades in the NZO and the IZL. Following a lead originally given in America in December 1941 by Hillel Kook, a former comrade of Stern's, Begin in October 1942 publicly called for the opening of a military front against Hitler in Western Europe, in order to rescue Jews.[140] Scheib, now the ideological spokesman of the remnants of the 'IZL in Israel', rejected this entirely. Considering the Allies 'a lost cause', they continued to adhere to the 'persecutor' and 'enemy' thesis. That line seemed to be reinforced by the anti-Semitic and anti-Zionist speech delivered by Lord Moyne in the House of Lords on 9 June 1942. The Allies, after all, were hardly fighting this war on behalf of the Jews. Why should the Jews fight for them? The Poles and the Czechs would not fight without a clear guarantee of independence after the war. It was not enough to fight 'because Hitler hates the Jews and has caused our nation so many casualties in the lands of the Diaspora'. Germany was merely another country where anti-Semitism had always been rife. Polish Jewry would have been exposed to the danger of Polish Nuremberg legislation had not war broken out in 1939. The whole world was anti-Semitic, but in England and America anti-Semitism was increasing. The leaders of the Jewish people, from the *Bund* to the Revisionists (*sic*) did not desire a state, but merely a solution to the problem posed by Jewish refugees through philanthropy. They were 'not fighting the war of redemption, but rather the war of the exile', a war in which there was 'no hope of victory' nor any 'interest' for the Jewish people.[141]

More realistically, the Revisionist IZL was aware of the nature of the Nazi foe, correctly estimating the important role the United States was to play in the Middle East and not forgetting to note that the Arabs were the main enemy of Zionism. True, the IZL's support for Britain was steadily eroding, mainly because of the local bureaucracy which favoured pan-Arabism. Nevertheless, opposition to conscription was becoming noticeably weaker. On 7 July 1942 the IZL high command announced (Order No.132) that 'if there are to be found among the ranks of the IZL and *Betar* men who will still be recruited into the army of the foreigner, they are to approach their immediate superiors and receive their permission for this'.[142] A 'general massacre' of the *Yishuv* amid an 'Arab uprising' was viewed as an inevitable corollary to an invasion by Rommel, and the IZL was in fact preparing for Massada. Force, the IZL stressed, was necessary to prevent 'immediate annihilation'. But, in contrast to the Stern group and in loyalty to Jabotinsky, it claimed that in the long run it was necessary for a Jewish majority to be attained by a Hebrew government.[143]

April 1942 saw the arrival in Palestine of Menachem Begin – the man who was to bring about a shift in the history of the IZL and, at the same time, take from *Lehi* the copyright over 'the revolt'. Before being appointed commander of the IZL on 1 December 1943, he served as the *Betar* commissioner in Palestine. Though he then expressed his bitterness at Britain's refusal to establish a Hebrew army, feeling that it was treating Zionism with scorn, he did not subscribe to Stern's notions of 'persecutor' and 'enemy'. For him, Germany was in 1942 the clear foe, and he yearned for 'a liberation of the world from the Hitlerian plague, also for the sake of the rescue of European Jewry'. A Hebrew air force could bomb Berlin, Munich and Nuremberg, in revenge for the fate of the Jews of Poland. He was dreaming of a Hebrew army of over 200,000 men from among the Polish refugees who had gone into exile in Soviet Asia. They would fight both in the Middle East and in Europe to liberate their brethren from the talons of the Nazis.[144] A month later came his call for 'a second front to rescue European Jewry'.[145] Immediately thereafter, in the wake of the first reports of the extermination of the Jews, Yaakov Meridor, the commander of the IZL, proposed that the High Commissioner set up vengeance units to operate behind the German army's lines.[146]

∗

At the beginning of September 1942 Yitzchak Shamir and Eliyahu Giladi escaped from prison and attempted to resurrect the 'IZL in Israel'. Together with Eldad, Prunin, Yehoshua Cohen, Tuvia Khanchinsky (Chen-Zion) and others who had no ideological doubts, they formed a religious group known as LAESH (*Le-Zikaron Avraham Stern* – in memory of Avraham Stern), but this decided to cease activities, lest it be wiped out.[147] This group, too, believed that both Britain and Germany were the prime enemies. England was the judge and Germany the executioner. Thus the concept of 'persecutor' and 'enemy' was not completely abandoned: 'There will yet arise neither one Hitler nor two, but rather a large number of Hitlers, or executioners. If we desire to solve thoroughly the question of anti-Semitism, we must uproot it. And its root is none other than that which is ruling our beloved land, our homeland.'[148] The LAESH group denied that it was about to unite with the 'IZL in Israel' – and indeed it was not prepared to do so until the second half of 1943.[149]

In order to reconstitute the 'IZL in Israel' a change in operative ideology was necessary, especially in connection with the search for a new ally. Only thus would it be possible to justify the basic assumption of its founding father. After hesitations and second thoughts, such an ally was found in Soviet Russia. Stern's followers would later pay for this shift by conceding some of his own basic assumptions.

PART THREE

# THE REAPPEARANCE OF *LEHI*

# 5

# The Rise of *Lehi*: An Ideological Reformulation?

Several circumstances seemed to promote the re-launching of Stern's organisation: Shamir and Giladi's escape from prison in September 1942; the growing realisation of the destruction of European Jewry; and the helplessness of the Zionist leadership – as indeed of the NZO and the IZL. Adhering to the old line, Friedman-Yellin and Eldad – the self-proclaimed ideological heirs of 'Yair' – still refused to concede that the Nazis were a greater enemy than the 'foreign ruler'. Shamir undoubtedly concurred with their priorities. The main task was now to destroy the British prisons before they destroyed the underground.[1] Not until November 1943, however, were Friedman-Yellin and his comrades able to escape from prison, and not until February–March 1944 could they realise their 'educational heritage' of 'death rather than imprisonment'. Meanwhile, in the late summer of 1943, the ideological ranks had to be reformed. This involved three sets of liquidations: of those who wished to return to the IZL (the Vilenchik affair);[2] of the internal nihilistic foe (Eliyahu Giladi); and of the enemy from their Revisionist past (Israel Pritzker).

The IZL too was busy reorganising itself and, although wounded by the split and the death of Raziel, was able to engage in ideological debate in the pages of *Betar*'s journal. Now, steeled by the news of the Holocaust, it termed the relationship between England and Zionism a 'total failure' and 'a catastrophe', akin to that of the Jews of Europe. Indeed the British bore 'direct responsibility' for the destruction of European Jewry, since they had not thrown open the gates of Palestine for rescue.[3] Instead, they were arming the Arabs, despite the latter's pro-German stand.[4] The absurd pro-Soviet orientation of *Ha-Shomer Ha-Tsair* ('unilateral Jewish love') was a futile alternative. The Soviet regime excelled in its hatred of Zionism, which it would not support at a peace conference. *Ha-Shomer Ha-Tsair* members were already being imprisoned in the liberated areas of Poland.[5]

The strident anti-British tone of these statements (not apparent in NZO writings) lent them some superficial resemblance to those of Stern. However, the IZL still refrained from attacking the NZO. Hence, the 'revolt' of February 1944 was still on the distant horizon.

True, as early as April 1943 Begin had begun to ask whether 'this generation of ours has stepped off the stage as a mere generation of the slaughtered, or will it make the effort to go down in the history of Israel as a generation of fighters and heroes? This is the Jewish "dilemma".' The White Paper had given the end of March 1944 as the term of the immigrant quota. There were huge numbers of refugees in Poland and the Balkans – possibly up to three million – who would be unable to reach Palestine. This 'immoral piece of paper' had to be torn up in a war.[6] But the nature of the struggle was as yet unexplained. 'Revolt' as such was not yet mentioned.

True radicalism did not begin to become evident until the Warsaw ghetto uprising of April 1943. The *Haganah* was now attacked for supporting the status quo, for allowing the White Paper – merely the English edition of the Nuremberg laws – to be turned into reality because of its lack of opposition. Begin refused to believe that there were not numerous Jewish survivors in Poland, and argued that it was the British who had issued 'a death sentence against our brethren in Europe, Hitler serving as the hangman who executes that sentence'. Indeed, the British were preparing for a 'slaughter' of the *Yishuv*, together with the Arab gangs, the Arab Legion and the Iraqi army, so as to create an Arab Palestine. For the very first time Begin called for a 'direct' war with all 'forces' and using all 'methods'. Now indeed was the time to 'cease chattering: "Everything after the War!"'[7] Some change was even apparent within the disintegrating NZO where in March and July 1943 calls were issued for the establishment of a temporary Hebrew government.[8] Dr B. Lubotsky – a member of the NZO supervisory committee for the IZL – stressed that the need for a unified, fighting nation had become much more urgent in the wake of the failure of the Bermuda Conference on refugees.[9] Here, then, was an indicator of the trend towards the unification of the underground movements within the NZO, which had been in disarray since Jabotinsky's death.

From within *Lehi*, Friedman-Yellin viewed these trends favourably. Although mocking Begin's 'lofty, almost revolutionary, phrases' ('Their venue proves they are not serious . . . he still thinks that the youth can be "vanquished" by an eloquent speech . . .'), he was otherwise prepared to be conciliatory. 'We must assist in every way the joining and linking of those already joined by God . . . The truth of the matter is that nothing separates them from us.' Indeed, he expected the Revisionist youth of *Betar* and the IZL to be ready to join the renewed *Lehi*. 'The owners of street-stands are no "enemy" at all. Perhaps some of them will understand that they are being led astray.'[10]

## THE LIQUIDATION OF ELIYAHU GILADI

To this day, the Eliyahu Giladi affair is one of the obscure chapters in *Lehi*'s history. All of the very little which is known of the man and his death comes from sources close to the *Lehi* leadership, which strives to depict the affair as an altogether unique chapter in the movement's chronicle. In fact, however, it seems to have been symptomatic of an extremist stream in the 'IZL in Israel', to which both Lavstein and Zetler belonged. They favoured uncontrolled terrorist radicalism, on the lines laid down by such Russian revolutionaries as Savinkov. It remained to be seen whether there was any place for such trends in the renewed organisation, which sincerely claimed to have learned the lessons of the failure of its predecessor.

Giladi's main failing was his inability to accept authority. According to Friedman-Yellin's later account, he was mainly influenced by the revolutionary nihilism of the nineteenth-century Russian revolutionaries, especially Nechayev and Pisarev. Giladi, he writes, was the true 'professional revolutionary', free 'of any loyalty to ideal or to man'. Confronted with his blows, the weak would collapse, whether inside or outside the underground. This attitude did not deter Shamir, who was indeed impressed by Giladi's personal qualities – 'imagination, daring, courage, a lack of any sense of fear' (he had participated in the 'expropriation' at the APC Bank in mid-September 1940). Accordingly, Shamir invited Giladi to escape with him. Unlike Friedman-Yellin, Shamir believed in Giladi's assurance that he would not act without consulting him first.[11]

What actually happened thereafter is not clear. It seems that in the spring of 1943 Giladi began to compete with Shamir for the command. Shamir wanted to get as many underground members released as possible and to engage in comprehensive propaganda activities. Giladi favoured immediate and bold financial 'expropriations'.[12] A second event which hastened his end was the suicide of his personal contact after a series of tortures (June 1943).[13] A third was his desire 'to liquidate' some of the heads of rival parties before beginning to take action against the British authorities. Another scheme provoked a death threat from Giladi to Shamir. Finally, his order to release Eliezer Ben-Ami from prison by means of a direct attack was considered suicidal. Now Friedman-Yellin warned Shamir that Giladi would cause disaster to the underground and to the entire Jewish people. He therefore had to be liquidated; otherwise *Lehi* would degenerate into a gang.[14]

Was Giladi really so great a threat? Or did his quarrel with Shamir in fact revolve around the question of who had the higher authority, rather than over the character of the war? Whatever the truth, the conclusion drawn within *Lehi* is instructive:

> Perhaps we made an overall error in not giving precedence to the moral value of a person, but rather to his professional value, or to the talent of his boldness, or to his adventurous tendencies. Neither boldness nor professionalism are main points with us. They are merely necessary and helpful means.[15]

### IN SEARCH OF AN IDEOLOGICAL IDENTITY

A study of its propaganda literature suggests that the reborn underground was prepared to draw organisational and operational – but not ideological – conclusions from the failure of the 'IZL in Israel'. As before, the source of all evil remained the loss of the people's faith in the messianic concept and the Davidic kingdom. All the old basic illusions were also said to persist: the dependence on British 'evil' and the Zionist fight for rights in the diaspora rather than for political independence.[16] Eldad – since November 1942 the prime *Lehi* ideologist – guaranteed the ideological continuity between the 'IZL in Israel' and *Lehi* for a considerable period, even though he became increasingly realistic. In fact, Eldad reformulated old ideas. He emphasised the influence of the Enlightenment and Emancipation (which had sapped the national will of the Jews), the missed historical opportunities of official Zionism, its essentially 'philanthropic' character and the ideological bankruptcy of left-wing Zionism.[17]

Above all, in the summer of 1943 *Lehi* had still not broken free from the doctrine of 'persecutor' and 'enemy'. Even after the extent of the Holocaust was revealed, *Lehi* refused to depict Hitler rather than England as the main foe. The Zionist movements 'were not capable of defending the Jews of Europe', whose plight might well have been worsened by the 'proclamations and recruitings of soldiers by the Agency and the NZO and the horror propaganda effort made since the very beginning of the War.' But 'there is an *Eretz Israel* front. The enemy is here as well, and here we must strike him' in 'a war of Gog and Magog', for it was 'Great Britain who has attacked Zion . . .' and not Hitler. The Arabs, too, were essentially 'a tool in the hands of the British inciters'. Hence, the IZL was criticised for overestimating the threat that they posed.[18]

What made it essential to forge a unique ideology, and to pose as the only real underground alternative, was the internal unrest in the IZL and the plan to put Begin in command. *Lehi* had now to stress its singularity and to attack with even greater ferocity not only Weizmann but also Jabotinsky, who had been imprisoned for years in his pro-English 'Zionist-in-exile' orientation in London. Nevertheless, *Lehi* ideologists still remained within the boundaries of Revisionist political culture with regard to the Arab question and socio-economic issues. In 1943, Friedman-Yellin was still far from painting a picture of the progressive Arab fighting against imperialism. His Arab was the backward son of the desert, lacking all national awareness, whom the English preferred to the more cultivated Jews.[19]

But it was not enough for *Lehi* merely to develop its own ideological character. Without an actual renewal of the struggle against England, there would be no value in reviving the underground as a political movement. As yet, however, the organisation was too weak, and the preparation of propaganda was required.[20] Contrary to the line adopted early in 1942, *Lehi* now decided to engage in a propaganda offensive before launching operations.

Significantly, particular attention was given to publicising *Lehi*'s views on the nature of terrorism, a subject on which Stern had in December 1941 been reticent. 'Terror', the movement declared, was 'whatever a person is compelled to do by means of sanctions'. Such a broad definition allowed the argument that much of the law was 'merely camouflage for a rule of terror'. Both the Government and the *Yishuv* – right and left to an equal degree – made use of disguised terrorism in order to enforce their laws. Mass murder, like the sinking of the *Struma*, was terrorism, but so too was the murder of an individual. Its justification had to lie in its contribution to the life-and-death struggle. *Lehi* was not interested in heroism for its own sake or in war as an end in itself. Its goal was victory. It thus abandoned Stern's view, which had glorified self-sacrifice as part of the inevitable redemption process. Instead, it presented a more pragmatic approach which viewed terrorism as necessary, even if it included an element of fraud rather than bravery, such as in the use of ambush. Moral considerations were of no account when millions had to be rescued. Like the pre-war IZL, *Lehi* cited the biblical Ehud ben Gera ('Gera' was Friedman-Yellin's alias) and Judith as precedents. They 'were clear-cut terrorists. They viewed deceit and murder as means of driving off danger and hastening victory, and used them in the name of the Lord God of Israel.' Admittedly, terrorism alone could not bring about a revolution. But the experience of the Russian social revolutionaries showed that it could play a part in the broader struggle by weakening the regime and contributing to revolutionary education. Furthermore, it would inform the entire world of the war of the Hebrew people, tell 'our miserable brethren' of the underground's fight against the 'occupant' (who was the real terrorist) and shake the *Yishuv* out of its complacency.[21]

That a revolutionary minority might succeed in its struggle was a lesson which *Lehi* derived from three models. The first was provided by Poland, where most of *Lehi*'s leaders had been born, and which also possessed its own tradition of messianism and failed revolts.[22] The second model, similarly favoured by all Revisionists, was Italy. *Lehi*'s specifications found a suitable match in the slogans of 'Young Italy' – 'the world is a battlefield', 'the main thing is not immediate success, the main thing is that we believe . . . Sometimes people accomplish more by their death than by living, and the memory of those who fall for their brethren can motivate an entire people for a long and decisive war.' Moreover, the Italian example provided an intimation of the outcome of the policy foolishly being advocated by Weizmann and Ben-Gurion; like them, Cavour (disregarding Mazzini's teachings) had been prepared to enter the Crimean war without any guarantees of substantial gain.[23] Finally, there was the model provided by the revolutionary socialists of Russia, starting with the Narodniks and ending with the Bolsheviks. Lenin and Trotsky had not been empowered to act for the Russian people; but had it not been for their underground war, the revolution of 1917 would never have taken place.[24]

None of the leaders thus cited (the catalogue was expanded by references to De Gaulle, Spartacus and Moses) had sought public approval before embarking on their course. The Zionist movement, on the other hand, transformed the liberation of the homeland into a topic for debate and for elections. Emphasising that fact, Eldad rejected Zionist democracy and therefore democracy in general. Moreover, he linked that issue for the first time to the rescue of European Jewry: 'The Jews of Poland should have been saved without asking them, the Jews of America must be rescued without asking them.' Reiterating the words of the maximalists of 1932, he stressed the right of the minority, representing 'the most vital force of the nation', to take decisions without consulting the majority. The minority expressed 'the best of the yearnings of the nation throughout the centuries', its messianic aspirations. *Lehi* was a numerical minority, but it was not a minority in the context of 'psychological, biological and cultural values'.[25]

PROBING TOWARDS THE USSR – STAGE 1

There remained the question of a foreign ally. On this issue, *Lehi* claimed to follow pragmatic rather than ideological considerations. Its anti-imperialist outlook was thus still a long way from its later pro-USSR orientation. Its true anchor was enmity to Britain. *Lehi* was willing to admit that the Hebrew people had 'painful national accounts' to settle with Nazi Germany, but the latter was mentioned in the same breath as the Soviet Union. Despite the insistence on total independence, feelers were being put out towards the United States – later disqualified because of its alliance with Britain – and Italy (before Mussolini's fall), both of which were neutral in their attitude towards Zionism. Turkey and India were also discussed. In fact, no option should be left unexplored. Weizmann and Jabotinsky had been mistaken to rely on the democracies, just as *Ha-Shomer Ha-Tsair* was mistaken to rely on the Soviet Union. Moreover, *Lehi* had not forgotten the Revisionist theory commending an alliance with the national religious minorities in the Middle East opposed to an Arab federation, nor the theory which viewed France as a potential ally because of its opposition to the Arabs.[26]

Urgently searching for potential allies, Friedman-Yellin first gave serious thought to the Soviet Union in September 1943, when diagnosing the budding Cold War. As before, his premise was anti-British. 'It is not Germany that at present upsets the statesmen of England and America when they think of the future. It is Russia that gives them no rest.' The danger of a third world war seemed 'very realistic'. Little was to be expected of a future peace conference, as force would decide the issue.[27] Against that background, *Lehi* gradually ceased bracketing Stalin with Hitler; henceforth, the latter would be referred to along with Britain and the United States. The argument now was that old divisions, like 'progressive' and 'reactionary', 'fascist' and 'democratic', were no longer valid: '"Bermuda" is the democratic reply to the Nazi "extermination programme"; they are merely two sides of the same coin.'[28]

It followed that a broader anti-imperialistic theory had to be formulated in order to justify the struggle against Britain. To that end, *Lehi* came to adopt Hans Kohn's idea of the struggle between imperialism and nationalism; the former encouraged the exploitation of one social stratum against another. That was why revolutionary insurrection was necessary.[29] *Lehi* applied that model to the British case. No people, it argued, had been more willing than the British to put into effect the doctrine of 'the supreme race'. Not even the Nazis were worse. 'A hatred of the Jews which reached its legalistic and political peak in Nazi Germany is realised personally and daily in the English. The Germans put their hatred into effect by means of law, the English by their very nature.' The reason was their fear of real Jewish strength. They had even sponsored an Arab nationalism, so that it would act as an obstacle to the Jews.[30]

*Lehi* historiography depicts the escape of 20 of the movement's members on the night of 31 October/1 November 1943 as a turning-point in its development – akin to the series of escapes of revolutionary socialists from the prisons of the Tsar in Siberia, or of the Polish freedom fighters from the 'Paviak'.[31] In one respect, at least, that estimate seems justified. Henceforth, a central role in the formulation of *Lehi* policy was to be played by Friedman-Yellin.[32] Once out of prison, he was to reformulate the old ideology on the basis of both 'The Principles of Revival' and the lessons learned from Nietszche, Lenin and Pilsudski.

Friedman-Yellin's first significant contribution to the evolution of *Lehi*'s thought came with the 'failure' of the Tehran Conference in early December 1943 and the advance of the Red Army towards Poland. Previously, the movement's analysts (including Friedman-Yellin himself) had generally assumed that, after the war, Russia would be the weakest of the world's three Great Powers and would be superseded in strength by Britain as well as the United States.[33] Now, however, Friedman-Yellin revised his view of Russia. Her victories in Eastern Europe constituted a legitimate expression of Soviet power; they would also intensify the pragmatism shown by the abolition of the Comintern. In return for abandoning revolution elsewhere, the Soviet regime demanded a free hand in Eastern and Southern Europe. Above all, the Red Army's advance also proclaimed Russia's might. She, and not England, might indeed become the decisive power in the world: Western Europe would be at her mercy, and the time was not far off when a Soviet army would reach the Atlantic Ocean and the Persian Gulf, and would not permit a British presence at Gibraltar and Suez.

Clearly, England was too weak – economically and politically – to withstand that challenge. Therein lay Zionism's opportunity. The movement might, for instance, attain an alliance with Indian nationalism against the British by demonstrating to Nehru and other Indian leaders that it was not 'a faithful servant, an actual agent of British Imperialism'. Russian hostility to Zionism could be overcome in the same way.[34] It was not very long before the assumption that the Soviet Union was more influenced by her national interests than by ideological considerations came to play a crucial role in *Lehi*'s ideology.

THE GENESIS OF A SHIFT ON THE INTERNAL FRONT? THE ATTITUDE
TO SETTLEMENT, TO THE *HISTADRUT* AND TO WORKERS

*Lehi* would never abandon its fundamental conception of a Hebrew liberation movement based on messianism and not on productivisation or emancipation. To that end, it similarly maintained that Hebrew

# א שעת=הכושר

1 The cartoon above appeared in 1939, captioned 'An Opportune Moment'.
Hitler to Mussolini: Now is the best time for action in Gibraltar – the British
Navy is busy hunting illegal immigrants (*Di Tat*, 1939). Below: Ernest Bevin
garbed as Athena, the Goddess of War, watches Weizmann, Sharett and
Ben-Gurion lead towards Israel a Trojan horse labelled 'The State of Israel',
'Partition Plan', 'Ceasefire', 'Arms Embargo' and 'Morrison Plan' (*Eretz
Israel*, Paris 1948)

ארץ ישראל

מדינת ישראל

תוכנית החלוקה

הפוגה

אמברגו על נשק

תוכנית מוריסון

אתנה (אלת המלחמה), בווין והסוס של טרויה!

2  Top, left to right: Uri Zvi Greenberg; Zeev Jabotinsky. Above, left to right: Uriel Heilperin (Yonatan Ratosh); Abba Achimeir and his sons

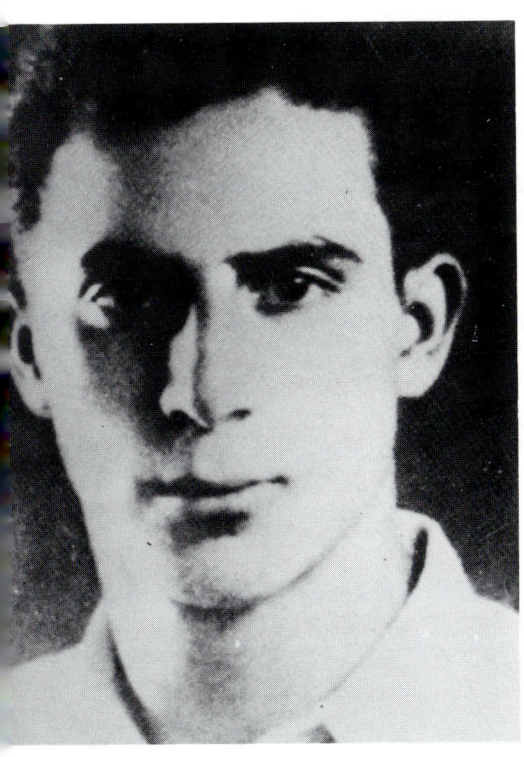

3  Top: Lord Moyne, Minister Resident in the Middle East. Above: the two
assassins, Eliahu Hakim (left) and Eliahaku Bet Tsouri (right)

e Nr. 1620 geh.

Deutsche Botschaft in der Türkei
Eing.: 18 JAN 1941
Anl.
J.-Nr. 27 Tr. 75 h/

Sehr geehrter Herr Botschafter!

In der Anlage übersende ich Ihnen:

1.) einen Brief, den der Chef der Sûreté Général in Syrien
Colombani an den General Dentz gerichtet hat. Roser teilt
mit, dass auf Grund dieses Briefes anscheinend eine weitere
Unterredung zwischen Colombani und Dentz stattgefunden hat.
C. ist der Ansicht, dass seine Zurückberufung durch die Zu-
sammenarbeit von G. Dentz (H.C.) und den Minister Pe........
begründet ist.

2.) eine Verfügung betr. Demobilmachung, die von den fran-
zösischen Militärbehörden in Syrien bei den Truppenteilen in
Umlauf gesetzt worden ist.

3.) einen Vorschlag der nationalen Militärorganisation in
Palästina zur Lösung der jüdischen Frage in Europa.

Mit einer Empfehlung

bin ich Ihr ergebener

1. 20. I.

4  First page of Stern's offer of alliance with Nazi Germany, January 1941

5 Avraham Stern ('Yair') alive (above) and dead (below, photographed by Sergeant Day). Right: Deputy Superintendent S. Schiff, Commander of the Jewish Police in Tel Aviv

6 Top left: 'Yair' Stern in pierrot costume. Top right: on his wedding day, 1936.
Above: with Polish immigrant pupils at Rehavia Gymnasium, Jerusalem 1926

7 Top: the bombing of the Military Paymaster's office, Tel Aviv 1947. Above: the
bombing of the Haifa Shipping Agency, 28 February 1947

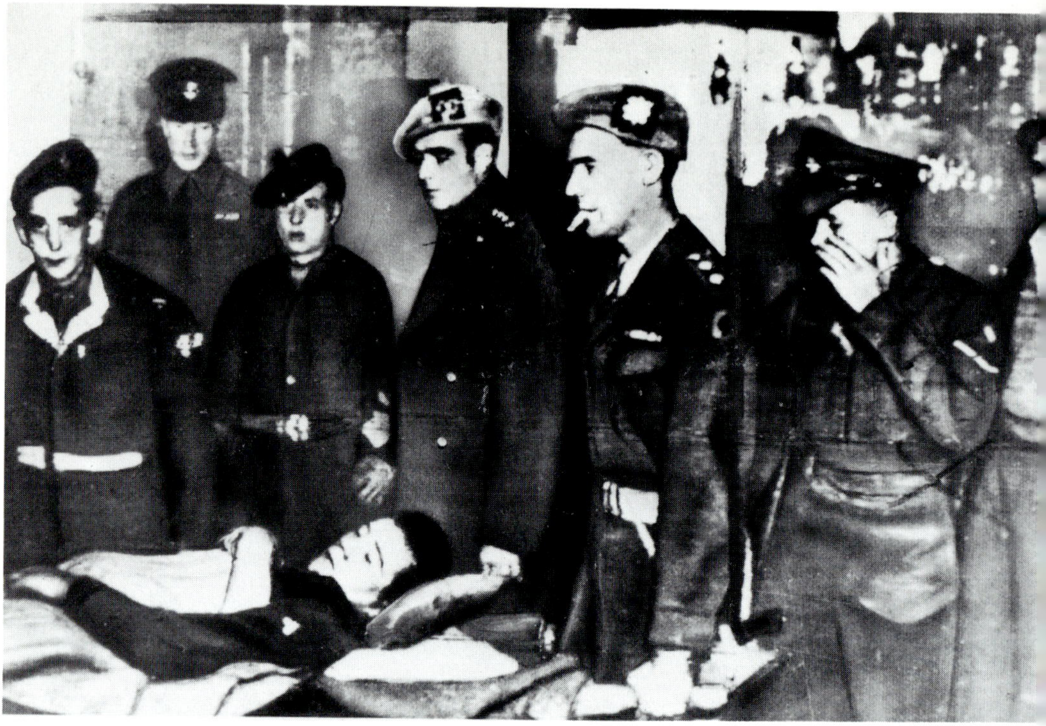

8 Above: After the bombing by *Lehi* of a café in Jerusalem, 1947. Below: a *Lehi* explosion near the Damascus Gate, Jerusalem 1948

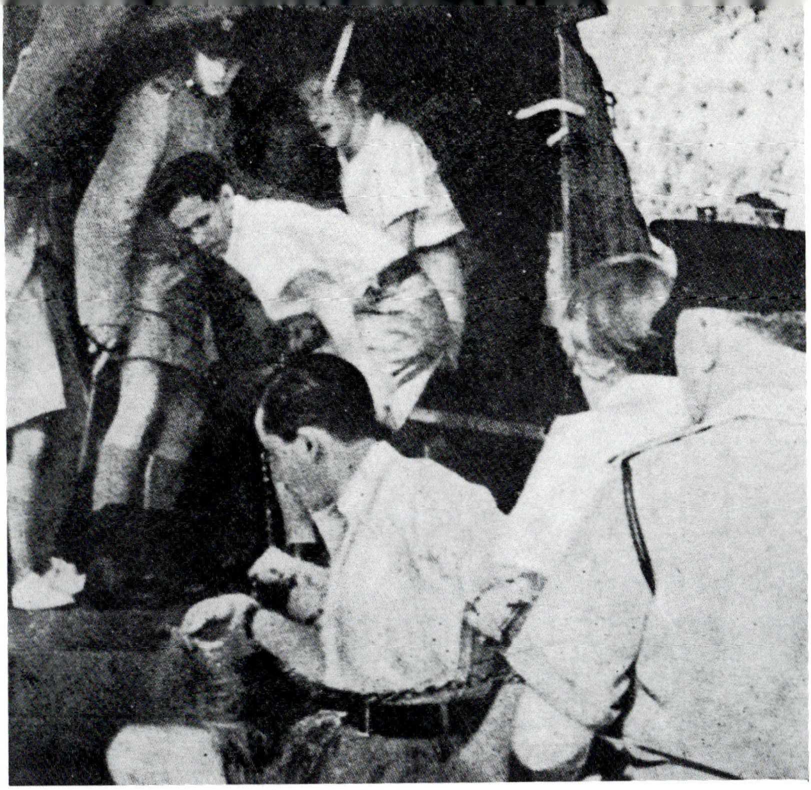

9  Above: *Lehi* members after their trial, Haifa 1946. Below: injured *Lehi* member Uzi captured by British security forces 1946

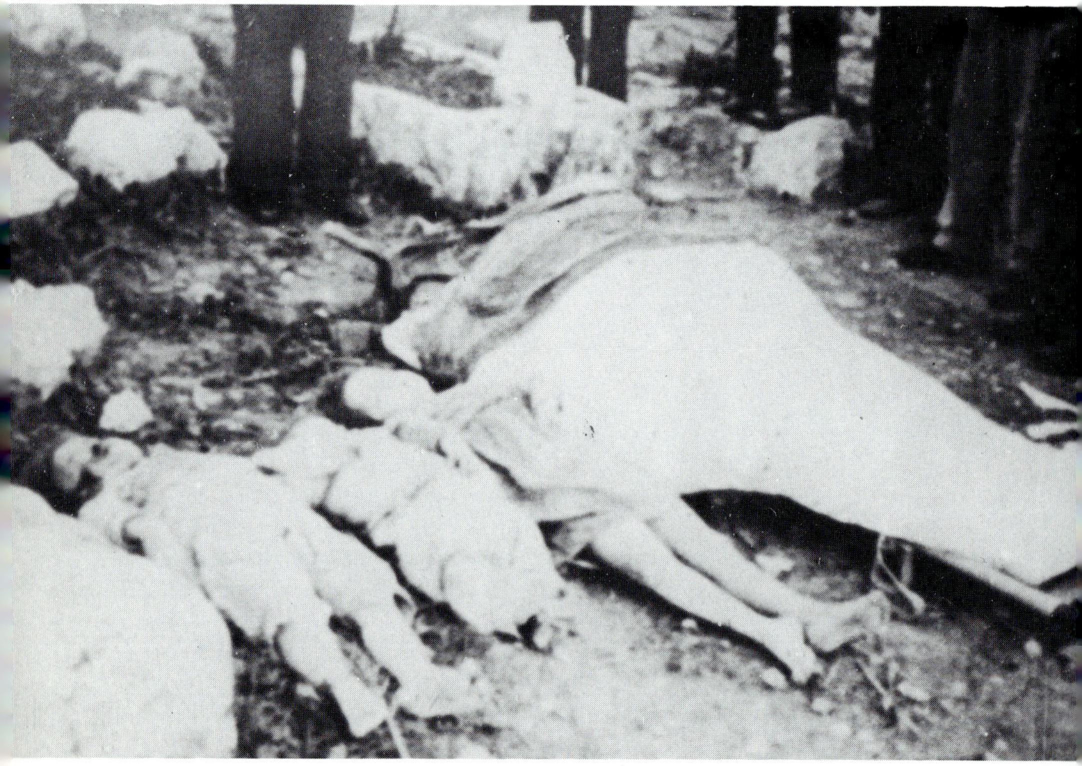

10  Top: the bombing of the Ritz Restaurant, Jerusalem, 13 November 1947.
Above: the massacre at Deir Yasin, 7 April 1948

11 Top: advice to Count Bernadotte, 1948: 'Get out of our country!' (signed
*Lehi*). Above: Count Bernadotte (in uniform) with UN officials, 1948

בריטאניה הודיעה על פינוי הארץ

הוא יוצא כאילו נכנס

12  Top: bombing of the oil refineries in Haifa, 30 March 1947. Above: Bevin
'goes out as if he is going in' (*Ha-Ma'as*, 1947)

13 The trial of Yellin-Mor and Shmuelevitch, 1949; leaving court (top); in court (centre); Eldad speaking, Shamir next to him (above left)

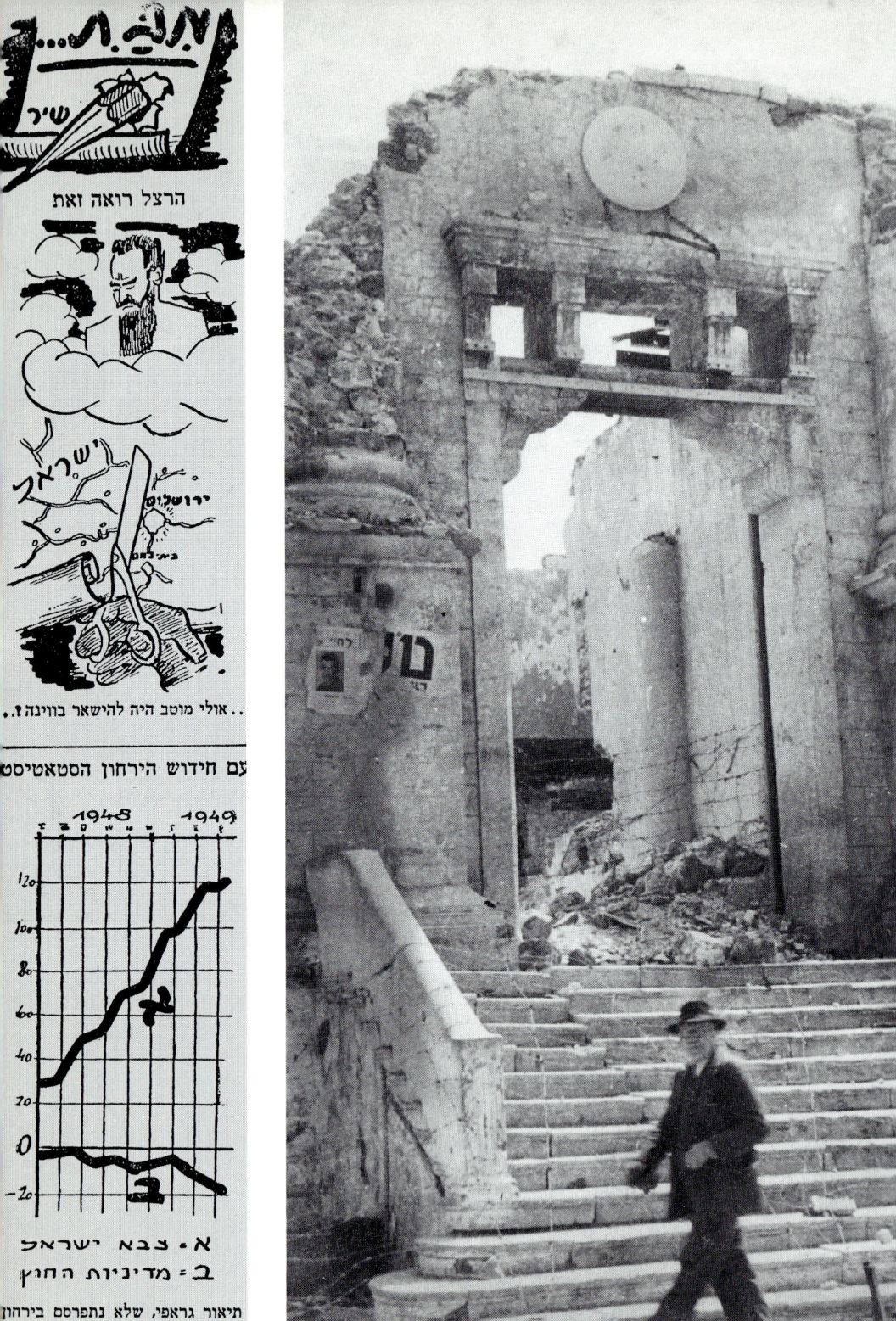

14  The bombing of the Sarayah in Jaffa, 4 January 1948 (above); cartoon
showing Herzl watching the partitioning of Eretz Israel and wondering if it
would be better to stay in Vienna (above left); the falling stock of a) the Israeli
Army; b) Israeli foreign policy (left)

15 Top: Geula Cohen, *Lehi* broadcaster. Above: 'God forbid!' Stalin offering his hand to Sharett, Weizmann and Silver (*Mivrak* 1948)

דייש

אם תתנהג יפה תקבל דולר בשביל גלידה.

16 Above: Uncle Sam advising Israel: 'If you behave, you will get a dollar for ice cream'. Below: Sharett, carrying the 'war for Jerusalem' colours towards the west, is corrected by the schoolboy: 'Mistake, Minister! My teacher says Jerusalem is in the east' (*Ha Ma'as*, 1949)

הוא יוצא ל„מלחמה"

דגל המלחמה למען ירושלים

מערב (ליק סאפס) | מזרח

שיר

הנער: טעות, השר! המורה אמר בכיתה שלי, שירושלים היא במזרח...

self-government would be achieved only by war and not by settlements or international recognition. Nevertheless, from September 1943 onwards Eldad was to strike a new chord in the series of articles which he published under the general title of 'Foundation Stones'. He now admitted that settlements in such places as Manara or in the south could have 'strategic value' and could provide 'a jumping-off point' for the conquest and liberation of the country. Even the *Histadrut* could play a strategic role by calling a general strike and paralysing the economic life of the country as part of the wider struggle against the foreign regime. The simple growth of the *Yishuv* in the form of settlements, economic enterprises, arms and immigrants was not in itself a sufficient path to liberation; neither would the Soviet Union be particularly impressed by the claimed similarity between the *kibbutzim* and the *kolhozi*. Nevertheless, all such enterprises could serve as useful 'supports' to the main struggle.[35]

To say this is not to suggest that *Lehi* had at this stage altered its fundamental principles. Faithful to Stern's teachings, the movement still regarded England as its main enemy. That it would remain so was proven by its most recent provocations: the incidents at Hulda, Ramat Ha-Kovesh and the trials of Jews for stealing arms.[36] A definite shift could, however, be noted in its other orientations. Notwithstanding *Lehi*'s continued reluctance to identify with the Marxist social and political order, its growing empathy with Soviet foreign policy was certainly bringing with it a readiness to concede possible Soviet lessons on revolutionary technique. Marxism, after all, viewed class conflict and revolution as a historical necessity while simultaneously demanding real action 'in both propaganda and deed, without waiting for necessarily overt public approval and for the masses to make a revolution'.

Still more striking were *Lehi*'s pronouncements on class issues. On the eve of its renewed war against England, and in order to increase its chance of success, the movement now sought to project a new image of freedom fighters favouring the struggle of the workers to improve their lot. This was not regarded as a complete *volte-face*, for *Lehi* proclaimed that while it did not share Achimeir's anti-socialist views (frequently expressed in the NZO organ), it had no ambitions of its own for social reform. It remained opposed to any approach based on a single social class and continued to support private enterprise. Nevertheless, the Hebrew state was to be the property of the entire nation and especially of the workers: 'The Hebrew nation in its homeland will be a nation of workers and farmers, otherwise it will not be able to live, otherwise it will not be able to survive.' The 'labouring man' would be at the heart of the concern of the Hebrew authorities.[37]

At a subsequent stage of *Lehi*'s history (and in particular during the Fighters Conference of 1949, by which time *Lehi* had definitely moved towards the left), statements such as these were retrospectively considered to have marked an ideological breakthrough.[38] That is an exaggeration. Clearly, *Lehi* was beginning to pride itself on its proletarian membership ('The most poverty-stricken of this *Yishuv* with neither home nor bed of their own, neither garment nor covering, with neither wages nor bread guaranteed . . . we have no material possession in this world; we merely conceive of the idea of freedom to which we have dedicated our lives'); certainly, it was attempting to detach the working class from its current political leadership. Nevertheless, in this matter (as in that of the shift towards the Soviet Union), the change in *Lehi*'s ideology was still in an embryonic stage. Even if it was putting out feelers to the left, on the eve of 1944 the movement was still anchored to the right.

What can be said about *Lehi*'s pronouncements on domestic social questions at this stage is that they provide evidence of an early attempt to pour national ideas into a conventional socialist mould, and thereby emphasise the movement's distinction from the IZL. Thus, *Lehi* even adapted the famous slogan from Marx's *Das Kapital*: 'Each gives to the nation according to his ability; each receives from the nation according to his needs.' Similar use was made of the notion of exploitation. As portrayed by *Lehi*, the exploiter was in this case the foreign regime, which was engaged in the systematic destruction of the Hebrew economy. Jewish history was pressed into similar service. In *Lehi*'s account, during past Jewish wars for freedom the upper classes had always acquiesced in national servitude; the fight had been led by the 'small person'. The Hasmonean army, for instance, had been composed of workers from Jerusalem and farmers from the villages suffering under the yoke of taxation who understood that only a war against the Hellenists would bring about both national and social liberation. Indeed, passivity in exile stemmed from the fact of the Hebrew people having been transformed from a nation of farmers and workers into one of peddlers.

Despite such socialist overtones, the Hebrew state of *Lehi*'s vision was based on the notion of *étatisme* and in substance was an integralist entity, recruiting all the resources of the nation for its needs. The proximity to classical Revisionist social ideology was still more evident in *Lehi*'s attitude to industrial disputes. Its stand was clearly non-socialist. There would be no government intervention on behalf of either side. Instead, through a system of 'compulsory arbitration', a strong nationalist movement would solve all problems of that nature in accordance with the national interest: keeping Hebrew industry from ruin, limiting the profits made by the employers to fair amounts (by imposing a Hebrew war tax on exaggerated profits) and also granting the workers' just demands. It was thus that the worker would benefit by participating in the war for national freedom.

From an ideological perspective, then, *Lehi* still had a long road to travel before it would formulate its own brand of National Bolshevism. However, the extent to which it was embarking on that route is best illustrated by comparisons with the contemporary situation within the IZL. The latter, unlike *Lehi*, was not engaged in seeking a world power as an ally, though its general leaning was towards the United States. Moreover, it seemed to have hardly any interest in social and economic matters. Finally, and despite the increasing unrest in its ranks generated by the revelation of the horrors of the Holocaust and the deterioration in relations between Britain and the *Yishuv*, the IZL had no apparent interest in fomenting a total confrontation with Britain. Its complaints were primarily aimed at the local administration and, at the most, at the British authorities in the Middle East. True, IZL propaganda did also equate the British with the Nazis – but by now that was hardly the expression of a separate ideological approach. What directly led to the IZL 'revolt' under Begin's leadership early in 1944 was the failure of the *Am Lohem* ('Fighting Nation') movement, which had striven to unite all the underground movements in the spirit of the IZL.[39]

*Lehi* had rejected the *Am Lohem* approach. Indeed, on the eve of 1944 the movement was in a mood of bitter self-chastisement. Internal weakness – 'the great and treacherous provocateurs in our midst' – had led to the failures of actions in the past. People had all too easily been allowed to leave the movement and betray it. Now there was a new resolve: 'Through our doorway one can only *enter*; there is no way out. We shall be brutal with our good men.'[40] In a broader sense, *Lehi* was closing accounts with Jabotinsky and his movement. He had erred in seeking legitimacy from the masses, believing in 'the good English', and proving juridically the validity of Zionism before the various investigatory committees. That is why

> he was doomed to die, not at the war front amongst those actively liberating the homeland in the field of Hebrew revolution, but rather like Herzl, his teacher at the lobbying front . . . [He] did not comprehend the only tongue of the twentieth century. He retreated . . . to Basle, London and Washington, while in the meantime the doctrine of Acre was coming into being.[41]

Ben Yosef and his comrades had already corrected his error. But the real test had now arrived.[42]

# *Lehi* Goes to War:
# The Assassination of Lord Moyne

## COMPETITION WITH THE IZL AS AN IDEOLOGICAL CATALYST

March 1944 marked two years since the death of Stern and also saw the IZL's declaration of its own 'revolt' under the leadership of Begin. For both reasons, that month ought to have witnessed the recommencement of *Lehi*'s war. The anniversary of Yair's death did indeed occasion the celebration of a one-time myth of heroism and foresightedness. But that success was offset by the discovery of the bomb which was meant to hit the British High Commissioner at the entrance to St George's Church, Jerusalem, on 3 February 1944. The truth of the matter was that *Lehi* was still a tiny movement which, although noticed by the British authorities, was hardly in a position to constitute a real threat.[1]

Despite these disadvantages, *Lehi* had to formulate a response to the IZL's 'revolt'. Its initial reaction was disdainful: it pointed out that the IZL's operations – such as the attack on the immigration office on 12 February – were paltry and symbolic affairs. Surely the youth would not be deluded, but would flock to *Lehi*'s ranks.[2] With the increase in IZL activities during the spring, however, this attitude was changed to one of grudging respect.[3] Temporarily despairing of its ability to persuade the public not to follow the policies pursued by Laval in France, *Lehi* now began to regard itself and the IZL as two wings of the same front. After all, both shared a common disdain for the official Zionist policy of negotiations with Britain for a handful of certificates or marginal changes in the boundaries of the 'Peel state'. Both, therefore, were in principle utterly opposed to the official policy of 'restraint'. What the public had to appreciate, *Lehi* maintained, was that England and Nazism were one and the same. 'Whilst Hitler conceived the idea of imprisoning Jews in compounds, it is England who has established just such a compound in our land.' The Jewish police in Tel Aviv were no different from those of the ghettos of Warsaw, Lodz and Cracow. England's ultimate objective was world domination, and to that end it sought to dominate Jewish industry and to impose a foreign culture on the entire *Yishuv*.[4]

One testimony to the intensity of emotions aroused by *Lehi*'s aggressive ideological assault on 'official' Zionism was provided on

12 February 1944 at the *Ha-Shomer Ha-Tsair* in Tel Aviv, where *Lehi* members attempted to distribute their propaganda. In the mêlée which ensued, one of the club guides was shot in the arm. According to Yellin-Mor's later account, the *Lehi* members involved were the victims of their own innocence. Not realising how much they were regarded as 'class enemies' by *Ha-Shomer Ha-Tsair*, they were forced to defend themselves when threatened with being turned over to the police and had only fired into the air. The *Lehi merkaz* ('centre', which discussed the incident on 14 February) attempted to make much the same point. The manifesto which it subsequently published was at pains to emphasise that *Lehi*'s only war was with the British rule; within the *Yishuv* it wished only to proclaim its ideology. *Lehi* also went on to express the hope that the public would repeat its right to promote its thinking and to defend its members against being turned over to the CID.[5]

*Lehi* considered this principle to have been accepted at a meeting which Revisionist activists subsequently arranged between the *Haganah* leader, Eliyahu Golomb, and Friedman-Yellin. Although the latter did agree to suspend *Lehi*'s propaganda activities within *Ha-Shomer Ha-Tsair* youth clubs, he had gained Golomb's recognition of its right to do so elsewhere. The *merkaz* was satisfied with this arrangement, which it thought a recognition on the *Haganah*'s part that *Lehi* was a responsible adversary which would not drag the community into civil war at the expense of its fight against the foreign foe.[6] Golomb's own report to the *Mapai* secretariat was entirely different. The attack on the club, he said, was a sign that *Lehi* 'intended to instil fear into the *Yishuv* and conquer its support by force of arms'. Convinced that 'they might bring upon us the greatest disaster' (and even 'attack people sitting at this very table'), Golomb insisted on the isolation of *Lehi*: 'the war has to be their disarmament wherever they appear in the Jewish public.' Golomb stopped short of suggesting that the *Haganah* co-operate with the British against *Lehi*, but Ben-Gurion was less restrained. Neither of them suggested placing a special unit at the disposal of the British police.[7]

Lord Moyne was appointed Minister Resident in the Middle East on 28 January 1944. The new appointee had long joined MacMichael and Churchill in *Lehi*'s rogues' gallery. In part, this was because of his role in the *Struma* incident and in part due to his support for the establishment of an Arab federation. Above all, however, there had been his speech in the House of Lords on 9 June 1942, when he had spoken of the 'purity' of the Arab race and had denigrated the attempts of the 'mixed' Jewish race to establish control over Palestine, Iraq and Syria. It is hardly surprising, therefore, that *Lehi* immediately regarded Moyne's new appointment as an omen that Britain was about to implement its anti-Zionist policy. Leaders of the movement had undoubtedly already hatched a plot to assassinate him.[8]

The 'official' Zionist leadership was in *Lehi*'s eyes clearly ill-fitted to meet the new challenge. Ben-Gurion's resignation from the chairmanship of the executive of the Jewish Agency in October 1943, together with his return to that office in January 1944, was considered to indicate the absence of any leadership worthy of the name. No replacements could be sought in the World Jewish Congress or the American Jewish Committee, nor even in the suggestion (voiced in circles close to the Revisionist movement) for the establishment of a 'Free Jewish Government'.[9]

> Today, we are the only [factor] in the Hebrew people which knows the objective . . . We represent the unconscious will of the entire people . . . We are just as entitled to declare ourselves to be the recognised and sovereign Hebrew government as were the band of Irish freedom-fighters who declared their sovereign rule in Easter 1916.

The innovation did not lie in *Lehi*'s ideology – indeed, *Lehi* deliberately refrained from issuing a declaration of its own on the grounds that the people were tired of empty pronouncements. What the movement had to do was prepare itself for armed struggle. In so doing, it followed Stern's revolutionary principle that without actual warfare no ideology could be authentic. It was this which, in Golomb's words, imparted a menacing tone to *Lehi*'s statement. Confident in its ultimate success, *Lehi* was prepared to suffer temporary unpopularity and to work in isolation.[10]

It is this conviction which also explains *Lehi*'s attitude towards the IZL, and particularly its rejection of Begin's somewhat patronising offer (made in the wake of the *Ha-Shomer Ha-Tsair* club incident) to offer *Lehi* the IZL's protection.[11] Believing that Begin was attempting to patch up a compromise between the activists among his youthful followers and those who 'sought only quiet', *Lehi* determined to intervene on behalf of the former. One reason was the (unfounded) suspicion that the IZL's 'revolt' was in any case only a sham – and that it in fact was designed to serve the interests of the British authorities.[12] Another was the bitterness aroused in *Lehi* ranks by the IZL's denigration (or at the very least, failure to acknowledge) the precedent for action established by Yair.[13] Yet a third, expressed most vividly by Eldad, was that the IZL's entire programme seemed awry. It made no sense for an underground movement to announce its programme for war, since the behaviour of the enemy and of the people could never be predicted.[14]

Notwithstanding its own claims to consistency, *Lehi* was beginning to change some of its positions drastically in response to both the dynamic of events and its competition with the IZL. One example is provided by its new-found preparedness to establish its own public hinterland, to be known as 'Supporters of the Freedom of Israel' (*Shoharei Herut Yisrael*) whose object was to mediate between the fighting underground and the masses. The formation of this body was more than just another exercise in propaganda. It reflected *Lehi*'s feeling that total war with Britain was now fast approaching and complemented a philosophy which envisioned a three-tiered battle consisting of: (a) terrorist activities, which would test the fighters, educate the people, wreak havoc on the enemy and direct attention to *Eretz Israel*; (b) wide-scale guerrilla activities and sabotage as a preparation for the rebellion; and (c) the final test of forces, in which the entire people would participate. Passage to the second and third stages necessitated public support, otherwise the fighting core would be permanently isolated; and such support could be garnered by a programme of education and indoctrination. In the first instance, the public had to be made aware of the enemy's true face and to be brought to hate him; it had then to be shown that *Lehi* was not just another party within the *Yishuv*, but its true representative.[15]

Similarly significant were the initial changes in *Lehi*'s attitude to the 'organised *Yishuv*' and particularly towards *Mapai*. *Lehi* was still far from changing its basic social perception and was by no means socialist or Marxist. Very much in keeping with the programme laid down by the 'IZL in Israel', it still regarded nationalism (guided by instinct) as the basis for all action, but it was now prepared to acknowledge that *Mapai* – for all its faults – had fulfilled a vital and 'historic' mission in preparing the community for war. The same was true of the *Haganah* which, although not prepared to launch offensive operations, had established a military framework, trained the youth in the use of weapons and stored up arms. The great question, however, was whether *Mapai* would not place so much value on its material assets that it would be incapable of following the Russian example of a scorched-earth policy when the time came to give true battle.[16]

But no change in attitude was discernible in *Lehi*'s positions *vis-à-vis* the IZL. Indeed, the Revisionists were entirely castigated; they claimed to be a revolutionary force but had allowed themselves to be dominated by 'the inertia of conditions'. Their principal errors lay in their reliance on the diaspora and in their belief in the 'scrap of paper' known as the Balfour Declaration. Equally misconceived was *Betar*'s assessment that the Arabs were the true enemy. They were neither that, nor the Jews' allies. They constituted a potential enemy for the rights over the land, but they were not at present to be fought because they did not control the country. Hence, *Lehi* did not (yet) advocate an alliance between Hebrews and Arabs against their common British foe; neither, at this stage, did it seek to initiate an Arab–Jewish war. 'By concentrating our war against the Arabs we shall only play into English hands, and give them an opportunity to arbitrate and thereby secure their own rule . . .The Arabs are no danger. The Hebrew *Yishuv* can easily deal with them by itself.'[17]

## BETWEEN THE EXTERNAL AND DOMESTIC FRONTS

For all its attempts to force a distinctive identity, *Lehi* was still uncertain of its own direction. Its one clear ambition was to drive a wedge between the *Yishuv* and England. This generated attempts to depict Britain's increasing problems in the international arena, but *Lehi* could not offer a comparable strong ally of his own choice. The United States, because of Roosevelt's unfavourable image and his pro-Saudi leanings, was not considered a potential adversary of Britain. In view of Stalin's anti-Zionism, the idea of an alliance with the USSR (as proposed by *Ha-Shomer Ha-Tsair*) seemed even more far-fetched. The only possible friend discerned in the external arena was Turkey, the wisdom of whose policy in both world wars was praised and whose territorial ambitions (which were said to include the acquisition of the oilfields of Mosul and Kirkuk in Iraq and of northern Syria) seemed to offer the possibility of an anti-British convergence of interests.[18]

On the domestic front, too *Lehi* seemed in very poor shape. One reason was the heavy toll in lives which its own decision to go to war with Britain was obviously taking. 'Elisha' Ahronson was killed in action on 19 March; as were 'Baruch' Rosenbaum on 3 April; and Lunz and Drucker ('Zion' and 'Eliezer') on 5 April. Six other *Lehi* members were arrested (including Eldad on 27 April). No less threatening was the danger from the 'organised' *Yishuv*. As early as February 1944, members of the executive of the Jewish Agency had suggested co-operating with the authorities against *Lehi* and the IZL. Rubashov (Shazar) raised the same idea at the meeting of the *Mapai* political committee on 27 March, where he was supported by Golda Meyerson, Shkolnik (Eshkol) and Loufban, all of whom were prepared to accept the risk of civil war. The notion was resisted by Ben-Gurion and, far more vigorously, by Katznelson and by Golomb (the latter arguing: 'They are . . . very Zionistic. Zionists who are prepared to sacrifice their lives . . . they are not very many; perhaps 200–300 or just 150 . . . It can also be a positive force').[19] Nevertheless, the

Zionist leadership could hardly remain inactive in the face of the challenge both to its own democratically confirmed leadership and to its policies. On 2 April it was decided to isolate the 'dissidents' both publicly and personally.[20]

Relationships reached a further crisis on 26 April, when – at the behest of the police – the Hebrew press published pictures of *Lehi* leaders and the rewards offered for their arrest. Writing to Golomb, Friedman-Yellin claimed that the very fact of publication had injected a 'change into the situation' since their last meeting in the wake of the *Ha-Shomer Ha-Tsair* club incident, when he had thought that a policy of co-existence had been established. 'In future', he warned, 'we shall be forced to determine our actions in the light of facts and not of words . . . We shall not lower our guard and will at every moment be prepared to return fire.' Golomb's reply was really menacing. What concerned him was neither the publications nor the police harrassment, but the fact that *Lehi* had executed some Jews whom it considered to be 'informers' and 'traitors' and had published a 'black list' of nine others. Any continuation of such actions, he wrote to Friedman-Yellin, would be considered 'a declaration of war. I therefore warn you! Do not follow that path, because in so doing you are embarking on the domestic war which we wanted to avoid.'[21]

Clearly, the 'organised *Yishuv*' approached the issue of its collaboration with the British against *Lehi* with deep misgivings. After all, it too harboured feelings of considerable bitterness in the light of the fact that 'the goverment fighting Hitler was in effect turning half of our people over to his hands'. There was also a determination not to permit a repetition of any attempt to 'exterminate Zionism', as had been attempted at Ramat Ha-Kovesh. But these sentiments were not automatically transmuted into a policy of political activism. For all their anger against the British, Ben-Gurion and his colleagues in the leadership knew the limits of their strength and concentrated on building the foundations for a future Jewish state. Moreover, at this stage, even the activists still believed in the possibility of co-operation with Britain. Therein, to their minds, lay *Lehi*'s true danger. There was no doubt that members of the movement were not simply a band of murderers, but true patriots. Nevertheless, their 'mad actions' were threatening to generate an Arab–British or Muslim–Christian anti-Semitic front which would destroy Zionism. Thus, members of *Lehi* were 'themselves' leading the *Yishuv* into war against their movement.[22]

Such sentiments were not restricted to the 'official' Zionist leadership. On the contrary, *Lehi* also came under verbal fire from the left and right fringes of the Jewish political spectrum in *Eretz Israel*. One instance, paticularly instructive in view of *Lehi*'s later alignment with communism, is provided by the movement's controversy with the Palestinian Communist Party (PKP) in 1944. The latter was unrestricted in its criticism of *Lehi*'s strategy and tactics. Insistent that *Lehi* was at root a fascist organisation (as evidenced by its attempts at alliance with Mussolini), the PKP poured scorn on the very idea that Yair's followers could gain the USSR's favour. Their apparent concern for the welfare of Arab labourers was also dismissed as no more than 'crocodile tears', and, as such, characteristic of fascists everywhere. If *Lehi* desired a Hebrew state, it was only in order to exploit the Arabs. Nehru appreciated the true facts of the situation. That was why – contrary to *Lehi*'s expectations – he was an anti-Zionist. The only way in which *Lehi* could possibly obtain Indian support was by first obtaining that of the Arab population and by showing consideration for its national aspirations.[23]

At the same time, *Lehi* was also criticised by Yonatan Ratosh, the founder of the right-wing 'Committee for the Solidification of Hebrew Youth' (better known as the 'Canaanites'). This was a more serious challenge, not least because Ratosh had himself been one of the formulators of Revisionist maximalism during the 1930s and had contributed to the crystallisation of the political thought of Stern and his successors. Impressed with the manner in which *Lehi* had apparently adopted his own political extremism, Ratosh now sought to influence its programme and to that end met Friedman-Yellin. It soon transpired that – notwithstanding *Lehi*'s refusal to adopt Ratosh's idiosyncratic 'Canaanite' outlook – there were few ideological differences between the two men; where they differed was on the action to be pursued. Friedman-Yellin insisted on the need for a programme of terrorism; Ratosh, however, saw this as a course which would force *Lehi* to remain a 'sect', supported by no more than a handful of the committed, who would increasingly be forced to direct their terrorism against those of their own number desirous of leaving *Lehi*'s ranks. In the absence of a union with the IZL, friction between the two movements would also become inevitable. His own advice was that *Lehi*, at the very least, co-ordinate its activities with those of the IZL. He also suggested that it concern itself with garnering public support, ironing out its ideological inconsistencies and seeking paths other than terrorism.[24]

*Lehi* did not directly respond to either Ratosh or the PKP, but it clearly did take to heart the signs of its own isolation. Indeed, these gave rise to increasing fears that *Lehi* was about to be betrayed by other groups in the Jewish community. Such fears further increased in May. For one thing, Golomb (who was under considerable British pressure to collaborate with the authorities against the 'dissidents') then wrote another threatening letter to Friedman-Yellin.[25] For another, between 26 April and 12 May, the Hebrew press again repeatedly published photographs of *Lehi* leaders, also advertising the police prices on their heads.

These developments did not deter *Lehi*; on the contrary (and as *Lehi*'s letters to the newspapers concerned pointed out), there was something flattering about the very fact of publication.[26] Hence, the movement refused to retract its positions. It continued to insist on the need for an active war against England; continued to justify its advocacy of terror before the bar of Jewish military history in *Eretz Israel*; remained confident that public pressure would force the 'official' leadership to adopt a more active stance; and even foresaw the imminence of a situation in which the old leaders would be replaced by others who were more attuned to the necessities and opportunities of the situation.[27] Thus, despite the apparently unfavourable domestic and external environment in which the movement found itself, *Lehi* was still convinced of the inevitability of its ultimate success.

### 'THE ACCUSED ACCUSE'

The arrest of its members in March–April 1944 provided *Lehi* with an excellent opportunity for publicity. This was grabbed. Determined not to repeat the mistakes previously made by the *Haganah*, the IZL (and, for that matter, also by the 'IZL in Israel'), the movement refused to resort to the device of employing attorneys who might secure a more lenient punishment than was expected. Instead, it would discard legal aid altogether; the defendants would conduct their own defence, would deny the right of the military court to try their cases and, in accordance with the Hague Convention, would demand the status of prisoners of war. Their trials would thus become a platform for *Lehi*'s propaganda.[28] Should the accused be condemned to death, *Lehi* would certainly have made its point. 'The gallows is the abyss above which it will no longer be possible to construct bridges of "understanding" and of compromise.'[29]

Proceedings opened at the end of May, when the first defendant was Zevi Tavori. He was followed by David Hameiri-Begin (cousin of the IZL commander), Hisya Shapira and Anshel Spielman. When called to answer the charges against them, all adopted an offensive stance, accusing England of aggression against the Jewish people and of intent to destroy the Zionist enterprise in the pursuit of imperialist aims. Their appearances demonstrated that, as far as *Lehi* was concerned, the principal ideological motif remained the depiction of

England as the main enemy. The revelations regarding the Holocaust of European Jewry, it transpired, had in no way lessened England's responsibility for Jewry's plight. *Lehi*'s aim remained 'ultimate salvation'; its objective was not the rescue of refugees but a war of liberation which would prevent the renewal of the diaspora through the establishment of 'the Kingdom of Israel'. This argument was put even more forcefully by Matityahu Shmuelevitch, who claimed that while from London's perspective England might appear as Dr Jekyll, its conduct in its overseas possessions showed it to be in fact Mr Hyde. Shmuelevitch also called as witnesses both the High Commissioner (MacMichael) and the chairman of the Jewish Agency executive (Ben-Gurion). The first was to be accused of dereliction of duty; the second was to be forced to confess that the entire *Yishuv* condemned Britain's Palestine policy.[30]

So considerable was the publicity accorded to the statements issued by the accused that the 'organised *Yishuv* felt in duty-bound to respond. Yisrael Galili, one of the leaders of the *Haganah* and of the *Ahdut Ha-Avodah* movement, admitted that he was extremely moved by Shmuelevitch's speech ('It was a proud appearance which imparts honour to the accused'). Nevertheless, he was afraid that the oratory of the *Lehi* defendants had distracted many people's minds 'from the dangerous and harmful actions of this band'. One thing which had to be remembered was that members of the *Haganah* and of the *Palmach* were undertaking work which was no less dangerous both in *Eretz Israel* and in the diaspora. The other – and more important – was that independence would in any case not be attained through acts of terror, but as a result of immigration, colonisation, a cultural renaissance and an intensification of 'the liberating force of socialist and nationalist content'.[31]

Only the IZL was virtually unstinting in its praise for *Lehi*'s stance during the period of the trials. Even though taking issue with some of the arguments put forward by the defendants (in respect to the war against British imperialism and the superiority of the Hebrew race), the IZL certainly agreed that they had been correct to depict the English as the guilty party. The IZL's own operations, it was argued, themselves demonstrated that the true conflict was not between Jew and Arab but between the Hebrew people and the 'repressive' authorities.[32] Eldad appreciated that the two movements were thus coming closer together – a process accelerated when the IZL's own military operations (and in particular its attack on the CID headquarters in Jerusalem on 15 July 1944) were severely criticised by Altman and other leaders of the NZO in terms which recollected their earlier protests against the Stern gang itself.[33] Nevertheless, the path to unity was still blocked by the opposition of Eldad's colleagues in *Lehi*'s 'centre', Friedman-Yellin and Shamir.

In the summer of 1944, one year after its reappearance, *Lehi* drew up a balance sheet of its progress. In general, its assessment was encouraging and the tone which infuses its pronouncements at this time is one of (perhaps premature) self-confidence. In part, this may be attributed to the Nietzschean teachings which had exerted so strong an influence on Eldad, especially, and which provided the foundation for the belief that the path to progress was to transmute necessity into will.[34] More immediately relevant, however, was the change in atmosphere which could be discerned in Anglo-Jewish relationships. The success of a liberation movement, *Lehi* argued,[35] was measured by its ability to recover from crises and to remain steadfast in its determination to achieve it goals. Military operations, too, had to be judged by psychological standards.

> The main aims of offensives during the stage of war in which we are presently situated is not to conquer the government but to undermine and weaken it: to shatter the nerves of the authorities and to undermine their sense of security; to destroy the quiet upon which a foreign dominion depends.

It was to *Lehi*'s credit (and not thanks to IZL) that the country now appeared to be under foreign conquest and that 'something had changed' in the attitudes of the *Yishuv* towards England. Indeed, during the past year *Lehi*'s status had been completely transformed. The trials had given the movement world-wide recognition; more particularly, it was recognised by all sectors of the *Yishuv* (including the working class) as representing a distinctive ideology. In short, it was no longer regarded as a terrorist 'sect' but as a real 'political movement'.

True, *Lehi*'s work was far from being complete. In particular, it still required a large measure of active popular support (as distinct from passive public sympathy). To that end, *Lehi* had to work towards a situation in which:

> The masses will regard our movement as the front-line troops of their own war . . . We have no intention of stooping to the level of the masses; we want to raise them to our standards by increasing revolutionary tension and by serving as exemplars . . . Like all revolutionary movements, ours is an avant-garde . . . which at the

appropriate moment has to be capable of drawing the masses in its wake and serving as their guide and activator.

The only bodies which might impede the attainment of *Lehi*'s aims were the IZL and the *Haganah*. The former, notwithstanding its show of symbolic attacks on Mandate targets, was surely prepared to repeat the cease-fire with the British of 1939. The latter, even though not constituting an 'army', seemed bent on launching a civil war against *Lehi*. Without forfeiting its own beliefs, *Lehi* would have to avoid that danger.

### THE BEGINNINGS OF THE 'LEFTWARD' TENDENCY IN DOMESTIC AND EXTERNAL AFFAIRS

In August 1944 *Lehi* could still not single out any ally which it hoped might support the struggle for Hebrew independence. But a cautious leaning towards the USSR was already becoming evident. As before, the prime investigator of this shift was Friedman-Yellin. Impressed with the Red Army's great victories (Russia's troops already occupied Bulgaria and had reached eastern Prussia and Russia seemed poised to take over all of Eastern Europe), he envisioned the possibility of a growing convergence of Soviet and Hebrew interests against the common British-imperial foe. After all, Allied unity was bound to break down, and the USSR had no longer any reason to regard Zionism as a threat to its influence. He also noted definite 'signs' of a change in the Soviet stance on questions of Palestinian concern. One was the cessation of Russian press attacks on the *Yishuv*; another the fact that Russian representatives were sitting at the same table with 'nationalist Jews'; a third, the opposition of the communist press, especially in the USA, to the White Paper; a fourth, the Russians' appointment of Dr Emil Zommerstein, a known Zionist leader, to membership of the 'Committee for the Liberation of Poland'; and a fifth, the permission granted for Zionist activity in Romania.[36]

Since *Lehi* was also planning its attacks on MacMichael (who was in fact the target of an assassination attempt on 8 August 1944) and on Lord Moyne, it was only natural that the movement should also praise the method of 'individual terrorism', which further generated sympathetic associations with Russia's use of that weapon. Citing examples from both before the First World War and during the Second World War, *Lehi* was at pains to point out the justice of its methods. In so doing, it poured scorn on its critics – both the *Ha-Shomer Ha-Tsair* and the NZO – charging that their opposition reflected timidity and ideological inconsistency.[37]

*Lehi* understood that, if it was to become a factor of importance in domestic and international affairs, it also had to devote attention to domestic political and social questions. Nevertheless, it argued that there was no reason to formulate an independent ideology in accordance with the conventional divisions between right and left. Since total priority had to be given to the struggle for national independence, its own position was '*étatist*'. It regarded the liquidation of foreign rule as the solution to class problems: independence would – at one and the same time – benefit the worker and industry (but no mention, it must be noted, was made of 'the industrialist'). Hence, what would be required was a planned economy; only that could prevent the country from falling prey to mass unemployment and could attract foreign investment. What interested *Lehi*, so the movement claimed, was not the interests of one class or another, but that of the country as a whole. Hence, it sought 'the just distribution of the slice of bread'.[38] In thus expressing its sympathy with the ambitions of the proletariat, however, *Lehi* was not adopting socialism. It was, rather, attempting to break out of its communal isolation and to put brakes on its own alignment with the IZL.

Particularly instructive, in this context, are the nuances and shifts in the positions adopted by Eldad. Early in the spring of 1945 he was – for the first time in *Lehi*'s history – to proclaim 'the class war' to be 'a fact of life'. He also gave due credit to the power and authority of organised labour, which he regarded as the nucleus of the fighting force required to bring about independence. Hence: 'If we have to choose between a people united but not prepared to fight (which is in fact Weizmann's aim) and a single class which fights the war of liberation – and intends to construct its own class state – then we prefer the war of the single class.'[39] These statements, it must be stressed, did not signify that Eldad was completely turning his back on his Revisionist traditions. As we shall see, in the Fighters' Conference of 1949 – by which time others in *Lehi* had formulated an ideology of National Bolshevism (namely, a combination of radical right ideology and leftist tendencies, such as a pro-Soviet orientation, national planning and nationalisation) – he was himself to retract some of his statements which could be interpreted as harbingers of that stance; even in 1945, he did not regard them as operational directives. That was why he still insisted that his own social outlook was determined neither by capitalism nor by socialism, but by the notions of social justice embedded in Israel's biblical texts. Nevertheless, a shift had taken place. *Lehi*, although still neutral where socialism was concerned, was now more sympathetic. Indeed, it really had no choice. In retrospect, the changes in its attitude towards social questions must be interpreted as a continuation of its attempt to forge an ideological identity of its own and to broaden the base of its popular appeal. The 'leftward' tendencies were thus designed to serve two purposes. One was to distinguish *Lehi* from the IZL (which, it claimed, had no social consciousness and which truly deserved the 'fascist' tag with which *Lehi* was itself frequently labelled); the other was to infiltrate its own nationalist ideology into Labour's ranks and thereby prod the working classes into a more 'activist' policy, without which there was no possibility of attaining what remained *Lehi*'s ultimate goal: national independence.

There are several indications of the extent to which *Lehi* was at this juncture attempting to reach some sort of accommodation with the 'organised *Yishuv*'. There was, for instance, its new-found preparedness to acknowledge the strategic value of 'settlements' and of the contribution which colonisation and immigration might make to the emergence of statehood. It was also prepared to declare (less than two months before the assassination of Lord Moyne) that it did not regard 'individual terror' as the sole means to the attainment of independence. ('Terror is just a small part of the front of war.') What *Lehi* sought, in fact, was a status of legitimacy – equivalent to that granted, for example, to the French *maquis*. Indeed, it considered itself to be a copy of the resistance led by De Gaulle. Like the Gaullists, *Lehi* too had grown out of the right, but was – similarly – prepared to submerge its own ideology within the common struggle for liberation. All it asked was that other sections of the community (and it had in mind particularly the *Ahdut Ha-Avodah* movement) adopt a similar attitude of 'live and let live'. Absolute unity was impossible; but the different streams within the community could still agree to fight their separate battles against the common foe and thereby avoid civil war.[40]

There was never very much hope that such an outcome could be attained. Golomb had already addressed an unequivocal warning to Friedman-Yellin.[41] Moreover, the official Zionist leadership was always conscious of the internal contradiction in *Lehi*'s advocacy of individual terror, on the one hand, and its support for colonisation and immigration, on the other.[42] Conscious of the fact, *Lehi* resorted to the tactic of appealing to the masses over the heads of the official leadership. One of its particular targets was the rank and file of the *Haganah*, whom it attempted to persuade not to carry out orders to participate in a 'saison' against the movement.[43] An alternative was to come to some sort of arrangement with the IZL.

ATTEMPTS AT UNITY WITH IZL

By the autumn of 1944, the IZL and *Lehi* seemed to be sharing much the same fate. Members of both organisations were being deported to

Africa; both were attempting to implement 'activist' policies; and both were coming under increasing pressure from the organised *Yishuv*'. Thus, for all the ideological and personal tensions which made the IZL and *Lehi* suspicious of each other, the time did appear ripe to explore the possibility of better relations. Especially was this so with the breakdown, in October 1944, of the talks with the leaders of the IZL and the *Haganah* – which had revealed how wide the differences between those two sides on matters of policy and outlook really were.[44]

Eldad, whose acquaintance with Begin dated back to their days together in the *Betar* movement in Poland, had late in 1943 suggested the formation of a common fighting force. He remained in occasional contact with Begin after the latter's subsequent appointment as commander of IZL, even going so far as to criticise him personally for the IZL's apology for the death of a British officer in March 1944. Although their talks sensitised both men to the ideological distance separating them, Begin responded to Eldad's overture by suggesting that *Lehi* 'return home' to the IZL.[45]

Eldad's subsequent imprisonment forced Begin to turn to Friedman-Yellin and Shamir, to whom he offered 'unity'. The *Lehi* leaders did not reject the offer entirely, but considered it premature. They thought it preferable that the talks concentrate on co-operation or co-ordination. Begin agreed, but on condition that *Lehi* withdraw its claims to be fighting against 'foreign rule' and 'British imperialism' (both fundamental terms in the movement's lexicon); instead, he suggested that the enemy be labelled 'repressive rule'. Friedman-Yellin was furious. Begin, he realised, remained wedded to Jabotinsky's formula of 'pressure'. He was even retracting from the IZL's position of 1938. If the war of liberation was to make any progress, he argued, no distinction could be made between the metropolitan and local centres of British decision-making. The war had to be carried to London itself. He also rejected Begin's demand that *Lehi* recognise Jabotinsky as its 'guide' (which implied a rejection of Stern's teachings), and the proposal that Begin himself should be given authority to arbitrate in any case of difference of opinion between the two movements. In fact (by Friedman-Yellin's account) the only point of agreement between the sides was that the Arabs be publicly informed that the Hebrew people's only war was with England, whom it wished to prevent exploiting Arab–Jewish differences for its own ends.[46]

Nevertheless, Begin came away from the talks in an optimistic frame of mind. On 23 July 1944 he informed an IZL parade that 'considerable progress has been made towards full understanding . . . In effect there is no great difference between the two fighting bodies in *Eretz Israel*, which should be united.'[47] How much he was mistaken became apparent with *Lehi*'s attempt on MacMichael's life on 8 August. Only now did Begin realise that *Lehi* had no interest in unity, but only in 'mutual support' during operations and in an exchange of information. This he considered insufficient; what he wanted was men, arms and control over *Lehi*'s activities. Accordingly, on 23 August, the IZL proposed the establishment of a joint operational body, and again suggested that Begin (who promised to be 'absolutely impartial') be empowered to arbitrate any differences which might arise between the two movements. Should *Lehi* reject this offer, it was decided, relations would remain as they were. Nevertheless, *Lehi* was to be asked to refrain from verbal attacks on the IZL and to agree to joint announcements.[48]

Insistent on its ideological independence, the *Lehi* 'centre' decided to reject the IZL's offer. Begin was bitterly disappointed. Once again he showed himself to be apparently insensitive to the mentality and ideology of *Lehi*'s leaders; his assumption was that the memories of past tensions between the two movements could be hidden beneath the slogan, 'we are brothers in arms'. Pronouncing 'the liquidation of the 1940 split' and a 'full unison of forces' to be 'an objective necessity', he claimed not to have heard from Stern (when they had met in Warsaw in September 1938) that there had existed any fundamental differences between him and Raziel. But *Lehi*'s leaders thought differently. To their mind, 'The split was inherent'. The most they would agree to was some measure of co-ordination in operational and propaganda matters. Begin had no choice but to accept this limited arrangement.[49]

Nevertheless, the two movements were moving closer together. Especially was this so after 8 October, when the authorities called on the *Yishuv* to co-operate with the police against them. At Begin's suggestion, leaders of *Lehi* and the IZL met again and formulated a joint manifesto which was published on 15 October. The terms of this document demonstrated that the sides were indeed not very far apart; they were even able to paper over their ideological differences without too much difficulty. While it is true that the manifesto accorded priority to action against 'repressive rule', room was also found for mention of 'foreign rule'. Deliberately, and for obvious reasons, no mention was made of Stern's opposition to enlistment. Instead, the manifesto stressed points of agreement. Furthermore, that document was itself part of a wider co-operative framework, at whose crux stood an operative clause which enjoined both parties to give the other at least one day's notice of an impending action.[50] When *Lehi* failed to fulfil this clause before Moyne's assassination, the agreement was to be put to its first test.

THE ATTACK ON LORD MOYNE AND ITS IMPLICATIONS

The assassination on 6 November 1944 in Cairo of Lord Moyne, Minister Resident in the Middle East, was the most extreme personal terrorist attack ever carried out by *Lehi*. Although other Zionist leaders who had personal contact with Moyne had never regarded him as in any way different from other British statesmen, *Lehi* had as early as February 1944 singled him out for special condemnation. In fact, the movement decided that it had no alternative but to attempt to assassinate him. It was realised that the success of that enterprise (especially if combined with the assassination of the High Commissioner) would be bound to generate draconian counter-measures on the part of the British (such as were indeed contemplated after Moyne's murder). But *Lehi*, as a small movement whose ambitions were totally disproportionate to its size, had no other way of giving expression to its outlook and transforming itself from a peripheral sect to a central party. Indeed, once its leadership had decided not to join forces with the IZL, *Lehi* had to redouble its efforts to stress its singularity. Distinctive ideological pronouncements would not suffice. Although the belief in the utility of 'personal terror' had been somewhat retracted since Stern's time, a dramatic operation was required.[51]

This was clearly necessary now that the IZL had intensified its own propaganda and operations. *Lehi*'s entire *raison d'être* lay in the inactivity of the IZL and its ideological weakness. *Lehi* had therefore to demonstrate that it was prepared to wage total war against British imperialism and to fight it outside *Eretz Israel* as well as within its borders. That posed certain operational difficulties – of which the most prominent was the impossibility of escape after the attack. Indeed, the assassination attempt thus amounted to a suicide mission. But this does not seem to have acted as a deterrent. Even if some of *Lehi*'s rank and file did express some despondency about the futility of waging a protracted and wasteful struggle, Eliahu Hakim and Eliahu Bet Tsouri, the two men selected to perpetrate the deed, did not share these sentiments.[52]

As soon as news of the assassination broke, *Lehi* published its justification for the action. Moyne's sins were catalogued in great detail and itemised in turn – from the *Patria* incident until his speech in the House of Lords in June 1942. Moyne, it was announced, had been responsible for delaying discussion on a pro-Zionist resolution in the American Congress; for destroying the economy of the country; for arms trials against the *Haganah*; for the expulsion of members of *Lehi* and the IZL to Eritrea and – ultimately – for the murder of millions of Jews in Europe. His appointment, indeed, had expressed Britain's wider imperial aims (a thesis which caused *Lehi* to attack Churchill too). England had no interest in a forward-looking Hebrew people, which would awaken the Middle East from its slumber and bring about England's exit from the region; instead, England's preference was for 'the downtrodden masses' and the 'exploitative princes', whom it hoped to unite in an Arab federation. The assassination, then, constituted a signal rather than an act of vengeance. It even gave early warning of a doctrine which *Lehi* was to develop in 1946: that all peoples of the region had a common interest in fighting the British foe.[53]

On the day of the assassination, the leadership of the *Yishuv* met in special session, where a decision was taken to co-operate fully with the authorities against the 'dissidents' in what was to be termed the 'saison'. The prime target was the larger organisation, which – after their meeting with Begin – Sneh and Golomb considered to be the greater danger to the 'organised *Yishuv*'. In fact, the *Haganah* kidnapped dozens of IZL members and only one *Lehi* member; moreover, while 700 IZL names were handed over to the authorities, no *Lehi* name is known to have been communicated. Eldad, who was then in prison, thought (as did the IZL internees) that Friedman-Yellin and Shamir had managed to frighten the *Haganah*. What he did not then know was that *Lehi* and the *Haganah* had in fact reached some form of agreement, formulated when Friedman-Yellin met Golomb in the wake of the kidnapping of 'Todi' Peli on 16 December 1944. The meeting had not been an easy one (as is illustrated by the fact that Friedman-Yellin placed a gun on the table); as he was later to recall, Friedman-Yellin considered himself to be caught in 'an awful dilemma'. He wanted at all costs to avoid a civil war, but nevertheless felt duty-bound to warn Golomb that *Lehi* would fight to the bitter end if it had to. Ultimately, and contrary to Eldad's later charges, Friedman-Yellin did not mean to implement a full 'union' with the *Haganah*, and any assurance that he might have given to that effect was merely tactical. He did, however, promise to refrain from further actions while Hakim and Bet Tsouri were still awaiting trial and (in response to a direct question from Golomb) not to make any attempts on Churchill's life. However, there was to be no relaxation in *Lehi*'s ideological struggle. *Lehi* was even more insistent than the IZL in denouncing the 'saison' and in castigating its perpetrators as 'Quislings', 'collaborators' and 'informers'.[54]

The assassination, then, did not generate any real change in *Lehi*'s ideology. On the contrary, and notwithstanding its feelers in the direction of new thought patterns (see below), that event was portrayed as evidence that *Lehi* was fulfilling the aims it had set. Not Hitler but the absence of a homeland was the nation's real tragedy; England could not be allowed sole control over *Eretz Israel*; *Lehi*'s true models were De Gaulle and Mikolajczyk.[55] Hakim and Bet Tsouri had proved as much. They had carried out their mission, and in their trial repeated the main lines of *Lehi*'s ideology (albeit with the addition of a 'Canaanite' leavening, perhaps understandable since Bet Tsouri was the principal speaker). The British government, they declared, was 'a gang of black-marketeers and exploiters', quite apart from being responsible for the deaths of millions of Jews 'who had drowned in a sea of blood and tears'.[56]

Even more important, from an ideological point of view, was the execution of the two accused on 22 March 1945. At long last, *Lehi* had martyrs of its own. Indeed, it was their execution which gave the assassination true meaning. First, it imbued the movement with a considerable degree of pride. ('There was meaning to their lives, and meaning to their deaths . . . They sacrificed themselves in war for the benefit of a better future and so that the light which signified the aspiration for freedom should never be extinguished from the heart of the nation.') Second, it provided *Lehi* with an opportunity to make explicit – and intentional – comparisons between England and Hitler. ('Like the German, his brother in race, the Englishman considers himself to be a member of a 'superior race' who has the right to rule over 'inferior' peoples.') Third, and equally important at the time, the assassination and its result had launched *Lehi* onto the path of success. *Lehi* had finally broken free of the shadow of IZL, the parent movement, and demonstrated its distinctiveness.[57]

Nevertheless, the extent of the breakthrough thus attained must not be exaggerated. Its international and diplomatic influence was certainly less than *Lehi* was later to claim. At most, Moyne's assassination might have exerted a long-term effect on the USSR (containing, as it did, a hint of a future Soviet–Hebrew community of interest against Britain). Otherwise, however, no influence is discernible. France's policy was not noticeably affected while Britain's, under Churchill's direction, in fact took an anti-Zionist turn. The Roosevelt administration, too, was not moved; Truman was to be swayed far more by the fate of the displaced persons (DPs) and Jewish electoral pressure.[58]

But there was one unexpected gain. Contrary to the fears originally expressed by the Jewish Agency's representatives in Cairo, the trial itself did not turn into an attack on Zionism as a whole. On the contrary, the British administration seemed to be in the dock. Egyptian public opinion had apparently taken to heart both the motives of the defendants and their heroism in refusing to shoot at the Egyptian policeman who arrested them. Even the judge seemed impartial – allowing the defendants far more freedom of speech than the British authorities would have wished – and the prosecutor unexpectedly generous, accusing Hakim and Bet Tsouri of acting against the best interests of the Zionist movement whose official leadership, he pointed out, had dissociated itself from their deed. Attorneys for the defence were particularly impressive, arguing that the defendants must have been influenced by the fate of their people, and that they both originated from 'eastern' lands.[59]

## THE ATTITUDE OF THE NATIONAL INSTITUTIONS
### AND THE AUTHORITIES TO THE MURDER OF MOYNE

Ever since the commencement of terrorist operations in February 1944, the 'organised *Yishuv*' had found itself in a dilemma. It is true that it had then rejected proposals that it co-operate with the British authorities against the 'dissidents', but the degree to which it felt that operations carried out by the IZL and *Lehi* were endangering its policy of political struggle had been communicated to Friedman-Yellin and Begin, both privately and in public. Moyne's murder brought matters to a head.

A special joint meeting of the Jewish Agency executive and of the *Va'ad Leumi* was held on the day of the murder. By a majority of ten votes to six (the latter comprising the General Zionists 'B', Mizrachi and *Ahdut Ha-Avodah*), a decision was taken to co-operate fully with the authorities.[60] Next day, Shertok met the new High Commissioner, Lord Gort, to whom he expressed the hopes that the *Yishuv* would manage to eradicate this evil from its midst and that the murder would not affect Britain's feelings and policy of justice towards the Jewish people. On 7 November, the national institutions publicly decried the 'base crime' and announced that they would co-operate with the authorities in eradicating terrorism.[61]

There followed a number of other meetings, at which the merits (or otherwise) of possible courses of action in collaboration with the Mandate authorities and against the 'dissidents' (no distinction being made between the IZL and *Lehi*) were thrashed out. On 8 November, the political committee of the *Mapai* party met, and Ben-Gurion called for 'controlled' co-operation with the authorities, warning against pushing the 'dissidents' too far.[62] Three days later, a similar discussion took place at a special meeting of the executive of the *Histadrut*, where debate was even more intense. Even those who opposed collaboration with the British authorities (notably, the *Ahdut Ha-Avodah* representatives) were prepared to support an independent Jewish operation against groups who were bluntly described as 'fascist'. Similarly, even those speakers (such as Golomb and Golda

Meyerson) who were prepared to admit that – on an individual basis – *Lehi* did contain some good and idealistic persons, felt that something had to be done. Ultimately, the executive ratified the motion to collaborate by a majority of 14 to four (the opponents consisting of *Ahdut Ha-Avodah* and the left *Poale Zion*).[63] Clearly, therefore, the resignations of Rabbi Fishman and Gruenbaum were less serious than might have been thought. The vast majority of the *Yishuv* leadership supported the 'saison', convinced that it was a moral as well as a political necessity.

Still more crucial was the meeting on 19 November of the Small Zionist Actions Committee, which – in between congresses – constituted the Zionist movement's highest parliamentary forum. Weizmann came to Palestine especially in order to address the body, and immediately made known just how angry and frustrated he was. Indeed, he seemed to have been more shocked by Moyne's murder than he had been in 1942 when told that his own son had been posted as missing in action. Citing his conversation with Churchill just two days before the murder, Weizmann claimed that the act had set back the attainment of Zionism's political aims. *Lehi* comprised 'men who possess neither patriotism nor understanding. I cannot understand [their] logic.'[64] Ben-Gurion agreed entirely, and laid out a plan for 'disgorging' terror by helping the authorities to break up the two 'dissident' movements. Indeed, he argued, only thus might the *Yishuv* avoid the two worse alternatives of civil war or subjection to the terrorists' will. Golomb took the same line. He too argued that the terrorists constituted 'the greatest danger to Israel'; the struggle was between Zionist democracy and Jewish Nazism. With that being the prevalent mood, it was useless for Gruenbaum to retort that the *Yishuv*'s own decisions to collaborate with the British were 'the greatest tragedy of the age'. Shertok probably spoke for the majority when depicting the 'saison' as an 'inevitability'. Golomb also noted *Lehi*'s intellectual indebtedness to Nietzsche's notions of the 'superior man'.[65]

This mood intensified once news arrived of the content of Churchill's own condemnatory speech in Parliament.[66] If a known friend of Zionism could speak in such terms, who knew the lengths to which Zionism's enemies in the British administration might now go? While it is true that *Mapai* supporters of the resolutions on collaboration still had to work hard in order to convince their domestic opponents, the extent to which they were carrying the day became evident at the special session of the sixth *Histadrut* conference (20–21 November), which conducted a public debate on the question of terror. This time, even the *Ahdut Ha-Avodah* and the left *Poale Zion* members supported the resolutions, which were carried unanimously.[67]

Collaboration with the British authorities was, indeed, soon truly under way. On 7 December, Weizmann informed Churchill that the names of 500 terrorists had been communicated to the police, and that half of the persons cited had already been arrested.[68] But whether such activity could in fact affect British policy remains doubtful. Aware of the contacts between the IZL, *Lehi* and the *Haganah*, and of Golomb's meetings with Friedman-Yellin, the CID had long believed that the Jewish Agency was prepared to protect the Stern gang, provided that it agreed to accept the Agency's orders and not interfere with its attempt to attain its wider aims. Officials in Cairo had similarly suspected that the Jewish Agency constituted a greater threat to British interests than did the 'dissidents'. After Moyne's murder, these sentiments did not die down. In fact, there was now an even greater tendency to lump all sections of the *Yishuv* together and not to put too much store by the 'saison'. 'It would be a logical attitude for HMG to hold the whole [Zionist] movement leaders responsible, and to impose sanctions accordingly.'[69]

Had these sentiments been translated into official policy, Zionist fortunes might have been brought to an even lower ebb. This is apparent from the advice tendered by J.S. Bennett, an outspoken enemy of Zionism and its ambitions, who maintained that eight of the 12 'charges' against Moyne that *Lehi* had publicised were also acceptable to official Zionist propaganda. To his mind, the Biltmore programme was no less 'inciting' than was the *Lehi* leaflet justifying Moyne's murder. He demanded that Weizmann repeat in public his earlier admission that it was a 'monstrous lie' to accuse Britain of responsibility for the Holocaust. His failure to do so merely showed that 'the *aims* of the terrorists are indistinguishable from those of the official Zionist movement. Only their methods differ.'[70] From the Zionist point of view, it was fortunate that Britain's official reaction to the Moyne murder was not determined by the likes of Bennett, but by Lord Gort, the Colonial Office and the Cabinet headed by Churchill. The latter rejected the draconian measures which their subordinates advised.[71]

### THE RENEWAL OF THE UNDERSTANDING WITH THE IZL

The murder of Moyne put a stop to co-ordination between the IZL and *Lehi*. But, despite the continuing personal debates and ideological differences between the leaders, the dynamic of events was nevertheless bringing the two organisations closer together. While it is true that *Lehi* could not acknowledge Begin's claim to have instigated the 'revolt', neither could it accept his call to bear in mind

Britain's war effort against Nazi Germany (a call which Begin himself in fact modified).[72] But the two organisations still shared a common view on the Arab question. More to the point, the IZL was also adopting an increasingly aggressive stance *vis-à-vis* the British, a position accentuated when it broke with the NZO in the wake of the action of 15 July 1944. Now, like *Lehi*, Begin also accused Britain of ultimate responsibility for the fate of European Jewry. Although claiming to be the true interpreter of Jabotinsky's theses, Begin's tone was thus very much harsher than his master's had been. Unlike Jabotinsky and the NZO, Begin did not aim at a Jewish dominion under British protection but at a Hebrew republic on the Irish model. England, he argued, sought to perpetuate the Jews' minority status within *Eretz Israel* and to award them little more than a 'Reservat' such as had been established in Lublin. England, he warned, had to make a choice: either she agreed to establish a Hebrew state or she had to attempt to expel and destroy the Jewish people.[73]

This did not mean that the two movements could therefore unite. Begin was not prepared to enrol *Lehi* as a unit within the IZL; he would only accept *Lehi* members on an individual basis. Moreover, the IZL – despite its declarations of unrestricted warfare against Britain – did not entirely give up hope that British policy might yet change (as it had done in the case of Ireland). Indeed, the IZL continued to decry a strategy of personal assassinations, arguing instead that Zionism would be fulfilled by 'a military and political war, a general uprising of the enslaved against the oppressors'.[74] *Lehi* members also had their reservations. They regarded their organisation as an underground political movement in possession of a distinct ideology, and saw themselves as catalysts of the IZL as well as the 'organised *Yishuv*'. Insistent on their independence, they therefore refused to be impressed even by the ideological split between the NZO and the IZL and by the increasingly militant character which Begin was imparting to his organisation.

Neither Begin's more sympathetic attitude towards Hakim and Bet Tsouri after their execution (a definite change from his earlier denunciation of Moyne's assassination),[75] nor even the experience of the 'saison', brought about a revision in this attitude. The IZL did not take sufficient account of the impression created on *Lehi* by the renewed experience of martyrdom; nor was Begin sufficiently sensitive to Friedman-Yellin's statement that *Lehi* represented a different ideological school. Had *Lehi* agreed to join the IZL, it would in fact have betrayed itself and its traditions, which its members now regarded as sacred. That was why *Lehi* refused to establish a joint tactical command with the IZL; this would have been the first step towards a union in which the larger organisation would necessarily have swallowed up the smaller. Instead, it constructed its own mythology of the past and the present. It regarded the Moyne assassination, together with the attempt on MacMichael's life and the trials, to have constituted a turning-point. 'These actions achieved what the Zionists never managed to attain in all their years of conferences and "political" work: they made the problem of *Eretz Israel* the boiling point of the Middle East and a nexus of world politics.'[76] Moreover, in *Lehi*'s eyes, the executions in Cairo had also served a further purpose. They had endowed *Lehi* with the right to assume what Yellin-Mor was later to call the 'representative' role hitherto claimed by Weizmann.[77] Unlike the IZL, *Lehi* was thus proclaiming its readiness to pursue its own foreign policy and to seek its own foreign ally.

Ultimately, as will be seen, that search was to lead *Lehi* in the direction of the left-wing spectrum of Jewish and international politics. In the meantime, however, its members still identified more with the IZL (for all its conservatism) than with any other grouping in the *Yishuv*. Much of the explanation is to be sought in the sympathy they felt for the larger organisation during the course of the 'saison', which was exclusively directed against the IZL and the consequences of which *Lehi* itself managed to avoid.[78] By the late spring of 1945, both movements were calling for the union of 'all the active forces in the nation'.[79] Golomb thought that the IZL had been too much weakened by the 'saison' to do anything effective; but Giles, the head of the CID, was less sanguine.[80] In the event, the latter was the better judge of the situation: between 12 and 22 May, the IZL carried out several raids. Moreover, with the end of the war in Europe (and with the publication of the full extent of the Holocaust), it also proclaimed its determination to tear up the White Paper of 1939. Furthermore, the IZL – unlike *Lehi* – called for the immediate establishment of a 'Provisional Hebrew Government', but, like *Lehi*, it now proclaimed the need to imitate the Czech model – to rise in revolt immediately and not to await a Great Power solution to the national question.[81]

It was this atmosphere which impelled the two movements, on 14 May 1945, to come to an agreement. They were to co-operate on 'the scale of war activities, their timing and general lines, which will be determined in the light of changing political needs by a "Combined Operational Centre" in accordance with the Political Council of the two bodies.'[82] The latter would also co-ordinate external political appearances. This, it must be stressed, was not an agreement providing for full union, but an attempt to collaborate on political and military issues. The extent to which the two organisations were still apart is shown by the fact that each was still to be responsible for its own political alignments, for internal and external propaganda, for its own funding, training and armament. Nevertheless, the agreement did also provide for a sharing of information, mutual support and even for an exchange of ideas on political and ideological matters. Should the latter indicate that their outlooks were 'similar' or 'identical', then organisational co-operation could be extended.

The change thus marked in relations between the IZL and *Lehi* cannot be exaggerated. For the first time since the 'revolt' had been declared 18 months previously, *Lehi* was prepared to recognise the 'legitimacy' of the IZL's war; moreover, the movement called on its members to do their utmost to befriend the IZL and to avoid any action which might cause it harm. In August 1945, the IZL and *Lehi* (in keeping with the entire Zionist movement) were prepared to give Britain's new Labour government a 'breathing space' in which to repeal the White Paper.[83] Meanwhile, on 23 July 1945, the two organisations had undertaken a joint operation when blowing up the bridge near Yavneh – which carried one of the British Empire's important lines of rail communication.

### THE DEVELOPMENT OF A PRO-SOVIET ORIENTATION AND INITIAL MOVES TOWARDS A CLOSER ALIGNMENT WITH THE LEFT IN THE *YISHUV*

*Lehi*'s world outlook was one of 'armed peace', contending that Great Powers – whether they liked it or not – ruled over the small peoples. World order was determined on the basis of 'interests' and the globe was divided into 'spheres of influence'. Only Hitler had departed from the rule that no 'final solutions' were possible in history when attempting to destroy entire races, and especially the Hebrew people.[84] Now that Hitler had been defeated, however, matters would revert to their former course. Small- and medium-sized peoples would refuse to act as 'placid bargaining counters'; instead, they would try to play one power against another. That being the case, it is hardly surprising that *Lehi* regarded the foundation of the United Nations Organisation at San Francisco as a 'show'. The fate of the world and its peoples would not be decided by such bodies (still less by the Arab League, whose foundation was not taken at all seriously) but by 'the big three' meeting at Yalta.[85]

The implications for *Eretz Israel* were self-evident. Clearly, Britain wished to remain in the country for ever. Moreover, since it wished to rule there without any international supervision, it had no real interest in the Mandate or the White Paper – nor even in the latter's promise of independence to 'the Palestinian nation'. Churchill's behaviour in

Greece showed how much British rule in the Middle East needed a strategic point on which to lean. Aware of their international weakness, the British wanted the Middle East to serve as their defensive shield against all potential enemies. Since Russia was already making moves in the direction of the region, *Lehi* anticipated a new set of anti-British alliances.[86]

That being the situation, Russia necessarily became a primary subject of *Lehi*'s interest, especially after the execution in Cairo. Writing during the Yalta conference, Friedman-Yellin painted a picture of perpetual Anglo-Russian conflict, the origins of which he traced to the times of Peter the Great and the Crimean war and which he claimed had reached a peak after the October Revolution. Even during the 1930s, Russia – and not the Axis powers – had been Britain's true enemy. Now 'the Russian giant' had proved its strength. Possessing the sympathy of 'the masses' in western and southern Europe, the Russians already had an alliance with France and influence in Norway. Their troops were stationed in Iran and at the Dardanelles. They were also poised to strike through Afghanistan at Britain's Indian Empire. Friedman-Yellin was convinced that Stalin would emerge victorious from Yalta, and publicly expressed his wish for that outcome.[87]

It was from that starting-point that *Lehi* moved to the articulation of a new alignment in Hebrew foreign policy. While the official Zionist leadership gave public expression to its pro-British orientation at the end of the war, and trusting that agreement between the three Great Powers would lead to the establishment of an independent Jewish state, *Lehi* was expressing its hope that the Soviet Union would come to constitute the ally of the Hebrew people.[88] True, the Russians had not yet themselves made any move in that direction; they might even have agreed to *Eretz Israel* being part of Britain's sphere of influence. But, even if that were the case, *Lehi*'s war against Britain could itself bring about a change in the Soviet attitude.[89] The Hebrew nation had to follow in the traditions of Bar-Kochba (who had attempted to exploit Roman–Parthian differences) and of David Ha-Reubeni (who had counted on Muslim–Christian antagonisms). As Eldad put it, *Lehi* rejected both the abstract idealism of Ahad Ha-Am and the materialism of orthodox Marxism. Instead, the liberation of the nation had to be built on 'the conjunction of historical events'.[90]

Indeed, like Friedman-Yellin, Eldad also began to pin his hopes on the Soviet Union. Moreover, he also found ideological grist to suit his mill. Writing at the time of the Yalta conference, he argued that Soviet Russia need no longer be depicted as the incarnation of Marxist orthodoxy. 'At her present stage of development, Soviet Russia may be embarking on the path of integrating new ideas: political and national values which attract material to them and which are not just forged as a result of material necessity.'[91] He also appreciated that, if *Lehi* was to attain a Soviet alliance, the movement had to modify its 'fascist' and Revisionist image by showing some evidence of a leftward shift in its social ideology. That was why he now attempted to weld his nationalism to socialism. He also prophesied that the communists and the bundists, who in the past had deliberately underplayed nationalism in left-wing ideology, would in the future liberate themselves from the fear and shame which had characterised their behaviour.[92]

As early as the last stages of the Second World War, *Lehi*'s leadership grasped that no closer association with left-wing groups in the *Yishuv* would be possible without the development of a pro-Soviet orientation. The opposite was also true: no such orientation was possible without a closer alignment with the *Yishuv* left. Initially, the latter was its prime motive (and, indeed, the pro-Soviet orientation was to prove justified within two years). Nevertheless, *Lehi* began, at the same time, to construct a distinctive ideology of National Bolshevism or leftist chauvinism. This development, it must be stressed, was not necessarily premeditated. Rather, it was the consequence of the dynamic of events and of a combination of processes which determined the way in which history unfolded.

# PART FOUR

# FROM LEGITIMACY TO DISBANDMENT, 1945–47

# 7

# From the United Hebrew Resistance Movement to the Fundamentals of Hebrew Foreign Policy

## THE UNITED HEBREW RESISTANCE MOVEMENT

With the end of the Second World War in the summer of 1945, the fate of Palestine had clearly reached a decisive stage. *Lehi*, however, saw no reason to change its basic tenets. As before, Britain remained the prime enemy. Its behaviour towards the Jews during the war – and especially the refusal to open the gates of Palestine to Jewish victims of Nazism – proved the folly of placing any hopes in a change in British policies. Moreover, Britain's attitude towards the Soviet Union – and especially the refusal to open a 'second front' in 1942 and 1943 – proved its cynicism. Fearful that an armed Anglo-American crusade against 'infidel Jewish communism' was imminent,[1] *Lehi* supported Stalin's policy of a division of the world into spheres of influence. Opposing what it considered to be British attempts to attain universal hegemony, it also supported communist gains in Eastern Europe and China. Within Palestine itself, the British had to be opposed by an all-out partisan war, on the lines of that so successfully waged in Europe against the Nazis.

*Lehi* realised that it lacked the public hinterland at the disposal of the official Jewish leadership in Palestine. Nevertheless, it remained optimistic that its policies could be successfully implemented. For one thing, it hoped to create precisely such a hinterland abroad;[2] for another, it felt that it was gaining some public legitimacy. The most important sign was its recent pact with the IZL whereby the two sides agreed to establish a joint political committee and operational centre. At the same time, they also reached some measure of tactical agreement. In the wake of its contacts with the IZL, *Lehi* decided to abandon the policy of 'individual terror' exemplified by the murder of Lord Moyne. Appreciating that to repeat such actions would only reinforce *Lehi*'s image as a minute faction, it instead decided to adopt the IZL's policy of large-scale attacks on British military installations. Its plan was now to confine British troops to their own enclaves ('ghettos') and to so disrupt British rule that the local administrators would themselves press their government to withdraw from the country.

It was at this juncture that Friedman-Yellin took upon himself what he termed the role of intermediary between the *Haganah* and the IZL. His task was facilitated by the British Labour government's announcement of September 1945 that it would continue the policies enunciated in the 1939 White Paper. Clearly, diplomacy alone would not shift that stand. Friedman-Yellin persuaded Begin that the *Haganah*, too, now appreciated the inevitability of an armed struggle against the British. He also concluded that Begin considered the advantages of tripartite co-operation between the three Jewish organisations out-weighed the drawbacks. Apart from providing retrospective justification for the IZL's dissociation from the organised *Yishuv*, an operational partnership would also forge ties with the grass-roots membership of the *Haganah* and the *Palmach*. Should their commands ever decide to break the agreement, they would find it difficult to explain why yesterday's allies had become today's foes.[3]

The secret negotiations were conducted by Sneh and Galilee, the leaders of the *Haganah*, on the one side and Begin and Friedman-Yellin on the other. They resulted in what was in effect an ad hoc basis for armed co-operation, not a full-fledged alliance. Although the parties did agree on the estabishment of a high command ('Command X') which was empowered to decide on the character of future joint operations, each of the parties nevertheless retained freedom of action with regard to operations designed to acquire arms or funds and to free prisoners. What is more, each side still retained its own ideological individuality.

This was true, in particular, of *Lehi*. Friedman-Yellin and Shamir did not join the United Hebrew Resistance Movement in order to see *Lehi* swallowed up by the *Haganah*. Rather, their primary purpose may have been tactical – to exploit the legitimacy which they now enjoyed in order to publicise their programme and to encourage their partners in the movement to adopt a more extreme anti-British stance.[4] Once the pact was signed, *Lehi* modified the tone of its verbal attacks on the Jewish Agency; but it still insisted on the primacy of a total struggle against the British. No people, it claimed, had ever won its independence through political negotiation alone (an argument contrary to 'official' Zionist doctrine); the true enemy of the Jewish people was not (as the IZL claimed) the British administration in Palestine, but the British government in London; no reliance could be placed on the hope, fondly harboured by the Jewish Agency, that 'friends' (meaning the British Labour Party) might eventually constitute that government.[5] In sum, Zionism had to concentrate on the expulsion of the foreign ruler from Palestine, not on the salvation of Holocaust survivors.[6] Moreover, the *Yishuv* had to be encouraged to believe in its inherent ability to accomplish that aim.

Actions – even when only moderately successful – thus became the subjects of *Lehi*'s praise. The release of prisoners from Atlit on 6 October 1945 was classed as 'a war operation of major importance'; the combined action against the railway network and *Lehi*'s unsuccessful action against the Haifa refinery installations on the night of 31 October was portrayed as an operation of supreme historic significance.[7] Equal importance was attached to the mass demonstration held in Tel Aviv on 14 November in protest against Bevin's infamous speech of the previous day. The fact that the clashes with the British authorities were violent (six persons were killed in Tel Aviv and another eight in separate incidents in the Sharon plain) was understood to justify *Lehi*'s long-held prognosis that the struggle for independence would become a phenomenon of 'the masses', whose resort to arms against the foreign foe would show that the fight against the British in Palestine was, together with events in India and Indonesia, just one more link in the world-wide struggle against the forces of imperialism.[8]

On the other hand, all suggestions of compromise with Britain were roundly condemned. *Lehi* poured scorn on Sneh's statement that he would support the retention of British bases in Palestine were Britain to grant the Jews independence.[9] It also castigated the establishment of the Anglo-American Committee of Enquiry on Palestine and – even more so – the readiness of the 'official' Zionist leadership to testify before its members. Resorting to one of its favourite historical analogies, *Lehi* argued that the entire episode was reminiscent of events during the second Commonwealth period. 'The choice is between the fate of the Hellenisers and those of the Maccabees.'[10] Within the former category came Ben-Gurion, whose 'sanctimonious' address to the 'twelve nobodies' of the committee had forfeited his claims to national leadership.[11] Indeed, neither *Lehi* nor the IZL had given its blessing to the memorandum presented on 25 March 1946 to the committee in the name of the United Hebrew Resistance Movement. Its declaration that 'we have no interest whatsoever in the weakening of Britain's position in the world, the Middle East, or in Palestine' negated everything that *Lehi* stood for.[12]

In order to hasten the inevitable historical process of total war against the British enemy, *Lehi* had meanwhile decided upon two parallel strategies of its own. One was to imitate the Leninist precedent and mobilise 'the Hebrew workers' (but not, one notes, the Hebrew working class) behind its own revolutionary leadership. This was a small, but nevertheless significant, step in the direction of what was eventually to become the ideology of National Bolshevism. *Lehi*, as it admitted, did not yet possess a full-blown social programme. But, in

contrast to the bourgeois mentality of the NZO, it did begin to advocate the participation of workers in the national economy. Hoping to
force a combination of the reorganised minority and the masses, it
declared itself opposed to class warfare and in favour of a fair profit for
both the factory worker and the factory owner.[13]

*Lehi*'s second strategy during this period was to work towards an
alliance with the Soviet Union, by publicly stressing its admiration of
the latter's strategic power and territorial contiguity. It will be recalled
that the search for an ally inimical to Britain had been proposed by
Stern in the summer of 1939. His followers attempted to avoid their
leader's failure – albeit without abandoning the fundamentalism of
1940. Thus, the coincidence of anti-British interests on the part of
both Russians and Jews had to be exploited. 'Gone is the time when
the Hebrew people was forced to be Britain's friend . . . We shall
choose our allies in accordance with [their] attitude towards us and
towards our struggle to establish our independence in our homeland.'[14]

In both cases, however, the key remained the pursuit of an active
armed fight against British rule in Palestine. Therein lay the point of
*Lehi*'s condemnation of *Ha-Shomer Ha-Tsair*'s policy of attempting to
win Russian support through the pursuit of what it termed a policy of
'philanthropy'.[15] Hence the importance attached to the eventual agreement of the United Hebrew Resistance Movement command that
(together with IZL) *Lehi* be permitted to carry out its first major
operation: the attack on British aircraft at three bases on 25 February
1946.[16] That action was followed by two others: 'Wingate night'
(27 March 1946, when the United Hebrew Resistance Movement
attempted – unsuccessfully – to beach an immigrant ship near Tel
Aviv); and – with better results – the IZL–*Lehi* attack on the railway
bridges at Na'aman and Yavneh (4 April 1946). Together, such actions
seemed to meet *Lehi*'s demands that direct strikes be launched against
the British Empire's lines of communication.

Nevertheless, even at this early stage, *Lehi*'s attitude towards the
United Hebrew Resistance Movement was one of dissatisfaction.
Basically, this was because the latter represented a multi-faceted
'compromise' – which itself could be none other than an intermediary
stage. As far as the 'official' Zionist leadership was concerned, the
movement was nothing but a façade, formed in order to mask its own
internal divisions and as a sop to embittered public sentiment. Moreover, its operational achievements had been minimal; its military
measures were still hesitant and inadequate. *Lehi*'s participation in
the Movement, therefore, had really been designed to strengthen the
forces of action against those of inertia; to prove to the public that the
ultimate objective was the most important factor; and – perhaps not

least – to attain domestic legitimacy. 'Through co-operation we in fact attain an admission of the credibility of an independent underground movement.'[17] Meanwhile, *Lehi*'s participation in the movement did not preclude criticism of its lack of achievements nor the dissemination of *Lehi*'s own propaganda.

As with the IZL, at no stage in the period of the United Hebrew Resistance Movement did *Lehi* ever ignore the fundamental ideological differences between itself and the 'organised *Yishuv*'. As in the past, shades of Achimeir, of the *Narodnaya Volya* of Mazzini and of Bolshevism remained apparent. *Lehi* opposed what it considered to be the movement's policy of 'half-hearted warfare'; that form of action negated the lesson of the struggles for national independence of the Irish, Poles, Americans and Italians in the past, and of India, Indonesia, Yugoslavia and France in the present. As Mazzini had taught: 'It was not enough that the idea be correct or that it be publicly proclaimed. It has to be expressed in actual life and implemented by actions which all can witness.' One such measure was 'individual terror' which – for all its drawbacks – did eliminate the most talented amongst the enemy and constituted 'a show of force'. Another – and more important – was partisan warfare, the objective of which was the creation 'of the essential preconditions for victory'. Most necessary of all, however, was 'mass warfare' – sustained public opposition to the foreign suzerain and its agencies. The latter would, and could, be attained by educating the public to regard *Lehi* as a viable alternative to the present leadership of the Jewish population of Palestine.

In general *Lehi* saw two possible circumstances which could facilitate victory over the British foe within the framework of the United Resistance Movement. One was 'a protracted struggle for liberation' which would turn the Palestine question into an 'open sore' in Britain's framework of imperial defence and affect her prestige. The second was 'a general uprising by the entire [Hebrew] nation'. Essential preconditions for the latter eventuality were: moral and material support for the underground on behalf of the majority of the population, who would thus show that they appreciated that Britain was their primary enemy; the existence of a 'core of fighters with considerable military potential' throughout the Hebrew diaspora; the undermining of the enemy's military rule; and the readiness to exploit immediate crises (world war, partial or total rebellion elsewhere in the Empire, severe economic crisis) which would prevent Britain from concentrating all its forces in *Eretz Israel*.[18]

It followed that 'the arrangement' (as the movement was now termed) could persist only as long as it served those purposes. In the absence of progress it would fall apart, and should only be regarded as

an interim measure 'which would not last many months'. Indeed, *Lehi*'s
own criticism did not await that outcome nor even the report of the
Anglo-American Committee. As early as mid-April 1946 an internal
memorandum reiterated *Lehi*'s own principles of action, stressing that
its prognosis of the international situation had been proved justified.
The prospect of Anglo-Russian co-operation had not materialised;
equally unfounded was the belief in the strength of the 'Anglo-
American alliance'. The United States, whose policies were guided by
economic interests, opposed both of its erstwhile allies and would eventually 'swallow up' the British Empire; Anglo-Russian conflict, too,
was inevitable, since the interests of the two powers were diametrically
opposed. The Middle East constituted a region of vital importance in
Russia's drive towards the Indian Ocean and the Soviets would support
any party which promised to undermine Britain's efforts to reinforce
her bases there. The Arab League, also opposed to the continuation of
British rule, might be supported by Soviet Russia. The Russians could
not, however, fail to ignore the 'official' Zionist leadership's protestations of basic loyalty to Britain provided the latter permitted Jewish
immigration and the establishment of a measure of Jewish independence. No wonder, therefore, that the Russians had not yet finalised
their attitude towards the Palestine question. Only 'independent and
free' action – as was advocated by *Lehi* – would bring her to do so.[19]

RELATIONS WITH THE IZL

The establishment of the United Hebrew Resistance Movement transformed the nature of the arrangement between the IZL and *Lehi*.
Henceforth, 'the political council' was the framework which co-
ordinated the two bodies' relationship with the movement. *Lehi* maintained that, apart from administrative problems, there were '*objective*'
circumstances which generated 'natural and inevitable tension' between the two units. One, as a revolutionary movement, propagated
'discipline through knowledge'; the other – a military organisation –
advocated 'discipline by virtue of command'. *Lehi* considered the IZL
to be moving closer towards its own ideology 'under pressure of our
information campaign', and Eldad, in particular, pressed for the
exploitation of such progress – even advocating (in a private letter to
Begin) the reconstitution of the two movements under a new joint
name.[20] But, notwithstanding Begin's ultimate willingness to compromise on certain issues, complete union proved impossible to attain.
    This became apparent during the course of a full review[21] of that
possibility (in which Eldad participated, even though he was at the
time in prison). It then became clear that:

Notwithstanding the *organisational* advantages which may ensue, the danger of ideological confusion and retreat is real and severe . . . Fundamental differences of outlook, should they arise within a unified framework, will eventually retard development . . . They will cause severe organisational damage, which will have a detrimental effect on the course of the external struggle and perhaps lead to its total cessation during the most critical period.

Of the several 'differences in outlook', five were paramount from *Lehi*'s viewpoint. First, it considered itself to be 'a political liberation movement with broad [ideological] horizons'. This was in contrast to the IZL, 'whose military props . . . narrow its field of vision . . . We aspire to a revolutionary movement untrammelled by the chains of "tradition"'. Second, *Lehi* saw itself as 'a sovereign and independent liberation movement' which 'cannot renounce the right of decision and absolute freedom of action'. Here, too, it differed with the IZL which – surprisingly – it considered to be part of the NZO. Indeed (with unknowing prescience), *Lehi* foresaw a situation in which the IZL might attain dominant influence over the NZO and yet, eventually, thereby be drawn into the 'party intrigue' that would erect a barrier between itself and the public which was to supply the rank and file of the liberation movement. Third, there was the distinctiveness of *Lehi*'s social programme. Even though its platform was in this respect self-confessedly inchoate, nevertheless, differences with IZL remained marked. 'The IZL has still not advanced beyond the stage of orthodox Revisionism, which in practice maintains equality of rights for all classes and in effect provides a crutch for a reactionary stance which is not only economically exploitative but also *anti-national* in its nature.' *Lehi*, on the other hand, insisted that 'the war for national liberation and social freedom are compatible'. Without enlisting Marx or Lenin (instead, like the Revisionists, *Lehi* referred to the Bible), it insisted that 'the working classes . . . had always and everywhere been the first to join the struggle for national freedom. So it will be here.' *Lehi*'s 'just social system' was that which had been proposed in 1943: a planned economy within the framework of an *étatist* regime.

Fourth, to these factors were added differences in foreign policy orientation. *Lehi* (unlike the IZL) could foresee no possibility of compromise or negotiation with the foreign suzerain in Palestine. Of its leaders, only Friedman-Yellin (at least so Eldad apologetically suspected) may at this stage have been prepared to see in Soviet Russia the key to the fulfilment of their hopes. But, in a general sense, all were certainly prepared to ally with any foreign power – provided only that it recognise the Jews' right to freedom and independence. That too, however, was at odds with the IZL who, because they refused to draw the ultimate conclusions from political analysis, were uneasy with *Lehi*'s anti-imperialism and its search for political ties in all directions.[22] Finally, *Lehi* accused the IZL of pursuing a cult of personalities 'whether dead [Jabotinsky and Raziel] or alive [Begin]'. Its own existence, it claimed, was 'based upon the supra-human ideal and not on the leadership of men . . . We do not embalm our fallen leaders and their teachings – even in the case of Yair . . . They serve as exemplars . . . not . . . instruments of internal warfare.'[23]

Of all the members of *Lehi*'s 'centre', Eldad was undoubtedly the most in favour of a union with the IZL, probably because his affinity with Revisionist maximalism was particularly strong. True, he was severely critical of what he called the IZL's 'legacy of Revisionist introversion', and hence was pained when the NZO returned to the Jewish Agency. He also urged the IZL to adopt a more open-minded attitude on other issues. 'Let us free ourselves of both the anti-Fascism of the left and the anti-Socialism of the right.' Nevertheless, before and after his release from imprisonment, he continued to press for union, both in conversations with his *Lehi* colleagues and in correspondence with Begin. Those efforts, it seems, were very nearly successful. According to Eldad's later account, the two sides were able to circumvent their principal differences: the IZL's demand to have Jabotinsky recognised as 'the father of the rebellion' and Begin's opposition to the designation of the struggle as an 'anti-imperialist' war. Eventually, he claims, Begin even agreed to the pro-Soviet orientation to be outlined in *Lehi*'s 'Fundamentals to Hebrew Foreign Policy' (see below). Where the talks broke down, however, was on matters of domestic ideology. Influenced by Friedman-Yellin, *Lehi* was increasingly turning leftwards – and becoming ever more suspicious that the IZL was only interested in union in order to blunt the military forced upon it by *Lehi*'s independence. Those feelings, combined with the heritage of mutual hatred, eventually won out. Friedman-Yellin was able to conclude that the majority of *Lehi* opposed the union.[24]

Notwithstanding the failure of the talks on union with IZL, *Lehi* could point to certain gains. Its membership had grown – and at no cost in quality; so too had its arsenal and (through what were euphemistically described as 'expropriations') its treasury. It had also managed to organise its friends and supporters; to despatch emissaries abroad; to publicise its view (both through the regular appearance in print of its own organ, *Ha-Ma'as*, and through its radio broadcasts); and to organise an embargo on government bonds which had led to the depreciation of their value.[25] *Lehi* was also in a position to forecast its function in the short-range future. Should the Anglo-American Committee present a totally negative report, its conclusions would unite the masses and silence the advocates of conciliation. But even were it to advocate such a partial solution as partition (a compromise which the 'official' Zionists would welcome gladly, notwithstanding their protestations to the contrary), *Lehi*'s mission would remain clear. It would constitute the only movement which had neither co-operated with the authorities nor forsaken its principles. Indeed, it would fight to prevent the imposition of partition and would thereby provide a magnet for a larger front of all persons who were 'zealous of the integrity of the Hebrew homeland'.[26]

The IZL's version of the circumstances which had brought about the failure of talks on union was entirely different. *Lehi*'s projection of supposed ideological differences between the two camps, it maintained, was no more than an insubstantive, smoke-screen. *Lehi*'s true colours had been shown during the 'saison', when its leadership – unlike the IZL – had bowed to the *Haganah*'s ultimatum and agreed to interrupt its struggle against the British, effectively maintaining a cease-fire for an entire year. What is more, there existed oral and written evidence that precisely the same people who were now preaching their supposed ideological differences with the IZL had, unbeknown to *Lehi*'s own rank and file, contemplated union with the *Haganah*. Even now, they were still keeping their followers misinformed. *Lehi*'s leaders did not admit that they had, of their own volition, agreed to abide by the IZL's principles with regard to military and political strategy – even agreeing to give up their own anti-imperialist socialist protestations and to describe them as 'communist slogans'. In fact, the IZL claimed, the only point of original disagreement between the two sides had been *Lehi*'s 'opportunistic' refusal to acknowledge Jabotinsky's unique and seminal contribution to the notion of the Hebrew liberation struggle.[27] Neither did they acknowledge the help which the IZL had given them in every sphere. Obsessed with the preservation of their own organisational framework, *Lehi*'s leaders had stooped to the furthest depths of falsehood and hatred. There was absolutely no foundation for their charge that the IZL's operations were purely 'demonstrative'. If anything, 'events had proved that the "faction" [that is, *Lehi*] had itself been constrained to accept the operational tactics of the *ma'amad* [IZL], to learn from its commanders and to follow in its paths'.[28] Nevertheless, *Lehi* was not forgiven for not co-operating with the IZL in its unsuccessful attempt to explode the oil refineries.

## THE DECLINE OF THE UNITED HEBREW RESISTANCE MOVEMENT

On 2 May 1946, the leadership of the United Hebrew Resistance Movement met to consider its response to the recently published report of the Anglo-American Committee on Palestine. Friedman-Yellin participated with some trepidation. Relations between *Lehi* and its partners in the movement had already become strained late in April, when the *Haganah* had condemned as 'stupid' and 'base' *Lehi*'s surprise attack on a detachment of British soldiers, who were murdered in their sleep.[29] He feared that the *Haganah* might withdraw from the Movement entirely. It was not the recommendations of the committee itself which would tempt them to do so; since its members had advocated that Palestine be neither Jewish nor Arab, their report was bound to be rejected. Far more dangerous was Attlee's subsequent declaration that his condition for the immediate immigration of 100,000 refugees was the disbandment of the *Yishuv*'s 'private armies' – a prospect which might lead to the 'legitimisation' of the *Haganah* and the exclusive pursuit of *Lehi* and the IZL. But to Friedman-Yellin's surprise, his suspicions proved unfounded. The meeting decided on a joint statement which spoke of the defence of Hebrew arms, a free homeland, Attlee's hypocrisy and the continuation – even after the admission of 100,000 refugees – of operations designed to further immigration, settlement and the acquisition of arms.[30]

Admittedly, *Lehi* did have to pay a stiff price for that show of unanimity. Specifically, it had to agree that the demand for the entry of 100,000 refugees take precedence over military operations, which would meanwhile be suspended. *Lehi*'s acceptance of that arrangement generated an unprecedented rift between its leadership and the rank and file, who considered it a betrayal of the basic principle that their movement would pursue an unceasing struggle for the total expulsion of the British.[31] But the tension was short-lived. On 12 June Bevin himself made it clear that Britain would only implement the Anglo-American recommendations *in toto*. His speech spurred the United Resistance Movement to immediate – and joint – action. On the night of 16–17 June (the 'Night of the Bridges') communications arteries throughout Palestine were attacked. Conceptually, the operation was a victory for the advocates of 'unceasing struggle'. Unfortunately for *Lehi*, however, the success was only philosophical. Its own part in the action (the attack on the Haifa railway yards) went awry: although considerable damage was caused, 11 of its men were killed and 23 were taken captive. For a small movement, this was a heavy blow; so much so that some of its members now advocated a return to individual terror.[32]

But the collapse of the United Hebrew Resistance Movement was not brought about by the weakness of *Lehi*. Rather, it was the direct consequence of the 'Black Sabbath' (29 June 1946, which *Lehi* compared to the worst pogroms), when British forces arrested and imprisoned several leaders of the *Haganah* and the Jewish Agency as well as a considerable number of prominent figures in local Jewish economic life. Stunned by the enormity of the action, much of the *Yishuv* expressed the opinion that nothing further was to be gained by pursuing a blatantly military strategy in co-operation with the IZL and *Lehi*. Instead, the struggle against Britain had to proceed along lines which were potentially less costly (such as pressure through 'illegal' immigration). Most important of all, Weizmann now managed to pressurise 'Command X' to cease its activities.[33]

With what virtually amounted to self-satisfaction, *Lehi* spurned that policy. The appropriate reaction to the British operation, it proclaimed in a series of broadsides, was increased resistance and total conflict, not pacifism. In retrospect, the 'Black Sabbath' constituted a victory for *Lehi*'s ideology. It had proved what the movement had throughout maintained – that the British were determined to conduct an all-out war against the *Yishuv*. It could therefore have been foreseen – and should have been anticipated by the 'official' leadership. Their failure to do so showed that they had no right to be called leaders at all. Ben-Gurion's so-called 'deep political wisdom' was especially scorned. He still did not realise that the British considered the *Haganah*, too, to be a 'terrorist' organisation. He and his colleagues were totally out of touch with reality. They had not waged a real war, but a 'struggle'; they had only initiated intermittent – and costly – sabotage operations instead of striking directly against the enemy's weakest point – the members of its armed forces. *Lehi* admitted that the moment for an 'overt and massive uprising' had not yet arrived. The people still had to wait until the necessary forces had crystallised and for the appropriate international constellation. Nevertheless: 'Men of political discernment and national pride do not today ask whether we should fight. Only fools and traitors object to [war].'[34] That the 'official' Zionist leadership subsequently condemned out of hand the IZL's blowing up of the King David Hotel on 22 July 1946 merely showed the extent of its pusillanimity.[35]

The counterpart to the renewed estrangement between the *Lehi* and the 'official' Zionist leadership was a somewhat closer alignment between *Lehi* and the IZL. Notwithstanding the acrimony which had characterised their exchanges the previous spring, when negotiations for their union had broken down, the two sides did evince some affinities. In a clear gesture of conciliation, for instance, *Lehi* was even prepared to acknowledge the sixth anniversary of Jabotinsky's death and to praise his 'fundamentally sound' ideas.[36] Operational circumstances further contributed to the change in the atmosphere. After the collapse of the United Hebrew Resistance Movement both organisations carried out many partisan actions (interrupted only during the month of the twenty-second Zionist congress in December 1946). Similarly, early in 1947, the two sides were united in their opposition to the notion that those of their members who were condemned to the gallows by the British authorities should ask for the King's pardon or accept any status other than prisoners of war. Indeed, with the executions of Gruner, Dresner, Alkoshi and Kashani on 16 April, together with the suicides in prison of Barazani and Feinstein one week later, the two sides could parade a similar martyrology. Hence, they were closer than ever before. It was at this stage (according to Eldad) that Begin was even prepared to accept *Lehi*'s 'Fundamentals of a Hebrew Foreign Policy', together with their pro-Soviet conclusions.[37] Nevertheless, the fundamental differences between the two camps were not thereby obliterated. As one IZL paper had earlier put it: 'Relations with the "faction" are not good and have recently considerably worsened. During the past months we have seen that hatred of the *ma'amad* [IZL] is truly a part of the "faction"'s ideology, and incitement against the *ma'amad* has become [its] method of education.'[38]

The true extent of the differences between *Lehi* and the IZL had become apparent after Bevin's announcement of 18 February 1947 that the London conference had failed and that Britain was turning the Palestine question over to the United Nations. Begin remained unconvinced of the sincerity of Britain's intention to terminate its rule in Palestine, considering Bevin's move an 'exercise'.[39] *Lehi* thought otherwise but, conscious that it was still very much a minority in the *Yishuv*, was fearful of the consequences. That explains why, in a meeting with Begin, Friedman-Yellin even advocated, albeit briefly, that the IZL and *Lehi* 'slow down the pace of the war and gain time to increase [our] strength'. Is not the impending British evacuation 'too early?' he asked. 'The underground movements have not yet reached the stage at which they can fill the administrative vacuum which will be created.' Begin's response is not known. But he clearly was not prepared to accept Friedman-Yellin's advice. Unlike *Lehi*, the IZL considered itself ready to replace the British administration should it indeed end. Moreover, provided that the *Yishuv* rallied around the flag of war, Begin would to that end even be prepared to co-operate with the Jewish Agency.[40]

THE PLAN FOR THE 'NEUTRALISATION' OF THE MIDDLE EAST

A new turning-point in the Palestine question had meanwhile been reached on 31 July 1946, with the publication of the Morrison–Grady Plan. From *Lehi*'s point of view (as well as that of the IZL and the *Yishuv* in general), this presented a particularly insidious danger. Since it proposed that the inhabitants of Palestine be granted nothing more than 'provincial autonomy', the plan in effect held out the prospect of a renewed British mandate over the country. Nevertheless, *Lehi* feared, the 'official' Zionist leaders might still find that particular plan acceptable. After all, they had already forsaken the path of armed struggle, embarking instead on the 'passive' routes of diplomacy, immigration and settlement. In true 'Quisling' fashion – and notwithstanding the persistence of Britain's actions against the *Yishuv* (Operation Shark (30 July–2 August); the deportations to Cyprus (12 August); and the searches in Dorot and Ruhama (28 August–2 September)) – they still refused to recognise the futility of their fundamentally pro-British orientation. Whereas the *Lehi*'s threat of retaliation had 'forced' the British to pardon the 18 fighters arrested during the raid against the Haifa railyards,[41] 'official' Zionism still insisted on 'restraint'. It was time that the *Yishuv* made a choice between the two courses.

As far as *Lehi* was concerned, the differences between the two sides were exemplified by proceedings at the twenty-second Zionist congress in December 1946. That gathering witnessed Sneh's 'public confession' (his declaration that 'Britain is the enemy of our desire for liberty' was in fact entirely consonant with *Lehi*'s own position)[42] and Weizmann's deposition from the presidency. Nevertheless, the congress did not generate the fundamental shift in strategy and orientation which *Lehi* considered imperative. Its proceedings reveal that debate concentrated on such 'peripheral' issues as the refugees, desert reclamation projects and the damage caused by the terrorist organisations (which the congress almost unanimously condemned).[43] There was no discussion of such basic questions as Britain's political, military and economic rule in the Middle East and of Palestine's place in present and future imperial designs.

Official Zionism thus still amounted to merely 'HIAS [Hebrew Sheltering and Immigrants Aid Society] sprinkled with a small measure of autonomy'. Before the congress, *Lehi* had suspected that the Jewish Agency was abandoning its own earlier resolution stipulating recognition of the need to establish 'a viable Jewish state' as a precondition for participating in negotiations. That charge, it transpired, was baseless.[44] Nevertheless, *Lehi* continued to warn that, in return for the sop of a 'federation', a 'mini-state' or a 'handful of immigration certificates', the Agency was probably prepared to accept the retention of British bases in Palestine. Subsequent developments seemed to confirm the justice of that prediction. How else was one to interpret Ben-Gurion's 'servile' choice of the 'back door' into the London round table conference of early 1947? How else could *Lehi* understand the news that, as a gesture to Britain, he had agreed to the interruption of 'illegal' immigration?[45] Still worse was its fear that General Barker (GOC Palestine) would impose Weizmann on Ben-Gurion.

Not unexpectedly, one alternative option advocated by *Lehi* was an increase in militant activities against the agents of British rule. Consequently, it had the previous summer turned down the *Haganah*'s request to extend the informal truce against Britain until 15 September 1946. Instead, it stepped up its campaign of terror. Martin, a key figure in the Jewish department of the CID, was killed on 9 September, and on the same day a bomb was planted at the CID's regional offices in Tel Aviv, killing Doran, an officer said to have impeded pre-war immigration from Romania.[46] Notwithstanding the condemnation of the Zionist congress, *Lehi* refused to apologise for those actions. On the contrary, it actively canvassed the delegates, demanding that they recognise the establishment of *Lehi* to have been a 'Copernican Revolution', comparable in Zionist history only with the appearance of Herzl himself.

Even more radical, however, was the simultaneous formulation of *Lehi*'s plan for the 'neutralisation of the Middle East'. Apparently initially drafted by Friedman-Yellin and Avraham Selman in September 1946,[47] this was indeed a far-reaching proposal. First, it did not limit *Lehi*'s demands to the ejection of Britain from Palestine alone, but proposed its expulsion from the entire Middle East. Indeed, it was claimed, only by refusing to host British military bases could the peoples of the region avoid being drawn into the horrendous third world war which current international tension showed to be imminent; only thus, moreover, could they freely develop their economic, military and cultural potential. It followed that *Lehi* did not project 'the neutralisation of the Middle East' as an exclusively Jewish interest; it would also benefit other forces – local, regional and international. Obviously, the plan included Transjordan, which was destined to be part of the Kingdom of Israel. Equally, of course, the plan would be opposed by the present clique of Arab heads of state – Nuri Sa'id, Abdullah, Sidqi Pasha and the 'presidents' of Syria and Lebanon. But it would be supported by other national minorities (the Kurds, the

Druze and Azerbaijanis), by 'the Arab masses' (especially in Egypt and Iraq) and, perhaps most important, by the Soviet Union.

As a method of side-stepping the thorny prospect of Jewish–Arab war, the 'neutralisation' plan was indeed an audacious leap in the dark.[48] But it is because of its proposed international alignment that it must command attention. *Lehi*, it must be stressed, did not blatantly equate 'neutralisation' with a Hebrew–Soviet alliance. Indeed, the statements on Palestine emanating from the USSR in the summer of 1946 were admitted to be still distinctly unfavourable from *Lehi*'s point of view (as Vladimir Lutzki's article had proved). But the 'neutralisation' plan did present a definite alternative to the pro-British orientation of 'official' Zionism. Indeed, the plan was founded on entirely different premises from those which seemed to be influencing the behaviour of the Jewish Agency and of the IZL (by whom it was also rejected outright).[49] One premise was the inevitable collapse of British power, whose shattered economy was unable to compete for markets against either the United States or the Soviet Union and whose people had been worn out by the Second World War. Another was the basically peaceful intentions of the Soviets who (so *Lehi* claimed) had themselves no need of the raw materials of the Middle East and would not invade the region unless provoked to do so by Western aggression.[50] When, on 12 September, Henry Wallace, the US Secretary of Commerce, delivered a speech which was believed to echo similar sentiments, even *Lehi*'s attitude towards the US underwent a temporary change.[51]

How much more important it was, therefore, to reject any policy which threatened to allow Britain to retain her military bases in the region. Indeed, only an intensification of the struggle against Britain could convince the Russians of the value of an alignment with a Jewish state. Hence, it had to be repeated, the campaign against Britain had to remain Zionism's single objective. Ever anxious to 'divide and rule', the British would exploit any available opportunity to set Jew against Jew (which explained the release of Shertok, Gruenbaum, Dov Joseph and Remez from prison on 5 November) and – needless to add – Jew against Arab (which was why the leaders of Arab 'gangs' had also been set free). *Lehi*, by contrast, declared itself prepared to go to almost any lengths to preclude both possibilities. If, at the same time, it could gain Russian support, then so much the better. Hence, it declared, were the communist party 'tomorrow' to decide to go underground and declare war on the foreign ruler, 'let no Hebrew dare to collaborate with the foreign ruler against the Communists, even though they oppose Zionism'. Moreover: 'If the Arabs tomorrow initiate war against the foreign ruler, let no Hebrew dare to co-operate with the foreign ruler, even though the Arabs object to our goals.'[52]

The extent to which *Lehi*'s domestic programmes were beginning to move towards what was later to become leftist chauvinism (or National Bolshevism) is illustrated by its reaction to two otherwise unimportant incidents in December 1946. One occurred at the Arab village of Salameh, which was raided by a *Haganah* unit in retaliation for the alleged Arab theft of a small-arms cache. The second took place in the Jewish settlement of Petach-Tikva, where several injuries were caused during a clash between members of the socialist *Histadrut* and those of the (Revisionist) 'National Organisation of Workers'. *Lehi*'s reaction to the first incident was one of outrage: the *Haganah*, it claimed, had perpetrated a 'provocation'. Worse still, it had become the cat's-paw of Britain, in whose interest alone it was to see 'the Hebrew war for liberation transmuted into a dispute between Hebrew and Arab'. With regard to the second incident, too, *Lehi* was outspoken. Blatantly supporting the Revisionist organisation, it claimed that the *Histadrut* was here too attempting to distract the Hebrew worker's attention from the true object of his struggle. 'The war for a crust of bread', it declared, 'and the war against the threat of unemployment, is today integral to the war against the foreign suzerain.'[53]

It is only as harbingers of things to come that such incidents merit attention. It must be stressed that, at this stage, *Lehi*'s domestic programme was far less clearly formulated than was its foreign policy. But the latter, as expressed in the plan for the 'neutralisation' of the Middle East, was by now quite firm, so much so that it was not even affected by Britain's announcement in February 1947 that it was turning the Palestine question over to the United Nations. On the contrary, the principal consequence of that development was that the 'neutralisation' plan was still further refined by Eldad, who then composed *Lehi*'s 'Fundamentals of Hebrew Foreign policy'.[54]

That document reconfirmed *Lehi*'s belief in the absolute incompatibility of Jewish and British interests and hence in the necessity for an armed struggle for Hebrew independence. It also insisted on the continued relevance of Yair's teaching that the *Yishuv* needed an international ally. 'Official' Zionism's collusion with Britain was therefore roundly condemned; so, too, were its contacts with the United States. Eldad placed little value on those approaches, and (unlike the 'official' Zionist leadership) had little faith in the ability of American Jewry to realise its potential political influence.[55] Instead, he looked eastwards – towards the communist bloc. Although the USSR could not yet be classed as an ally there was no question of its potential contribution to Jewish national progress. *Lehi*'s proposal to 'neutralise' the Middle East would facilitate that development, not least because it would obviate the Soviets' understandable fear that a Jewish state allied to Britain would become a tool of anti-Russian imperialism. Echoing Friedman-Yellin's conviction that Russia's strategy was fundamentally 'defensive' in orientation, Eldad was certain that 'Russia will assist Jewish emigration from the ports of Romania, Bulgaria and Yugoslavia, at least provided [such emigration] will be anti-British.' Russia will have to be assured:

> that on the morrow of their arrival the new immigrants will not be employed in British bases or establish British ports. The question is whether the *Yishuv* will not appear to be behind a movement whose 'Sieff Institute' in Rehovot is working on chemical inventions which will be handed over to Britain. For Russia cannot yet be certain that such inventions will not be put to use against her.[56]

As portrayed by both Friedman-Yellin and Eldad, the plan to 'neutralise' the Middle East became a panacea. Its publication would help the Russians determine their own policy and thus look more favourably on the *Histadrut* and the *kibbutzim*; it would also win acceptance in such other world flash-points as Germany and China. In both Eldad's and Friedman-Yellin's versions, moreover, it could even incorporate the 'Arab' factor. *Lehi*'s views, unlike those of the IZL, which still remained wedded to the Revisionist disdain of Arab impotence, had been undergoing change ever since 1944. With the formulation of its blatantly 'anti-imperialist' programme, these changes were now made plain. Arab–Jewish conflict was not as inevitable as the British conspired to make it; instead, the two sides could co-operate against the common foe. The *Yishuv* should stimulate the rebellion of the Arab masses inside and outside Palestine against the British lackeys by whom they were held in chains; it should also offer those at present residing in Palestine and Transjordan Jabotinsky's old option of 'full civil rights'. Naturally, the British would do everything possible to prevent any such understanding. But until a final settlement was attained, Arabs and Jews could agree to refrain from attacks on each other and to co-operate against their mutual (British) enemy.[57] Interestingly, nevertheless, the 'neutralisation' plan was not anti-American. On the contrary, it favoured (albeit temporarily) American economic involvement. However, American Jewry was not considered to be an important factor in the movement's progress. All really depended on whether American Jews would support Henry Wallace and his pro-Russian policies.[58]

# Towards the United Nations

*Lehi* was profoundly distrustful of Bevin's announcement of 18 February 1947 that the British government had decided to turn the Palestine question over to the UN. That, transparently, was nothing more than a typically British 'plot'. 'It was designed to strengthen Britain's position in the Middle East and to dissuade the Egyptian Premier, Nukrashi Pasha, from implementing his threat to take the Anglo-Egyptian dispute to the United Nations. Thus, *Lehi* contested the official Zionist analysis, which regarded Britain's departure from Palestine as an inexorable consequence of its impending withdrawal from India and Egypt. Those events, it prophesied, would only strengthen Britain's resolve to tighten its hold on Palestine, which would constitute its most important *place d'armés* between the Mediterranean and the Persian Gulf. Furthermore, *Lehi* foresaw a situation in which the British would encourage 'Abdullah's armies' to march on Damascus and Aleppo. By thus extending the borders of the Hashemite monarchy to Turkey, the British hoped to bolster its anti-Soviet front. Indeed, it was to precisely the same end that Britain was at this time constructing new military barracks in Palestine itself and bringing fresh divisions to serve there.[1]

It followed that there was no reason to lessen *Lehi*'s military operations against the British. If anything, the desire to attract Russian attention to *Lehi*'s own 'neutralisation' plan demanded that such activities be intensified. The expulsion of the immigrant ship *Hayyim Arlozoroff* on 27 February 1947 provided the pretext. Two days later, explosions were set off at the offices of the British shipping company in Haifa and the military paymaster; attacks were also made against the tax assessors' office as well as military posts in Jerusalem, Haifa and Tel Aviv. A week later, the target was the Colonial Office in London, the military camp at Pardes Hanah (9 March) and subsequently (13–14 March) trains transporting British material at various points in the country.[2] More important than the material impact of those actions was their pyschological effect. Coinciding with the IZL's attack on the British officers' club in Jerusalem on 1 March (which resulted in 12 fatalities) and the subsequent British imposition of martial law in Tel Aviv and northern Jerusalem, they gave the impression that the Anglo-Jewish wars of *Lehi*'s prediction had materialised. Indeed, the movement regarded with satisfaction both the intensification of the struggle and the fortitude with which it considered the *Yishuv* had exploited Britain's political weaknesses in order to force the revocation of martial law only 15 days after it was imposed.[3]

On 11 March, while martial law was still in force, the *Lehi* command made a remarkable approach to the *Haganah* and, by extension, to the executive of the Jewish Agency. Provided that the latter embarked on a course of 'total' civil rebellion and 'active reaction and opposition to all [British] decrees, expulsions, military orders etc.', *Lehi* declared itself prepared 'to accept some measure of the yoke of discipline'.[4] Whether or not a favourable response was expected to this offer must be left an open question. Nevertheless, it remains a telling indication of *Lehi*'s own self-image. Unlike the IZL, *Lehi* (at least, in theory) did not consider itself an alternative to the authority of the official Zionist leadership. Instead, it perceived its true role to be that of a catalyst in framing their opinion. Thus seen, the object of its approach to the Jewish Agency seems to have been to strengthen those elements in that body whom *Lehi* considered to be unbending in their opposition to Britain, and to weaken the influence of those whom it considered 'waverers', 'weaklings' and 'compromisers'. Altogether, the *Yishuv* had to be made to realise its own inherent strength and thus to abandon the 'Ben-Gurion policy' of accommodation with the British. In the face of Jewish resolve, Britain would indeed ultimately relent – and even the pressure exerted by the boatloads of 'illegal' immigrants contributed to the struggle.[5]

It is against that background of combined suspicion and confidence that *Lehi*'s attitude towards the forthcoming debates on Palestine at the UN can best be understood. What *Lehi* feared most was a latter-day version of the conferences at Evian (1938) and Bermuda (1943). Appeals based on humanitarian grounds by Jewish representatives who projected the image of spokesmen for a community of refugees would necessarily invite a non-Zionist solution. Far better just to announce that: 'The Hebrew nation wants its homeland.' The nations of the world, *Lehi* proclaimed: 'will speak with our fighters, not with our refugees. Instead of turning our fighters here into refugees, we should turn our refugees in the Diaspora into fighters.'[6]

Besides, *Lehi* doubted whether the UN constituted the most decisive of forums for the resolution of international affairs. In a world dominated by the Cold War between the United States and Russia, the influence of the UN *per se* was bound to be minimal. Hence, the official Zionists were wasting their efforts preparing their case for presentation there. They could not possibly influence affairs behind the scenes, which is where final decisions would be taken. Ultimately, they would find themselves in the position of Haile Selassie in the 1930s, who had been betrayed by his nominal supporters at the very time that he was appealing to the League of Nations. A realistic appraisal showed that there was no substance to the 'democracy' of the UN, since many of its members were not at all independent. No count of votes could be taken seriously; a great power could always 'fix' a majority or – failing that – ignore the majority by exercising its powers of delay or veto. Everyone knows that in the final analysis the UN will act upon decisions taken by the British Chiefs of Staff and the American stockholders of oil shares.'[7] The latter reference was not incidental. *Lehi* was intensely afraid of American military might and the strength of the dollar. It feared that, confronted with those forces, the 'official' Zionist leadership might be tempted to succumb to American imperialism. Instead of dealing with the Americans on a basis of national give and take, they might accept American hand-outs, in return for which the Jews (like the Greeks and Turks) would have to pay the military and political price of adhesion to an anti-Soviet bloc. That was a danger to be avoided at all costs:

> The Hebrew nation neither wants nor is able to become America's political and military partner in a front directed at the Soviet Union . . . We have no interest in a war against the Soviet regime. We have no interest in a war against the Russian people and none in a war against the Soviet state.

Quite apart from endangering 'the millions of our brethren in Russia and the countries under her influence', any such course would also bring disaster on the *Yishuv* itself. Should the Jewish Agency decide upon a 'Western' orientation it would forfeit any claim to be considered representative of the Hebrew people. Far more appropriate was the action taken by *Lehi* itself which, parallel to its ideological attacks on Britain, also increased its terrorist campaign. Particular attention was paid to targets considered to be of imperial significance. Thus, on 31 March, 20,000 tons of oil were destroyed at the Haifa refineries. The action, it was proclaimed, did not merely strike at British rule in Palestine but also at the wealth of the Empire.[8]

TOWARDS THE GROMYKO DECLARATION OF 14 MAY 1947

Notwithstanding its attitude to the UN, *Lehi* did not altogether disdain the United Nations nor reject the notion of participating in its deliberations. Indeed, instead of advocating a boycott of the United Nations Special Commission on Palestine (UNSCOP), established on

14 May 1947, *Lehi* insisted that the Jews make a 'factual' presentation before that body. One advantage which could thus be gained was essentially propagandist in form. It provided an opportunity for publicising the demand for international acknowledgement of the national rights of the entire Hebrew people and of *Eretz Israel* as its homeland.[9]

Second, and more important, a forum of that sort would also facilitate *Lehi*'s efforts to generate a change in the policy of the USSR. Hitherto, it was admitted, the attitude of the Russians had not been as favourable as *Lehi* would have wished; although acknowledging the national rights of the Jewish people, they had not specified *Eretz Israel* as its homeland. The composition of the proposed UN Commission, however, signified a possible change in that position. Unlike all of its predecessors, that body was not a mere tool of the imperialist powers. For the very first time, a voice in Palestinian affairs was also given to representatives of 'independent' nations sympathetic to the USSR or under its influence. One was Czechoslovakia, where the communist Clement Gottwald was already acting as Prime Minister; another was Yugoslavia, whose strained relations with the USSR were not to become public knowledge until one year later. This, then, was an opportunity not to be missed.[10] *Lehi*'s response was to align itself totally with those communist movements that were elsewhere (as in Greece and Burma) fighting for their national freedom. Their leaders were 'serious people'; unlike those of the *Yishuv* they had not stopped their hunger strikes after only four days but had persisted until the bitter end.[11]

The shift in Soviet policy towards Palestine signified by Gromyko's announcement of 14 May 1947 seemed to reward *Lehi* for its labours. True, the announcement itself did not contain all that *Lehi* desired. Gromyko favoured, in the first instance, a bi-national Jewish and Arab state; only if that solution should prove impractical did he advocate the division of the country into two separate entities. Nevertheless, his statement did recognise the principle of Hebrew rights to an independent homeland, and thus signified a shift in Soviet policy.

In analysing the possible reasons for that change, *Lehi* acknowledged the relevance of several circumstances over which it had itself exercised no influence. Within the Soviet Union, it noted, the authorities were quite independently promoting a revival of the Russian people's own national heroes (a category which included the Ukrainian Bogdan Khmelnitsky and even the Hebrew Bar-Kochba, played in Yiddish, as well as Ivan the Terrible and Peter the Great); they were also advocating – and, in the Armenian case, also implementing – the repatriation of peoples to their historic homelands. Both positions dovetailed nicely with parallel Hebrew aspirations regarding *Eretz Israel*. To that had to be added the Russians' undoubted sympathy for the victims of the Holocaust; their desire to gain the support of the Jewish communities in Western Europe and the United States in their struggle for peace and against imperialsim; and their 'realistic' appraisal of both the Hebrew presence in Palestine and of the total degree to which such Arab states as Saudi Arabia and Transjordan were sub-servient to the Anglo-Saxon powers.

Ultimately, however, those had only been contributory factors in the Russian decision. Their importance was by far outweighed by the influence exerted on Russian attitudes by recent demonstrations of the strength and determination of *Lehi*'s own freedom fighters. Indeed, it had been the evidence of *Lehi*'s anti-imperialism and pro-Soviet orientation which had finally convinced the Kremlin to support the Hebrew cause. Only those who did not want to acknowledge this 'deep connection' failed to see it. In return for Stalin's gesture, it was now incumbent upon the radical underground to intensify its campaign against Britain, and especially against Bevin, whose pseudo-socialism had to be exposed for the sham that it was.[12]

*Lehi*'s supposedly unique 'contribution' to the Gromyko announce-ment eventually became part of the movement's mythology, spawning several variants and embellishments.[13] In the early summer of 1947, too, the emphasis was on exclusivity. Intentionally deaf to the *Haganah*'s counter-argument that a 'handful of terrorists' could not possibly have won Russian approval (especially not if they had previously shown themselves ready to co-operate with the fascists),[14] *Lehi* refused to acknowledge that any other sector of the *Yishuv* might claim a share in the triumph, portraying it as uniquely its own. 'Neither the *Histadrut* nor the Hebrew "Socialist" movements could possibly have aroused Gromyko's interest . . . Nor [could] the thirty years' history of Hebrew *kolkhozi* in the Jezreel Valley.'[15] There, indeed, lay the essential point. *Lehi* was intransigent in its opposition to any policy which might perpetuate a British presence in Palestine. For that reason, it continued to pour scorn on the 'official' Zionist leaders. Ignorant of the fact that Ben-Gurion was in contact with the Russians,[16] *Lehi* persisted in believing that he and his colleagues were still tied to a pro-Western policy which refused to recognise the necessity for a full-scale war against the British. That policy, the movement claimed, would prove disastrous: bound to be rejected by the Anglo-Saxon powers, it would also miss the historic opportunity to take advantage of the support of the Soviet Union and her allies. In sum: 'Ben-Gurion and his agencies are jeopardising the nation's interest. The masses must defeat them before they can do any further harm.'[17]

Of the several themes which lace *Lehi*'s pronouncements on the Gromyko statement and its implications, two are particularly worthy of attention. One, already foreshadowed in earlier writings, emphasised the pernicious consequences which would result were Ben-Gurion to continue to advocate a bargain with the British whereby they retained their military bases within a truncated Jewish state. Any such state would constitute nothing more than another Transjordan – a slave to British political and military imperialism and, necessarily therefore, an obvious target of Soviet attack on the very outbreak of a third world war. Only short-sightedness, born of a personal craving for the trappings of ministerial office, could allow that possibility. *Lehi* would fight against it. 'We shall continue to shoot at every Briton in the land today so that we shall not tomorrow have to fire on Russians and on Jews living in Russian areas.'[18]

The second theme, although less explicit, was in many respects still more dramatic. The evidence indicates that Gromyko's announcement increased the pressure within *Lehi* to adopt a more left-wing orientation in internal affairs. Without precisely committing themselves, exponents of that view showed that they were prepared to portray the future regime of the Hebrew state in terms which they thought might please the Kremlin. Thus, for the very first time, *Lehi* announced that a developed *Eretz Israel* 'also raises the status of the working class, and permits a regime which at any rate will not be antagonistic towards Soviet Russia'.[19]

## LEHI AND UNSCOP, STAGE 1: TACKLING THE ARAB QUESTION

In July 1947 *Lehi* presented its memorandum to UNSCOP.[20] Compiled by Friedman-Yellin, the document summarised the movement's ideology and policies as they had crystallised during the past year. Its principal purpose was to project the image of a progressive and leftist Hebrew national movement, possessed of deep historical roots in *Eretz Israel*, which had consistently and unprecedentedly been tricked by the British but which now stood a good chance of being favoured by the Soviet leadership.

Of the eight individual sections of the memorandum, the first (entitled 'The Homeland and the Nation') set out to demonstrate that the Hebrew people had always striven for their liberation from foreign dominion – often alone. In keeping with standard Zionist polemic, *Lehi* also posited the eternal continuity in the Jews' mystical attachment to *Eretz Israel*, a land which (it emphasised) had never been entirely devoid of Jewish inhabitants. The messianic idea had continued to inspire Jews even during the darkest days of the Holocaust;

all that had been accomplished since the 1880s was the result of the Jews' 'limitless love' of their land, as well as 'the forces of science and the sweat of the masses'. It followed that *Lehi*'s underground war against Britain did not articulate the fantasies of a few extremist hotheads. Rather, it was the result of a contradiction between the ambitions of the nation for its liberation and the interests of a foreign power.

The memorandum next turned its attention to those interests, devoting its next four sections to an analysis of Britain's policies towards Palestine. The first, entitled 'Roots of British Rule in Palestine', demonstrated the cynicism which had always characterised those policies. Originally, it argued, Britain had supported the Ottoman Empire in order to exploit its material resources. Subsequently, it had planned to control Palestine through the medium of Arab chieftains and heads of families who had no interest in their peoples' welfare. Since Zionism aspired to raise the living standards of the inhabitants of the region, it necessarily constituted a threat to Britain's strategic interests. That was why 'immediately' after 1917, British 'agents' had instigated unceasing efforts to impede the progress of the Jewish people. Britain's nominal support for the establishment of a Jewish 'national home', a theme developed in the section entitled 'Thirty Years of British Rule in Palestine', was itself in accord with that policy. Its purpose had been to generate tension between the Arab and Jewish sectors of the population which, in classic imperial style, the British could then divide and rule. Indeed, they had consistently attempted to do so. Posing as supposedly impartial arbitrators between the two peoples, the British had used the spectre of Jewish dominion in Palestine as a weapon with which to distract Arabs inside and outside Palestine from their more pressing problems. Britain had also deliberately inflated the 'threat' of Jewish immigration, against which it had also incited the 1936 Arab riots.

One purpose of this presentation was to convince the members of UNSCOP that an Arab–Jewish conflict, far from being inherent in the Palestinian situation, was in fact a British creation. (To that end, *Lehi* disguised from UNSCOP the fact that the IZL – its forebear – had between 1936 and 1939 instigated a campaign of counter-terror against the Arabs: its only comment on the episode was that 'The Jewish reaction to hostilities of Arabs incited by British agents was an open dispute with Arabs'.) Another purpose was to stress the singularity of *Lehi*'s decision to raise the standard of revolt. Its rebellion, it maintained, was directed against the entire tenor of Britain's 'bloody rule' and not just against the specifics of the 1939 White Paper. This theme was further developed in the section entitled: 'The Rule of Subjection

Revealed – the Genesis of the War of Liberation.' Unlike the 'established' leadership of the *Yishuv*, it argued, *Lehi* had appreciated the depths of British cruelty and the impossibility of co-operation with the Mandatory Power. This had become apparent during the Holocaust, for which the British were 'no less' responsible than the Germans. After all, while 'the Nazis established the concentration camps and gas chambers', it was the British who 'drove masses of Jews' into them.

Under the rubric 'The Foreign Ruler's Policy of Economic Destruction', the memorandum next turned its attention to what *Lehi* perceived to be the economic consequences of the British Mandate. These, it argued, were uniformly detrimental. The British had done nothing to benefit the economy of the country. On the contrary, they had exploited its natural resources and thus deprived it of its wealth while their officials lined their own pockets. A battery of statistics were marshalled in order to prove that Britain was bent on destroying the economic base of the *Yishuv*. By encouraging the influx of unnecessary imports, it had produced an unfavourable balance of payments, offset only by the enlistment of Jewish capital from abroad; by freezing Palestine's sterling assets in London, it had hampered investment; by the imposition of heavy taxes, it had also deprived the country of liquidity. Worse still, an increasing proportion of the revenues thus raised (40 per cent in the financial year 1945/46) had been 'wasted' on expenses related to 'internal security'. Far less had been devoted to 'constructive' investments in public works and development.

In an independent Hebrew state, it was claimed, these proportions would be reversed. At the same time, import policies would be rationalised and the present high cost of living and level of wages thereby reduced. It is indicative of *Lehi*'s social policies at this time that the memorandum adopted an even-handed approach to the labour conflicts which had resulted from the present situation. Notwithstanding its generally favourable attitude towards the working classes, the movement preferred to place the entire responsibility for social conflict at Britain's door, claiming that 'right' was on the side of both employers and employed. It did, however, promise a reversal of Britain's present policy of distributing economic concessions without consideration of Palestine's own interest. The 'scandalous' petroleum concessions granted to the Anglo-Iranian and Anglo-Iraqi oil companies and to the Trans-Arabian Pipeline Company would certainly be revoked. After all, the projected pipelines from Iran and Saudi Arabia to Haifa served only Britain's imperial needs. They also signified the extent to which Palestine was being turned into a British base against Russia. That thesis was further strengthened by reference to British propaganda in the Middle East, which was trying to convince the 'reactionary' Arab governments that the 'Bolsheviks' of Russia were bent on destroying Islam and therefore had to be attacked.

The falsehood of that particular charge constituted the brunt of the next section of the memorandum, entitled 'The End of British Rule and the Evacuation of British Forces – Also for the Sake of World Peace'. It was not the Russians, the document argued, who harboured aggressive designs but the British. Having sacrificed millions of its citizens in the recent war, Russia was intent on reconstruction. The only reason it was amassing troops in its southern borders was to deter the British threat. Only thus, indeed, could Russia avert the danger of a new world war and the terrible destruction that it would cause. *Lehi*'s fears of yet another Holocaust may have been sincerely generated by the recent tragedy of European Jewry. But in raising that spectre the movement also clearly wished to gain Russian support. Although still protesting at the lack of foundation in British (and American) fears that a Hebrew state would constitute a Bolshevik Trojan horse in the Middle East, *Lehi* was certainly framing its arguments with an eye to possible Russian reactions. Indeed, one of the memorandum's main objectives was to gain Soviet support for a Hebrew state within its historic boundaries.

Precisely what those boundaries would be was beyond question and was clearly spelled out in the final section of the memorandum: 'The Positive Solution – Independence'. Although *Lehi* had retreated from its original claim to the Euphrates as the border of the projected 'Kingdom of Israel', in other respects it remained uncompromisingly loyal to the classic Revisionist map. Despite all the transformations in its foreign policy orientations, that part of its programme remained stable. Specifically, the Hebrew nation possessed 'historic rights' to the eastern bank of the Jordan; those were as inherent as were the rights of the Poles, Belo-Russians and the Russians to their own traditional homelands. Consequently, both sides of the Jordan river had to be under exclusive and independent Hebrew control. The Hashemite kingdom, in consequence, had to be dismantled; according to Friedman-Yellin, the Arab inhabitants of the region (like those of the west bank) had to be transferred elsewhere.

In respect to his social conceptions, too, Friedman-Yellin had not yet freed himself from those of classic Revisionism. Like the latter, he claimed Jewish responsibility for the very first socialist laws (a mandatory day of rest; the prohibition of interest on loans; the emancipation of slaves); he also promised that 'the Hebrew people . . . will construct in our free land a social regime founded upon the principles of the equality of men, the destruction of class barriers and the prohibition of poverty and penury'. But in describing that regime he coined the phrase 'people's democracy'. In origin, the choice of the term may have been designed to help *Lehi* manoeuvre between its wish to impress the Yugoslav and Czech representatives on UNSCOP and the charge that *Eretz Israel* would become part of the Soviet sphere of influence. It was not directed at the Arabs, but at Jews then relegated to a second-class status in both the DP camps and the Middle East.

As to the present Arab inhabitants of *Eretz Israel*, the memorandum attempted to ease UNSCOP's fears. The Arabs, it claimed, had nothing to fear from massive Jewish immigration. Like the Jewish Agency (whose arguments on this subject before the Anglo-American Committee *Lehi* cited), *Lehi* maintained that the economic potential of the country – both agriculturally and industrially – was large enough to satisfy both peoples, who were capable of co-operation. Arab enmity, the memorandum repeated, was nothing but a British fabrication. One example, Friedman-Yellin suggested, was provided by their partnership in the Jerusalem municipality; another (underlined in the memorandum) by the practical support which they were beginning to give to the Jewish underground. Truth to tell, neither example was well chosen. The situation in Jerusalem was more complicated then *Lehi* suggested, and the only specific instance it could cite of Arab support for the underground was the assistance which the Abu Gosh family (because of its feud with the Husseinis) had given to Geulah Cohen in her escape from prison on 13 April 1947. But in thus subordinating facts to its ideology, *Lehi* was pursuing a characteristic line. Here, too, the purpose of the memorandum was to enlist Russian support for the establishment of an independent Hebrew state. Hence the forecast that: 'With the extension of the war against British Imperialism, co-operation with the Arabs will not be restricted to *Eretz Israel* alone. It will also extend to the Arabs in neighbouring lands, who will support independence for *Eretz Israel* and its neighbours.'

The precise status of the Palestinian Arabs in a future Jewish state presented more delicate problems. It is apparent from the last section of the memorandum that contemporary circumstances demanded some revisions in the formula originally adopted by Stern and Eldad. In 1943 *Lehi* had called Jabotinsky to order when he had apparently promised the Arabs a bi-national state. Now, however, Friedman-Yellin adopted a more cautious phraseology, which assured the Arabs of 'cultural independence' and in parts even promised them equal political rights ('The Arabs will participate in the political life of the state in proportion to their numbers and capabilities.'). How that aim would be accomplished was not specified. Nevertheless, Friedman-

Yellin could promise that 'There is no possibility that the Jews would subject the Arabs or exercise political repression'. Themselves the victims of persecution, Jews could not possibly become persecutors. Besides – and more pragmatically – they would not welcome a situation in which 'a portion of the populace will be dissatisfied and provide a pretext for foreign intervention'.

Despite such protestations, the *Lehi* memorandum provided several indications of its ideological stand on this question. One is to be found in its favourable references to the concept of a population transfer and, as Stern had suggested, a population exchange. On this point, the memorandum also argued the irrelevance of both the Czech and Yugoslavian multi-national examples. In neither case did the relevant nationalities possess territories other than those in which they were then residing. 'The Arabs of *Eretz Israel*, on the other hand, are not a specific people. They are part of the great Arab nation, whose lands are divided only because of foreign intervention and the competition between ruling dynasties.' Only the Sudetens in pre-war Czechoslovakia provided a possible precedent. Unlike the Slavs, they had not then constituted a 'political-administrative separate entity'.

Equally significant was the opposition that the memorandum expressed to the possibilities of either a bi-national state or partition, both of which (it noted) were opposed by the Arabs themselves. The first, it maintained, was inherently 'undemocratic', since it proposed to divide administrative responsibilities on a 'racial' basis and discounted both the wishes of the population and the credentials of the candidates for office. It also ruled out the possibility that political parties (socialist as well as conservative) might be composed of both elements of the population. Partition was disqualified for different reasons. Quite apart from the consideration that the present generation possessed no authority to dispose of lands which also belonged to future generations, neither of the two proposed states would be economically viable. One would possess an industrial surplus, the other a deficit. Moreover, far from facilitating good relations between the prospective neighbours, partition would worsen them. Both states would maintain large armies and both would devote huge budgets to their maintenance (a situation bound to be exploited by the British). Within each state, 'irredentism' would flourish; so too would reactionary and fascist parties which would thrive on economic distress and national disappointment, and would seek foreign allies. Last, but not least important, partition would preclude the ability of the new state to absorb new immigrants. It would therefore condemn the denizens of the DP camps in Europe in their entirety, and the Jews of the Middle East, to 'physical destruction'.

It is instructive to compare the policies and programmes which *Lehi* thus outlined to UNSCOP with those which the IZL presented to the same body. The comparison underscores the extent of the affinity which the two underground movements had come to share in matters both operational and ideological. The IZL of 1947 was not the IZL of 1944. In part, the change may have been due to the ideological influences exerted by *Lehi*. What must also be taken into account, however, is the escalation generated by the intensification of the struggle against the British. In 1947, the IZL too – at least outwardly – feared that the British might wish to continue their control over the entire Middle East. Its principal differences with *Lehi* were now reduced to two major issues: one concerned the possibility of a pro-Soviet orientation in foreign policy; the other the domestic role of the separate underground movements. Whereas *Lehi* considered itself a catalyst in the *Yishuv*, the IZL regarded itself as a possible alternative leadership. It was the latter consideration which dominated the character of Begin's meetings with the chairman of UNSCOP, Judge Sandstrom, and his aides, Bunche and Ho.

The proximity of the positions adopted by *Lehi* and the IZL is illustrated in their joint denial of the existence of an Arab–Palestinian national movement. Indeed, like *Lehi*, the IZL insisted that 'most' local Arabs desired to join the Jews in the march forward towards 'political freedom and social progress'. Arab land sales to Jews (including that by Abdullah in Transjordan in 1932) provided one indication; so, too, did their co-operation in the Haifa municipality. Altogether, Arab–Jewish tensions (themselves artificially exaggerated by British propaganda) were 'considerably less serious' than intra-Arab conflicts. The armed struggle against the British had brought the two sides even closer together; notwithstanding the conflicts 'organised' (sic) by the British, they had even co-operated in prison.

Unlike *Lehi*, the IZL was concerned that the Jews would constitute a demographic minority *vis-à-vis* the 'non-Jewish' majority. Its own solution, however, was not to adopt Jabotinsky's original proposal for shared rule ('a Jewish president and Arab vice-president, in turns'). Neither did it echo the 'population transfer' advocated by *Lehi*, nor even the latter's 'readiness' to accommodate the progressive Arab peoples in its proposed plan for the 'neutralisation' of the Middle East. Instead of imitating such far-reaching projects based on a truly international perspective, the IZL proposed what Jabotinksy had called the 'repatriation' of Jews abroad to their homeland. The numbers required, it argued, would not be considerable. After all, it claimed, the existing demographic statistics were incorrect. Indeed, they had been deliberately falsified by the British.[21]

### *LEHI* AND UNSCOP, STAGE 2: DISAPPOINTMENT

In the final pages of its memorandum to UNSCOP, *Lehi* had adopted a tone of cautious optimism. The movement still suspected that British delaying tactics would prevent the UN from voting in favour of Hebrew independence: in which case, it warned, the Hebrew people would exercise their own veto. Nevertheless, it considered the intervention of the world organisation constituted an 'important stage' in its struggle, especially in view of the appointment of 'non-partisan' (namely, Czech and Yugoslavian) representatives to UNSCOP itself. In support of that contention, *Lehi*'s 'centre' was even prepared to adopt a somewhat lower military profile between 28 June and 18 July 1947, while UNSCOP was in session. Replying to their internal critics, the leaders of the movement later claimed that there had been no reason to jeopardise UNSCOP's activities by demonstrations of force. After all, UNSCOP was already aware of the underground's existence and strength.[22]

That tone soon changed. Indeed, *Lehi* had begun to criticise UNSCOP while its hearings were still in progress. The commissioners, it maintained, had bowed to British pressure even before commencing their work and thus connived in a plot to conceal the necessity for British withdrawal. Only that could explain UNSCOP's failure to demand that the Mandatory Power cease 'hostile activities' against the *Yishuv*; its refusal to inspect the 'concentration camps' on Cyprus and to take evidence from the underground movements; its failure to demand the unconditional reversal of the death sentence passed on three IZL members in June 1947; and its silence in the face of the 'scandal' of Major Farran's murder of a *Lehi* member, Alexander Rubowitz. The committee had squandered the 'moral credit' which the UN had extended to it. In part, this was due to the suspected 'Anglo-Saxon' leanings of its chairman (who, having once served as a judge in Egypt, was feared to be in the employ of the British CID); more generally, it was because its other members had also failed to preserve their impartiality in the face of the Cold War.[23]

Besides, it appears that from *Lehi*'s point of view the most important development of the summer of 1947 was not the appointment of UNSCOP but the consequences of Gromyko's announcement the previous May. That indeed was a true 'turning-point'. It would open a new chapter for the 'millions of Jews living in the sphere of Soviet influence and, within a few years, for the Jews of Russia itself'. More generally, it would also encourage 'other peoples and many other movements in the world to take a stand favourable to us'. As a result of Gromyko's announcement, the Hebrew people had ceased to be thrown at the mercies of the Anglo-Saxons and deprived of all political choice. This was a breakthrough of historic significance, and a hurdle which – once surmounted – would open up various other possibilities.

Judged by those standards, the resolutions to be adopted at the UN were largely irrelevant. Unlike the Jewish Agency, *Lehi* refused to consider the UN 'a high court'. The decisions of that body (even UNSCOP's majority report in favour of partition) would only result in a 'compromise', and thus give birth to a truncated Hebrew state which would in fact become an Anglo-Saxon base. The state itself would wipe out the 'dissidents'; thereafter, its official leadership would itself perish in the expected world war. Hence, it was at that stage that the 'Hebrew Liberation Movement' had to act not merely as an underground, but as a legal party which would work towards the attainment of domestic power. Otherwise, the Hebrew state would become nothing more than a kind of 'Palestine Dominion' in alliance with the Anglo-Saxon powers. India provided just such a model, since the Congress Party of that country was unwilling to separate from Britain. *Lehi*'s ideal, in that particular case, was the anti-British forces, such as were represented by Subhas Chandra Bose's Indian National Army and Jaya Prakash Narayan, whom it hoped would gain power in India. As far as *Lehi* was concerned, the fact that they had collaborated with Japan and Germany during the Second World War was only to their credit.[24]

Meanwhile, *Lehi* still had much work to do. Specifically, it had to intensify its efforts to attain a more 'maximalist' Soviet pronouncement which would grant the future Hebrew state its historic borders. It was in pursuit of this aim that *Lehi* intensified its pro-Soviet campaign, most particularly by taking Russia's side in the Cold War. The Marshall Plan, *Lehi* maintained, was no more than a capitalist tool, designed to increase the markets (and hence the profits) of such magnates as Rockefeller and Ford. Indeed, because it was aimed at all European countries, including those within the Soviet sphere, the Marshall Plan was even worse than the Truman Doctrine. It would be used to unify Germany and thus to create a new international danger; it would also so divide east from west that it would destroy the UN. Gone, then, were the days when *Lehi* had been prepared to accept American economic penetration of *Eretz Israel* and the Middle East. Instead, *Lehi* now emphasised the fact that the American economy (like the British) was one of free enterprise which promoted economic exploitation.[25] This did not imply that *Lehi* had become a Soviet tool (on the contrary, it promised, the Hebrew underground would fight against all foreign bases), but it did intensify its orientation towards communism and the crystallisation of its brand of leftist chauvinism. Therein lay the significance of its praise for the PKP, the only local party (apart from *Lehi* itself) to have condemned outright before UNSCOP the 'crime' of British rule in *Eretz Israel*.


RENEWED CRISES IN RELATIONS BETWEEN *LEHI* AND THE IZL

Their joint struggle against the British necessarily generated an affinity between *Lehi* and the IZL. Both were sceptical of the results to be expected from UNSCOP. Most likely, the IZL prophesied, the commissioners would be able to free themselves of their competing Cold War allegiances and therefore they would advocate a solution along the lines suggested by the Morrison–Grady Plan or by Bevin's 'cantonisation' plan. Similarly, both sides opposed the policies of the Jewish Agency, with the IZL (very much like *Lehi*) pouring scorn on Shertok's assessment that Jews and Arabs would not be able to co-operate within the framework of an independent state. Such announcements, it claimed, merely legitimised Britain's contention that the extension of its rule was necessary to prevent civil war.[26] Operational circumstances brought the two sides even closer together, particularly after the execution of four IZL members and the suicides of Feinstein and Barazani in April 1947.

Nevertheless, these events could not conceal their ideological and political differences. For one thing, the IZL did not support *Lehi*'s plan for the pro-Soviet 'neutralisation' of the Middle East. If anything, it was inclined to hope for eventual American support. Neither did it share *Lehi*'s belief that Jews and non-Jews in the Middle East were partners in the struggle against imperialism. Even Gromyko's announcement, although admitted to be 'a most valuable develop-ment', did not arouse the 'sentimental' enthusiasm which it was accorded in *Lehi* circles. What mattered, the IZL maintained, was the content of that message – which left much to be desired. Consequently, it would be a mistake to place blind faith in the support of Soviet Russia.[27] On domestic issues, too, the two sides differed. Encouraged by the fact that most of the candidates to the twenty-second Zionist congress had favoured 'activist' slogans, the IZL also adopted a more ambitious programme. Unlike *Lehi*, it demanded the establishment of a 'democratic' Hebrew government, projecting itself as the potential national leadership.[28]

The sense of isolation thus generated in *Lehi* was compounded by the more spectacular successes of the IZL. In the sphere of military operations, the most striking was the IZL break-in to the Acre prison on 4 May 1947.[29] On the diplomatic front, it was their meeting with the chairman of UNSCOP and his aides, to whom Begin expounded the classic Jabotinsky thesis that *Eretz Israel* was large enough to accom-

modate both Arabs and Jews, and that the permanent government of
the new state would include Arab ministers.[30] Although the *Lehi*
'centre' did call upon its members to curb their 'envy' of such developments, as well as their jealousy of the IZL's greater numbers and
larger budget, competition between the two movements could hardly
be avoided. Indeed, their relations reached a new low in July 1947,
when the IZL was particularly anxious to attain UNSCOP's intervention on behalf of three of its members who had been condemned to
death. After a special meeting, *Lehi* agreed to the temporary cessation
of its own activities; but this promise was not kept. In retaliation for
the murder of Alexander Rubowitz, *Lehi* itself attempted to capture
British hostages. On 28 June 1947, it announced its intention of
providing armed protection for those of its members who were sticking
up posters in Tel Aviv, an action which (according to Begin) possibly
caused the unexpected intervention of an armed British escort and
thus foiled the IZL's attempt to capture British officers who could
have been exchanged for its three condemned men. Whatever the
truth of the charges, the IZL's conclusion was unequivocal:

> The incident is a very sad one and proves the utter impracticality of
> any 'arrangement' with the 'faction' [that is, *Lehi*] . . . the only
> conclusion which can be drawn from this shameful episode is that
> total separation is preferable to the mirage of 'arrangements' which
> are trodden underfoot by the 'faction' every time they are put to
> the test.[31]

As is so often the case in such matters, those charges were met in
kind. Thus, *Lehi* did not merely attempt to explain and thereby justify
its actions in the particular case, it also indulged in wider invective,
accusing the IZL of 'provocation' and also recalling the latter's co-
operation with the British enemy in 1940–42. In that atmosphere, the
chances of a successful renewal of unity talks between the two sides
were very slim indeed, particularly in view of Shamir's imprisonment.
His absence left Friedman-Yellin in a strong position within *Lehi*.
Unlike Eldad, Friedman-Yellin had already decided upon a 'leftist'
orientation and on the 'abandonment' of the 'pure' nationalist line
contained in 'The Principles of Revival'. Against Eldad's opposition,
he was therefore able to carry the day and reject any offer of union
with the IZL.[32]

## LEHI AND THE 'OFFICIAL' ZIONIST LEADERSHIP AFTER UNSCOP

*Lehi* considered itself to be somewhat closer to the *Haganah* than was
the IZL. In part, it believed, this was because of the residual sympathy

which it still enjoyed among the *Haganah* rank and file; in part, because the latter feared *Lehi*'s retaliation to any hostile action; in part (and more pragmatically) because the IZL probably had higher priority on the *Haganah*'s list of targets.[33] Such circumstances induced *Lehi* to adopt an attitude of restraint *vis-à-vis* the *Haganah*. Nevertheless, because it considered its differences with the Jewish Agency to be greater than those with the IZL, it was the former which became the principal target of its own invective. The Agency, *Lehi* maintained, had adopted an altogether incorrect policy with regard to UNSCOP. Instead of emphasising the extent to which *Eretz Israel*, on both sides of the Jordan, had become a 'massive' military base, the Agency had wasted its efforts on arguments with the Arabs and on castigating the White Paper. In *Lehi*'s eyes, the report which UNSCOP published on 1 September 1947 merely underlined the Agency's failure and the bankruptcy of Ben-Gurion's strategy of 'mutual interests' with Britain. Although UNSCOP had advocated the end of the British Mandate, its partition proposal was unacceptable. First, a confined Hebrew state would not be able to meet the demographic and economic requirements of the masses of Jews waiting to enter it. Second, it would in any case fall prey to British designs. Entirely out of touch with the inner circle of Jewish Agency decision-makers (who by this stage were already giving priority to the forthcoming conflict against the Arabs), *Lehi* continued to be tied to the principles which it had cultivated during seven long years of struggle: Britain was the only enemy; a Hebrew state had to be established within the nation's historic borders; the Arabs could be manipulated to the benefit of the Zionists. If the 'official' Zionist leadership thought otherwise, then the reason lay in the fact that 'elderly leaders and technocrats had been overcome by weariness'.[34]

If any single event brought the debate between *Lehi* and the Jewish Agency to a head it was that of the *Exodus*, most of whose 'illegal' passengers were deported to Cyprus just two days after their arrival at Haifa on 18 July 1947. Notwithstanding its admiration for the 'illegals' themselves, *Lehi* refused to consider the *Exodus* as anything other than a symbol. Of itself, it maintained, the struggle for immigration was only marginally more effective against British rule than were the speeches delivered by Ben-Gurion and Shertok, and even the strikes and protest demonstrations organised by the Agency. Consequently, *Lehi* launched into an unrestrained and unprecedented attack on the latter's entire immigration policy. Unlike the British authorities (who by this time did consider the influx of 'illegal immigrants' to be as influential as terrorist activities),[35] *Lehi* could not see how the arrival of an occasional ship could generate a fundamental change in the situation. If anything, the concentration on immigration merely diverted attention from other and more constructive activities. It also deluded the *Yishuv* into believing – absolutely incorrectly – in the 'activism' of its official leadership. In actual fact, the latter were no more than 'cowards and faint-hearts'.[36]

The depths of *Lehi*'s opposition to the Jewish Agency and its policies is illustrated by two further aspects of its propaganda at this time. First, it again found itself in alignment with the IZL, supporting the latter during the period of the 'minor season' which followed the hanging of three British sergeants in July 1947, and issuing 'final warnings' to those members of the Agency whom it termed 'the tools of Bevin and Cunningham'.[37] Second, it made blatant use of an analogy culled from the recent Jewish past. Specifically, *Lehi* categorised the Agency as a *Judenrat*, whose treasonable methods were comparable to those adopted by the Nazi-appointed masters of the Vilna ghetto who had betrayed their co-religionists in the name of 'responsibility'.[38] Possibly, this startling comparison might be attributed to *Lehi*'s fears that the *Haganah* was indeed planning a St. Bartholomew's Day Massacre against the 'dissidents' (although, even so, it must be pointed out that *Lehi*'s use of the *Judenrat* motif was far more explicit than that of the IZL).[39] Alternatively, or perhaps in addition, *Lehi* appreciated the deficiencies in its analogy, but could see no other way of legitimising its own position.

Whichever was the case, *Lehi*'s attacks on the Agency were unrestrained. It poured scorn on the *Haganah* actions against the radar station on Mount Carmel on 19 July 1947 and a deportation ship in Haifa four days later.[40] It even went as far as to ascribe the Agency's opposition to the 'dissidents' to 'economic egoism'. Leftists as well as capitalists, it claimed, were primarily interested in maintaining their own standards of living. *Lehi* advocated an entirely different – indeed National Bolshevik – approach. 'The Hebrew people is in a state of war . . . and if our war demands a regime of *military and political Communism*, if it means hunger – then we shall accept it.' (My emphasis.) Moreover, *Lehi* would not even desist from civil war, promising that all traitors and informers would meet the fate meted out to the Vichy collaborators.[41]

### BETWEEN THE CHALLENGE OF SOCIALISM AND THE COMPLEX OF FASCISM

As we have seen, *Lehi*'s foreign policy leaned increasingly towards the Soviet Union and left-wing movements of national liberation. But that orientation was still absent from its internal policy. As long as

*Ha-Shomer Ha-Tsair*, the Palestine Communist Party (PKP), or the latter's off-shoot, the Union for Communist Education (later the Hebrew Communist Party), did not join the war against the British, *Lehi* found itself unable to adopt their left-wing social and economic ideology. This lack of symmetry apparently disturbed the left-wing faction in the movement and generated an internal debate on the issue.

The principal spokesmen for the 'conservative' wing, which advocated a leftward orientation in foreign policy alone, was Eldad. In principle, he argued, there was no need for *Lehi* to take a definitive stand on the nature of the future regime to be established in a Hebrew state. 'The Hebrew people', he claimed, 'will be free to establish the regime appropriate to its wishes and needs.' Hence, matters could change. *Lehi*, after all, was 'a dynamic movement, not a party' and still in the process of change. 'We grew out of instinct, and then through the wisdom which confirmed it.' Moreover, 'We are attaining self-knowledge, we are divesting ourselves of all that is foreign and superfluous.'

With that premise at hand, Eldad went on to be still more flexible. In consideration of the 'conservative' wing within *Lehi*, he was insistent that the movement would remain faithful to Yair's original teachings. But those, he pointed out, had really only been concerned with the question of the freedom of the homeland from foreign rule, to be attained by gaining the support of political allies. They did not mean that *Lehi* could not 'divest' itself of the blind anti-socialism inculcated by Achimeir and Uri Zvi Greenberg. Fundamentally, he pointed out, socialism and nationalism were not incompatible. Nor, indeed, were socialism and Judaism (indeed, he exclaimed, any such contention was 'Absurd! Judaism is not tied to any particular social and economic system').[42]

Marxism, Eldad admitted, was a different matter since its conflict with Judaism was basic. But even in that case some balance was required. Jabotinsky's equation of socialism and Marxism was too simple. Besides, Marxism's benefits could not be denied. For all its faults, it had 'laid bare the exploitative character of capitalism, whereby the few reap profits from the labour of the masses'. Thanks to Marxism, moreover, 'the twentieth century had become that of the workers and the peasants, like it or not'. The fact that the working class was not at present in the vanguard of the struggle for Hebrew national liberation was unfortunate. All it indicated was that 'we do not yet possess a true proletariat, and the workers in the *kibbutzim* and towns are by nature intelligentsia and petit-bourgeois'. But that could also change. Should the workers and peasants indeed manage to break down 'the ghetto', then they would be in a position 'to determine the nature of the regime'. Explicit anti-socialism, therefore, was out of the question, 'Because there is no doubt that in one way or another the world is marching towards Socialism: that is, towards the equitable distribution of property and profits'.

To say this was not to advocate that *Lehi* declared itself socialist. However much the movement might have been groping towards its later version of National Bolshevism, the steps were still tentative. Eldad admitted that he was not himself a socialist, principally because, in his view, the issues it raised were not the most pressing of the moment; they were subsidiary, he claimed, to the Hebrew struggle for national liberation. Neither, he contended, was *Lehi* as a whole socialist.

> Neither in our publication ['Fundamentals of Hebrew Foreign Policy'] nor in any of our conversations with various people, even those from the Communist sector of the world, have we ever projected ourselves as Socialists. We would not do so because we are sincere to our basic principles. We are fighting for the freedom of the Hebrew people in its homeland, and that problem pushes all others aside.

Russia itself did not demand a pro-socialist declaration as the price for its support. *Lehi*'s proposal to 'neutralise' the Middle East coincided with the interests of the Soviet Union; it was not dictated by them. Therein lay the 'fundamental difference' between *Lehi* and the communists, who formulated their every move in accordance with their perception of what was good for Russia rather than what was good for the Hebrew nation.[43]

While the question of socialism was a matter of internal *Lehi* concern, and was treated as such, the charge that the movement was fascist necessitated a public reply. Always favoured by *Ha-Shomer Ha-Tsair*, that accusation had become especially pronounced towards the end of the period of the 'United Hebrew Resistance Movement'. It was then recalled that 'the dissidents' (in this respect, no distinction being made between the IZL and *Lehi*) had begun to emerge at precisely the period when world-wide fascism had been at its peak.[44] *Lehi*'s 'social phraseology' reminded *Ha-Shomer Ha-Tsair* of Gregor Strasser's Social Opposition within the Nazi party. The Soviet Union would not support a *Lehi* which ignored the Arab right to national socialism.

In some respects, *Lehi* was flattered by the accusation, which it regarded as a sign of the extent to which it presented a challenge to *Ha-Shomer Ha-Tsair*. Nevertheless, of course, it completely denied the charge, which it considered to be nothing but a salve to *Ha-Shomer*

*Ha-Tsair*'s own 'polluted conscience'. How, otherwise, could the latter have explained the fact that its own 'constructive activity' was being undertaken at the price of 'an agreement with British imperialism and its military bases'? Probably because it was itself hoping for the support of left-wing elements in the *Yishuv*, *Lehi* was prepared to accept the Marxist definition of fascism as: 'All forms of regime . . . which do not serve the interests of the masses – and especially of the working and peasant classes.' But that description did not apply to *Lehi* itself. Not one magnate supported the movement, most of whose members were workers and affiliated with the *Histadrut*. Truth to tell, the boot was on the other foot. It was *Lehi* that was doing the most to help Russia by fighting against the British Mandate. Conversely, Weizmann (*Ha-Shomer Ha-Tsair*'s hero) and the *Histadrut* were indebted to foreign capital. Finally, there was something particularly incongruous in *Ha-Shomer Ha-Tsair*'s opposition to *Lehi*'s use of force and terror. When had true Leninists ever objected to such methods?[45]

Eldad was fully aware that the real reason that *Lehi* was labelled 'fascist' was because of its Revisionist origins. In response to that challenge he set out to defend Jabotinsky and his movement. Far from being a fascist, Eldad claimed, Jabotinsky had been a 'faithful servant' of liberalism and a sworn opponent of totalitarianism. Revisionism was not fascist, but the movement of the Hebrew middle class, and in that respect akin to Mazzini's movement for Italian liberation. The greatest mistake of Jabotinsky's life – his belief in Britain and the possibility of their common interests – had stemmed from his love of democracy. If he had failed it was because of the unholy alliance which had been forged against him by Zionist social democracy and British imperialism. That, however, could now be defeated by an alternative combination of the ideas of Borochov and Nordau, supplemented by Russian assistance. In thus rebuffing the charge of fascism, Eldad moved even closer to National Bolshevism. Indeed, he claimed that his somewhat fanciful scenario was already on the verge of realisation. For one thing, 'the *Ahdut Ha-Avodah* movement' was beginning to move in the direction of a national liberation movement led by workers; for another, the communist movement was beginning (albeit slowly and incompletely) to free itself from its hatred of Zion.[46]

Under what circumstances, then, could fascism exist in *Eretz Israel*? The answer, according to Eldad, was if the country were to be divided into two states. That situation would generate a 'red revolution', nurtured on the national despondency and economic hardship which a state based on the Morrison–Grady Plan would bring about. The reaction would be a counter-revolution enhanced by military assistance.

Thus, a partitioned state would result in a threefold slaughter: civil war; conflict between the two divided states; and world war.

It was not *Lehi* that was laying the groundwork for that eventuality, but (as had been the case in pre-war Europe), the social democrats. *Lehi* was spearheading the struggle against the only form of fascism which at that time existed in *Eretz Israel* – that cultivated by British imperialists, including such leftists as Richard Crossman, who (in classic Leninist fashion) were themselves promoting 'a higher form of capitalism'. Instead of combating that evil, the Hebrew workers' movement (so-called) was fighting the 'dissidents'. 'Wasn't that precisely how the Social-Democrats had behaved in Germany? Didn't the Vichyists do exactly the same when attacking the "Reds" and partisans?'[47] It was in the absence of a direct response to those questions that *Lehi* embarked on its own course of unity. Specifically, it entered into negotiation with both the Cominform and the Palestine Communist Party (PKP).

### THE FAILURE OF CONTACTS WITH THE PKP AND THE COMINFORM

In retrospect, an aura of inevitability pervades *Lehi*'s earliest attempts to establish contacts with the PKP and the Cominform. In part, those efforts were the consequence of the movement's confidence in both Soviet Russia's victory in the world struggle and its support for the Hebrew liberation movement. In part, they were also the result of *Lehi*'s increasing tendency towards a left-wing orientation in domestic affairs. Both developments, as we have seen, increased in tempo after the Gromyko announcement of May 1947, causing *Lehi* to yoke together extreme nationalism and support for the eastern bloc: two positions which had hitherto been regarded as absolutely contradictory.

The initial talks were held between Eldad and Avraham Selman (representing *Lehi*), and David Levinger, secretary of the communist party in Pilsen, Czechoslovakia (who represented the Cominform), and Meir Wilner and Aliosha Gozhansky (of the PKP).[48] Eldad took the opportunity to ask that the Cominform permit *Lehi* to organise Jewish youth in communist countries for the fight against British imperialism in *Eretz Israel* and against French imperialism in Syria and Lebanon. He also reviewed and summarised *Lehi*'s policies, explaining both its desire for the 'neutralisation' of the Middle East and opposition to foreign bases. To judge by the only available record of the conversation, not everything Eldad said could have pleased his audience. He did not hide *Lehi*'s denial of Arab national rights in *Eretz Israel*; neither did he conceal the contradictions in its economic programme (a seemingly impossible combination of both nationalisation and private enterprise). Equally unpalatable must have been his repetition of the *Lehi* slogan that political freedom must precede social freedom.

What Eldad hoped would be more attractive were *Lehi*'s foreign policies. There existed, he claimed, 'a complete identity of interests' not only between the Hebrew people and 'the Arab people', but also with those 'of the Soviet Union, the east European democracies and every people, person or party fighting for freedom and progress'. Thus, he painted a picture of a 'combined anti-Imperialist front, consisting of progressive forces amongst the local and world-wide Hebrew people, amongst the non-Jewish inhabitants of the country, amongst the peoples of the Near East and – in general – the progress and freedom-loving powers and peoples'. He admitted that there were some snags. The effectiveness of that front would depend on the support ('moral, political and other') which it would receive from the USSR and the east European bloc. It might also be opposed by the United States. Nevertheless, it was precisely with regard to the dangers posed by the latter power that *Lehi* could play a role. By so undermining British strategic plans in *Eretz Israel*, the movement would be able to convince the United States that it had itself best be cautious.[49]

In immediately practical terms, these approaches were unsuccessful. However much the two sides may have sought common ground for tactical co-operation, the ideological chasm between the PKP and *Lehi* was too deep to be bridged. Nevertheless, the contacts were not altogether without result; they stimulated a public confrontation which helped to refine and define *Lehi*'s own position.

The opening shot in that particular confrontation was fired soon after the talks (and perhaps for the purpose of denying their existence) by Esther Wilenska, one of the dominant figures in the PKP. After Gromyko's announcement, and in order to deny *Lehi* any credit for it, she wrote a stinging attack on the movement. Not unexpectedly, she called up some uncomfortable ghosts from *Lehi*'s cupboard – most prominently, the 'IZL in Israel' which had expressed opposition in principle to the war against Hitler and Mussolini. She also recalled Eldad's more recent praise of the Italian dictator. *Lehi*, she went on, was a fundamentally Revisionist movement. It still worshipped Jabotinsky; laid claim to Jewish dominion over both banks of the Jordan; and ignored the national rights of the Palestinian Arabs. The latter, she wrote, would never accept *Lehi*'s offer of 'cultural autonomy' or transfer, an offer which unmasked the *herrenvolk* nature of its programme. Equally castigated was *Lehi*'s proclaimed 'neutrality' and 'even-handedness' in social affairs. Like *Ha-Shomer Ha-Tsair*, Wilenska did not trust the sincerity of *Lehi*'s sympathy for the worker.

Nor did she fail to attack the movement for its readiness to agree to the intrusion of American capital into the Middle East. Does *Lehi* know nothing, she asked, of the links between 'economic and political dependency', or about the extent to which the peoples of the area were becoming enslaved by the American dollar, or about Anglo-American co-operation for the purposes of both economic exploitation and political subjection?[50]

*Lehi*'s response, again composed by Eldad,[51] was measured. It began by praising the communist organ, *Kol Ha'am*. Unlike *Mishmar* and *Davar*, it had 'consistently' called upon the worker to resist the temptation to shift his attention from the struggle against imperialism to the conflict with the Arabs or other Jews. The remainder of the reply, however, was less flattering. The charge that 'IZL in Israel' had sabotaged the war against the Axis powers, Eldad asserted, was misdirected. It could be levelled against the Soviets (the Molotov–Ribbentrop pact), as well as numerous leaders of the liberation struggle in the Far East. Wilenska's attack on *Lehi*'s Arab policies, he claimed, was similarly uncalled-for. For one thing, the Arab inhabitants of *Eretz Israel* (which is how *Lehi* preferred to define them) were part of the greater Arab nation; for another, 'transfer' had in fact been proposed as a secondary option, to be implemented only if the Arabs themselves so desired.[52] Besides, was not the Soviet Union itself in favour of that policy, encouraging population transfers in Poland and possibly elsewhere?

The remainder of Wilenska's charges were dealt with even more forcefully. *Lehi*, Eldad insisted, was not 'neutral' as regards the working class. Most of its members were themselves workers, and if *Lehi* did not concern itself with the day-to-day state of relations beween employer and employed it was because it was following guidelines laid down by Lenin and most recently reiterated by the leader of the Syrian communists. The latter had taught that 'in enslaved countries it is necessary to establish an alliance amongst all the classes against British rule, which prevents the development of the country'. *Lehi* (to take another analogy) was following the precedent of the French *maquis*. It constituted a fighting underground movement and not a trade union. In its war against British rule, the bourgeoisie, the workers and the Arabs were all its 'allies'.

Finally, there were Wilenska's strictures on *Lehi*'s foreign policy orientations. Eldad admitted that he was not opposed to American capital investment. However, he most vehemently denied that *Lehi* therefore favoured American imperialism. The one had nothing to do with the other (as was shown by the fact that the Bulgarians favoured American investments and the Hungarians had been prepared to sign economic agreements with England).[53] Neither was *Lehi*'s support of the Soviet Union merely a response to public pressure. The movement had in fact supported that orientation at an early stage; moreover, it had done so on the basis of a 'scientific' study of Hebrew interests. Therein lay its difference with the PKP which, therefore, could not be considered a potential partner for *Lehi* in the future Hebrew state. Far better, from that point of view, was the Union for Communist Education (after October 1947 known as the Hebrew Communist Party), which had split from the PKP in 1945. Admittedly, the latter proposed a programme at variance with *Lehi*'s, advocating the establishment of two states which would combine in a federal arrangement. But at least its members 'had begun to think their Hebrew communism independently . . . and on the basis of a consideration of national interests'.[54]

In the summer of 1947 *Lehi* had reached its climax from all possible points of view: ideological, political and military. Its war against the British (during the course of which it had launched 112 terrorist actions between 26 October 1946 and 14 September 1947) was about to come to an end. But its primary suppositions and policies made no such promise, even though an Arab–Jewish war was on the point of eruption. *Lehi* had been quick to overcome the surprise of 29 November 1947 and its repercussions. Nevertheless, its decline was about to begin.

PART FIVE

# *LEHI* IN DECLINE, 1947–49

# 9

# Towards Jewish–Arab War

The first signs of impending Jewish–Arab war became apparent on 10 August 1947, when four Jews were murdered and seven injured at the Gan Hawai restaurant in Tel Aviv. That incident was followed by clashes beween Jews and Arabs on the borders of Tel Aviv and Jaffa and by reprisals on the part of the *Haganah*, during the course of which an Arab mother and her seven children were killed in the orchards of Abu-Laban (Pardes Katz). *Lehi*'s Arab policy, as formulated by Friedman-Yellin, was now put to the test. Its reaction was to call on the public to avoid war. Responsibility for the clashes, it maintained, lay with the 'imperialist meddlers' of Britain, who had incited the Arab actions and who needed a Jewish–Arab war in order demonstrate that the continued presence of the British army was necessary to preserve law and order. *Lehi* itself advocated an alternative relationship: 'The guilty will be punished but the innocent will not be harmed.'[1]

The essential distinction between the British and the Arabs, Friedman-Yellin maintained, was that whereas the former were truly enemies, the latter were only 'rivals'. It was the Englishman Houston Stewart Chamberlain, *Lehi* was to note, who had inspired the ideology of racial hatred which had found expression in Nazi Germany; indeed, English history was replete with examples of quotidian anti-Semitism and it was clear that – whatever the United Nations might decide – the British would not leave *Eretz Israel* 'until we force them to do so'.[2] However, 'Our Arab neighbour is not our enemy; he is not a stranger in this land. He dwells amongst us and will continue to do so after the last British soldier has left this land.' It followed that a 'military' resolution of Arab–Jewish relationships, as advocated by the *Haganah* was inappropriate. Instead, 'political solutions' had to be found. Although Arab–Jewish rivalries were admitted to exist, *Lehi* believed that they could – and would – be resolved in a political fashion 'through understanding reached by a perception of common interests'. This did not imply that *Lehi* was prepared to retract its statement to UNSCOP that 'there is no Palestinian nation'. Neither did it provide a blue-print for the manner in which a future solution would ultimately be attained. Nevertheless, the principle was clear. 'Every Arab [here] is a resident . . . There is no race war between us. We recognise the right of the

Arab to live here and are not entitled to take away his life.' The *sulhah* (peace) reached after the riots in Tel Aviv and Jaffa proved that mutual understanding was possible.[3] The *Yishuv* had to avoid falling into the sort of 'trap' which had enabled the British to divide and thereby rule India and had generated the horrors of civil war between Muslims and Hindus. The solution preferred by *Lehi* was demonstrated by the resolution of the Serbo-Croat or Ukrainian–Polish conflicts.[4] Instead of initiating a series of reprisals which would only inflame feelings and lead the country into a spiral of hostility, *Lehi* advocated a more controlled response to Arab attacks. It did justify the *Haganah* action at Abu-Laban, but warned that the main aim must always be kept in view.[5]

Thus seen, the present situation even held out the prospect of wider co-operation with the Arab states themselves. After all, did not the latter also thirst for freedom from the thrall of British imperialism? Even Egyptian nationalism could thus be praised. Following the line already set down in its plan for the neutralisation of the Middle East, *Lehi* called for a 'combined political action' which might realise the common interests of Jew and Arab in 'independence and development'. It also castigated Ben-Gurion and Weizmann, who had followed British dictates when restricting their contacts with the Arab states to the 'poisoned' channels provided by the Colonial Office. Instead of showing sensitivity to the current situation, it charged, Ben-Gurion was diverting the attention of the Zionist Greater Actions Committee at Zurich to attacks on the 'dissidents'.[6]

However much *Lehi* might scorn those attacks, it could not ignore them. Indeed its own isolation, compounded by its absolute rejection of the UNSCOP report, was now painfully apparent. Comprising no more than 300 members, the movement was seriously deficient in operational and propaganda resources. Thus weakened, it fell back on two avenues. One was increasing alignment with the IZL which – despite its ideological differences with *Lehi* – did at least share the latter's belief in the need for a total fight against Britain and a campaign against her transparent design to retain control over a divided Palestine. Indeed, the common demands for the release of the underground internees in Africa and for the immediate immigration of the Jewish DPs in Cyprus and Europe provided a practical programme for co-operation between the two movements.[7] *Lehi*'s second response to its isolation was to strengthen its pro-Soviet orientation. Deliberately, albeit cautiously, *Lehi* now appealed to the USSR to exercise its power of veto in the UN against the 'puppet' state which Ben-Gurion was about to establish and which the majority Anglo-Saxon bloc at the UN was to foist upon the Hebrew people. Indeed, so obsessive was

*Lehi*'s drive to gain Russian support that it now retracted its readiness to receive American economic assistance, accusing Marshall, the US Secretary of State, of attempting to 'purchase countries with budgets'.[8]

On 26 September 1947, Creech-Jones, the British Colonial Secretary, announced that – in the absence of an agreement to implement the UNSCOP report – Britain would withdraw its army and administration from Palestine. *Lehi* regarded that announcement as a tactical move, designed only to frighten the Jews, incite the Arabs and squeeze further funds out of the USA. Nevertheless – and notwithstanding its own promises to hound the British out of the country – *Lehi* did agree to the Jewish Agency's request that it call a temporary halt to its own activities. On 2 October, *Lehi* published its decision to 'refrain from warlike activities' until the end of the current UN session when, it presumed, the British lie would be exposed.[9] But, despite this move (the third occasion on which it had agreed to a halt in its anti-British activities), *Lehi* assured its members that its basic ideology had not changed.[10] Neither were its fundamental beliefs affected by the growing signs that the Arabs were themselves preparing for a war against the Jews. *Lehi* continued to believe that the announcements issued by the Arab League gatherings at Sofar and Alei in September and October 1947 were inspired by the British. They did not represent the true feelings of the Arab masses who, *Lehi* warned, if they listened to their 'leaders', would only find themselves doubly enslaved by imperialism.[11] *Lehi*'s greatest regret was that 'there exist no Arab "dissidents" who might turn their backs on Abdullah, the British slave, and the Mufti, who has sold out to the American dollar . . . There is no doubt that we could have forged [bonds of] common freedom with Arab freedom fighters, whatever tomorrow's fate between us.'

In the absence of such a development, however, *Lehi* found itself fighting a war on four fronts: against the British ('from the minister in Downing Street to the policeman on Allenby Street in Tel Aviv'); against the Arab leadership (although not, it stressed, the Arab masses); against the 'official' Zionist leadership (although, again, not the wider Jewish public); and – most recently – against American imperialists. *Lehi* was to continue to wage all these wars until the very end. As a movement of principles, it could not admit that changing historical circumstances had flown in the face of its ideology. Even when, in November 1947, *Lehi* felt it imperative to initiate a reprisal action (against a group of Arabs who had 'informed' on one of its units near Ra'anana and caused the death of its members at British hands), its basic position did not shift. 'We call upon our Arab brothers to drive out from their midst all the hired traitors who seek to generate hatred between us and yourselves and thereby provide the British with a pretext for remaining in our land as guardians of the peace.'[12]

### THE RESPONSE TO THE ANNOUNCEMENTS BY JOHNSON AND TZARAPKIN (10 AND 12 OCTOBER 1947)

During the second week of October 1947, both the American and Soviet representatives at the UN announced their governments' support of the partition proposal. *Lehi* accorded the two statements entirely different receptions. The American announcement was a 'betrayal'. Gained at 'great cost', it in fact constituted a regression from America's earlier support for the Balfour Declaration and the Biltmore Programme, and was the result of nothing more than Jewish electoral pressure and domestic squabbles between Truman and Marshall. The Russian announcement was entirely different. It expressed 'a feeling of justice, a recognition of a particular reality, or of a far-sighted and rational calculation of her interests in the Middle East'. Whatever the case, Russia had not betrayed the Hebrew people. On the contrary, 'the USSR wrought a fundamental change in her attitude towards the link between the Hebrew people and the Hebrew home-land'. *Lehi* was convinced that 'the masses of the Hebrew people had instinctively welcomed with enthusiasm the Soviet announcement – despite its acceptance of "partition"'. It was only the Jewish Agency which continued 'to walk in step with the British and Americans on the march towards retreat and betrayal'.[13] Ben-Gurion, of course, was the worst offender. He, 'the buffoon', was only interested in becoming 'the prime minister of a Morrison–Grady state'. *Lehi* predicted that he would run its politics on the lines adopted by Tsaldaris, the Greek dictator, 'and would establish draconian laws and hang rebels'. But other parties too (the list included the *Ahdut Ha-Avodah* movement, *Ha-Shomer Ha-Tsair* and even the PKP) had fallen prey to the mirage of partition. In fact, only the IZL had not.[14]

This line hardened immediately before and after the crucial UN vote of 29 November. *Lehi* continued to doubt the possibility of true American–Soviet co-operation on the Palestine question and to stress the differences which it thought to exist in the policies of the two powers.[15] It also announced its own support for the Soviet bloc ('a world which strives for peace and construction') rather than the West ('a world of exploitation and aggression'). Such support, how-ever, was not the result of sentiment, but of *realpolitik*. That, too (so *Lehi* maintained) was the basis of the Soviet attitude. Russia is interested in:

a real force . . . which can guarantee neutrality and peace, which can withstand the total conquest of the Anglo-Saxons . . . which can oppose Imperialism and be truly independent . . . That is why it wants to see the Hebrew state in possession of [a] maximum of territory and independence.[16]

Not the least of the faults of the Jewish Agency was that it failed to appreciate that situation. Concomitantly, therefore, *Lehi* adopted an increasingly bitter tone towards the Agency's representatives at the UN, whom it accused of 'selling the majority of the homeland at an open and public auction'. Shertok, in particular, was made a target of abuse. According to *Lehi* caricature, the welcome accorded him on his return from Lake Success was even more grotesque than that received by Chamberlain when he had returned to London from Munich in 1938.[17] At the same time, *Lehi*'s personal attacks on Ben-Gurion reached a new pitch. *Lehi* was especially incensed by Ben-Gurion's 'persecution' of 'the dissidents', mainly since (so it believed) its positions in fact accorded with Ben-Gurion's own best interests.

Does he really want his own partition plan to represent the extreme position of the Hebrew people? . . . Does not far-sighted political realism demand the invention of separatists, if they are not already in existence, rather than the destruction of those who do exist?

The real source of Ben-Gurion's attempt to destroy his adversaries lay in his megalomania. He must therefore be considered 'a sinner, a fool and also . . . a failure'. Otherwise, how was it possible to understand the fact that 'he stretches out a hand to Abdullah but not to the dissidents'?[18]

## *LEHI* AT THE BEGINNING OF WAR: THE PROBLEM AND ITS SOLUTION

On the day after the UN decision of 29 November, *Lehi*'s stand *vis-à-vis* the 'official' Jewish leadership underwent a change. For the first time, the movement announced its preparedness to 'acknowledge and accept the discipline of Hebrew independence . . . We did not recognise an Agency, we shall accept a government; we did not recognise a *Haganah*, we shall recognise an army.' This announcement was less unconditional than it at first appeared. In fact, *Lehi* promised to support a future government 'provided . . . it will be independent and free'. Nevertheless, it was a far-reaching declaration – and one which certainly exceeded the position simultaneously adopted by the IZL.[19]

One operational corollary of *Lehi*'s position was the disbandment of its independent 'fighting unit'. Indeed, in his capacity as head of *Lehi*'s 'centre', Friedman-Yellin gave precisely such an order (excluding only the Jerusalem front).[20] But this did not portend amity. The order caused a deep internal rift within the *Lehi* ranks which (Eldad relates) lasted for a month until the command to disband was ultimately rescinded.[21] Moreover, the 'centre' in any case strenuously resisted the *Haganah*'s call that it lay down its arms and join the common ranks. There still did not exist, *Lehi* pointed out, 'Hebrew rule, a Hebrew state or a Hebrew army'. On the pretext that the *Haganah* was in any case failing to respond to murderous British assaults, it therefore undertook a series of independent actions, beginning with the attack (on 6 December 1947) on the Jerusalem offices of the Husseini newspaper *Al Wahda*.[22]

At one level, such operations indicate *Lehi*'s growing realisation that some measure of armed conflict with the Arabs was inevitable.[23] Equally, however, they indicated its perception of its position within the *Yishuv*. *Haganah* intelligence feared that *Lehi* would become a 'fifth column', and obtain from the Soviets the arms which, in 1940, it had failed to acquire from the Italians. For its part, *Lehi* was still profoundly distrustful of the 'official' Jewish agencies and still committed to its own maximalist Revisionist ideology which discounted their right to positions of leadership. Fearful that the Jewish Agency was in fact planning its own version of the St. Bartholomew's Day Massacre, *Lehi* announced that it would not disband.[24] It also stepped up even further its personal attacks on Ben-Gurion, who was portrayed as the principal obstacle to the formation of a united Hebrew front.[25]

The news that *Mapai* might wish to conduct elections to an 'Assembly' as early as March (and hence before the final British withdrawal) was particularly castigated. Elections under the shadow of the British 'tommy guns', *Lehi* declared, stood no chance of being democratic. Indeed, they would only lead to the establishment of a local version of the *Judenrat* which had ruled over the Jews in the Vilna ghetto.[26] The true colours of the Agency, *Lehi* declared, were shown when it agreed to the diversion of the two *Pan* ships carrying 'illegal' immigrants to Cyprus. In Washington, Shertok was selling out on *aliyah* from Eastern Europe; and in London and Jerusalem, his colleagues were selling out on the entire state. 'He who shouted "Biltmore" and intended partition – has in the depths of his heart agreed to the Morrison plan cooked up in the British kitchen.'[27]

Its analysis and description of the 'official' leadership showed *Lehi* to be still tied to perceptions forged during the very different circumstances of 1946–47. It continued to believe that this leadership had followed an entirely misconceived policy with regard to Britain, whose impending withdrawal from Palestine (so *Lehi* maintained) owed nothing whatsoever to the Agency's own actions. It had been brought about solely by American and Russian pressures, which had themselves been triggered by the activities of the underground.[28] Similarly consistent was *Lehi*'s belief that Britain remained the primary enemy of the Jews and that the 'mini-state' which the Jews were about to establish would 'not withstand the test of the ideology of freedom fighters [nor] of the realisation of Zionism'.

Nevertheless, *Lehi* did appreciate that circumstances had changed, in some respects fundamentally. Hence, unlike the IZL, *Lehi* did not in principle oppose the establishment of the intended state within six months; neither did it deny that – with the British withdrawal – 'most of the political point of our actions would have evaporated'. Again the comparision with the IZL is instructive. *Lehi* was far quicker to consider its future in terms of a political party. It was also prepared to admit – albeit only in internal memoranda – that it had in the past made mistakes. 'Our movement often erred in its first stages when acting in accordance with its sacred principles rather than tailoring them to contemporary circumstances.'[29]

In general, the movement thus became torn between its own radical ideology and practicality. The former was apparent in its continuing opposition to American 'imperialism' and its continuing belief in Russian favour. The latter was apparent in its realisation that it did not itself possess the military power necessary to accomplish its territorial ends (the conquest of Nablus, Hebron, Jerusalem and Amman was now advocated on strategic rather than ideological grounds).[30] More importantly, it had also to admit the bankruptcy of its previous belief that 'there would be no Hebrew–Arab front'. Ultimately, *Lehi* was prepared to concede that: 'If it should prove possible – and it is possible – to reach an agreement with the *Haganah* with regard to the Arab front, we shall agree. Because today there are not many differences respecting behaviour *vis-à-vis* the Arabs.' That there still did exist some residual tensions was revealed by the next sentence: 'We shall not agree to forego actions against the British, should they prove necessary.'[31]

### *LEHI* JOINS THE WAR: A FAILURE OF IDEOLOGY?

Not until 4 January 1948 did *Lehi* admit that it was undertaking assaults on specifically Arab targets.[32] In effect, however, its ideological position with regard to the prospect of Jewish–Arab conflict had begun to shift somewhat earlier. It had already claimed to have anticipated the slaughter of 41 Jewish port workers in Haifa at the end of December

1947; and was now to argue that – in view of the incitement of the Arab masses by British 'agents' and their 'effendi' slaves – 'the only option remaining . . . is that chosen by the Hasmoneans in Edom: the path of war and conquest'.[33] By this time, even Friedman-Yellin had become sceptical about the possibility of successful propaganda among the Arabs, whom he categorised as 'primitive'. He still decried plain 'revenge' on the part of the Jews, but he was prepared to sanction 'punitive action which is the result of consideration and debate and carried out by persons subject to public criticism'. The new tone is evident in *Lehi*'s justification for its action in the Romema quarter of Jerusalem in January 1948: 'If you wish to live in peace', *Lehi* now informed the Arabs, '– then live. If you wish to leave in peace and tranquility – then leave. But if you wish neither: *then you shall leave in fear and haste.*'[34]

This view affected *Lehi*'s perception of the strategy to be pursued during the war. First, the Jews must take the initiative. Although *Lehi* did not underestimate the possible consequences of a Syrian invasion (which, typically, it attributed to British machinations), it remained convinced of the *Yishuv*'s ability to conduct a successful and lengthy campaign. The failures characteristic of the first months of the fighting were therefore all the fault of the 'official' leaders, who were still pursuing a policy of 'restraint'. The Jews should not rely upon an international force to save them but launch attacks on 'the bases and troops of the Arab rioters with the utmost force and speed'. *Lehi*, like the IZL, now believed that the ultimate decision would be reached on the battlefield. Ignoring all the logistical and organisational difficulties which were still hampering the *Haganah*'s activities, it therefore demanded that the war be carried to the Arab regions of the country.[35]

When, in March 1948, Arab–Jewish hostilities increased in Haifa, *Lehi* urged that the advantages of that situation be pressed home. There is no room for 'courtly behaviour', the movement averred. The Arab enemy has to be hit in places where it hurts him most. 'And if he has shown weakness in Haifa, he should not be left in peace there. Let his trade be destroyed and his tens of thousnds forced to flee. Let them become a burden in Nablus, Nazareth and Jenin.'[36]

The strategy thus advocated clearly differed from that originally proposed in *Lehi*'s plan for the neutralisation of the Middle East. Although the movement did hope that its projection of an anti-imperialist front comprising both the Hebrew state and its Arab neighbours could still reach fruition (indeed, the riots in Baghdad against the Anglo-Iraqi treaty of January 1948, together with the resignation of Saleh Jaber, seemed to confirm that possibility),[37] its attitude to the 'Arab question' within *Eretz Israel* was hereafter effectively divorced from the original 'neutralisation' plan. In addition, there were other changes. Indicating the Trieste model of 1947, *Lehi* no longer believed in the possibility of neutrality 'in the full sense of the term . . . Like it or not, we shall be forced to take sides with one or the other [great power] long before we are ready to do so'.[38]

There was no doubt about *Lehi*'s own preferred alignment. For some time the movement had been proclaiming its support for the USSR and its hostility towards the USA. Indeed, the latter increased in January 1948 with the announcement of George Kennan's appointment to high office in the State Department and reached new heights the following month when Warren Austin, the American representative in the Security Council, proposed sending another commission of enquiry to Palestine.[39] When, in March, the United States seemed to forsake partition in favour of the establishment of 'trusteeship', *Lehi* was not surprised. After all, America had never been a true supporter of Hebrew independence; her main object now was to provide a breathing-space for Britain's Arab allies. It is hardly surprising that Eldad should have privately expressed his readiness to support the USSR in the event of a war with the USA.[40]

Furthermore, throughout this period, *Lehi*'s hatred of Britain, and its suspicion that London still harboured imperialist designs in Palestine, did not wane, 'No state is blacker than Britain; none more reactionary. She wants to destroy us plain and simple, and Truman looks on and takes refuge in an embargo.' Unlike the Russians, who were apparently prepared to consider the Arab marauders as 'war criminals', Britain was concerned only for the integrity of its oil supplies. 'She has already signed one agreement with Iraq and will conclude others with Amman, Damascus, Cairo, Riyad and Sa'ana.' Palestine might become a second Spain.[41] Under those circumstances, there was no point in the Agency's claims that the Jews, not the Arabs, were the true representatives of Western culture and democracy in the region. It would be far better to show the extent to which they, too, could interfere with Western oil supplies (as by attacks on the Haifa refineries) and – above all – to align with their friends in the Kremlin.[42]

Friedman-Yellin was at pains to point out that *Lehi*'s support for the USSR did not imply commitment to communist ideology. Instead, and in an effort to improve the movement's image within the *Yishuv*, he emphasised *Lehi*'s own brand of ideology. This, he explained, owed nothing to 'foreign' influences, but reflected ideas which Stern had outlined over seven years before and to which *Lehi* had remained steadfast ever since. Basically, *Lehi* advocated a hybrid of 'people's democracy' and national fervour. The first element was apparent from the sources of *Lehi*'s popular support which, Friedman-Yellin claimed,

were located in the poorest areas of Jewish settlement. The second
was apparent in *Lehi*'s insistence that national revolution had to
precede social transformation.

Therein, stressed Friedman-Yellin, lay the essential difference between *Lehi* and the other forces of the right (namely, the Revisionists).
The latter, he claimed, 'call upon the people to forget "class interests".
But they direct that appeal to one class alone, the class of the poor and
the sufferers . . . They want to perpetuate inequality.' And it was
because they knew that *Lehi* would always fight for a just society that
they accused the movement of being 'communists'. 'Those who incite
and frighten [the people] with cries of "Communism" and "Marxism"
are unwittingly ratifying one of Marx's own laws: all agents of exploitation dig their own graves.'[43]

This attitude also necessarily required further attacks on the 'old
leadership' of the so-called left. Not only had the latter failed in the
determination of the war strategy, it had also failed to organise the rear.
Instead of condemning such British outrages as the attack on the offices
of the *Palestine Post*, the 'official' leadership was covering up for the
British. Instead of encouraging the *Yishuv* to rely on its own financial and
military resources, it was requesting armed and economic assistance
from abroad. The conclusion was self-evident: 'The true danger to the
Hebrew public stems from the fact that in this fateful hour it is led by old
and weak leaders who are afraid of assuming the burdens which the
times demand. The time has come to establish a new leadership.'[44]

### MILITARY AND POLITICAL FAILURES – TACTICAL ERRORS
### OR STRATEGIC BLUNDERS?

*Lehi*'s failure of enmity towards Britain reached new heights after 22
February 1948, when a British gang of soldiers exploded a bomb in
Ben Yehuda Street in Jerusalem, killing 50 Jews and wounding many
more. Besides decrying British terror and calling for a declaration
of all-out and open war against the enemy, *Lehi* also castigated the
*Haganah* and Ben-Gurion. The former were not supplying the *Yishuv*
with the necessary defences; the latter was totally unsuited to take
charge of the nation's security.[45] These charges increased in intensity
one week later when, in response to a *Lehi* attack on a British military
train near Rehovot, British soldiers turned over ten *Haganah*
members in Tel Aviv to local Arabs, who killed them. Once again,
according to *Lehi*, the fault lay with the *Haganah*'s 'passivity' towards
British rule. Its leaders had still not freed themselves from the state of
mind inculcated by thousands of years of the diaspora and 30 years of
the Mandate. Oblivious to the fact that the leaders of the *Haganah*

had, as early as January 1948, already concluded an agreement for the supply of Czech arms and were also taking steps to bypass the American embargo. *Lehi* accused them of failing in their duty to apply to the USSR for assistance. Indeed, it called upon each member of the *Haganah* to support (at least 'secretly') *Lehi*'s own political programme.[46]

By this stage, *Lehi* was already taking its own steps towards political organisation, apparently in anticipation of the imminent disbandment of its forces and its transformation into a 'legal' political party. The new cells addressed several inquiries to the 'centre', asking for explanations for the failure to unite all of the *Yishuv*'s fighting forces. One immediate reason, the 'centre' responded, was the pointlessness of the idea. Since neither the *Haganah* nor the Jewish Agency possessed either a grand military strategy or a plan, co-operation would serve no purpose. But to this were added more fundamental arguments. *Lehi* recalled that the *Haganah* had itself suggested a form of unity at the very outbreak of the war of independence. *Lehi* had rejected the proposal for two reasons. First, it could not agree to the *Haganah*'s condition that no attacks be made on either the Arab Legion or the British forces (a demand quite unacceptable in view of British support for the Arab side); second, the proposal had amounted to nothing but a military alliance. By thus ruling out the necessity for prior political agreement, the *Haganah* had in fact misrepresented *Lehi*'s entire structure. Unlike both the IZL and the *Haganah*, *Lehi* was 'not itself a military organisation but a political movement. Our fighting unit is but one of the instruments which operates in accordance with the instructions of our movement and in line with its political directives.'[47]

*Lehi* claimed to identify with such oppressed peoples as the Malaysians and Indonesians, who were fighting for their freedom from the 'Imperialist International'. But by adopting this ideological stance, *Lehi* in effect intensified its own isolation. Indeed, in April 1948 it was even to be deserted by its only ally, the small *Tenu'at Ha'am* (People's Movement) whose founder, Dr B. Lubotsky had for some time been editor of the *Lehi* newspaper *Mivrak*. The reasons for the split were ideological. *Tenu'at Ha'am* maintained that the very process of sovereign organisation within the *Yishuv* was revolutionary and anti-imperialist. *Lehi*, it charged, should therefore accept the authority of the Temporary People's Council (to be established by Ben-Gurion on 11 April) and – moreover – temper its leftward 'diversion'.[48] Other and earlier attacks on the movement had been equally forthright. Throughout the early months of 1948 *Lehi* had been severely criticised by both the left (of 'fascism') and the right (of 'communism').

*Lehi*'s response was characteristically original: the movement put on a show of absolute self-confidence. History, it claimed, had vindicated the extent to which its earlier prognoses had been correct: the Hebrew people's interests were indeed incompatible with those of British imperialism; on the other hand, and as *Lehi* had foretold, it had been possible to align them with those of the USSR. Altogether, 'our basic premises have become common coin'. The true reason for the antagonism towards *Lehi* was the fear of its opponents that, when the time for democratic and independent elections came, the voters would decide in its favour. Ben-Gurion's 'provisional government' would be transitory. Once the state was established, the masses would hand over the leadership to the freedom fighters.[49]

That such was likely to be the case was also made apparent by the 'muddle' which characterised the situation created by the *Yishuv*'s existing leadership. *Lehi* would itself reap the fruits of this situation.

> The public is beginning to understand and recover. It has lost its blind faith in the national institutions, the directed press, and empty slogans. What is apparent is an appreciation of the political thought of the liberation movement; the appearance of our fighters and their spiritual valour inspires honour . . . A new force has appeared in the streets and is taking root.[50]

The explosion at the Jewish Agency buildings in Jerusalem on 11 March showed the true extent of the *Haganah*'s failure; so too did the destruction of the convoy at Nebi Daniel at the end of the month and the series of simultaneous military reverses in Jerusalem (which, it was claimed, had only been saved by the actions of *Lehi* and the IZL). Clearly, Ben-Gurion had to resign. Wilfully or otherwise, he had made entirely the wrong strategic choices. Instead of waging 'war' he had 'played with the blood of hundreds of Hebrew youth'. He and 'the ruling clique' in *Mapai* were interested only in the perpetuity of their own control over 'the Morrison state'. That is why they had not taken the opportunity, during the very first stages of the Arab 'riots', to instil 'fear and awe' into the enemy and thereby cause the Arabs' confused and panic-stricken flight. We cannot, declared *Lehi*, countenance a situation in which 'the post of commander in chief should be held by a confused and deranged man with no experience of military affairs, and who lives day and night in fear of both the dissidents and the threats of [*Mapam*]'.[51] There was, argued *Lehi*, no doubt that Ben-Gurion would lead the Hebrew youth 'from slaughter to slaughter' until 'final surrender'. Especially criminal were the hopes which he seemed to be placing on internal disunity in the Arab camp – which was united in its opposition to the Hebrew cause. Similarly false was the trust which the Jewish Agency seemed to have placed in the possibility of a cease-fire, which in fact would only perpetuate Arab superiority. *Lehi*, for all its continued faith in the USSR, did not think that even the Russians would undertake tasks which the *Yishuv* had to accomplish for itself. The decision of 29 November had merely supplied 'moral support'. In short, 'no force but ourselves can implement the principle of Hebrew independence'. Following the example set by the communist General Markos in Greece, the Jews ought not to await international recognition of the Hebrew state but immediately declare its establishment.[52]

The war strategy thus proclaimed was the direct product of *Lehi*'s ideology. Troubled by what it considered to be the 'cancer' eating away at the Hebrew people in their exile, the movement called for the dissolution of the diaspora. That task, however, necessitated the 'living space' necessary to absorb 'many millions'. It followed that there could be no territorial concessions and certainly no agreement to partition. 'From the historical perspective, to acquiesce in partition is to sign a death warrant . . . we shall become another element in the melting pot of races and peoples who are decaying in the declining Levant.' *Lehi* aspired to the creation of a 'mighty state' which, by the full exploitation of its oil, its agriculture, its trade and its industry could command all the historic pathways of the region. The borders it required stretched 'from the sea to the desert, from the Nile to the Euphrates'.[53] Once again, the contrast with the strategy adopted by *Mapai* was plain. In accepting partition (and declaring the ridiculous territory thus received to constitute a 'state'), the latter were preparing the Jewish people for another ghetto, under the tutelage of British and American imperialism. *Lehi*, on the other hand, was building the bridge to be crossed by the Messiah, who would be accompanied on his journey by all the enemies of imperialism.[54] That was why *Lehi* would have nothing to do with the Temporary People's Council set up on 11 April 1948. Responding to Ben-Gurion's speech announcing its establishment (which it described as 'absurd verbiage and mutual deception'), the movement declared:

> Ideals had to be fought for. How could [Ben-Gurion] talk of peace and in the same breath offer [Richard] Crossman bases? We must prevent the surrender by Ben-Gurion and the Social-Democrats of both right and left. The youth will continue to fight even if ordered by its Pétains to surrender.[55]

DEIR YASIN AS A HIGH POINT AND A TURNING-POINT IN THE WAR

On 7 April 1948, IZL and *Lehi* units launched a joint attack on the Arab village of Deir Yasin near Jerusalem. During the course of its conquest, 240 Arabs were killed. The reaction of the Jewish Agency was particularly fierce. Meeting on 20 January, the executive of that body had already expressed its concern that, even at so late an hour, the 'dissidents' still refused to accept the Agency's authority. In addition, Ben-Gurion was especially troubled by the possibility that the Arab Legion might intervene in the fighting between Jews and Arabs in Palestine. It was with both concerns in mind that the entire Agency executive accepted Ben-Gurion's motion to condemn the Deir Yasin 'massacre' and that Ben-Gurion himself sent a telegram of apology to King Abdullah of Jordan.[56]

It was at this stage that *Lehi* itself launched a propaganda offensive. Its initial account of the Deir Yasin incident had been laconic, juxtaposing the report of 240 Arab deaths with the news that 170 Arabs had been killed in the *Haganah*'s conquest of the Kastel. In response to Ben-Gurion's telegram to Abdullah, however, the movement moved on to the offensive. It published the letter from Shaltiél (the *Haganah* commander in Jerusalem) to the IZL and *Lehi* informing them that the conquest of Deir Yasin formed part of a wider plan of conquest; it claimed that the attack on the village had sown fear and terror among neighbouring Arabs; it rebuffed the accusation of looting with the counter-accusation that the *Histadrut* concern, 'Solel Boneh', had likewise pillaged; it denied that Arab corpses at Deir Yasin had been defiled; above all, *Lehi* attacked – on principle – the notion of an apology to the United States and Britain (who 'had stood idly by while millions of our brothers were slaughtered in Europe') and denigrated the notion of apologising to the Arab rioters who had been murdering and raping Jews for years, especially since the Arab Legion had itself slaughtered Jewish convoys at both Beit-Naballah (on 14 December 1947) and Wadi Rushmeiah (17 January 1948). *Lehi* was prepared to express its 'deep' sorrow for the number of Arab deaths, but disclaimed responsibility for them. Like the IZL, *Lehi* claimed that the battle of Deir Yasin had been characterised by 'heavy fighting. Our troops were attacked by rifle and machine-guns from almost every house.' Both also pointed out the relatively high rate of their own casualties (attributed to the fact that they had deliberately foresworn the advantages of surprise), the large number of weapons that they had captured, and the number of Iraqis and Syrians among the casualties, which indicated that they were 'units of the regular army encamped there'.[57]

More fundamental were the prognoses which *Lehi* made in the wake of Deir Yasin. At this level, it is possible to discern two conflicting elements, both reflections of its previous ideological positions. One, a derivative of the 'right-wing' orientation outlined by Stern and now promulgated by Eldad, regarded a clash between the Hebrew and

Arab worlds as unavoidable. The other, however, remained faithful to the 'leftist' programme outlined less than two years earlier and insisted that – notwithstanding Deir Yasin – 'There will still be found Arabs who will understand that their true enemy is foreign Imperialism, that we must overcome the differences between us . . . in the face of the common enemy.' Characteristically, advocates of the left-wing position in *Lehi* not only regarded the Arabs of Palestine itself as possible candidates for such a partnership. They also looked to the masses of Egypt and Iraq 'who know that they are being sent to *Eretz Israel*, not to defend their homeland, but in order to divert their attention from the poverty and exploitation in their own lands'. Above all, they argued that Hebrew independence had to be an organic part of a new international and ideological order, in which the Hebrew people had to stand against the imperialists and Anglo-Saxon powers and alongside the Soviet Union.[58]

The divergences in these two orientations were first dealt with as a matter of principle in March 1949, when Friedman-Yellin and Eldad clashed on the issue during the Fighters' Conference being held in Ramat Gan.[59] But (as Eldad testifies) Friedman-Yellin had privately reacted much earlier. Immediately after Deir Yasin he apparently wrote an abrasive letter to Yehoshua Zetler, the *Lehi* commander in Jerusalem. This revealed the extent to which Deir Yasin had become the touchstone of *Lehi*'s internal ideological debate. It also indicated just how much had changed in Friedman-Yellin's views on the Arabs and Soviets since the days of 1938–39, when he had fully supported maximalist Revisionism and IZL's anti-Arab programme. There were, he now stated, three major reasons which moved him to condemn the Deir Yasin operation as a 'massacre'. First, 'it will spoil our image *in the eyes of the Soviet Union*, with whom we hope finally to establish ties'. Second, 'It was indeed too cruel an action, and the murder of women, etc. is shocking'. Third, 'Co-operation with the IZL did not have the formal approval of the "centre"'. The contrast with Eldad's position was stark. The latter was to regard Deir Yasin as an authentic expression of *Lehi* as a right-wing political movement; it articulated the need to 'transform Jerusalem into the Archimedean point of the Hebrew revolution'. In general, Eldad now wished to restrict *Lehi*'s movement to the left to tactical matters, and was therefore quite flattered by Friedman-Yellin's charge that he had encouraged Zetler to establish an independent, and competing, 'centre' in Jerusalem. Specifically, Eldad was convinced that '*without Deir Yasin the State of Israel could never have been established*'.[60]

Notwithstanding these differences, *Lehi* remained united in its other views, as became apparent in the wake of the slaughter of 76 members of the Hadassah convoy to Mount Scopus, just four days after Deir Yasin. Both wings of the movement denied the Jewish Agency's charge that the Arab perpetrators of the outrage had been motivated by 'revenge'. Instead, they regarded the Hadassah incident as yet another example of Britain's complicity with the Arab side in the fighting and of the *Haganah*'s own dereliction of duty.[61]

Such was the intensity of *Lehi*'s animosity towards the 'official' leadership of the Agency that the movement was unable to come to terms with the fact that the war was taking a new course. It failed to recognise the operational turning-point reached after Operation Nahshon, early in April, when the *Haganah* moved onto the offensive. Similarly, it failed to appreciate the political importance of the establishment of the People's Executive and the People's Council, both of which constituted the first steps on the road to the establishment of an independent provisional Jewish government. *Lehi* expressed its satisfaction with the welcome string of *Haganah* military successes, but it regarded these as merely affirmations of the justice of its own principles. The Hebrew people had still to be on guard against the possibility that their 'official' leaders would succumb to British or American intervention. They had also to assert their willingness to fight. Provided that they followed the principles laid down by *Lehi*, the nation would emerge victorious.[62]

### THE IZL AGAINST *LEHI*

During the winter of 1947–48, the IZL seemed to be adopting positions close to those of *Lehi*. For one thing, *Herut* (the IZL newspaper) was then stressing its alienation from the 'rich' and its own character as a *'movement with roots among the masses'*. For another, it also expressed opinions close to *Lehi*'s on its relationship towards the two great powers. Like *Lehi*, the IZL accused the USA of 'the cruel curtailment of our country' and was sure that the USSR 'would not stand aside should an attempt be made to destroy the Hebrew people, the only democratic force in the Middle East'. To say that is not to suggest that the IZL was therefore prepared to underwrite *Lehi*'s plan for the 'neutralisation' of the Middle East. On the contrary, *Herut* stressed that 'this is not a question of one ideology or another. It is one of the natural relations between objective partners'.[63] Moreover, unlike *Lehi*, the IZL did not believe in the possibility of future co-operation between the Hebrew nation and 'anti-imperialist' Arabs. But the affinity between the two movements was nevertheless close. The IZL also doubted whether the British were sincere in their decision to withdraw from *Eretz Israel* and regarded them and the Arabs as the common strategic foe. It also rejected the idea of partition; demanded that a Jewish state be established on both banks of the river Jordan; and – like *Lehi* – was caustic in its criticisms of Ben-Gurion and his 'ghetto-like' policies of appeasement and defence. The leaders of the Jewish Agency, declared *Herut*, had missed every opportunity to establish the Hebrew state. The people would pay for those mistakes with rivers of blood 'until it will shake itself free, establish a new fighting leadership and go forth from slavery to freedom'.[64]

Notwithstanding such declarations, *Lehi* refused to regard the IZL as an ally. To do so, the movement feared, might jeopardise its own ideological distinctiveness. Instead, in March 1948, it stepped up its verbal attacks on the IZL – whose political conception, it claimed, 'was no better than that of the Jewish Agency'. To that end, *Lehi* called attention to the fact that (with only occasional exceptions) the IZL stopped fighting the British after 29 November 1947, concentrating instead on the war against the Arabs. *Lehi* also pounced on the fact that the IZL employed the term 'Nazo-British' rather than 'British imperialists' in order to describe their enemy. This showed that 'there existed no essential distinction between the IZL and the Jewish Agency or the *Haganah*'. Indeed, *Lehi*'s ideological and political claims could not even be satisfied by the IZL's assurance that it would not disband its forces until the territorial integrity of the homeland had been assured.[65]

The tension between the two movements reached a new level of intensity after 7 March 1948, when the *Haganah* and the IZL agreed on operational co-operation.[66] Even though this accord was followed by the joint IZL–*Lehi* venture at Deir-Yasin, their mutual acrimony intensified, again scaling new heights after the IZL's mismanaged attack on Jaffa in April 1948. *Lehi* was in any case annoyed that its own forces were not invited to participate in the latter operation; it also accused the IZL of retreating as soon as British forces had intervened in the fighting. Jaffa, it claimed, was a missed opportunity. The IZL had possessed the chance to prove that what was at stake was a Jewish–British war and to strike at the British who 'no longer wish to spill their own blood'. But instead of fighting the British forces, the IZL had fallen prey to the *Haganah*'s way of thinking.[67]

Even fiercer were *Lehi*'s criticisms of the IZL–*Haganah* agreement. Among themselves, individual members of *Lehi* accepted the possibility that they too might have to become parties to that accord.[68] In public, however, they attacked it outright. Unlike the IZL, *Lehi* refused to promise to consult the Jewish Agency before carrying out anti-British operations and accused the IZL of giving the anti-Arab front higher priority than the anti-British front. Its own actions, it declared, were directed against both the British and their Arab agents, and were the consequence of 'the Anglo-Arab onslaught against the Hebrew people'. Furthermore, *Lehi* continued to reject the possibility of operational co-operation with the *Haganah* as long as Ben-Gurion remained at the helm of the Jewish Agency.[69]

Equally hostile was the IZL response, delivered at the very height of its battle for Jaffa. In response to *Lehi*'s charges of 'inconsistency', the IZL reminded the smaller movement that Friedman-Yellin had himself earlier agreed with Golomb to a six months' truce in activities against the British. It also denied the accusation that the IZL–*Haganah* agreement would be exploited by the British. The IZL, Begin claimed, had signed the 'arrangement' of 'its own free will', in a spirit of the 'highest patriotism' and by virtue of its own moral strength. '*Lehi*', he protested, 'had no right to project an all-knowing image. In fact, its recent political assessments had proven to be seriously mistaken.' Just five months before, *Lehi* had believed the British to be packing their bags and had, consequently, decided to emerge from the underground and become a legal political party. The IZL, however, was less sanguine. Its agreement with the *Haganah* was purely 'military' in nature: 'The nation faces a war for survival, whose peak has yet to be reached. A unity of forces was vital. The entire people demanded it, and we carried out the will of the people.' Besides, the continuation of the 'arrangement' depended upon political circumstances. Within six days it would be known whether an independent Hebrew government would be established or whether the Agency would give in to the British.[70]

## *LEHI* FACES THE TEST OF THE CHANGE IN THE WAR:
### THE ESTABLISHMENT OF THE PEOPLE'S COUNCIL

Given its own basic principles, it is no wonder that – as late as one month before Israel's declaration of independence – *Lehi* was still extremely sceptical about the possibility of the establishment of a Jewish state. In large part, and as had always been the case, this was because the movement continued to doubt whether the British would indeed withdraw their forces from Palestine. In fact, *Lehi* considered Britain still to be 'the enemy with a capital letter "E"'. Britain certainly posed a greater threat to the Hebrew nation than did the Arabs, who were in effect merely Britain's agents. As much as was indicated by the speed with which the British had rushed reinforcements to Jaffa after the IZL attack on that town. Once entrenched there, *Lehi* averred, they would seize other strategic points in the country and thus impose the Morrison–Grady proposal. Thereafter, Britain would turn *Eretz*

*Israel* into 'a battlefield in the third world war' and use Hebrew youth as 'cannon-fodder in the Imperialist fight'.[71]

Second only to the British were the Americans, whose various concessions to Zionism were illusory. Altogether, *Lehi* considered the United States to be 'the most aggressive factor in the contemporary international arena'. The US government was attempting to persuade most of the nations of the world 'to encircle the Soviet Union', and had turned Britain into its 'instrument'. *Lehi* sincerely believed that, in an effort to maintain Anglo-Saxon superiority in *Eretz Israel*, the United States would even send troops to the region. Thus, the fate awaiting the Hebrew state was that which had already befallen Greece. Here, too, the Americans would pressurise the Jews while the British persuaded the Arabs.[72]

At bottom, however, it was the Jewish Agency which was responsible for the present sorry condition of the *Yishuv*. Thanks to the leadership of that body, the struggle for independence had all but failed. The drive for immigration had yielded few results; land settlement had ground to a halt; and the economy was in decline. Only the war waged by the underground movements had given birth to Hebrew sovereignty. But this achievement was endangered by the policy of 'restraint' now being pursued even by the IZL, whose co-operation with the *Haganah* undoubtedly heralded a new wave of anti-*Lehi* persecutions.[73]

No less significant were the actions of the new People's Council – whose very choice of that title instead of 'government' showed that it was nothing but a *Judenrat* led by 'defeatists'.[74] The latter were already running cap in hand after the forces of 'international reaction' and 'neo-fascism'. In short, Ben-Gurion and his supporters were nothing but the slaves of Bevin and Marshall. As much was revealed by the *Haganah*'s withdrawal from Dier Muhsein (8 April) and – under British pressure – from the Sheik Jerah quarter of Jerusalem (which had been captured on 26 April). In thus bowing to British wishes, they were in fact restricting their operations to the 'Morrison state'.[75]

In general, the Agency's strategy was mistaken. It had not forged alliances with such other minorities in the area as the Lebanese Christians and the Kurds ('who are our natural allies'); neither had Ben-Gurion turned the country into a 'massive arsenal'. Above all, neither he nor *Mapam* had appealed for help to 'the progressive forces of the world', a category which included – apart from the Soviet Union – thousands of Spanish republicans, Greek and Yugoslavian refugees, and Czech and Polish members of the 'International Brigade', all of whom were eager to strike a blow against fascism. The counter-argument, that a pro-Soviet orientation would harm American Jewry, entirely failed to see that the fate of world Jewry was at stake.

From Lenin's teachings we should learn that there exists no common bridge between progress and its opposite; no compromise is possible between constructive communism and destructive fascism. Sooner or later we shall have to participate in this wider struggle. And we have to realise that while the victory of one of those sides means our *destruction*, the victory of the other ensures the continued life of Jewry and the realisation of its ambitions.

Convinced that the Soviet Union would emerge successful from the present international struggle, *Lehi* wished to see the Hebrew nation among the new family of peoples which the USSR would lead.[76] That aim could not be accomplished, said Eldad, simply by joining Ben-Gurion in celebrating 1 May. 'So long as the flag of freedom is not flying here, the red flag will be just an empty slogan.' *Lehi* demanded that the existing workers' parties realise their responsibilities by channelling the war effort against such British targets as the High Commissioner's residence, Rafiah and Sheik Jerah.[77]

These exhortations increased in stridency with the approach of 15 May. On the one hand, *Lehi* emphasised that 'total' war against the Arab mercenaries of Britain was an integral part of the struggle against imperialism itself. It thus accommodated classical Revisionist ideology within its own brand of anti-imperialism. Without the conquest of Jenin and Nablus, it claimed, the Jewish position in Mishmar ha-Emek would be untenable; Jerusalem, Beit Sha'an and the potash works would not be safe as long as a hired Arab ruler sat in Amman.[78] *Lehi*, therefore, refused to acknowledge that the borders of 'partition' were in any way sacred. On the contrary, once the first shots in the war of independence had been fired, that entire concept had lost whatever legal and moral force it might once have had. The Arabs had to be defeated, and *Lehi* was confident that they would be defeated provided the Jews took the initiative. If there were to be a 'permanent settlement' between the two peoples it had now to be based on the principle of demographic exchange (a concept somewhat different from that proposed in *Lehi*'s memorandum to UNSCOP). The tens of thousands of Arabs who had fled of their own volition would be replaced by the Jews of the Arab lands. In that way, the barrier to a covenant of friendship with the Arab peoples would be removed. Their bitterness and hatred had to be directed towards the British and their own appointed leaders.[79]

It followed that *Lehi* itself could sanction no cessation in its own anti-British activities. In fact, it renewed them just ten days before the expiration of the Mandate, when members of the movement attacked a British unit at Gan Hayyim, killing one officer and six of his men. This, *Lehi* explained, was no mere 'provocation' (as the *Haganah* charged) but a calculated effort to dissuade the British from returning to Palestine and hindering the establishment of Hebrew independence there. 'He who fears to harm the British is also afraid to fight for a free Hebrew port.' Every young man who spoke about activism and anti-imperialism could ensure that the Sixth Airborne Division would not stand at the gates of the military compound in Sarona.[80]

Given that background, it is not surprising that *Lehi* rejected the suggestion that it join forces with the *Haganah* and attempt to influence the latter organisation from within. In fact, the period witnessed an intensification of tension between the two organisations. The *Haganah* took the first steps, by arresting four *Lehi* personnel in Haifa and impounding a stock of explosives. *Lehi* reacted in kind. Three days later it fulfilled its warning that 'civil war is a double-edged sword . . . we shall respond to force with force and to violence with violence. There will be no return to the days of 1942.' It captured four of the *Haganah*'s commanders, including Yosef Rokhel (Avidar), head of its quartermaster's unit, and refused to release them until its own men had been returned.[81]

Even then, *Lehi*'s personal abuse of Ben-Gurion (now nicknamed 'Ben-Mugion' – that is, 'Son of Fear') did not abate. If anything, the movement's radical nationalism and pro-Soviet orientation made its rejection of Ben-Gurion's claims to leadership absolute. He and his supporters were now even accused of being unpatriotic, and entirely lacking on both a broad national outlook and a correct understanding of international affairs. They would again surrender, as they had already done over the Biltmore Programme and the 'Black Sabbath'. As late as 5 May, *Lehi* did not believe that Ben-Gurion intended to declare the establishment of a state. Even if he did so, it was thought, he would only set up a dictatorship, as Pétain had done in France. Therein lay the point in his dismissal of Yisrael Galili of *Mapam*, his formal deputy at the head of the *Haganah*. Ben-Gurion, claimed *Lehi*, appreciated that his long-standing partnership with the latter party had spoiled his image in the eyes of such 'reactionaries' as Truman, Marshall, Churchill, Bevin and Bidault. The reason was that, while *Mapam*'s leadership was ready to follow Ben-Gurion's lead in surrendering, the rank and file opposed that position. Having already got rid of Sneh, Ben-Gurion now wished to disband the *Palmach*, and thus remove the last 'activist' obstacle to his rule with the help of British bayonets. His actions showed that he was still a prisoner of his 'diaspora mentality' and quite incapable of assimilating the forces contributing to renewed Hebrew sovereignty. That, too, was why he was refusing to give the order to cross the partition boundaries and take western Galilee and the west bank – although both operations could be accomplished with comparative ease.[82]

Thus it was that *Lehi*'s feelings on the eve of independence constituted a mixture of apprehension and hope. Its apprehensions stemmed from the anticipation of further evidence of British treachery and the Jewish Agency's pusillanimity. The first was to become apparent when the British, having indeed withdrawn their administration from Palestine, used their army to enforce the Morrison–Grady Plan as a step towards renewing their control over the country.[83] The Jewish Agency's pusillanimity was to be shown by its agreeing to serve as the guardian of Britain's positions between the Mediterranean and the Persian Gulf. Thus, *Lehi*'s greatest fear that the Agency would not rise to the exceptional occasion which history had provided was realised. Instead of seizing that opportunity, the Jewish Agency had reached an agreement with Abdullah. 'The Hebrew nation will not forgive its leaders for this stupidity, this crime. Neither this generation, nor those to come, can ever forgive them.'[84]

The other side of the coin was compounded of several favourable factors. One was *Lehi*'s belief in the justice of its own cause and in the movement's ability to serve as a catalyst which would excite the minds of Hebrew youth and stimulate their fervour, thus bringing about their inevitable victory over their domestic and foreign foes. The second cause for *Lehi*'s optimism was its estimate of the disunity of the Arab states, whose mutual suspicions were analysed with some glee.[85] The third was its confidence in Russian support, now made apparent by Soviet broadcasts which reported the Arab defeats and prophesied their continuation.[86]

Ultimately, it was in the latter mood that *Lehi* prepared itself to meet the challenges posed by the establishment of the state and its invasion by the armies of the Arab state. The movement was still confident of its ability to implement both the internal and the external aspects of its ideology, its attitude being reminiscent of that of National Bolshevism. As much is apparent from a letter which, just two months earlier, Friedman-Yellin had addressed to the *Lehi* representative in Czechoslovakia, asking that he strengthen his ties with the new communist administration, and pointing out that 'they should be interested in assisting us'. The leader of *Lehi*'s 'centre' did not consider his movement to be in any way in decline. On the contrary, he was convinced of its future strength: 'We could become one of the most decisive forces, a fighting unit of thousands, and not of a few men. Many of the Palmach people who are now in distress would join us . . . The problem is arms. Could we but overcome that difficulty – the outlook would be very bright.'[87]

# The Invasion of the Arab States

In one sense, *Lehi* accepted the establishment of the state as a fact, its only regret being that independence had not been declared 20 years earlier: after all, the Mandate had always been 'one big lie', as was the international code of honour which had imposed it on a 'righteous' Britain.[1] Nevertheless, so ideological a movement as *Lehi* could hardly have been expected to change its position overnight merely because independence had been declared. More significant was the fact that it was *Lehi*'s old domestic adversaries who now constituted the new state's leadership.

Such shifts as *Lehi* made, therefore, were only operational. On 29 May the 'Fighting Unit' was disbanded, and at the end of August *Lehi* set out to become a legal political movement. But these moves did not imply a fundamental ideological change. *Lehi* considered that Ben-Gurion's motives were suspect (asking which was dominant: 'his delusions of grandeur and his cravings for ministerial office, or his weak-kneed fear of "sanctions"'); moreover, there was nothing in *Mapai*'s historical record that could inspire confidence. On the contrary: 'We shall not tire of calling on the public to bring down this rule', especially as it had 'relinquished' most of the homeland, collaborated with imperialism and had forfeited Jerusalem to foreign rule. Unless the entire country was liberated, the state of Israel would be condemned to repeated attacks. Geography, history and strategy dictated that course, 'if we do not wish the State of Israel to remain a short episode in the national chronicle'.[2]

Abdullah's invasion only strengthened *Lehi*'s opinion that Britain was the main danger. In May, the British were charged with responsibility for the fall of the Etzion bloc. June, when Adolf Eichmann was rumoured to be visiting Cairo with British support, saw the reappearance of the 'Nazo-British' formulation. 'It is difficult to understand why Eichmann is considered worse than Clayton, for example. Clayton intended to do to us exactly what Eichmann did. But it is not a question of who is worse. The point is that they are one and the same.'[3]

As to the other powers, *Lehi* attributed America's recognition of Israel to her acknowledgement of the superiority of the Hebrew forces, but warned that the United States could not be relied upon. The US position could always change again in response to elections.

Ultimately, only the 'neutralisation' plan could ensure that Hebrew youth would not become cannon fodder in the next world war.[4] The slight delay in the Soviet recognition of Israel generated some confusion. *Lehi*'s explanation was the Israeli government's own uncertain attitude with regard to the British army of conquest. The USSR could hardly have been expected to rush to recognise Israel at a time when tens of thousands of British troops were still stationed there and thus in a position to wrest rights to land, sea and air bases. Under those circumstances, Israel was no better than Abdullah's state.[5] When the USSR's recognition was eventually announced (on 18 May), *Lehi* explained this event in terms which were both practical and related to principles. Russia, *Lehi* declared, would help the new state to remain neutral and to resist the establishment of foreign bases on her soil; Russia would also release its own 'embargo on the Jewish soil' by permitting the emigration of those Soviet Jews who wished to go to the new state. The Russians had no illusions about the pro-Western leanings of most of Israel's leaders; nevertheless, the election of the pro-British Weizmann as president was a serious political error. 'Should such mistakes be multiplied, we could lose the USSR's support.'[6] Meanwhile, *Lehi* demanded that Stalin should be forced to 'balance' such measures by arms supplies of its own.[7]

*Lehi* regarded Britain's temporary retention of Haifa as a bad omen. If the Government of Israel did not stand on guard, *Lehi* would have to do so. 'This will not be a rebellion against the Hebrew government, since no government can demand the loyalty of its citizens while it is itself relinquishing its own powers and authorities.' Although *Lehi* units were already joining the national army, this was no idle threat – as future events were to show. *Mivrak* openly proclaimed: 'The choice is between war against the enemy and internal unity, or submission to the foreign foe and domestic strife.'[8]

However, in *Lehi*'s view, the situation in Jerusalem (likened to that in Stalingrad during the Second World War) was always to be the true barometer of success in the war of independence. Hence, despite the enlistment of *Lehi* members in the army, the movement diverted many of its men to the city. But its forces were too few to influence the campaign there. Consequently, and characteristically, it resorted to verbal attacks on 'the inactivity and carelessness of both the *Haganah* and IZL leaders during the first days of the fighting, when they refused to co-operate with *Lehi* who had plunged deep into enemy territory'. Irrespective of the situation in Sheik Jerah and Ramat Rahel, *Lehi* itself wanted to liberate the Old City, and pressed Shaltiél (the Israel Defence Force commander in Jerusalem) to launch an immediate attack. But the latter refused to place at *Lehi*'s disposal the heavy weapons required for an independent action, and did not heed its warnings that the Jewish quarter was in danger.[9] When the Old City did fall, *Lehi* refused to accept that event as history's final judgement. 'There exists an ancient *will*, which neither desert marauders nor domestic misfits can overcome.' The true fault lay with those who had relinquished Jerusalem and agreed to its internationalisation.[10]

Neither in its hypotheses nor in its operational policy did *Lehi* turn over a new leaf in its relations with the Provisional Government. Ben-Gurion's announcement that he was instituting 'emergency decrees' seemed to threaten *Lehi*'s very existence, and certainly reinforced the belief that he was assuming dictatorial powers in order to establish single-party rule at the expense of all his domestic foes. *Lehi* promised that, if it was made the target of these emergency decrees, it would fight against them with all its might.[11] On 20 May it also explicitly proclaimed that it would not recognise the authority of the Provisional Government beyond the borders assigned to the Jewish state by the UN decision of 29 November 1947. This was a far-reaching decision, which was eventually to bring about *Lehi*'s demise. Its most dramatic effect was on the life of Count Bernadotte who – on the same day – was appointed mediator in the Palestine conflict by the UN Secretary-General. As early as the first week in June *Lehi* strongly denied the Provisional Government's announcement that the movement had disbanded once its men had joined the national army on 29 May. *Lehi* proclaimed that it would continue to retain its independence and appeal for public assistance, both at home and abroad, within the boundaries of the present state as well as in those territories of the homeland which the Provisional Government had relinquished of its own volition.[12]

Since *Lehi* refused to accept the partition borders, the movement also opposed any cease-fire on the basis of the situation on 14 May. The Arabs had to be returned to their deserts. The USSR, it claimed, was also interested in a Hebrew state in its 'natural borders': stretching from the Mediterranean to the desert.[13] Consequently, *Lehi* was aghast at the possibility that the Provisional Government might agree to a cease-fire. To stop the war now, it claimed, would be to grant the Arabs an advantage and thus to cause further casualties in a month's time. Hence, *Lehi* called upon the troops at the front to refuse to lay down their arms and to inform their officers of their decision to continue the war under all circumstances and at any price. 'Those who conclude political deals are also trading in your blood.'[14] To this was added, on the following day, a call for the public to elect a new leadership which would replace that which was at present advocating submission.[15]

*Lehi*, then, did emerge from the underground, but changed only its outward form; it refused to transform its ideology or its politics. The 'centre' announced that *Lehi* would remain a revolutionary movement. Those about to be conscripted in the national army were explicitly told that they were enlisting 'in the service of the movement'; their task was to disseminate within their units their readiness to fight to the end and not to relinquish any territory. Indeed, the present war was just an intermediate phase, and the experience gained would later be put to use when the time came to liberate the entire homeland. Thus, only *Lehi*'s means had changed, not its ends. Its weapons would be political 'wherever the problems were political, but military wherever an alternative Israeli army would not be available to solve the problems'. In other words, its men were enlisting on condition that its maximalist national ideology would be fully implemented. They were certainly not joining the ranks of the *Haganah*, which had 'departed the stage', taking its 'foolish ideology' with it.[16]

### THE CHANGE ON THE ARAB QUESTION

In the wake of the invasion of the Arab states, *Lehi* retracted its previous support for the Egyptian liberation movement. Instead, it adopted an anti-imperialist line which negated Arab national feeling and described Arab leaders as British lackeys. To this was added the Revisionist argument which took issue with the demographic statistics compiled by the Mandate authorities. Jews, *Lehi* claimed, constituted a third of the population within the 'natural borders' of the homeland (that is, between the Litani, the Euphrates, and the Nile) and 47 per cent of the inhabitants west of the Jordan. Their colonising and military potential exceeded that of any other group. Thus, within three years, the Arabs would no longer possess a majority – even within the 'natural' boundaries.[17] As for the 'progressive' Arab forces – with whose assistance *Lehi* still hoped to save its own 'neutralisation' plan – they seemed to be non-existent. *Lehi* expressed its readiness to co-operate with the Arab masses against their leaders; but could find no evidence that its ambitions were reciprocated. On the contrary, the unalterable fact was that the new Hebrew state was confronted by a united Arab front.[18]

It is no wonder that, even at this stage, *Lehi* adopted a definitively negative attitude with regard to the repatriation of Arab refugees. Specifically, the movement opposed the return of 20,000 refugees to Haifa. Although prepared to grant Arabs already resident in the country equality of rights and obligations, *Lehi* doubted whether they would be prepared to accept such burdens as a special war tax (of the sort imposed on Egyptian and Syrian Jews). It was more likely that at least some of the repatriated refugees would become a fifth column who, 'at every moment of weakness will dare to rise up against us, as befits their Levantine, cowardly and treacherous character'. Only after the war could the Arab return to his place; provided he fulfilled his obligations, he would then receive equal rights.[19] The only group which *Lehi* was prepared to look upon with favour were the Lebanese Falangists, rumoured to be preparing to announce the establishment of an independent Christian republic and thereby break the Arab ranks. *Lehi* believed that the Falange (like *Lehi*) were moving from fascism to a left-wing ideology and also attracting the support of members of the Greek Orthodox Church and the Protestants, thus constituting a large majority in Lebanon.[20]

All this did not imply that *Lehi*'s attitude towards the Arabs was taking a 'Revisionist' turn. Quite the opposite is revealed by the movement's response to articles written at this time by two major Revisionist ideologists: Wolfgang von Weisel and Abba Achimeir. *Lehi* accused the former of betraying Jabotinsky's principles when advocating a 'deal' whereby Israel would help Abdullah to take Damascus if he relinquished western Palestine. Apart from falling into a British trap, this plan constituted a betrayal of the principle that the Hebrew state had a right to possession of both banks of the Jordan. Achimeir, on the other hand, was accused of showing too much interest in the welfare of the effendis, and thereby of betraying that of the fellahin. This, too, ignored Jabotinsky's teachings on the subject.[21]

The truth is that *Lehi*'s attitude was not determined either by its position on the eastern bank of the Jordan or with regard to class differentials within the Arab community. After Deir Yasin, especially, it was at odds with the communists on both issues and drawing closer to the positions of the IZL and the Revisionists. What mattered for *Lehi* was that the nation now faced a struggle for its very survival. Increasingly, therefore, it reverted to premises which had originally been postulated by Stern, and for which the tone of its 'anti-imperialist' ideology was merely a cover. It was on that basis that *Lehi* advocated that local Arab property be confiscated in order to finance the expenses of those families whose menfolk were enlisted. Totally unacceptable was the Provisional Government's action in registering such property as 'enemy possessions'. Local Arabs must be made to pay compensation for the war declared by the Arab states in which they had been called to participate. They must be told that their property would not be returned.[22]

Thus *Lehi*'s references to the 'progressive' Arab forces who figured so prominently in its original 'neutralisation' plan became increasingly rare. Indeed, none occur in its publications between 18 May and 1 July, and are only fleeting thereafter. The programme which the movement issued in mid-July (see below) did again refer to the 'neutralisation' plan as a basic ideological plank, and promise 'equality of rights to all citizens of the country without distinction of religion or nationality'. But what followed was in contradiction to that proclamation, and demonstrated the extent of the influence of the war:

> *Lehi* regards the exchange of the Arab population of *Eretz Israel* and the Jews of Arab countries as the best solution to the problem of relations between the Hebrew people and the Arabs. This solution will obviate the danger of blood rivalries; facilitate peace between neighbouring states; and deprive imperialism of the weapon of incitement to national and racial hatred. The efficacy of this solution has been proven by the experience of many peoples in our age.[23]

There was no better illustration of the extent to which, from a political and ideological point of view, *Lehi* was becoming part of the rightwing camp in Israel. Unlike *Al ha-Mishmar* (*Mapam*'s organ), *Lehi* refused to consider that a flourishing Arab community within Israel would foil the imperialist attempt to erect a barrier of blood between Jews and Arabs. On the contrary, its role was likened to that fulfilled by the Sudetens in Czechoslovakia in 1938. Unlike *Maki* (the Communist Party), it also refused to set too much store by the incipient organisation of an anti-Husseini 'League for National [Arab] Liberation' in Nazareth. Although this circumstance did perhaps foreshadow some change, it could not completely revolutionise the situation. The Arab social structure was still patriarchal and lacked any industrial proletariat. Its rulers still relied on imperialist bayonets.[24]

In effect *Lehi* admitted that its previous hopes for the emergence of a 'progressive' Arab sector had been misplaced. Above all, it refused to relinquish complete Hebrew control over the entire homeland. Even if the 'League for National Liberation' did manage to establish an independent Arab unit within the Mandate borders, it would still have to be a subject entity. 'Does there indeed exist an Arab nation in *Eretz Israel* which can establish a state here? Is it not clear that any Arab state to be established here would only be a fiction, and a base for the re-establishment of Imperialist rule?'[25]

At most, *Lehi* was prepared to see the 'League' establish a 'democractic' government *after* the Hebrews had reconquered their entire homeland – and thereby prevent Abdullah's acquisition of that portion of the west bank assigned to the Arabs by the partition proposal of 29 November.[26] But that was its only 'concession'. Otherwise

– both before and after the cease-fire – *Lehi* was adamant in its opposition to the formation of a local Arab force which threatened to establish an independent Arab state. Right up until its disbandment, the movement also fostered the image of the local Arabs as a defeatist community which, although desirous of peace, possessed no self-confidence in the surrounding cliques of effendis and kings. In the last analysis, *Lehi* considered that the true solution of the problem posed by the Arabs was to be found in their mass flight from the country in which the 'Kingdom of Israel' would again be established.[27]

## TOWARDS THE FIRST CEASE-FIRE

*Lehi*'s opposition to the cease-fire of 11 June increased as the date approached. A truce could only be signed, it claimed, when the army of Israel was stationed in the vicinity of Amman, Damascus and the eastern bank of the Suez Canal, as befitted a fighting people who had 'powerful allies' in the world (namely, the USSR). Under the present circumstances, the cease-fire was tantamount to leading the nation to slaughter. It would also tie the new state 'to the chariot of the dollar' and thereby perhaps even lead Russia to withdraw its recognition. Altogether, in agreeing to the cease-fire, the Provisional Government had acquiesced in a second Munich; it had been 'dragged along' on Bevin's coat-tails and had not shown any independence. Its members were no better than Pétain and Laval (who now reappeared as *Lehi*'s models for Ben-Gurion and Weizmann). Once victory in the war had been achieved, a domestic revolution would have to take place. The old guard had to be replaced by a new regime of young people. Otherwise, foreign rule would be renewed.[28]

Although *Lehi* openly sided with the eastern bloc, it did not link its appeal for that alignment with one for social revolution. One reason was the fact that the states of Eastern Europe had themselves not yet fully implemented socialist policies, and were considered to be in a 'transitional stage'. Another was *Lehi*'s own need to find a balance between its leanings towards the right and the left. Eldad may have been particularly sensitive to the latter point, and seems to have attempted to put a brake on *Lehi*'s leftward tendencies. Instead, he attempted to reinstate some of the motifs which characterised the Revisionism upon which he had been raised.[29] More than any other member of *Lehi*, however, Eldad considered the cease-fire a betrayal. Indeed, inspired by its own largely eschatological view of events, the movement found the truce incomprehensible. Having renewed the glorious fighting traditions of the Maccabees, the Sicarii and Bar-Kochba, the entire nation was ready to continue the war, whatever the cost. Only the 'worm-like leaders' of the Provisional Government pleaded shortages of arms, oil and money. But the fact was that there were no such shortages. The claim was a blatant lie, and just proved how unfit these 'mercenaries of Bevin and Abdullah' were to rule.[30]

At a meeting with divisional commanders on 18 June, Ben-Gurion described the cease-fire as 'a blessing' (in Mosheh Carmel's term). The fighting thus far had revealed serious weaknesses in Israel's military capabilities; these had to be repaired before the war was renewed. The Israel Defence Force (IDF) had first to defeat the Arab Legion and then deal with the Lebanese army and the Syrians. 'The war for Jerusalem and its environs', he added, 'quite apart from its sentimental aspects, is the war for the entire country. If we win here, we can say that we have been victorious.'[31]

*Lehi* was unaware of the problems which Ben-Gurion faced at that stage of the fighting, and of his overall strategy. Like the IZL, it judged him by the gauge of the past – which was no longer relevant. Indulging in fantasy, it regarded Jerusalem as another Stalingrad – except that the Provisional Government (unlike the Russians in the case of Stalingrad) was deliberately undermining the morale of its inhabitants. That is why they were not being supplied with all the required assistance. Eldad was convinced that 'only the distant hills of Moab in the east would have halted the great victory parade of the tens of thousands of Jerusalem's soldiers'.[32]

In sum, following the best of Revisionist traditions, *Lehi* considered the leadership to be the root of all evil. It also defended the right of the *Palmach* to its independence, and opposed Ben-Gurion's attempt to disband that force on the grounds that it was little more than *Mapam*'s private army.[33] *Lehi*'s right to retain the independence of its own units in Jerusalem was even more justified. Because of Ben-Gurion's limited political aims, especially his readiness to leave Jerusalem outside the borders of Israel, *Lehi* could not abide his plan to unite all fighting forces within a single army subject to his own authority. Confrontation was just a matter of time.[34]

## THE *ALTALENA* EPISODE

The fusion of all forces in a single national army proved to be a more complicated issue for the IZL than for *Lehi*. The IZL and the *Haganah* had reached an agreement in principle on the matter on 27 April; and in Jerusalem on 13 May. However, the IZL did not finally agree to disband until 1 June, when it also undertook to place all of its arms at the disposal of the Israeli government and to cease its activities within the area of the state of Israel '*and all areas under the*

*Government's jurisdiction*' (para. 6). In order to facilitate the conscription of its troops to the IDF, an IZL command was to operate for
only one month. The *'Altalena* episode' was the result of misunder-
standings not only between the IZL commander and the authorities
representing the IDF and the Ministry of Defence, but also – perhaps
principally – between the IZL command in Israel and the IZL leaders
in the European diaspora.[35]

Shertok raised the issue of the *Altalena* (the IZL ship which carried
armaments and almost 1,000 men) in the Cabinet as early as 20 June.
Ben-Gurion recalled the IZL's undertaking of 1 June; Shertok advised
dispersing the IZL; Bentov advocated the arrest of Begin. Ben-
Gurion was also inclined to use force. The government announcement
published on the following day declared that the arrival of the ship
constituted a blatant breach of national law, of the agreement with the
IZL and of the government's international commitments. The IZL
published a counter-manifesto. On 22 June, Ben-Gurion informed the
government that the ship had reached Kfar Vitkin, and that many
former IZL members had deserted their unit and were making their
way to the coast. He regarded such actions as mutiny. Gruenbaum,
the Minister of the Interior (who had previously resigned over the
'saison'), advocated a compromise; but the notion was rejected by
Ben-Gurion, who had the support of *Mapam*, Shertok and Kaplan.
That day, violent clashes took place, during which 18 members of IZL
lost their lives and the ship was sunk by IDF artillery. Although the
IZL immediately gave in, Begin on the same day delivered a public
address in which he claimed that he 'could in a moment have killed the
Prime Minister, had he wished to do so'. The Provisional State Council
met to discuss the matter on 24 June. When voting took place, 24
members supported the government, four opposed (three from the
Revisionist Party and one from the *Mizrachi*), five abstained. The
*Mizrachi* and *Ha-Poel Ha-Mizrachi* ministers resigned.[36]

*Lehi* supported the IZL over the *'Altalena* episode' as a matter of
course. Notwithstanding their separate existence, the two movements
had in any case been drawing closer together (in part because the *Lehi*
leadership was becoming increasingly appreciative of the IZL's ideological pragmatism, as evinced by the IZL's appeal to the USSR to help
Israel overcome the American embargo).[37] Ben-Gurion's 'madness' in
firing on the *Altalena* (an action subsequently compared to Nero's
insane conflagration of Rome and the Tsar's victory over the battleship
*Potemkin* in 1905) sealed the bond. His only purpose, *Lehi* claimed,

was to demonstrate his loyalty to the Anglo-Saxon bloc. He hopes
that Bevin and Marshall will now agree to leave him the title and

domestic rulership. Before the defeatist Government informs the public of its agreement to a surrender, Ben-Gurion wants to destroy any force which would refuse to accept subjugation.[38]

*Lehi* immediately discerned a link beween the *Altalena* incident and the Bernadotte mission. Both demonstrated the extent to which the Hebrew people were on the verge of renewed subservience to foreign rule.[39] Clearly, the Provisional Government was totally bankrupt: 'This is a comedy, not sovereignty'. Had the government insisted on true sovereignty and stood firmly against Bernadotte, all public opinion would have supported it and demanded that the IZL hand over the arms on the *Altalena*. In the present circumstances, however, the government had committed a 'crime'. Instead of diverting at least 20 per cent of those weapons to the liberation of the Old City of Jerusalem (as Galili had promised), it would hand them over to Bernadotte's agents. In so doing, it was making necessary further sacrifices.[40] The fact that Ben-Gurion had blown up the ship, even though promised 80 per cent of its cargo of arms, was for Eldad ample demonstration of the Prime Minister's readiness to accept an imposed surrender. Indeed, and as one *Lehi* pamphlet explicitly proclaimed, 'Ben-Gurion is signing with Hebrew blood the document of surrender prepared by Bernadotte'.[41]

Clearly *Lehi* considered that the fate meted out to the IZL (some of whose members were also arrested in the wake of the *Altalena* incident) would also be its own. 'Today the IZL; tomorrow *Lehi*; and the day after, the *Palmach*.' The government had embarked on 'a dangerous path'; instilling fear in the population; dividing the military from the civilians; and therefore necessitating a revival of the underground.

The greater the suppression, the greater will be the explosion. The results will also be the more terrible. You may disband those organisations which have emerged from the underground. You can arrest their fighters . . . but it will do no good. It is precisely those Socialists who have learnt a chapter in historical dialectics who should understand that it is not men who give birth to facts, but the opposite. And the fact of suppression will give birth to other men who will fight it.[42]

The reference to 'socialist' was deliberate. Believing that the Provisional Government was leading the people in the pro-imperialist direction already followed by Greece, *Lehi* thrust itself into the vanguard of revolutionary activity. Hence, it exploited the opportunity provided by the *Altalena* to proclaim once again that Israel must cease enslaving itself to the West and join the eastern bloc. Britain, it warned, intended to use its bases in Palestine as a springboard for an attack on the Caucasus and the bombing of Russia. *Lehi*'s own mission was now – more than ever before – to act as the Soviets' agency in the region.[43] *Lehi* was certainly better equipped to fulfil that role than were the local left-wing *Mapam* party (whose representatives had already accepted ministerial office) or Ben-Gurion – the so-called leader of the working classes. The latter was deliberately avoiding an exchange of diplomatic representatives with the USSR, but had received the temporary American representative at the very height of the *Altalena* affair. Hebrew workers had to decide 'whether . . . to fight imperialism or join *Mapai*'s "Social-Democrat-Reform" bandwagon'. 'If you refuse to go the treacherous way of French social-democracy . . . be with *Lehi* . . . Transform the workers' councils into weapons of war against Anglo-Saxon Imperialism and its servants.'[44] For a short spell, *Lehi* tried to issue a call for the establishment of a 'common front' on the lines of the 'Hebrew Resistance Movement'.[45] But it was really too late for that. Although the IZL did show some pro-Soviet leanings in the wake of the *Altalena* affair,[46] and although *Lehi* did defend those IZL leaders who had been arrested, the two organisations remained apart. The IZL called members of the Provisional Government 'Hebrew Tsaldarites'. Yet *Lehi* felt itself to be almost entirely isolated – a position which forced it to rely on its own resources. At this stage, *Lehi* even doubted whether its men had to take an oath of allegiance to the IDF; they should swear only to 'the freedom of Israel' and not to any institution.[47]

### TOWARDS THE END OF THE FIRST CEASE-FIRE

While the cease-fire was in progress, *Lehi* demanded that the fighting be renewed. Even though the last British soldiers had left Haifa (a circumstance which justified *Lehi*'s earlier teachings), the presence of the Arab Legion under British command proved that the homeland had not been liberated. This had to be the next step. Thousands of soldiers, together with the necessary supplies, had to be sent to Jerusalem. Victory there would ensure victory everywhere. Notwithstanding the fear and defeatism of their leaders, the Hebrew people possessed the potential to reach the Nile and the Euphrates. They need not fear the 'Arab–British Legion'. 'It is only an Arab robot who sits in the tanks which the British have left behind . . . We shall blow up the British armour and the entire country – yes, the *entire* country – will be ours.'[48]

In principle, *Lehi* rejected the government's claim that the cease-fire had provided the breathing-space necessary for the reorganisation of the army. The opposite was the case. It was the Arabs who were making the best use of the respite, in order to tighten the ring around Jerusalem. The government, however, had spent the time in blowing up the *Altalena* and carrying out mass arrests. The army was in chaos; the air was thick with rumours and threats of mass resignations of the senior staff – which had resulted from Ben-Gurion's attempts to politicise the IDF. So weak-kneed was the present leadership that it was even prepared to sacrifice Jerusalem. The heads of the religious parties – whose attachment to the Holy City might have been expected to have been greater – were no better than their colleagues. They, too, refused to acknowledge that the Messiah was on his way.[49] In fact, the entire cease-fire was a British–Arab plot, designed to further the implementation of the 'Morrison Plan'. Without in any way supervising Arab activities, it imposed restrictions on Jewish immigration and on the import of Jewish supplies; involved the forfeiture of Jerusalem; and psychologically undermined the foundations of the Hebrew army.[50]

Under those circumstances, the inhabitants of Jerusalem had certainly to oust their present governors (Joseph and Shaltiél) and bring to power new leaders who would liberate the city. Moreover, since the Arabs were persistently violating the cease-fire, *Lehi* called for the incessant bombing of the Old City of Jerusalem. Otherwise, it warned, its 100,000 Jewish inhabitants would probably be slaughtered. On the very day that the fighting was renewed, Eldad publicly warned that 'any Jew who signs a document of surrender not necessitated by military decision and disaster – deserves death as a traitor'.[51] Meanwhile, *Lehi* itself made use of the cease-fire in order to demonstrate that its underground strength – in Jerusalem at least – was still as great as ever. It executed Rosa Beizer for being a 'British agent'.[52]

### 'THE TEN DAYS BATTLE' (9–19 JULY 1948)

*Lehi* attributed Israel's victories during the short spell of fighting after the first cease-fire to the fighters themselves. They had won despite the government. Indeed, the IDF owed its success in the central front to the commando forces of *Lehi* and *Palmach*, who had executed a pincer movement around Jerusalem and (notwithstanding the *Altalena* affair) had effected an amicable conjunction of forces.[53]

These victories had two principal effects. First, they generated a further hardening of *Lehi*'s positions, especially those relating to the Arab refugees (who were now advised to apply to their 'benefactor', Bevin, so that he could arrange for them to be sent as colonists to one of the British territories or to Madagascar)[54] and to the borders. The movement now called for the enemy to be driven from the entire land 'at least as far as the Jordan'. The Hebrew youth had now to put pressure on its leaders to 'finally throw into the garbage the borders of the mini-state delineated by the gentiles of the UN and to return to the eternal borders delineated by the God of Israel'.[55] To this was added an increase in *Lehi*'s self-confidence. By the middle of August 1948, the movement was already celebrating victory. The only danger was political: the reaction of the government to the Security Council's call for an unlimited cease-fire. To *Lehi*'s mind this was a purely imperialist device; it could only lead to economic as well as military 'disaster'. Moreover, there was no need to accept it. 'Our situation now is not at all as it was in 1938. Today we possess strength and are able to create facts.'[56]

Needless to say, *Lehi* could give the government no credit whatsoever for the victories. On the contrary, it portrayed the 'old leadership' as being responsible even for *Lehi*'s own failure to effect a forced entry into the Old City of Jerusalem. It claimed that the collection of party hacks who currently controlled the country were likely to sacrifice all the gains which had been made and thereby renew the threat of a 'Morrison-Bernadotte' Plan which had no right to be revived. Reverting to the maximalist Revisionist positions preached by U.Z. Greenberg, Eldad proclaimed that 'The path of Hebrew liberation will be that of liberation throughout the world: the path of blood. A conquered land is holier than one bought for money.'[57]

Because of that outlook *Lehi* could not agree to a second cease-fire (which was compared to the truce in the war against Britain in the summer of 1946). For one thing, such a cease-fire would merely sacrifice Jerusalem (where even now a smiling Shaltiél was being photographed alongside Abdullah El-Tal, the Jordanian military governor of the Old City). For another, a cease-fire raised the spectre of a renewed Western imperialist plot. The extent to which the forces of reaction were on the march had been shown by the attack on the life of the Italian communist leader, Palmiro Togliatti, on 14 July. 'Berlin, Trieste, *Eretz Israel*, Malaya, Korea – all these, "hot spots" are interconnected.'[58]

### LEHI AND THE SECOND CEASE-FIRE

Until the very last moment, *Lehi* hoped that the cease-fire would be prevented from coming into effect by the Arab refusal to honour it. In addition, throughout the period which followed the *Altalena* incident, *Lehi* lived in fear that it would be the next target of Ben-Gurion's attack; as early as July 1948 members were warned of the possibility that the 'government of dictators' would attempt to destroy the movement in Jerusalem.[59] An equally important subject of concern was the prospect that the Provisional Government would enslave the nation to 'western imperialism', in the guise of the American dollar and the oil companies, once work at the Haifa refineries had been renewed. Indeed, it was said that a secret agreement with the Americans had already been reached. In return for a massive American loan and acceptance to the UN, Israel would virtually become an American protectorate.[60] *Lehi* argued that Israel would not attain true independence until it had freed itself of the yoke of the West and aligned with the East. That was why it found so obnoxious Ben-Gurion's suggestion of some sort of political co-operation with Transjordan. The movement's immediate response was that 'any agreement with Abdullah is a British trap'. The proper solution was complete victory over the enemy and compromise only with the 'truly progressive' forces in the Arab world.[61]

This background explains the continued support which *Lehi* had been extending ever since 1946 to Henry Wallace, the leader of the American Progressive Party and an opponent of Truman's Cold War policy. In July 1948 a *Lehi* representative named Jerry Geisler (Nicolas Kinsberg) was invited to address the Progressive Party. He decried Anglo-Saxon imperialism, demanded that all foreign forces be removed from the Middle East and asked that Wallace help Israel to resist any attempt to impose territorial concessions on it for the sake of foreign bases.[62]

But the high-point of *Lehi*'s activities during the second cease-fire was its demand that the Provisional Government publicly declare Jerusalem's incorporation within the territory of the state. To that end, it even issued a real and deliberate threat. 'The Government of Israel faces the choice: either to make use of the fighters for the liberation of Jerusalem or to face a bloody civil war.'[63] Although demanding co-operation with the IZL, the *Lehi* commander in Jerusalem, Yehoshua Zetler, was prepared to back up that challenge. He promised that *Lehi* would be ready 'to intensify underground activities and mount immediate actions once [the Government declares] the demilitarisation of the city or its internationalisation'.[64] Early in August, *Lehi* welcomed Shaltiél's replacement by Dayan as commander of the Jerusalem district, especially as he pursued a more activist policy. But it did not retract its unfavourable opinion of Dov Joseph, who was appointed the city's military governor. 'His true function . . . is not to prepare for the annexation to the State of Israel of the capital but its transfer to the auspices of the cross.'[65]

THE ATTITUDE TOWARDS *MAPAM*, THE 'HEBREW COMMUNIST
PARTY' AND TO *MAKI*, THE 'COMMUNIST PARTY OF ISRAEL'

A review of *Lehi*'s attitude towards the Israeli left illuminates the movement's ideology at this juncture. Although the movement did stress its differences with the parties of the left, it also sought some contact with them. Its purpose was dual: it wished to avoid falling into the arms of the rightist *Herut* movement; at the same time, it also wanted to become the focus of the Israeli left's identification with the Soviet Union on the basis of its own ideology of National Bolshevism.

As early as January 1948, Friedman-Yellin had suggested the formation of a political bloc comprising the most outstanding of the leaders of the three underground movements. Dr M. Sneh, who was soon to join the *Mapam* party, rejected this proposal on the grounds that their history of mutual tensions would make it impossible for the persons involved to formulate a unified policy. In particular he feared that Begin's self-righteousness and social conservatism would lead to a bitter debate and to a form of local 'Pilsudskism' which would result in a split. Nevertheless, during the spring of 1948, by which time Sneh had joined *Mapam*, he did hold weekly meetings with Friedman-Yellin in which (so both Friedman-Yellin and Eldad relate) he 'persistently' flattered *Lehi*.[66] Moreover, *Lehi* certainly found itself in agreement with some of Sneh's public positions, particularly when he announced his opposition to Western imperialism and advocated a pro-Soviet orientation.[67]

On the other hand, *Lehi*'s ideological differences with *Mapam* were deep. Once *Ha-Shomer Ha-Tsair* and the *Ahdut ha-Avodah* movement had combined, *Lehi* claimed, internal opposition in both parties had weakened. Both had ceased to compete for the soul of the Hebrew youth, instead following a policy of revolution in theory but of surrender in practice. *Mapam* was interested only in ministerial posts. Hence, the *Palmach* had not dared openly to criticise Ben-Gurion's strategic follies and demand his resignation from the Defence portfolio. That, too, explained *Mapam*'s behaviour during and after the *Altalena* affair. The party had completely failed to realise that Ben-Gurion had tricked them when using the *Palmach* against the IZL. In fact, the *Palmach* was itself next on Ben-Gurion's list of targets. Instead of aligning themselves with the communists and the forces of progress (namely *Lehi*), *Mapam* was now being enticed by the prospect of co-operation with *Mapai*, which represented social democracy. It had a flawed understanding of the ideological divisions in the world struggle.

Social-Democracy is today in the vanguard of reaction and Imperialism throughout the world. Leon Blum, [Guiseppe] Saragat and their like are no less the enemies of the Soviet Union and of the progressive parties than are De Gaulle, Franco, Truman and Marshall. Is the situation any different in *Eretz Israel*? Certainly not.

*Lehi*'s inner hope was that the youth of *Mapam* would discover its revolutionary roots and reject the *petit-bourgeois* mentality of its leaders and their leanings towards imperialism.[68]

What brought this animosity to a head was the question of the Arab refugees, which became a public issue during the second cease-fire. On 22 July *Al ha-Mishmar* demanded a government announcement to the effect that the property and rights of the Arabs would be preserved, should they wish to return after the war. *Lehi* was astounded: that was precisely the demand of the Arab League! How could *Mapam* be so sure that, on their return, the refugees would suddenly become loyal citizens? Experience and common sense indicated quite the opposite. 'The Arabs can easily be incited to rebel, and logic teaches that in the contest between imperialism and ourselves for influence over the Arabs, it is imperialism which will win, not us.' Imperialism aimed to create anew a large Arab minority in the low-lands and to exploit it in the same way that the Nazis had exploited the German minority in Czechoslovakia. Instead of depriving imperialism of this card 'once and for all', *Mapam* rushed to return it. 'Does not [*Al ha-Mishmar*] understand that as long as Imperialism exists, and as long as Hebrew independence persists, they will be at war – whatever its form?[69]

It was thus that the Arab question now became the focus of disagreement between *Lehi* and *Mapam*, rather than (as in the past) the relationship with imperialism and the subject of obedience to the official Zionist leadership. *Lehi* now maintained that *Mapam*'s 'original' sin lay in its retroactive agreement to partition (on which, Galili had predicted during the period of the United Hebrew Resistance Movement, the Zionist movement would be sundered). *Mapam*'s mistake, similarly, lay in its inability to see the connecton between the situation within *Eretz Israel* and the wider world.

No progressive rule can be established in one part of *Eretz Israel* without a revolution throughout the Middle East . . . No rule of progressive Arabs can presently be established in a part of *Eretz Israel*. We do not deny the existence of some progressive circles amongst Arabs inside and outside the country; but as a political force they are inconsequential.

Partition, therefore, was impracticable.[70]

Precisely the same issue (together with the question of socio-economic relevance) divided *Lehi* from the 'Hebrew Communist Party' and from the PKP (which, with the establishment of the state, had changed its name to *Maki*). Relations with the latter, especially, were characterised by the same degree of conflict as had marked their ideological confrontations during the previous summer. *Maki* was attacked because it still referred to *Lehi* as 'fascists' and because it had not acknowledged its own collaboration with the foreign suzerain against which *Lehi* had fought. *Maki* was also scorned for its attempts to gain public favour by attacking 'the forces of progress' (meaning, *Lehi*) within the country instead of uniting with them. That was what distinguished the leaders of *Maki* from Maurice Thorez and Palmiro Togliatti, the communist leaders of France and Italy. The present circumstances dictated three vital conclusions. First, that Anglo-Saxon imperialism constituted the prime enemy of the Jewish people, as well as of the Soviet Union and of democratic and progressive forces throughout the world; second, that every inch of the historic Hebrew homeland not wrested by force from the effendis and the Arab kings would become an Anglo-Saxon base; third, that the Provisional Government was inclined towards the West and ready to compromise with Abdullah and Britain.

*Maki*'s leaders recognised none of these facts; consequently, their efforts to claim a monopoly of Soviet support were totally unwarranted. Not surprisingly, therefore, they had still not been accepted by the Cominform. 'We believe that the Soviet Union is interested in organic allies rather than in . . . those who suffer from an inferiority complex.'[71] The PKP has misled the Soviet Union by adopting 'formalistic' conclusions which negated Marxist-Leninist dialectics. Mikunis, their leader, suffered from 'characteristic inferiority', whereas *Lehi* dared to fight for the independence of the entire homeland and to deny 'the British concoction of a special Arab reality in *Eretz Israel*'.[72]

*Lehi* hoped to establish better relations with the 'Hebrew Communist Party', which had split from the PKP in 1945. True, the two were not in any way identical. *Lehi* itself (as its own programme showed – see below), did not adopt Marxist – or even socialist – principles; the 'Hebrew Communist Party', for its part, had also long shown its opposition to *Lehi*'s positions and politics. As early as 1946 the Hebrew communists had opposed the United Hebrew Resistance Movement, supported the notion of self-determination for both Arabs and Jews (following B. Leontiev in *Pravda* on 30 September 1946), and described the gains of the Revisionists at the twenty-second Zionist congress as a circumstance which also strengthened 'the terrorist organisations'.[73] At the end of March 1948, they also criticised *Lehi* for ignoring the national rights of the Arabs and for harbouring designs of conquest and territorial expansion.[74]

Nevertheless, *Lehi* did consider that some basis for co-operation existed. After all, at its founding conference in October 1947, the 'Hebrew Communist Party' had expressed its 'horror' at the revival of the partition proposal (its own proposal being for a federated Arab–Jewish independent state with a right to separation) and had warned against 'the efforts of the leadership of the *Yishuv* to retain the alliance with British Imperialism or to establish an alliance with American Imperialism'.[75] *Lehi* hoped to exploit this opportunity. It called upon the Hebrew communists to define their borders and immediately to recognise Nablus and Amman (as well as Jerusalem) as Hebrew. In return, *Lehi* promised to move towards whatever form of regime the Hebrew communists would hope to establish in 'the great Hebrew republic': a regime of nationalisation of all the country's resources and products or a regime of a classless society.[76]

### *LEHI*'S RELATIONSHIP WITH THE IZL AND CLASSIC REVISIONISM: THE FIRST PROGRAMME

As we have seen, throughout the *Altalena* episode, *Lehi* supported the IZL. At bottom, however, Eldad thought that Begin had not gone far enough. Hence his later criticisms of Begin's 'surrender' and of his unpreparedness to follow the 'revolutionary path' to victory. Precisely what Eldad had in mind became clear when he tried to convince Begin to commit 700 IZL fighters to join 300 *Lehi* men in an attack on Arab positions in and around Jerusalem. But while Eldad saw 'external conquest' as the key to success and public esteem, Begin (so Eldad relates) was inclined to attempt to gain domestic power before taking any other steps. That was why the IZL commander was not a true revolutionary on the Leninist model.[77]

Nevertheless, it was during this period that the right wing of *Lehi* intensified a process which had already begun in 1943 and 1946, reverting in no small degree to Jabotinsky's ideology. As much became apparent in the eulogies published in August 1948, on the eighth anniversary of Jabotinsky's death. These played down Jabotinsky's liberalism (especially with regard to the Arab question) and even excused his declaration of a 'community of interests' between the Jews and the British. More important than these failings, it now appeared, was Jabotinsky's nationalism – the fact that (unlike Ben-Gurion and Weizmann) he did not represent or address just one party, but the entire people. That was why he deserved to become part of the national pantheon. He had returned to the Zionist movement the magic Herzlian term 'The Jewish State' and aroused in the masses the desire to employ Hebrew military force to attain that end. In an unprecedented attempt at apologetics, which did not even mention the fact that *Lehi* was born out of Stern's rebellion against Jabotinsky's political teachings, Eldad also suggested distinguishing between 'the core' and 'the shell' of Jabotinsky's teachings. On questions of foreign and social policy, *Lehi* had indeed followed its own path; nevertheless, Jabotinsky still deserved to be recognised as a national leader and an inspiration of the very first rank: 'If Jabotinsky did not manage to bring about the Hebrew revolution, that was because . . . he did not consider western liberalism and democracy merely as means, but as *ideals*. And that was his greatest and most tragic mistake.'[78]

The operational importance of this ideological perspective became apparent when a group (whom Eldad referred to as constituting a 39-man 'council') met in order to draft *Lehi*'s programme in the summer of 1948. Although this body did strive to effect a compromise between the right and left wings of the movement, and thereby to bring *Lehi* into conformity with the 'people's democracies', it was in fact the right-wing leanings which became most apparent. True, the programme did not speak of the establishment of the Third Temple; but it did promise to promote the liberation of the entire homeland throughout its natural and historic borders; to establish (in line with 'The Principles of Revival' of 1940–41) a 'kingdom' and 'mastery'; it was also announced that the 'entire' people 'carries the burden of the War of Liberation'.

The principal innovation lay in the field of domestic policy (para. 7); here too the contrast between the programme and the 'IZL in Israel' was particularly marked. Under Klausner's influence, the latter had spoken in only the most general terms about the promotion of a 'just society . . . in the spirit of the morality of Israel and prophetic justice'. *Lehi*, however, strove to formulate a new socio-economic ideology which was National Bolshevik in nature. The programme made no reference to the subject of class warfare; but (like Revisionism) it projected the state as the sole prism determining national life in all its expressions. Hence, the programme spoke of national planning; the sequestration of property under foreign ownership; the nationalisation of the country's resources, basic industries, sources of energy and public services; it also proclaimed that foreign commerce would be under government supervision and that private enterprise would be encouraged only within the framework of the state's economic planning. All this fitted in nicely with the present transitory nature of the 'people's democracies', which permitted private initiative for the time being, and the beliefs of *Lehi* rightist wing.

In addition, the programme promised to raise Jewish funds abroad; to promote the development of modern agriculture; to take surplus and unused land from large land-holders for the purposes of the colonising projects which were planned; to give national assistance to the small farmer, to the worker and to the agricultural co-operatives; to exploit water resources and to give prominence to the preservation of land. Unlike Stern, *Lehi* called for the establishment of a 'united workers federation' in order 'to safeguard the worker's professional interests and to prevent competition between one labourer and another; it will also become a powerful weapon in the war for national and social liberation'. Finally, there followed a number of other promises: of work for each citizen; to uproot black-marketeering and poverty; of housing for everyone in need; of a progressive form of taxation; of free national education at all levels; of progress in every scientific field; often the provision of free medical services; of compulsory national insurance; of the promotion of a higher birth-rate. If this sounded like a dictatorial and corporatist regime, *Lehi* never denied the fact.[79]

There were also innovations in those sections of the programme that dealt with foreign affairs. Like Stern in his day, *Lehi* now aimed to turn the Hebrew people into a 'military, political, cultural and economic force of first-rate importance in the Orient and along the shores of the Mediterranean'. But to this it added a pro-communist anti-imperialist thrust, which Stern had never known but which now became fundamental: 'The aim of Hebrew foreign policy is to free the entire homeland from Imperialism . . . and to ensure its political and economic independence.' Similarly innovation was the attention which *Lehi* now paid to the Middle East in its search for allies in that struggle, its plans for the neutralisation of the region, and its inclination towards the eastern bloc (even though the USSR was not explicitly mentioned), in the hope that its position on the Arab question would be accepted.

Clearly, *Lehi*'s programme was less influenced by 'The Principle of Revival' than by the establishment of 'people's democracies' in eastern Europe under Soviet aegis. To this must be added its attempts to achieve some alignment with the communist parties in Israel itself (which eventually combined in December 1948, only to split again later) and the 'cosmetic changes which some of *Lehi*'s representatives in Eastern Europe felt it necessary to make to the original programme.[80]

Nevertheless, in the summer of 1948, *Lehi* generally found itself closer to the *Herut* movement, founded by the IZL. Admittedly, the residue of tensions dating from their past relationships still prevented the two movements from appearing on a common political platform;

so, too, did personal antagonisms and continued ideological differences between Begin and Friedman-Yellin. Begin might have been pragmatically inclined to accept Eldad's version of an orientation which favoured the USSR; but he could not agree to the notions of a 'people's democracy' or National Bolshevism advocated by the left wing in *Lehi*. Nevertheless, *Lehi* and the IZL did feel an affinity born of their common fate as groups of hounded 'dissidents'; their shared radical nationalism, which aimed at the liberation of the entire historic homeland; and the history of their joint efforts to expel the British from the country. To this was later added the IZL's recognition of the vital role played by the USSR in Israel's establishment.[81]

The state of relations between *Lehi* and the IZL at this stage can best be ascertained by comparing the former's programme with the proposals earlier published by the *Herut* movement.[82] Their common adherence to Revisionist postulates is clearly illustrated by their shared commitment to Israel's 'historic' borders. Both aimed at the establishment of Hebrew dominion over both banks of the Jordan. Similarly, because both movements gave priority to national issues over the class struggle, both came to be regarded in the public mind as segments of the radical right.[83]

Otherwise, however, their programmes differed in two central areas. One concerned the nature of the regime which they wished to promote. *Herut* spoke of the establishment of a 'new society' based on 'true democracy'; *Lehi*, however, avoided the latter term, principally because of its insistence that 'domestic policy must take second place to the needs of the war of liberation'. It was in line with this fundamental lack of commitment to democracy that *Lehi* adopted the term 'Kingdom of Israel', coined by Stern and U.Z. Greenberg, and spoke of 'mastery [*adnut*]'. Both demanded nationalisation; but *Lehi* insisted on fulfilling the Communist Manifesto's promise to prevent 'the exploitation of man by man'. Equally significant were the differences in their foreign policies. On the Arab question, *Herut* (unlike *Lehi*) did not make any reference whatsoever to the possibility of a demographic exchange between the Arab population of Israel and the Jews of Oriental lands; instead, it referred only to 'absolute equality of rights in all areas of life'. Similarly, and again unlike *Lehi*, *Herut* did not consider the 'neutralisation' of the Middle East to be an indispensable prerequisite for the avoidance of a third world war. Its foreign policy orientation, therefore, was far from being pro-Soviet. Indeed, it hinted that the USA was the power to be identified with.

*Herut* published no reaction to *Lehi*'s programme; *Mapam*, however, responded in the sharpest of terms. Two subjects were singled out for particular attack. One was *Lehi*'s 'hypocritical' position on the Arab question (that is, the promise of 'full rights' after expulsion); the other was its economic proposals. There was nothing socialist about *Lehi*'s notions of a planned economy; since the entire purpose of its programme was not the welfare of the working class but the attainment of national ambitions, *Lehi* had in fact revealed its truly 'fascist' face. When subjected to intensive examination (as was the case), *Mapam* found internal contradictions in some of *Lehi*'s proposals and – more to the point – fundamental flaws in others. In sum, the programme as a whole did not convey the image of 'a revolutionary leftist movement of the camp of progressive forces'. Quite the contrary:

> There are two possibilities. One is that *Lehi*'s 'Programme' is a mechanistic and childish mélange of slogans, which its editors picked up wherever they could . . . The other is that the 'Programme' is a well thought out document, and constructed with a single purpose in mind. But if the latter is the case, then the conception is anti-proletarian and the purpose is fascism.

Hence, there was now a way in which *Lehi*'s programme could form the basis of an alliance with the Soviet Union and with the revolutionary anti-imperialist movements.[84]

Although few contemporary observers realised the fact, *Lehi* was soon to be on the verge of a split between its right and left wings.[85] Hence, its programme was construed as a temporary compromise between positions which were supposed to be ironed out at a subsequent conference. Even so, as it stood, the programme revealed conceptions which are anti-democratic and anti-liberal. It was founded on the belief that there exists common ground between the basic postulates of the radical right (which stress the organic and biological unity of the nation and the primacy of *raison d'état*) and the tactical conceptions of the 'people's democracies' which were to act as the agent of the Soviet Union. In fact, the ideology of National Bolshevism (that is, leftist chauvinism) was too revolutionary and too Utopian for the Israeli political system, and hence gained few adherents. Sooner or later, its supporters had to find their place within the framework of more conventional political opinions and within political parties whose place on the right–left spectrum was more clearly defined. National Bolshevism could find no place in the socio-political conception of the 'people's democracies' which were then in the process of rapid Sovietization. Even less could it find institutional expression in the liberal democracy of the state of Israel.

# The Murder of Count Bernadotte

Count Folke Bernadotte was appointed the United Nations mediator on the Palestine question on 20 May 1948; *Lehi* first referred to the appointment on 1 June and its tone was *a priori* hostile.[1] In part, this was because of the obvious discrepancy in his aims and those of the movement; while *Lehi* dreamed of Jewish Legions parading through Amman, Bernadotte aimed at the restriction of the Jews to just a small portion of the west bank of the Jordan. More fundamentally, however, *Lehi* suspected Bernadotte's credentials. He was, after all, the emissary of the United Nations, an organisation which did not have the best interests of the Hebrew people at heart. That also made him an agent of Anglo-Saxon imperialism; as much was indicated by the proposed composition of his staff, which was to comprise American, French, Belgian and Swedish officers but not Poles, Romanians, Hungarians, Yugoslavs and Bulgarians. Hence, Bernadotte was the enemy of all those who – like *Lehi* – regarded a pro-Soviet policy as the only guarantee of Israel's survival. Because the Provisional Government obviously thought otherwise, its members were to be condemned. Shertok's agreement to a cease-fire during the course of secret negotiations with the mediator proved to *Lehi* that the government of Israel was set on the path of compromise and surrender. Hence the warning issued as early as 6 June:

> Should the Government of Israel agree to Bernadotte's 'inter-pretation' with regard to immigration and supply to Jerusalem; should it agree to the composition of the team of observers as proposed by the Count with a pedigree; then it would indicate that the Government has sacrificed its independence even before becoming independent. It would have unconditionally surrendered to the Imperialist enemy.[2]

*Lehi*'s criticisms of all who collaborated with Bernadotte became increasingly strident during the next few days. Its attacks on the Provisional Government were particularly vicious. Ministers were accused of helping the Arab war effort by agreeing to the incarceration of Jewish immigrants of military age in 'concentration camps'; of violating Israel's own declaration of independence by being pro-American instead on non-aligned; and of agreeing to the eventual resuscitation of the Morrison–Grady Plan, whereby *Eretz Israel* would be divided between 'two Abdullahs, one Arab and the other Jewish', both of whom would owe allegiance to the same British master. Instead of seizing the glorious military opportunities now available, Ben-Gurion and his minions were simply succumbing to Bernadotte's dictates. In so doing, they were sharing his responsibility for the destruction of the Hebrew national entity. The proper course would have been to pronounce Israel's non-recognition of the UN's framework of supervisors, and to expel them.[3]

*Lehi* claimed that the fact that the Provisional Government did not act thus merely revealed the extent to which its members still held to the same views as had characterised their behaviour during the period before the State of Israel existed. They failed to appreciate that Bernadotte's mission was not truly mediatory; his objective was to save the Arab states and to implement British plans. Hence, 'whoever accepts [Bernadotte's invitation] to a conference at Rhodes accepts another Munich; it is like going to Berchtesgaden'. Bernadotte was in fact making Bevin's work easier. In the not too distant past, the latter had needed tens of thousands of troops and millions of pounds sterling. Now, his mission was being accomplished by just a handful of officers.[4]

Interwoven with some of these prognoses of doom were more explicit threats. Most were directed against the members of the Provisional Government. ('There is a limit to treachery and a border to discipline . . . the fighting youth will cast off the yoke of the discipline of the surrenderers.')[5] In addition, however, *Lehi* also cast its net wider. Together with the IZL, *Lehi* informed American correspondents that it would violate the cease-fire by murdering foreign observers.[6]

In effect, these attacks were misplaced. The Provisional Government was not at all subservient to Bernadotte's wishes. Cabinet protocols as well as Bernadotte's diary reveal that quite the opposite was the case. Ben-Gurion and Shertok showed themmselves well aware of the dangers inherent in Bernadotte's mission as early as their first meeting with the mediator and his aides on 6 June. They then rejected out of hand both the Arab demands and the mediator's interpretation of the Security Council's decisions with regard to the immigration of combatants and men of military age. Similarly, the ministers were no less concerned than *Lehi* about the fate of Jerusalem. Where they differed, however, was in their estimate of the need for a cease-fire. Unlike *Lehi*, Ben-Gurion and his military advisers believed that a temporary halt in the fighting would serve Israel's interests, enabling it to re-equip its forces and train its troops. That was why, on 8–9 June, they accepted Bernadotte's proposal for a cease-fire. But, as the plan of operations which Ben-Gurion submitted for Cabinet approval on 14 June showed, he intended to make use of this respite in every way possible.[7]

In many respects, indeed, the government's true positions were not very different from those advocated by *Lehi*. Shertok, for instance, no less than *Lehi*, believed that the Arab question could not be 'turned back' now that several parts of the country had been deserted by their Arab inhabitants. Like *Lehi*, moreover, Ben-Gurion believed that the fate of the country could be settled only by military force and that both the Arab Legion and the Egyptian army could be destroyed. He was as intent as was *Lehi* on achieving victory in Jerusalem; on retaining the southern Negev; and on securing Jewish control over the western Galilee. His attitude was equally forthright towards Britain, which he described as 'our most dreadful difficulty'.[8]

Even had *Lehi* known of these declarations, it is doubtful whether its criticisms of the Provisional Government would have relented. The principal reason for its criticisms lay in Ben-Gurion's refusal to translate his feelings into foreign policy orientations. For tactical reasons, themselves born of the fact that Israel was barely one month old, Ben-Gurion could at the most only proclaim a policy of neutrality in world affairs and of reliance on the United Nations. Israel, he felt, could not afford to disassociate itself publicly from Bernadotte's policy of supervision.[9] *Lehi*, however (no less than *Mapam* and *Maki*),[10] insisted on a public stance in favour of the USSR. Convinced of the coincidence of Russian and Israeli interests, the movement considered that Ben-Gurion was playing into the hands of the Anglo-Saxon imperialists who were intent on Russia's destruction. In so doing, he had relinquished all sovereignty, and had transferred true authority in the country (especially in matters of immigration and of military action) to Bernadotte himself:

> As long as Ben-Gurion has not arrested Bernadotte on a charge of hostile activity against Hebrew independence, or as long as Bernadotte has not arrested Ben-Gurion on charges of resisting those who 'repair' that independence – then we still have to write 'Minister', 'Government' and 'State' in inverted commas, and the word 'independence' in double inverted commas.[11]

The conclusion was clear. Since the state of Israel itself did not stand upright (*Lehi* predicted that the government would yet agree to an embargo on arms to Jerusalem), it had no right to claim authority over any man. No one had the right to command soldiers to implement the orders of Bernadotte and his aides.[12]

## BERNADOTTE'S FIRST PLAN

From the start, Bernadotte had looked with disfavour on the UN decision of 29 November 1947. It had brought about war and had delineated artificial borders. He preferred a unified Arab–Jewish state, in which the Jews would possess extraordinary rights. To his mind, the *Altalena* episode had weakened the Israeli case; he was also sure that the government of Israel would become even more uncertain of its ability to emerge victorious from the war. He therefore thought that the leaders of the state would be more amenable to negotiation. Nevertheless, he was also aware of their need to be cautious in respect to his proposals for a final solution because of domestic opposition (although he expected trouble in that quarter from the IZL rather than from *Lehi*).

In formulating his proposals for the future of Palestine, Bernadotte was undoubtedly influenced by Britain's global interests in the Cold War. That explains his wish to make Abdullah the dominant ruler of a unified state of Palestine and Transjordan, which would conduct joint policy in the fields of economics, development, defence and foreign affairs. A central council would direct the affairs of this 'union'. The two states, one Jewish and the other Arab, would possess internal independence; each would have the right to scrutinise the other's immigration policy, as would the UN's Economic and Social Council. The mediator was inclined to hand the Negev over to the Arab state, in return for which the Jewish state would receive the western Galilee. He suggested that Jerusalem be included in the Arab state, with autonomy for the city's Jewish inhabitants; Haifa and Lydda would be free ports; the status of Jaffa would have to be ascertained. Bernadotte even suggested that his proposals be subjected to a referendum, so that responsibility for their implementation would not fall on the Great Powers.[13]

These proposals were finally formulated by Bernadotte's aides between 24 and 27 June; they reached Ben-Gurion on 29 June. His immediate reaction was totally negative: 'Whoever suspected that he [Bernadotte] was Bevin's agent – was not entirely wrong.'[14] Consequently, Ben-Gurion's own recommendation to his colleagues was to renew the war, in which the Arab states would be defeated. An alliance with the Arabs, he claimed, would be possible only under conditions of Israeli superiority. In subsequent debate, several members of the Israeli cabinet were inclined to accept at least some of the mediator's proposals as bases for negotiations, partly because they feared the consequences of breaking off negotiations, partly because they were not yet confident of Israel's military capabilities. Hence, the discussion was not entirely one-sided. Nevertheless, no minister advised accepting Bernadotte's proposals in their original form. Indeed, all were aware that domestic pressure would not permit them to do so. They were particularly senstive – not to *Lehi* – but to the 'poisonous' propaganda being put out by the IZL against the government with regard to Jerusalem.[15] Ultimately, in a closed session of the Provisional State Council held on 5 July, the vast majority of representatives accepted Shertok's resolution to reject Bernadotte's proposals.[16]

*Lehi* itself knew no details of the cabinet debate. Indeed, it was reduced to learning the specifics of Bernadotte's proposals from such suspect sources as the Lebanese Falangists.[17] Nevertheless, uncertainty only made the movement even more apprehensive. Convinced that pressure exerted on the government would result in the establishment of 'a sort of Luxembourg in Arab–Nazi arms', *Lehi* regarded even the agreement to go to Rhodes as a surrender. 'Those who go to Rhodes should know: their surrender commits only themselves . . . They received no mandate . . . Laval was not saved by the legal cover of the Pétain government.'[18]

As the above quotation shows, *Lehi*'s virtually instinctive response to the Bernadotte proposals (as it knew them) was to step up its attacks on the Provisional Government. In addition, however, the movement also adopted two other courses. One was to stress the extent to which the proposals increased the need for a pro-Soviet alignment (so much so that, when Yugoslavia seceded from the Cominform, *Lehi* unhesitatingly sided with the USSR).[19] Another was to vilify Bernadotte's mission itself. True, at this stage, *Lehi* called for the liquidation of the process of mediation rather than of the mediator; but the personal element in its pronouncements was nevertheless emphatic. In general, Sweden's neutrality was called into question: after all, had it not during the Second World War granted the Nazis passage over Swedish territory during their attack on the USSR and supplied them with steel? Could Russia now be sure that Stockholm would not become a base for atomic attacks on Warsaw, Kaliningrad, Riga, Tallinn, Leningrad and even Moscow itself? More specifically, there was Bernadotte's own background. Surely it was no coincidence that he had been selected as a mediator after the Nazi defeat by Himmler, the head of the Gestapo? Was it not also significant that the Swedish roots of this Count went back no more than 150 years? He was the scion of a family which had betrayed its benefactor, the Emperor Napoleon. Altogether, therefore, he was not to be trusted, and possessed no sense of history. His proposals with regard to Jerusalem merely showed as much. 'Just as you [Bernadotte] can offer Jerusalem to Abdullah; we can offer Stockholm to the Russians.'[20]

Ultimately, *Lehi* was to find fault with virtually all of Bernadotte's proposals. One (para. 9 in his original document) spoke of the 'unrestricted' right of return of the Arab refugees, whom he estimated to number a quarter of a million persons. Another, rumoured to have been proposed later as a 'sweetener', was his readiness to provide 'international guarantees' for Israel's security. *Lehi* regarded the first as impracticable, querying how one could verify that every Arab who declared himself to be a 'refugee' was indeed so, and not just an unemployed Egyptian, Syrian or Iraqi who had heard that there was food and work in Palestine; and as for the second, given the Jewish people's experience during the Holocaust, it considered this to be an insult.

> Guarantees never saved anybody. That is the lesson which we have learned from our own bloody experience . . . Only the naive can be trapped by guarantees given during the period of the cold war . . . The [Arab] Legion must be hit first, and then we shall grant guarantees to the Arab minority . . . The only guarantee in which we trust is our own military might . . .[21]

An earlier and more fundamental point of issue, however, was that portion of Bernadotte's proposals which affected the future of Jerusalem. *Lehi* (like Ben-Gurion) considered the status of the city to be the crux and symbol of the entire subject of Hebrew independence. As Eldad put it as early as 6 July, without sovereignty over Jerusalem, Israel would possess no real sovereignty at all. That Israel's leaders 'despite their talk of sovereignty, did not think it treachery to hand over Jerusalem to foreign rule' was, he claimed, the result of the fact that they had no 'free subjective will'. Indeed, resorting to the teachings propounded by Yair and Ratosh – and which he had himself proclaimed in 'Foundation Stones' in 1943 – Eldad claimed that Israel's leaders were still 'Zionists' of the old school; they aimed at a 'secure haven' guaranteed by international law rather than at true freedom. 'That is why they subject Israel's fate to the will of foreign inter-cessionaries . . . As long as the State of Israel is not founded upon the subjective Hebrew will for freedom, it is nothing but a "state of the plain" . . . the target of foreign intrigue . . . a colony.'[22]

It followed that Bernadotte's mission had made even plainer the coincidence of Israel's and Russia's interests. Not only had his mediation permitted the Arabs to improve their military position; as reports from Moscow radio showed, it had also injected American troops into *Eretz Israel*. One of Israel's answers had to be 'a massive and daring' counter-attack, which would encompass the entire area between the Litani river, Amman and the Suez Canal. ('If we win, the

[Western] Powers will have to accept the *fait accompli* despite themselves.')[23] Another, allied to the first, had to be the tightening of ties with the USSR. *Lehi* noted with deep satisfaction Russia's critical attitude towards Bernadotte's mission in the Security Council on 7 July, and especially Gromyko's open accusation that the mediator's proposals had been inspired by the British Foreign Office. In return, *Lehi* was itself prepared to publish a sensational report that another party to Bernadotte's proposals had been the Aramco Oil Company and to support Russia's stand in the Berlin crisis.[24] *Lehi* was thus implementing one of the principles laid down by Stern (paras. 7 and 9 of 'The Principles of Revival') – an 'alliance' for the purpose of realising Hebrew 'rule'. 'For the past nine months, Russia has been demanding for Israel more than Israel herself . . . She has not done so out of the goodness of her heart . . . it is in her interest that there should exist here an Israel as large as possible, as powerful as possible.'[25] This had special importance in view of *Lehi*'s conviction that a third world war was imminent.

THE SECOND CEASE-FIRE AND THE MEDIATION OF THE UN

Following a series of clear Israeli victories, the second cease-fire entered into effect on 19 July. *Lehi* was again aghast, and renewed its attacks on Bernadotte and his domestic and foreign allies. The mediator, the movement warned, would do double damage: repatriating the Arab refugees and preventing the immigration of Jewish exiles from Cyprus. His mission was simply an extension of British plans, and a precursor to restored British rule. However, Ben-Gurion's policy of acquiescence in foreign rule would fail. The models provided by Greece and China proved that: 'A domestic regime of slavery, which opposes the interests of its people and country and sells its independence to foreigners, becomes confused when confronted with revolutionary movements of liberation who know exactly what their goals are.'[26]

If the depth of *Lehi*'s animosity towards Ben-Gurion at this stage is to be properly understood, due recognition must be given to the fact that the movement had no means of judging precisely what the government's true positions were. Its only gauge was the public announcements of individual ministers.[27] These, however, were invariably tactical in nature and designed only to buy the time thought necessary for Israel's ultimate victory. True, some members of the government (notably Kaplan, Levin, Shapira, Rosenblueth [Rosen] and Remez) were reluctant to resume the fighting; others were prepared to advocate a policy of moderation on certain issues. One that was advocated strongly (for example, by Bentov of *Mapam*) was the search for 'allies' among Arab opposition groups in Iraq, Egypt and Syria. Other issues included the cessation of 'expulsions' of Arab inhabitants of conquered territories and a 'free-state' in the Arab area of Palestine. Most were ready to accept a Jewish state in part of Palestine. But, with regard to the main points of Bernadotte's proposals, the government was unanimous. In this respect – although the movement had no way of knowing it – Shertok and Ben-Gurion were quite as adamant as was *Lehi*. Addressing the Provisional State Council on 29 July, Shertok rejected in their entirety Bernadotte's proposals to internationalise Jerusalem and restore the Arab refugees. In his speech to the Provisional Government early in August, Ben-Gurion was even more forthright. Indeed, he expressly stated that in the current circumstances war was more desirable than peace and that he intended to annex Jerusalem and its approach road. Had Latrun been in Israeli hands, he would have proposed that the seat of the Provisional Government be moved to Jerusalem from Tel Aviv immediately the cease-fire was over.[28]

Totally unaware of these positions – and basically mistrustful of persons by whom the movement had been persistently persecuted during the past decade – *Lehi* could only draw conclusions from what it saw. And what it saw, it found intensely dangerous. Indeed, its patience ebbed the longer Bernadotte's mission lasted and his original proposals remained on the agenda. It imagined that thousands of foreign troops were on their way to supervise the demilitarisation of Jerusalem and to relieve its Hebrew fighters of their arms. Quite mistakenly, even Bernard (Dov) Joseph's appointment as military governor of the city was regarded as a prelude to that activity; his meeting with Bernadotte in Jerusalem on 3 August was regarded as an act of 'collaboration', worthy of a lineal descendant of Pontius Pilate or of MacMichael.[29] Even the credit given to Shertok for having 'slapped Bernadotte in the face' on 5 August (when Israel explicitly rejected the proposal to demilitarise Jerusalem) was short-lived. After all, there had been no change in the basic circumstances which had given rise to the mission and to the government's retreats. The arrival of 19 American officers, under the command of a general, was regarded as the harbinger of 'an army of conquest'. Truman would not rest until he could use Haifa as a base for attacks on Russia in time of war.[30]

The welcome accorded to the first Soviet representative to arrive in Israel, Pavel Yerashov, was entirely different. This, indeed, was a 'festival', the credit for which *Lehi* considered to be entirely its own. It was not thanks to Ya'ari, *Mapam*'s leader ('the hypocrite'), nor to Mikunis, the communist leader ('the fellow-traveller'), that Russia had become Israel's ally. The Soviets themselves had adopted this course because they had seen – realistically – 'that every independent Hebrew in *Eretz Israel* is a guarantee of the country's liberation from being a political, economic and military base for Imperialism . . . It is on the bridge of this supreme interest that we meet with Soviet Russia.' It had been 'the war of liberation of the Hebrew underground' that had paved the way for Yerashov's arrival. His appearance was a 'true testimony' to the sovereignty of Israel.[31]

*Lehi*'s first open confrontation with Bernadotte took place on 10 August. During the mediator's meeting with Shertok, Joseph, Ben-Zvi and Daniel Oster (the mayor of Jerusalem), members of the movement demonstrated outside the Belgian consulate, waving placards which declared: 'Stockholm is Yours; Jerusalem is Ours!' and 'Your Work is in Vain; we are Here!' In itself, this was (as Joseph put it) no more than 'a theatrical demonstration . . . quite useless';[32] but it was mentioned at the cabinet meeting the next day. Ben-Gurion then said that *Lehi* might wish to kidnap Bernadotte, and not merely to demonstrate against him, and that would be 'a serious matter'. However, most of the meeting was taken up with a discussion on relations with the IZL and on the state of the negotiations which Gruenbaum, the Minister of the Interior, was conducting with its members (particularly in regard to their status in Jerusalem). Notwithstanding Ben-Gurion's advocacy of a hard line against 'the dissidents' – who aimed to play the role fulfilled by General Zeligowski in Vilna in 1920 – Gruenbaum (who was supported by ministers representing the *Mizrachi*, *Agudat Yisrael* and the General Zionists) eventually won the cabinet's approval to continue his efforts to reach agreement, and the decision to use force against the IZL was thus shelved. Unwittingly, the government had thus given *Lehi* a free hand to act against Bernadotte.[33]

True to its own ideological principles, *Lehi* at this stage still gave absolute priority to the political struggle against foreign and domestic foes. Nevertheless, it could not entirely ignore the need for social liberation. Hence, it appended to its anti-imperialist demonstration against Bernadotte on 10 August a social offensive. Essentially, this followed the lines of its National Bolshevik 'Programme', declared in July 1948 (see above, Chapter 10); the only difference was that *Lehi* now concentrated its attack on the *Histadrut* which, it claimed, did not truly represent workers' interests. In part, this was because of the structure of the organisation, which was itself a large-scale employer and enslaved its workers to such corporations as *Solel Boneh*, *Egged*, *Dan* and *Tenuvah*. In part, it was because of the *Histadrut*'s refusal to discuss the 'awful deprivations' of the families of the fighters. This was entirely consistent with its earlier subservience to British imperialism. Clearly, in the new state of Israel, 'the Hebrew hired worker would be the first to suffer from the restriction of the homeland's territory and from the establishment of imperialist-Abdullist homelands within its borders'. Their task was to establish 'fresh' trade unions 'which would represent the true interests of the masses of workers'.[34]

In 1940, *Lehi* stated, neither *Pravda* nor *Izvestia* had hesitated to publish vitriolic criticism of the production facilities of industry and commerce. The Soviet government had known that the Nazis were recording every disorder with *schadenfreude*, but had nevertheless had no fear of telling the truth. 'But in Israel the Government is afraid of creating a "bad impression".'[35] Its subservience to Bernadotte merely indicated the extent to which that was so.[36]

*Lehi*'s attacks on Bernadotte's mission relented somewhat between 12 August and 6 September, when the mediator himself was absent from the country. But they could never entirely cease. Now, as ever, the movement lived in an atmosphere of revolutionary urgency and of imminent transformation. All the greater, therefore, was its frustration at the cease-fire, which was depriving Israel of the victories which would have made its dreams come true. Instead of sitting back, the government should be seizing the day. Why did the Minister of the Interior speak of the immigration of a million Jews within a decade, instead of within two years? Clearly, the government was interested in freezing the *status quo* and, thereby, in perpetuating its own links to the 'dollar government' of the United States. The latter's perfidy was shown by Marshall's declaration that Israel's economy was 'still sound', and that it did not need an American loan. Obviously, he wanted Israel to be so weakened that (like France, Italy and Greece) it would truly be subservient to American wishes, and would therefore serve as a base for imperialist aggression against Soviet Russia. Israel had to confound this design by immediately renewing the attack on Abdullah.[37]

IN THE SHADOW OF BERNADOTTE'S SECOND PLAN

During Bernadotte's absence from the region, significant modifications were introduced into his mediatory proposals. The changes, initiated at the secret instigation of the British Foreign Office, and agreed to by the American administration, were designed to serve the interests of British imperial defence. Israel, they stipulated, was to be independent and not part of a 'union' with Jordan. Moreover, although the western Galilee was to be ceded to Israel, it was to give up the southern Negev; to agree to Jerusalem being an international city (and not, as formerly proposed, part of Abdullah's kingdom); to agree to Haifa becoming a free port; and to repatriate (or provide compensation for) the Arab refugees. The details of this proposal were finally formulated by Bernadotte's aides on 16 September, one day before the mediator was himself assassinated.[38]

One of the principal justifications, in British eyes, for these changes, was the danger that Israel might fall under communist influence. *Lehi* and the IZL, which were already believed to be receiving assistance from 'Soviet forces' and endangering the rule of the Provisional Government, were considered to be spear-heading that threat.[39] Ironically, however, *Lehi* itself was totally unaware of the new proposals. In the event, such ignorance was of no consequence. Knowledge of the changes could not have intensified the movement's opposition to Bernadotte's mediation, since even his original suggestions had fallen far short of *Lehi*'s minimum demands. As we have seen, *Lehi* had already reached the conclusion that Bernadotte was a tool of Western imperialism, and that his proposals had been inspired by American oil interests.[40] Soviet Russia, therefore, constituted the sole source of possible support. The delicate question of the Russian government's refusal to permit the emigration to Israel of her Jewish population was carefully avoided. Instead, *Lehi* focused its attention on the 'sham Zionism' of American and British Jewry, who limited themselves to making the financial contributions which enabled *Mapai* to rule.[41]

Bernadotte himself returned to the Middle East on 6 September. A victim of his own over-confidence, he truly believed that he possessed the abilities required to bring about a peace settlement between Jews and Arabs. Such hurdles as still existed, he was convinced, were entirely of Israel's making. Whereas the Arabs had 'complete' confidence in his mediation (an impression confirmed after his meeting with Azzam Pasha, the Secretary-General of the Arab league on 6 September), the Jews were intent on war. His mistrust of Israel increased even further when he learned from Azzam and from the Syrian Prime Minister that the Jews regarded him as an Anglo-Saxon agent, and that the government of Israel had therefore attempted to bypass him as a mediator and to negotiate directly with their Arab foes.[42]

*Lehi*'s attacks on Bernadotte were resumed as soon as he returned to the region. Indeed, the demand that his mediation be stopped now assumed a tone of even greater urgency. The cease-fire that Bernadotte had imposed was working to Israel's disadvantage. ('Today we are still sufficiently strong to attain a military victory; we will soon have no choice but to rely on Bernadotte's mediation.') Moreover, the balance of his mediatory proposals – even though their details were not made public – was also obviously shifting in the Arab's favour. A third reason was that, even before an agreement had been reached, Bernadotte seemed to be controlling Israel's destiny. The most recent example was provided by the State Department's announcement that it would not permit Jews of military age to immigrate to Israel from the DP camps under American control in Austria and Germany. This, claimed *Lehi*, clearly implied that 'Bevin's certificates' would be replaced by those to be issued by Bernadotte. 'The People want to know: Who governs us? Is it Ben-Gurion or Bernadotte? The Provisional Government or the UN?' One conclusion was that pressure had to be exerted on the Israeli government itself to become master of its own house by renewing the war. Another, even more ominous, was to bring the mediator and his observers to a state of 'political and practical bankruptcy . . . It is an urgent command to banish Bernadotte and his observers. And any hand which fulfils that command will be blessed.'[43]

By this time, the Provisional Government's patience had become exhausted, and on the night of 7 September military police raided a *Lehi* camp at Sheikh Munis ('Ramat Ya'ir'). *Lehi*'s reaction was immediate. It accused the government of 'running amok like savages', and compared the raid to the worst excesses of the British Mandatory authorities. Undeterred, *Lehi* also intensified even further its attacks on Ben-Gurion's policies, domestic as well as foreign. The government clearly had no concern whatsoever for the true interests of the worker; instead, it was only interested in its own existence. 'A fundamental change could occur only if the citizen stood by those who prefer the interests of the people to those of the party machine.' A 'revolution' was therefore required. Indeed, it had become vital in view of Ben-Gurion's tendencies towards totalitarianism. Despite the youth of the state, it had already witnessed political arrests and show trials. *Lehi* would not be surprised if executions were soon to follow. 'The people's affairs cannot be entrusted to those who are complex-ridden. The nation must entrust its affairs to healthy people.'[44] Clearly, *Lehi* now feared that the Provisional Government was about to decide on the movement's final elimination.

Another sign that such was indeed the case occurred on 10 September, when the editor and publisher of *Mivrak*, its daily newspaper, were arrested on charges of disregarding the censor's orders. Once again, *Lehi*'s reaction was vicious. The Provisional Government, it claimed, was laying the foundations for its rule 'for a thousand years'. That was why it was arresting those whom it accused of avoiding conscription; that was why it was enlising boys only 14 [sic] years old; that was why it was enlarging the government bureaucracy. It was even less concerned with the welfare of the masses than were the current dictators of Greece, Nationalist China and Spain. Like them, moreover, the Provisional Government was working only for American recognition and support. True, there had so far been no massacre of 'non-Western democrats'. But the tendency was nevertheless plain. The government's entire objective was to bring about a situation in which Marshall, Bevin and Bernadotte could declare: 'Yes, the state of Israel is a strong and faithful fortress against Russia.'[45] As for itself, *Lehi* was proud of the fact that the July issue of the *Middle East Journal* (published in Washington and believed to be a semi-official publication) had noted its own links with communism.[46]

Matters reached a crescendo in the days which immediately preceded Bernadotte's murder. Two days before the event, *Lehi* called on 'the fighting Hebrew youth' (that is, the troops of the IDF) to put an end to the destructive cease-fire and to take its officers out for one 'last and decisive' battle. At the same time, it also advocated that Bernadotte and his observers be banished from the country.[47] To this was added, on the very day that Bernadotte was murdered, an attack on the Provisional Government the tone of which was unprecedented even by *Lehi*'s own standards. As though it had nothing more to lose, *Mivrak* vilified the state's official leadership, root and branch. The country, it claimed, was being led by a 'dictatorship of the party machine . . . an absolutely reactionary dictatorship'. Its sole interest was to enlarge the base of its 'monopolistic' stranglehold on the country's economy and thereby to serve the narrow interests of the class of which it was composed. It possessed no ideology worthy of the name, nor even any true national goals.

> It will arouse the youth against her [Israel] and thus deprive her of the biological continuity vital for the persistence of any rule and regime . . . she will increasingly be forced to resort to the assistance of a foreign power . . . *she will be forced to enslave herself to the yoke of Anglo-American Imperialism.*[48]

Judged by these words, the assassination of Bernadotte can be seen to have served two of *Lehi*'s purposes. First, it removed the problems caused by the mediator who, as an agent of imperialism, threatened to make Israel its slave. Second, however, it was also directed against the rule of the Provisional Government, which was colluding with the foreign mediator. These were by no means new messages; they accorded with *Lehi*'s doctrines as propounded before the establishment of the state (which explains why even *Lehi*'s 'class' criticisms of the government were not truly socialist in flavour; as in its programme, they were entirely subordinate to its fundamental nationalist aims).

But their publication on the day of the murder invested them with an operational significance of the very first order.

On the day before his murder, Bernadotte tabled an amended version of his second plan for solving the Arab–Jewish dispute. But, as has been seen, this remained faithful to the British strategic interests by which it was inspired.[49] As such, it did not even meet the wishes of the Israeli government, let alone those of *Lehi*. Even had the movement possessed advance information of the changes in the programme, it is highly unlikely that it would have been satisfied by them. To that extent, Bernadotte's assassination was inevitable. All that remained undetermined were its timing and location. These were provided by Bernadotte himself. Wishing to visit UN observers and prepare for the removal of his staff to Government House, he arrived in Jerusalem on 17 September.

THE ASSASSINATION AND ITS CONSEQUENCES

The assassination had been decided upon by all members of *Lehi*'s 'centre', Eldad, Shamir and Yellin-Mor, on 9 September. It was carried out by Yehoshua Cohen, who was one of Yair's earliest followers and who had recently been released from a British prison, on the afternoon of Friday, 17 September in the middle of Jerusalem.

As far as Bernadotte's proposals were concerned, the assassination of the mediator himself was largely inconsequential. It was not his death that prevented the implementation of his plans but four other circumstances: the IDF's victories in the Negev between 15 and 20 October; the fact that the United States dropped its support for Bernadotte's plans; Soviet opposition; and Arab opposition.[50] The real impact of the assassination was felt in Israel's domestic life and, particularly, with regard to *Lehi*. Accordingly, it is to that sphere that attention must be devoted.

*Lehi* tried to deny responsibility for Bernadotte's death. Indeed, anticipating the government's reaction, the movement warned that 'Whoever touches us will not be cleared of guilt. We shall cut off the hand raised against us.'[51] Insisting on its own innocence, *Lehi* in fact projected a form of dualism: within Israel itself, it was now a legitimate political movement; it had remained an underground movement only in those territories not under explicit government control. Bernadotte's assassins, it claimed, belonged to what *Lehi* portrayed as a separate organisation – *Hazit ha-Moledet* (the Homeland Front).[52]

The latter group (formed in 1942 in Bulgaria by a coalition of resistance fighters against the Nazis, and within which communist influence had become dominant by 1944) had indeed published an inflammatory leaflet. But *Lehi*'s claim that it constituted an independent organisation was patently misleading. The tone of that leaflet is itself suffused with notions and phrases taken directly from *Lehi*'s own lexicon. The *Hazit*, it announced, had been formed in order to fight against 'any foreign ruler, any mediator, and body, whatever its mantle of authority, whose foot will tread on this land. *Hazit ha-Moledet* will fight against anyone who opposes the liberation of the country, of Jerusalem its capital and against the people's redemption.' This declaration had been followed by an indictment of Bernadotte (described as 'a British agent. His entire plan accorded with the Anglo-Saxon programme, which aims to suppress our sovereignty and turn the country into a narrow ghetto') and by a catalogue of the Provisional Government's policy of appeasement, past and present.

> As long as we have the slightest suspicion that the leaders are bent on concessions and on a cessation of the fighting in return for a 'mini-state' deprived of existence and sustenance – *we shall exist! we shall be the guarantee!* against the surrender . . . of the sovereignty of our people in its entire homeland.[53]

The government did not accept *Lehi*'s argument. Ben-Gurion, as his diary reveals, had for some time been aware of the danger that *Lehi* presented, and especially of the movement's intention to blunt any attempt to establish an international jurisdiction over Jerusalem.[54] Once news of the murder was announced, Isser Harel (the head of the Secret Service) immediately singled out as suspects the brothers Yehoshua and Menahem Cohen, the former's wife and Efraim Zetler – all residents of Kfar Sabah and all *Lehi* members.[55] Similarly, neither Joseph nor Dayan (respectively, military governor and military commander of Jerusalem) had any doubt that *Lehi* (even more than the IZL) must have been behind the assassination. Within hours of the event, Joseph and Dayan had agreed to mount a large-scale military operation which would result in the arrest of all *Lehi*'s members. Joseph then had a meeting with Ben-Gurion, Rosenblueth (the Minister of Justice), Kaplan (the Minister of Finance) and senior IDF officers. All agreed to commence arrests immediately and to disarm anyone resisting arrest. The next day, forces surrounded the *Lehi* camp in Jerusalem, whence 40 members were taken to prison without a fight. A further 144 *Lehi* personnel were arrested in Jerusalem and 62 others in Tel Aviv and elsewhere.[56]

Ben-Gurion's actions undoubtedly accorded with the consensus of domestic political opinion. As much became apparent at the meeting of the Provisional State Council on 23 September. Ben-Gurion himself spoke against *Lehi* in the strongest of terms. Bernadotte's assassination, he declared, showed not a whit of 'patriotism'. On the contrary, it had done enormous harm to Israel, to the national reputation and to the sanctity of Jerusalem. Whatever the government's differences of opinion with the mediator (and he made no attempt to conceal the existence and extent of these differences), he still had the greatest respect for a man who – like Colonel Serot, who was also murdered – had saved many Jewish lives during the Nazi period. His opinions were shared by virtually every other representative of the Israeli political spectrum. Even though the Revisionist opposition spokesman spoke in glowing terms of the contributions that the 'dissidents' had made to the establishment of the state, he also denounced the assassination. So too did Mikunis of *Maki*. Indeed, the latter thought it especially necessary to do so in the light of *Lehi*'s claims to have a pro-Soviet orientation and to be the country's true representative of communism. That, he claimed, was totally unfounded. Like the IZL (which he also attacked), *Lehi* was nothing but 'a private army of the Jewish bourgeoisie . . . an anti-proletarian organisation with all the trappings of fascism'. The assassination itself was a blatant 'provocation' to the government and, instead of harming imperialism, had 'opened up greater opportunities for Anglo-American intervention'. At the conclusion of the debate, the Council unanimously approved the goverment's 'Order for the Prevention of Terrorism'.[57]

*Lehi* did not remain silent. Quite a few of its members (including Shamir and Eldad; but not Friedman-Yellin) avoided arrest and published a manifesto which declared that the government's decision to outlaw the movement was not a response to Bernadotte's assassination: it had preceded that event. The proof lay in the incident at Ramat Ya'ir. As it had done before the assassination, *Lehi* maintained that the government of Israel was more repressive than that of Greece. It could not even abide by its own earlier recognition of *Lehi* as a legitimate political organisation. The 'centre' demanded the cancellation of the decision of 20 September, the release of all its men who had not been charged, and the return of its impounded property. Otherwise, it warned, it retained 'the right to take all appropriate steps'.[58] These, it promised, would be principally directed against foreign foes. However, 'We shall not harm Jews unless they force us to defend ourselves'. The 'centre' announced that it was releasing from all obligation those of its members who had joined *Lehi* because it was a legitimate movement. All others were explicitly informed: 'The war of liberation goes on!'[59]

By this time, *Lehi* was obviously in no position to carry out its threats. Nevertheless, it remained defiant. Bernadotte's assassination and its own subsequent liquidation as a political movement, it announced, had marked a turn for the better, not for the worse. It had released the movement from the need to recognise the government's surrender of territory. At most, the government could arrest a few hundred men; it could never break the backbone of the nation, which was made of the 'steel of clear, consistent and correct political thought . . . *As long as one of us remains* this wonder will once again rise up, as it did in the winter of 1942'. *Lehi* would only disband if 'a different spirit' were to enlighten the Provisional Government and put a stop to its fidelity to imperialism, Abdullah and the United Nations. But the movement was under no illusions that this was about to happen. *Mapai*, it contended, had not yet decided who to choose as its ally: Abdullah, 'the servant of imperialism' or the 'Nazi' Mufti.[60]

# Between the Trial and the Split

## LEHI – A NEW UNDERGROUND MOVEMENT?

*Lehi*'s 'centre' was convinced that the authorities had decided on a 'new regime' against the movement. That was evident from the government's attempts to isolate the 'fighting unit' in Jerusalem; from the publicity given to the arrest of *Lehi* members; from the searches in Ramat Ya'ir; and from the censorship of *Mivrak*.[1] This impression seemed to be confirmed on 14 October when Friedman-Yellin and Shmuelevitch, who had been arrested in Haifa a fortnight previously, were charged with being leaders of what the emergency decrees categorised as a terrorist organisation.[2] Although several other imprisoned members of *Lehi* were released (and many others escaped confinement) over 100 were still held captive. On 29 October two young women accused of posting *Ha-Ma'as* ('The Deed') were also placed on trial.

This crisis in *Lehi*'s fortunes occurred at a time when the government of Israel was taking decisive steps to expand the country's borders. True, no substantial territorial gains were made on the eastern front – which is where *Lehi* would have most liked to see the army in operation and where Ben-Gurion himself originally wished to make a move.[3] But the Egyptian threat in the south was utterly repulsed in a series of IDF actions undertaken between 15 and 20 October. Indeed, the southern map of Israel was thereby entirely altered – to the extent that General Templer, the Vice-Chief of the British Imperial General Staff, feared that Israel's victories would deprive the West of the opportunity to use the Negev as a base from which to launch strategic bombers against the Soviet Union's 'Achilles' heel' in the Caucasus.[4]

Prominent in *Lehi*'s thinking during this period was the tendency to cease activities designed to bring about its transformation into a legal political party. Instead, the movement reverted to an underground mentality. Not unwittingly, it now revived Yair's newspaper, *Ba-Makhteret* (In the Underground) and preached the virtues of individual acts of terror. 'Acts of terror are carried out by a tiny number of people, who do not need to rely on a large political movement.' Ben-Gurion, it claimed, had 'decided to shut our mouths, and to get rid of a serious force which might endanger his conspiracy with America, his plots with Abdullah and his efforts to establish a rule of dictatorship and exploitation within the state'.[5]

Thus, notwithstanding Israel's gains, *Lehi*'s mission had not been completed. Indeed, it continued to revolve around its three traditional axes. One was the complete liberation of the homeland. 'British gendarmes', argued *Lehi*, were still present in several parts of the country, and the danger of a British invasion, or of penetration by other agents of Western imperialism in the form of officials of the oil companies, had not been removed. *Lehi* considered itself to be the only barrier to that eventuality. Second, the movement also saw itself as still responsible for the destruction of imperialism in the neighbouring countries of the Middle East. 'Our movement will therefore strike at the cells of Imperialism in Cyprus, Sinai, Egypt, Syria, Lebanon and Iraq.' The 'neutralisation plan' constituted the solution to 'the rotten feudal regimes' of the Arab lands. Finally, *Lehi* still remained faithful to its programme of the previous July on domestic affairs. Indeed, *Mapai*'s tendencies to weaken the *Histadrut* (a charge also made by *Mapam*) now made it even more imperative to insist on new ideology. This was to take the form of 'large-scale nationalisation, supervision and planning, and the destruction of poverty . . . [Otherwise] A regime of suppression and exploitation would enfeeble the powers of self-rule and the state's fighting strength.'[6]

The upshot was a feeling that *Lehi* had no choice but to retreat into the background. Although the movement appreciated that its emphasis had now to be placed on political rather than military activities, and indeed hoped to revive its legal status, the imminence of international and domestic dangers really left it no option but to follow its own path.

We shall therefore intensify conspiratorial activity and tighten our ranks even more . . . he who lacks the strength, and can no longer suffer the wounds of the underground, will leave the underground. Those who remain will continue the war with greater force and greater courage . . . even within the State of Israel.[7]

The tone of self-righteousness which infuses such statements was intensified by the movement's internal efforts to justify and explain its present position. Essentially, these consisted of arguments designed to demonstrate that the assassination of Bernadotte, like the earlier assassination of Moyne, had in fact saved the Zionist movement from itself. Just as the establishment of Israel would not have come about without *Lehi*'s war against the British, so the state's recent military victories were only made possible by the assassination of Bernadotte. That act had shown the government just how feeble its previous positions had been, and had therefore forced it to concentrate, not on peripheral and 'quantitative' gains, but on intrinsic and 'qualitative' achievements. *Lehi*'s response to the charge that it had adopted a strategy of 'individual terror' was thus simple: 'an early individual war against UN observers can in certain circumstances prevent the need for a bloody confrontation with an international army at a later stage.'[8]

Such statements were, of course, solely for internal consumption. Outwardly, *Lehi* denied all responsibility for Bernadotte's assassination which, it claimed, had 'surprised' the movement as much as the government. Altogether, it attempted to project the image of a movement against which the authorities were waging a vendetta.

> It is a short step from confrontations with the members of the underground (which are inevitable) to the spilling of blood, to civil war and to the establishment of a repressive and dictatorial regime which will injure the entire public . . . public leaders have a duty to demand from the Government a decision which is just, democratic, logical and commmensurate with the national and sovereign interest.[9]

In several respects, however, *Lehi* could now only present a façade. Its organisational infrastructure was entirely upset by the enforcement of the emergency decrees between 20 September 1948 and the elections of January 1949. Its ideological axioms, too, did not seem to be standing the test of time. The justice of its pro-Soviet orientation was placed in jeopardy by Ilya Ehrenburg's article in *Pravda* on 21 September, which disavowed any Soviet support for Zionism; the 'League for National Liberation' affiliated with *Maki*, and thus showed that the Arab communists would insist on an independent Palestinian state and would not be content with *Lehi*'s offer of a shadow sovereignty under Israeli protection; neither could *Lehi* hope to stand in the vanguard of a united workers' front. In December 1948, *Kol Ha-Am* announced *Maki*'s union with the 'Hebrew Communist Party' also.[10]

Summarising the year's activities, Eldad refused to acknowledge such setbacks. In retrospect, he even justified Friedman-Yellin's original decision to legitimise the movement and overlooked the internal dispute to which it had given rise. At the same time, however, he attempted to remain faithful to *Lehi*'s original principles and thus to have matters both ways. *Lehi* now wanted to be recognised as a legitimate political movement within the boundaries of the state but to be given freedom of action beyond those borders.[11]

## THE 'SEIZURE OF POWER' AND THE 'PERMANENT REVOLUTION WITH ALL MEANS' AS UNIFYING CONCEPTS

The discussion between *Lehi* leaders on 27 October 1948 illustrates the movement's state of mind at that time. In essence, they had three possible courses of action. One was to become an entirely legal party; a second was to follow the illegal path of underground activity; the third was to follow the hybrid policy earlier outlined by Eldad.

In one extreme variant, the arguments in favour of *Lehi* remaining an exclusively underground movement were doctrinal: 'We must establish within the State an underground in all its forms. But only an underground . . . an unarmed underground party is just cosmetic, and no one pays any attention to it.'[12] But this seems to have been an isolated viewpoint. Most of the arguments against becoming a fully legal party were organisational. 'This method of activity does not suit our character.' In open elections, *Lehi* could hope to gain no more than five per cent of the votes of the electorate; the only way to save the movement from stagnation 'and to increase our strength as *an independent political force with international weight* was to persist with clandestine operations throughout the Middle East and to establish a new underground centre of operations somewhere in Europe. This course, it was claimed, would receive the backing of the Soviet Union.

Notwithstanding the explicit pro-Soviet orientation thus implied in 'illegality' (a matter itself disputed), its principal opponents were to be found in *Lehi*'s pro-communist wing. Their position was largely derivative of their political education. Only legal status would enable the movement to attain mass support by implementing its programme, which resembled that of the communist parties of Czechoslovakia and Poland. *Lehi*, in fact (even if it changed its name), had to follow an ideology which was entirely communist and a foreign policy orientation which was pro-Soviet rather than pro-Russian. It certainly could not remain a mixture of various ideological hues.

But the predominant tendency was to bypass the ideological hurdle. Due to the actions which the government had already taken, it was the organisational question which was paramount. That was why at this stage no voices were raised against the *Lehi* programme of the previous July. Both right and left wings of the movement were united in their ambition to seize power, even though the road to that objective seemed a lengthy one.[13] Both also appreciated that the government, basking in the reflected glory of newly established independence and recent military victories, would enjoy a large measure of public support.

That being the case, there was clearly no place for an armed underground within the state of Israel (although it remained true, of course, that *Lehi* did have to persist in its world-wide armed struggle against Western imperialism). Instead, it was advocated that *Lehi* place its faith entirely in the alternative of absolute legality. *Lehi*, thus seen, had to work towards a situation whereby it would indeed be in a position to manipulate the levers of state power. Only when in control of the armed forces, the administrative bureaucracy and the economy would *Lehi* be able to realise its national ambitions to the full.[14]

Yet another alternative was the bifurcated orientation which, while not entirely rejecting the underground bases of the movement, emphasised the present need for political activity. What had to be established was a series of 'cells', such as those formed by contemporary communist parties abroad, 'so that when the time comes we shall be ready to capture power, which is the only way that we can implement our ideas'. This approach did not suggest that what *Lehi* had in mind was an orderly attainment of office through the conventional parliamentary process. On the contrary, what it preached was the need to project *Lehi* as a '*revolutionary* movement', ready to seize power by whatever means were appropriate. In other words, it was *Lehi*'s continued mission to be the *avant-garde* of national transformation. This did not mean that it had to be communist; neither did it necessarily have openly to proclaim its outright support for the Soviet Union. *Lehi* did indeed have to place its faith in the masses of workers, but its foreign policy orientation had to follow national interests and not to echo 'sentiments and preconceptions'.[15]

This range of views represented an attempt to bridge ideological differences which had in the past been neglected. Typically, *Lehi*'s right-wing spokesmen were especially adamant in the claim that: 'the social question has propelled the movement into a sterile debate which has generated much tension and upset unity . . . It has created something of an "appendix" to *Lehi* . . . We must beware of creating a connection between the social question and that of orientation.' They sought to identify a framework of 'orthodox' formulae which would concentrate on the movement's national objectives. These could allow it to tolerate the communists (provided they accepted the relevant axioms) but did not allow for the acceptance of a Marxist philosophy, which was alien to the 'spirit of Israel'. 'I do not think that a return to the status of a legal party – with the burden of a social dispute – will endear us to the masses. Quite the opposite.'

In sum, then, the meeting clarified the problems of *Lehi*'s future existence from an ideological as well as an organisational point of view. The movement had four basic options: (1) Our task is solely to expel the British, and nothing more. (2) Lehi has a special mission, as stated in its Programme. (3) A permanent revolution by all means. (4) To work only to seize power.'[16] But the time had not yet come to choose between these courses. Instead, because of the impending trial of Friedman-Yellin and Shmuelevitch, and the amnesty granted by the government in advance of the forthcoming elections, attention was focused on organisational matters. This enabled *Lehi* to postpone, temporarily, a basic ideological debate. Indeed, no such debate was to take place until the movement's first – and last – conference.

The prospect of the trial of two of its leaders provided *Lehi* with an excuse to issue what it termed 'a final warning' to the government.[17] In fact, however, this was an idle threat as *Lehi* was not prepared to undertake against the government of Israel the measures which it threatened. Quite the opposite was the case. An 'internal memorandum' issued the following month emphasised the extent to which the movement was now drawing a distinction between the sovereign government of Israel and Britain as the Mandatory Power. It had waged war against Britain, but was not prepared to do so against the state of Israel. On the contrary, it wished to respect the laws of the independent state since 'they may tomorrow protect us'. 'Struggle', therefore, could not mean armed resistance; instead, it had to take the form of propaganda and political action – even if the latter did have to take place in underground conditions. From this it followed that no point could be served by the assassination of such targets as UN observers. Indeed, what remained of *Lehi*'s 'centre' explicitly appealed to its followers to desist from all such actions. 'Our movement opposes independent or terrorist actions under present circumstances, since they injure both the state and our ambitions.' Should any member of *Lehi* disagree, 'he had better defect from us and not interfere with actions which we are undertaking in accordance with the lines set down by the movement'.

In effect, *Lehi* had thus made a complete volte-face. Confronted by the government's harsh reaction to Bernadotte's murder and its refusal to distinguish between *Lehi* and the 'Homeland Front', it was attempting to turn over a new leaf. 'We have first and foremost to fight for legality. The very fact of that struggle shows that we honour the law and that the foundations of the State are dear to us . . . We must now display civilian heroism.'[18] The latter did not consist of armed activities, but of standing firm under trial and proudly acknowledging membership of the movement and affiliation with its aims. It now remained to be seen whether Friedman-Yellin and Shmuelevitch would live up to those standards.

THE TRIAL OF FRIEDMAN-YELLIN AND SHMUELEVITCH –
A DISRUPTIVE FORCE OR A CATALYST FOR UNITY?

The trial of Friedman-Yellin and Shmuelevitch opened on 5 December 1948 and ended on 25 January 1949 (the day of the elections to the first Knesset). Before the trial started there had been some attempts at

compromise. On 28 October, Eldad met Shaul Avigur, the deputy
Minister of Defence, and assured him that *Lehi* was 'sincerely' interested in a return to legal status. He also disclaimed all knowledge of
Bernadotte's murderers (a disclaimer which Avigur did not accept).
These manoeuvres failed, as did the attempts by both the military
lawyer (Hoter-Yishai) and the head of the Secret Service (Isser Harel)
to dissuade Ben-Gurion from proceeding with the trial. As Ben-
Gurion recorded in his diary: 'I told Isser that there is no possibility of
that. We must here discuss the uprooting of terror and the underground.'[19]

The trial opened on 5 December at a special military court in Acre,
and received detailed press coverage. In his opening address, Hoter-
Yishai claimed that on 17 September *Lehi* had launched a 'Pearl
Harbour' attack. 'While its representatives were conducting negotiations with the government institutions, it had in territory under the
sovereign control of the Government of Israel attacked an emissary of
the UNO and the head of the International Red Cross.'[20] He cited
documents culled from *Lehi* sources (including an incriminating letter
written by Zetler on 15 August) as evidence that *Lehi* had indeed
planned the assassination.

Such accusations, countered Friedman-Yellin, were a 'libel'.
Bernadotte, he showed, had been vilified in other sections of the press
while *Lehi* – as was demonstrated by its negotiations with various
municipal authorities and its letter to the Minister of the Interior of
28 August – had declared its intention of acting as a legal movement.
The prosecution's attitude towards *Lehi*, he claimed, was no different
to that of medieval Christian disputants against Judaism. Words were
taken out of context, and mere rhetoric was treated as though it were
a statement of intent. In fact, in the coastal plain *Lehi* had ceased all
underground activity after 15 May. If it had retained its independence
in Jerusalem thereafter, that was only because it feared (as did all the
inhabitants) that the government was about to relinquish Hebrew
control over the city. *Lehi*'s actions had been akin to those of Zeligowski
in Vilna and D'Annunzio in Fiume. Even so, not a hair of Ben-
Gurion's head had been harmed. Why should *Lehi* stand trial? Had
not the IZL also retained its independence? Had not the government
forces fired on the *Altalena*? Had not Bernadotte refused to reveal his
knowledge of Nazi atrocities and wished to hand Jerusalem over to
Abdullah? Had not the first political murder in *Eretz Israel* been
committed in 1924 (against De Haan) by persons (namely Ben-Zvi)
who were now *Mapai* leaders? Even if some affinities did exist between
*Lehi* and the 'Homeland Front', the two were not identical.[22]

Friedman-Yellin's arguments were repeated in a public bulletin issued by *Lehi* at the close of the prosecution's presentation. Had the trial been conducted under democratic laws and in a regular court, it announced, the prosecution would have had to admit that, due to lack of evidence, it was withdrawing charges. 'But the law is not democratic. It is retroactive, and enjoins the accused to prove that he is not . . . an elephant . . . a camel . . . a terrorist. This is in the best traditions of the Nazis and of the British.' Clearly the prosecution was acting under the instructions of a gang in the Secret Service who were motivated by their personal hatred of *Lehi*. 'Ever since the days of the British their consciences have not been clean, and they are exploiting an excuse to destroy *Lehi* . . . to find favour in the eyes of foreigners.' What is more, they were clearly taking the opportunity provided by the trial to get rid of one of their opponents before the forthcoming elections.[23]

Under cross-examination by Advocate Seligman (on behalf of the defence), Friedman-Yellin denied that he had been on his way to Moscow at the time of his arrest, or that he had known about the money found hidden in his home, or that he had been about to flee to Moscow by way of Czechoslovakia ('I am not the sort of person to run'). He also repeated the reasons for *Lehi*'s actions in Jerusalem, pointing out that it had been an article in *Davar* that had aroused his fears for the future of the city. *Lehi*, he claimed, had become a legal movement after 14 May; thereafter, it had acted solely in accordance with the laws of historical determinism. He also noted that criticisms of the government had not emanated solely from *Lehi* sources. In sum, the world had witnessed numerous criticisms of authority, none of which had led to arrests and trials for treason. The only bases for comparison were the Dreyfus trial and that carried out in Nazi Germany in the wake of the Reichstag fire.

When Shmuelevitch took the stand, he repeated most of his leader's arguments. The only point on which he substantively differed was in his argument that the present trial was in fact an even greater travesty of justice than that carried out by the Nazis after the Reichstag fire. Shmuelevitch also cited newspaper articles to prove that the government had been criticised by a wide spectrum of public opinion; he also denied any direct affinity between *Lehi* and the 'Homeland Front' (although he did admit that the latter had copied some of *Lehi*'s pronouncements). *Lehi*'s 'revolutionary' nature, he claimed, did not testify to its tendency to violence but to its wish to generate a million new immigrants within three years.[24]

Evidence for the prosecution was presented by a number of current and former ministers and their deputies. First among them was Levi Eshkol, the deputy Minister of Defence, who denied that the

government had either singled out *Lehi* for particular persecution or
acted provocatively towards the movement. Despite the government's
attempts to reach a compromise with *Lehi*, it had proved to be 'a
serious internal enemy'. Gruenbaum, the Minister of the Interior
(who had in fact prevented government action against *Lehi* and had
expressed his faith in the possibility of an agreement), denied the
accusation that the government had planned a 'St Bartholomew's Day
Massacre', but said that no co-operation had been possible with 'dissidents' who had retained their arms. Using the same arguments in his
own earlier testimony, Pinhas Rosen (the Minister of Justice) had
already gone one stage further. In his opinion, *Lehi* did not deserve to
sit on the Provisional State Council. Indeed, none of the other parties
would have agreed to its presence.[25]

The high point of the trial was reached during the testimony presented by Yisrael Galili, the former deputy Minister of Defence and head
of the *Haganah* command. He gave a long historical excursus on the
origins of *Lehi* and on his own contacts with the movement. His object
was to demonstrate that, far from contributing to the eventual triumph
of Zionism, *Lehi* had in fact impeded its progress. In pursuit of its own
aims, the movement had implicitly co-operated with the British and
had shown itself prepared even to work with Nazi Germany. In fact,
'throughout the years of its existence, Lehi did enormous harm to the
process whereby the *Haganah* had amassed its strength . . . which
saved the people of Israel'. According to Galili, the trend set when
*Lehi* deliberately attempted to demoralise the *Yishuv* had still not
ceased. It still believed in Lenin's dictum that 'The worse matters are,
the better our position' (a charge which Friedman-Yellin did not
deny). Indeed, it represented a potential fifth column, especially in
view of its blatant pro-Soviet stance and, even more so, its earlier
support of the Axis powers.

Eldad considered Galili's evidence to be largely irrelevant and in
many important respects (for example, with regard to developments
after the 'Black Sabbath') inaccurate too.[26] But it was more difficult to
dismiss the evidence of the last witness, General David Shaltiél, who
had commanded the Jerusalem district between mid-February and
early August 1948. He stated that *Lehi* had exercised a deleterious
effect on the *Haganah*'s operations in Jerusalem. He particularly
castigated the attack on Deir-Yasin, *Lehi*'s refusal to co-operate in
the main Kastel operation, and Zetler's 'absurd' suggestion that *Lehi*
exercise joint command with the *Haganah*. Altogether, he declared,
matters would have been easier had *Lehi* not been around.[27]

It was at this stage in the trial that, on 7 January 1949, the first
announcement was made of *Lehi*'s candidates for election to the first

Knesset within the framework of the 'Fighters' Party'. Friedman-Yellin and Shmuelevitch headed the list (so that they would be released if elected), and they were followed by Yaakov Banai (formerly commander of the 'Fighting Unit' and the person responsible, until Bernadotte's assassination, for *Lehi* members in the IDF), Geulah Cohen, H. Shabtai and Yusuf Abu-Gosh. The government's decision (taken against Ben-Gurion's initial disinclination) to permit *Lehi* to contest the elections was itself a concessionary move. So, too, was Hoter-Yishai's announcement on 11 January that a committee would be established to examine the petitions of *Lehi* members for release from imprisonment.[28] Nevertheless, *Lehi* stepped up its attacks on the government and on its conduct of the trial. The latter, declared *Ha-Ma'as*, was designed as a sop to to the Western powers, who were demanding some 'sacrifice'. A leaflet signed by the 'Homeland Front' went even further. Noting the release of several Britons accused of espionage (among them Sylvester, who was implicated in the explosion in Ben-Yehudah Street in Jerusalem), the 'Front' vowed to wreak vengeance. It similarly swore to put an end to Ben-Gurion's collusion with Abdullah, Bevin and Bunche.[29]

Summing up the case for the prosecution on 19 January 1949, Hoter-Yishai denied the charge that certain sectors of the government had hatched a detailed plan to destroy *Lehi* and that Bernadotte's assassination had just been a pretext. He attributed that view to the movement's paranoia, born of its underground existence. In fact, he went on, *Lehi* remained an underground, and its supposedly 'legal' activities (clubs, newspaper, and so on), were a sham. The movement had always attempted to thwart the official Zionist enterprise, preferring its own interest to that of the nation as a whole. Furthermore, the programmatic similarities between *Lehi* and the 'Homeland Front' were clear; *Lehi* had never condemned Bernadotte's murder – indeed, it was clearly responsible for that act.[30]

The court handed down its verdict on 10 February, after elections to the Knesset had taken place. In every substantive respect, the opinion of the judges accorded with that of the prosecution. Especially damning was that portion of the verdict devoted to a description of *Lehi*'s 'character'. This utterly rejected *Lehi*'s claim that it had been responsible for the 'expulsion' of the British; it also itemised the evidence which proved that – even after the declaration of the state of Israel – the movement had continued to function as an underground bent on forcing its will on the entire nation. In fact, the court declared, *Lehi*'s character stood in stark opposition to the principles of democracy. As for Bernadotte's murder, that could only have been perpetrated by persons with substantial underground experience. Members of the 'Homeland Front' came from the ranks of the IZL and *Lehi*, more probably the latter.

That being the case, the court saw fit to commit Friedman-Yellin to eight years' imprisonment and Shmuelevitch to five years, both with special conditions. However, it was also prepared to recognise that there were extenuating circumstances, principal among which were the facts that *Lehi*'s underground activities had begun during the Mandate period and that its members now proclaimed their wish to be free and law-abiding citizens. Hence, the court was prepared to remit the sentences passed, provided that the accused undertook to abide by four conditions. They would each sign a declaration acknowledging that it was an offence to support an underground inside or outside the country; they would appeal to *Lehi*'s members abroad to cease underground activities; they would personally undertake not to participate in any such activity; they would agree to accept police supervision for the next two years.[31]

### THE ELECTIONS TO THE FIRST KNESSET

Despite the damage caused to its image by the trial, *Lehi* pressed ahead with its propaganda before the elections. Since all of the contending parties presented platforms which promised further expansion of the borders, mass immigration, economic prosperity and social justice, the 'Fighters' Party' sought to find unique ground in its opposition to the emergency decrees. These, it noted, had been passed with the support of all the other parties. *Lehi* alone had claimed them to be undemocratic, placing Israel in the same category as Greece, Spain and Malaya. Clearly *Mapai* had insisted on this legislation in order both to gag its opponents and to prepare the ground for an alliance with Abdullah and the Western powers. Indeed, these constituted two sides of the same coin. Since the government was now (as before) prepared for territorial concessions, it had to anticipate opposition. It could only deal with this by ruling through emergency decree.[32]

What was most striking about *Lehi*'s announcements in advance of the elections was the moderation of its ideological tone. Indeed, the 'Fighters' Party' deliberately avoided taking a stand on any of the major doctrinal issues which its members had themselves debated in order to blur their image of an ideologically confused party. In an attempt to make a virtue out of necessity, they insisted on their 'practicality'. They were not, they claimed, wedded to any particular class; even more remarkably (in view of *Lehi*'s previous pronouncements) neither were they wedded to any particular foreign policy orientation. Even where the question of the party's attitude towards the Soviet Union was concerned, the line adopted leaned far more towards the position of Eldad than that of Friedman-Yellin. Thus the 1946 plan for the 'neutralisation' of the Middle East was now revived.

The renewed emphasis on Hebrew sovereignty on both banks of the Jordan was not incidental. On the contrary, Transjordan was now proclaimed to be 'the vital life-line of the entire country', essential for its industrial development and economic well-being. It followed that *Lehi* was under no circumstances prepared to accept further rule there by Britain's puppet, Abdullah. Indeed, *Lehi* insisted that the war had to be continued against both Jordan and Iraq, although it was prepared to agree to peace with an Egypt free of Britain. Entirely absent from the Fighters' programme was any reference to *Lehi*'s previous hopes that an Arab Palestinian unit might be created in that area. Now, the movement openly ridiculed *Mapam*'s hopes that 'the great Arab proletariat' might come to rule parts of the west bank.[33]

While the 'Fighters' Party' saw no need to make any further response to this openly Revisionist line on the Arab question, its position regarding a pragmatic foreign policy orientation and neutrality were different matters. Eldad rejected Lubotsky's charge that the two were incompatible. Stressing that the USSR, unlike the imperialistic powers, had no interest whatsoever in expansion, Eldad posited the clear possibility of the fusion of Israeli and Russian aims. Furthermore, and in a clear attempt to win the favour of the left wing of the movement in anticipation of the coming split, he also declared that a policy of neutrality could serve a wider purpose: 'An alliance with the Arab states on the basis of their *freedom* from Imperialist rule.'[34]

But despite all its efforts, the 'Fighters' Party' failed to carry its message to the people. It received only 5,363 votes (1.22 per cent of the total), only 190 more than the Women's International Zionist Organisation (WIZO) and far fewer than opponents such as *Herut* (whose results were also disappointing), *Mapam* and *Maki*. One consequence of these results was that *Herut* attempted to improve its relations with the 'Fighters' Party'. (After all, the contribution to Israel's liberation of the IZL as well as of *Lehi* had been denigrated at Friedman-Yellin's trial; moreover, in view of the election results, *Herut* now had little to fear from *Lehi*.)[35] Another, as we have seen, was that the court, which announced its verdict on Friedman-Yellin and Shmuelevitch after the election results were known, could afford to be magnanimous. The Provisional State Council authorised their pardon, which was even defended by their arch-enemy, Weizmann.[36]

THE CONVENTION OF THE 'FIGHTERS' PARTY'

A convention of the 'Fighters' Party' was held from 24 to 25 February, in preparation for the party's conference. Its two programmatic addresses, delivered by Friedman-Yellin and Eldad, showed their ideological and political points of agreement – and their differences.

Not without purpose, Friedman-Yellin's speech was devoted to 'problems of regime and of society'. The choice of subject was revealing. The left wing of the movement now acknowledged that the party's future needs would not be met only by high-minded references to 'the integrity of the homeland and the liberation of the nation'. In Friedman-Yellin's view, the party had now to fuse its national aspirations with its social ambitions. These were not contradictory; instead, 'they complemented each other as do man's two legs'.

Neither the left nor the right in Israeli politics, Friedman-Yellin claimed, had attained the correct synthesis. The Labour movement had not thought in political categories. It was a party of those who aimed at 'individual redemption'. Hence, it had become enmeshed in inner contradictions: in theory it had declared war on the bourgeoisie; but in practice it had signed a pact with the non-national elements in the population in return for their financial support. Even worse, in theory Labour had waged war for the destruction of capitalism and the construction of a new social order. In practice, however, it had compromised with the worst form of capitalism – 'with the imperialism which rules our land and also suppresses other peoples'. The Revisionist movement, on the other hand, could have performed a 'historical mission' had it attacked Labour's practice rather than its theory. Instead, it had become a militantly anti-socialist force. Thus the conflict between the Labour and Revisionist movements had focused on the dichotomy between the national aim and social liberation. Had a synthesis been found earlier, declared Friedman-Yellin, 'The war of liberation would have broken out sooner and its results would have been more considerable'.

At this stage, Friedman-Yellin went on to claim that ever since the days of Yair *Lehi* had aimed at precisely that synthesis. Indeed, he cited texts and incidents in order to demonstrate that Stern's philosophy – although necessarily incomplete – had not been anti-socialist. If anything, it had been 'anti-anti-Socialist . . . opposed to a view of Socialism as a fundamentally anti-national outlook. It contains hints of other facets too – there is no reason why nationalism and Socialism cannot co-exist.' Clearly projecting his own perspectives of 1949 back into *Lehi*'s past, Friedman-Yellin argued that the movement had always attempted to follow that path. To that end, he was even prepared to quote at length from 'The Class War and the War of Liberation', written in 1945 by his most serious ideological opponent, Eldad. Although he did not acknowledge the latter's authorship, he did reiterate the message of his work: the negation of the class war in both its Revisionist and *Histadrut* versions in favour of 'the unity of the national and class war'.

The way to implement that programme under the new conditions of statehood was, first of all, for the 'Fighters' Party' to throw itself into the socio-economic life of the nation. It could no longer sit on the fence where social matters were concerned for fear of losing support for its national programme. It had, rather, to harness its energies to the day-to-day struggle for housing, conditions of labour, fair rents, proper investment, strikes, foreign trade, exchange controls and the like. In an attempt to deflect the criticism launched against *Lehi*'s programme of the previous July by both *Mapam* and the Marxist wing of his own membership, Friedman-Yellin advocated that 'Everything must be directed and planned, and the planning – let there be no question – must be Socialist'. *Mapai* and *Mapam*, he claimed, were both ideologically bankrupt. Even worse was the situation of the *Herut* movement, which had been lavish in making promises which only a ruling party could hope to keep. All a 'Fighters' Party' had to do was make a clear stand; it would then experience no difficulty in attracting support.[37]

Friedman-Yellin was followed by Eldad, who addressed the gathering on the subject of 'national foundations'. Like Friedman-Yellin, Eldad denied that there was any dichotomy between the struggle for national liberation and that for social equality. He also rejected the suggestion that *Lehi* housed two different schools of thought – the communist, represented by Friedman-Yellin, and the fascist, represented by Eldad himself. On most major issues, they were in agreement. Where they differed, however, was in their perspective. Eldad maintained that he had no need to learn the principles of socialism from the pages of *Kol Ha-Am* or *Al ha-Mishmar*, still less from Marx. The Bible contained all he needed to know. Moses had been the greatest exponent of the principles of social justice, to which the later prophets had added the notion of an international struggle for the attainment of that goal. All had been great Hebrew patriots and all had attacked social systems in surrounding countries. *Lehi* had to continue that tradition. It did not aim to create a 'cosmopolitan' Jew, divorced from his roots – which is all that official Zionism had accomplished.

Eldad, too, claimed to stand resolutely in Yair's shadow, but he did not quote from 'The Principles of Revival'. Rather, he cited his own

'Foundation Stones' (1943), and disclosed the impact made on him by Schopenhauer, Berdichevsky and Nietzsche when emphasising the centrality of man. But he knew that he was arousing antagonism when citing such nationalist slogans as 'the chosen people'. His reason for doing so was his fear that Friedman-Yellin and his supporters (and even more so those who stood still further to the left of the movement's political spectrum) had in mind the establishment of another Uganda or Birobizhan. Thus, he deliberately added to his repertoire another symbol: that of 'the Jacob's ladder', the highest rung of which reached to heaven but whose base was on earth, on *Eretz Israel. Lehi*'s

> first task is to conquer this land so that the ladder might stand on it firmly. And this ladder cannot stand on a divided state. We need a large territory for this great nation . . . 'on land' also means the order and regime of this country: nature, security, independence, social justice . . . This is the dialectic of Jacob's dream which preceded the dialectic of Marx.[38]

It was symbolic that the gathering had opened on 24 February, the anniversary of Stern's death (25 *Shevat*). It was also the day that Israel signed an armistice agreement with Egypt. In its concluding resolutions, the meeting protested against the fact that the government had 'relinquished territory conquered by Israel's soldiers' (especially since the Knesset had not been consulted) and called on the party organs not to accept the partition of the country but to fight 'with all available means' for its unification. Special mention was made of the reunification of Jerusalem. Furthermore, the meeting also sent greetings to all the nations and governments which had supported the struggle of the people of Israel 'and especially to the USSR and the lands of people's democracy'. Reference was also made to *Lehi*'s belief that 'barriers to the free emigration of all Jews who wish to leave will be removed'. The gathering promised that in any event it would support the true neutrality of the state of Israel and oppose all forms of imperialism. Finally, the meeting also congratulated Friedman-Yellin on his election to the Knesset and on his courage in supporting the candidacy of Professor Y. Klausner for president rather than Weizmann.

But this show of unity was deceptive. In effect, the party had still not managed to unify its own doctrines. As much was apparent as early as 9 March, when Friedman-Yellin first addressed the Knesset. What he then presented was a programme which, in effect, compounded part of the social and political philosophies of *Mapam* and *Maki* with the security and political doctrines of the *Herut* movement. He accused Sharett of aiming to reach agreements with the feudal regimes at present in control of the Arab countries and of forfeiting the goodwill of the USSR. True to the spirit of *Lehi*, he posited the connection between foreign and economic policies. Israel's absorptive capacity, he claimed, was dependent on the extent of the country's borders. Hence, the latter had to be expanded and all development projects had to be directed towards a complete transformation of the existing social system. Nevertheless, unlike *Maki*, he did not oppose the government's acceptance of an American loan. Instead, and like *Mapam*, he abstained.[39]

Throughout the next two years, Friedman-Yellin's addresses to the Knesset were to veer between those two conflicting poles. In retrospect, it appears that an ideology which attempted to fuse integral nationalism and socialism, and which called to mind the National Bolshevism of Weimar, really left no other choice. But that attempt at fusion, although designed to stress the uniqueness of the 'Fighters' Party' was inherently unstable. Ultimately, and paradoxically, it was to be torn asunder by a stronger political and ideological reality.

THE FIRST (AND LAST) CONFERENCE OF THE 'FIGHTERS' PARTY'

In the light of the party's disastrous showing in the elections, a measure of ideological and organisational stock-taking was clearly called for. Consequently, a conference of the 'Fighters Party' was held behind closed doors from 20 to 27 March 1949 in the presence of 120 delegates.

The opening address was delivered by Yitzchak Shamir, a former member of *Lehi*'s 'centre'. His message was that: 'This conference must decide what we want. It has to decide not what we *are* today as a result of various developments, but what we want *to become*.' Shamir himself, it must be remembered, was not by nature an ideologue. What is more, he had been out of the country between the summer of 1946 and May 1948 – precisely the period when *Lehi* had wrestled with the social and political consequences of its pro-Soviet orientation. Perhaps for both reasons, he did not address himself to the questions of society and regime which, he claimed, the movement had in any case not enjoyed the leisure and will to examine in sufficient depth. Nevertheless, he did acknowledge the challenge which *Lehi* now faced. Having always concentrated its efforts on the defeat of Britain, 'the direct enemy', *Lehi* had not equipped itself to deal with the Arab question. Furthermore, how was the battle against imperialism to be waged now that the government of Israel constituted a new factor in the political equation? In effect, he thus returned to the dilemma of the previous summer. Was *Lehi* to 'wage war against the Government of Israel, if so – how and when, in what way and in what form? As an underground movement or as a party? Is there any other way?'[40]

The first delegate to address these issues was Pinhas Ginosar, representing the extreme Marxist section of the party, as opposed to the moderate left represented by Friedman-Yellin and Shamir. Immediate priority, Ginosar agreed, had to be accorded to national issues: 'The completion of the national revolution, the integrity of the homeland, the gathering in of the exiles and liberation from the bonds of American imperialism which have begun to hold us in chains.' In foreign affairs, the party had to aim at neutralisation by generating 'social ferment' in neighbouring Arab states. Ultimately, however, the party's ambition had to be to create a fully socialist state. There was no hope that this form of regime would be established by the existing workers' parties. Indeed, Ginosar was scathing in his attacks on *Mapai* and *Mapam*, which he depicted as having in effect represented the bourgeois interests of, respectively, their own massive economic plants and the middle-income farmers ever since the days of the Mandate (which explained why they had been able to co-operate with British imperialism).

Up to that point in his speech, Ginosar was largely in agreement with the sentiments that Friedman-Yellin had expressed in his address to the party gathering the previous month. He too, moreover, regarded *Mapai*, *Mapam* and *Herut* as parties on the verge of disintegration and thus foresaw a great future for the 'Fighters' Party'. Thereafter, however, the paths projected by the two men differed. Ginosar, who within a few weeks was to formulate his own theory of National Bolshevism, presented a far more activist programme than did Friedman-Yellin. He called on the 'Fighters' Party' to enter the *Histadrut* 'with the clear ambition of assuming leadership, for as a collectivity we have the greatest amount of revolutionary experience in *Eretz Israel*'.

In operational terms, this meant undertaking two tasks. One was ideological: the clear announcement of the message that only a true workers' regime could entirely unify the homeland, gather in the exiles and free the Middle East from the yoke of imperialism. The second was organisational: 'reaching out to the people' by encouraging unionisation, assisting strikers, lecturing to workers, and involvement in the poor communities and those of the new immigrants. By so doing, 'We shall prepare the ground for the days of revolutionary opportunity, days which may be closer than we realise'.

Having thus outlined his differences with Friedman-Yellin, Ginosar then proceeded to take issue with Eldad as well. Specifically, he objected to the picture portrayed in his 'Jacob's ladder'. For one thing, he protested, Judaism was itself not cut of one cloth, and contained more than the prophetic tradition of which Eldad had spoken. Second, and more important, he rejected the notion of superiority inherent in Eldad's references to 'the chosen people'. 'If I wish to build a co-operative society in *Eretz Israel*, I cannot claim: I have received the idea of justice from the prophets or the Sicarii . . . we have to learn from those who laid the scientific foundations of social and political science.'[41]

During the debate which followed this address, several speakers highlighted the differences in the positions presented by Ginosar, Friedman-Yellin and Eldad on both organisational and ideological issues. Others, however, attempted to formulate a compromise. Particularly prominent in this respect was Mordechai Shalev, who spoke after Dr Helman, Dr Sabo and Abrasha Selman, each of whom had suggested various ways of bridging the gap between the contending sides. Summarising the previous discussion, Shalev suggested that the movement incorporate the ideological views advocated by both its right and left wings. It would aim at a proletarian revolution on socialist lines, but at the same time would not fudge Hebrew distinctiveness. After all, he argued, no individual or nation had ever created anything without a sense of mission. Socrates used to address the Athenians as 'the best of persons' and in Russia reference was made to 'the mission of the Russian people'. In the main, however, he concentrated on the question of organisation. On this issue, he rejected the position of Friedman-Yellin – 'a classless and mass movement which aims at rule' – as well as that presented by Ginosar – 'a mass and class movement which aims at rule'. Instead, he suggested adopting Eldad's organisational solution: 'an educational and political core which will crystallise *Lehi*'s ideological foundations, adapt them from time to time in accordance with changing circumstances, and when the time is ripe become a mass movement'.[42]

Ultimately, however, the attempt at compromise was doomed to failure. As speaker after speaker took the floor, it became clear that the party was deeply divided on both the ideological and the organisational issues which constituted the core of debate. True, the majority of delegates did support the form of National Bolshevism advocated by Shamir and Friedman-Yellin and encapsulated in the phrase 'national communism within Biblical borders'. But a minority were clearly and adamantly right wing (much more so than Eldad), and were even prepared to disband *Lehi* altogether. Such was the stand taken by Y.L. Schneersohn, Eliyahu Amikam, Geulah Cohen and Avraham Rosenfeld. Each denied Friedman-Yellin's thesis that Yair had been a closet socialist. Instead, they contended that a Marxist

platform (even such as had been advocated in *Lehi*'s earlier Programme) did not speak to specifically Hebrew interests, and advocated
an ultra-nationalist approach such as was portrayed in the writings of
Uri Zvi Greenberg of *Herut*. Moreover, differences on organisational
matters continued to preclude unity among the delegates on the
movement's left wing. They could still not decide whether they were
now to constitute a sect or a party and, if the latter, whether their base
was to be broad or narrow.[43]

Before a vote was taken, each of the three leaders who had guided
*Lehi* 's fortunes during the Mandate period addressed the delegates.
The first was Shamir. Speaking 'with emotion and dread', he attacked
those who considered an internal split to be inevitable. That view, he
claimed, was born of 'hysteria' – of precisely the same sort as had
generated the split of 1940. As in his first speech, Shamir did not devote
himself particularly to matters of ideology. Although he insisted that
there existed a large measure of common ideological ground between
the rival factions, the main focus of his speech was on operational
matters. Accordingly, while admitting that he had learned much from
Uri Zvi Greenberg's 'vision', he denied that *Lehi* had anything to
learn from Greenberg regarding its fulfilment. Similarly, he disputed
the claim that it was *Lehi*'s 'mission' to promote revolution in the
neighbouring Arab countries. 'The only legitimate mission is . . . that
this great [Hebrew] people will grow, expand and build its own life and
sovereignty.' In the same tone, he launched into a diatribe against the
'intelligentsia' in his own movement who advocated acts which they
did not possess the means to carry out. It followed that the party could
not be reduced to 'a narrow core'. If it was to seize whatever opportunities were offered to attain its ends, it required (on the model of
ELAS, the Greek communist underground):

> a discernible, united, disciplined and organised force, capable of
> attaining the means necessary for the implementation of revolution
> . . . We must create a strong organisational mechanism which will
> attempt to incorporate the masses, which will strive towards and
> believe in its success in increasing its strength, and which will
> encompass wider circles in order to fulfil its vision.

Shamir's tone was predominantly pragmatic. He accepted the
argument that *Lehi* was in favour of 'national maximalism and the
search for social justice'. But although Shamir did have left-wing
tendencies, he was not a doctrinaire Marxist. The national element in
his philosophy was far more authentic than was its socialist component.
Moreover, and perhaps because he was already disappointed with
the Soviet Union's attitude towards Israel, Shamir warned against

accepting the explicitly pro-Soviet orientation advocated even by *Lehi*'s moderate right wing. 'I think we are exaggerating in this matter. I believe that in the present situation we must principally emphasise neutrality and not a permanent link with a particular bloc in the world.'[44]

Eldad, the next speaker to address the conference, criticised Shamir for not dealing with what he considered to be the main issues of ideological content. Of his own positions, he left no doubt. He attempted to rectify the obviously negative impression created by his 'Jacob's ladder' address. At various points in his speech, he also hinted that he was prepared to reach a compromise on the basis of *Lehi*'s July programme. Nevertheless, there were four issues on which he insisted. One was his utter opposition to imperialism and (quite contrary to Shamir) his demand that *Lehi* adopt the explicit pro-Soviet stand advocated by Friedman-Yellin and Ginosar. A second was his interpretation of the July programme which, he argued, accorded priority to national liberation over social liberation. The third of Eldad's criticisms of Friedman-Yellin emanated from the others. He feared that *Lehi* might be forced to choose between national liberation and social liberation as a result of an economic crisis or unemployment. The Labour movement would blame the bourgeoisie and demand nationalisation. A revolution would then break out:

> A very strange situation will be created . . . Fearing that a revolution might ensue, the bourgeoisie will speak of borders and conquest, and the IZL movement will then hitch itself to the bourgeoisie's bandwagon and turn into the bourgeoisie's army . . . And what will the *Lehi* party do then – betray the workers' party or side with the bourgeoisie?[45]

Finally, and most important of all, Eldad referred to the organisational issue. While Friedman-Yellin wanted to see the establishment of a workers' party, Eldad did not believe in its future. Principally, this was because (unlike Friedman-Yellin) he did not believe that *Mapai* and *Mapam* were about to disintegrate. Hence, 'Either we establish a mass party which wants to seize power, or I establish a framework which in the present circumstances undertakes educational work.'[46]

In his own concluding speech, Friedman-Yellin sought to preserve the unity of the movement. Accordingly, he praised both Eldad's part in formulating *Lehi*'s ideology and Shamir's role in providing it with a toughness of fibre. He also considered that the gap between the positions advocated by the extreme left and right wings of the party could easily be bridged. After all, the former adhered to the principle of 'territorial integrity' while the latter supported socialism. In fact, both elements were vital components of the movement's ideology. Thus, Friedman-Yellin insisted on the continued viability of the 'classic' *Lehi* approach, which regarded the homeland as the principal focal point. Indeed, in contrast to his own earlier statements, he even expressed a favourable view of the present state of Israel ('the Archimedean point') which, notwithstanding its 'bad' leaders, provided a base for mass immigration and maintained a large army. On the other hand, the national element had to be complemented by the social. The mission of the 'Fighters' was not only the liberation of the homeland. 'It is also our mission to fill this homeland with content – a content which is economic, social, spiritual and cultural.'

It is interesting that Friedman-Yellin was not oblivious to the possibility of a break with the USSR ('whether due to a misunderstanding or because of Russia's interests'). Even more significant are his views on the Arab question. Indeed, during the course of his address Friedman-Yellin for the first time revealed his differences with Eldad and Zetler over Deir Yasin. The path to a new age in the Middle East, he implied, was not to be sought by such actions, but by giving encouragement to the establishment of socialist and neutral states in Arab lands.

Altogether, Friedman-Yellin attempted to remain faithful to *Lehi*'s programme of the previous July. Thus he insisted on the need to work towards the formulation of a socialist mode of state and economic planning, on the lines of the 'people's democracies' in their transitional stages. This form of state socialism, he insisted, was different from that proposed by Shalev (the funds raised in America were to be spent on national projects, such as the absorption of immigrants, and were not to be paid to the workers). It also differed from the 'revolutionary socialism' proposed by Edelstein (Eshed) and Ginosar – which he termed 'sheer demagogy'.

On the organisational question, too, Friedman-Yellin expressed definite views. Convinced that a 'club' was not enough ('we also need an instrument'), Friedman-Yellin was far more optimistic than Eldad. Although he did not, on this occasion, speak of the impending disintegration of the large parties, he did speak of the possibility of an association with *Mapam* ('the camp containing the *Palmach*'). Altogether, 'even though few in number, we must strive for expansion . . . it will bring closer the day of the entire homeland's liberation'.[47]

Although the speakers seem to have been divided more by organisational issues than by those of ideology, the 'political committee' of the conference presented two separate resolutions. The first, tabled by Friedman-Yellin, voiced the views of the majority and received 14 votes; the second, tabled by Eldad, received only six votes.

It is interesting to compare these two resolutions with *Lehi*'s previous programme. The majority decision, for instance, certainly leaned far more to the left wing of the party than had the earlier document. Thus it made no reference to 'historical natural' borders, instead it employed the new phrase 'the entire homeland' (but did retain the reference to Uri Zvi Greenberg's call for Hebrew 'mastery' (*adnut*)). On the other hand, the resolution was far more specific in its call for the establishment of a 'socialist' regime (whereas the July programme had spoken of 'national ownership of the country's resources and means of production'). Similarly, the new resolution spoke of the 'identity' between the workers' struggle for their true interests and the national fight for political liberation. Some of these changes might have been generated by a wish to draw somewhat closer to *Mapam*, as may have been also the explicit reference to the *Histadrut* as 'the sole unit of professional organisation'. Whatever the case, it is also noteworthy that the new resolution had some significant omissions: no mention was made of the pronounced right-wing call for population exchanges; the code-word 'neutralisation' was absent and the notion was only alluded to; similarly dropped (perhaps under Shamir's influence) was the original programme's reference to an alliance with 'the eastern bloc'.[48]

In presenting his own resolution, Eldad categorically rejected the left-wing leaning of Friedman-Yellin's resolution. For one thing, he declared, it obfuscated the true identity of *Lehi*, which had to be based on an explicitly national programme. That was why he deliberately retained the programme's original reference to the establishment of a Hebrew 'monarchy' (*malkhut*) which had been dropped in the majority resolution. Socialism and a class war, he argued, would simply burden the movement with excess baggage. In fact, the resolution tabled by Friedman-Yellin was a recipe for decline; it lacked all the necessary ingredients of independence, philosophy, strategy and tactics. In that sense, it bore comparison with the infamous 'Uganda' resolution tabled by the sixth Zionist congress in 1903. 'The workers will not come [to us] if we declare a thousand times that we are Marxists. We do not believe in the possibility of a large workers' party.' Along the same lines was the statement that: 'Present circumstances do not permit *Lehi* to establish a mass party, with the aim of attaining rule without detriment to its own principles. We therefore propose the establishment of an educational-political party, which will turn into a mass party when circumstances are right.'[49]

The minority resolution took Shamir, at least, by surprise. Considering the majority resolution 'the most faithful expression of what is common to us all', he thought that the minority proposal had no other purpose than 'to divide the movement'. Shamir rejected the notion that there was anything substantively different in the majority's definition of the objective, and hence considered the 'Uganda' analogy entirely irrelevant. After all, Eldad had himself concurred with the previous programme which had also declared *Lehi* to be a *'political liberation movement'*. It was an insult to say now that the majority resolution was so concerned with social issues that it was not sufficiently nationalist. The minority was suffering from a 'nightmare complex'. The struggle for the defence of the rights of the Hebrew workers must be considered 'a part of' and 'identical' with that for national liberation.

In the light of these observations, Shamir concluded that Eldad sought to divide the movement on the organisational question rather than that of ideology. And on the organisational issue, Shamir's attack on Eldad was quite blunt. The path which he had mapped out could only lead to disaster. It would result in the creation of 'a tiny group which will bring out some good newspapers, but that will be their only activity; they won't even have enough people to distribute the papers'. Shamir claimed that his objective was not to establish a mass party 'overnight' but to lay the foundations for its existence.[50]

In the plenum, too, Eldad was defeated. The majority resolution was passed by 49 votes to 13 (with 25 abstentions); the minority resolution was defeated by 41 to 19 (with 27 abstentions). Eldad took his defeat badly. He considered the majority resolution to have 'fudged' the movement's aims; to have encouraged introspection; and to have raised the 'mirage' of its growth. Nevertheless, for the sake of party unity, Eldad and his group had chosen to abstain on the majority resolution rather than vote against. Clearly, the ideology of National Bolshevism had ceased to be a unifying force. The remainder of the conference was devoted to the passage of largely ceremonial resolutions. These spoke of the dangers inherent in the spread of British imperialism and of the American economic monopoly; deplored the UN armistice commission as an imperialist tool and the plan to form regional blocs under NATO influence as a threat which could involve Israel in war; rejected the armistice agreements signed with the neighbouring Arab countries, since they had forfeited portions of the homeland to 'backward' regimes which were tools in the enemy's hands; called on the Arab masses to bring down their 'enslaving' governments; expressed horror at the anti-Jewish persecutions in Arab lands (but did not call for population transfers, only for the free immigration of Jews to Israel); expressed sorrow at the 'impediments' which in the 'People's democracies' lands had been placed on the free emigration of Jews to Israel; supported the settlement of barren land; and protested at the continued retention of the emergency decrees.[51]

THE DISSOLUTION OF THE 'FIGHTERS' PARTY'

Effective dissolution was now just a matter of days. The press was soon reporting the final departure of Eldad and his faction, and their accusations of treachery. Eldad was himself ordered to appear before an internal court for having published *Sulam*, but he refused.[52] In a public speech, he accused Friedman-Yellin of being associated with the Hebrew communists and claimed that after the conference the majority of Fighters had rejected the party's new socialist programme. In effect, Eldad maintained, Friedman-Yellin had betrayed Yair's ideology and had established a neo-Marxist party. In response, an internal Fighters' court decided to expel Eldad and his supporters from the party; they were found guilty of fomenting internal discord and of retaining a Revisionist mentality which attached no importance to socialism.[53]

Despite the split, the leaders of the Fighters put a bold face on matters, hailing the Chinese communist model. Friedman-Yellin, for instance, was sure that 'from the point of view of political theory, ours is the most complete and strongest of all movements'. He claimed that *Herut* and – even more so – *Mapam* were terrified of the Fighters. Shamir, too, was convinced of the inevitability of a clash with imperialism, and equally sure of the Fighters' ultimate success.[54] That tone also infused the Fighters' propaganda on the eve of the seventh *Histadrut* convention, which met at the end of May 1949. Here, too, what was emphasised was the party's illusion of a possible 'fusion' of its two ideals: integral nationalism and socialism. Hence it spoke of combining

the people's war for political independence throughout the homeland with the class war for a regime of creativity and labour . . . for the establishment of a socialist regime in which the people will own the national resources and means of production, of equality and the prevention of the exploitation of man by man.[55]

For the moment, domestic concerns had to give way to the need to fight the forces of foreign imperialism. Friedman-Yellin was particularly perturbed by the possibility that the impending implementation of the Marshall Plan might lead to an imperialist hegemony over the Middle East, as a result of which Israel's present borders would be frozen. The most effective response, he thought, was not the austerity programme proposed by the government, but the encouragement of massive immigration and of land settlement (such as was signified by the foundation of the Fighters' own agricultural settlement which they named Neveh Yair). Another side of the same coin was the danger of a renewed attack on Israel by a combination of Arab and Anglo-Saxon forces. All Fighters, so the party claimed, were united in their determination to 'repel the invaders and free the homeland'. Hence, all opposed the Lausanne Conciliation Conference; all opposed the notion that the Arab refugees might be permitted to return; all opposed the government's lack of an independent foreign policy; and all, on the other hand, supported the notion that Israel had to seek to increase the similarities between her own interests and those of the 'people's democracies' and, in particular, Soviet Russia.[56]

Even more outspoken was the notion of National Bolshevism as formulated at this time by Ginosar. True, Ginosar did not hesitate to criticise Stalin himself for having denied the existence of a separate Jewish nationality as early as 1912; nor did he spare Soviet Russia for its support of the Arabs; for its attempt to distinguish between the Jewish people in the diaspora and the Hebrew nation in its homeland; and for its conception that the state of Israel had to be confined to its present borders. Nevertheless, he argued, gone were the times when dichotomy had existed between Soviet and Zionist interests. Now that the Hebrew liberation movement had proved to be imperialism's 'most terrible foe', there exists 'a basis for co-operation and identity between the movement for Hebrew revival and the socialist revolution'. Such had been the case in Italy, where (he claimed) the workers' movement had taken root in the work of Garibaldi and Mazzini; such was the case in Russia, where Lenin had considered himself to have continued the work of the *Narodnaya Volya*; such was the case in China, where Mao Tse-tung saw himself as an extension of Sun Yat-sen; and such – most important of all – had been the case within Soviet Russia during the Second World War, when 'what had been made plain was the identity between true nationalism and true socialism'. Ginosar was convinced that precisely the same model would be implemented within Israel.[57] An essential prerequisite to that end was massive immigration of the poor, which would emphasise the contradiction between labour and capital. Only with such an influx would Israeli society be revolutionised and its regime transformed.[58]

In the circumstances, this was nothing more than an experimental ideology. Its implementation would have demanded considerable organisational strength; it also required the benefit of stronger proofs. These could not be supplied either by reference to incidents culled from *Lehi*'s own history (such as the assassination of Lord Moyne, taken as an exemplar of anti-imperialist warfare), or by resort to ideological debates with Eldad and his faction.[59] The only circumstance which might have improved the Fighters' image – in their own eyes and those of the public – was the fulfilment of their own prophecies of doom. What they needed, in fact, was both a collapse of Israel's economic and social framework and the outbreak of a war at Arab instigation with imperialist support. In the absence of such events – despite weekly forecasts of their imminence – a party with so experimental an ideology had no chance of continued existence. At the same time, the internal gulf within the party itself between the moderate left and the Marxist left widened.

Friedman-Yellin was to serve as the Fighters' representative in the first Knesset until the summer of 1951; but signs of the party's dissolution were apparent much earlier. As early as November 1949 Avraham Selman, who was responsible for the movement's affairs abroad and in the *Histadrut*, accused his colleagues of organisational, political and moral failure. There was, he claimed, no 'political programme, no instruction and no strategic direction'. In effect, the leadership had no right to its position and had forfeited the moral validity of the decision to expel Eldad and his faction. Since (in his opinion) most of the rank and file had left the party because of the failure of the 'centre' to provide a unifying focus, he advised the members of the 'centre' to resign and to leave the fate of the party in the hands of the conference. When his appeal met with no response, Selman himself resigned. The Marxists on the movement's left wing soon drew their own conclusions. 'We can only hope that there will be some point in your existence and activity. To our regret, we see no chance of that.'[60]

Nevertheless, Friedman-Yellin himself remained optimistic. In both his public appearances in the Knesset and in the Fighters' publications, he continued to retain the façade of a unified party with a single ideological message. Thus, encouraged by the victory of communism in Soviet Russia, in Eastern Europe and – most recently – in China, he continued to support the establishment of a socialist regime and a classless society. He denied charges that he was himself veering between *Herut* and *Mapam*, claiming that that impression resulted from a mistaken view of the concept of the 'complete fusion' of the national and social aspects of the war of liberation. Nevertheless, that Friedman-Yellin was himself beginning to show signs of strain is apparent from his admission that the outcome of the struggle was by no means certain.[61]

Some of the Fighters' leaders were even more sceptical. On the eve of his own departure from the party, Ginosar maintained that the 'Hebrew Revolutionary Movement' (that is, the 'Fighters' Party') is 'in a condition of acute dissolution, with a fall in tension and lack of activity'. The fault, he argued, lay with *Lehi*'s failure to seize the historic opportunity afforded it to become 'a revolutionary party in possession of weight and influence' when the British had left the country. To Ginosar's mind, the principal fault had lain with the conference. Notwithstanding the majority resolution, Eldad's group had prevented the Fighters from defining their position on socialism with sufficient precision. What was now needed was a clearly defined socialist party 'with a connection to the symbols of the international working class, viz.: the red flag and the *Internationale* hymn, because they articulate the ambitions and vision of the class for a post-revolutionary world'.

The passage from a petit bourgeoisie party into a workers' party would not be easy. 'Before all else we must rid ourselves of . . . a narrow nationalist outlook which does not recognise that nationalism and internationalism are two sides of the same coin and from a mystical conception of national needs.' The latter had been instilled by Eldad who ('in a somewhat confused fashion') had propounded an anti-rational outlook with a strong Nietzschean streak which had been at odds with the historical materialism simultaneously preached in, for instance, *The War on Fascism*. Eldad's responsibility, therefore, was twofold. Not only had he generated internal dissension; he had also 'impeded' the consistent development of the movement's political thought and the recognition that 'our actions and conceptions rest on the pillars of historical materialism'.

Ginosar himself called for the party to stand 'with both legs' on the Marxist world-view, both because it was scientific and because it was the philosophy of the fighting working class and of consistent freedom fighters all over the world. In order to become the true party of the working classes, the Fighters had to concentrate their attacks – not on *Herut* but on *Mapam*. Although himself undoubtedly influenced by some of *Mapam*'s thinkers,[62] Ginosar was convinced that the latter party as a whole did not meet the people's needs on matters of national and social liberation; its impending entry into the government would assuredly lead to its own breakup. Advantage must also be taken of the defections from *Herut*'s ranks.

There were two concrete issues on which Ginosar was deliberately explicit, because he recognised them as constituting litmus tests of his brand of 'communist nationalism'. The first was the attitude to be adopted towards the Arab question. He rejected 'the nationalist approach which would regard them as inferior' and which would deny them their wish to establish, for instance, an Arab university. The second issue was that of terrorism. Here, too, he was adamant. He opposed the revival of that tactic, recently proposed in Fighters' circles when the UN suggested appointing the Colombian, Alberto Gonzales Fernandez its commissioner in Jerusalem. Instead, he favoured *Herut*'s suggestion that Fernandez be boycotted: 'Have we not learned enough of the lessons of the past? . . . We have simply forgotten that there are political and public means of struggle which are vastly more consequential than assassination.'[63]

Notwithstanding the force of these arguments, it was clear that they represented only the views of the Marxist left in the party. Even after the expulsion of Eldad and his group, the Fighters were still not a united party. Some of the members despaired that they could ever turn the masses, who were perceived to be by nature conservative, into a revolutionary and fighting force. Accordingly, and as before, reliance had to be placed 'on a small handful of idealistic fighters'.[64] Others, it transpired, were still opposed to socialism. *Lehi*, they insisted, '*Had been born, created, had acted and fought as a movement for national liberation.*'[65]

One last attempt to forge a sense of party unity was made in February and March 1950, when two meetings of the Fighters' council were held within a single week. The main items on the agenda were the future of the party in the light of the 'incitement and vilification' of its defectors and their condemnation. The council decided on the adoption of new methods, and to that end bestowed on Friedman-Yellin 'unlimited powers' for a period of six months. Comparing the present crisis to that which had befallen the movement in the winter of 1942, Friedman-Yellin was himself convinced that it, too, could be overcome. Indeed, the Fighters did close ranks on the burning issue of Israel's foreign policy. Moreover, and for the very first time, the USSR was also condemned for having voted at the UN in favour of the internationalisation of Jerusalem.[66]

Friedman-Yellin tried to comfort his comrades with the thought that 'rottenness had affected only the fringes of the camp'.[67] But he was really whistling in the dark. Within three months, *La-Haver* had ceased to appear; within another year, the Knesset had been dissolved, new elections had been announced and the party leader (Friedman-Yellin, who had now changed his name to Yellin-Mor) was no longer a member of the country's legislature. The Fighters' failure was dual: organisational and ideological. For one thing, it had fallen between several stools in its struggle for Israeli public opinion. In addition, it had also failed to hold onto its own original members. Henceforth, the latter either ceased to play active political roles or had dispersed among the wide spectrum of political parties (a spectrum which ranged from *Maki*, *Mapam* and *Mapai* to *Herut*), whose positions they had wished to undermine and to inherit. In retrospect, this failure does seem to have been predictable. Eldad had read the signs while Yellin-Mor and Shamir indulged in organisational and ideological fantasies. In summary, three points must be made. First, that the revolutionary experiment undertaken by the Fighters, a party which attempted to forge a unique brand of National Bolshevism, was too novel to succeed; second, that the movement possessed too few followers, and that even those it did have were subject to pressure by other parties; and third, that historical reality made no haste to suit itself to the Fighters' own ideological and political needs.

# Conclusion

To read the accounts compiled by former members of *Lehi* is to gain an impression that, in conjunction with the IZL, their movement was responsible for 'expelling' the British from Palestine in 1947–48. That position is not viable. At the most, *Lehi* (again, together with the IZL) can be depicted as a catalyst in the processes whereby Anglo-Zionist relations deteriorated and Britain's withdrawal from Palestine became inevitable. But it cannot claim exclusive credit for that outcome – nor even for the fact that the USSR was supportive of the young state. In effect, *Lehi* accounts of the end of the Mandate constitute a distortion, and are negated by a detailed study of the relevant documents. They take no account of the fact that immediately after the Second World War the British were themselves in any case dismantling their empire (even in India and Egypt). Neither do they acknowledge the influences exerted on Britain's Palestine policy in the Mandate's final years by American pressure and the plight of Jewish refugees in Europe.

Equally misleading is the failure of *Lehi*'s hagiography to note the manner whereby the 'organised *Yishuv*' harnessed its own strength for what turned out to be the decisive confrontation – not against the British, but against the Arabs. Indeed, contrary to the programme advocated by both the IZL and *Lehi*, the majority of the mandatory *Yishuv* then decided to concentrate on the crystallisation of its own power under British protection and thus prepare for its struggle against the long-term Arab foe. In retrospect, that proved to be a decisive strategy, which rendered the extreme political solutions that *Lehi* proposed entirely inappropriate. The events of 1939–41 did not necessitate – even had they made possible – the establishment of a 'Kingdom of Israel' under Axis protection; neither did the Soviet victories of 1944–45 require the foundation of a 'people's democracy' under Stalinist auspices in 1949, even had the Russians been amenable to that option.

Given the minor extent of *Lehi*'s operational successes, the true interest of the movement's history must be deemed to lie elsewhere – in the uniquely diverse and tortuous path of its ideological development. Throughout its existence, *Lehi* experienced perpetual tensions between its ideology and changing circumstances. Furthermore, it was at once both innovative and eclectic. It was this which endowed the movement with an importance and strength which bore no correlation to either the direct impact of its military operations or its numerical following (which amounted to about 200 persons when *Lehi* was formed and some 800 when it disbanded).

Existing literature on *Lehi* has hitherto failed to focus on that aspect of the movement's character. Broadly defined, the available historiography falls into two categories. The first consists of memoirs written by persons who were themselves members of the movement. Like all examples of the genre, such works aim to provide justifications for the course adopted by their authors. Concentrating on tales of partisan and terrorist operations, they largely ignore the chronology of the movement's emergence and its subsequent ideological and political developments. It is hardly surprising that they also tend to bring the story of *Lehi* to a close on 29 May 1948, with the disbandment of the 'Fighting Unit', and refrain from discussing the movement's subsequent decline and split, which take the shine off its heroic image.[1] The second category of literature consists of works written by persons who were opponents of *Lehi*. One example is provided by Niv's history of the IZL, which regards *Lehi* as a marginal group and therefore pays little attention either to the differences of opinion among the movement's members or to its mistakes. Although the works compiled by the 'organised *Yishuv*' are written from a completely different ideological perspective, they adopt the same attitude. Pre-eminent among works of this type is Slutsky's *History of the Haganah*, which utterly rejects *Lehi*'s principles and methods.

The present work has attempted to chart a different and less biased course. Utilising the substantial body of writings by *Lehi*'s formative thinkers, it has concentrated on the movement's various – sometimes substantial – ideological transformations, between its origins and the conclusion of the Fighters' conference. Only from that perspective, it argues, can historians understand both the motives which generated the emergence of the movement and its subsequent changes in course. No less significantly, it is also ideological circumstances that explain the fundamental internal divisions which characterised *Lehi* and ultimately precluded its ability to survive the period of its war against the British Mandate.

### FROM MAXIMALIST REVISIONISM TO 'THE IZL IN ISRAEL'

The embryonic stage of *Lehi*'s history is intimately bound up with the name of Avraham Stern. Justifiable though that association is, it must also be noted that Stern was not the first to rebel against the philosophy of Revisionism's founders. In fact, the ideological and political bases for the split of 1940 had been laid as early as the 1920s by Achimeir,

Yeivin, and U.Z. Greenberg and by Ratosh during the 1930s. Still more decisively, the seeds then sown had taken further root throughout the crucial decade spanned by the Arab riots of 1929 and the British White Paper of May 1939; it was during those years that a break between Jabotinsky and the maximalists within his movement had become unavoidable. Less and less were the latter prepared to countenance Jabotinsky's support of Western democracy, his pro-British orientation and his apparent ambition – not to replace England, but to succeed Weizmann. Thus, the more Anglo-Zionist relations deteriorated, the greater became the maximalists' revulsion against the official *Yishuv* policy of 'self-restraint'. Instead, it was the need for a complete break with Britain and a war of independence (ideas preached by Achimeir and Ratosh) that were bound to become the focus of thought in Revisionism as a whole, and in the IZL in particular. True, as early as 1936 Jabotinsky was himself evincing increasing sympathy for the anti-British sentiments of his more radical followers.[2] Nevertheless, his world-view and attitudes – quite apart from his statements – were never as extreme as those of the maximalist Revisionists. As much is indicated by their contrasting attitudes to what became known as the 'Italian option'. Jabotinsky brandished this as a tactic; but Achimeir, Ratosh and Stern regarded it as a strategic alternative, to which U.Z. Greenberg, from the wings, imparted an eschatological and messianic flavour.[3]

Thus seen, Stern was only the last (if also the most crucial) link in the process whereby the revolutionary ideas implicit in some of Jabotinsky's own teachings were translated into a more distilled philosophy of revolutionary deeds. Stern, in fact, built on foundations laid by others. One of his mentors was Achimeir, whose distinction as a theoretician lay in the fact that he was the first to question the validity of Jabotinsky's teaching that Revisionism was an opposition and not a revolutionary liberation movement on the models of the European right. Another was Ratosh, who (once Achimeir's image had been tarnished by his physical and psychological frailty in prison) had inculcated similar ideas concerning the need for a revolutionary minority which would activate the masses towards a seizure of power. It was thus that Ratosh became the key link connecting Achimeir, the verbal revolutionary who instilled social-Darwinist ideas and the need for force, and Stern, the practical revolutionary. Ratosh also moulded Achimeir's sporadic notions into a more concrete form. In his hands they became a sort of codex, endowed with what had been absent under Achimeir: a broad programmatic charter affecting every sphere of life and possessing a corporative perspective on economic and social affairs. Finally, Ratosh was also more precise in his delineation of the appropriate moment for the creation of a springboard for revolutionary fulfilment, the anticipation of which had always motivated Revisionism's various wings. Stern had only to specify that, with the drastic enfeeblement of Britain's position at the outbreak of the Second World War, the moment for armed military action had indeed arrived. Moreover, Hitler's victories during the early stages of the war confirmed who the ally in that struggle had to be.

In sum, then, Stern's contribution was to act as a catalyst. He did so in both an organisational and an ideological context. Altogether, he may be classed as one of those right-wing and radical political leaders who, having failed to impose their outlook on existing political reality, was constrained to establish an alternative framework for action in order to attain their goals. Stern's original aim had been to seize high command of the IZL.[4] Frustrated in that ambition, he established 'the underground of revolutionaries'. At the same time, he also formulated 'The Principles of the Revival'. In this document, he signified the ideological crystallisation of integral nationalism which, influenced by both maximalist Revisionism and the classic European revolutionary nationalists (Mazzini, Garibaldi, Pilsudski, Casement and, above all, the heroes of *Narodnaya Volya*), he endowed with a character of revolutionary operationalism. Therein lay the basis for such formulations as 'Perpetual war against all who threaten to impede attainment of the goal', and 'the creation of alliances with all who are interested in the organisation's struggle, and who are prepared to give it direct assistance'.

Thus presented, Stern's political thinking did not comprise only messianic fatalism. Although strongly influenced by the ancient Jewish legend of Messiah ben Yoseph and by Maimonides, Stern also projected an image of rationality. Therein, to his mind, lay the logic in the search for an alignment with Nazi Germany (whose anti-Semitism even Jabotinsky had not considered to be a revolutionary departure in the Jewish experience); therein, too, lay the legitimacy of his distinction between the two classes of adversaries whom he labelled 'persecutor' and 'enemy'. Nazism fell under the former category and hence could be regarded as a possible negotiating partner. On the other hand, since Britain was the foreign power exercising control over the Hebrew homeland, it constituted an 'enemy' with whom no compromise was possible.[5]

### THE BEGINNING OF THE TURN TO THE LEFT

The failure of Stern's strategy did not dishearten his disciples. They regarded it as a tactical setback, which did not detract from their outlook of ideological wholeness or its meta-historical correctness. It was thus only natural that they would again try their hand at political intrigue, assisted by the myth of the founding father which they cease- lessly cultivated. But this time the search for a suitable ally involved changes in the hallowed ideology.[6] Although continuing fully to delegitimise its political rivals, *Lehi* attempted to break out of the political isolation in which it found itself during the mid-term period of 1943–45. It did so by retreating further from classical Revisionism. Thus, *Lehi* gradually adopted a favourable attitude towards land settle- ment and the *Histadrut* as organic elements in the war of liberation; it also divested itself of anti-socialist assumptions and acknowledged the proletariat to be the class which carried the principal burden of that war.

Quite apart from the pressures exerted by *Lehi*'s own organisational and ideological weaknesses, such changes were also the result of pres- sing political needs. These became especially marked in 1944 when the IZL, now under Begin's command, renewed its military campaign, and when the armed clash with the left took place at the *Ha-Shomer Ha-Tsair* club. Both events forced *Lehi*'s leaders to intensify their efforts, not only to achieve further military successes, but also to strive for ideological originality. As a result, the movement gradually formu- lated a new ideology, reminiscent of Weimar's National Bolshevism, which yoked together right-wing nationalism and such leftist tendencies as nationalisation, state planning and, above all, a pro-Soviet inter- national orientation.

It did not occur to *Lehi*'s leaders that they were moving towards a theory of National Bolshevism. Rather, they convinced themselves that they were engaged in a legitimate attempt to develop ideas implicit in Stern's own teachings. Nevertheless, the shift away from original Revisionist positions was marked. For one thing, *Lehi* was to abandon Jabotinsky's former hatred of communism[7] and, instead, to preach that the USSR's foreign policy would permanently work to the benefit of the creation of a greater Hebrew state. Therein, it claimed, lay the justification for its own 'neutralisation plan' of 1946 and the true inter- pretation of such developments as Gromyko's statement, Tzarapkin's message, Russia's struggle against the Bernadotte plan and – especially – the delivery of Czech arms at the height of Israel's war of indepen- dence. Simultaneously, *Lehi* also changed its domestic objectives, eventually moving towards a recognition of the centrality of the work- ing class in the war for national liberation. This process began with Eldad's series of programmatic articles entitled 'Foundation Stones' and was extended by Friedman-Yellin's contacts with Golomb. But such were the dynamics generated by the dramatic events of the period that by 1947–48 *Lehi* had been forced to step up the pace of its

shift to the left, both ideologically and politically. It even openly advocated the establishment of an Israeli 'people's democracy' which,
since it would also allow private enterprise, was understood to be the
only regime capable of solving the new state's enormous domestic and
foreign problems.

The changes in *Lehi*'s outlook did not reflect opportunism. Rather,
they articulated a sincere intellectual attempt to construct a new ideology, one which tried to fuse nationalism and communism into an
organic ideological system and stand the test of the regime to which it
gave rise.[8] Ultimately, however, that attempt was doomed to failure.
This became apparent with the final split between the right and left
wings of the movement at the conference of the 'Fighters' Party'. It
then transpired that the compromise attained in the programme of the
summer of 1948 was a temporary arrangement rather than a long-term
*modus vivendi*. In ideological terms, *Lehi* still had to choose between
right and left; moreover, on matters of organisation, the Fighters had
to decide whether they were to constitute an independent political
party or nothing more than an educational society. In numerical
terms, it was the left wing which prevailed; considerably strengthened
by the return of those *Lehi* members who had been exiled to Africa,
Friedman-Yellin's followers voted to continue to support an experimental model of putative 'national communism' and to retain their
party identity. But that proved to be a Pyrrhic victory. In an atmosphere now clouded by mutual distrust, the right wing – led by Eldad –
began to revert to maximalist Revisionism and 'The Principles of
Revival'. Eventually, then, the Fighters simply disintegrated. Each
member chose his own course and decided when to embark on it.

### *LEHI*'S MODELS AND THEIR IMITATION

Throughout its history, *Lehi* derived enormous inspiration from the
heroic episodes known to have occurred during the second Jewish
Commonwealth. It also tended to position itself within the main-
stream of Jewish messianic movements. But to the outsider, the movement appears to be (at the most) a link in the history of Revisionist
Zionism.[9] This was true even during its National Bolshevik period,
when *Lehi* adopted positions on socio-economic and international
affairs that had been an anathema not only to the founders of maximalist Revisionism, but even to Jabotinsky himself. Then, too, *Lehi*
(and, right up until its dissolution, the 'Fighters Party' itself) still
continued to maintain ideas which were fundamental to maximalism.
Among the latter were the territorial commitment to the notion of a
'Greater Land of Israel' (although references to the 'Kingdom of

Israel' were now dropped), and the conviction that the Palestinian Arabs constituted a minority undeserving of equal rights.

Chronologically, *Lehi*'s history can be divided into four broad periods. The first ended with Stern's own death; the second spans the interim years of 1943–45, when the movement was in search of an identity; the third (1946–47) covers the time when its pro-Soviet orientation was in the process of formulation; the fourth (1948–49) is that which has here been termed the period of National Bolshevism. What unites all periods is the élitism and apocalyptic radicalism which *Lehi* had inherited from its spiritual teachers in maximalist Revisionism and which maintained that the 'Kingdom of Israel' had to be attained by all possible means. What distinguishes them are the models which *Lehi* regarded as the most suitable for imitation.

During the first – embryonic – period, Stern attempted to adopt a model that combined Bar-Kochba, NILI and the integral nationalism of inter-war Europe, and to implement it by allying with the Axis powers. Shattered by historical reality, that conception was abandoned by Stern's followers during *Lehi*'s second period. It was not then, however, immediately replaced. All that was left to them was the general precedent of freedom fighters struggling for their liberation (in the main, the cited paradigms were the anti-Nazi undergrounds, but reference was also made to some nineteenth-century underground movements in Italy, Poland and India). During the third period, *Lehi*'s model was still in the process of formulation. Although showing a definite leaning towards a pro-Soviet position, it was still restricted to 'neutralisation', on the assumption that the USSR would be satisfied with that stance. What characterises the fourth period, when the ideal finally ripened, was that a 'people's democracy' constituted the solution that the Soviets themselves desired in the Middle East.[10] It followed that it was also the one desirable for the emerging Israeli nation.

Whence did *Lehi* derive the model for this new formula? Clearly, its closest affinities were with the Weimar theoreticians of German National Bolshevism (such as Moeller van den Bruck, Karl Otto Paetel and Ernst Niekisch) – who had also believed in their ability to bridge the enormous gap dividing right from left. But it would be wrong to assume that *Lehi* had learned the lessons of National Bolshevik failures in Germany.[11] Rather, its prime inspiration, as early as 1943–44, was Russia's experiences during the Second World War. It was these that had validated both the theory and the practice of the fusion of communism and nationalism. A second series of models was provided by the East European 'people's democracies' and by communist China. A third consisted of the *Ahdut Ha-Avodah* movement, the Hebrew

Communist Party, the PKP and *Maki* during Israel's own war of independence.

It is the breadth of those influences and models which allow *Lehi* to stand comparison with other radical and revolutionary minority movements that have aspired to spearhead extreme national liberation movements. Indeed, at various stages, *Lehi* explicitly cited (in addition to the above) the inspiration provided by the Irish Republican Brotherhood and the extreme Indian nationalist groups led by Subhas Chandra Bose and Prakash Jaya Narayan; after 1947, it also referred to the struggles against foreign domination being waged by Greek and Malayan communists. It is true that, following the precedents established by those and other groupings, *Lehi* also resorted to acts of individual terror, but it must not be judged as simply a terrorist movement. Its own view was that terrorism was only a necessary means towards the attainment of what was essentially a political goal. Indeed, *Lehi*'s underground activities would have been unnecessary had its parent Revisionist movement, or the IZL, become a truly fighting liberation force against Britain. Stern's successors understood that it was not enough to read the writings of the fathers of Russian terrorism – Savinkov, Spiridonova, Figner, Gershuni and so on; nor was it sufficient simply to imitate their terrorist activities. In order to deserve their own designation as revolutionaries, they had to prepare a more comprehensive social and political theory and to demonstrate more realism – *vis-à-vis* both the *Yishuv*'s domestic political framework and the international system. By 1944 Lehi had definitely abandoned the view that its role in history would end once it had written a glorious page along the lines of the Massada. Henceforth, it sought political success. In its formula of National Bolshevism it thought (totally incorrectly, as matters turned out) that it had found the means of attaining that objective.

## SELF-IMAGE AND PUBLIC IMAGE

Throughout, *Lehi* was forced to wrestle with the dissonance between its heroic self-image as a movement of national liberation and the public view that the movement comprised a ragtag of radical right-wing fanatics. Even during Stern's days, the movement had tried to combat the public perception that it was fascist by projecting itself as an organisation above association with any particular party. That effort failed. So too did its attempt to capitalise on the opportunities provided by the establishment of the 'United Hebrew Resistance Movement'. Always an *ad hoc* arrangement, that alignment with the *Haganah* and the IZL did nothing to gain *Lehi* public acceptance.

As soon as it fell apart, *Lehi* once again found itself isolated and (unwillingly) closer to the IZL in operational matters. Moreover, once it became apparent that the IZL and *Lehi* could not themselves fully unite, the situation – from *Lehi*'s viewpoint – became even worse. Its members, too, were now tarnished with the stigma of 'dissidents' hurled against the IZL.[12]

In terms of public support, however, the refinement of *Lehi*'s left-wing image in the wake of its 'neutralisation' formula of September 1946 and Gromyko's announcement of May 1947 was no more helpful.[13] True, *Lehi* did then try to break out of its isolation through communication with Mosheh Sneh, with *Maki* and with the Hebrew Communist Party. But the differences between *Lehi* and these parties on such crucial issues as the Arab question and whether priority was to be given to Marxism or nationalism were too pronounced to permit such contacts to be fruitful. What is more, *Lehi* still remained beyond the pale of the *Yishuv*'s accepted political spectrum. Admittedly, the leaders of the national religious parties and the General Zionists were prepared to stand by *Lehi* (and the IZL) during the critical days of 1944 and 1948. But even their position was purely emotional and, in the main, the consequence of their fear of a civil war in the *Yishuv*. *Lehi* was still believed to have overstepped the boundaries of discipline demanded by consensus within the *Yishuv* and the Zionist movement. Furthermore, and notwithstanding its national communist slogans, it was thought to have remained stranded on the radical right.

This situation was further exacerbated with the outbreak of Israel's war of independence. It then became starkly apparent that, with the conclusion of the British Mandate, the movement had lost its *raison d'être*. Not only had it erred in its prognosis that the war could be averted; it also seemed plagued by ideological and organisational confusion. On the one hand, it aligned with the IZL on such episodes as the slaughter at the oil refineries, Deir Yasin and the *Altalena*. Like the IZL, it also tended to minimise the value of the military operations undertaken by the official leadership against Israel's Arab enemies and their British allies. On the other hand, however, the public image it projected was one of a movement which supported a platform of national communism full of National Bolshevik formulae. It was thus deprived of the ability to present itself to the public as a homogeneous unit. Neither the left nor the right took its new image seriously. The left continued to regard *Lehi* as a right-wing – even fascist – organisation; the right's attitude was one of pity for the fact that *Lehi* – notwithstanding its own abject failure – was denying its origins.

Only for as long as the underground conditions persisted could *Lehi* dismiss its numerical inferiority as less important than its superior understanding of the political situation. That thesis was untenable in an independent and democratic environment. From that viewpoint Bernadotte's assassination, too, turned out to be a tactical and strategic blunder. Instead of arousing in either Israel or the eastern bloc the enthusiasm which *Lehi* had anticipated, the assassination was utterly condemned by the entire political community – including the IZL (now the *Herut* movement) and the Revisionist party. It also brought about *Lehi*'s effective delegitimisation. Particularly damaging was the fact that the trial of Friedman-Yellin and Shmuelevitch (at which *Lehi* and its entire history effectively stood in the dock) took place on the very eve of the elections to the Knesset. *Lehi* emerged as a movement that had failed to liberate itself from archaic notions which – although perhaps understandable during the Mandate period – were utterly inappropriate in the democratic reality of the new state of Israel. It also appeared to be working against the normalisation of the young state. The vast majority of voters considered it a group which the government had outlawed, and which could make no constructive contribution. By 1949, all that the Fighters had to offer were prophecies of doom – that the government would succumb to the pressures of a severe international crisis or deep economic recession. When those forecasts, too, proved unfounded, the party's disbandment immediately ensued.

Even before that demise, however, *Lehi* had really only been able to hope to draw potential support from the subculture of the Revisionist movement – and *Herut*, under Begin's more conventional style of Revisionist leadership, captured that particular ground. The alternative, that the 'Fighters' Party' might find a common language with the country's existing left-wing political bodies, was precluded by its attitude toward the Arab issue. This was the true gauge of its leanings. Once applied, that litmus test revealed that – notwithstanding the movement's protestations of National Bolshevism – on this central issue *Lehi* was still unable to dissociate itself from its roots in maximalist Revisionism. True, Friedman-Yellin did now preach a doctrine which Stern would never have contemplated, envisioning an alliance between all the 'progressive' peoples of the Middle East who had overthrown their feudal overlords. But not even the Marxist left within *Lehi* could up to the last moment forgo the refusal to grant political rights to the Palestinian Arabs or the claim to Transjordan. Indeed, the former were altogether ignored. This was an entirely different attitude from that adopted, for instance, by the Hebrew communists – who did accept the principle of a Palestinian Arab state and its federation with its Jewish counterpart. It was also a less flexible position than that adopted by *Herut* which (faithful to Jabotinsky's teachings) advocated both full equal rights and an alliance with the Arab peoples.

## IDEOLOGICAL LEADERSHIP AND PRAGMATIC LEADERSHIP

All of *Lehi*'s leaders were of Polish origin and all were influenced by the revival of their country of birth under Pilsudski. But whereas Stern was only influenced by Pilsudski's achievements, his successors – particularly Friedman-Yellin and Eldad – took more note of the fact that, judged from the perspective of events of 1939–41, the Polish marshal had been a failure. Consequently, they consciously attempted to avoid his mistakes and thereby bridge the gap between their ideals and the means at their disposal.

How they might do so was, however, to become a bone of bitter contention. Until 29 November 1947, when it became clear that *Lehi*'s war against the British was drawing to a close, the leaders of the movement were able to work in unison. Thereafter, however, the bonds which held them together swiftly loosened. Forced to address the fundamental social questions which the total war against the British had hitherto enabled them to avoid, their differences became decisive. It was then, too, that the contrasting extent of their respective commitment to *Lehi*'s brand of National Bolshevism became most marked.

That commitment was particularly strong in the case of Friedman-Yellin. Admittedly, his ideas were rooted in maximalist Revisionism; but even before joining this political stream he had made it plain that he did not consider his affiliation to the NZO to be the result of dry dogmatism. Rather, it was the consequence of pragmatic considerations:

> Our position on all questions does not result from any principles, from a world-view which is embalmed in a book; but from life, and in the light of the one and only goal before our spirit – the salvation of Israel in the land of Israel. Today, at the moment of construction, we oppose socialism; and tomorrow we shall oppose and fight fascism – should such a movement come into existence – if it threatens to impede the fulfilment of our ideas.[14]

Moreover, although Friedman-Yellin was utterly opposed to 'socialist injections' into the *Betar* idea, his mind had always been open to additional ideological developments. That remained the case in 1943, when *Lehi* was reconstructed. By that time even the hard core of that stream within Revisionism had learned its lesson. Now, even Achimeir seemed to have been influenced by the National Bolshevik 'turnabout' seemingly effected by Stalin during the Second World War, and had accordingly praised the national heroes of feudal Russia:

> Whoever fights Germany is our ally . . . It is because of Germany that we are enthusiastic about the Soviet regime. Only that regime possesses the ability to wipe out tens of millions of Germans. We

pray for socialist experiments in Germany. We are troubled by the thought that Germany might suffer a British and American occupation. We pray for an occupation by the Red Army; for what do we care?[15]

Friedman-Yellin's distinction lay in the fact that, just one year later, he showed himself prepared to go beyond the original dogmatism of his intellectual forebears, and gradually to adopt a National Bolshevik model. Not only did he consider this to be a formula which, in view of the radical changes that had taken place in the international system, might facilitate a new orientation in foreign policy. He also regarded it as representative of a new socio-economic theory in domestic affairs. Quite apart from considerations of personal rivalry and different temperaments, it was this theory which prevented him from aspiring to the union with the IZL desired by Eldad. Indeed, the more that the National Bolshevik model became central, the more did the partnership between the two men become difficult.

Principally this was because Eldad's thinking always remained firmly rooted in maximalist Revisionism. True, he was in extreme circumstances forced into a secret statement that – in the event of a third world war – he would be prepared to fight alongside the USSR.[16] But his temporary open-mindedness to formulae reminiscent of National Bolshevism was probably the result of a pragmatic consideration: the failure of the attempts to attain unity with the IZL and Begin's demand that 'we start from afresh' rather than 'unite'. The implication was that Begin and the revived IZL were also representing a version of the radical right and competing for the same audience as was *Lehi*. Consequently, steps had to be taken to ensure that the latter would possess an independent ideology. Otherwise, there would be no justification for its separate existence. Moreover, Eldad was also convinced that the USSR would be the victorious power – an opinion which he continued to hold right through the split of 1949.

Even so, Eldad was not prepared to forgo some of his ingrained positions only where questions of foreign policy were concerned. On issues which concerned the regime and society, he very soon reverted to his ideological origins. Even though (unlike U.Z. Greenberg, Achimeir and Yeivin) he did not join *Herut*, he did disseminate Stern's radical ideas through *Sulam* – a forum which, although devoid of any electoral prospects, continued to function until the 1960s. This, it appears, was not a coincidental development. Eldad's roots in maximalist Revisionism were always deeper than those of Friedman-Yellin and were based upon an eschatological, messianic and Hassidic conception which he had obtained from two sources: one was U.Z.

Greenberg; the other was Berdichevsky, who had demanded a complete 'change of values' in Judaism. It had been Berdichevsky – and not Herzl or Jabotinsky – whom Eldad had in the 1930s considered to be the 'great rebel':

> Berdichevsky took his manifesto for the revolt of the Hebrew people from the school of the German scholar, Nietzsche. There is no deed but that which springs from a deep and courageous will which exerts a power of persuasion over the spirit. The atrophy of will and the hyperatrophy of spirit is the national malaise . . . will is more important than spirit. Beauty has precedence over pure research; a healthy body has precedence over a refined intellect. Laughter has precedence over a sigh, the future is more important than the past. We must shake off the burden of the past, of the Exile . . . burn the rotten old before the entry of the new . . . True, we do carry Samson who has taught us laughter and how to sharpen swords; true we do have *Betar*, in whom the will to build has precedence over any nitpicking . . . [sic] But we still have much to learn from the great rebel, Berdichevsky.[17]

In Eldad's view, only Max Nordau had achieved a full synthesis between Berdichevsky and Nietzsche; that was because he represented the diametric opposite to the destructive teaching of Ahad Ha-Am and of his pupil, Weizmann, who had aspired to a grocery store rather than a state. Eldad's attitude towards Jabotinsky, on the other hand, was ambivalent – especially after the world *Betar* convention in Warsaw in 1938. In practice, he despaired of him only after the outbreak of the Second World War.[18] At the same time, he formulated his own basic world-view, under the influence of the German philosophers Schopenhauer and Nietzsche. It was from the latter that he inherited the fundamental notions of the instinct, the will and voluntarism; that will has precedence over intellect, and that will animates life.[19]

Yitzchak Shamir, the third of the leading figures in the 'Fighters' Party', falls into a somewhat different category. Imprisoned between 1946 and 1948, he had been absent from the arena of ideological confrontation in those years. Since he was in any case not particularly troubled by such matters, he regarded his party's uncertainties as (at best) pragmatic.

Two episodes in Shamir's life substantiate this view. One occurred when he joined Stern – at precisely the time when the latter decided to continue his pro-German orientation, notwithstanding the failure of Lubenchik's mission in 1941; the second was his late affiliation with the *Herut* movement (in 1970). Similarly, at the time of the Fighters' convention – and even subsequently – Shamir made it plain that, as far as his world-view was concerned, the conjunction of communism and nationalism was not organically strong enough. Moreover, his socialism was just a means to the attainment of his goal. As a man of terrorist action, Shamir was often dismissive of intellectuals such as Eldad, who paid no attention to the limitations imposed by reality. He could not see eye to eye with a communist leader who subordinated his own considerations to those of the USSR. Nevertheless, Shamir did consider the models of Russia's Communist Party and of the 'people's democracies' relevant to the state of Israel and the transformation which it was undergoing. 'Only the working class is able to mobilise the strength which will bring about the complete fulfilment of revolutionary changes.'[20] It would be an exaggeration to say that Shamir's alignment with Friedman-Yellin was entirely organisational (although it is true that Shamir could conceive of no future for himself without party activity). But whether he could ever have worked in harness with Eldad – even had the latter agreed to continue within the party – must be considered doubtful. At bottom, Eldad regarded ideology as a vital instrument for the fulfilment of his political aspirations. Shamir, it seems, did not.

Ultimately, however, *Lehi*'s failure was one not of leadership, but of ideology. For one thing, its programme of National Bolshevism caused too many internal divisions to constitute an effective basis for power. For another, it was formulated too late to have a public impact. Third, and even had neither of those conditions prevailed, it was in any case too revolutionary for the taste of the Israeli electorate, which preferred a political system with which it was already familiar. All in all, then, once the state of Israel was established *Lehi* really no longer had any role to play. The political and ideological spectrum was too crowded to permit the continuation of the movement – however new and manipulative its form.[21] Since it remained essentially wedded to ideas derivative of the radical right, the 'Fighters' Party' necessarily appealed to only a minority of the electorate. Indeed, the only other party with which it might have aligned was the *Herut* movement, which had itself grown out of maximalist Revisionism. But to have done so would have necessitated a disavowal of the very National Bolshevik formulae which lent *Lehi* any distinction.

In the event, the problem thus posed proved too great for *Lehi* to wrestle with. Those of its members who did attach importance to the socialist element in their programme were forced to seek refuge in the (Zionist or non-Zionist) parties of the left. Others either moved over to *Herut* or – like Eldad – retreated into a form of self-imposed political isolation. Neither option left any room for the survival of an independent 'Fighters' Party'. Thus it was that *Lehi* found itself declining and then disappearing from view in the revived state of Israel.

# Notes

## INTRODUCTION (pp. 1–8)

1. Cf. Z. Jabotinsky, 'The Igniter' (1912) in *Notes*, pp. 13–17; 'An Exemplary Leader' (Dr Herzl) (1904) in ibid., pp. 221–3; 'Leader?' (1934) in *Memoirs of a Contemporary*, pp. 213–17. Apart from Jabotinsky's own writings I rely, in this summary, on Y. Shavit, *From Majority to a State. The Revisionist Movement : The Plan for the Colonisatory Regime and Social Ideas* (Tel Aviv, 1978); see also his *Jabotinsky and the Revisionist Movement, 1925–1948* (London, 1988). J.B. Shechtman, *The Vladimir Jabotinsky Story* (New York, London and Tel Aviv, 1959–61): Vol. 1, *Rebel and Statesman*; Vol. 2, *Fighter and Prophet*.
2. Z. Jabotinsky, 'What Do the Zionist Revisionists Want?' idem, *On the Way to Statehood* (Jerusalem, 1953), pp. 297–8.
3. Z. Jabotinsky, 'How Does a State Colonise?' *Ha-Zafon*, 24 June 1927, 15 July 1927; idem, 'Old Zionism', *Raasvet*, 16 Aug. 1925.
4. Cf. his speech to the XVII Zionist Congress in 1931: *Stenographisches protokoll der verhandlungen des XVII Zionistenkongresses*, Basel, 30 June–17 July 1931 (London, 1931), s. 170–1.
5. Z. Jabotinsky, 'England and Us', *Raasvet*, 25 March 1928. He enlisted J. Wedgewood to disseminate the pamphlet but it made little impression on policy-makers in either the Foreign Office or the Colonial Office. Cf. J. Wedgewood, *The Seventh Dominion* (London, 1928).
6. A. Achimeir (1896–1962), b. Russia, emigrated to Palestine 1912 for two years and again in 1925. Developed an intense hatred of Soviet Russia, and sympathy towards fascist Italy. His PhD thesis was on Spengler and Russia.
7. Z. Jabotinsky at the 4th World Conference of the Zionist Revisionists, Prague, 17 Aug. 1930. *Speeches 1927–1940* (Jerusalem, 1948), p. 103.
8. Cf. 'The Idea of Betar' (1934) in *On the Way to Statehood*, pp. 23–4.
9. Uri Zvi Greenberg (1896–1980), b. Poland. Served in the Austrian Army in the First World War and afterwards witnessed a pogrom in Lvov (1919). After leaving *Ahdut Ha-Avodah* joined the Revisionists in 1930.
10. Y.H. Yeivin (1891–1970), b. Russia. Served as a surgeon in the Russian Army in the First World War.
11. Z. Jabotinsky, 'Aliyah', *Ha-Aretz* (14 Nov. 1919) and 'M. Nordau' (20 Jan. 1929) in Y. Nedava (ed.), *Zionist Revisionism Crystallised: Collected Articles from Raasvet 1925–29* (Tel Aviv, 1985), pp. 35–8; 'Declaration at a Press Conference in Bucharest', *Unzer Velt*, 25 Nov. 1938. On Zangwill's influence, 'A Talk with Zangwill' (21 July 1939), *Memoirs of a Contemporary*, pp. 253–63.
12. Z. Jabotinsky, 'On the Zionist "NEP" (Second Time)', *Doar Ha-Yom*, 23 March 1928; idem, 'Jews and Fascism. Some Remarks and a Warning', *Jewish Daily Bulletin*, 11 April 1935; Jabotinsky to Jacoby, 4 Oct. 1933, Collection of Letters, Jabotinsky Institute.
13. Cf. their debate in *Ha-Aretz*: 4 Jan. 1980; 11 Jan. 1980; 8 Feb. 1980. S. Avineri, *The Making of Modern Zionism* (New York, 1981), pp. 159–86.
14. Leonard Stein, an adviser to the Jewish Agency in London, estimated the NZO's membership at no more than 150,000. Arthur [Lourie] to M. Shertok, 24 June 1938, CZA S25/2090.
15. J.B. Shechtman, *The Vladimir Jabotinsky Story* (Tel Aviv, 1959–61), Vol. 3, pp. 130–2.

CHAPTER 1 (pp.11–29)

1. 'If I am not for myself, who will be?' *Ha-Aretz*, 15 Nov. 1927.
2. Achimeir to Jabotinsky, 25 Oct. 1928, The Achimeir Files, Jabotinsky Institute (hereafter JI). See also 'On Contemporary Questions . . . Concerning the arrival of our *Il Duce*', *Doar Ha-Yom*, 10 Oct. 1928; Shavit, *From Majority to a State* (Tel Aviv, 1978), pp. 231–2.
3. A. Achimeir, 'On the Way to Dissolution', *Doar Ha-Yom*, 31 July 1929; 'In the Light of Circumstances', ibid., 9 Aug. 1929.
4. A. Achimeir, 'Not as the Sons of Kushites', ibid., 21 Aug. 1929.
5. Jabotinsky's speech of 30 July 1929, in *Speeches, 1927–1940* (Jerusalem, 1948), p. 76.
6. Ibid., pp. 93–4 (at a gathering in Paris, 29 Aug. 1929).
7. [Anonymous] 'The Other Way' (editorial), *Doar Ha-Yom*, 29 Sept. 1929. Cf. also B. Weinstein, ibid., 22 Aug. 1929 and 5 Sept. 1929.
8. Z. Jabotinsky, 'Our Situation', ibid., 4 Oct. 1929, including a section from the will of his 'Samson'; A. Achimeir, 'The Official and the Rabbi', ibid., 22 Dec. 1929. Jabotinsky, 'The British May do Anything' – his speech to the *Yishuv* concerning the situation in the Zionist movement (in Beit Ha'am in Tel Aviv), *Doar Ha-Yom*, 24 Dec. 1929, as reported by Shechtman, op. cit., II, pp. 163–4. As a result of this speech, he was no longer permitted to return to Palestine by the authorities.
9. The title of an unsigned article, ibid., 1 April 1930; H. Yeivin, 'The Evil Decree and Hypocrisy', ibid., 4 April 1930. Only a fortnight before Achimeir and Yeivin had extolled the memory of Balfour, who had just died. Achimeir asked why the Greek people were privileged to have Byron's heart buried on Greek soil, while the Jews were not privileged to have Balfour's brain buried in Palestine; A. Achimeir, 'The Lessing of our Political Renaissance', ibid., 20 March 1930.
10. U.Z. Greenberg, *Book of Indictment and Faith* (Jerusalem, 1937), pp. 53–8. Greenberg's poems show signs of these trends even before the events of 1929, in 'In the Vision of one of the Legions' (1928) and 'House Dog' (1929). H. Hever, 'The Beginnings of Political Poems in Palestinian Hebrew Poetry', unpubl. diss., Jerusalem (1984), Part IV.
11. Ibid. This was also the message conveyed by his articles in *Doar Ha-Yom*, such that on 28 May 1930, 'Do not adjust, Jews!'.
12. Ibid. The term 'betrayal' was frequently used by Greenberg, such as when he compared the role of the hated Jewish Agency towards the British with that of the *Yevsektzia* in the service of the Comintern; Greenberg, 'Blood Guilt: Deceit', ibid., 26 May 1930. See also Stern's motto: 'A Jewish soldier prays with a rifle [for your good,/may the rifle be more pleasant to you than a melodious lyre!'] in Greenberg, *A Buffer Zone and the Speech of a Son of Blood* (Sadan ed., Jerusalem, 1930), pp. 5–6. See the motto of the poem 'To Gangs of Madmen' in his *Book of Poems* (Sulam ed., 1950), p. 31.
13. A. Achimeir, 'Desert and Eden', *Doar Ha-Yom*, 4 April 1929.
14. A. Achimeir, 'The Bridge of Iron', ibid.
15. A. Achimeir, 'Shall We Miss the Opportunity?', ibid., 24 Sept. 1929.
16. Z. Jabotinsky, 'Is There No Choice?', *Doar Ha-Yom*, 6 Aug. 1930.
17. Z. Jabotinsky, *Speeches, 1927–1940*, pp. 102–3. At the Fourth Revisionist Convention in Prague on 10 Aug. 1930.
18. A. Achimeir, 'From Now On', *Doar Ha-Yom*, 26 May 1930.
19. H. Yeivin, 'The Despicable Wisdom of Silence', *Doar Ha-Yom*, 28 May 1930.
20. A. Achimeir, 'A Letter to Zionist Youth', ibid., 21 Oct. 1930; '*Sinn Fein*', ibid., 28 Oct. 1930; '*Haat Masari, Bas!*' (Arabic – Give enough money!), ibid., 30 Oct. 1930 and Y. Pograbinsky, 'They Return to Their Vomit', ibid., 7 Nov. 1930; H. Rosenblum, 'The End of the Jewish State!', ibid., 10 Oct. 1930.
21. *Doar Ha-Yom*, 10 Oct. 1930.
22. Jabotinsky to Avraham Weinshal, 29 Dec. 1930. Collection of Letters, JI; Z. Jabotinsky, 'The Last Attempt', ibid., 31 Dec. 1930; Shechtman, op. cit., Vol. II, p. 37.
23. Z. Jabotinsky, 'A Round Table With the Arabs', *Ha'am*, 24 March 1931 (*On the Way to Statehood*, pp. 245–7, 248–9).

24. A. Achimeir, 'Rome and Jerusalem', *Ha'am*, 8 May 1931.
25. Jabotinsky to Lichtheim, 20 March 1931, JI; Shechtman, op. cit., Vol. II, p. 191.
26. Z. Jabotinsky, *Speeches, 1927–1940*, pp. 118–19, 131.
27. U.Z. Greenberg, 'And After the Word of the King . . .', *Ha'am*, 16 July 1931. Greenberg was the second candidate of the Revisionists (Jabotinsky being the first candidate).
28. *Sicarii* – originally Jewish terrorists of the Second Temple period, so called from the dagger (Lat. *sicus*) which they carried under their cloaks to murder collaborators with Rome. The League was founded in the wake of a series of protests against the population census of October 1931 and after a demonstrative blowing of the *shofar* by Mosheh Segal at the close of the Day of Atonement on 2 Oct. 1931, a practice which the British outlawed as provocative. See Y. Orenstein, *In Chains – from the Memoirs of a Fighter* (Tel Aviv, 1973), pp.56–61; Achimeir against the census, *Doar Ha-Yom* (12 July 1930) and *Hazit Ha-Am* (18 Nov. 1931). The name *Brit Ha-Biryonim* (League of the *Sicarii*) was given by Greenberg via his emissary, Yeivin. Orenstein, op. cit., p. 58.
29. The only source for this is Orenstein's book; fragments of memoirs collected by Y. Achimeir and S. Schatzky in *We are Sicarii* (Hebrew; Tel Aviv, 1972) confirm his version.
30. Contrary to Orenstein's hypothesis, op. cit., p. 60.
31. H. Yeivin, 'To Prisoners of Zion – a Revolutionary Act', *The Yishuv and the Census*, a one-time publication, 22 Oct. 1931. For a summary of the activity against the census see *Mishmar Ha-Umma*, 24 Dec. 1931.
32. Jabotinsky to Lichtheim, 3–6 July 1931, JI.
33. Z. Jabotinsky, '*Oyfn Pripitshek* (At the Fireside) – The New Alphabet', *On the Way to Statehood*, pp. 93–4 (printed for the first time in *Haynt* (Warsaw), 16 Oct. 1931.
34. 'Serious Rioting at the Hebrew University', *Hazit Ha-Am*, No. 3, 12 Feb. 1932. 'After the Rioting at the University', ibid., No. 4, 16 Feb. 1932. The handbill distributed by the Revisionist students was published in Weinshal's biography of 'Yair', though he did not take part in the events: *The Blood on the Threshold* (Tel Aviv, 1978), p. 69.
35. H. Yeivin, 'We – the Representatives of the People', *Hazit Ha-Am*, No. 2, 5 Feb. 1932.
36. Z. Jabotinsky, 'On Adventurism', *Hazit Ha'am*, 11 March 1932 (omitted in *On the Way to Statehood*, p. 28, but adduced by Achimeir and Schatzky, ibid., p. 161) (*Haynt*, 26 Feb. 1932).
37. Z. Jabotinsky, 'On Adventurism', ibid., pp. 28, 30; Abba Sikra, 'The Murder in Kefar Hasidim', ibid., 15 March 1932.
38. Z. Jabotinsky, 'Orientation', *Hazit Ha-Am*, No. 17, 1 April 1932 (*Haynt*, 18–20 March 1932).
39. Z. Jabotinsky, 'Geneva (the Thoughts of Another)', *Hazit Ha-Am*, No. 20, 15 April 1932 (*Haynt*, 8 April 1932).
40. 'Chapters . . . We shall learn Holy Hate . . .', *Ha-Biryon*, No. 5, Nissan 11.
41. The National Convention of the Palestine Revisionist Movement. Jabotinsky's letter, 'The Revisionist Way in Palestine – the Active Way' (begun 22 April) *Hazit Ha-Am*, No. 22, 29 April 1932 (cf. a somewhat differfent version in *Doar Ha-Yom*, 26 April 1932, and the protocol in the Jabotinsky Institute: C/10/10.
42. Jabotinsky to Weinstein, 26 May 1932; Y. Achimeir and S. Schatzky, (above, n. 29), pp. 165–6. Also his letter to Freulich, 29 July 1932, ibid., p. 166.
43. H. Yeivin, 'Of Our Simple Truth', *Hazit Ha-Am*, No. 30, 17 June 1932; Abba Sikra, 'The Financial Blockade', ibid.
44. Abba Sikra, 'The Problems of the World Convention of the Revisionist Movement', ibid., No. 38, 15 July 1932.
45. A. Achimeir, 'Gorgulov', ibid., No. 43, 2 Aug. 1932.
46. *Davar*, 8 Sept. 1933, with slight changes from the original version preserved in the State Archives, in the files of the 'League of *Sicarii* trial, and also in A. Achimeir, *Brit Ha-Biryonim*, pp. 217–23 (with slight differences in wording).
47. Jabotinsky on the nature of *Betar*, Paris, 7 July 1932, *Hazit Ha-Am*, No. 42, 29 July 1932.
48. Z. Jabotinsky, 'The Meaning of Adventurism', ibid., No. 44, 5 Aug. 1932 (*Raasvet*,

24 July 1932).

49. Jabotinsky to Yeivin, 9 Aug. 1932. First published in B. Lubotsky, *The Life Style of a Fighting Zionist* (Jerusalem, 1947), pp. 227–9.

50. H. Yeivin, 'Opposition or Liberation Movement? (On the Eve of the Convention)', ibid., No. 50, 26 Aug. 1932. Cf. also his article 'The State Under Way or the Way to a State?', ibid., 5 Aug. 1932.

51. Z. Jabotinsky, *Speeches, 1927–1940*, pp. 137–47 (28 Aug. 1932), especially p. 146.

52. Ibid., as well as Z. Jabotinsky, 'The Fifth Convention', *Hazit Ha-Am*, No. 55, 13 Sept. 1932 (*Raasvet* 28 Aug. 1932); 'The Legion', *On the Way to Statehood*, pp. 33–8 (30 Sept. 1932).

53. Achimeir's speech in *Hazit Ha-Am*, No. 55, 13 Sept. 1932. At the convention, the section from attorney E.Z. Cohen's speech in praise of Hitler was also read out. In his article 'An Evaluation of the Convention' (*Hazit Ha'am*, 7 Oct. 1932; *Raasvet*, 25 Sept. 1932), Jabotinsky declared that Achimeir's group was 'one of the healthiest phenomena' and that it was necessary to wait and see how it consolidated.

54. Jabotinsky's reply, *Speeches*, pp. 151–5 (1 Sept. 1932). Achimeir's summing up after the convention made no attempt to hide his faction's open admiration for Italian fascism; when Attorney L. Carpi of Milan, who saluted the convention with a fascist-style raised hand, entered the hall 'we jumped up from our seats and raised our arms in his honour', A. Zir [Achimeir], 'A Review of the Convention', *Hazit Ha-Am*, No. 57, 20 Sept. 1932.

55. A. Achimeir, 'In Short', in *A Betar Guide, A Platform for Ideology and Education*, publ. by Betar in Poland, No. 1, Sept. 1932 (ed. I. Remba).

56. H. Yeivin, 'We fight the People's War', *Hazit Ha-Am*, 29 July 1932.

57. A. Shamai [Achimeir], 'Strewn and Scattered, Helsinki in 1932', *Hazit Ha-Am*, 16 Aug. 1932.

58. A. Achimeir, 'Romantic Realism or Realistic Romanticism', *Hazit Ha-Am*, No. 59, 30 Sept. 1932.

59. Marginal (?), 'The Movement in 1932', ibid., 30 Sept. 1932.

60. 'People's Diary, They will not Rise, if they are Driven by a Whip' (anon.), ibid., No. 77, 3 Feb. 1933. Cf. also the comparison by A. Mistakel (A. Achimeir) of Nazism and fascism: 'The Origin of Hitlerism', *Betar*, I, Jan.–June 1933, pp.188–91. For Achimeir's deep hatred of communism cf. his declaration that the day of the collapse of the Red Army (10 Aug. 1920) should be treated as a holiday, for otherwise it would have been necessary for the Jewish state to have been built in Birobidzhan: A. Achimeir, 'From the Land of Beggardom and Bankruptcy', *Hazit Ha-Am*, 6 Jan. 1933.

61. Abba Sikra, 'Exilic or Political Intelligence', *Hazit Ha-Am*, No. 78, 16 Feb. 1933.

62. Z. Jabotinsky, 'Germany', *Hazit Ha-Am*, No. 79, 24 Feb. 1933 (*Moment*, 19 Feb. 1933).

63. H. Yeivin, 'When Will We Learn?', *Hazit Ha-Am*, No. 82, 17 March 1933.

64. 'Towards Katowicz' (anon.), *Hazit Ha-Am*, 10 March 1933.

65. A. Sikra, 'The Third Zionist Organisation', *Hazit Ha-Am*, No. 84, 28 March 1933; Shechtman, op. cit., Vol. II, pp. 221ff.

66. 'People's Diary, Kernel and Shell' (anon.), *Hazit Ha-Am*, No. 85, 31 March 1933.

67. The main headline, ibid., 31 March 1933; Z. Jabotinsky, 'A Dictator? On the Contrary', ibid., No. 86, 28 April 1933 (*Moment*, 16 April 1933). Achimeir claimed that it was not Hitler who invented anti-Semitism, but rather Wagner and Gobineau. In Germany it existed only theoretically. In America it was actual: A. Mistakel, 'The Origin of Hitlerism', ibid., pp. 391–5; A. Amar [Achimeir], 'Prohibition', ibid., 31 March 1933.

68. 'People's Diary: Germany Against Judaea!' (anon.), ibid., 7 April 1933.

69. Jabotinsky's radio speech in Warsaw on 26 April, *Hazit Ha-Am*, 5 May 1933; Z. Jabotinsky, *Letters*, p. 311 (17 May 1933).

70. *Hazit Ha-Am*, No. 92, 19 May 1933; No. 94, 26 May 1933.

71. Z. Jabotinsky, 'The Revisionist movement and Germany', *Hazit Ha-Am*, No. 91, 12 May 1933 (*Die Welt*, 5 May 1933) and his 'No, to the end!' in *By Storm*, pp. 189–95 (*Doar Ha-Yom*, 3 May 1933).

72. A bold headline ran above that article, 'The Announcement by the Commissariat of

Financial Matters in the Revisionist Movement', ibid., 16 June 1933, and see Greenberg's articles, 'From Week to Week' on 9 and 18 June, ibid.

73. Y. Pograbinsky, 'The Stalin–Ben-Gurion–Hitler Alliance', ibid., 16 June 1933.

74. The main headline in *Hazit Ha-Am*, No. 93, 26 May 1933 was 'The Jewish S.D.
Sabotages our War Against Nazism. The Mapai Diplomat Plots to undermine the War
Against Hitler', ibid., No. 95, 9 June 1933. The quotations were collected by H. Ben-
Meir [Schorer], *The Arlosoroff Murder. Material for the Public Trial.* Cf. also the
Prosecution Documents I, II, VI and IX cited in *Ha-Yarden*, 11 May 1934 and 13 June
1934.

75. H. Yeivin, 'Towards a Red Dictatorship?', *Hazit Ha-Am*, 18 Aug. 1933.

76. 'Regards from Achimeir on the occasion of a visit to the grave of Sarah Aharonson
(from the Jaffa gaol)', ibid., No. 120, 18 Oct. 1933.

77. H. Yeivin, 'We – and Events – The Legions Once Again on the Agenda', ibid., No. 126,
8 Nov. 1933; Yeivin, 'Without Depair and Laxness', ibid., No. 134, 6 Dec. 1933.

78. Achimeir, who was sentenced to 21 months' imprisonment, was released in August
1935; in March that year Orenstein and Dviri were released. Svorai and Katznelson
were acquitted. Yeivin was sentenced to four months.

79. A. Stawskai, 'They Are Worse than the Nazis', ibid., No. 146, 8 Jan. 1934. Ben-
Gurion, for his part, did not hesitate to call Jabotinsky 'Vladimir Hitler' and his
supporters 'Hitler's deputies amongst the Jews', *Davar*, 21 March 1933; *Ha-Medina*,
No. 11, 23 April 1933.

80. Jabotinsky secretly tried to have Achimeir's imprisonment curtailed, Jabotinsky to
Weinshal, 13 Dec. 1934. JI.

81. *Haganah History* (hereafter HH), [book] II, p. 426ff., p. 574ff. and pp. 1167–70.

82. Cf. H.S. Ha-Levi (a member of *Suhba*) in *Ha-Metsuda* (The Fortress), (Tel Aviv,
1978), p. 12, and D. Niv, *Battle for Freedom. The IZL* (Tel Aviv, 1965), Vol. I, p. 156ff.

83. A. [Yeivin], 'Our Holy Destiny', in H.S. Ha-Levi, ed., *Ha-Metsuda* I, pp. 17–18; This
edition seems to have come out in the summer of 1932. Cf. also his article, 'The Lesson
of August 1929', where he calls for the prevention of a pogrom by means of a strong
defence, ibid., II, p. 24.

84. Infantrist (D. Raziel), 'In the memory of a Friend (Meir Alhasid, who died an
"unimportant death")', ibid., p. 19.

85. A. [Yeivin], 'The Pacifism of German Jewish Youth', ibid., pp. 19–20.

86. A. Yeivin, 'The Lesson of August 1929', ibid., p. 24.

87. *Ha-Metsuda* I, p. 24. The poem was written under the inspiration of *Nebi Musa*, the
Arab festival serving as warning of the possibility of rioting in the spring of 1932.

88. The Recluse [J. Klausner], 'The Defeated Bar-Kochba', *Ha-Metsuda* III, p. 31, and
the Introduction, p. 14. Klausner never hesitated to make his historical researches
available to Revisionist politics. Cf. J. Klausner, *The Founders of the State of Israel*,
Essays on Zionist Leaders in the Previous Generation, 2nd ed., 1955, p. 249. On the
other hand, he claimed he never joined the Revisionist movement because of the
emphasis it placed on force, rather than spirit, even when there was no need: J.
Klausner, *When a Nation Fights for its Freedom*, 2nd ed., 1939. 'In Lieu of an Introduction', p. x; similarly his apology for Elazar Ben-Yair's final speech, ibid., p. 152;
cf. J. Klausner, *The Idea was There from the Start* (Hebrew; Jerusalem, 1931).

89. A. [Yeivin], 'The Bar-Kochba Revolt', *Ha-Metsuda*, III, pp. 31–2.

90. Dated 4 Oct. 1929, the letter is in the possession of Roni Zamir (Burstein).

91. H. Kalay's testimony to Y. Slutsky, *Haganah* Archives (HA).

92. 'Reality is as our ambitions are able to shape it . . . To strive means the willingness to
make every sacrifice on the way to the goal. A person striving with all his strength will
attain his goal despite the difficulties he encounters.' A. Stern to Roni Burstein,
26 Nov. 1930. The collection of letters is in Roni Zamir's possession.

93. S.[tern], 'Israel in the Diaspora (a Historical Survey), *Ha-Metsuda*, III, pp. 19–20.
Stern is careful to use the term 'the Jewish people'.

94. S.[tern], 'We and Our Neighbours', *Ha-Metsuda*, pp. 40–41. Stern correctly diagnosed
the rise of Arab radicalism, but did not fully appreciate its anti-British nature. Cf.
Y. Porath, *From Riots to Rebellion* (Heb. ed.), p. 156.

95. Yair [A. Stern] 'We Live Underground' (written 1933), in his *Book of Poems* (Sulam ed., Jerusalem, 1950), p. 24.
96. A. Stern to H.S. HaLevi, 15 Feb. 1934, *Ha-Umma* (The Nation).
97. A. Stern to Roni Burstein, 9 Jan. 1935, in possession of R. Zamir.
98. A. Shiri, 'The International Political Situation', *Ha-Yarden*, 1 March 1934.
99. A. Yacobovsky, 'A Press Conference with Jabotinsky, the Leader, concerning the Concept "Fascism" (12 Jan. 1935)', *Ha-Yarden*, 18 Feb. 1935.
100. S. Yitzhaki, 'Italy Awaits a Jewish State in Palestine in Another Ten Years', *Ha-Yarden*, 31 March 1935 (quoting *Popolo d'Italia* and *Regime Fascista*); Ts. Kolitz, 'In the Name of Rabbi Jesus of Rome', ibid., 12 April 1935; Kolitz, 'D'annunzio Wants to Die', ibid., 5 March 1935; Y. Dillion, 'The Jews in Italy', ibid., 15 April 1935; M. Even-Sapir, 'Fascistic Policy on a European Scale', ibid., 14 March 1935; Ts. Kolitz, 'The Evolution of a Jewish Army', ibid., 1 Aug. 1935.
101. R., 'Jabotinsky speaks before National Youth', *Ha-Yarden*, 25 Aug. 1935. Cf. also Y. Shavit, 'Between Pilsudski and Mickiewicz: Policy and Messianism in Zionist Revisionism in a Context of Polish Culture, and its Relationship to Poland', *Zionism* (Tel Aviv, 1985), X, pp. 7–31 (Hebrew).
102. For his support of Mussolini cf. I. Eldad's introduction to Stern's book of poems (1950), p. 5 (*Hegionot Israel*, p. 270); F. Gervasi, 'Terror in Palestine, *Collier's*, 11 Aug. 1945, p. 64; A. Koestler, 'Middle East Underground', *Contact*, May 1946, p. 53; Y. Ratosh, *Earliest Days* (Tel Aviv, 1980), p. 24. His support of Pilsudski is related in the testimony of his disciples such as that of Zelnik as told to B. Gurewitch, 1 Oct. 1950, the Weinshal Files, Yair File, JI, as well as the testimony of H. Kalay in HH.
103. Cf. A. Stern's book of poems (1950), p. 106.
104. Abba Sikra, 'Silently (The Diaspora in 1935)', *Ha-Yarden*, 27 Sept. 1935; 'Polish Jewry in Trouble' (anon.), ibid.
105. 'As a Sign of the Liquidation of the Diaspora. Jabotinsky Opens the First Congress in Vienna', *Ha-Yarden*, 8 Sept. 1935. Compare *Speeches, 1927–1940*, p. 186.
106. 'Ways of National Liberation, A Speech by the Representative of the Extremists, P. Haller', *Ha-Yarden*, 24 Sept. 1935. For Haller's view of Revisionism, see Paul Haller, *Nationalrevolutionärer Zionismus, Untersuchung und Proklamation* (Wien, 1938).
107. U. Heilperin, 'The War of Hegemony in the Near East, III. Stroke of Death', *Ha-Yarden*, 25 Aug. 1935; U.H. [eilperin?], '"The Establishment of the Legislative Council Will Not Lead to Non-Cooperation" says Weizmann on the Platform of Official Zionism', ibid., 29 Aug. 1935.
108. Dr A. Altman, 'Africa for the Africans', ibid., 29 Aug. 1935; Y. Ben-Menashe [Altman], 'The Political Hour, Italy and the League of Nations', ibid.; A. Peren (Heilperin), 'The Political Hour, The Concession Awaits its Hour', ibid., 6 Sept. 1935.
109. U. Heilperin, 'The War for Hegemony in the Near East, IV. On the Bayonets of the British Army', ibid., 4 Sept. 1935.
110. A. Achimeir, 'Patriarchal Rights', *Ha-Yarden*, 8 Sept. 1935; U.H.[eilperin], 'Non-British Colonial Office', ibid., 11 Sept. 1935 and the article praising Mustafa Kemal, 'The dictator who did more for his people than any democrat', A.A.[chimeir], 'Mustafa Kemal', ibid., 29 Aug. 1935.
111. B.M. [Altman?], 'The Political Hour, Europe', *Ha-Yarden*, 25 Sept. 1935; 'The *Volkischer Beobachter* concerning Lucerne', ibid.
112. Cf. the testimony of H. Kalay to B. Gurewitch and Y. Slutsky in the Jabotinsky Institute, as well as to B. Nadel, in the possession of David Stern.
113. A. Achimeir, 'The Ways of the Fourth Commissioner', *Ha-Yarden*, 1 Sept. 1935.
114. Its participants engaged in 'kissing the whip'; they also claimed that Ben-Gurion had said that there was no possibility of overthrowing Hitler! Cf. Ben-Gurion, *Memoirs*, II, pp. 395–6, where he condemned the Nazi regime at the nineteenth congress, both directly and indirectly. P.Y. [Y. Pograbinsky], 'Of the Results of the Lucerne Congress', *Ha-Yarden*, 12 Sept. 1935; 'Lucerne and Nuremberg' (anon.), ibid., 22 Sept. 1935; 'The Transfer Statistically – Germany takes 65 per cent, the Transfer People –

55.5 per cent, Yaakobi's Boycott at the NZO congress', ibid.
115. 'Lucerne and Nuremberg', ibid.
116. M.S. 'In the Year 1935', ibid., 28 Sept. 1935; Dr M. Shamir, 'A Sound From Germany – The Trumpet of Messiah', ibid., 25 Aug. 1935.
117. There is more regarding his cautious attitude to fascism in his letter to the Naval School in Civitavecchia, 20 Nov. 1934.
118. Jabotinsky's pluralistic approach to the ideological dispute in his movement – for which he paid dearly in 1940 – stemmed, of course, from his belief that he could control the maximalists after their downfall subsequent to their trials. Cf., for example, 'The Head of *Betar* addresses *Betar* Members' of 24 Jan. 1934, in *Diary of Orders*, the memoranda and instructions given by the *Betar* authority in Poland, 1 Feb. 1934; photographed by H. Ben-Yeruham, *The Great Libel* (Tel Aviv, 1982), p. 210.
119. Jabotinsky to Achimeir, 12 Nov. 1935, secret, in Z. Jabotinsky, *Letters*, pp. 25–6. It is interesting that he did find common ground with Achimeir (because of martyrology), but not with Greenberg or Yeivin. Jabotinsky to Achimeir, 4 Dec. 1935, ibid., pp. 27–9.

CHAPTER 2 (pp.30–55)

1. Cf. my article 'Weizmann, Jabotinsky and the Arab Question – the Peel Affair, *Jerusalem Quarterly*, 26 (1983), p. 110; Z. Jabotinsky, 'A Horrible Threat', *Ha-Yarden*, 7 March 1936.
2. Z. Jabotinsky, 'Make an End!', *Ha-Yarden*, 1 May 1936 (*Moment*, 26 April 1936); Jabotinsky to Raphael Rosov, 28 April 1936, JI.
3. D. Niv, *Battle for Freedom. The IZL* (Tel Aviv, 1965), Vol. I, p. 268ff.
4. A. Achimeir and Z. Jabotinsky at the fourth session (8 June 1936) of the fourth national convention of *Brit-Trumpeldor* in Poland (Lectures, Debates and Resolutions), 7–9 June 1936, edited by Y. Wirnik and I. Epstein (Warsaw, June 1936), pp. 16–19; Z. Jabotinsky, 'How Long is the *Yishuv* to Restrain Itself?', *Ha-Yarden*, 12 July 1936. (*Moment*, 26 June 1936); A. Achimeir, 'Heroes – not Saints!' *Ha-Yarden*, 12 July 1936.
5. A. Achimeir, 'Alcazar and Self-Restraint', ibid., 16 Nov. 1936. Idem, 'They Care for Madrid and We – for Jerusalem', ibid., 27 Nov. 1936. Niv, op. cit. I, p. 242.
6. See, for example, Z. Jabotinsky, 'Poland will assist and be assisted in the Evacuation Plan', speech at the Institute for the Research of National Problems, Oct. 1936, *Speeches 1927–40*, p. 220. Cf. also Jabotinsky's letter to Altman of 20 Sept. 1936 concerning the need to find a 'fulcrum' other than England, and even against England when necessary, JI.
7. On the 'policy of alliances' there exists Shechtman's Revisionist version, III, pp. 115–27; also B. Akzin, 'Jabotinsky's Foreign Policy', *Gesher* (1960), pp. 36–58, which is basically apologetic. However, cf. E. Melzer, 'Polish Diplomacy and the Problems of Jewish Emigration 1935–1937', *Gal'ed* I (Tel Aviv, 1973), p. 216, idem, 'The Ruling Party and the Jews in Poland (1937–1939), *Gal'ed*, IV–V (Tel Aviv, 1978), p. 410. Cf. also Z. Jabotinsky, *A Jewish State – A Solution to the Jewish Problem* (Tel Aviv, 1937), Ch. 14.
8. Jabotinsky, *Speeches*, II, pp. 233–71.
9. HH, II, p. 731. There is a description of the entire affair in Ch. 38, ibid., and in D. Niv, op. cit., I, p. 279ff.
10. Niv, ibid., p. 301.
11. 'To the Faithful to the Oath!', Niv, I, p. 298. Eliav (*Wanted*, p. 40). There seems to be a degree of exaggeration in the attempt to discern here the buds of the split of 1940.
12. 'Instructions Regarding the Organisation'. Niv, op. cit., I, p. 301; HH, II, p. 1054. It is interesting to note that in the basic leaflet the expression used is 'Jewish state', not 'Kingdom of Israel' – another indication of the acceptance of Jabotinsky's authority.
13. A letter from 'the opponents of a split' (that is, opponents of fusion with the *Haganah*) to Colonel Patterson in 1937, unsigned and undated, 'Yair's Milk Churn' (his private archive) (hereafter YCA), file 1.
14. Niv, op. cit., I, p. 301. Bitker was the former *Betar* commissioner in China and the commander of the Jewish unit in the international force in Shanghai.
15. Weinschal, *The Blood on the Threshold*, p. 96. Kalay told Weinschal (5 Aug. 1953) that

Jabotinsky reacted scornfully at their first meeting and asked: 'Who is this little fellow?' while Stern trembled.

16. Cf. Niv, op. cit., II, p. 20, and HH, II, B., pp. 1054–6.
17. M.A. Perlmutter, 'Natural Zionism', *Sadan*, Organ of National Pioneers, single issue, Editor-in-Chief, S. Biggelman, April 1937, pp. 3, 5.
18. A. Selman, 'Zionism and Anti-Semitism', ibid., pp. 7–8. *Sadan* was suspected by the British of being a fascist and terrorist group. Cf. 'Memorandum' in English by a high-ranking British official in YCA, file 108.
19. Avigdor Kipnis, 'Towards the Necessary Shift', *Sadan*, pp. 8–9. On Achimeir's influence, Y. Achimeir and S. Schatzky, eds., *We Are Sicarii*, pp. 147–8.
20. Cf. Niv, op. cit., II, p. 20. HH, II, pp. 1054–6.
21. M.H. (editorial article), 'No!', *Ha-Yarden*, 9 July 1937. 'The Speech in Alexandria', ibid., Shechtman, op. cit., III, pp. 68–70. Cf. Akzin's testimony concerning Jabotinsky's original agreement to partition as a first stage in the formation of the state. B. Akzin, 'The Foreign Policy of Jabotinsky', pp. 52–3. Akzin was, at the time, the deputy president of the NZO.
22. Dr A. Altman, 'We Came First and will Leave Last', *Ha-Yarden*, 16 July 1937.
23. U. Heilperin (Y. Ratosh), *Our Eyes are Lifted Up to Domination. The Liberation Movement's Front of Tomorrow* (Tel Aviv, 1937), I, 'The Report of the Royal Commission', and II, 'England has Raised the Question', *Ha-Yarden*, 16 July 1937, pp. 14–20 and 17 Nov. 1937; pp. 22, 25.
24. *Ha-Yarden*, editorial article signed by Altman on 19 Nov. 1937 and interview given by Jabotinsky to the JTA on 17 Nov., Niv, op. cit., II, pp. 49–50, 53.
25. *Our Eyes Are Lifted Up to Domination*, pp. 47, 50; 'The Banner of the Demand for Domination' (17 Dec. 1937).
26. His speech before the NZO consultation, ibid., pp. 5–8; Proposed Resolutions, pp. 8–14.
27. Ibid., p. 12. Cf. also his article (signed by U. Hal) 'Messianic Days', *Mishmar Ha'am*, 29 Oct. 1937.
28. *Our Eyes are Lifted Up to Domination*, pp. 13–14. Shortly afterwards in his 'Speech to the Members of the Sect', Heilperin argued that such a 'sect' rather than the IZL would be the new kernel of the liberation movement. They of course needed 'the power . . . and the support of the masses at the crucial hour', but only if the aims of such a group were to be proclaimed clearly and simply, with a 'flag waving high'. 'Speech to members of the Faction' (Conclusion); *Our Eyes are Lifted Up to Domination*, pp. 58–60.
29. N. Yellin-Mor, *The Fighters for the Freedom of Israel. People, Ideas, Deeds* (Haifa, 1974) pp. 45–7. It is doubtful if Stern actually thought that way as early as 1937, especially with regard to the left. For Heilperin's influence cf. also Y. Eliav, *Wanted*, p. 66.
30. In *For the Homeland*, a one-time publication, 14 Jan. 1938.
31. Shechtman introduced him to a number of high-ranking officers in the ministries of Foreign Affairs, War and the Interior. According to Shechtman, Stern made an 'excellent' impression, and was promised that arms and ammunition would be made available to the IZL for cash and on a payment plan. This deal – later described by *Lehi* as Stern's independent move – came through only in the spring of 1939, too late to be effective. One of the officials – Victor Drimer, the deputy director of Jewish affairs in the Foreign Ministry – was impressed by the national-romantic education Stern had enjoyed in his youth in Poland, and by his admiration of Slowacki, Poland's national poet, and of Pilsudski and Adam Skwarczynsky. Here stood before him a 'fanatic supporter' of the idea of the conquest of Palestine by means of a 'self-executed bloody effort', 'a Jewish prophet, poet soldier and a quiet and cold statesman'. V. Drimer, *Memoirs, Historical Writings* (Polish; Paris, 1968), pp. 70–1, 76–7.
32. Z. Jabotinsky, *Speeches 1927–1940*, pp. 291–302. Also *Ha-Degel* (The Flag), single issue, 25 Feb. 1938. M. Giora (Elimelekh) views this Convention as the inception of the split between Jabotinsky and the IZL: 'The IZL, Trial and Moral', *Keshet* (Autumn 1974), p. 74; Y. Ratosh, *Earliest Days*, p. 18.
33. Y. Ratosh, *Earliest Days*, p. 17.

34. Uriel Heilperin, 'A Platform for the World Convention', *Ha-Medina, Betar* bi-weekly, No. 10, 12 July 1938 (Warsaw), in full in 3/1/2/2, JI; and 'What Will *Betar*'s Answer Be?', *Metsuda* (June 1938), pp. 6–9.
35. 'A Platform for the World Convention', *Ha-Medina*, ibid., 12 July 1938.
36. Ibid., p. 5.
37. For details of the influence of the fascist corporatist regime in Italy, see Y. Shavit, *From Majority to a State*, p. 227ff.
38. HH, II, pp. 1056, 1255; Niv, op. cit., II, pp. 27–9; Ben-Gurion, *Memoirs*, III (Tel Aviv, 1973), p. 164.
39. Cf. Y. Eliav, *Wanted*, pp. 53–5.
40. 'Passive Defence and Active Defence', (early 1938), in *Ba-Herev*, May 1942, an issue dedicated to the first anniversary of the death of the commander-in-chief, David Raziel, pp. 4–5; quoted in part by Niv, op. cit., II, pp. 41–2.
41. Jabotinsky to Moshe Rosenberg, 18 March, 1938, JI.
42. Thus, the HH, II, pp. 809–10, 1058–9, contrary to Niv, op. cit., II, p. 61ff., who accepts the official IZL version. Compare, however, the contemporary estimate in the MacDonald–Jabotinsky conversation of 26 June 1938 (the eve of the Ben-Yosef execution), CO/733/379/75561/3, PRO.
43. U.Z. Greenberg, *The Book of Indictment and Faith* (Jerusalem and Tel Aviv, 1937), p. 169.
44. *Ha-Yarden*, 22 Jan. 1937 and see the similar reaction of Klausner, ibid.
45. Cf. Y. Weinshal, *The First Conqueror of the Mountain* (Tel Aviv, 1968), pp. 72–3.
46. Jabotinsky to Israel Rozov, 28 June 1938, JI.
47. 'In the Shadow of the Scaffold!' (undated), 'Sons of the Zealots' (29 June 1938); CZA S25/2091.
48. Niv, op. cit., II, pp. 71–2, Y. Shavit, *Self-Restraint or Reaction. The Dispute in the Jewish Yishuv between 1936 and 1939* (Ramat-Gan, 1983), pp. 124, 127.
49. Jabotinsky to Haskel, 9 Aug. 1938, and Jabotinsky to the Revisionist movement in Palestine, 28 Aug. 1938 both in JI.
50. Jabotinsky to Haskel, 9 July 1938, JI.
51. ('Yair' to Raziel), 19 Aug. 1938. A Conversation with 'Pitt' (Jabotinsky), from YCA, file 5.
52. For the agreement, see Niv, op. cit., II, pp. 113–14. It was negotiated by S. Yunitchman and H. Lubinsky, supported by Rosenberg, Yunitchman and Haichman, and opposed by Katznelson and A. Stern. See also HH, II, pp. 1064–6 and Ben-Gurion, *Memoirs*, V, p. 220. On Raziel's resignation: his letter to 'Yair', unsigned and undated (Oct. 1938), from YCA, file 106.
53. Speech, summer of 1938; from YCA. The speaker may have been Stern himself. 'The War of Liberation Goes On!', *National Bulletin*, No. 1.
54. Scheib (Eldad), *First Tithe, Memoirs and Lessons* (Jerusalem, 1960), p. 72.
55. 'The Authorities are Preparing the Second Jewish Execution', *National Bulletin*, No. 5 (undated). Compare M. Sharett, *Political Diary*, III, 1938 (Tel Aviv, 1972), p. 236.
56. *The Records of the World Convention of Betar, Warsaw, 11–16 September 1938* (Bucharest, 1940), pp. 58–60. Jabotinsky was also challenged by Aryeh Kutscher and Israel Scheib. Kutscher, representing the Rosh Pina platoon, attacked the NZO for deserting them, and accused the Revisionist leadership in Palestine of being neo-Weizmannists. He demanded that *Betar* adopt 'insurrection and the revolutionary act' and insisted that the Arabs had to be fought and broken. *The Records*, pp. 65–6. In his book (A. Kotzer, *Red Carpet. My Life with Yair*, p. 100) Kutscher attributes to himself even stronger language.
57. *The Records*, pp. 61–2.
58. Ibid., p. 74. In the original the quotation does not appear.
59. Scheib, op. cit., p. 25.
60. Ibid., p. 26. Cf. also A. Kotzer, op. cit., pp. 104, 106–8.
61. *The Records*, pp. 90–4.
62. Ibid., pp. 98–9, 102–3.
63. Niv, op. cit., II, pp. 190–1, and the *Ayala Lubinsky Volume* (Tel Aviv, 1960), pp. 23,

36, 45, 50, 78–80.

64. *The Book of Indictment and Faith*, pp. 163–4. *Liberated Jerusalem*, No. 1, pp. 13–14.
65. *Liberated Jerusalem*, No. 3, 11 Oct. 1938.
66. Jabotinsky to the Executive of the NZO, 14 Oct. 1938, JI.
67. D. Vardi, 'The Political Hour', *Ha-Yarden*, 7 Oct. 1938.
68. A Ma'aravi [Achimeir], 'The Lists of Anti-Ma, Disciples of Bethmann-Hollweg', *Ha-Yarden*, 21 Oct. 1938. His basic assumption was that 'a real force does not need signatures', ibid.; A. Ma'aravi [Achimeir], 'The Lists of Anti-Ma, Czech Self-Restraint', *Ha-Yarden*, 11 Nov. 1938.
69. U.Z. Greenberg, 'Bankruptcy or Bar Giora', *Al Mishmar Ha-Uma* (On the Nation's Guard) [1938], p. 21.
70. Jabotinsky to the IZL Command, 15 Nov. 1938 (To the Peak of the Matter), JI, and in YCA, file 15.
71. Infantryman (D. Raziel), 'At This Time of the Year', *Ba-Herev*, Nov. 1938.
72. Y.H. (Yeivin), 'Seychelles and Acre', *Ha-Yarden*, 16 Dec. 1938.
73. Cf. D. Niv, op. cit., II, pp. 171–4; Y. Banai, *Unknown Soldiers*, pp. 22–4; Y. Eliav, *Wanted*, pp. 84–8.
74. Dr S. Yunitchman, 'Towards the National Convention, A Debate on our Future', *Ha-Yarden*, 6 Jan. 1939.
75. Dr Y. Yeivin, 'The Fateful Question', *Ha-Mashkif*, 13 Jan. 1939.
76. Yunitchman, 'Towards . . .'; —, 'One Does not Plough with a Sword, Neither does One Fight with a Pen' (reply–reflections), *Ha-Mashkif*, 20 Jan. 1939. Cf. also B. Elitsedek, 'The Revisionist Movement Remains Faithful to Itself', ibid., 20 Jan. 1939; Dr M. Luria, 'The Tasks Before the NZO Convention', ibid.; Naphtali ben Israel, 'On the War of Liberation (on the basis of Freedom of Debate)', *Ha-Mashkif*, 20 and 27 Jan. 1939.
77. Z. Jabotinsky, 'The Eleventh Hour', *Ha-Makshif*, 27 Jan. 1939 (*Moment*, 18 Jan. 1939).
78. Cf. Circular No. 5 of the *Betar* authorities dated 10 Feb. 1939 (Ben-Yeruham, *The Betar Book*, Vol. II, p. 906); Shechtman, op. cit., III, pp. 238–40.
79. Niv, op. cit., II, pp. 184–6. Jabotinsky also refused to transfer matters of illegal immigration to the IZL command. Raziel to Jabotinsky, HA, 8/21a.
80. Bulletin of Command, No. 1/39, dated March 1939, in *Ba-Herev*, April 1939.
81. *Di Tat*, No. 20 (55), 10 March 1939, in HH, III, pp. 62–3.
82. IZL: 'Wait, Methods of Realisation and Objective Possibilities', *Di Tat* No. 20. For more about the aid offered by Germany to the Arab terror, cf. an IZL Memorandum to Knickerbocker (undated), YCA, file 95. See also Dr S. Klinger, 'Great International and Zionist Politics', *Ha-Mashkif*, 31 March 1939, and Dr W. von Weisel, 'England's Policy in the Middle East', ibid., 26 April 1939. Cf. the memorandum on Turkey in French, dated 17 Dec. 1938, YCA, file 9.
83. Shechtman, op. cit., III, p. 240 (citing the testimony of Lily Strassmann). In the IZL propaganda publications in English, an attempt was still being made at this time to convince England of IZL loyalty. Cf. *Sentinel*, No. 3, 17 Feb. 1939; No. 8, 24 Feb. 1939.
84. B.H. (D. Raziel) to A.F. Giles, 29 Dec. 1938, YCA, file 8.
85. Shechtman, op. cit., III, pp. 235–6.
86. Eliav, *Wanted*, pp. 83–7; Haichman in oral testimony to the writer. The 'accord', if such a thing ever existed, was never written down. According to Mark Kahan, Colonel Galadik was the commander of the IZL course (*The Ayala Lubinsky Volume*, p. 85) – otherwise he served as the head of the training wing of the Polish infantry. The IZL commander on the course was Mordechai Strelitz, and his deputy, S. Katz; Niv, op. cit., II, p. 172. It should be recalled that the *Haganah*, too, benefited from the assistance of the Polish Government; HH, II, p. 999.
87. M.A. Perlmutter, '"Heil Hitler" in Jewish Jerusalem', *Ha-Yom*, 1 March 1939. The Jewish Agency's Press Office reported on this matter to the Executive the very same day: 'Such "fragrance" has never before appeared in any Jewish newspaper in the world, not even in any Revisionist newspaper'. Gravitsky to the Executive, CZA S25/2091. Nevertheless, it must be admitted that this was an unusually extreme reaction. More characteristic were articles such as that written by Dr W. von Weisel,

'German Plans', *Ha-Makshif*, 20 Feb. 1939, in its strong line against Hitler.

88. Jabotinsky to Shechtman, 28 Feb. 1939, JI.
89. Z. Jabotinsky, 'And Now – We Need a Programme', *Ha-Makshif*, 3 April 1939 (*Moment*, 26 March 1939).
90. Idem, 'Tonight', ibid., 9 April 1939 (*Moment*, 7 April 1939).
91. Untitled, A[vida]n, *Ba-Herev*, April 1939.
92. 'Maimonides, *Mishneh Torah*, laws of Kings, chapters 5–7, 11–12,' ibid.
93. Raziel to Jabotinsky, 28 March 1939, HA 21a/8.
94. Jabotinsky to Raziel, 1 April 1939, JI, Raziel to Jabotinsky, 3 April 1939, HA 21a/8. Jabotinsky foresaw a Muslim *jihad* supported by the Axis powers. Jabotinsky to Albert Sarraut, 18 April 1939, JI.
95. Raziel to Jabotinsky, 7 May 1939, HA. Cf. also the correspondence between Raziel and Yunitchman from April 1939 (Raziel's replies dated 10 and 18 April) in YCA, file 16, which testifies to the state of tension between them.
96. Untitled memorandum opening with the words 'The I[rgun] is an independent body . . .', YCA, file 96. Cf. also the memoranda in German about bacteriological warfare, dated 13 Feb. 1939, ibid.
97. Z. Jabotinsky, 'A Few Paces before the Intersection', *Ha-Mashkif*, 18 May 1939 (*Moment*, 7 May 1939; *der Nayer Veg*, 14 May 1939, Kovna; and *The Jewish Herald*, Johannesburg, 19 May 1939).
98. U.Z. Greenberg, 'Our Cry: Acre and Gaza!', *Ha-Mashkif*, 18 May 1939 (*Moment*, 7 May 1939). Acre was the site of Ben Yosef's hanging; at Gaza the body of the illegal immigrant who had been shot on board the boat *Agius Nicholaus* by British guards on 31 March 1939 was washed ashore.
99. Scheib, *First Tithe*, pp. 33–4.
100. Jabotinsky to the IZL Executive, 8 May 1939, JI, and *Speeches*, p. 340.
101. Jabotinsky to the NZO Executive, 8 May 1939, JI.
102. Jabotinsky to A. Zacharyta, 12 May 1939, JI.
103. 'To All IZL Members, 27th of *Iyar* 5699 (June 1939) – National Headquarters', YCA.
104. Z. Jabotinsky, 'The Insult', *Ha-Mashkif*, 29 March 1939 (*Moment*, 19 May 1939).
105. Z. Jabotinsky, 'From My Diary. The results of the White Paper', *Ha-Mashkif*, 22 May 1939; see also letters in JI.
106. Niv, op. cit., II, pp. 238–40. Jabotinsky's demands aroused dissatisfaction in the IZL, ibid., p. 240.
107. Cf. the IZL leaflet in HH, III, p. 58. Similarly, 'Bir Ades' in material for *Ba-Herev* in YCA file 86. The leaflet regarding Bir Ades also appears in *Liberated Jerusalem*, No. 22 (30), p. 7 (23 June 1939).
108. 'The Most Important Aim – Changing Jewish nature', ibid. In its broadcasts the IZL would claim that King David and Judas Maccabbaeus were religious, but they also knew how to spill the blood of the enemy 'like water for the glory and liberty of Israel': 'The Voice of Zion at War, The Voice of Liberated Zion' [July 1939?], YCA file 93.
109. 'From a State to a Ghetto', unsigned and undated, JI, P. 233a. Opposing the leaflet put out by Buber, Berl Katznelson and Mania Schohat (7 July 1939), 'Thou Shalt Not Kill!', they adduced as models Moses, Deborah and Isaiah: Deut. 20:3–4, 16; Judges 5:31; Isaiah 66:16. 'The Voice of Zion at War, the Voice of Liberated Zion' [July 1939?], YCA, file 93.
110. Y. Eliav, *Wanted*, p. 90ff. Niv, op. cit., p. 240ff. Cf. also 'An Order' [to Raziel], 24 June 1939, JI; *Liberated Jerusalem*, No. 21 (29), 16 June 1939, 'Chronicles', p. 5; the IZL in Palestine, High Command, Bulletin No. 2, 9 June 1939, YCA, file 93.
111. Z. Jabotinsky, 'A White Paper on Diaspora Jewry', *Ha-Mashkif*, 9 June 1939 (*Moment*, 4 June 1939); Jabotinsky to Haskel, 5 June 1939, JI.
112. Jabotinsky to the NZO *Nesiut* (Executive), 7 June 1939, JI.
113. Jabotinsky to the NZO *Nesiut*, 24 June 1939, JI.
114. Jabotinsky to Shofman, 9 June 1939, JI; Shechtman, op. cit., III, pp. 120–24. Z. Jabotinsky, 'The Tension Drops', *Ha-Mashkif*, 18 June 1939 (*Moment*, 9 June 1939 —, 'They have been Chloroformed', ibid., 16 June 1939 (*Moment*, 11 June 1939). Jabotinsky to the NZO *Nesiut*, 7 June 1939, ibid., Jabotinsky to Haskel, 15 July 1939,

ibid.
115. 'From a State to a Ghetto', *Ha-Makshif*, 28 July 1939.
116. *Di Tat*, 17 May 1939, No. 25, and also 23 May 1939.
117. P.223/3A, JI.
118. 'The Five Years that are Liable to be Shorter', *Liberated Jerusalem*, No. 18(26), 26 May 1939, p. 31 and 'Chronica', ibid., p. 403; 'The Interest of the State', ibid., No. 24 (32), 7 July 1939, pp. 1–3. The term 'innocent' is mentioned explicitly.
119. 'Accursed is he who performs God's work Deceitfully, and Accursed is he who Keeps his Sword from Blood!', *Rak Kach* (Only Thus), 18 July 1939, 'The IZL in Palestine'. Cf. also 'The Devil Laughed', an IZL broadcast (a debate with M. Assaf); cf. Y. Shavit, *Self Restraint or Reaction*, pp. 142–5), JI 2/3/4k. *Rak Kach*. 'Jews! The IZL in Palestine' (6 Aug. 1939).
120. 'Regarding the Crimes of the Agency', JI, P.233. He seems to have been the author.
121. The writer quotes from the anthology: B.Z. Herzl, *Zionism, A Political Edition*, ed. B. Netanyahu (Jerusalem, 1937), pp. 269–70. Cf. also B.Z. Herzl, *Facing a People and the World*, II, *Zionist Speeches and Articles, 1899–1904* (The Zionist Library, Jerusalem, 1961), pp. 271–4; Usishkin's letter, ibid., p. 270. The quotation was also acceptable to Jabotinksy who viewed himself as Herzl's successor. Cf. 'Zionism and Palestine' (written 1905) in Z. Jabotinsky, *First Zionist Writings* (Jerusalem, 1949), p. 123.
122. Cf., for example, the memorandum opening with the words 'The I[rgun] is an independent body', YCA, file 96.
123. 'Jews, Jewish Youth in the Homeland!' (undated), P.233/4a, JI.
124. Jabotinsky to Kopelevich, 28 July 1939, JI.
125. Jabotinsky to the NZO Executive, 1 Aug. 1939, JI.
126. Jabotinsky to the NZO Executive, 3 Aug. 1939, JI.
127. E. Katz, 'Freedom Fighters of Israel (Lehi)', in *The Freedom Fighters of Israel* (Tel Aviv, 1955), pp. 239–40.
128. Jabotinsky to the NZO Executive, 7 Aug. 1939 (Conversations with Sternheim (Stern) Refaeli and 'friends from the USA').
129. Jabotinsky to the NZO Committee of Deputies in Palestine, 21 Aug. 1939, JI.
130. 'Jewish "I.R.A." Fights for Sovereign Palestine', by Morris Gilbert, excerpt from the *New York World Telegram*, 13 July 1939, in the Golomb files in HH, file 11.
131. P.223/3A, JI (no date).
132. 'A Message from the Head of the IZL High Command to the Yishuv', *Omer La-Am* (Speaking to the People), an evening newspaper, 29 July 1939. According to A. Haichman, a member of the command, the writer was Dr Yeivin and not H. Strelitz, the head of the Command.
133. Ibid.
134. Ibid.
135. 'Principles and Conclusions', signed E.B.Y., ibid. Most of the article was not published in *Lehi Ketavim* (Writings), I, pp. 123–4.
136. 'Principles and Conclusions', ibid.
137. 'We and the Arabs' (anon.), ibid.
138. 'From the Writings of Josef Pilsudski. How to Educate a Nation towards a War of National Liberation', *Omer La-Am*, 29 July 1939.
139. 'Hitler Enters Danzig', headline in *Omer La-Am*, 29 July 1939.
140. The leaflet is cited in Weinshal's book, p. 135.
141. According to HH, which also quotes a letter from Raziel to Jabotinsky, 17 Nov. 1939.
142. Shavit, ibid., p. 404. For his students' version, see Niv, op. cit., II, pp. 279–81; Shechtman, op. cit., III, pp. 263–5; H. Ben-Yeruham, op. cit., II, pp. 971–2. Cable to the NZO Executive 24 Aug. 1939, JI; Shechtman, op. cit., III, pp. 130–2.

## CHAPTER 3 (pp.59–76)

1. Eliav, *Wanted*, p. 148; Niv, op. cit., III, p. 37. Also, *Irgunpress* (IZL organ in English from August 1939), No. 1/5, pp. 2–3, 5–8.

2. IZL leaflet, 21 July 1939; collection of IZL leaflets, JI.
3. 'Do not Stand by Your Neighbour's Blood' (30 July 1939), ibid.
4. 'The Geneva Congress', IZL leaflet, undated (end August 1939), ibid.
5. Jabotinsky to Anatole de Monsie, 2 Sept. 1939; *Letters*, pp. 111–13; *The Jewish War Front* (London, 1940); letter to Akzin of 18 Sept. 1939 in Niv, op. cit., III, p. 108. Jabotinsky spoke of an army rather than a legion, and an IZL delegation was working to that end in the USA.
6. The letter was sent by D. Raziel, Y. Gurion and M. Ginsberg from 'Yair's Pitcher' (YCA), published in Y. Gurion, *Arieh Posek. His Life and Achievements* (Hebrew: Tel Aviv, 1957).
7. National Command Communiqué No. 107, Sept. 1939, YCA.
8. 'The Word of the IZL to the Hebrew *Yishuv*', *Rak Kach* (Only Thus), CZA, S25/2091. According to the *Palestine Post*, in PRO, FO/371/23240 and Niv, op. cit., III, p.37, the date of the pamphlet was 11 September.
9. 'To the Commanding Officers of *Ha-Tekuma*, *Rak Kach*, Sept. 1939. *Ha-Tekuma*(The Resurrection) was the inner circle of IZL officers before the split in April 1937.
10. 'Current Events', (unsigned), *Ba-Herev* (By the Sword), Sept. 1939.
11. 'A General Discussion of the Situation: (a) Recruitment; (b) What are the Economic Possibilities at this Time?' and 'Our Task', YCA, file 26.
12. 'The Vision of Our Faith', *Ba-Herev*, Sept. 1939, showing clear signs of the influence of Stern and Yeivin.
13. 'The Wars and the IZL', ibid.
14. Jabotinsky to Haskel, 22 Sept. 1939, JI; to the Committee of Deputies, 29 Sept. 1939, JI.
15. Jabotinsky to the *Betar* Commission (Raziel), 25 Sept. 1939, JI.
16. Raziel to Jabotinsky, 22 Oct 1939, HA 21/8a. 'Elements of the New *Betar* Regulations' (undated; Sept. 1939?), YCA.
17. The Agreement ('Programme A') was photographed from YCA, file 28: 'The B.H.–A.S. Accord' (B.H. = Ben-Hanania (Raziel); A.S. = Alan Saunders). The stipulations are written in his handwriting. The document was photographed in Amira Stern's MA thesis on the subject of 'Yair's "Milk Churn"', Hebrew University's School of Archives, 1984, p. 195. Cf. also Eliav, *Wanted*, pp. 152–3, and Niv, op. cit., II, p. 236 and III, p. 21; Y. Orenstein, *In Chains*, pp. 140–43; HH, III, p. 1680.
18. 'Current Events', by Bo'az (?), undated (Oct. 1939), p. 2, 'A Kind of Summary', by Bo'az, pp. 4–5. Collection of IZL leaflets, JI.
19. Yohanan, 'Our Task at This Hour', ibid.; D.S. (untitled), *Ba-Herev*, ibid., p. 10.
20. B. Katznelson, 'Conversations with Jabotinsky in the Autumn of 1939', *Molad* 18, No. 146–7, Oct. 1960, pp, 438–47.
21. Jabotinsky, *The Jewish War Front*, Ch. 17, pp. 15, 19–20, 31, 33–4; Ch. 15 and pp. 179–87. The book was translated into Hebrew in 1941 by Dr Y.H. Yeivin, who doubtless disagreed with a significant proportion of its basic assumptions.
22. Ibid., pp. 192–6, 200–2.
23. Ibid., pp. 214, 220–24.
24. Ibid., pp. 216–18.
25. Ibid., p. 237.
26. Z. Jabotinsky, 'All in All', *Ha-Mashkif*, 5 March 1940.
27. Jabotinsky to Y. Mirlman, 16 April 1940; to Yakov Dam, 16 April 1940; to Haskel, 18 April 1940, JI.
28. Jabotinsky to Akzin, 9 May 1940, JI.
29. Jabotinsky to Churchill, 12 May 1940. JI. On 17 May 1940 Jabotinsky also asked Sir Archibald Sinclair, the Secretary of State for Air in Churchill's government, to help in purifying the 'vengeful atmosphere' created in Palestine by the Mandatory Government.
30. 'Revolutionary Zionism' (undated and anonymous), YCA, file 105; 'The NZO Whither? The Conclusions of the Maximalist Faction Concerning the Situation within the Movement', internal leaflet, 19 Oct. 1939, HA; and 'The Error in Tactics, Revolution and Evolution When?' Ibid., p. 3.

31. 'The Two Souls of the Revisionist Movement', ibid., p. 4.
32. 'Summary', ibid., pp. 6–7.
33. 'The Agreement – Beginning of the End' (anon. and undated), YCA, file 28 [Oct.–Nov. 1939?]. It seems to have been published after the publication of Bulletin No. 33 of the 'Committee of Deputies', 19 Oct. 1939; and Niv, op. cit., III, p. 15. For the agreement between the 'Faction of Allegation and Faith' and Stern and his followers, cf. also '(Explanations of the Inner Line)', undated, (anon.), YCA, file 100. Ultimately, the agreement between Altman and Rutenberg became void when the latter resigned because of illness.
34. 'Evolutionism – Failure or Obliteration', p. 8, YCA, ibid. Cf. also Ben-Zeruya, 'Organisation and Tactics', *Ha-Mashkif*, 17 Nov. 1939, which also discusses the constant struggle within the Revisionist movement between evolutionist and revolutionary tactical viewpoints, and praises *Betar* and *Hazit Ha'am* as expressions of revolutionary tactics, which were viewed by the opposite camp as 'monstrous, disgusting and harmful'. The clash between the two always produced chaos within the party. For strong maximalist opposition to communism as an ideology, cf., for example, Dr Y.H. (Yeivin), *The Decline of Marxism and its Causes*, published by *Le-Om* (Nation), Jerusalem, undated (1940), pp. 3–15.
35. 'The NZO Whither? Our Path', pp. 8–9.
36. 'Our War' and 'Our Approach', internal leaflets put out by the 'Faction of Allegation and Faith'. It should be remembered that Akiva Brun, the head of the National Workers' Union (NWU), was one of the leaders of the Faction. E. Katz, 'Freedom Fighters of Israel', in *The Freedom Fighters of Israel* (Tel Aviv, 1955), pp. 237–8.
37. The IZL Centre in Palestine, Bulletin of the National Command, No. 108, 5 Nov. 1939, YCA, file 46. Nevertheless, even while attacking the 'Committee of Deputies', the IZL was willing to stand by it in labour disputes, warning that Palestine could become a second Spain with the left playing the role of the supporters of Stalin. See 'To the *Yishuv*!', 14 Jan. 1941, Collection of IZL leaflets, JI. 'To the Jewish *Yishuv*', 16 Jan. 1941, ibid. The ideological heritage of activist Revisionism in socio-economic affairs would accompany both the IZL and Stern's group for a long time. *Lehi* was only gradually to free itself of this heritage.
38. 'Zealotry', 14 Dec. 1939(?), JI. IZL propaganda material in HA's IZL Archives (apparently material confiscated at the time of the *Altalena* affair). An explanation of 'Because' starts with Jabotinsky's *Autobiography* (Hebrew; Jerusalem, 1947), pp. 24–5. Poland's military defeat, however, was ultimately explained by the fact that she had been stabbed in the back by Russia. 'The Defeat of Poland', 10 March 1940, leaflets for IZL propagandists.
39. 'Spring is Approaching . . .', 9 Feb. 1940 (?), ibid., HA. At this time British intelligence received information from a source with contacts in the Jewish Agency that Revisionism was not a type of Nazism, and that it did not harbour Gestapo agents (as had been speculated); rather, it constituted 'Jewish fascism'. Secret information, 1939–42, CZA, S25/4351. As early as the summer of 1938, the authorities in Palestine had noted the fascist, pro-Italian and anti-*Mapai* nature of the NZO and the IZL: 'Note on Present Position in Regard to the Revisionists', Secret No. 2, August 1938: MacMichael to MacDonald, 10 Sept. 1938. Annex 1, in PRO, CO/733386/75866.
40. The land laws divided Palestine into three areas, of which only a small part was open to Jewish settlement. This procedure had already been anticipated in the 1939 White Paper.
41. 'Concerning Events', 10 March 1940, leaflets for propagandists, 1939–40, issued by the Information Department of the IZL for use in schools and youth movements, JI, 21-4/12. See also Bulletin of the National Command, No. 110, 28 Feb. 1940. YCA, file 46.
42. D. Niv, op. cit., III, pp. 38–9 (citing testimony of H. Kalay collected in the HA and JI).
43. A Haichman to the author, 14 Nov. 1985. Haichman often spoke with Stern in Mazra, where he was angered by Stern's repeated references to Germany's victories. Cf. also the testimony of B. Lubotzky in D. Niv, op. cit., III, p. 46. German submarines sank 229 ships between September 1939 and May 1940.

44. 'To Our Mothers', *You Shall Live Forever*, pp. 105–14, in various versions. 'The Messiah' (fragment), ibid., pp. 130–31. Cf. also Y. Eliav, op. cit., pp. 151–2, and A. Kotzer, *Red Carpet*, p. 178.

45. According to Weinshal (*The Blood on the Threshold*, p. 155), Stern conversed with unspecified 'communists' in Mazra. He is also known to have conversed with Yizhaki, one of the leaders of *Po'alei Zion Semol* (Left Zionist Workers), but it is extremely unlikely that this had any ideological significance. It would seem that such reports reflect an attempt to recast events in the light of *Lehi*'s later leftist tendencies. Eliav, op. cit., p. 156. Another testimony (A. Haichman) says Stern met in Mazra with a detained German officer.

46. 'Minority and Dominion', 10 March 1940. Cf. 'The Minority and its Struggle for Power', *Ba-Herev* (May 1940?). Cf. also M. Giora, 'The IZL Trial and Lesson', *Keshet*, 65, Autumn 1975, who attributes the 'doctrine of the few' to Heilperin (Ratosh), p. 74. In fact, Achimeir and Yeivin had expounded it earlier.

47. 'The Front and the Hinterland', parts 1–4, *Ba-Herev*, (May 1940?).

48. 'In the *Yishuv*, ibid.

49. 'Towards the Decisive Battle', ibid.; 'Leftists Raise Their Eyes to . . . Jabotinksy', ibid.

50. 'The Aim of the War for the Jewish People', ibid.

51. 'Recruiting the Hinterland', ibid.

52. Niv, op. cit., III, p. 43. HH III, pp. 474–5, has a different version, whereby Raziel did not withdraw his resignation, but transferred the command to lower-ranking officers, supporters of Altman.

53. National High Command Communiqué No. 111, 31 May 1940. 'To All IZL Members', YCA, file 46.

54. Jabotinsky to Yitzchak Ben-Ami (a member of the IZL mission to the USA), 27 May 1940, JI.

55. Jabotinsky to Alexander Raphaeli (a member of the IZL mission to the USA), 12 June 1940, ibid.

56. Jabotinsky to Lord Lothian, 21 June 1940; to Duff Cooper; and to Beneš, 3 July 1940, JI. For the negotiations between the Agency and the authorities on the establishment of a Jewish army: Y. Gelber, *The History of Volunteering* (Hebrew; Jerusalem, 1979), who disproves Jabotinsky's claims. Also Shechtman, op. cit., III, pp. 156–7, who does not present a true picture of the Jabotinsky–Lothian contacts.

57. Haichman's testimony to the author, 14 Nov. 1985, claims that Raziel erred in not explaining to his comrades the advantages of an agreement with England.

58. That dating is, however, open to question. Stern's original intention was to take control of the *Irgun* both ideologically and administratively. The split developed because he was supported by only a portion of the IZL's membership and half of its command.

59. Command Communiqué, No. 112, in *Lehi, Ketavim*, I, pp. 17–18; Niv, op. cit., III, pp. 45–6.

60. Jabotinsky to Altman, 29 June 1940, 5 July 1940, JI.

61. The letter is unsigned and without an address; it appears in the second edition of Weinschal's book, *The Blood on the Threshold*, between pp. 165 and 168.

62. For the text, see Niv, op. cit., III, pp. 43–4. Both telegrams are dated 15 and not 17 July, JI. Compare HH III, p. 475 and Niv, pp. 44–5. The former cites testimony by Moshe Rotstein, the British intelligence agent; Niv relies on the testimonies of the IZL members opposing Stern. The attempt to organise a political movement failed completely, apparently because of the reservations of Achimeir, Greenberg and Yeivin concerning the terrorist nature of 'the IZL in Israel'. The links between 'the 'IZL in Israel' and the 'Faction of Allegation and Faith' are still obscure, because of the lack of sources.

63. Jabotinsky to Dr Y. Mirlman, 18 June 1940 and 27 July 1940; Z. Jabotinsky, *Letters*, pp. 213–15. Strangely, the president of the NZO expected the Soviets to agree to a Jewish army while they were still allied to Hitler. Jabotinsky to Abrahams, 18 July 1940, JI.

64. Stern to Merlin, 22 July 1940, unsigned and unaddressed, YCA, file 40. Yellin-Mor

(op. cit., p. 67), quoting passages convenient for him from this letter, mistakenly writes 22 August. At the same time, Altman was also being attacked by the maximalist Dr Moshe Cohen who – like Stern – felt that Altman was collaborating with the authorities, especially with the chief secretary, Sir John MacPherson. This collaboration had begun with the *Bank Ha-Poalim* robbery affair in September 1937, and he was accused of misusing NZO funds, a lack of moral ability and judgement, and of having an extravagant lifestyle at the expense of the movement. 'The Committee of Deputies' was nothing but *Zubatovshchina*, and Altman himself was nothing but a provocateur and police agent. See 'A Gangster as Leader' (unsigned), printed in Palestine (July 1940).

65. Stern to Merlin, 22 July 1940, YCA, file 40; cf. Yellin-Mor, op. cit., pp. 66–7, who deliberately overlooks the main disagreements on the question of foreign orientation, which prevented the survival of a united IZL. Merlin, for his part, refused to support Stern (despite additional cables to him on 3 Sept. and 30 Oct. 1940) because he had understood that Stern did not present him with the real reasons or with the ideological ones. Merlin to Stern, 19 Dec. 1940, YCA, file 46.

66. Raziel (to Hillel Kook), unsigned and undated, HA 8/21a.

67. Ibid. Raziel noted the letter he had received after his release, signed by Kalay (winter–spring 1940). The letter itself has not been recovered. It was 'full of tricks', and he was well aware who was behind it. The letter marked a turning-point for the worse in his relations with Stern.

68. Raziel to Kook, ibid.

69. Ibid.

70. Eri Jabotinsky to Raphael Rozov, 9 Aug. 1940, p. 201, JI.

71. For the most part, the young rank and file members did not know the details of the question of foreign orientation. Contrast E. Lankin, *The Story of the Commander of the Altalena* (Hebrew; 3rd edition, Tel Aviv, 1974), p. 53, and the testimony of B. Lubotzki, Niv, op. cit., III, p. 46.

72. Weinshal, *The Blood on the Threshold*, pp. 168–9.


CHAPTER 4 (pp.77–108)

1. 'What do we want?' Most of this is published in Y. Weinschal, *The Blood on the Threshold* (Hebrew; 1978 ed.), pp. 98–9. The source is to be found in YCA, file 98.

2. Ratosh was to point out Stern's ideological dependence on Jabotinsky and questioned the justification for the new movement. He would certainly not join it, though he sought collaboration with Stern, in order to influence it. Heilperin [Ratosh] to Stern, 28 Aug. 1940. In Yonathan Ratosh [Uriel Shelah], *Letters, 1937–1980* (Hebrew; ed. Y. Amrami [Yoel], Tel Aviv, 1986), pp. 53 and 56–7.

3. Order No. 12, 22 July 1940, HA, Ba/1.

4. Order No. 115, 29 Aug. 1940. Cf. HH, III, p. 477.

5. 'The H[igh] C[ommand] of 'the [IZL] in Israel'. No. 1. 'From the Eve of the New Year 5701 (3 September 1940)', *Ketavim*, I, pp. 19–20. YCA, file 49.

6. According to Niv, op. cit., III, pp. 174–5.

7. For Ratosh's scepticism, see his *Letters*, op. cit., p. 52.

8. On Stern's attitude towards Jabotinsky and his book, see Y. Weinschal, *The Blood on the Threshold*, p. 59.

9. Some former members of the Stern group (such as Eliav, op. cit., pp. 188–9), were later to claim that the Hebrew letter *aleph* could be read as a code for 'English' and not only 'Italians'. In the light of the document at our disposal, that claim does not stand up to critical investigation. Italy is explicitly mentioned in the document reproduced in A. Amichal-Yeivin, *In Purple: the Life of Yair – Avraham Stern* (Hebrew; Tel Aviv, 1968), p. 313.

10. The Hebrew fleet would be a quarter of the size of Italy's merchant and battle fleet. Cf. the original document in JI.

11. This paragraph is missing from the other version in JI, as are the last two paragraphs.

12. Cf. L. Hirszowicz, *The Third Reich and the Arab World* (Hebrew; Tel Aviv, 1965),

pp. 95–103. Information given to American intelligence by the British in 1944 tells of contacts between Stern and Italian intelligence officers in Beirut, who agreed to finance anti-British operations for a sum of $2,000 per month(!). Cf. Research and Analysis Branch, 'R & N. No. 2717, Aims and Activities of the Stern Group in Palestine', 1 Dec. 1944. Secret. (National Archives, Washington.)

13. 'Of Fate and War', *Ba-Mahteret*, A, Sept.–Oct. 1940, *Ketavim*, 1, pp. 23–4.

14. P.S. O'Hegarty, 'The Triumph of *Sinn Fein* (The 1916 Uprising)', *Ba-Mahteret*, Issue 5, ibid., pp. 53–6. A comparison of the myth with the academic-historical description is instructive. Cf. W.I. Thompson, *The Imagination of an Insurrection: Dublin. Easter 1916* (N.Y., 1967); C. Townsend, *Political Violence in Ireland since 1848* (Oxford, 1983), pp. 298–321; F.X. Martin, 'The Evolution of a Myth – The Easter Rising. Dublin 1916', in E. Kamenka (ed.), *Nationalism: The Nature and Evolution of an Idea* (N.Y., 1976), pp. 57–80.

15. 'Aspirations of the Organization', undated and unsigned, YCA, file 99.

16. Document, undated and unsigned, containing 14 paragraphs, YCA, file 101.

17. Document unsigned, untitled and undated, beginning with the words: 'In case political rule can be neither altered nor cancelled . . .', YCA, file 106. Appears to date from summer 1940. For the influence of *Narodnaya Volya*, cf. I. Tvuah to B. Gurevich, 9 June 1953, Weinschal files, JI.

18. From *Ba-Makhteret*, Issue 2, p. 18. Omitted from *Ketavim*, I.

19. The proposal of Hanoch Kalay. Undated. Includes 14 principles. YCA, file 37.

20. Principle 16 of 'the Principles of Revival', Issue 2, *Ba-Mahterets*, Oct.–Nov. 1940. Cf. the original in YCA, file 89.

21. Principle 13 in Kalay's version. YCA, file 37.

22. The Editor's reply to letters, *Ba-Mahteret*, 6, Feb.–March 1941, pp. 71–2; HH III, p. 495 exaggerates in making a complete mockery of 'The Principles of Revival'.

23. For the use of the term 'integral nationalism', cf. J.J. Linz, 'Political Space and Fascism as a Latecomer . . .', in S.U. Larsen et al. (eds.), *Who Were the Fascists?* (Bergen, 1980), p. 154. For a definition of the term 'radical right', cf. S.G. Payne, *Fascism, Comparison and Definition* (Madison, Wisconsinm, 1980), pp. 14–21. Payne's distinctions are problematic from the standpoint of 'the IZL in Israel'. On Stern's being a fascist or tending to fascism, see the explicit remarks in A. Koestler, 'Middle East Underground', *Contact*, May 1946, p. 53; F. Gervasi, 'Terror in Palestine', *Collier's*, 11 Aug. 1945, p. 64.

24. *Hedim* (Echoes), I, 1 Nov. 1941, *Ketavim*, I, p. 29 (*Ba-Mahteret*, 2).

25. 'A Uniform National Front', ibid., p. 30. Cf. also Stern, 'Present Tactics: a [party] movement desirous of redeeming the *nation* must be free of the fetters of the reality of the *Yishuv* . . .', *Sulam*, X, No. 6–7, Dec. 1958–Jan. 1959.

26. 'Weizmann Teaches the Jews Morality', *Ketavim*, I, p. 30; 'We are with England Unconditionally', ibid.; 'Patria', ibid., pp. 31–2.; 'The White Paper Lives and Breathes!', *Hedim*, II, ibid., pp. 39–40; 'This is No Time to Announce the Aims of the War', ibid., p. 41; 'At the Gates of Disappointment', ibid., pp. 41–2; 'The Volunteer Army of Eretz Israel', ibid.

27. Dr Yeivin, 'The Start of the Movement for the Kingdom of Israel. Yair: Bar Mitzva to his Death', *Sulam*, 11 (71), VI, Feb.–March 1955, p. 21.

28. 'The Messianic Movements in Israel. I', by S[tern]., *Ba-Mahteret*, Issue 4, *Ketavim*, I, pp. 47–8.

29. 'The Messianic Movement in Israel. II', *Ba-Mahteret*, Issue 5, ibid., pp. 55–6. The source is from Maimonides, *Ha-Yad Ha Hazaka*, Laws of Kings, Ch. 2.

30. Y. Orenstein, *In Chains*, p. 156.

31. *Hedim*, V, 'Jew-haters and Zion-lovers'. *Ba-Mahteret*, Issue 4, pp. 48–9. In the wake of Dr David Lazar's article, 'Lovers of Zion – True and False', *Ha-Aretz*, 23 Jan. 1941.

32. Internal Information leaflet No. 3, Dec. 1940–Jan. 1941.' In the Yishuv', YCA, file 91. *Hedim*, IV, 'Some Activity Somewhere', *Ketavim*, I, pp. 57–8.

33. 'Those Who Walk in Darkness' by R.[?], ibid., pp. 45–6. 'The U.S.A. is Condemned Because America's Aid to England is given for Commercial Reasons', ibid., *Hedim*, V, 'Lithuanian "Zionism" and Jewish Zionism', *Ba-Mahteret*, Issue 5, Jan.–Feb. 1941,

ibid., pp. 58–60 (cf. 'The Lithuanian Liberation Movement in America', by G.W., *Ha-Aretz*, 2 Feb. 1941, 7 April 1941).

34. *Hedim*, 'Pithom and Ramses in Democratic Switzerland', *Ketavim*, I, p. 46; 'Democratic Antisesmitism', ibid.

35. 'Exile and Redemption (Concerning the Ghetto)', *Ba-Mahteret*, Issue 6, pp. 20–23. This article was omitted from *Ketavim*. Cf. YCA, file 89; and also 'Police, Theatre and Cinema in the Ghetto', *Ha-Aretz*, 13 March 1941. The aforementioned article was based on this information.

36. 'Enthusiasm', by 'a Zealot' [?], *Ketavim*, I, pp. 66–7, 69–72. For a later repetition of the same theme, see 'Under the sign of the end', from Yair, 25 Shevat (early Feb.) 1944, *Ketavim*, I, pp. 393–6. According to Yellin-Mor (p. 76) Stern dictated this article to him in summer 1941. For the doctrine of 'persecutor' and 'enemy' cf. the testimony of Moshe Svorai: Y. Banai, *Unknown Soldiers*, p. 72.

37. Weinschal, *The Blood on The Threshold*, p. 173.

38. Y. Eliav, *Wanted*, pp. 187–8. The man – Suleiman Kheidar, a Shi'ite Muslim from Baalbek who later converted to Judaism. David Siton, *In Light and in Secret* (*Pages from the Diary of a Detainee*), (Jerusalem, 1978), pp. 128–31.

39. Cf. O.W. von Hentig, *Mein Leben. Eine Dienstreise* (Goettingen, 1962), pp. 338–9. Von Hentig (who died in 1984) was interviewed later by Israeli scholars and journalists. Cf. recently S. Shamgar, 'When the Reich Representative in Beirut met with "a Jewish Terrorist from Palestine" ', *Yediot Aharonot* Supplement, '7 Days', 15 July 1983, p. 22. The German diplomat recalled Lubenchik proposing 'to collaborate [with Germany] against his own people'. Cf. also H. Canaan, *Two Hundred Days of Anxiety, Eretz-Israel vs. Rommel's Army*, (Tel Aviv, undated, 1974?). Von Hentig supported a Jewish state in the 1930s, but had little influence over the decision-making process in Nazi Germany, despite being the head of the Department of the Levant in the Foreign Office, since he was a non-Nazi and a survivor from the Second Reich and Weimar eras. D. Yisraeli, *The Third Reich and Eretz Israel* (Hebrew; Ramat Gan, 1974). pp. 173–4.

40. Canaan, op. cit., p. 59. 'The German (or Sternist) Memorandum' is adduced as Appendix 11 in Yisraeli, op. cit., pp. 315–17: 'The Basic Outline of the Proposal of the *IZL* in Eretz Israel Concerning the Solution of the Jewish Question in Europe and the Active Participation of the IZL in the War on the Side of Germany'. Secret, Constaninople 11 January 1941.

41. See my *In the Struggle for a State. Zionist Politics, 1936–1948* (Hebrew; Jersualem, 1984), p. 309.

42. M. Domarus, *Hitler. Reden und Proklamationen, 1932–1945*, II Band (Munich, 1963), p. 1065; A. Hitler, *My New Order*, ed. with commentary by Raul de Rousy de Sales (N.Y., 1941), p. 872.

43. Yisraeli, op. cit., pp. 309–10.

44. Abba Sikra, 'Twarda and Gilboa (Two Sessions with Yair)', *Herut*, 17 May 1949.

45. Weinschal, *The Blood on the Threshold*, p. 184–5, 194–5, Cf. also the mystic apologetics of Sh. Ben-Dov, *The Redemption of Isral and the Crisis of the State* (Hebrew; Safed, 1960), pp. 301–2; I. Eldad, 'Who and What were Yair and the Lehi?', *Sulam*, XIII, 1962, Nos 3–4 (135–6). Eldad relies on the same informaton concerning the Lubenchik report as was available to Eliav (*Wanted*, pp. 190–91).

46. More serious was the threat posed by the German plan (voiced as early as 1938, repeated in Hitler's conversations with Mussolini in June 1940, formalised the next month, and not officially cancelled until February 1942) to make Madagascar the location of Jewish 're-settlement'. This certainly undermined Stern's basic premise that 'the persecutor' would help him to wage war against 'the enemy'. See Y. Orenstein, *In Chains*, pp. 147–8 and the testimony of H. Kalay to Y. Slutsky, 1959). HA. According to Yellin-Mor (*Etgar*, 25 Jan. 1962) 'Yair' still believed in the Madagascar option in the summer of 1941.

On the 'Madagascar plan' itself, see L. Yachil, 'Madagascar – an Imaginary Solution to the Jewish Question', *Yalkut Moreshet* XIX (1975), pp. 159–78. Cf. also Y. Arad, I. Gutman and A. Margaliot (eds.), *Selected Documents Concerning the Destruction of*

*German, Austrian, Polish and Soviet Jewry* (Jerusalem, 1978), No. 88. Cf. also the findings of the American Jewish Committee who sensed the danger of an enforced migration to Madagascar: E. Hevesi, 'Hitler's Plan for Madagascar', *Contemporary Jewish Record* (August 1941), pp. 381–94. Also C.R. Browning, *The Final Solution and the German Foreign Office* (London and N.Y., 1978), pp. 35–43.

47. *The Voice of Zion at War, The Voice of Zion being Set Free*. The Radio of the IZL, 10 May. YCA, file 94.

48. The NZO had ordered recruitment for the British army in a resolution of 25 September 1940, but this coercive move had been opposed by the high command of the IZL. At the *Betar* convention of December 1940, and very much under pressure from the imminent schism, it was agreed to support recruitment on an individual basis only. See HH, III, pp. 479–81; and also the *Betar* convention which was held in Tel Aviv, CZA, S25/2090. Niv, III, pp. 129–31.

     The Jewish section of the Palestine Communist Party (PKP) also opposed recruitment for what was to remain an 'imperialist war' until Hitler's invasion of the Soviet Union in June 1941. At this stage no serious discussions were possible between the right-wing, anti-Arab 'IZL in Israel' and the Marxist, anti-Zionist and pro-Arab PKP. This would only become possible in 1947, under entirely different conditions.

49. 'In the Revisionist Camp. Review of the Period from January 1 1941 to June 15 1941.' HA, 2/B. Among those arrested was Yehoshua Zetler, and with him Y. Polani and M. Svorai, who managed to escape. See also E. Golomb, *Concealment and Daring* (Hebrew; Tel Aviv, 1955), II, p. 260ff.

50. 'The Quisling of our Land', *Ha-Aretz*, 12 May 1941. It should be noted that at the time fairly free use was made of the term 'Quisling' in the *Yishuv*. 'The *Yishuv* – towards an overt, serious split?', *Ha-Aretz*, 15 May 1941; and HH, III, pp. 221–2.

51. M[eridor?] to Shu'ali, 12 May 1941. The Galili Archives, H.A.

52. *The Voice of Zion at War. The Voice of Zion Being Set Free*. 14 June 1941. *Ketavim*, I, pp. 73–5. Cf. also the Shai's interpretation of Stern's search for a 'moral justification' for his anti-British line. 'In the Revisionist Camp', ibid.

53. *The Voice of Zion at War, the Voice of Zion Being Set Free*, *Ketavim*, I, p. 83 (apparently June–July 1941).

54. Ibid, pp. 86–7.

55. Ibid.

56. The testimony of H. Kalay, HA; also Weinschal, op. cit., p. 207. H. Canaan, *Two Hundred Days of Anxiety*, pp. 46–7.

57. The testimony of H. Kalay concerning the convention of late November 1941, in HA. Cf. Banai, pp. 70–71, Weinschal, op. cit., pp. 196–209. Eliav, op. cit. p. 192. Niv, op. cit., III, p.183.

58. Stern's image as Shabbetai Zvi was mentioned in the *Ha-Boker* newspaper the day after his assassination. It quoted his acquaintances who related that as a youth in Suwalki he had played the part of Shabbetei Zvi in Zulawaski's play on this topic, and was swept up by the idea. According to the newspaper, this was no coincidence (cf. also Weinschal, op. cit., p. 28).

59. A. Amichal-Yeivin, pp. 224–5.

60. Yellin-Mor, p. 78. With minor alterations this appears in *Etgar*, 25 Jan. 1962.

61. Yellin-Mor, pp. 23–33, 78–9.

62. Y. Banai, *Unknown Soldiers*, pp. 20, 22, 35, 44, 56–7.

63. Scheib, *First Tithe*, p. xli.

64. M. Begin, to S. Yunitchman, Vilna, 8 Jan. 1940, JI, Yunitchman Files, p. 106. Begin was not precise. While Jabotinsky had indeed opposed the 'mixed battalion', he had none the less supported joining up on the side of the allies, even though the principle of a Hebrew army was not conceded.

65. I. Scheib, 'At a Junction (A Hebrew Battaltion at this Hour)', *Ha-Medina* (Kovna), Nos. 1 and 2, 17 and 23 Feb. 1940.

66. *First Tithe*, pp. 62–3.

67. I. Ben-David [Scheib], 'Was Delayed', *Ha-Mashkif*, 11 July 1941.

68. I. Ben-David [Scheib], 'In Favour of Practical Zionism', *Ha-Mashkif*, 1 Aug. 1941.

69. I. Scheib, *Principles*, p. 7. I am indebted to Dr Eldad (Schieb) for having made available to me the manuscript. On the meaning of the term *geza* (race) in Revisionism, cf. Z. Jabotinsky, 'Lecture on Jewish History' (May 1932), in his *Nation and Society* (Hebrew; Jerusalem, 1959), pp. 161–2.

70. B. Ha-Cohen [Lubotsky], 'Towards a New Zionist Doctrine', *Ha-Mashkif*, 22 Aug. 1941 and E. Jabotinsky to A. Stern (n.d.), YCA, file 40.

71. 'Read and Hand to Your Friend! Do Not Deny the Truth!', No. 5. The original is from Feb.–March 1941, ibid.

72. Order No. 120, 22 Jan. 1941, HA 8/1.

73. 'Information', *Ba-Herev*, Feb.–March 1941.

74. Order No. 117, 5 July 1942; HH, III, pp. 479–81. Not even the fall of Tobruk changed the IZL's view. 'After the Drafts', *Ba-Herev*, Feb.–March 1941.

75. 'The Schism and its Aftermath', *Ba-Herev* (undated: Dec. 1940) by Avishua[?].

76. 'On Guard', *Ba-Herev*, March–April 1941, p. 1; 'The Balkans', ibid., pp. 1–2; 'The Changes in Libya', ibid., p. 2 and a group of news items, 6–7 Aug. 1941, The Revisionist Camp, IZL file 53, HA.

77. 'The Chances in Libya', *Ba-Herev*, March–April 1941, p. 2.

78. 'On the Death of the Leader', ibid. (undated: Dec. 1940–Jan. 1941).

79. Political Office Information, NZO, the Presidency. Internal Distribution. 3 June 1941. *Ba-Herev*, July–Aug. 1941. Y. W[einschal], 'He', *Ha-Hevra*, I, 13 June 1941, p. 195.

80. The Revisionist movement and the O[rganization], undated and unsigned (apparently April 1941). YCA, file 103.

81. Lehi, *Ketavim*, I, pp. 103–4.

82. 'Few Against Many', in 'The Miracle of Hannukah', *Lehi* publications file, HA.

83. 'Those Who Suffer in Sadness', 'A Smile', ibid.

84. 'The Bearer of the Destiny', 'The Individual and the Community after the War', ibid.

85. Eliav, *Wanted*, p. 193. This was Oliver Lyttleton and not Richard Casey, as was presumed by Yellin-Mor, p. 10 and Banai, p. 79.

86. 'IZL in Israel', the High Command (undated). Magnes Archives, P3 2317; the General Archives for Jewish History, Jerusalem.

87. On the failure of the conspiracy see I. Eldad, op. cit., pp. 75–6. Eliav, op. cit., pp. 207–11. For the story of the affair see 'How the Freedom Fighters Fell', *Ketavim*, I, Jan.–Feb. 1944, pp.345–52. For the trial of Lavstein and Svorai, see ibid., pp. 351–62; Y. Banai, op. cit., pp. 90–94, 110–11. Cf. also the report of the inspector-general of the police, Saunders, of 20 February 1942 to the chief secretary, Most Secret. HA, A 51/8 B. The report is entirely based on Morton's version, which he wrote in his position as head of the CID in the Lydda district: *Just the Job. Some Experiences of a Colonial Policeman* (London, 1957), p. 145; see further, Eldad, op. cit., pp. 79–81; Yellin-Mor, op. cit., pp. 85–6; Y. Banai, op. cit., pp.112–13.

88. Agency Executive Protocol, 25 Jan. 1942, No. 22, Vol. 34, CZA; M. Sharett, *Political Diary*, V. (Hebrew; Tel Aviv, 1979), pp. 287–8. One week later Shertok was to become very disturbed when *The Times* referred to Stern as the 'Quisling of Palestine'. Here the Government was trying to show that 'the Jews were not all angels . . .'. See Agency Executive Protocol, 1 Feb. 1942. *Political Diary*, ibid., p. 210.

89. Y. Ben-Zvi to M. Shertok, undated. Internal; not for publication. CZA, S25/4765. *Mapai* central committee, 28 Jan. 1942, LPA, 23/42.

90. *Mapai* central committee session, 28 Jan. 1942, LPA.

91. Editorials in *Ha-Mashkif*, 11 and 21 Jan. 1942.

92. Different pictures were published in subsequent editions, on 3 Feb., on 30 April and four more times during May.

93. Political Office, Information, NZO, The Presidency, Internal Distribution. In the *Yishuv* and around 'the Stern group'. 1 March 1942.

94. 'The Kidnappers', *Ha-Mashkif*, 3 March 1942; adduced in the second edition of Weinschal's book (opposite p. 243). British intelligence translated these fliers in their entirety. See Weekly Intelligence Summary, No. 14, 25 Feb. 1942, PRO, WO/169/434.

95. 'A Voice from the Depths . . .', undated, JI K4/13/1.

96. 'Avraham Stern, Martyr; Avraham Amper, Martyr; Zelig Zack, Martyr', *Ba-Herev*,

Feb.–March 1942, p. 8; 'The *Struma* Affair', ibid., 'Our Front', ibid.

97. Opposed to the further recruitment of the Jews of the *Yishuv* to the British army, Eri turned down an offer to join the presidency of the NZO. See his letter to the NZO presidency (undated; summer–autumn 1942), Eri Jabotinsky Files, Container 5, Revisionist movement and *Eretz Israel* file, 1938–50, JI.

98. 'Our Front', *Ba-Herev*, Feb.–March 1942, p. 2. Eri Jabotinsky was particularly outspoken in defence of Stern, whose attempts to ally with Germany he completely ignored. See 24 March 1942, E. Jabotinsky to the Editor of *Zionviews*, CZA, A226/62.

99. Intelligence, Palestine and Transjordan. GSI No. 4/23. Headquarters British Forces, Palestine, 15 Sept., 1939. Political Situation. WO/169/148; Note of an interview with Mr Jabotinsky (6 Sept. 1939), PRO CO/733/401/75266; WO/169/148, Lt. Col. Norton, GSI No. 4/23 29 March 1940. Weekly Political Intelligence Summary, No. 31. (31 July 1940), PRO, FO/371/25235.

100. GSI, 23 July 1940, Political Situation, Jewish (C) Revisionists, ibid.

101. GSI AD/I/3/6 5 Sept. 1940. Political Situation, Jews. d. Revisionist National Army or IZL; ibid.

102. GSI, 18 Sept. 1940, ibid., GSI, 4 Oct. 1940, (b) Revisionists, ibid.

103. Internal Security, 15 Nov. 1940; 27 Nov. 1940, ibid.

104. Weekly Political Intelligence Summary No. 68, 22 Jan. 1941; No. 72, 10 Feb. 1941, PRO, FO/371/29315. PICME to GH MEF, PIC/190/31. Most Secret 6/43/53, 13 May 1943. Wartime Activities of the NZO or the Revisionist Party. FO/921/58.

105. WO/208/1560/PRO Syria *3*, Report No. 526, 7 June 1941.

106. No. 625, Oct. 1941, ibid.

107. 'A Note on Jewish Illegal Organisations, their Activities and Finances'; Secret. Enclosure in MacMichael to Moyne, 16 Oct. 1941. FO/371/31378/E2026. Moyne was very worried by the extreme approach which had developed in the political stand taken by front-ranking Zionist leaders, as he explained in a special memorandum to members of the War Cabinet in September 1941. Cf. G. Cohen, *Churchill and the Question of Palestine, 1939–1942* (Hebrew; Jerusalem, 1976), pp. 90–3.

108. MacMichael to Moyne, 16 Oct. 1941, ibid.

109. MS 5 Dec. 1941. Security Summary M.E. No. 2; No. 8; 24 Dec. 1941, ibid.

110. Weekly Intelligence Review, No. 9, 21 Jan. 1942, WO/169/4334.

111. HH, III, pp. 141, 1630. CID, Palestine, A. Saunders, inspector-general to Chief Secretary. 30 Jan. 1942. Jewish Affairs. Secret. CO/733/445/75969/1.

112. Monthly Summary, 16 March 1942 1–31 Jan. 1942. WO/169/4334.

113. GOC Palestine to WO C-in-C ME. Jewish Organisations. Stern Group. 12 Feb. 1942. CO/733/445/759691/1. Weekly Intelligence Summary, 18 Feb. 1942. No. 13. WO/169/4334.

114. Security Summary, No. 24, 26 Feb. 1942 WO/208/1561.

115. HC to SSC, tel. No. 230. 24 Feb. 1942. CO/733/445.

116. Most Secret, Security Summary, Middle East, No. 6, 30 April 1942. WO/208/1561; No. 43, ibid., 25 May 1942.

117. Ibid, No. 51, 4 June 1942; No. 53, 11 June 1942; No. 55, 18 June 1942; No. 61, 13 July 1942. WO/169/4334.

118. 'The Man in the Attic', *He-Hazit*, I, June–July 1943, *Ketavim*, I, p. 125 (according to Eldad, the writer was E. Katz.

119. Together with Zack and Amper. Jan./Feb. 1943–Jan./Feb. 1944, *Ha'Ma'as* (The Deed), a newspaper for *Lehi* youth; *Ketavim*, I, pp. 328 and 345ff.

120. Yair. *Yair*, 25 Shevet 5702–25 Shevet 5704 (Feb. 1942–Feb. 1944). Ibid. pp. 371–2.

121. [Eldad], 'His Life and Death', ibid., pp. 375–6.

122. Ibid., pp.377–80.

123. [Eldad], 'His Image', ibid., pp. 379–81.

124. Ibid., pp. 382–3.

125. 'His Road to Independence', ibid., pp. 383–6.

126. 'The Leader', ibid., pp. 395–6; Yellin-Mor, op. cit., pp.83–4. Cf. also Kalay's testimony in HA that 'Yair' was the victim of an idea he did not create.

127. A letter to the editors of *He-Hazit*, *Ba-Herev*, March–April 1944, pp. 27–8.

128. 'A Reply to the Dissidents. C. Revolutionary History', ibid., p. 35.
129. The term was first used by Maurice Barrès; for a definition see above, n. 23.
130. 'Of His Sayings', *Yair*. *Ketavim*, I, pp. 397–8. 'In My Blood You Will Ever Live', p. 145.
131. Stern was influenced by Klausner's writings and messianic exegesis. He deliberately chose the name 'Yair', intending to continue in the footsteps of the hero of Massada. *Ketavim*, II, p. 377.
132. The Meeting of Y.S. [Yitzchak Sadeh] with 'Yair' (15) 19 Oct. 1941, HA, A 8/51c.
133. Following 'Headings for a Lecture' found in the possession of M. Svorai at the time of his arrest in Jan. 1942 and read out at his trial on 27 April 1942 *Ketavim*, I, p. 357.
134. YCA, file 56, untitled, signed 'Aryeh' (Kotzer – so Eldad supposes). Yet, for Stern, victory for the underground within the *Yishuv* would be achieved through an alternative foreign policy, when the international constellation seemed right, rather than by exploitation of the social question, which required a much larger organisation. In any case, Stern himself was not much interested in social issues, and paid only lip-service to the concept of a 'just regime'. See 'The IZL in Israel', *Ketavim*, I, p. 102.
135. Scheib, *First Tithe*, p. 83; Yellin-Mor, op. cit., p. 85.
136. *The Voice of the Hebrew Underground, The Voice of the Freedom Fighters of Israel*. Undated, 'The IZL in Israel', *Lehi* leaflet file, HA (No. 241); Eldad, op. cit., p. 81.
137. 'To the Youth and the Hebrew Nation in Eretz Israel', *Ketavim*, I, pp. 110–11 4 Aug. 1942).
138. Arrested members of 'the IZL in Israel' claimed that the officer who dealt with them was named Brigadier Ballantine. I have not been able to trace an officer of that name. The affair was recounted for the first time in *Ha-Ma'as*, XXIV, Oct.–Nov. 1946, *Ketavim*, II, pp. 265–8. See also M. Shmuelvitch, *In Red Days*, pp. 22–32. Yellin-Mor exaggerates when he claims that the authorities were in trouble and so made that proposal: op. cit., pp. 95–100.
139. A Selman, 'From the Detainees of Mazra to Moshe Shertok, Nov. 1942: CZA, S25/7915. Shertok handed the letter over to Ben-Gurion, Dov Joseph, Reuven Zaslani and Teddy Kollek: M.S. to T.K., 24 Nov. 1942, ibid.
140. Cf. 'X', 'If not now, then when? On the Hebrew Army Affair', *Ha-Madrich*, Officers' Forum, Internal, No. 6, Oct. 1942, pp. 49–51. —, 'American Methods of Propaganda for the Hebrew Army', ibid., pp. 46–9. M. Ben-Zeev [M. Begin], 'Plans for a Zionist Programme', ibid., pp.53–6. Main headline, *Herut*, No. 4, 1 May 1942.
141. [Eldad], 'The Second Front of the Hebrew People', *Ketavim*, I, pp. 111–14. For a different interpretation of Moyne's speech, see B. Wasserstein, 'New Light on the Moyne Murder', *Midstream*, XXVI, 3 (March 1980), pp. 30–8.
142. *Herut*, No. 5, 24 May 1942. HH, III, pp. 481, 1682.
143. 'Zionism as grasped by the heart [IZL]', *Ba-Herev*, March–April 1942.
144. M. Ben-Zeev [Begin], '1917–1942', *Ha-Madrich*, Officers' Forum, Internal, No. 8, Vol. B, Sept. 1942, pp. 10–13.
145. M. Ben-Zeev [Begin], 'Plans for a Zionist Programme', ibid.
146. HH, III, pp. 486, 1864.
147. Niv, op. cit., III, pp. 194–5. Circular. 'Brothers Lehi!', undated, YHA, file 29.
148. Circular to the Organisation LHB, Dec. 1942, ibid. Internal Circular to *Lehi* Brethren (20 Nov. 1942), ibid. 'Tuvia Group' [Khanchinsky-Chen-Zion] was the first to use the name '*Lehi*'.
149. Internal Circular To *Lehi* Brethren, 14 Jan. 1943, ibid.

## CHAPTER 5 (pp.111–121)

1. [N. Friedman-Yellin], 'To Liquidate the Prisons!' (Jan. 1943), from a lost leaflet, *Ba-Mahteret* in *Ketavim*, I, pp. 151–4. See also Yellin-Mor, op. cit., p. 125 and Friedman-Yellin to Eldad, undated [summer 1943], YHA, file 52.
2. The Shai claimed that Giladi had been the main participant in Vilenchik's assassination on 25 Feb. 1943; 13 May 1943, HA 5/8a. *Ha-Mashkif* (4 March 1943) accused *Mapai* of responsibility.

3. 'Yes, Rescue is Possible!', *Herut*, 7, 1 Feb. 1943; 'The Positive and the Negative at Biltmore', *Herut*, 8, 15 Feb. 1943.
4. 'A New Ally', *Herut*, 7, 1 Feb. 1943. 'Iraq intends to achieve a Pan-Arab Union with British Encouragement', ibid.
5. M. Ben Zeev [Begin], 'Russia and Zionism', *Ha-Madrich*, Forum for Commanding Officers, Internal, No. 3, Vol. 11, Feb. 1943.
6. M. Ben Zeev [Begin], 'The Main Question', *Ha-Madrich*, April 1942, pp. 224–6.
7. M. Ben Zeev [Begin], 'In the Days of Confusion', *Ha-Madrich*, May 1943, pp. 4–7; 'The British Regime Prepares for a Slaughter of Jews in *Eretz Israel*', *Herut*, 13, 17 May 1943.
8. A. Weinschal, 'Don't Be Late', *Ha-Hevrah*, 39, pp. 499–500, and also his open letter to Ben-Gurion, ibid., 41, pp. 534–5.
9. B. Ha-Cohen [Lubotsky], 'Water Up to the Nose', *Ha-Mashkif*, 17 May 1943. See also U. Avneri [Osterman], 'A Total Disavowal', ibid.
10. Friedman-Yellin to Eldad, undated (spring 1943), YHA, file 52.
11. Yellin-Mor, pp. 101–2, 108.
12. As was carried out in the army paymaster's office in Haifa. Banai, pp. 141–2.
13. Banai, p. 145; Yellin-Mor, p. 124.
14. In general the sources are identical, but hostile to Giladi. Shamir brought the decision to kill his rival before the 13 responsible leaders of *Lehi* after he had already been liquidated, claiming that he was ready to be tried for this. *A posteriori*, the decision received unanimous approval. Aryeh Kotzer (*Red Carpet*, pp. 140–89, 255) relates the opposite: he claims that the atmosphere hostile to Giladi was generated by his girlfriend, that his utterances reflected no more than childish boasting, and that his liquidation was 'a crime'. The affair is so obscure that even the exact date of Giladi's liquidation is unknown.
15. From an unpublished issue of *He-Hazit* (apparently too bold to be printed), 8, HH, *Lehi* Printed Matter. Cf. also Y. Okev, 'The Black Deed' (Dec. 1948–Jan. 1949), pp. 14–15.
16. 'The Front', *He-Hazit*, 1, June–July 1943, *Ketavim*, 1, p. 121.
17. 'Foundation Stones, I', *Ha-Hevrah*, 43, ibid., pp. 127–9.
18. 'The Man in the Attic', *He-Hazit*, 1, June-July 1943, ibid., pp. 123–5; [Avidan], 'The Other Side of the Coin', ibid., pp. 133–4; 'The Front', ibid., pp. 135–6.
19. Eldad, 'Foundation Stones, II, Palestine and *Eretz Israel*, ibid., pp. 137–8; [N. Friedman-Yellin], 'England, Zionism and the Hebrew Freedom Movement between Two World Wars', ibid., pp. 139–41.
20. 'A Statement for Internal Consumption', ibid., p. 171.
21. 'Terrorism', *He-Hazit*, II, ibid., pp. 141–4.
22. 'The Underground, Propaganda for the Public', *He-Hazit*, IV, Sept.–Oct. 1943, ibid., pp. 193–4; 'Foundation Stones, IV: Of a Minority and a Majority', ibid., p. 194.
23. 'Thus People Fought for Freedom: Thought and Deed in the Rebirth of Italy' (copied from M. Beilinson's book, *In the Days of the Rebirth of Italy*, 1930), ibid., pp. 233–6. According to Friedman-Yellin, Lilian Voinitz's book on the liberation of Italy, *Insurrection*, served as an important educational volume in the *Lehi*. Yellin-Mor, p. 362; 'Foundation Stones, IV', *Ketavim*, I, p. 199.
24. 'The Underground, Propaganda for the Public', *He-Hazit*, V, ibid., p. 217.
25. [Eldad], 'Foundation Stones, IV: Of a Minority and a Majority', ibid., pp. 199–202.
26. 'A Short Outline of Hebrew Diplomacy in our Time', ibid., pp. 143–6 (apparently written by Friedman-Yellin).
27. 'The Illusion: The Peace Conference', ibid., pp. 161–6. In his memoirs (pp. 345–6), Yellin-Mor subsequently dated the shift in his views on the Soviet Union to the article he wrote three months later, entitled 'Political Articles. Between the Baltic and the Adriatic Seas', *Ketavim*, I, pp. 303–8.
28. 'The Great Longing', ibid., p. 167.
29. 'From Other Sources', ibid., pp. 169–70; in H. Kohn, *Nationalism and Imperialism in the Hitherto East* (London, 1932).
30. 'Who is he? Is it not yet clear?', *Ketavim*, I, pp. 173–4.

31. 'Twenty Escaped from the Latrun Concentration Camp', *He-Hazit*, V, ibid., pp. 237–42.
32. Born in Grodno (Poland) in 1913, Friedman-Yellin had been one of Stern's closest assistants in inter-war Poland.
33. [Friedman-Yellin], 'Political Articles: Anglo-French Relations in the Shade of Lebanon', ibid., pp. 225–30.
34. [Friedman-Yellin], 'Political Articles', ibid., pp. 303–8; 'The Sinking of Great Britain', ibid., pp. 309–12. Nehru is cited in *He-Hazit*, VII, January 1944, ibid., pp. 313–16. Nehru's *Letters from Prison* had shortly before this been published by Ha-Kibbutz Ha-Meuhad.
35. 'Zionism of Construction, Political Zionism and a War of Liberation', *Ketavim*, I, pp. 255–7.
36. 'Public Opinion and Public Support for the Freedom Movement', *He-Hazit*, VI, ibid., pp. 261–3.
37. 'The Hebrew Worker', ibid., pp. 293–300.
38. See below, Chapter 12. M. Getter, 'The Ideology of the *Lehi* Movement', (unpublished MA thesis, Tel Aviv University, 1967), pp. 178ff, argues that this article typifies *Lehi*'s movement towards the left. That is not so; as will be seen, the shift did not occur until later.
39. Y. Shavit, 'Begin's Road to Revolt (1938–44)', in *The Mythologies of the Right Wing*, pp. 125–52, deals with the IZL's hesitations regarding 'the revolt'. For the *Am Lohem* affair cf. HH III, pp. 490ff., and Bauer, *Diplomacy and Resistance*, pp. 267–8. Also Eldad, *First Tithe*, pp. 93–4.
40. 'Confessions', pp. 4–12 of an unprinted issue of *He-Hazit* (early 1944); HA, file of *Lehi* printed matter.
41. 'The Three Mournings of Tammuz', ibid.
42. 'On the Zionist Front (a tragi-comic script)', ibid. Somewhere deep in its political consciousness it appreciated that it owed its origins to Jabotinsky, even though its members had revolted against him. An illustration of *Lehi*'s ambivalence is provided by Eldad's 'Zeev Jabotinksy: Three Years Since His Passing' (ibid., pp. 147–8), whose tone is generally one of admiration. Jabotinsky is criticised on only two points. First, he was not sufficiently brutal; second, he had guaranteed the Arabs equal status in the future Hebrew state.

## CHAPTER 6 (pp. 122–147)

1. On the creation of the Yair myth see 'March 1942–March 1944' (Hebrew), *Ketavim*, I, pp. 325–8; on the attempt on the life of the High Commissioner: IGP, CID (A.F. Giles) to Chief Secretary, 18 Feb. 1944, Secret, Jewish Affairs, The Revisionist Party, Intelligence Summary No. 3/44, PRO, FO 921/153.

   British intelligence had first warned of the renewal of the Stern gang's activities as early as 10 Aug. 1943 (PRO, WO 208/1562 No. 143) and first referred to *Lehi* by its new name on 30 Aug. 1943 (ibid., No. 146). Its estimates of *Lehi*'s membership (some 2,000 (!) in March 1944) were clearly exaggerated. Compare ibid., No. 171 with R. Newton's report in Hall to Attlee, Bevin and Morrison, 17 Oct. 1945, PRO, FO 371/4380/E8197/G.
2. 'Three Choices' *Ketavim* I, pp. 327–30. Eldad later claimed that the IZL did indeed fear mass defections to the *Lehi*. See 'Who and What were Ya'ir and Lehi', *Sulam*, April 1959, p. 28.
3. 'The Front', *He-Hazit*, 8, Feb.–March 1944; *Ketavim*, I, pp. 409–12.
4. 'The Palestinian Compound', *Ketavim*, I, pp. 329–32. *Lehi* seems also to have been influenced by the emphasis placed on the motif of the Holocaust in the IZL's declaration of its rebellion. See, for example, *He-Hazit*, ibid., pp. 409–12.
5. For conflicting accounts of this incident, see Yellin-Mor, pp. 147–8 and op. cit., *Mishmar*, 13 and 18 Feb. 1944. *Lehi*'s manifesto in YHA, file 49, *Ketavim*, I, pp. 343–4 and Appendix B in Giles to Chief Secretary, 18 Feb. 1944, PRO, FO 921/153.
6. Yellin-Mor, op. cit., pp. 147–50.
7. Meeting of *Mapai* secretariat, 17 Feb. 1944, LPA.

8. For Lord Moyne's appointment, see 'Internal memorandum to the Supporters of Israel's Liberation', I (Feb. 1944), *Ketavim*, I, pp. 458–60. In fact, recent research suggests that Moyne was no worse than other British decision-makers. He supported partition and the establishment of a Jewish state. See N. Katzburg, *The Palestine Problem in British Policy, 1940–1945* (Hebrew; Jerusalem, 1978), pp. 103–4 and M.J. Cohen, *Palestine, Retreat from the Mandate, 1936–45* (London, 1978), pp. 169–70.

9. 'A Leadership for the People' *He-Hazit*, 8 (March–April 1944), *Ketavim*, I, pp. 417–18 and *Ha-Hevrah*, No. 44 (July 1943), ibid., pp. 578–9.

10. Ibid., pp. 419–20.

11. *Herut*, 27, 28 Feb. 1944.

12. The suspicion was voiced in A. Selman to 'Itamar', 5 May 1944, HA, Golomb files, No. 13. Compare, however, Giles to Chief Secretary, 18 Feb. 1944, n.1 above.

13. See Banai, *Unknown Soldiers*, pp. 175–6 and 'Elisha', (Y. Aharonson), 'Thoughts of a Hebrew Revolutionary', March 1944, *Ketavim*, I, pp. 479–80. For examples of IZL counter-propaganda, see, for example, the 'announcement' of 27 March 1944 in *Ba-Herev*, April 1944, esp. pp. 33–4.

14. Eldad, *First Tithe*, pp. 112–13.

15. On the imminence of war, see 'Means', *Ketavim*, I, pp. 450–1 and 'Towards Coming Events', ibid., p. 460. On the 'Supporters', see 'Internal memorandum to the Supporters of the Freedom of Israel', 1, March 1944, ibid., pp. 443–8. In fact, nothing came of this idea and the memorandum itself remained an isolated pamphlet.

16. ['Elisha'], 'From the Thoughts of a Hebrew Revolutionary' (March 1944), ibid., pp. 473, 480–83. Far different – and much less complementary – was the attitude towards the *Ahdut Ha-Avodah* movement, which had recently separated from *Mapai* and seemed to be moving leftwards, towards *Ha-Shomer Ha-Tsair* and *Poale Zion Smol*. See 'Split in *Mapai*', *He-Hazit*, 11, June–July 1944, *Ketavim*, I, pp. 633–4 and Banai, op. cit., p. 185.

17. 'Thoughts of a Hebrew Revolutionary', *Ketavim*, I, pp. 481–3.

18. 'Political Notes – Turkey's Attitude', ibid., pp. 425–30 and (on the USSR), 'Astrology and Biology: A Dialogue', ibid., p. 435.

19. Meeting of the *Mapai* political committee, Givat Brenner, 27 March 1944, LPA.

20. See Heller, *The Struggle for Statehood*, pp. 392–5 and HH, III, p. 532.

21. 'Gera' [Shimon] to Golomb, 11 May 1944, YHA, file 15 and Golomb to 'Shimon' [Friedman-Yellin], 16 May 1944, HA. 'Dissidents', 8/21a; also HH, III, p. 517. On the 'Black List', see *Ketavim*, I, pp. 521–32. Two executions (of Flesh and Gutovich, respectively) had been carried out on 31 March and 10 May 1944.

22. 'Letters to an imprisoned comrade' [that is, to Y. Galili], no date, *Le-Haver* ('Ha-Haganah'), March 1944, I, pp. 8–10, 13–17.

23. 'Asher' [Hanoch Bzhozah], '"Fighters of Israel" or Enemies of Israel: Sternism without a Mask.' Socialist Union for a National Policy. People and World (March 1944), pp. 2–16. See Also B. Haifai [Balti], 'On "Zion in the Underground"', *Kol Ha-Am*, 16 August 1944, who claimed that Stern had met with Mussolini in 1936.

24. [Y. Ratosh], 'Letter to the Fighters for the Freedom of Israel' (Spring 1944). See also his memoirs, *Earliest Days* (Hebrew; Tel Aviv, 1980), pp. 17–18, 22–28.

25. Golomb to 'Shimon' [Friedman-Yellin], 16 May 1944, HA file 8/21a.

26. 'Letter to the Newspaper Editors', 16 May 1944, *Ketavim*, I, pp. 487–8.

27. See, for example, the articles entitled 'The Enforcement of the National Will', 'The Ledger of Time', and 'More on National Discipline and Rule' in ibid., pp. 571–4 and 581–4. On the Jewish tradition of activist warfare in the homeland (as opposed to defensive warfare in the diaspora): [Friedman-Yellin], 'Defensive War or Patriotic War?', ibid., pp. 513–16 (ms in YHA, file 52).

28. Eldad, *First Tithe*, pp. 134ff and Yellin-Mor, *Lehi*, p. 165. On the demand to be treated as prisoners of war, see 'Our Demand: A War Trial', *Ketavim*, I, pp. 605–8.

29. 'Gallows', *He-Hazit*, 11 (June–Aug. 1944), *Ketavim*, I, pp. 629–32. For indications of the process whereby one of the defendants (Shmuelevitch) convinced himself to face the gallows, see 'Two Letters from the Condemned Cell to Rabbi Aryie Levine', ibid., pp. 643–4.

30. Shmuelevitch was tried on 26–27 June 1944 and, although condemned to death for shooting policemen, was pardoned on 6 July. For the proceedings of the case, see ibid., pp. 755–66 and Shmuelevitch's own memoirs, *In Red Days* (1949 ed.). On the trials of Tavori (29 May), Hameiri-Begin (13–14 June), Shapira (19 June) and Spielman (20 June), see *Ketavim*, I, pp. 743–54. Tavori was sentenced to seven years' imprisonment, Hameiri-Begin to 12, Shapira to four and Spielman to ten.
31. 'Letter to a Comrade in Jail', op. cit., pp. 29–33; see also 'Bulletin of the *Ahdut Ha-Avodah* Movement', 15 Sept. 1944) (internal, not for sale).
32. 'The Trials', *Herut*, 29, 9 July 1944. According to Begin (*The Revolt* [Hebrew], p. 334), the IZL offered to spring Shmuelevitch from prison, but he was meanwhile pardoned.
33. *Ha-Mashkif*, leading article, 16 July 1944. For Eldad's contacts with Begin at this time, and his criticism of some of Begin's attitudes, see *First Tithe*, p. 116.
34. [Y. Sheib], 'Core and Peel in Nietzsche's Teaching', *Ketavim*, I, pp. 785–8.
35. 'Dangers', 'Mood' and 'Where Do We Stand' in *Ha-Mahteret* (internal), (July 1944), pp. 3–10, 10–16 and 16–27. HA. Lehi file, printed matter.
36. [Friedman-Yellin], 'Political Notes – Decisions in Europe', *He-Hazit*, 13 Sept. 1944, *Ketavim*, I, pp. 703–8 and Yellin-Mor, *Lehi*, pp. 346–7. Earlier intimations – in 'On Political Understanding', *Ketavim*, I, pp. 659–64.
37. See the articles 'A Helpful Debate', 'An Addition to the Theory of Terrorism', 'How Did they React' and 'Towards a Good Year', in *Ketavim*, I, pp. 621–8, 669–72, 677–80 and 683–4.
38. 'Foreign Rule – A Parasite on the Body of the Nation' and 'On the Slice of Bread', ibid., pp. 651–3 and 697–8.
39. [Eldad], 'The Class War and the War of Liberation', *He-Hazit*, 17, April 1945, *Ketavim*, I, pp. 901–6. The attribution to Eldad's authorship was made by Ginosar in the 'Fighters' Conference' of 1949; see *Protocol* (1949), p. 12.
40. 'We shall Fight the Enemy Everywhere'; 'The Road to Liberation – Immigration and Policy, a Hebrew Policy, War Against Foreign Rule' (Sept. 1944); 'What is Gaulleism?', *Ketavim*, I, pp. 715–18; 722–34; 799–802.
41. 6 Sept. 1944, HA 21/8.
42. Bauer, *Diplomacy and Resistance* [Hebrew], pp. 272–8. Compare the assurances received by Weizmann in his meeting with Churchill on 4 Nov. 1944, Weizmann, *Letters*, Vol. 21, No. 225.
43. 'Letter: To Every Faithful Hebrew, To All the Organised Hebrew Youth in the Homeland' (Oct. 1944); and 'The Word of Those who Pass Through Fire and Water', *Ketavim*, I, pp. 765–72.
44. For the Sneh-Begin talks on 8 Oct. 1944, see HH, III, pp. 1887–93 and Begin, *The Revolt* (Hebrew), pp. 197–9. For the talks between Begin (and Lankin) and Golomb on 31 Oct. see Lev-Ami, 'Protocols of the IZL, July–November 1944', *Ha-Zionut*, Vol. 4 (Hebrew), pp. 432–40.
45. Eldad, *First Tithe*, pp. 97–8, 115–16.
46. Yellin-Mor, *Lehi*, pp. 178–81. In *The Revolt*, Begin makes no mention of the negotiations with Lehi. See, however, his *In the Underground*, I, pp. 90–2. Friedman-Yellin's recollection of the agreement concerning an announcement to the Arabs might be incorrect, and perhaps refers to a later agreement. Little information can be gleaned from Begin's 'To Our Arab Neighbours', *Herut*, 34 (15 Sept. 1944). See also below.
47. Lev-Ami, *Protocols*, pp. 394–5.
48. Meeting of IZL command on 23 Aug. 1944, Lev-Ami, ibid., pp. 408–9.
49. Meeting of IZL command, 1 Sept. 1944; Begin to Friedman-Yellin, 4 Sept. 1944, and meeting of IZL command, 29 Sept. 1944: all in Lev-Ami, *Protocols*, pp. 412–18.
50. The manifesto, 'The IZL in *Eretz Israel*, Lehi–Manifesto', in *Ketavim*, I, pp. 719–20. On the background, see Yellin-Mor, *Lehi*, pp. 209, 230–31; HH, III, p. 533 and (for the meeting of the IZL command on 16 Oct. 1944) Lev-Ami, *Protocols*, pp. 423–4.
51. In *Lehi* (pp. 211–12), Yellin-Mor maintains that Stern had comtemplated the assassination of the Minister-Resident as early as 1941.
52. Bet Tsouri, the elder of the two, had also come under the 'Canaanite' influence of Ratosh's brothers. See Amir, 'The Harp and the Sword' (Hebrew), *Keshet*, 18(i),

(1975), pp. 41, 43. For details of the mission, see Frank, *The Deed* (New York, 1963). For one example of rank-and-file despondency, see Eli, *We have Enlisted for Life* (Hebrew; Tel Aviv, 1969), pp. 115–16.

53. 'Hebrews in the Homeland' (Nov. 1944) and 'The Front' (Dec. 1944), in, respectively, *Ketavim*, I, pp. 737–8 and 809–10. The attacks on Churchill were uncalled for. In fact, it was he who (unknown to anyone in the *Yishuv*) prevented the initiation of extreme measures after the assassination. Cf. Y. Gelber, 'Zionists and British in Palestine in the Shadow of Jewish Revolt, 1942–1944', *Ha-Zionut* (Hebrew), Vol. 7, p. 392; M.J. Cohen, 'The Moyne Assassination: A Political Analysis', *Middle Eastern Studies*, XV (Oct. 1979), pp. 358–83; and the War Office to C-in-C, Middle East, 18 Nov. 1944, Top Secret, Immediate, PRO, WO/208/1706.

54. For examples of such broadsides, whose prime target was Weizmann, see 'In the Rear', *He-Hazit*, 15, *Ketavim*, I, pp. 811–18; 'Learn Hebrew', ibid., pp. 835–6. Eldad was throughout opposed to any agreement with the *Haganah* (although not to a cessation of operations), and claims that he did not learn about it until he came across a copy of *He-Hazit* (whose original I have been unable to trace). See Eldad, *First Tithe*, pp. 170–2 and Begin, *The Revolt* (Hebrew), p. 208. Friedman-Yellin's version is in *Lehi*, pp. 233–9, 264. See also HH, Vol. III, p. 517.

55. 'One against the Other' (Nov. 1944), *Ketavim*, I, pp. 807–8.

56. Although the court forbade publication of the statements by the accused, their speeches were reported to Friedman-Yellin by Gerold Frank (see Yellin-Mor, *Lehi*, pp. 250–51) and published by *Lehi* in March 1945 (see *Ketavim*, I, pp. 925–30). For the backgrounds of the two accused see Frank, *The Deed*.

57. For illustrations of these themes, see 'Hebrews in the Homeland!' (April 1945), *Ketavim*, I, pp. 937–8; 'In the Light of the Gallows', ibid., p. 939; 'Thus they went to the Gallows', ibid., pp. 969–70; and 'With Much Love and Anger', ibid., p. 952.

58. See C.E. Boehlen, *Witness to History* (New York, 1973), pp. 370–1 and B. Wasserstein, 'New Light on the Moyne Murder', *Midstream*, XXVI (1981), p. 38. For the claim to possible influence on the Soviets, see Yellin-Mor, *Lehi*, p. 347.

59. On initial Jewish Agency fears, see N. Wilensky to M. Shertok, 27 Dec. 1944, CZA, S25/5676. For a later report, see M. Kapeliuk (*Davar* correspondent in Cairo) to Ben-Gurion, 25 Feb. 1945, ibid. He added: 'If we had a few boys like these [Hakim and Bet Tsouri] we would get rid of the English.

60. Heller, *The Struggle for Statehood*, p. 68, n. 131 and Cohen, *Moyne*, pp. 367–8. No protocol has survived, and information on the meeting is gleaned from British intelligence sources. Rabbi Fishman thereafter resigned for the space of two weeks, as did Gruenbaum (apparently at the beginning of November, returning to the Agency executive only in March). See Bauer, *Diplomacy and Resistance* (Hebrew), p. 278, n. 46.

61. Shertok read the announcements (accepted unopposed) at the second of the two Jewish Agency executive meetings held on 7 November, See *Jewish Agency Protocols*, Nos. 14, 15.

62. This was in response to Shaul Meirov who, while admitting collaboration to be a serious matter, could see no other option. See protocol in LPA, 44/26 pp. 22–40.

63. Protocol in Archive of the *Histadrut* executive.

64. Protocol of the speech in CZA, S25/1804; see also Heller, op. cit., pp. 411–15. For Weizmann's address to the executive of the Jewish Agency on 19 Nov. and 16 Dec., see Protocols Nos. 17 and 23, Vol. 44, CZA, ibid.

65. Ibid.

66. Delivered on 17 Nov. See *Hansard, House of Commons Debates*, 5th Series, Vol. 404, col. 2242.

67. See *The Sixth Histadrut Conference, 20–21 November 1944* (Tel Aviv, 1944), p. 42.

68. Weizmann, *Letters*, Vol. 21, No. 235. Police records give the precise numbers as 561 and 284. See Cohen, 'Moyne', p. 369.

69. See minute by J.S. Bennett, 22 Nov. 1944, Top Secret, PRO, WO/208/1562. For earlier assessments, see PIC Paper No. 57, Secret, PIC/335, 'The Possibility of IZL Having Joined Forces with Haganah', PIC ME, 19 July 1944, (c), PRO, FO/921/153.

The British authorities closely followed the intensification of terrorist activities in 1944, and translated into English several of the 'dissident' leaflets. Many were enclosed in the fortnightly reports submitted by Major H. Hanluke, Defence Security Officer. See PRO, WO/169/1581.

70. J.S. Bennett to Sir W. Croft, 2 Dec. 1944, PRO, FO/921/154. Croft agreed to this suggestion, but was overruled by the High Commissioner, who argued (inter alia) against paying *Lehi* the compliment of arguing with the movement. See Shaw to Croft, 22 Dec. 1944, Secret, ibid.

71. Hoffman, *British Strategy*, pp. 67–74.

72. Compare '1939–1944', *Herut*, 33, 1 Sept. 1944, 'Only a fighting people merits independence', ibid., 34, 15 Sept. 1944, 'The war effort', ibid., 37, 31 Oct. 1944.

73. '*Eretz Israel* – an open wound in the body of the British Empire?', *Herut*, 33, 1 Sept. 1944. Note that while the *Lehi* had earlier planned to assassinate MacMichael, IZL planned to kidnap him. Cf. meetings of the IZL command, 2 and 8 Aug. 1944 in Lev-Ami, 'Protcols', p. 398 and 'Information in the path of the police', *Herut*, ibid.

74. 'Not to give in', *Herut*, 38, 16 Nov. 1944. See also M. Begin, *In the Underground*, (Hebrew), Vol. 1, p. 165 fn., and *Sekirah* (Most Secret), Nov. 1944), p. 5 in JI C4 – 2/2/12. For Begin's hopes of an eventual change in Britain's attitude see 'A Reply to Winston Churchill' (Nov. 1944), *In the Underground*, I, pp. 189–96.

75. Compare *Sekirah*, ibid., with the leaflet issued in Feb. 1945 (*In the Underground*, I, pp. 221–3); 'Failure', *Herut*, 39, 3 Dec. 1944; and 'The bloodthirsty rulers have sinned', *Herut*, 46, April 1945.

76. 'Three Years' (Nov. 1944), *Ketavim*, I, p. 856; 'The Two Condemned', *He-Hazit*, 16 (Nov. 1944), ibid., pp. 857–60 and 'The Front', ibid., pp. 859–62.

77. Yellin-Mor, *Lehi*, p.234.

78. On the effect of the 'saison' on the IZL compare the meeting of IZL commanders on 1 Nov. 1944 in Lev-Ami, 'Protocols', p. 429 and 'There will be no civil war', *Herut*, 39, 3 Dec. 1944. See also HH, III, pp. 540–41.

79. 'Manifesto' (May 1945), *Ketavim*, I, pp. 1021–2.

80. Compare Golomb in the *Va'ad Leumi* on 4 June 1945 (CZA, S25/952) with Giles to Shaw, 24 April 1945, Secret. PRO, CO/733/457/75156/151J.

81. 'The Czech example', *Herut*, 49 (Aug. 1945); and 'Memorandum' (June 1945), Begin, *In the Underground*, I, pp. 262–8.

82. 'Announcement' (internal; Sept. 1945), *Ketavim*, I, pp. 1023–4. The IZL claimed that it was wooed by *Lehi*. See *Sekirah* (internal, May 1946), in HA, IZL archive.

83. Although the IZL and *Lehi* were not at all confident that Labour would do so. See *Lehi* 'manifesto' (Aug. 1945), in HA, collection of *Lehi* leaflets; and compare the somewhat less abrasive IZL 'manifesto' of the same period in Begin, *In the Underground*, I, p. 275.

84. This is an interesting viewpoint; it marks *Lehi*'s final break with Stern's philosophy of 'the enemy' which it and 'the IZL in Israel' had followed for many years. See 'In the period of decisions', *He-Hazit*, 16 (Feb. 1945), *Ketavim*, I, pp. 867–72.

85. 'In preparation for the show at San Francisco', *Ketavim*, I, pp. 945–6; 'Middle Eastern Affairs', ibid., pp. 946–8.

86. '*Eretz Israel* in Britain's political system', *He-Hazit*, 17 (March 1945), ibid., pp. 911–12.

87. (Friedman-Yellin), 'A summary of Anglo-Russian relations up to the Crimean Conference', *He-Hazit*, 17, ibid., pp. 919–20. The alternative, of course, was to look for American support; but *Lehi* was correct not to do so. On his return from Yalta, Roosevelt declared that he had learned more about the Middle East in five minutes of talk with Ibn Saud than from all his correspondence with the Zionists. See 'Affairs connected with *Eretz Israel*, ibid., pp. 948–50; 'Excitement and Indifference', ibid., p. 901.

88. See, for example, Sneh's article in *Ha-Aretz*, 27 April 1945, and the reactions in *Ketavim*, I, pp. 1009–10.

89. 'When "masteries" were willed to the Gentiles', *He-Hazit*, 18 (April 1945), ibid., pp. 965–6. It is interesting that although *Lehi* was by this time already recognising the inevitability of a war against the Arabs, it did not yet attempt to portray an alliance

with the Soviets as the key to a solution of the Arab question. See '"Scorched Earth" – a dangerous interpretation', ibid., pp. 985–8; and 'In a straight line' (April 1945), ibid., p. 1012.

90. (Eldad), 'The historic and historic-philosophic debate', *He-Hazit* 16 (Feb. 1945), ibid., pp. 873–5.
91. Ibid., p. 874.
92. 'The chosen people, in a religious, historical and philosophical light', *He-Hazit*, 18 (April 1945), ibid., pp. 962–4.

## CHAPTER 7 (pp. 151–167)

1. 'In the Underground'. Strictly internal. Information material (June–July 1945). *Ketavim*, II, p. 21.
2. Ibid., p. 30.
3. Yellin-Mor, op. cit., p. 269; cf. Begin in *Sekirah*, 25 Sept. 1946. JI K4-12/2/2.
4. D. Horovitz, *A State in the Making* (Hebrew; Jerusalem, 1952), p. 9.
5. 'Only in War will we Reach our Goal', *Ha-Ma'as*, 1 (Oct. 1945), *Ketavim*, II, pp. 33–4.
6. 'This is not the Decision' *Ha-Ma'as*, ibid., pp. 39–40.
7. 'Britain's Wicked Force will not stop the Nation's War for Liberty', *Ha-Ma'as*, II (Dec. 1946), ibid., pp. 45–6.
8. The Voice of the Hebrew Underground, 'To Tel-Aviv the Faithful', Dec. 1945, ibid., pp. 53–6.
9. 'Our Homeland will not be an Imperialist Base', ibid., pp. 51–2.
10. 'The Days were those of Channukah', *Ha-Ma'as*, 3 (Dec. 1945), ibid., p. 64.
11. 'The Failure of Appearances', *Ha-Ma'as*, 6 (April 1946), ibid., pp. 115–16. For the speech, see *Ba-Ma'arakhah*, V, pp. 31–9.
12. The text of the Memorandum in PRO, CO/733/463/75872. Cf. p. 4 of that document with the version in Yellin-Mor, op cit., p. 304. On the origins of the wording see HH, p. 1734. Unlike *Lehi*, the IZL presented its own memorandum to the committee. JI 1/15/4.
13. 'Let the Hebrew Worker be Among those who Rule the Economy', *Ketavim*, II, pp. 81–2.
14. Idem. Soviet valour against Nazism was adopted as an exemplar, even though the Indian struggle against Britain – because the more relevant – was still the more favoured example; ibid., pp. 83–4.
15. The reference is to 'League V (Victory)', *Ha-Ma'as*, 4 (Feb. 1946), ibid., pp. 102–21.
16. Ibid., pp. 105–6.
17. 'The Zionists and "United Hebrew Resistance Movement"', ibid., pp. 10–20.
18. [Shlomo Edelstein] (Haggai Eshed), *The Goal – the Enemy – the War* (n.d., early 1946), pp. 11–38; (Eldad), ibid., pp. 1–11.
19. 'Words of Explanation'; strictly internal; April 1948, *Lehi* file, printed matter, HA, pp. 1–10.
20. Dated April 1946; IZL Archives HA. Cf. his *First Tithe*, pp. 286–90.
21. 'Between Us and the IZL', information material, April 1946.
22. This charge was somewhat misplaced. The IZL was not in fact the anti-Russian and pro-American organisation of *Lehi*'s caricature. See, respectively, *Herut*, 56, March 1946 and *Sekirah*, strictly secret, May 1946. JI 2/2/12 – K4.
23. 'Between Us and the IZL', (above, n. 21), pp. 22–6.
24. *First Tithe*, pp. 286–90.
25. 'What have we Gained during the [past] Half Year?', information material, April 1946, pp. 26–30. Much of *Lehi*'s funds came from robberies (euphemistically termed 'expropriations') which had brought in some 81,000 Palestine pounds. Cf. Yellin-Mor, pp. 443–6.
26. Information material, pp. 30–33.
27. IZL. Command communiqué No. 15, June 1946. 'On the Union talks between Ourselves and the *Lehi*'. JI; poster collection.
28. *Sekirah*. Internal. IZL Archive, HA. Begin's publications of the 1950s, issued at a time when he sought to bring former members of *Lehi* into his fold, contain no

references to this embarrassing review. See also *Sekirah*, 25 Sept. 1946, where it is claimed that documents have been discovered which prove *Lehi*'s efforts to unite with the *Haganah*. JI 2/2/12 – K4.

29. *Lehi*'s response was that the 'battle' had been planned in retaliation for the murder of Jews in Tel Aviv and elsewhere. See also the recollection of the operation's commander, Y. Banai, in *Unknown Soldiers*, p. 403.

30. Yellin-Mor, pp. 308–12.

31. Idem. The *merkaz* admitted the contradiction, but maintained that there was in any case not 'the faintest chance' that the British would accept the implied deal. Eli, *We Have Enlisted for Life*, pp. 163–4.

32. *Ba-Mahteret*, *Ketavim*, II, pp. 203–5 and Shamir's later recollections in *Ha-Ma'as*, 6 (88), 16 June 1949. In May 1946, the *Haganah* estimated that the total membership of *Lehi* was only 300. Memorandum, 22 May 1946, HA, 21/8b.

33. Y. Heller, 'From the Black Sabbath to Partition: The summer of 1946 as a Turning-Point in the Political History of Zionism', *Zion* (Hebrew), Vol. 43 (1978), pp. 331–5; M.J. Cohen, *Palestine and the Great Powers*, pp. 84–90.

34. 'How to Fight at This Hour', *Ha-Ma'as*, July 1946, *Ketavim*, II, pp. 135–62; see also the various articles of the same period in ibid., pp. 129–42 and 'Ha-Shabbat Ha-Gedolah' [the Great Sabbath], *Ba-Mahteret*, strictly internal (late Aug.–late Sept. 1946), ibid., pp. 206–7.

35. 'Accompanied Victims', *Ha-Ma'as*, 11, 1 July 1946, ibid., pp. 145–6. Unlike the IZL, *Lehi* did express its sympathy with the Arab victims of the explosion: 'they are not our enemies and we shall not hate them. They are only tools of a regime which is also foreign to them.' Idem, July 1946 (see also Yellin-Mor's memoirs, p. 327).

36. 'Z. Jabotinsky [In Memoriam]', *Ha-Ma'as*, 11, Aug. 1946, *Ketavim*, II, pp. 147–8. The reference is all the more instructive when it is noted that the IZL itself did not mention this particular anniversary, choosing instead commemorating the death of Raziel. See *Herut*, 58, May 1946.

37. Eldad, op. cit., pp. 289–90. On reactions to the trials of Gruner compare M. Begin, *In the Underground* (Hebrew), II, pp. 341–2 and N. Levitzki in *Koteret Rashit*, No. 72, 19 April 1984. On Barazani and Feinstein, *Ha-Ma'as*, 42, *Ketavim*, II, pp. 465–6.

38. *Sekirah*, 25 Sept. 1946, JI, 2/2/12 – K4.

39. *Herut*, 69, Feb. 1947.

40. *Herut* 66. According to his own later account (pp. 397–8; not substantiated by any contemporay source), Friedman-Yellin soon changed his mind.

41. For threats of retaliation should the 18 be executed see *Ha-Ma'as* 13, July 1946 (3), *Ketavim*, II, pp. 153–4 and 14, Aug. 1946 (1), pp. 159–60.

42. However, Sneh still opposed *Lehi*'s operational strategy. See his speech, delivered on 13 Dec. 1946, in *Protocol of the 22nd Zionist Congress, Basel; 9–24 December 1946* (Jerusalem, n.d.), pp. 190–99, and his letter to Ben-Gurion of 21 Sept. 1946, in HH, III, 3, pp. 1933–4.

43. Examples of various broadsides against the Jewish Agency, in *Ha-Ma'as*, 15, Sept. 1946 (2), *Ketavim*, II, pp. 161–2 and *Ba-Mahteret* (Sept. 1946), p. 208. In fact, Weizmann was never ready to compromise. See, for example, his rejection of the Morrison-Grady plan in his letter to Chief Rabbi Herzog of 21 July 1946, in *Letters and Papers of Chaim Weizmann*, Vol. 22 (Jerusalem, 1979), No. 193.

44. For Ben-Gurion's justification of his action see protocol of the Jewish Agency executive, 20 Jan. 1947, CZA. Compare *Lehi*'s reaction in *Ha-Ma'as*, 33, Feb. 1947 (3), *Ketavim*, II, pp. 341–60.

45. 'A Warning in Good Time', *Ha-Ma'as*, 34, Feb. 1947 (3), ibid., pp. 389–92. Attempts at 'illegal' immigration were halted between 7 Dec. 1946 and 9 Feb. 1947. *Ha-Ma'as*, 30 (2), ibid., pp. 333–4.

46. Yellin-Mor, op. cit., p. 358; HH, III, pp. 906–8.

47. Yellin-Mor, op. cit., pp. 349–50; for the plan itself see 'A Liberation Plan versus a Liquidation Conspiracy', *Ha-Ma'as*, 15, Sept. 1946 (2), *Ketavim*, II, pp. 157–60.

48. As such, its omissions were also significant. In order to retain the possibility of French support, the plan deliberately avoided mention of Syria and Lebanon. In order not to

injure the claim to a Jewish state 'within its historical borders', it also refrains from discussing the issue of the Arab Palestinians. Instead, it appeals only to the 'masses' of Egypt and Iraq. *Ha-Ma'as*, 15, Sept. 1946 (2), *Ketavim*, II, pp. 161–2 and pp. 247–8.

49. See *Herut*, 62, end Sept. 1946. Cf. Lutski's article in PRO, FO/371/1525/43/E 6969.
50. *Ketavim*, II, pp. 175–6 and 249–56.
51. 'Political Review', ibid., pp. 217–18. However, the image was spoilt when Truman sacked Wallace just a few days later.
52. 'In the Market of Collaboration', *Ha-Ma'as*, 25, ibid., pp. 293–4. Always sensitive to the precedent of Muslim and Hindu strife in India. *Lehi* did not discard the possibility of Arab-Jewish conflict. It did, however, definitely tend to play it down and was even prepared to admit that 'We and the Arabs can discuss natural rights in this land'. Compare *Ha-Ma'as*, 24, Oct. 1946, ibid., pp. 265–6 and *Eshnav*, 143 (27 Nov. 1946) pp. 1–2 and 146 (17 Dec. 1946), pp. 1–2.
53. 'Basel – Salameh – Petach-Tikva', *Ha-Ma'as*, Dec. 1946 (4), *Ketavim*, II, pp. 305–6; cf. IZL's reaction in *Herut* 66 and 67, Dec. 1946 and that of the *Haganah* in *Eshnav*, 17 Dec. 1946, p. 1. The incident in Petach-Tikva, which commenced on 5 Dec. 1946, was far less serious than those which had occurred during the 1930s.
54. *Ketavim*, II, pp. 340–61. Eldad's authorship is attested by E. Katz, op. cit., p. 336; Friedman-Yellin drafted the section of the document on the Arab issue.
55. *Ketavim*, II, pp. 335–6.
56. Ibid., p. 350. In fact, throughout this period, the Russians were assisting emigration from Romania and Bulgaria. Compare HH, III, 3, pp. 1908–14 and Holman to FO, 8 May and 20 June 1946, PRO, FO 371/52522 No. 589 and 52531 No. 779.
57. *Ketavim*, II, pp. 357–8. See also 'First Principles' in *The Goal – the Enemy – the War*, p. 9.
58. *Ketavim*, II, pp. 355–6.

CHAPTER 8 (pp. 168–192)

1. 'In the Meantime'; *Ketavim*, II, pp. 423–4.
2. See *Lehi*'s announcements of March, 1947, ibid., pp. 425–6 and 327–8, and Yellin-Mor, op. cit., pp. 401–2.
3. 'Martial Law – A British Failure', *Ha-Ma'as*, 38, April 1947 (1), *Ketavim*, II, pp. 429–30. On the imposition of martial law and on the reasons for its revocation see HH, III, pp. 916–17; and M.J. Cohen, *Palestine and the Great Powers, 1945–1948* (Princeton, 1982), p. 238–42.
4. Yellin-Mor, op. cit., and CZA, S25/5677.
5. *Ha-Ma'as*, 37, *Ketavim* II, pp. 410–20.
6. 'Towards the UN', *Ha-Ma'as*, 36, March 1947 (1), ibid., pp. 417–18. The IZL's attitude was broadly the same. See *Herut*, 69, Feb. 1947.
7. 'The Spectacles of that Few', *Ha-Ma'as*, 43, May 1947 (3), *Ketavim*, II, pp. 469–72.
8. See 'The Light of the Dollar and its Shadow', *Ha-Ma'as*, 39, April 1947 (2), ibid., pp. 435–6 and the 'announcement' of April 1947, ibid., pp. 455–6.
9. 'Towards the Commission for Establishing facts', *Ha-Ma'as*, 44, May 1947 (4), ibid., pp. 473–4.
10. 'Manifesto', ibid., pp. 477–8 and Yellin-Mor, p. 417. According to the latter, *Lehi* also conducted preliminary enquiries with the Yugoslavian representative on UNSCOP.
11. 'In the Margins of a Fighting World', 6 (3), ibid., pp. 475–6.
12. 'Many Walls have been Shattered', *Ha-Ma'as* 45, June 1947 (1), ibid., pp. 481–4. It is instructive to note that *Lehi* did not refer to Achimeir's far cooler reception of Gromyko's announcement. Indeed, the latter still maintained a pro-Western orientation, predicting that an upswing in immigration would signify a turn in the tide. See *Ha-Mashkif*, 22 May 1947.
13. In his memoirs, Yellin-Mor cites two additional items. One is an undated conversation in Paris between Betty Knut ('Iranda'), a former member of the French resistance, and Molotov, who was her mother's cousin (pp. 383–4); another is a conversation between Yitzchak Merkin and Georgi Dimitrov, leader of the Bulgarian Communist Party and one of Stalin's associates (pp. 387–90).

14. These arguments were put forward in *Ba-Mahaneh*, 141 (16 June 1947), pp. 8–9 and – still more forcefully – by spokesmen for *Ha-Shomer Ha-Tsair* in *Mishmar*, 16 and 27 May 1947. Note that the IZL also claimed credit for Gromyko's announcement: see Begin, *In the Underground*, III, pp. 98–9.
15. *Ha-Ma'as*, 48, June 1947 (1), *Ketavim*, II, pp. 481–4.
16. On which see Ben-Gurion's report to the Jewish Agency executive, on 22 May 1947, CZA, No. 28, Vol. 51.
17. 'Ben-Gurion is Preparing a Total failure', *Ha-Ma'as* 46, June 1947 (2), *Ketavim*, II, pp. 485–6.
18. *Ha-Ma'as* 47, July 1947 (1), ibid., pp. 525–8.
19. 'Orientation on What and on Whom?', *Ha-Ma'as*, 48, July 1947 (2), ibid., pp. 529–30.
20. The full title of the document was 'For Justice, Freedom and Peace' (Hebrew), dated July 1947. For text see *Ketavim*, II, pp. 533–85, from which all succeeding quotations are taken.
21. Begin's memorandum to UNSCOP, *In the Underground*, III, pp. 159, 175–6. See also his *The Revolt* (Hebrew), p. 372. On the demographic statistics, see also S. Katz, *Day of Fire* (Hebrew; Tel Aviv, 1966), pp. 283–90.
22. See, for example, *Ha-Ma'as*, nos. 49(3) and 50(4), Aug. 1947, *Ketavim*, II, pp. 589–94.
23. *Ba-Makhteret* (internal information leaflet), Aug. 1947, ibid., pp. 645–7. The 'centre' also admitted that in any case it hardly possessed the strength to carry out many operations.
24. Ibid., p. 610.
25. *Ba-Makhteret*, internal memorandum, Aug. 1947, ibid., pp. 599–600.
26. *Dapim*, June 1947, in Begin, *In the Underground*, III, pp. 114–15 and 129–30.
27. *Herut*, 74, June 1947.
28. Begin, *In the Underground*, III, pamphlet (n.d., March 1947?), pp. 32–6; *Herut*, 71, April 1947.
29. Yellin-Mor (op. cit., pp. 414–16) later claimed that this was originally intended to be a joint *Lehi*-IZL operation, but that Begin asked for the IZL to be given a free hand. Begin's own memoirs do not recall this aspect of the planning.
30. For a report see *Sekirah*, 23 June 1947, in Begin, op. cit., III, pp. 134–49.
31. Announcement; Top Secret; July 1947. Most of this document is absent from Begin's later summary of his writings (op. cit., III, p. 150), probably because at the time of their publication he wished to mend fences with ex-members of *Lehi* and attract them to his *Herut* party. On *Lehi*'s earlier calls to its members to restrain their envy of the IZL, see *Ba-Makhteret*, *Ketavim*, II, pp. 613–14.
32. *Ba-Makhteret* (internal information leaflet), Aug. 1947, *Ketavim* II, pp. 656–8. On Friedman-Yellin's position see *Sulam*, April 1949, p. 46; cf. Eldad's memoirs, pp. 289–90.
33. *Ketavim*, II, pp. 647–8.
34. 'We will defend the Integrity of the Homeland', *Ha-Ma'as*, 59, Sept. 1947 (4), ibid., pp. 717–18.
35. W. Roger Louis, *The British Empire in the Middle East, 1945–1951* (Oxford, 1984), p. 384. A turning-point was reached in the summer of 1946, when the number of immigrants broke the barrier of 1,500 permitted under the White Paper, HH, III, pp. 1135ff.
36. 'To the Youth', Aug. 1947, *Ketavim*, II, p. 660; *Ha-Ma'as*, 52, August 1947, ibid., pp. 661–2.
37. 'On the Verge of the Precipice', ibid., pp. 663–4. Indeed, in its defence of the hanging of the sergeants *Lehi* was even more forthcoming than the IZL who subsequently (in an internal leaflet) admitted that its first pronouncement on the 'illegality' and 'terrorism' of the British had been 'somewhat exaggerated'. Compare *Ha-Ma'as*, Aug. 1947, with Begin, *In the Underground*, III, p. 235.
38. 'Thus Wrote the *Judenrat* in Wilna'; *Ha-Ma'as*, Aug. 1947, quoting from the Judenrat newspaper first published in 1946 by Ruzka Korchak, *Flames in Ashes* (Hebrew); *Ketavim*, II, p. 659.

39. Eldad, op. cit., pp. 296–310 claims that Ben-Gurion had given the signal for action against 300–400 'dissident' leaders. See, however, Ben-Gurion's particularly aggressive speech to the 'National Council' on 1 April 1947, *Ba-Ma'arakhah*, V, pp. 159–60, 167–9.

40. 'For Abhorrence'; *Ketavim*, II, pp. 671–2.

41. *Ha-Ma'as*, 54, Aug. 1947 (3), ibid., pp. 673–6; and *Lehi*'s 'announcement', Aug. 1947, ibid., pp. 681–2.

42. Eldad, *First Tithe*, pp. 300–304; see also his letter to an old colleague (Moshe Svorai), dated May 1947, in *Ketavim*, II, p. 617. For attacks on the anti-socialism of Achimeir see *Ha-Mashkif*, 17 Feb. 1947, and 'Gandhi and Dr. Achimeir', *Ha-Ma'as*, 45(1), ibid., pp. 483–4.

43. 'Our Attitude to Socialism', ibid., pp. 618–22. For one 'conservative' reaction, see Svorai's reply, dated July 1947, YHA, file 47. Svorai revealed that several of his *Lehi* comrades in prison were under the impression that 'socialism is already part of our ideology', and that he was personally opposed to that development which might necessitate a choice between the war for national liberation and communism or socialism.

44. See, for example, Y. Ben-Zakkai (Ronkin), *Against the Terrorist Groups. The IZL and Lehi – Their Paths and their Outlooks* (Hebrew; published by *Ha-Shomer Ha-Tsair*, Tel Aviv, 1946).

45. [Eldad], *War Against Fascism* (Hebrew), *Lehi* publication, July 1947; *Ketavim*, II, pp. 623–5. In a private communication to the author, Eldad testified to his authorship.

46. Ibid., p. 634.

47. Ibid., pp. 635–40.

48. 'Review of the Substance of *Lehi*' (summary of conversation); signed by A. Selman, n.d., JI/47 10/4-/-K5. The contacts were first arranged by Zvi Nadav, Selman's friend, who was active in 'League V'. After the meeting, Wilner was criticised in the central committee of his party for having been in contact with representatives of a 'Fascist-reactionary-nationalist' body. Nevertheless, contacts apparently continued until the Deir Yasin episode of April 1948, when Wilner informed Selman that they would not be renewed. Cf. H. Canaan, in *Ha-Aretz* supplement, 7 Sept. 1973.

49. Idem.

50. E. Wilenska, 'On the Road of Lehi', *Kol Ha-Am*, 15 Aug. 1947.

51. *A Reply to Esther Wilenska* (Hebrew), *Lehi* publication, Sept. 1947, *Ketavim*, II, pp. 705–14.

52. This was not altogether true. Although the formula adopted by Jabotinsky in 1940, it had been rejected by Eldad in 1943. However, in 1947 it clearly served tactical purposes.

53. An earlier article in *Ha-Ma'as* (58), ibid., pp. 703–4, had cited with some glee a speech by Georgi Dimitrov, general secretary of the Bulgarian Communist Party, who had invited American capitalists to invest in his country.

54. Ibid., p. 714.

CHAPTER 9 (pp. 195–216)

1. 'No Arab-Hebrew War', *Ha-Ma'as*, 15 Aug. 1947; *Ketavim*, II, pp. 683–4. It was Friedman-Yellin who determined that 'there will be no Arab front'. Eldad, on the other hand, demanded that *Lehi* prepare its operational and information sections for such an eventuality, *First Tithe*, pp. 321–2.

2. 'The Thames Flowing to the Rhine', *Ha-Ma'as*, 60, Sept. 1947, *Ketavim*, II, pp. 721–4 and No. 61, ibid., pp. 729–30.

3. 'Defeat the Enemy Conspiracy' and 'Between Enemy and Rival', *Ha-Ma'as*, 56(a) and 57(b), Aug. 1947, *Ketavim*, II, pp. 689–90 and 697–8.

4. *Ha-Ma'as*, 61, ibid., pp. 729–30.

5. *Ha-Ma'as*, 56, ibid. For Wilner's attack on this stand, *Kol Ha-Am*, 15 and 17 Aug. 1947.

6. This charge was misplaced. In fact, Ben-Gurion did warn of an impending Arab attack. See CZA S5/320. For *Lehi*'s support for Egyptian nationalism, see 'For Egypt's

Independence', *Ha-Ma'as*, 58, Sept. 1947, *Ketavim*, II, pp. 701–2 and Friedman-Yellin's memoirs, pp. 425–6.

7. 'We Will Fight for the Integrity of the Fatherland', *Ha-Ma'as*, 59, Sept. 1947, *Ketavim*, II, pp. 717–18. See also the unsigned letter of the same period in YHA file 47.

8. 'The Right and Power of the Veto', *Ha-Ma'as*, 72, Sept. 1947, *Ketavim*, II, pp. 733–6.

9. Ibid., pp. 737–8. An internal memorandum proclaimed the Creech-Jones announcement to be 'a very important strategic victory'. (Ibid., p. 738.) For Friedman-Yellin's later testimony on the meeting between Begin, Scheib and the Jewish Agency, see HH, III, p. 931. There are grounds for believing that *Lehi*'s decision to comply with the cease-fire was in part caused by its financial difficulties. On the day that its manifesto was published, *Lehi* 'expropriated' 45,000 Palestine pounds from a branch of Barclays Bank.

10. Friedman-Yellin, op. cit., p. 740 and *Ha-Ma'as*, 63, Oct. 1947, *Ketavim*, II, pp. 741–4.

11. 'Against the Arab Threat', ibid., pp. 741–2. The Jewish Agency likewise exaggerated the extent of British influence on these gatherings; see M.J. Cohen, *Palestine and the Great Powers*, pp. 319–20. Indeed, Ben-Gurion, too, maintained that the actions of the British Government were directed against both the Arabs and the Jews. See his speech of 29 Oct. in *Ba-Ma'arakhah*, Vol. 5, pp. 242–3.

12. See manifesto dated 21 Nov. 1947; *Ketavim*, II, pp. 1085–6.

13. 'The Declaration of Hope and the Declaration of Treason', *Ha-Ma'as*, 64(b) (Oct. 1947), ibid., pp. 745–6; 'The Danger of India and the Danger of Greece', ibid., pp. 757–8.

14. Ibid., pp. 747–8; see also *Herut* Nos. 77–80 (Oct.–Nov. 1947). *Lehi*'s proposed borders were those outlined by Yair: the Euphrates and the Nile Valley. See *Hazit ha-No'ar*, 4 (Dec. 1947), *Ketavim*, II, pp. 795–6.

15. See, for example, ibid., pp. 791–2, where the Hebrew press is accused of concealing the fact that the American representative on the UN Commission was attempting to decrease the area of the Jewish state, while his Russian counterpart was attempting to increase it.

16. 'The Serious, the Wicked and the Ridiculous', *Ha-Ma'as*, 68(b) (Dec. 1947), *Ketavim*, II, pp. 813–16. Avidan warned Friedman-Yellin of the consequences of too close an alignment with the USSR. 'By portraying the Russian Bolsheviks as meek lambs, we shall raise a generation of misguided and blind fanatics' (undated letter, Avidan Archives).

17. *Ha-Ma'as*, ibid.

18. 'Without Heart, Without Brain, Without Success', *Ha-Ma'as*, 6 (Oct. 1947), *Ketavim*, II, pp. 761–4. On relations between the *Haganah* and the 'dissidents' during this period, HH, II, pp. 958–9 and protocol of meeting of Jewish Agency executive, 2 Nov. 1947, CZA, Vol. 52 No. 8.

19. Compare Eldad's article ('For a Change in Internal Relations') in *Ha-Ma'as*, 69 (Dec. 1947), *Ketavim*, II, pp. 817–18, with Begin's in *Herut*, 82 (Dec. 1947) and the review cited in *Ba-Makhteret*, Vol. 3, pp. 105–7. In general, Yellin-Mor, op. cit., p. 433.

20. As far as Friedman-Yellin was himself concerned, this was not altogether a drastic step. See *Lehi* statement of 4 Dec. 1947, *Ketavim*, II, pp. 825–6.

21. Eldad, op. cit., pp. 321–2.

22. *Lehi* statement, 7 Dec. 1947, *Ketavim*, II, pp. 827–8; see also Friedman-Yellin's retrospective (and somewhat different) justification in his memoirs, p. 434.

23. Signs of such a realisation are evident in *Ha-Ma'as*, 71 (Dec. 1947), *Ketavim*, II, pp. 833–4 and 835–6. For the contemporary position adopted by the *Haganah*, HH, III, p. 1415.

24. 'When will dissidence be Liquidated?', *Ha-Ma'as*, 67 (Dec. 1947), *Ketavim*, II, pp. 789–90. See also Katriel Katz's speech at the meeting of *Mapai* delegates, 17 Dec. 1947, LPA.

25. 'In the Battles for the Freedom of Israel', *Ketavim*, II, pp. 831–2. Weizmann was similarly described: 'Weizmann and Farran', ibid.

26. Ibid., pp. 829–30.

27. 'Nothing New under the Sun', *Ha-Ma'as*, 71 (Dec. 1947), ibid., pp. 833–6. Cf.

M. Barak in *Mivrak*, 20 Dec. 1947.

28. [Eldad], 'How We Succeeded', ibid., pp. 842–3.
29. Ibid., p. 844.
30. Ibid., pp. 842–3.
31. Ibid., pp. 847–8. This statement contained a barely concealed reference to the manner whereby in Jan. 1948 the head of *Lehi*'s 'centre' had decided (without due judicial process) to sentence to death Judah Aryeh Levi, who was in charge of *Lehi*'s arms store, but who after the incident of 29 Nov. decided to join the *Haganah*. On this incident see the *Lehi* memorandum, 'strictly internal', in *Ba-Makhteret*, 5 (Jan. 1948), HA, 27/a 8 and Y. Okev (B. Lubotsky), *Ha-Ma'as Ha-Shahor* (Jan. 1949), pp. 24–9.
32. Information Dept. announcement, *Ketavim*, II, pp. 847–8 and HH, III, p. 1373. The announcement was occasioned by the *Lehi* attack on the 'Sarayah' controlled by the Husseinis in Jaffa, which served as a base for terrorist operations. In fact, there had been seven previous *Lehi* actions (including two against the Arab Legion).
33. *Hazit Ha-No'ar*, 5 (Jan. 1948), *Ketavim*, II, 851–2. On the Haifa incident (initiated when an IZL bomb killed six Arabs) see M. Barak in *Mivrak*, 31 Dec. 1947 and the IZL broadcast of 4 Jan. 1948 in Begin, *Ba-Makhteret*, 4, pp. 136–8.
34. *Mivrak*, 4 Jan. 1948, HH, 3, p. 1383. On the action itself, see also Y. Levi, *Jerusalem in the War of Independence* (Hebrew; Tel Aviv, 1986), pp. 136–8. Friedman-Yellin's views are in *Mivrak*, 2 Jan. 1948. Nevertheless, it should be noted that *Lehi* did make one more (unsuccessful) appeal to the Arabs in Feb. 1948; see *Ketavim*, II, pp. 1095–6 and Yellin-Mor, op. cit., pp. 438–9.
35. 'On the Situation: War or Retaliation?', *Ketavim*, II, pp. 887–90; see also *Ha-Ma'as*, Nos. 73–4 (Jan. 1948), ibid., pp. 879–80, 881–2 and *Mivrak*, 4 Jan. 1948.
36. 'We Aborted the Conspiracy in Haifa', *Ha-Ma'as*, 76 (March 1948), *Ketavim*, II, pp. 913–16.
37. See M. Barak in *Mivrak*, 22 Jan. 1948, also noting the simultaneous riots in Egypt.
38. *Mivrak*, 17 Jan. 1948; emphasis in original.
39. See, for example, *Mivrak*, 15 Jan. 1948 and the earlier statements in idem, 25 Dec. 1947, and 3 and 4 Jan. 1948. For reactions to Warren Austin's statement, see *Ha-Ma'as* (March 1948), *Ketavim*, II, pp. 935–6 and *Shikuf* (internal), ibid., pp. 937–9 (cf. Ganin, op. cit., p. 152). At the same time, *Lehi* stepped up its attacks on Truman. One new element in *Lehi*'s propaganda at this time was its sympathy for the social regimes in the communist bloc (A. Almagor, *Mivrak*, 26 Jan. 1948). Nevertheless, *Lehi* had already strongly denied reports, emanating from the IZL, that it had joined the communists. See 'How *Lehi* is Being Disintegrated', *Ketavim*, II, pp. 883–4. It also denied that it had concluded a secret agreement with the USSR.
40. Y. Netanyah [Eldad], 'Who Surrenders to Whom?', *Mivrak*, 26 March 1948. *Lehi* later feared that the United States was even prepared to send troops to impose a trusteeship. *Mivrak*, 5 and 7 April 1948. Eldad to Gepner, Jan. 1948; M. Getter, 'The Ideology of the *Lehi* Movement' (unpublished MA thesis, Tel Aviv University, 1964), p. 56, n. 40.
41. Britain was castigated in articles by M. Barak in *Mivrak*, 19 Jan. 1948 and A. Almagor, idem, 20 Jan. 1948. See also *Ketavim*, II, pp. 909–14. On the other hand, *Lehi* writers constantly reported signs of apparent Russian favour. See, for example, *Mivrak*, 1 and 6 Feb. 1948.
42. E. Amikam, *Mivrak*, 13 Feb. 1948. Indeed, such was the degree of *Lehi*'s alignment that the movement accepted with equanimity the news of Masaryk's suicide. *Mivrak*, 11 March and 2 April 1948.
43. See Friedman-Yellin's statement in *Ketavim*, II, pp. 915–16. In his memoirs, Yellin-Mor admits it was written in a mood of bitterness.
44. M. Barak in *Mivrak*, 16 Feb. 1948 and *Ha-Ma'as*, 77 (March 1948), *Ketavim*, II, pp. 925–8.
45. M. Barak, 'Let the Crime in Jerusalem be a Turning-Point in our Life', *Mivrak*, 22 Feb. 1948 and pamphlet of same date in *Ketavim*, II, pp. 913–14.
46. 'A Fighting Leadership for a Fighting People', ibid., pp. 919–24. In fact, in the wake of the Tel Aviv incident, the *Haganah* did tighten its defences. See HH, III, p. 1450. On the Czech arms deal, see ibid., pp. 1525ff.

47. See the 'political diary', entitled 'The Military Organisation and the Political Movement', issued for internal use in March 1948, *Ketavim*, II, pp. 945–8.
48. *Mivrak*, 2, 4 and 9 April. Lubotsky claimed that another reason was the murder of Levi. B. Eliav, *Memoirs from the Right Wing* (Hebrew; Tel Aviv, 1990), pp. 177–8. See also above, n. 31.
49. *Ba-Makhteret* (internal: March 1948), *Ketavim*, II, pp. 955–9. Cf. Shikuf, 4 (March 1948), pp. 8–10, internal, HA.
50. *Ketavim*, II, pp. 960–2. For reactions to the bombing of the Jewish Agency, see ibid., pp. 963–6; on the situation in Jerusalem, *Ha-Ma'as*, 78, ibid., pp. 969–70; for exaggerated accounts of *Lehi*'s contribution to the city's defence, ibid., pp. 969–74.
51. 'Take Off the Mask', ibid., pp. 979–80.
52. M. Barak, 'Cowards', *Mivrak*, 24 March 1948. In fact, *Lehi*'s accusations against Ben-Gurion were unwarranted. He was convinced that the British were behind the Arab invasion and did now consider the military struggle to be more important than the diplomatic campaign. See, for example, his letter to Shertok, 27 Feb. 1948, in *Political and Diplomatic Documents: December 1947–May 1948* (ed. G. Yogev; Jerusalem, 1979), No. 228.
53. *Shikuf*, 4 (March 1948), pp. 1–5; HA.
54. 'What is Today's Market-Price for a "State"?', *Ha-Ma'as*, 79 (March 1948); *Ketavim*, II, pp. 977–8.
55. M. Barak, 'Orientation on Peace', *Mivrak*, 9 April 1948, responding to Ben-Gurion's speech two days earlier to the Zionist Executive (for which see *Ba-Ma'arakhah*, 5, pp. 302–9).
56. See meetings of the Jewish Agency executive; 29 Feb., 17 March and 11 April 1948, CZA, Vol. 53, Nos. 31, 34 and 35/36.
57. See *Lehi* and IZL announcements of April 1948 in *Ketavim*, II, pp. 989–92 and 282–5; also M. Begin, *In the Underground*, 4, pp. 274–7. Compare the subsequent accounts in HH, III, p. 1547; D. Niv, *History of IZL*, 5 (Tel Aviv, 1980), pp. 78–94; and B. Morris, *The Birth of the Palestinian Refugee Problem* (Cambridge, 1986), pp. 113–15.
58. 'Against Armistice', *Ha-Ma'as*, 80 (April 1948), *Ketavim*, II, pp. 985–6 and M. Barak in *Mivrak*, 16 April 1948.
59. See the protocol of that meeting in P. Ginosar (ed.), *Lehi Revealed: Minutes of the Conference of the Fighters for the Freedom of Israel (March 1949)* (Hebrew; Ramat Gan, 1985), pp. 50, 59.
60. Eldad, *First Tithe*, pp. 334–5, from which the citations from Friedman-Yellin's letter to Zetler are also taken. I have not been able to locate the original.
61. *Mivrak*, 14 and 15 April 1948, and the *Lehi* broadcast entitled 'The Freedom of Jerusalem' in file of *Lehi* broadcasts, HA. For British views of the Hadassah incident, see Intelligence Report for 7–19 April (No. 66); PRO, WO/275/64.
62. *Ha-Ma'as*, 81 (April 1948); *Ketavim*, II, pp. 995–6.
63. *Herut*, 82 (Dec. 1947) and 85 (Feb. 1948).
64. *Herut*, 94 (April 1948); see also idem, Nos. 92 (March 1948) and 93 (April 1948) and M. Begin, op. cit., 4, pp. 259–63, 269–71.
65. 'The Military Organisation and the Political Movement', *Ketavim*, II, pp. 949–51. For the IZL's response to such charges, and especially its anger at the tone with which *Lehi* attacked its 'mistake' after 29 Nov., see, for example, *Herut*, 88 (Feb. 1948), Begin, op. cit., pp. 178–9.
66. For text, see Begin, *The Revolt* (Hebrew; Tel Aviv, 1950), pp. 423–4. The agreement was ratified by the Greater Zionist Action Committee on 12 April by a majority of 39 to 32; *Mapai, Mapam* and *Aliyah Hadashah* voted against.
67. See transcript of *Lehi* broadcast of 29 April 1948 in HA and *Ketavim*, II, pp. 1016–17; also Eldad, *First Tithe*, p. 334. On the Jaffa battle itself (where the IZL sustained 30 fatal casualties), compare Begin, *In the Underground*, 4, pp. 308–9 and *The Revolt* (Hebrew), pp. 433–69 with HH, III, pp. 1551–3 and 1575–7.
68. Although not without giving up the anti-British front. See 'Gera' (Friedman-Yellin) to 'Dan' (Blau), 10 March 1948, YHA file 47.
69. *Lehi* announcements of 7 and 9 March 1948, *Ketavim*, II, pp. 953–4. See also ibid.,

pp. 1015–16.

70. IZL broadcast, 30 April 1948, in Begin, *In the Underground*, pp. 316–18.
71. *Ketavim*, II, pp. 1017–18. Also *Ha-Ma'as*, 81 (April 1948), ibid., pp. 995–6; *Shikuf*, 5 (April 1948), ibid., pp. 1001–4.
72. *Mivrak*, 18 April 1948 (2nd ed.), and 19, 21 and 23 April.
73. *Lehi* announcement, 4 May 1948, *Ketavim*, II, p. 1019. Nevertheless, *Lehi* promised that it would concentrate its operations against the British, 'the Arabs' principal props'. See also ibid., pp. 1023–4.
74. *Mivrak*, 23 April 1948.
75. *Lehi* broadcast, 18 Nissan, HA, and *Mivrak*, 18 and 24 April 1948, and *Lehi* broadcast of latter date. *Ketavim*, II, pp. 1009–10.
76. Y. Nov, 'Orientation of Surrender', *Mivrak*, 23 April 1948.
77. Y. Netanyah [Eldad], *Mivrak*, 29 April 1948. Nevertheless, it is indicative of *Lehi*'s internal tensions that the same newspaper also published an article praising Marx and Engels by M.A. Yaffe; ibid., see also *Lehi* broadcast, *Ketavim*, II, pp. 1018–20.
78. 'On the Debris of Lies', *Ha-Ma'as*, 82(c), ibid., pp. 1023–4. This was of course a far cry from the position then adopted by *Mapam*, which envisioned a new relationship with the Arabs growing out of the ruins of their settlements. See *Mivrak*, 5 May 1948.
79. B. Shemer (Friedman-Yellin), *Mivrak*, 7 May 1948.
80. *Lehi* broadcast, *Ketavim*, II, pp. 1026–7 and that of 3 May 1948 in HA.
81. The *Haganah* prisoners never forgot their captors' 'zoological' hatred of the British, nor their belief that 'there is no need to fight the Arabs'. HH, III, pp. 1546, 1809; D. Ben-Gurion, *The Restored State* (Hebrew), 1 (Tel Aviv, 1969), p. 104; Y. Avidar, *The Road to the IDF* (Hebrew; Tel Aviv, 1970), p. 104.
82. *Mivrak*, 5, 6 and 7 May 1948; also *Lehi* broadcasts of 5 and 8 May 1948, HA. Nevertheless, it must be noted that, in defending the *Palmach*, *Lehi* did not retract its opposition to either *Mapam* or *Ha-Shomer Ha-Tsair*. Although recognising the need for a communist opposition to Ben-Gurion's 'reactionary, right-wing, fascist and Bevin-like regime', *Lehi* did not feel that either party could fulfil that function. See Y. Yanai, *Mivrak*, 7 May 1948.
83. *Lehi* broadcast, 13 May 1948, *Ketavim*, II, pp. 1029–30.
84. M. Barak in *Mivrak*, 9 and 11 May 1948 and *Lehi* broadcast, 13 May 1948, ibid., pp. 1029–30. Cf. A. Shlaim, *Collusion Across the Jordan: King Abdullah, the Zionist Movement and the Partition of Palestine* (Oxford, 1988).
85. 'Arab "harmony"', *Mivrak*, 13 May 1948.
86. *Lehi* greeted these reports with particular enthusiasm; see *Mivrak*, 12 May 1948.
87. 'G[era]' (Friedman-Yellin) to 'Dan' (David Blau), 10 March 1948, YHA file 47. Ben-Gurion at this period categorised Friedman-Yellin as a 'Bolshevik' and considered *Lehi* to have 'serious links' with Russia. See entry dated 21 March 1948 in D. Ben-Gurion, *The War of Independence: Ben-Gurion's War Diary*, eds. G. Rivlin and E. Oren (Hebrew, Tel Aviv, 1982), p. 315.

CHAPTER 10 (pp. 217–238)

1. 'Y. Netanyah' (Eldad), 'Thank goodness we are Rid of Them', *Mivrak*, 14 May 1948.
2. 'B. Shemer' (Friedman-Yellin), 'Frankness in Fog', idem. See also 'The Voice of *Lehi*', 16 May 1948, *Ketavim*, II, pp. 1033–4.
3. *Lehi* broadcast, 7 June 1948, HA. File of *Lehi* broadcasts.
4. *Ketavim*, II, pp. 1036–37; *Lehi*'s broadcast, 23 May 1948, HA.
5. *Mivrak*, 17 May 1948.
6. 'The Voice of *Lehi*', 17 and 18 May 1948, *Ketavim*, II, pp. 1035–9; see also M. Barak, *Or Le-Yom*, of both dates. *Lehi* demanded that Weizmann be put on trial for (a) 'fighting against' attempts to save Polish Jewry and (b) 'misleading' the Hebrew people to believe in Britain's friendship.
7. *Mivrak*, 29 May 1948.
8. M. Barak, *Mivrak*, 19 May 1948; see also *Ketavim*, II, pp. 1039–40.
9. See *Lehi* broadcast of 19 May (*Ketavim*, II, pp. 1041–2) and Friedman-Yellin's words of

29 May (ibid., pp. 1053–6), also the attack on Shaltiél in *Mivrak*, 4 June 1948. According to M. Bar-Zohar, *Ben-Gurion* (Hebrew; Tel Aviv, 1987), III, p. 835), *Lehi* aimed to destroy the Mosque of Omar; this is not confirmed in *Lehi* sources, although Eldad did warn that 'the destruction of our temple will also lead to the destruction of the temples of the [Arab] marauders', *Mivrak*, 29 May 1948. *Lehi*'s casualties in the Jerusalem battles amounted to four killed and 32 wounded. See *Lehi* broadcast, 20 May 1948, HA, ibid.

10. Eldad, 'The Old City will be New', *Mivrak*, 29 May 1948.

11. *Lehi* broadcast, 20 May 1948, pp. 2–3; HA, ibid.

12. *Mivrak*, 6 June 1948.

13. M. Barak, *Mivrak*, 24 and 26 May 1948, and B. Shemer, ibid., 28 May 1948.

14. *Lehi* radio broadcast, 30 May 1948, HA.

15. M. Barak, *Or Le-Yom*, 31 May 1948.

16. See Friedman-Yellin's address to conscripts in *Ketavim*, II, pp. 1053–6 and *Lehi* announcement of 22 May 1948, ibid., pp. 1051–2.

17. *Mivrak*, 16 May 1948; see the IZL's similar estimates in M. Begin, *In the Underground*, III, pp. 143, 180–2. *Lehi* found further evidence in the very fact of the Arab invasion itself.

18. *Lehi* broadcast, 18(?) May 1948, *Ketavim*, II, pp. 1050–1.

19. *Lehi* broadcast, 19 May 1948.

20. *Mivrak*, 27 May and 25 July 1948.

21. Avner in *Mivrak*, 5 June 1948, responding to articles by von Weisel and Achimeir in *Ha-Mashkif* of the previous day.

22. *Lehi* broadcast, 5 June 1948, *Ketavim*, II, p. 1065. See also 'Yonah''s reaction to the news that the villages of Gilboa had been cleared of their Arab inhabitants, *Mivrak*, 13 June 1948.

23. *Lehi*'s Programme, dated July 1948, in HA, file of printed matter, *Lehi*. Compare *Lehi* broadcast, 22 July 1948, paras. 2 and 9, ibid.

24. B. Shemer, 'A Distorted Plan', *Mivrak*, 29 Aug. 1948.

25. See *Mivrak* 17 and 24 July 1948; compare the reaction in *Kol Ha-Am* 12 July and 2 Aug. 1948. In general, see Y. Porath, 'The League for National Liberation; Its Foundation, Content and Dispersal', *Asian and African Studies*, Vol. 4 (1968), pp. 1–21.

26. *Mivrak*, 16 and 18 Aug. 1948. See also Bernadotte, *To Jerusalem*, pp. 141–2.

27. *Mivrak*, 7, 13 and 15 Sept. 1948. The attempt to enlist the Abu Gosh family was based on its hatred of the Husseinis, and was also helped by bribery. YHA file 69.

28. B. Shemer in *Mivrak*, 11 June 1948. See also *Lehi*'s views on the cease-fire in *Ketavim*, II, pp. 1067–8.

29. See, for example, his articles on the festival of Pentecost and on the 'Ba'al Shem Tov' (the founder of the Hasidic sect) in *Mivrak*, 11 June 1948.

30. *Mivrak*, 17 June 1948.

31. D. Ben-Gurion, *The Restored State of Israel* (Hebrew; Tel Aviv, 1969), pp. 170–75; compare his address to the *Mapai* council on the following day, ibid., pp. 175–9.

32. *Mivrak*, 18 June 1948.

33. Compare Ben-Gurion's case in his address to the *Mapai* council, in *The Restored State*, pp. 177–9.

34. *Lehi* broadcast, 20 June 1948. See Shaltiél's defence of his actions, for example, before the 'Council of Five' early in July 1948: A. Shapira, *The Army Controversy 1948. Ben-Gurion's Struggle for Control* (Hebrew; Tel Aviv, 1985), pp. 89–101.

35. Cf. E. Tavin, *The Second Front: The IZL in Europe 1946–1948* (Hebrew; Tel Aviv, 1973). The '*Altalena* episode' still awaits objective treatment; it has hitherto been the subject of polemic by Nakdimon and Brenner. For the agreement of 1 June, see HH, III, p. 1557 and D. Niv, *History of the IZL*, Pt. 6 (Tel Aviv, 1980), p. 214.

36. Protocols of meetings of the Provisional State Council, No. 5 (23 June 1948), pp. 12–39 and No. 6 (24 June 1948), pp. 4 and 7. For the pressures put on Begin by his extremist followers see S. Katz, *Days of Fire*, p. 415; Begin's address of 22 June in JA, C 5/20/4.

37. See *Ha-Herut* ('The Daily newspaper of Fighting Jerusalem'), No. 1, 1 June 1948.

38. *Lehi* broadcast, 22 June 1948, HA; 'Historical Questions', *Mivrak*, 23 June 1948. On tension between former *Lehi* members, and their officers in the IDF, see protocol of

*Lehi* trial, 5 Jan. 1949, JI, H 4/48/3/13.

39. M. Barak in *Mivrak*, 22 June 1948.
40. *Mivrak*, 23 June 1948. The paper's black-bordered headline of the same date read: 'The House of Israel mourns the burning of the "Altalena" and the loss of weapons and fighters.' In retrospect, both *Lehi* and the IZL exaggerated the strategic importance of the *Altalena*'s arms (see *Mivrak*, 27 June 1948 and Begin's *The Revolt* (Hebrew), p. 247). Supplies from Czechoslovakia had already been arriving since April; further-more, it was later estimated that 'the vast majority' of the weapons on the ship did eventually reach the IDF's stores. See P. Vazeh, *The Goal – Supplies* (Hebrew; Tel Aviv, 1966), p. 277.
41. See also *Lehi* broadcast of 24 June 1948 and Y. Netanyah [Eldad], 'Smoke in the Eyes', in *Mivrak*, 25 June 1948.
42. *Lehi* broadcast, 24 June 1948, HA.
43. 'Yeruba'al' in *Mivrak*, 22 June 1948. *Lehi*'s claims were not far off the mark; see the report of the conversation between General Templer (Vice-Chief of the Imperial General Staff) and the American Ambassador in London at the end of October 1948, cited in my article 'Failure of a a Mission: Bernadotte and Palestine, 1948', *Journal of Contemporary History* (1979), p. 527. At this time, the American Vice-Consul in Jerusalem was already reporting that the Russians were sending *Lehi* arms and money via Poland (Burdett to Marshall, 24 June 1948, Secret tel., *FRUS*, 1948, Vol. 5, Pt. 2, pp. 1141–2); he also suspected Begin of being pro-Soviet.
44. *Mivrak* 22 June 1948 and *Lehi* broadcast 24 June 1948. In fact, the Russians themselves placed more store by *Maki* ('The Communist Party of Israel', until the foundation of the state known as the PKP). See the report of the press conference held by Mikunis in Prague on 22 June 1948 in Ro'i, *Decision-Making in Practice*, pp. 160–1.
45. *Lehi* broadcast, 26 June 1948, HA.
46. 'Yehoash' in *Ha-Herut*, No. 19, 24 June, 1948.
47. *Lehi* broadcast, 26 June 1948 and M. Barak in *Mivrak*, 28 June 1948.
48. *Lehi* broadcast, 30 June 1948 and *Mivrak* (2nd ed.) of the same day.
49. *Lehi* broadcasts of 4 and 6 July 1948.
50. 'Lehi on the Ceasefire' June 1948, *Ketavim*, II, pp. 1067–8.
51. 'Y. Netanyah', 'Deserving of Death', *Mivrak*, 9 July 1948. In fact, members of the Cabinet (Shertok, Shapira and Rabbi Levin) were prepared to accept the demilitarisa-tion of Jerusalem. See Ben-Gurion's record of the Cabinet meeting of 7 July 1948 in *The Restored State*, I, pp. 221–3.
52. *Lehi* announcement, June 1948, File of *Lehi* announcements, HA and M. Barak in *Mivrak*, 20 July, 1948.
53. *Lehi* broadcast, 11 July 1948, HA.
54. *Mivrak*, 15 July 1948.
55. *Lehi* broadcasts of July 1948, HA.
56. 'Yeruba'al' and M. Barak, *Mivrak*, 15 July 1948. This, of course, was to ignore the strategic realities of the situation, especially in Jerusalem; on which see Ben-Gurion, *The Restored State*, I, pp. 234–8 (meeting of the Provisional State Council, 16–18 July) and D. Joseph, *The Faithful City* (Hebrew; Tel Aviv, 1960), pp. 253–6.
57. 'Y. Netanyah' in *Mivrak*, 16 July 1948; see also *Lehi* broadcasts of 17 and 19 July 1948, HA.
58. 'We are not "Greeners" in Ceasefires'; *Mivrak*, 18 July 1948.
59. *Lehi* broadcast, 21 July 1948, reporting that D. Joseph had informed *Lehi* representa-tives: 'Your good times have ended; be prepared for bad times'.
60. See the report in *Mivrak*, 24 July 1948 by its American correspondent, B. Orni, and Eldad ('Netanyah') in *Mivrak*, 30 July 1948.
61. *Lehi* broadcast, 24 July 1948, HA. For Ben-Gurion's suggestion see Protocol of the State Council, session 11, 22 July 1948, p. 10.
62. *Mivrak*, 25 and 27 July 1948. Otherwise, however, Geisler accomplished little. Indeed, he came into conflict with the *Lehi* delegation to the United States. See 'Hori' (B. Gepner) to the *Merkaz*, 30 July 1948, YHA file 47. In general, *Lehi* activities in the USA were not conspicuously successful. During a period of 11 months only 40,000

dollars had been collected (principally, it was claimed, because *Lehi* had a communist image) and most of that was spent on propaganda and administration. See 'Hori' to 'Michael' (Shamir), 16 May 1948, idem.

63. M. Barak in *Mivrak*, 26 and 27 July 1948 and *Lehi* broadcast, 27 July 1948.
64. See his letter to Friedman-Yellin (late July ?), which was later brought in evidence by the prosecution in the *Lehi* trial. JI H 8/48/3/18. The letter also indicates the extent to which *Lehi* was torn between tendencies towards legitimacy and underground activity, as well as the danger of duplication, which confused and annoyed Zetler.
65. *Lehi* broadcast, 31 July 1948 and M. Barak in *Mivrak*, 2 Aug. 1948.
66. Yellin-Mor, *Lehi*, pp. 457–8; Eldad, *First Tithe*, p. 337.
67. See, for example, Sneh's address to the unity conference of the *Ahdut ha-Avodah* movement and *Ha-Shomer Ha-Tsair*, Tel Aviv, 23–24 Jan. 1948, pp. 42–5 and his articles in *Al ha-Mishmar*, 23 July and 13 Aug. 1948.
68. *Mivrak*, 28 June 1948 and *Lehi* broadcast, 28 July 1948. Compare A. Shapira, *The Army Controversy*, pp. 55–6, 59.
69. *Mivrak*, 22 July 1948.
70. *Mivrak*, 29 Aug. 1948. Compare Shertok to Shitrit, 8 Aug. 1948, in *Political and Diplomatic Documents, December 1947–May 1948* (Hebrew; Jerusalem, 1979), No. 436.
71. *Mivrak*, 31 July 1948 and *Lehi* broadcast, 23 Aug. 1948, HA.
72. For an attack on *Lehi*, see, for example, *Kol ha-Am*, 11 May 1948; *Lehi*'s response in a broadcast, 25 Aug. 1948. HA. However, it should be noted that *Kol ha-Am* made less frequent attacks on *Lehi* than on the IZL.
73. See *Ahdut* Nos. 4 (April 1946), 10 (Oct. 1946) and 11 (Nov. 1946).
74. S. Ettinger's defiance of *Lehi* in *Iggeret le-Haver* (Bulletin for Party members), 31 March 1948, internal, issued by the secretariat of the Central Committee of the Party; for members only. In Files of the Hebrew Communists, *Kadesh* 1272, The National Library, Jerusalem.
75. *Ahdut*, No. 25, 9 Oct. 1947. However, the conference also denounced *Lehi*'s method of struggle.
76. *Lehi* broadcast, 1 Aug. 1948. HA.
77. *First Tithe*, pp. 362–4.
78. *Mivrak*, 6 Aug. 1948; see also *Lehi* broadcast, 5 Aug. 1948, HA.
79. *Lehi, Programme* (July–Aug. 1948).
80. See, for example, the letters from 'Zamir' (David Blau, in Prague) to 'G' [Friedman-Yellin], 14 Aug. 1948 and n.d., YHA file 47. 'You will see some 'cosmetic changes' here . . . such as the paragraph on strikes. But we saw no other possibility and I do not think there is any danger involved.' See also 'Avraham' to the *Merkaz*, n.d., ibid. On *Lehi*'s intense interest in events in Eastern Europe during this period, see, for example, *Mivrak*, 6 Aug. 1948.
81. See, for example, *Ha-Herut*, 10 Aug. 1948.
82. Published in *Herut*, No. 99, 15 June 1948. For the view of the NZO, as expressed in its conference in Paris that summer, see *Ha-Mashkif*, 26 May and 16, 17 and 21 June 1948.
83. In fact, however, there were shades of differences in their socio-economic programmes. Unlike *Lehi*, *Herut* never advocated – in so many words – a 'planned economy' (even though it may have had something of the sort in mind). On the other hand, *Lehi*'s programme seems to suggest that the welfare of the worker is merely a stage in the struggle against imperialism rather than, as in *Herut*'s case, an end in itself.
84. Z. Abramovitz in *Al ha-Mishmar*, 3 Sept. 1948. Although *Mapam* and the communist parties were unable to align, they did share a common resistance to *Lehi*'s claims to be considered a party of the left. Even after the latter split in March 1949, they accepted its members only on an individual basis, demanding that they first renounce *Lehi*'s previous postulates.
85. One of the few exceptions is to be found in a report dated 15 Sept. 1948 to the *Herut* Party, where note is taken of a faction headed by Y.L. Schneersohn, who is said to have wished to align with *Herut*, against the views of Scheib who is described as an anti-Marxist, who supports 'popular Socialism and religion'. JI 2/12/5. For an example of more right-wing views see 'Eliyahu' (probably Amikam, the editor of *Mivrak*), *The*

*Road to the Kingdom of Israel* (Hebrew; Jerusalem, July 1948), who advocates transferring the crux of the movement's activities to the diaspora and decries all attempts to achieve power as a legal party through the democratic process. 'It is impossible to be loyal in practice both to the Kingdom of Israel and to 'the government of Israel', and we must choose between them.' (The document was adduced as evidence in the trial of *Lehi* members; see JI H 7/3/48/13, pp. 43–9). The movement rejected this extremist view, even when its fortunes were at their lowest ebb.

## CHAPTER 11 (pp. 239–255)

1. M. Barak, 'Bernadotte Made Haste to Come', *Mivrak*, 1 June 1948. On the mission in general see J. Heller, 'A Failure of a Mission: Bernadotte and Palestine, 1948', *Journal of Contemporary History* (1979), pp. 515–34. On the formulation of his various plans by his aides, see Sune O. Persson, *Mediation and Assassination: Count Bernadotte's Mission to Palestine in 1948* (London, 1979).
2. *Lehi* broadcast, 'Bernadotte's Officers are Enemy Agents', 6 June 1948, *Ketavim*, II, p. 1066.
3. M. Barak, 'Before the Certain "Aye"', *Mivrak*, 9 June 1948; *Lehi* broadcasts, 10 and 15 June 1948; HA.
4. *Lehi* broadcast, 16 June 1948. See also M. Barak, 'Through the Back Door', *Mivrak*, 16 June 1948; 'The Appetite of the Great Pig', ibid. and 'Not to laugh, not to rejoice', ibid., 17 June 1948.
5. *Lehi* broadcasts, 9 and 10 June 1948, HA.
6. *Mivrak*, 11 June 1948, citing UP. The State Department, at least, took this threat seriously. See Memorandum by Lovett to Clifford, 28 June 1948, *FRUS*, op. cit., pp. 1154–5.
7. See Protocol of the third meeting of the Provisional State Council, 3 June 1948, pp. 3–26; *Documents on the Foreign Policy of Israel*, Vol. 1, *14 May–30 September* (ed. Y. Freundlich; Jerusalem, 1981), No. 151; D. Ben-Gurion, *The Restored State of Israel*, pp. 143–5, 151–6, and 161–3. For Bernadotte's own impressions, see his *To Jerusalem* (Hebrew; Jerusalem, 1952), pp. 38–9, 48–9, 74–5, 77–8.
8. Ben-Gurion, op. cit., pp. 163–7, protocol of Provisional Government meeting of 16 June. *Lehi* would have been equally surprised to know of Weizmann's antipathy towards Bernadotte, whom he called 'just a stooge of the British'. See *Letters and Papers of Chaim Weizmann: Letters*, Vol. 23, No. 207.
9. Protocol of the fourth meeting of the Provisional State Council, 17 June 1948, pp. 3–5 and 28–34. Cf. Shertok's address, pp. 5–8.
10. See the words of their representatives in idem, pp. 12–21.
11. M. Barak, 'Two who Returned Empty-Handed', *Mivrak*, 20 June 1948. Friedman-Yellin appealed to American Zionist leaders to bestir themselves and to condemn Ben-Gurion's pro-Western orienation. See leaflet (no date; 20 June 1948?) issued by the American Friends of the F.F.I. Stern Group, JI.
12. *Lehi* broadcast, 21 June 1948, HA. In 'On the Margins of Ben-Gurion's Speech' (*Mivrak*, 21 June 1948), *Lehi* wondered whether those fighting in Jerusalem were doing so for the liberation of the city, or for Bernadotte.
13. Bernadotte, *To Jerusalem* (Hebrew), pp. 99–109; see also Heller, op. cit. (note 1, above).
14. Ben-Gurion, op. cit., p. 200.
15. For the debate see idem, pp. 208, 213–21. For an example of IZL propaganda, claiming credit for all Israel's military successes hitherto, see 'Jeruba'al', 'Who Saved the City?', *Ha-Herut*, No. 21, 27 June 1948.
16. Eighth meeting of the Provisional State Council, 5 July 1948, pp. 4–18. The resolution was passed by a majority of 24, with four abstentions.
17. 'Headline', *Mivrak*, 28 June 1948.
18. 'A.S.', 'After the Publication of the Bevin-Truman-Bernadotte Plan', *Mivrak*, 5 July 1948. See also *Lehi* broadcast of 3 July 1948.
19. 'Jeruba'al', 'Yugoslavia at the Crossroads', *Mivrak*, 1 July 1948.

20. *Lehi* broadcasts, 5 and 6 July 1948; compare anon., 'The Swedish Count and the Jerusalem Sage', *Mivrak*, 7 July 1948. See also M. Barak, 'During the Last Hours', *Mivrak*, 7 July 1948.

21. M. Barak, 'International Guarantees', *Mivrak*, 14 July 1948. On the Arab refugee issue, see *Lehi* broadcast, 14 July 1948, HA.

22. 'Jeruba'al', 'A Zionist State or a Sovereign One?', *Mivrak*, 5 July 1948.

23. Reports from Moscow radio, idem, and M. Barak, 'To the Memory of Ben-Yosef', idem; M. Barak, 'To Reject!' *Mivrak*, 16 July 1948.

24. On these see, respectively, *Lehi* broadcast, 8 July 1948, *Ketavim*, II, pp. 1073–4; anon., 'The Diplomats of the Oil Moguls Participated in the Formulation of the Bernadotte Programme', *Mivrak*, 8 July 1948; and T. Yisraeli, 'What is Happening in Berlin? The Siege on the Centre of Aggression and Anglo-American Intrigues in Germany', ibid.

25. M. Barak, 'Do not Betray an Ally', *Mivrak*, 8 July 1948. See also *Lehi* announcement, 9 July 1948, *Ketavim*, II, p. 1079. By comparison, the IZL had considerably moderated its pro-Soviet stance. See, for example, Ben-Barukh, 'How Did he Dare?', *Ha-Herut*, No. 35, 13 July 1948 and 'Yeho'ash', 'The Hands are those of Jacob and the Voice that of Esau', ibid., No. 43, 23 July 1948.

26. *Lehi* broadcast, 31 July 1948, HA.

27. See, for example, the reaction in *Lehi*'s broadcast of 4 Aug. 1948 to Ben-Gurion's interview with a French journalist, where he declared his preference for 'a small territory acquired through decision or agreement with the Arabs' over 'a large territory acquired through force'.

28. See Protocol of the twelfth meeting of the Provisional State Council, 29 July 1948, pp. 5–31; and (on the Cabinet meeting of 1 Aug.), Ben-Gurion, *The Restored State*, pp. 247–52. At this time the CIA was taking a greater interest in the two movements than it had done previously. See 'Report by the Central Intelligence Agency', 27 July 1948, *FRUS*, op. cit., pp. 1241, 1245, where the IZL's strength is estimated at no fewer than 12,000 [sic] men and *Lehi*'s at 800 (an increase of 100 per cent in the past six months).

29. See various articles in *Mivrak* of the same date and *Lehi* broadcast of 5 Aug. 1948. For a completely different estimate of Joseph's position, see Bernadotte, *To Jerusalem* (Hebrew), p. 160 and Dov Joseph, *Faithful City*, pp. 304–5.

30. 'The American Army of Conquest: Here it Comes', *Mivrak*, 8 Aug. 1948. On the meeting of 5 Aug., *Lehi* broadcast, 7 Aug. 1948, HA. Cf. Bernadotte, op. cit., pp. 162–4, and *Documents on the Foreign Policy of Israel*, Vol. 1, No. 424.

31. M. Barak, 'Welcome to the Soviet Representative', *Mivrak*, 8 Aug. 1948 and anon., 'The Soviet Representative and the American "Representative"', ibid., 9 Aug. 1948. The IZL declared that its own actions (the Acre break-out and the hanging of the sergeants) had been responsible for the Soviet attitude. See 'The USSR and Israel', *Ha-Herut*, 10 Aug. 1948; for the reactions of *Mapam* and *Maki* see *Al Ha-Mishmar*, 9–10 Aug. 1948; Sneh's announcement, ibid., 15 Aug. 1948; *Kol Ha-Am*, 9 Aug. 1948 and special supplement, ibid., 13 Aug. 1948.

32. Joseph, *The Faithful City*, pp. 305–6.

33. Ben-Gurion, The Restored State of Israel, pp. 281–4.

34. *Lehi* broadcast, 11 Aug. 1948.

35. B. Shemer (Friedman-Yellin), 'Small Change', *Mivrak*, 3 Sept. 1948.

36. See, for example, *Lehi* broadcasts, 19 and 24 Aug. 1948, HA.

37. B. Oren, 'And So – Aliyah "Chet"', *Mivrak*, 24 Aug. 1948, and *Lehi* broadcast, 26 Aug. 1948, HA.

38. C.P.(48) 207, 24 Aug. 1948, Memorandum by E. Bevin, Top Secret; PRO, CAB 129/29; Secret, C.M. 57th Conclusions, Cabinet 57 (48), 26 Aug. 1948; CAB 128/13, ibid. See also Marshall to Douglas, 1 Sept. 1948, Top Secret. Urgent. *FRUS*, op. cit., p. 1369. The Government of Israel learned of the new proposals through its representative in Sweden as early as 2 Sept. See *Documents on the Foreign Policy of Israel*, (Hebrew), Vol. 1, No. 487.

39. Department of State Comments on NSC (National Security Council) 27. Top Secret;

30 Aug. 1948, *FRUS*, op. cit., pp. 1360–3.

40. This charge was repeated in *Lehi*'s broadcast of 29 Aug. 1948 (HA), which claimed that the oil companies were behind the idea of repatriating the same Arab refugees whom they had earlier incited to fight the Jews.

41. Y. Netanyah, 'the Dread of "Dual Loyalty"', *Mivrak*, 3 Sept. 1948. Nevertheless, *Lehi* was also critical of other Israeli parties. Even the Revisionists were prepared to concur with the division of Jerusalem. See M. Barak, 'A Division which Has no Luck', *Mivrak*, 2 Sept. 1948.

42. Bernadotte, *To Jerusalem* (Hebrew), pp. 175, 182. According to the same account, Bernadotte's assessments of the two sides were shared by Trygve Lie, the UN Secretary-General, ibid., p. 177.

43. M. Barak, 'Bernadotte's Travels', *Mivrak*, 6 Sept. 1948. In the subsequent trial for Bernadotte's murder, the article was adduced by the military prosecutor as evidence of *Lehi*'s responsibility. See also *Lehi* broadcast, 5 Sept. 1948, HA.

44. B. Shemer, 'A Torch for a Soul', *Mivrak*, 10 Sept. 1948. See also *Lehi* broadcast, 7 Sept. 1948, HA; 'The Heroes of the Ceasefire at Work', *Mivrak*, 8 Sept. 1948; *Lehi In Jerusalem*, leaflet, 8 Sept. 1948 (file of *Lehi* leaflets; HA); and M. Barak, 'Another Glorious Bastion', *Mivrak*, 8 Sept. 1948.

45. Amiel, 'Athens and Jerusalem: Israel's Ministers in the Wake of Sofoulis and Tsaldaris', *Mivrak*, 12 Sept. 1948. Censored passages were also published in *Tenu'at Lehi Bulletin*, No. 1, 14 Sept. 1948; file of publications and printed matter, HA.

46. See M. Ebon, 'The Communist Tactic in Palestine', *Middle East Journal*, July 1948, pp. 255–69.

47. *Lehi* broadcast, 15 Sept. 1948 and 'To Banish Bernadotte', *Mivrak*, 15 Sept. 1948.

48. Y. Schinar, 'The Israeli Dictatorship and the Dollar Enslavement', *Mivrak*, 17 Sept. 1948.

49. See Bevin's remarks in the Cabinet on 21 Sept. 1948; PRO, CAB 129/29. The details were largely the work of Bernadotte's aides. See *To Jerusalem*, pp. 186–93; S. Persson, passim.

50. See my article, op. cit. (above, n. 1). The American Ambassador did consider that Soviet Russia had instigated the murder (MacDonald to Secretary of State, 22 Sept. 1948, No. 123. 867N. 01/S-2248. National Archives Washington). But this accusation was denied by the Russians themselves.

51. *Lehi* broadcast, Sept. 1948; HA. Compare, however, American Friends of the F.F.I. Stern Group, press release, 21 Sept. 1948, in which Bernadotte's death was seen as inevitable, and where *Lehi*'s own responsibility is not explicitly denied.

52. On 19 Sept., Begin published a manifesto which also placed 'direct responsibility' on *Hazit ha-Moledet*, adding that the British and the Government were 'indirectly responsible'. Cf. M. Begin, 'Who is Responsible for Bernadotte's Death?'

53. *Hazit ha-Moledet*, Sept. 1948. Eldad has informed me that the name of the organisation was suggested by Friedman-Yellin.

54. D. Ben-Gurion, *The War of Independence. Ben-Gurion's War Diary*, eds. G. Rivlin and E. Oren (Hebrew; Tel Aviv, 1982), p. 644 (entry for 11 Aug. 1948).

55. He also reported his suspicions to Ben-Gurion, ibid., p. 704. Several details of *Lehi*'s plans to murder Bernadotte were subsequently published in a pamphlet prepared by the Israeli Secret Service (the Shai) on the occasion of the *Lehi* conference the following year: 'Fighters! Why are we fighting? An Open Letter to a member of "The Fighters"', March 1949, HA; file of *Lehi* publications.

56. Ibid., pp. 700–9 and D. Joseph, *The Faithful City*, pp. 309, 312. At the same time, the opportunity was also taken to take other steps against the IZL, which was suspected of planning to take Jerusalem and declare the establishment of a 'Kingdom of Judaea' there unless the city was annexed. On 19 Sept., a majority of Cabinet members supported Ben-Gurion's demand that the laws of the state with respect to the army, conscription and arms apply to all residents and visitors to Jerusalem; and on the following day the IZL was given an ultimatum to disband within 24 hours. D. Ben-Gurion, *The Restored State*, pp. 284–5. For its part, the IZL claimed that it had disbanded in order to avoid bloodshed: *Ha-Herut*, No. 95, 22 Sept. 1948.

57. Provisional State Council, nineteenth session, pp. 4, 21–2. *Mapam* was entirely in agreement with the tone of the debate; see A. Benshalom, 'Our Affairs. Separatism is at an End', *Al Ha-Mishmar*, 24 Sept. 1948. The Revisionists, however, were more ambivalent. Some members of the party were unhappy at the way their representatives had voted. See M. Grossman, 'Internal Opposition and Foreign Policy', *Ha-Mashkif*, 1 Oct. 1948.
58. Manifesto, published by the *Lehi* 'centre', Sept. 1948. On 20 Sept. The government declared *Lehi* to be a terrorist organisation.
59. 'The War of Liberation Goes On', *Ha-Ma'as*, Sept. 1948. After Friedman-Yellin's arrest on 30 Sept., Shamir and Eldad even claimed that the 'centre' was itself preventing action by elements even more extreme. 'As long as you [meaning, Ben-Gurion] do not go completely mad, and do not perpetrate provocative and foolish acts, we shall continue as before on the external front.' 'They have Again "Done Away" with Lehi', *Ha-Ma'as*, No. 83, Oct. 1948.
60. Idem.

## CHAPTER 12 (pp. 256–284)

1. The Secretariat of the *Lehi* Movement, *Bulletin* No. 1, 14 Sept. 1948.
2. Friedman-Yellin was about to travel to Czechosolvakia, and had in his possession a considerable sum of money and a small arms cache. *Ha'aretz*, 1 Oct. 1948 and 15 Dec. 1948 and Ben-Gurion, *War Diary*, pp. 724, 729.
3. On 26 Sept., Ben-Gurion proposed that the Provisional Government give the order to conquer the majority of Judea; but most members of the Cabinet opposed this plan, principally because of the atmosphere of opposition to Israel created in several European states by Bernadotte's assassination. See Ben-Gurion, *The Restored State*, p. 288.
4. See the report of a conversation between Templer and the American Ambassador in London, 29 Oct. 1948, *FRUS*, 1948, V, pp. 1530–3.
5. 'Why have we been cast into the underground?', *Ba-Makhteret*, strictly internal bulletin, Nov. 1948, pp. 4–6, HA.
6. 'Our future mission', ibid., pp. 6–9.
7. 'Our present task', ibid., pp. 9–10.
8. 'Provocateurs' (Thoughts in the wake of the assassination of Bernadotte), ibid., pp. 11–13.
9. *Lehi* memorandum, Nov. 1948, Seligman file, JI H 13/3/48a.
10. On these events, see *Kol Ha-Am*, 22 Sept. 1948, 6, 15 and 22 Oct. 1948, and 10 Dec. 1948.
11. (Eldad), *From Underground to Underground (5708 in the History of the Movement)*, (Hebrew; no date, [October 1948]), pp. 15–16, 21. YHA file 87.
12. The Protocol itself is located in YHA file 35.
13. Ibid., pp. 3–6. Indeed, a protracted struggle, it was argued could work in *Lehi*'s favour. 'It would be a disaster for us were we to receive 50 per cent in elections now. We would sink under the burden of victory.' *Lehi*, in fact, had to concentrate on educating the masses to its ideas and to leave it to history to bring about its inevitable victory. 'Hedai' (Hayyim Dviri), pp. 13–15.
14. Ibid, pp. 16–18. According to the protocol, 'Pinhas', was the only participant who doubted the USSR's loyalty to Zionism and feared that the Russians might support the Arabs, notwithstanding *Lehi*'s pro-Soviet stand.
15. Ibid., pp. 6–11.
16. Ibid., pp. 16–18.
17. *Lehi* 'Last warning' Nov. 1948, Collection of *Lehi* printed materials, CZA. Compare Friedman-Yellin's bitter letter to the Minister of the Interior (dated 8 Nov. 1948), in which he claims that the Provisional Government is treating him 'far more bluntly' than Pilsudski in Poland had done, adding that the Government had apparently learned from the Nazis. He further added that the Arab states would certainly use the example of 'the orders for the prevention of terrorism' to destroy their own Jews.

He insisted that the elections be postponed until after the trial, in order to allow for *Lehi*'s free participation, that is after its members had been set free and its property had been released. JA 8/48/3 13H.

18. Internal leaflet, Dec. 1948.
19. Ben-Gurion, *War Diary*, p. 838 (22 Nov. 1948); for the previous attempts at compromise, ibid., pp. 752, 783, and 802–4.
20. The protocol of the trial (other than the secret sessions) is located in the files of Advocate Seligman, JI, H 148/3/13 (the above quotation is from p. 6). Seligman acted as legal adviser to the accused, who otherwise conducted their own defence.
21. Ibid., p. 177 and *Ha-Aretz*, 9 Dec. 1948.
22. Protocol, pp. 320ff. At this juncture in the proceedings, the prosecution raised the issue of *Lehi*'s espionage department ('Department vav') and the court retired into closed session for a discussion of *Lehi*'s espionage in the IDF's stores – which Friedman-Yellin denied. This session is not recorded in the protocol, but see *Ha-Aretz*, 30 Dec. 1948.
23. 'With a clear conscience and a fearful heart', *Ha-Ma'as*, Dec. 1947 (bulletin).
24. Protocol, ibid., p. 522.
25. Ibid., pp. 804–8 (Eshkol), pp. 860–84 (Rosen) and 1028–75 (Gruenbaum).
26. Compare Eldad MS in YHA file 87 with Galili testimony, Protocol, pp. 1028–75.
27. Ibid., pp. 1296–403.
28. On the latter see *Ha-Aretz*, 12 Jan. 1949. For Ben-Gurion's initial opposition to the appearance of the 'Fighters' Party in the elections, *War Diary*, p. 923. The government eventually decided that were the party to be disqualified, *Lehi* would adopt the more disastrous course of underground activity.
29. 'Trial or Perversion?' *Ha-Ma'as*, Jan. 1949, CZA. 'The Homeland Front will not Betray', ibid., Jan. 1949.
30. *Ha-Aretz*, 23 Jan. 1949.
31. For the verdict see JI, 7/48/3/13H.
32. 'What is the election struggle about?', no date (Jan. 1949).
33. 'What peace and what war?', *Ha-Ma'as*, special edition, Jan. 1949. Eldad's authorship is evident from the MS of this article in YHA file 87.
34. 'Between Orientation and Neutralisation', ibid.; see also Eldad's draft in YHA *ibid.* For Lubotsky's charge see 'Lehi', *Ha-Dor*, 6 Jan. 1949.
35. See the leading article in *Herut*, 13 Feb. 1949 and the favourable article on 'Yair' published in the same newspaper on 29 Feb. 1949.
36. Weizmann to Lady Bonham-Carter, 13 March 1949, *Letters and Papers of Chaim Weizmann*, Vol. XXIII (Jerusalem, 1980), p. 308. Nevertheless, the Fighters' Party did not cease its attacks on Weizmann. See 'On the hysterical reaction', *Ha Ma'as*, 3 (105), p. 5.
37. For the protocol of the speech, see YHA file 4; cf. Friedman-Yellin's more balanced view of Stern's socialism in his memoirs (p. 48).
38. For the protocol of Eldad's address see *Protocol*, ibid. An expanded and revised version is in 'Jacob's Ladder', *Sulam*, 1 May 1949, pp. 4–5.
39. *Proceedings of the First Knesset*; tenth session, 9 March 1949, pp. 89–92.
40. A copy of the conference proceedings is located in HA, where Shamir's speech is found on pp. 4–8. It has been published in P. Ginosar (ed.), *Lehi Revealed: Minutes of the Conference of the Fighters for the Freedom of Israel* (Hebrew; Ramat Gan, 1985), where the speech is on pp. 44–52.
41. Ginosar, op. cit., pp. 56–61 (pp. 11–14 in the original). Ginosar had become a Marxist while in exile in Kenya. See R. Anbar, *Yehudah Ben-David. A Freedom Fighter for Israel* (Hebrew; Jerusalem, 1973), p. 80. In his speech, Ginosar mentioned Darwin, Lisenko and Mitshurin.
42. Ginosar, op. cit., pp. 72–6; in the original, pp. 23–6.
43. Ginosar, op. cit., pp. 78–89; in the original, pp. 27–37. See also P. Ginosar, in *Yehudah Ben-David*, p. 62.
44. Ginosar. op cit., pp. 89–104; in the original, pp. 37–47. For the small extent to which Shamir was influenced by socialist ideas see Y. Shamir, in *Yehudah Ben-David*, p. 62.
45. Nevertheless, Eldad did admit that Friedman-Yellin's Knesset appearances had

certainly created 'a great impression'.

46. Ginosar, op. cit., pp. 104–13; in the original, pp. 47–52.
47. Friedman-Yellin's speech in Ginosar, op. cit., pp. 113–26; in the original, pp. 52–60.
48. For the majority resolution, see Ginosar, pp. 127–8; in the original, pp. 61–2.
49. The minority resolution is in Ginosar, pp. 128–30; in the original, pp. 62–3.
50. Ginosar, op. cit., pp. 128–30 (in the original, pp. 64–5). Compare Friedman-Yellin's summary, where it is precisely the classless aspect which is emphasised. Ginosar, pp. 39–41; in the original, pp. 1–2.
51. Ginosar, pp. 133–5; in the original; pp. 65–7.
52. *Ma'ariv* and *Yedi'ot Aharonot*, 29 April 1949. In a council meeting, Friedman-Yellin claimed that until 29 Nov. 1947 Eldad had supported *Lehi*'s political principles and actions, and had sometimes been even more extreme than were Shamir and himself in drawing conclusions. See *La-Haver*, internal bulletin, No. 4 (June 1949), pp. 1–2.
53. *Ma'ariv*, 13 May 1949. For the views of the two sides, compare Eldad, 'The Crisis in the Underground Movement', *Sulam*, May 1949, pp. 5–7 and Friedman-Yellin's address to the council of the 'Fighters', reported in *La-Haver*, No. 4, 1949, pp. 1–2.
54. See the report of Friedman-Yellin's address to the Tel Aviv branch of the party on 28 April 1949 in *La-Haver*, No. 2, pp. 1–4 and Shamir's address to the same group on 4 May 1949, 'The Totality of the Idea and of the Deed', *La-Haver*, No. 3, pp. 1–5.
55. 'The Word of the "Fighters" to the Histradrut Convention', May 1949.
56. For examples of such views see, for instance, the various articles written by Friedman-Yellin (using several different names) during this period, such as N. Mor, 'Britain in *Eretz Israel*', *Ha-Ma'as*, 4 (86), June 1949, p. 2; Friedman-Yellin, 'Report on the Political Situation to the Party Council; 4 June 1949', *La-Haver*, No. 4 (June 1949), pp. 1–5; N. Yellin-Mor, 'Lausanne too will not bring a solution', *Ha-Ma'as*, 2 (84), May 1949, p. 3.
57. P. Ginosar, 'The October Revolution and the Movement for Hebrew Revival'; idem (pseud. 'Ben-Rachel'), 'The 32nd Anniversary of the October Revolution', both in *Ha-Ma'as*, 4 (106), 2 Nov. 1949, pp. 4, 8. Ginosar later joined *Mapam* and thereafter (with Dr Sneh), *Maki*. See P. Ginosar, in *Yehudah ben David*, p. 82.
58. See (anon), 'Demagogy or Stupidity', *Ha-Ma'as*, 3 (105), p. 8; Y. Ben-Eliyahu, 'The State on the verge of Winter', ibid.; M. Ben Ya'akov, 'There is no escape from the Necessary', *Ha-Ma'as*, 4 (106).
59. For examples of both tactics see, for example, 'Five Years Ago Lord Moyne was executed in Cairo. The Meaning of the Verdict', *Ha-Ma'as*, 7 (89), p. 5; David [Ginosar], '*Lehi* – 1949', ibid., 20 (102).
60. Selman to Friedman-Yellin, 13 Nov. 1949 (copy to Shamir), JI, Selman File, p. 257; and 'Haggai' (Shlomo Edelstein) and 'Amnon' (Pinhas Ginosar) to the *merkaz* of the Fighters' Party, 22 Jan. 1950, ibid. Ginosar later claimed that 'one of the reasons for the early dissolution was the fact that Gera [Friedman-Yellin] and Michael [Shamir] were suspicious of the Marxist left in their party . . .', P. Ginosar, op. cit. p. 33. See also the report in *Al Ha-Mishmar* of 12 Feb. 1950, that the left wing had accused the leadership of retaining its Revisionist tendencies.
61. Friedman-Yellin (?), 'Proposals for the Analysis of the Problems which Face Us', (n.d.), pp. a–f, p. 21; YHA file 29.
62. Especially M. Sneh. See, for example, the latter's articles 'Europe of the United States' and 'The Demonstration and the Issues', *Al Ha-Mishmar*, 30 Sept. and 28 Oct. 1949.
63. (P. Ginosar), 'Towards the Eradication of the Crisis', YHA file 29, pp. 1–14.
64. Anon., 'On the Party's Path', ibid., pp. 14–15. In this view, even the use of democratic methods had to be avoided.
65. Anon., 'On *Lehi*'s Path', ibid., pp. 16–21.
66. 'The Fifth Session of the Council', *La-Haver*, internal, n.d. (March 1950), pp. 1–2.
67. 'Gera', 'An Answer to a Comrade', ibid., pp. 3–5. Also pointed out was the fact that dissension had begun to affect the apex of the regime, including *Mapam*; Anon., 'The Crisis of the Present Regime', *La-Haver*, 9, 17 March 1950.

CONCLUSION (pp. 285–299)

1. There has recently been a surge in *Lehi* hagiography. Compare H. Dviri *Unforgettable Spring Day* (Hebrew; Tel Aviv, 1986); Y. Gilboa (Polani), *In Fields of Fear* (Hebrew; Tel Aviv, 1986); A. Amichal-Yeivin, *In Purple: The Life of Yair – Avraham Stern* (Hebrew; Tel Aviv, 1986).

2. Thus, in September 1936 he had stated that: 'In general, it would not be wise "to place all our eggs in one basket"', Jabotinsky, *Speeches* (Hebrew), II, p. 205. Also noteworthy is the fact that he did not protest when in the same year, Achimeir proclaimed (in a tone which was to become characteristic of *Lehi* in the future) that: 'British Nazism is more dangerous than Teuton Nazism . . .', N.F. (namely, Natan Friedman), 'Abba Achimeir in Poland', *Ha-Medinah*, 5, (41), 6 April 1936 (Hebrew).

3. See Y. Heller, 'Ends and Means: The Ideological and Political debate between Jabotinsky and Achimeir, 1928–1933' (Hebrew), *Zion*, 52 (1987), pp. 315–69; Y. Shavit, '"Until a Faithful Prophet Should Arise" – U.Z. Greenberg's Status as an Eschatological Poet', in Shavit, *The Mythologies of the Zionist Right Wing* (Hebrew; Bet Berl, 1986), pp. 180–206.

4. It was in this connection that he considered Achimeir as a candidate to organise the public hinterland of his organisation in 1941. Compare Abba Sikra, 'Twarda' and 'Gilboa', *Herut*, 27 May 1949.

5. Compare Y. Shavit, '*Lehi* – Between Idealism and Opportunism. On the Status of *Lehi* as an Underground Organisation and as an Ideological Group' (Hebrew), in Shavit, op. cit., pp. 156, 159.

6. Without succumbing to the same mistakes as had been made by the revered founding-father. This explains the care and caution which his successors showed in formulating their pro-Soviet orientation before Gromyko's announcement – but not thereafter. Compare Eldad, *First Tithe*, pp. 302–4 with pp. 329–31.

7. 'Communism must work toward the destruction of the Jewish sources of our capital and construction, since its entire foundation, root and essence is the class war against the bourgeoisie.' 'Zion and Communism' (Hebrew), *Hazit Ha-Am*, 27, 3 June 1932 (*Haynt*, 24–26 May 1932), also printed in Jabotinsky, *On the Way to Statehood* (Hebrew), p. 66.

8. Shavit, '*Lehi* (above note 5), pp. 170–74. While some of the versions of National Bolshevism might be characterised as opportunistic, that designation does not fit their cumulative effect.

9. 'The IZL in Israel' recalls two similar enterprises in Vichy France. The first was undertaken by the pupils of Edyah Gurevitch (Horon; who had left the Revisionist movement after the establishment of the NZO), George Blumberg and Leon Yehoshua, who aspired to establish a Hebrew state in the Middle East by allying with Vichy France – because the latter was anti-British. Only in 1942, when the anti-Jewish persecutions in France increased and Jews were transported to the east, did they appreciate that there was no point in hoping for an objective alliance with Vichy. They then joined the anti-Nazi underground. See Y. Porath's recent biography of Ratosh, *The Life of Uriel Shelah* (Hebrew; Tel Aviv, 1989), p. 157. The second effort was made by the *Masadah* group founded by Yitzchak Kedmi-Cohen, who was also one of Jabotinsky's disciples. In 1943 he suggested to Marshal Pétain, the Vichy leader, the establishment of a Hebrew state in the Middle East. This would have been allied with the Axis powers against Britain and Russia, would solve the Jewish problem, and would secure the Axis powers' interests respecting oil and trade in a better manner than the current Vichy methods. Kedmi-Cohen's life shortly thereafter came to an end at Auschwitz. Compare M. Marrus and R.A. Paxton, *Vichy France and the Jews* (New York, 1981). In both cases, the groups concerned were tiny.

10. Nevertheless, notwithstanding *Lehi*'s pretentions, the USSR itself regarded the PKP and *Maki* – not *Lehi* – as the most faithful representatives of its ideology. Compare two examples out of many in R'oi, *Soviet Decision-Making in Practice*, pp. 161–2, 212–16. Such was *Lehi*'s need of firm models if it was to attain legitimacy that it was even forced to contend that Hakim and Bet Tsouri had displayed greater heroism than

had the Warsaw ghetto fighters, since the latter really had no choice. Compare Y. Achidov [Eldad], 'Five Years After the Warsaw Ghetto Uprising. The Day of the Gallows and the Night of Rebellion (In Memory of Hakim and Bet Tsouri and In Memory of the Warsaw Ghetto Heroes)', *Mivrak*, 16 April 1948.

11. Compare the following studies: A. Ascher and G. Lewy, 'National Bolshevism in Weimar Germany. Alliance of Political Extremes against Democracy', *Social Research*, XXIII, 2 (1956), pp. 450–80; L. Dupeux, *Stratégie communiste et dynamique conservatrice; Essai sur les différents sens de l'expression 'National-Bolchevisme' en Allemagne. 1919–1933* (Lille and Paris, 1976); K. von Klemperer, 'Towards a Fourth Reich? The History of National Bolshevism in Germany', *Review of Politics*, XXII, 2 (1951) pp. 191–210; O.E. Schueddekopf, *Linke Leute von rechts. Die national-revolutionaeren Minderheiten und der Kommunismus in der Weimarer Republik* (Stuttgart, 1960).

12. That was precisely why both organisations were, at different times, hounded by the 'national agencies' and their emissaries – the *Haganah* and the *Palmach*. Compare, for instance, 'Jewish Terrorist Gangs in Palestine', 15 Jan. 1945, in T. Kollek to R. Moore, 21 Jan. 1945, RG 226, Records of the Office of Strategic Services, Entry 190 – Box 73/ Cairo-SI-OP-7 (Operations – Jewish Agency), National Archives, Washington.

13. Eldad, *First Tithe*, pp. 170–82. Eldad was on this occasion a party to those contacts via his conversations with Dan Ram. These were the consequence of his wish to draw closer to the *Ahdut Ha-Avodah* movement, because of the latter's anti-imperialist activism.

14. N. Friedman, 'The First Principle: A Single Miracle', (Hebrew), *Ha-Medinah*, 2 (20), 6 Jan. 1935. On the beginnings of the influence which maximalism exerted on Friedman-Yellin compare idem, 'Tomorrow's Perspective' (Yiddish), *Ha-Medinah*, 6 (53), 5 Sept. 1937, pp. 5, 7.

15. Abba Sikra, 'What do we Care?' (Hebrew), *Ha-Madrich*, II, book 14 (April 1943), pp. 222–4. At this stage, Friedman-Yellin was full of admiration for Achimeir. Compare his letter to Eldad, above (Chapter 5, note 2). Begin never experienced that sort of transformation. Compare M. Ben-Ze'ev [Begin], 'Russia and Zionism' (Hebrew), ibid., book 13 (Feb. 1943), pp. 197–204.

16. Compare his letter to the *Lehi* emissiary in the USA, Benjamin Gepner, dated January 1948: 'There is no doubt that there will be a world war between the USSR [on the one side] and the USA and Britain [on the other]. We shall fight on the side of the USSR.' Cited in M. Getter, 'The Ideology of the Freedom Fighters of Israel ("Lehi")' (Hebrew; unpublished MA thesis, Tel Aviv University, 1967), p. 56, note 40. Geulah Cohen ('Tirzah'), felt a similar affinity with (Israeli) communism. Compare her letter to Pinhas Ginosar ('Amnon'), 19 June 1948: 'It is precisely that which was the most natural to do *which has not been done at all* [emphasis in original] by the Communist Party. It is very difficult to draw it into action. From a propaganda point of view that is very good; they write just like Lehi; really. But they are not Lehi.' My thanks to Dr P. Ginosar for allowing me to quote from this letter.

17. B. [that is, Y.] Scheib, 'Berdichevsky the Rebel [To mark the 60th anniversary of his birth]' (Hebrew), *Metzudah*, II, No. 3, May 1937, p. 31. Compare idem, 'Schopenhauer and Judaism [To mark the 70th anniversary of his death]' (Hebrew), ibid., pp. 31–3.

18. Y. Scheib, 'Fom Ahad Ha'am to Max Nordau', (Hebrew), *Ha-Medinah*, 3 (76), 20 Jan. 1939, p. 2; idem, 'R. Shimon Bar Yohai: To Mark the Visit of the Head of *Betar* to Poland' (Hebrew), ibid., 18 (91), 12 May 1939, p. 1.

19. Eldad's doctoral thesis, on Von Hartmann, concerns the attempt of this German philospher to unite Schopenhauer's irrational voluntarism with Hegel's intellectualism. See I. Scheib, *Der Voluntarismus Eduard Hartmann's in der Abghängigkeit von Schopenhauer*, Dissertation, Universität Wien (1933). The same ideas were expressed in Eldad's interview with the author, 11 Sept. 1986.

20. Y. Shamir, 'The Changes and their Subject' (Hebrew), *Ha-Ma'as* (1949), fourth year, 7 (89), 23 June 1949, p. 2.

21. Compare here the Fighters' failed attempts at land settlement: H. Shalem, *To the Negev* (Hebrew: Tel Aviv, 1989).

# Bibliography

PRIMARY SOURCES

## Archives

### Yair House Archives (YHA)
*(Tel Aviv)*
Lehi collection (107 files).
The 'Fighters' Party' collection (39 files).

### Yair Milk Churn Archives
### (in possession of David Stern, Tel Aviv)
Correspondence and memoranda on activities (files 1–45).
Command announcements (files 46–9).
Organisation (files 50–64).
Instructions (files 65–80).
Publications (files 81–92).
Broadcastings (files 93–4).
Articles and memoranda (files 95–107).
Intelligence (files 108–14).
Codes (files 115–17).
Notes (files 118–22).
Additional documents (files 123–37).
Poems (files 138–40).

### Jabotinsky Institute (JI)
*(Tel Aviv)*
Abba Achimeir (42 files).
Menachem Begin (315 files).
Brit Ha-Birionim (8 files).
Yaakov Cohen (604 files).
Irgun Zvai Leumi (IZL) (400 files).
Eri Jabotinsky (145 files) World Revisionist Alliance.
Zeev Jabotinsky Collection of letters (560 files).
Leaflets collection.
*Lehi* (70 files).
Martyrs (88 files).
Avraham Selman (10 files).
Joseph Shechtman (15 files).
Avraham Stern (17 files).
Yaakov Weinschal (120 files).
World Revisionist Alliance, the Executive (Paris and London).
Max Zeligman (81 files).

### Haganah Archives (HA)
*(Tel Aviv)*
Haganah Intelligence Service – General and 'Dissidents'.
Haganah Publications.
IZL Publications.
Leaflets files.
Lehi Publications.

### Histadrut Archives
*(Tel Aviv)*
The Executive files.
The Secretariat files.

### Labour Party Archives (LPA)
*(Bet Berl)*
Mapai Centre files.
The Secretariat and the Political Committee files.

### Central Zionist Archives (CZA)
*(Jerusalem)*
The Political Department (S25).
Protocols of the Jewish Agency Executive (S100).
Protocols of the National Committee (J1).
Protocols of the Small Zionist Action Committee (S25, S5).

### Public Record Office (PRO)
*(London)*
Colonial Office (CO), CO/733, 814.
Foreign Office (FO), FO/371.
Minister Resident in the Middle East, FO/921.
War Office (WO), WO/208, 169.

### National Archives
*(Washington)*
Office of Strategic Services (OSS).

### Institute of Contemporary Jewry, Oral History Division
B. Akzin.
B. Lubotsky.

## Published Sources

### Daily Newspapers and Periodicals

*Al Ha-Mishmar* (Mishmar) (Mapam).
*Ba-Mahane* (Haganah).
*Betar* (Revisionist).
*Bh-Herev* (IZL).
*Dapim* (IZL).
*Davar* (Histadrut).
*Der Nayer Weg* (Revisionist).
*Di-Tat* (IZL).
*Doar Ha-Yom* (Revisionist 1928–31).
*Ha'am* (Revisionist).
*Ha-Aretz* (Liberal).
*Ha-Birion* (Revisionist Maximalist).
*Ha-Herut* (IZL).
*Ha-Hevra* (Revisionist).
*Ha-Ma'as* (*Lehi*).
*Ha-Madrich. Bamat Mefakdim* (*Betar*).
*Ha-Mashkif* (Revisionist).
*Ha-Medina* (Revisionist).
*Ha-Metzuda* (IZL).
*Ha-Yarden* (Revisionist).
*Haynt* (General Zionist).
*Hazit Ha-Am* (Maximalist Revisionist).
*Hazit Ha-Noar* (*Lehi*).
*He-Hazit* (*Lehi*).
*Herut* (IZL).
*Jerosolima Wyzwolona* (IZL).
*The Jewish Herald* (Revisionist).
*Kol Ha-Am* (Communist).
*Le-Haver* (*Lehi*).
*Metzudah* (*Betar*).
*Mivrak* (*Lehi*).
*Moment* (Revisionist from 1932).
*Omer La-Am* (IZL).
*Raasvet* (Revisionist).
*Sadan* (Maximalist Revisionist).
*Sentinel* (IZL).
*Shikuf* (*Lehi*).
*Sulam* (Eldad's organ after the split).
*Undzer Velt* (Revisionist).

### Books and Articles

A. Achimeir, *Brit Ha-Birionim* (Hebrew), Tel Aviv, 1966).
Y. Achimeir and S. Schatzky, *We Are Sicarii* (Tel Aviv, 1972).
A. Amir, 'The Harp and the Sword', *Keshet*, Vol. 18, No. 1 (1975), pp. 5–43.
R. Anbar, *Yehuda Ben-David. A Freedom Fighter for Israel* (Hebrew, Jerusalem, 1973).
Asher (Hanoch Bzhozah), *Fighters of Israel or Enemies of Israel. Sternism without a Mask* (Socialist Union for National Policy People and World, March 1944).

S. Avineri, *The Making of Modern Zionism* (New York, 1981).
Y. Banai, *Unknown Soldiers* (Hebrew, Tel Aviv [1958]).
M. Begin, *The Revolt. The Memoirs of the Commander of the IZL* (Hebrew, Tel Aviv, 1950) (English ed. London, 1951).
D. Ben-Gurion, *Ba-Ma'arakha*, Vols. 1–5 (Hebrew, Tel Aviv, 1957).
— *Memoirs*, Vol. 2 (1934–35), Vol. 3 (1936), Vol. 5 (1938) (Hebrew, Tel Aviv, 1972–82).
— *The Restored State of Israel* (Hebrew, Tel Aviv, 1969, English ed., *Israel – A Personal History*, London 1970).
— *The War of Independence. Ben-Gurion's War Diary* (eds. G. Rivlin and E. Oren) (Hebrew, Tel Aviv, 1982).
H. Ben-Meir (Schorer), *The Arlosoroff Murder. Material for the Public Trial* (Hebrew, Tel Aviv, 1934).
H. Ben-Yeruham, *The Betar Book. History and Sources*. Vols. 1–2 (Hebrew, Tel Aviv, 1969–76).
— *The Great Libel* (Hebrew, Jerusalem, 1982).
Y. Ben-Zakkai (Ronkin), *Against the Terrorist Groups. The IZL and Lehi – Their Paths and Their Outlooks* (Hebrew, Tel Aviv).
F. Bernadotte, *To Jerusalem* (London, 1951).
C. Bohlen, *Witness to History* (New York, 1973).
*Documents on the Foreign Policy of Israel, Vol. 1, 14 May 1948–30 September 1948* (ed. Y. Freundlich) (Jerusalem, 1981).
W.T. Drymmer, 'Zagadnienie Zydowskie', *Zeszyty Historyczne*, XIII (1968), pp. 55–77.
H. Dviri, *Unforgettable Spring Day* (Hebrew, Tel Aviv, 1986).
I. Eldad (Scheib), *Der Voluntarismus Eduard Hartmann's in der Abhängigkeit von Schopenhauer*, Dissertation, Universitat Wien [1933].
— *First Tithe. Memoirs and Lessons* (Hebrew, Jerusalem, 1950).
— 'Who and What were Yair and Lehi?', *Sulam*, Vol. 10, No. 9, 1959, pp. 5–50.
—*Hegionot Israel* (Hebrew, Tel Aviv, 1980).
Eli [D. Shomron], *We Have Enlisted for Life* (Hebrew, Tel Aviv, 1969).
Y. Eliav, *Wanted* (Hebrew, Tel Aviv, 1983) (English ed., New York, 1984).
*Foreign Relations of the United States, Vol. V: The Near East, South Asia and Africa, Part Two* (Washington, 1976).

P. Ginosar, ed., *Lehi Revealed. Minutes of the Conference of the Fighters for the Freedom of Israel. March 1949* (Ramat Gan, 1985).

M. Giora (Elimelech), 'The IZL. Trial and Moral', *Keshet*, 65, (Hebrew, 1974), pp. 60–77.

U.Z. Greenberg, *A Buffer Zone and the Speech of a Son of Blood* (Hebrew, Jerusalem, 1930).

— *Book of Indictment and Faith* (Hebrew, Jerusalem, 1937).

Y. Gurion, *Arieh Posek. His Life and Achievements* (Hebrew, Tel Aviv, 1957).

P. Haller, *Nationalrevolutionaerer Zionismus. Untersuchung und Proklamation* (Wien, 1957).

J. Heller, ed., *In the Struggle for a State. Zionist Politics, 1936–1948* (Hebrew, Jerusalem, 1985).

B.Z. Herzl, *Zionism, A Political Edition* (ed. B. Netanyahu) (Hebrew, Jerusalem, 1937).

— *Facing a People and the World* (Hebrew, Jerusalem, 1961).

B. Hoffman, *The Failure of British Military Strategy within Palestine 1939–1947* (Hebrew, Ramat Gan, 1983).

Z. Jabotinsky, *Speeches, 1927–1940* (Hebrew, Jerusalem, 1948).

— *On the Way to Statehood* (Hebrew, Jerusalem, 1953).

— *Letters* (Hebrew, Tel Aviv, n.d.).

— *Notes* (Hebrew, Tel Aviv, n.d.).

— *Memoirs of a Contemporary* (Hebrew, Tel Aviv, n.d.).

— *A Jewish State – A Solution to the Jewish Problem* (Hebrew, 1937).

— *The Jewish War Front* (London, 1940).

— *First Zionist Writings* (Hebrew, Jerusalem, 1949).

D. Joseph, *The Faithful City. The Siege of Jerusalem 1948* (London, 1960, Hebrew, Jerusalem, 1960).

E. Katz 'The Freedom Fighters of Israel (Lehi)' in S. Friedman (publisher), *The Freedom Fighters of Israel* (Hebrew, no editor, Tel Aviv, 1955).

S. Katz, *Days of Fire* (Inside the Miracle) (Hebrew, Tel Aviv, 1966, English ed., London, 1968).

A. Kotzer, *Red Carpet. My Life with Yair* (Hebrew, n.d., no place of publication [1975]).

S. Lev-Ami, ed., 'Protocols of the IZL Command July–November 1944', *Ha-Zionut*, Vol. 5 (1976), pp. 391–454.

*The Ayala Lubinsky Volume* (Hebrew, no editor, Tel Aviv, 1960).

B. Lubotsky, ed., *The Life Style of a Fighting Zionist. The Life of E. Washitz* (Hebrew, Jerusalem, 1947).

— *Memoirs from the Right Wing* (Hebrew, Tel Aviv, 1990).

— (Y. Okev) *The Black Deed* (Oz ed., 1949).

*Lohamei Herut Israel. Ketavim (Writings)* (Hebrew, no editor, Tel Aviv, 1959–60).

Y. Nedava, ed., *Zionist Revisionism Crystallised: Collected Articles from Raasvet 1925–29* (Hebrew, Tel Aviv, 1985).

Y. Orenstein, *In Chains. From the Memoirs of a Fighter* (Hebrew, Tel Aviv, 1973).

*Political and Diplomatic Documents* (December 1947–May 1948) (ed. G. Yogev) (Jerusalem, 1979).

*Proceedings of the First Knesset* (Hebrew, Jerusalem, 1949–51).

*Protocol of the 22nd Zionist Congress. Basel, 9–24 December 1946* (Jerusalem, n.d.).

*Protocols of the Provisional State Council. 1948–1949.* 2 Vols (Hebrew, Jerusalem, 1949).

Y. Ratosh (U. Heilperin), *Our Eyes Are Lifted Up to Domination. The Liberation Movement's Front of Tomorrow* (Tel Aviv, 1937).

— *Earliest Days* (Hebrew, Tel Aviv, 1980).

Shapira A., ed., *The Army Controversy 1948. Ben-Gurion's Struggle for Control* (Hebrew, Tel Aviv, 1985).

M. Sharett, *Political Diary, Vols. 3, 5* (1938, 1940–42) (Hebrew, Tel Aviv, 1972, 1979).

M. Shmuelevitch, *In Red Days* (Tel Aviv, 1949).

A. Stern (Yair), *Book of Poems* (Sulam ed., Jerusalem, 1950).

— *You Shall Live for Ever*. Avraham Stern (Yair) Poems (ed. A. Spielman) (Hebrew, n.d.).

P. Vazeh, *The Goal – Supplies* (Hebrew, Tel Aviv, 1966).

C. Weizmann, *The Letters and Papers*, Vols. 22–23 (Jerusalem, 1979).

N. Yellin-Mor (Friedman-Yellin), *The Fighters for the Freedom of Israel. People, Ideas, Deeds* (Ramat Gan, 1974) (French ed., [Yalin-Mor] Paris, 1978).

## SECONDARY SOURCES

B. Akzin, 'The Foreign Policy of Jabotinsky', *Gesher* 6 (2) (1960), pp. 36–58.

A. Amichal-Yeivin, *In Purple. The Life of Yair–Avraham Stern* (Hebrew, Tel Aviv, 1986).

A. Ascher and G. Lewy, 'National Bolshevism in Weimar Germany. Alliance of Political Extremes against Democracy' *Social Research*, XXIII, 2 (1956), pp. 450–80.

Y. Bauer, *From Diplomacy to Resistance. Jewish Palestine, 1939–1945* (Hebrew, Merchavia, 1963, English ed., Philadelphia, 1970).

M.J. Cohen, *Palestine. Retreat from the Mandate. The Making of British Policy 1936–45* (London, 1978).

— *Palestine and the Great Powers 1945–1948* (Princeton, 1982).

— 'The Moyne Assassination: A Political Analysis', *Middle Eastern Studies*, XV (October 1979), pp. 358–73.

L. Dupeux, *Stratégie communiste et dynamique conservatrice: Essai sur les différents sens de l'espression 'Nationale-Bolchevisme' en Allemagne, 1919–1933* (Lille and Paris, 1976).

M. Ebon, 'The Communist Tactic in Palestine', *Middle East Journal* (July 1948).

G. Frank, *The Deed* (New York, 1963).

Y. Gelber, 'Zionists and British in Palestine in the Shadow of Jewish Revolt 1942–1944', *Ha-Zionut*, Vol. 7 (1982), pp. 324–96.

J. Heller, 'Weizmann, Jabotinsky and the Arab Question – The Peel Affair', *Jerusalem Quarterly*, 26 (1982), pp. 109–26.

— 'From the Black Sabbath to Partition. Summer 1946 as a Turning-Point in the Political History of Zionism', *Zion* (Hebrew), Vol. 43 (1978), pp. 314–61.

— 'A Failure of a Mission: Bernadotte and Palestine, 1948', *Journal of Contemporary History*, XIV (July 1979), pp. 515–34.

N. Katzburg, *The Palestine Problem in British Policy, 1940–1945* (Hebrew, Jerusalem, 1978).

J. Klausner, *The Founders of the State of Israel. Essays on Zionist Leaders in the Previous Generation* (Hebrew, 2nd ed., Jerusalem, 1955).

— *When a Nation Fights for its Freedom* (Hebrew, 2nd ed., 1939).

K. von Klemperer, 'Towards a Fourth Reich? The History of National Bolshevism in Germany', *Review of Politics*, XXII, 2 (1951), pp. 191–210.

W. Roger Louis, *The British Empire in the Middle East, 1945–1951* (Oxford, 1984).

M. Marrus and R.A. Paxton, *Vichy France and the Jews* (New York, 1981).

E. Melzer, 'Polish Diplomacy and the Problem of Jewish Immigration 1935–1937', *Gal'ed*, I, (Hebrew, Tel Aviv, 1973), pp. 211–49.

— 'The Ruling Party and the Jews of Poland, 1937–1939', *Gal'ed*, VI–V (Hebrew, Tel Aviv, 1978), pp. 397–426.

B. Morris, *The Birth of the Palestinian Refugee Problem* (Cambridge, 1986).

D. Niv, *Battle for Freedom. The Irgun Zvai Leumi*, 5 Vols. (1931–1948) (Tel Aviv, 1965–80).

S.O. Persson, *Mediation and Assassination: Count Bernadotte's Mission to Palestine in 1948* (London, 1979).

Y. Porath, *From Riots to Rebellion. The Palestinian Arab National Movement, 1929–1939* (Hebrew ed., 1978, English ed., 1977).

— *The Life of Uriel Shelah (Yonathan Ratosh)* (Hebrew, Tel Aviv, 1989).

— 'The League for National Liberation: Its Foundation, Content and Dispersal', *Asian and African Studies*, Vol. 4 (1968).

Y. Ro'i, *Soviet Decision-Making in Practice. Soviet-Israeli Relations 1947–1953* (New Brunswick, 1980).

O.-E. Schueddekopf, *Linke Leute von rechts. Die nationalrevolutionaeren Minderheiten und der Kommunismus in der Weimarer Republik* (Stuttgart, 1960).

H. Shalem, *To the Negev* (Hebrew, Tel Aviv, 1988).

Y. Shavit, *From Majority to a State. The Revisionist Movement: The Plan for the Colonisatory Regime and Social Ideas* (Hebrew, Tel Aviv, 1978).

— *Jabotinsky and the Revisionist Movement* (London, 1988).

— 'Between Pilsudski and Mickiewicz: Policy and Messianism in Zionist Revisionism', *Ha-Zionut*, Vol. 10 (1985), pp. 7–31 (in English: *Studies in Zionism*, Vol. 6, No. 2 [1985], pp. 229–46).

— *Self-Restraint or Reaction. The Dispute in the Jewish Yishuv between 1936 and 1939* (Hebrew, Ramat Gan, 1983).

— *The Mythologies of the Zionist Right Wing* (Hebrew, Bet Berl [1986]).

— '"Until a Faithful Prophet Should Arise"' – U.Z. Greenberg's 'Status as an Eschatological Poet', in *The Mythologies of the Zionist Right Wing* (Hebrew, Bet Berl [1986]), pp. 180–206.

— 'Lehi – Between Idealism and Opportunism. On the Status of Lehi as an Underground Organisation and as an Ideological Group', in *The Mythologies of the Zionist Right Wing* (Hebrew, Bet Berl [1986], pp. 153–79.

J.B. Shechtman *The Vladimir Jabotinsky Story* (Hebrew & English, New York, London and Tel Aviv, 3 vols., 1959–61).

A Shlaim, *Collusion Across the Jordan. King Abdullah, the Zionist Movement and the Partition of Palestine* (Oxford, 1988).

Y. Slutsky, *History of the Haganah*. Vol. 2 (parts 1–3): *From Defence to Struggle: (1920–1939)*, Vol. 3 (parts 1–3) (Hebrew, 1959–63), *From Resistance to War (1939–1948)* (Hebrew, 1972).

B. Wasserstein, 'New Light on the Moyne Murder', *Midstream*, XXVI (March, 1980) (also in *The Jewish Historical Society in England. Transactions. Sessions 1978–1980*, Vol. XXVII and *Miscellanies. Part XII* (London, 1982), pp. 72–83.

Y. Weinschal, *The Blood on the Threshold. The Story of the Life and Death of Yair – Avraham Stern* (Hebrew, Tel Aviv, 2nd ed., 1978).

— *The First Conqueror of the Mountain* (Hebrew, Tel Aviv, 1968).

# Index